In accordance with the latest syllabus prescribed by the Council for the Indian Certificate of Secondary Education Examination, New Delhi.

A TEXT BOOK OF
ICSE COMMERCIAL STUDIES

CLASS X

AUTHORS

A. GHOSH **A. BANERJEE**

Advisory Member
Chetan Tiwari
M. Com., M.Sc., B.Ed.,
Principal St. Anthony's School, Kurseong

OSWAL PUBLISHERS
1/12 Sahitya Kunj, M. G. Road, Agra-282 002

No part of this book can be reproduced in any form or by any means without the prior written permission of the publisher.

Edition : 2021

ISBN : 978-93-89937-98-5

OSWAL PUBLISHERS

Head office : 1/12, Sahitya Kunj, M. G. Road, Agra-282 002
Phone : (0562) 2527771-4, +91 75340 77222
E-mail : contact@oswalpublishers.com
Website : www.oswalpublishers.com
Printed at

Preface

We feel immense pleasure in introducing the thoroughly revised edition of Commercial Studies text book for ICSE Class X. This edition strictly adheres to the latest syllabus prescribed by the Council for the Indian School Certificate Examination, New Delhi.

The text book has been carefully designed so as to be useful for scholars as well as for the students with preliminary knowledge of the subject. The topics have been fully explained so that each reader can acquire the relevant knowledge as per their requirements.

Philosophy of this book

The concepts have been explained in simple language, easy conversational text with familiar examples, without making any sacrifice in the depth or precision.

The subject matter dealt in this book is self-explanatory to enable the students to understand the fundamental concepts and principles of Commerce easily.

'Lesson at a Glance' given at the end of each chapter will help students in quick revision before the examination.

The Project work/Assignments given at the end of chapters have been designed specifically for ICSE students to generate a practical aptitude towards the subject.

Sufficient short questions and essay type questions, on the pattern suggested by the council, are given at the end of each chapter to enhance the ability of a students to understand the text clearly and develop the skills to answer accurately.

In spite of our best efforts, the possibilities of some errors of omission and commission cannot be ruled out. Constructive suggestions will be appreciated and thankfully acknowledged.

—PUBLISHER

SYLLABUS CLASS X
COMMERCIAL STUDIES

There will be **one** written paper of **two** hours duration carrying 80 marks and Internal Assessment of 20 marks.

The paper will be divided into **two** sections A and B.

Section A (Compulsory) will consist of questions requiring short answers and will cover the entire syllabus. There will be no choice of questions.

Section B will consist of questions, which will require detailed answers. There will be a choice and candidates will be required to answer **four** questions from this section.

1. **Stakeholders in Commercial Organisations**

    (a) Meaning of stakeholder, types : Internal (shareholder, employee and employer—meaning of each) and External stakeholders (supplier, creditor, government and society–meaning of each); difference between internal and external stakeholders.

    (b) Expectations of employers (owners and managers), employees, creditors and suppliers, government and society from a commercial organization.

2. **Marketing and Sales**

    (a) Marketing

    Meaning and objectives of marketing. Difference between marketing and sales.

    (b) Product and service

    Meaning and difference between a product and a service (with examples).

    (c) Pricing

    Meaning and objectives

    (d) Advertising and Sales promotion

    Advertising : meaning, importance of advertising, merits and demerits, difference between advertising and publicity. Advertising Agency; meaning and functions only, Social advertising media–Concept and examples only.

    Sales promotion – meaning and techniques; difference between advertising and sales promotion.

    (e) Consumer Protection

    Consumer Protection Act (2019); features of the Act, rights of a consumer, Consumer exploitation; meaning and types, Importance of consumer awareness.

    (f) E–commerce

    Introduction and benefits over traditional methods of transactions, E-tailing, E-advertising, E-marketing and E-security (meaning only). ERP and its modules (brief concept).

3. **Finance and Accounting**

    (a) Capital and Revenue

    Capital and revenue receipts, capital and revenue expenditure (meaning, difference and examples) deferred revenue expenditure (meaning and examples)

    (b) Final accounts of Sole Proprietorship

- Meaning and **preparation of Trading account, profit and Loss account and Balance sheet** based on the given trial balance with the adjustment of closing stock only.
- (Preparation of manufacturing account, profit and loss on sale of assets, intangible and fictitious assets, prepaid and accrued expenses and incomes are excluded.)

(c) Costs

Fundamental concept of Cost Classification of costs–based on behaviour (fixed, variable, semi-variable), nature (direct, indirect).

(d) Budgeting

Meaning and utility of budgeting; comparison between budgeting and forecasting; types of budgets; sales, production, cash, purchase and master–meaning only.

(e) Sources of Finance

(i) Capital Market

Meaning and functions of Capital Market.

(ii) Sources of raising capital

Long term : Meaning of shares (Types; preference and equity) and debentures, differences between the two.

Short term : loans from commercial banks (cash credit, overdraft, discounting of bills—meaning only).

4. **Human Resources**

(a) Recruitment, selection and training

(i) Recruitment – meaning; sources : internal and external; advantages and disadvantages of internal and external sources.

(ii) Selection – meaning and steps, types of selection tests.

(iii) Training – meaning, objectives and methods of training (on the job and off the job).

(b) Industrial relations and trade unions

Industrial relations : meaning and objectives; Trade Unions; Meaning and Functions.

(c) Social Security

Concept of Social Security; brief reference to Provident Fund, Gratuity, Pension, Group Insurance and Maternity Benefits. New Pension Scheme. (Acts are not required).

5. **Logistics**

Meaning of logistics and its classification

(a) Transportation

Modes of transportation : land (road and rail), air and water; merits and demerits of each.

(b) Warehousing

Meaning, importance and types (public, private and bonded–meaning only).

(c) Insurance

Meaning; Types of insurance : Life insurance, General insurance; (Fire, Health and Marine–meaning only) principles of insurance.

6. **Banking**

    (i) Central Bank

    Central Bank; Meaning and functions, Difference between the Central Bank and Commercial Banks.

    (ii) Internet Banking

    Modes of transferring money / Net Banking: NEFT, RTGS, IMPS, mobile wallets: meaning only.

    ATM, Credit & Debit cards- meaning & difference, caution to be taken while using these cards.

    (iii) Financial fraudulent practices

    Credit card fraud, false accounting, insurance fraud, intellectual property fraud, Internet and cyber fraud. A brief understanding of these types of financial fraud.

7. **Government initiatives in Environment Protection**

    (i) *Environment (Protection) Act, 1986—Features of the act.*

    (ii) *Central Pollution Control Board— Functions only.*

INTERNAL ASSESSMENT

A minimum of three assignments are to be done during the year, as assigned by the teacher.

EVALUATION

The project work is to be evaluated by the subject teacher and by an External Examiner. The External Examiner shall be nominated by the Head of the school and may be a teacher from the faculty, **but not teaching the subject in the relevant section/class.** For example, a teacher of Commerce/Accounts of Class XI may be deputed to be the External Examiner for Class X Commercial Studies project work.

The Internal Examiner and the External Examiner will assess the candidate's work independently.

Award of marks **(20 Marks)**

Subject Teacher (Internal Examiner)   10 Marks

External Examiner   10 Marks

The total mark obtained out of 20 are to be sent to the Council by the Head of the school.

The Head of the school will be responsible for the online entry of marks on the Council's CAREERS portal by the due date.

CONTENTS

1. Stakeholders in Commercial Organisations — 9–22
2. Marketing: Meaning and Objectives — 23–29
3. Product and Service — 30–37
4. Pricing — 38–41
5. Advertising — 42–51
6. Sales Promotion — 52–55
7. Consumer Protection — 56–67
8. E-Commerce — 68–74
9. Capital and Revenue — 75–79
10. Final Accounts of a Sole trader — 80–101
11. Fundamental Concept of Costs — 102–110
12. Budgeting — 111–118
13. Sources of Finance — 119–125
14. Recruitment and Selection — 126–139
15. Training of Employees — 140–151
16. Industrial Relations and Trade Unions — 152–158
17. Social Security — 159–169
18. Logistics: An Overview — 170–172
19. Transportation — 173–182
20. Warehousing — 183–189
21. Insurance — 190–201
22. Banking — 202–215
23. Banking Transactions — 216–229
24. Financial Fraudulent Practices — 230–232
25. Government Initiatives in Environment Protection — 233–236

CHAPTER-01
Stakeholders in Commercial Organisations

STAKEHOLDERS

The term 'stakeholder' has been derived from the word 'stake', which means an interest or expected benefit. Stakeholders, therefore, refer to all those individuals, groups and institutions which have a stake in the functioning and performance of a commercial organisation or a business enterprise. A person is said to be a stakeholder when that person has an interest in the organisation, especially because he/she has invested money in it.

- *Meaning of Stakeholders*
- *Internal Stakeholders–employers, employees and shareholders*
- *External Stakeholders–suppliers, creditors, distributors, society and government.*
- *Difference between internal and external stakeholders.*
- *Expectations of Stakeholders—employers, employees, creditors, suppliers, government and society from a commercial organisation.*

Thus, stakeholders are the individuals or groups that are directly or indirectly affected by an organisation's decisions and actions. Stakeholders include owners/shareholders, employees, suppliers, distributors, general public, labour unions, financial institutions and government. Conventionally, the customers also come into the purview of stakeholders but in the contemporary competitive environment, the customers have the option to switch over to other organisations, thereby, remaining unaffected from organisation's action and decisions.

The primary task for any business today is to define its stakeholders and their expectations. Conventionally, most business organisations primarily thought of their owners/shareholders, *i.e.*, they were concerned only about the profits, applying the traditional rule of minimum investment and maximum return. In today's competitive business scenario, however, no business organisation can grow until and unless its stakeholders, *i.e.*, employees, suppliers, distributors, general public, labour unions, creditors, financial institutions and government are satisfied. Thus, if these stakeholders of an organisation, *e.g.*, Reliance Industries, are unhappy, Reliance cannot earn large profits for shareholders. Hence, it becomes rather mandatory for any business organisation today to atleast satisfy the minimum expectations of its stakeholders.

The organisation can deliver to any stakeholder a minimum level, a performance level or an extraordinary level of satisfaction. In setting these levels, the organisation must be careful not to violate the sense of fairness among stakeholders about the relative treatment they are getting.

There is a dynamic relationship connecting the stakeholder groups. A growing organisation caters to high level of employee satisfaction which leads employees to direct their energies towards continuous improvements, look for new breakthroughs and innovate. Consequently, higher quality services and products are produced which deliver higher degree of customer satisfaction. Customer satisfaction leads to repeated business which means growth and profits. This in return gives higher satisfaction to owners/shareholders. This cycles back and permits building a qualitative environment for employees. The same can be applied for suppliers, distributors, financial institutions, government, labour unions and general public.

The dynamic relationship mentioned above is shown below through diagram:

DISTINCTION BETWEEN STAKEHOLDERS AND SHAREHOLDERS

It should be understood that, stakeholder is a much wider term than shareholder. In a joint stock company, the persons and groups who have the shares of the company are known as shareholders. They contribute to the company's share capital and assume risk of loss. In addition to shareholders; customers, creditors, employees, government and others also have a stake in the company. All these are known as stakeholders.

The term shareholders is used only in connection with a joint stock company but the term stakeholders is used in connection with all business enterprises—sole proprietor-ship, partnership, joint stock company, etc.

DISTINCTION BETWEEN STAKEHOLDERS AND CUSTOMERS

As mentioned in the beginning of this chapter, if we look from conventional point of view, even the customer constitutes the stakeholders group. Any individual/group who is affected by the decisions of the organisation is a stakeholder. The customer is also affected by the decisions of the organisation but unlike other stakeholders, customer has wide options and can switch over to other product or organisation the very moment his/her interest is affected adversely, which is not very pleasing for suppliers, distributors, etc.

Basis of Distinction	Stakeholders	Customers
Financial Stake	As per meaning, stakeholders have a financial stake in a business firm.	Customers do not have financial stake in a business firm.

Basis of Distinction	Stakeholders	Customers
Supply of Capital	Human as well as financial capital is supplied by the stakeholders.	They do not supply any kind of capital to the organisation.
Risk Taking	They bear the risks of the organisation.	They do not bear the risk of the organisation.
Product and Market Orientation	Tastes of stakeholders do not influence the manufacturing of the products.	Products are manufactured according to the tastes of the customers. Therefore, market orientation is necessary to satisfy customers.
Sharing of Profits	They share profits in the form of interest, dividend, wages, salaries etc.	They do not share profits.
Participation in Management	Stakeholders, such as owners, participate in the management of an organisation.	They do not participate in the management of an organisation.

INTERNAL AND EXTERNAL STAKEHOLDERS

Stakeholders can be grouped as internal stakeholders and external stakeholders. Internal stakeholders are those groups or individuals which form the organisation themselves and these include employers, shareholders, owners, managers and employees. External stakeholders are those individuals or groups which are outside the organisation, such as suppliers, distributors, labour unions, creditors, general public and government.

Internal Stakeholders

1. Employers:
This group of stakeholders is constituted by the shareholders/owners and managers/board of directors. The decisions taken by the managers can affect the shareholders/owners and the managers themselves too. If the managers of any organisation decide to add a product to their range of products, it requires more money and it may prove fruitful or it may not. If it does not, definitely it will affect the profits of the organisation which will result in the loss to owners of the organisation and will also have a negative impact on other stakeholders. Similarly, the governing structure of public limited companies allows shareholders to influence a company by exercising their voting rights which again can affect the various stakeholders.

2. Employees:
An employee is an individual who is hired by an employer to do a specific job. The level of satisfaction of employees must be taken due care of, because it generates high morale and motivation. If the employees do not get proper remuneration, have poor working conditions or have inadequate social security; it will affect the

profitability of the organisation and can also create distress amongst employees which can be harmful for the public image of any organisation and can adversely affect the stakeholders including employees themselves.

3. Shareholders:
Shareholder is an individual who owns one or more equity shares of a particular company. Basically shareholders are partial owners of the company and hence, they are entitled to a certain share of the profit. This share of the profit is given to them on the pre-existing agreement depending on the increased valuation of the company's stock. As owners, shareholders can also incur losses when the company does. They may also have voting rights equal to the percentage of their ownership.

External Stakeholders

1. Suppliers:
Every organisation buys inputs, raw materials, services, energy, equipments and labour and uses them to produce output. What the organisation brings in from outside and what it does with what it brings in, will determine both the quality and the price of its final product. Organisations are, therefore, dependent upon suppliers and also, the suppliers are dependent upon organisations for orders. Any decision taken by the organisation can demotivate indigenous suppliers, deregulate the supply schedule, block their money and can affect them. On the other hand, any decision taken by the suppliers can affect the production process of an organisation.

2. Creditors and Financial Institutions:
Creditors and financial institutions disburse loans and advances to earn interest and hence, generate profit. These loans are given to the organisation keeping in view its past performance and future prospects. Any decisions taken by the organisation which reduces its cash flow, definitely affect the repayment of loans and payment of interest to creditors and financial institutions.

3. Distributors/Retailers:
Organisations require channels to distribute their product to the end user. This work is done by distributors and retailers. Any decision taken by the organisation can affect them. *For example*, if an organisation decides to open more outlets for its products or services in the same locality, it will adversely affect the existing retailers because their sales would be reduced. The same thing is true for the distributors.

4. Society:
Activities of organisations affect the society also, hence, every organisation has social responsibilities too. Organisations should not misuse natural resources. They should help in avoiding class conflicts, protect natural environment and should not engage in any kind of activity which proves detrimental to the interest of the general public. Taxes and duties paid by these organizations form a major part of government revenue, which is spent on public in providing basic amenities, social projects, etc. Thus, any decision taken by organisation can affect the society also.

5. Government:
It becomes the duty of any organisation to obey the rules laid down by the government, pay taxes and duties timely to the government and not to enter into

contracts with enemy countries through illegal channels. Hence, any decision taken by organisation can affect Government also.

From the above discussion, it is evident that any decision taken by the organisation can affect the stakeholders, which in turn affects the growth and profitability of the organisation itself. Due care should be taken of the expectations of internal as well as external stakeholders as they affect the growth, profitability and public image of an organisation.

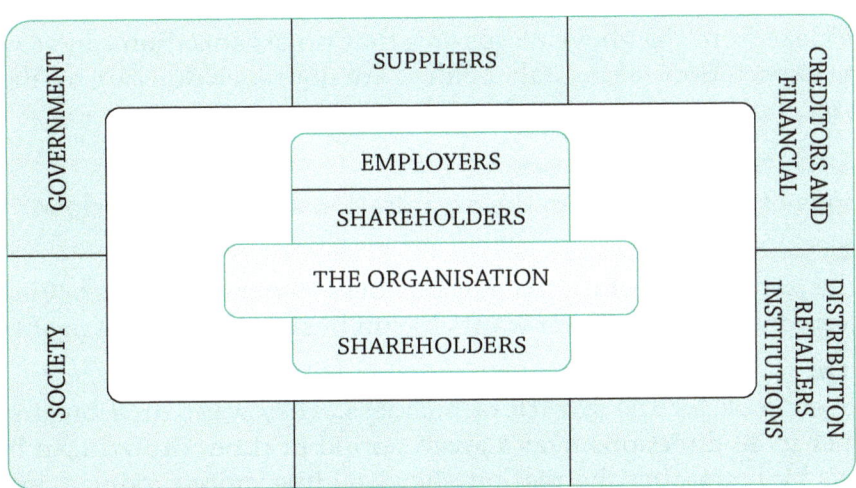

DIFFERENCE BETWEEN INTERNAL AND EXTERNAL STAKEHOLDERS

Owing to complexity of the business environment it is sometimes difficult to differentiate between an internal and an external stakeholder. However, the following table points out to the differences in detail:

Basis of Distinction	Internal Stakeholders	External Stakeholders
Nature	The individuals who are directly a part of the organisation are called internal stakeholders.	The parties or the groups who are not a part of the organisation but are affected by its activities, are called the external stakeholders.
Nature of Impact	Internal stakeholders have direct impact on the company.	External stakeholders have indirect impact on the company.
Who are They?	The people who serves the company.	The people who are affected by the functioning of the company.
Employed by the Entity?	Yes.	No.
Responsibility of the Company towards them	The company has primary responsibility towards internal stakeholders.	The company has secondary responsibility towards external stakeholders.

Basis of Distinction	Internal Stakeholders	External Stakeholders
Example	Employees, Owners, Board of Directors, Managers, etc.	Suppliers, creditors, customers, competitors, government and the society in general.

EXPECTATIONS OF STAKEHOLDERS

It is quite clear from the above discussion that no organisation can grow and earn profits if the expectations of its stakeholders are not taken due care of. Expectations of various stakeholders are discussed as follows:

(A) Expectations of Employers

Expectations of employers from the organisation are discussed below:

1. Profit:
Profit is the primary expectation of any business owner or manager. It is the reward of an entrepreneur. Every owner wants to run business and make profits.

2. Growth:
All employers look for the growth of business. They want their business to grow and prosper in all directions over a given period of time. Growth can be achieved in business by increasing the market share, adding more products, expansion of markets, cutting down of costs and increasing the productivity.

3. Market Leadership:
To become the leader of the market, is another expectation of employers. To attain a niche in the market, innovation is an important factor. Innovation may be in the field of advertising, finance, product etc.

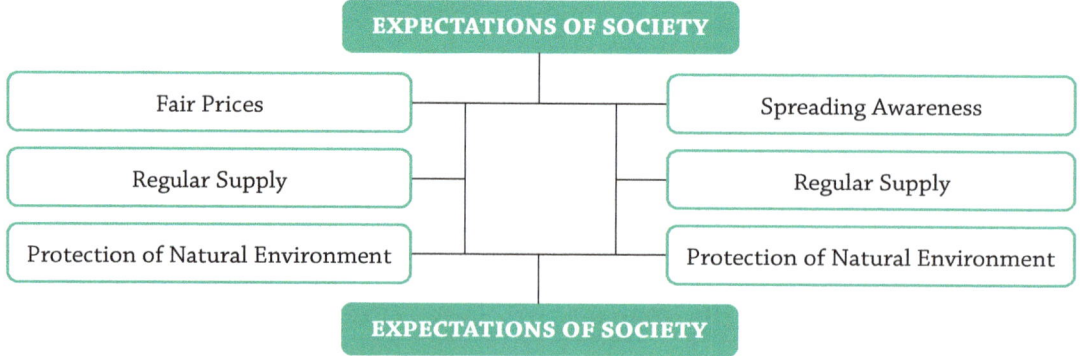

4. Expectations from Suppliers:
Owners and managers expect their suppliers to supply the goods regularly or whenever required, so that the production process is not hindered. They also expect suppliers to charge reasonable prices and sell goods to them (employers) on easy terms of credit.

5. Expectations from Employees:
Employers expect employees to be faithful to the organisation, so that the secrets of the organisation are not disclosed to the competitors. Employers expect serious and

devoted efforts from employees towards their work in return for the remuneration and services/amenities provided to them.

6. Expectations from Government:
Employers, *i.e.*, owners and managers expect government to formulate such policies which are favorable for the business environment. They expect that domestic industries be given cover in form of loans, subsidized technological import etc. to face the threat and competition from foreign companies or organisations. They expect the government to levy taxes in a manner which is not too harsh for the employers.

7. Expectations from Creditors:
Owners and managers expect creditors and financial institutions to grant loans and advances at reasonable rate of interest, *i.e.*, creditors should not take undue advantage of situation at the time of crisis of cash inflow.

(B) Expectations of Employees
Expectations of employees from the organisation are discussed below:

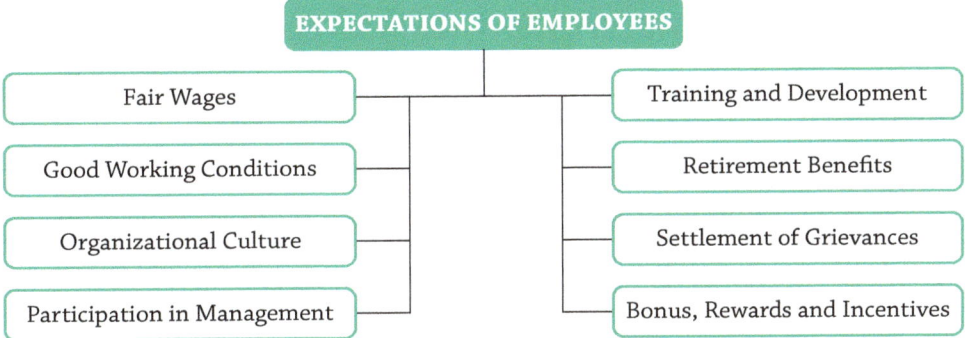

1. Fair Wages:
Employees of an organisation expect fair remuneration for the work done by them. If the workers or employees do not get salaries or wages proportionate to work done by them, their efficiency will be affected which in turn would result in lower product quality and disloyalty to the organisation in terms of continuity with the job. The moment the employee gets proper and better remuneration in some other organisation, he will leave his job from the present organisation.

2. Good Working Conditions:
Employees of an organisation expect their working conditions to be proper. It means, that the environment in which the employees work, should be such that they are able to work with their full potential. For example, the employee working in a shoe unit during summers with fan or cooler will have higher efficiency than the employee working without fan or cooler. Similarly, proper sitting place, canteen and water facilities should be provided to the employees. Employees also expect that immediate and proper treatment should be given to them at the time of accidents.

3. Organizational Culture:
Employees expect that the organizational ambiance and culture should be amicable. They expect that the relationship between boss and subordinate should not be

autocratic and imposed. If it is imposed, employees will work unwillingly and this will definitely affect their efficiency and quality of work.

4. Participation in Management:
Employees expect that their demands should be considered favorably. To communicate their demands to top level management or Board of Directors, they expect that a person (employee) representing them should hold a post on top level management.

5. Training and Development:
Employees dislike remaining stuck to the same position forever. Instead, they want themselves to go on to the superior position for which they require proper training. Employees expect the organisation to look into this need and make proper arrangements for their training and development. They also expect to get their due promotions.

6. Retirement Benefits:
Employees expect that once they are old and are retired from the job, there should be sufficient income for them in the form of pension, provident fund and gratuity to comfortably live the rest of their life. It is not only in case of retirement, but also in case of premature death of an employee. They expect that job on compensatory ground should be provided to their dependent so that the family members of deceased do not starve.

7. Settlement of Grievances:
Grievance means 'cause for complaints or annoyance'. Employees expect that their grievances are handled immediately with sincerity of purpose and an intention to resolve it. They expect that their grievances are resolved at the lowest admissible level so that it does not take far too long a time to get resolved.

8. Bonus, Rewards and Incentives:
Employees expect that any extra work will be properly rewarded by the organisation. Additionally, if organisation earns some extra profits, it would be shared with them as bonus.

(C) Expectations of Suppliers

Expectations of suppliers from the organisation are discussed below:

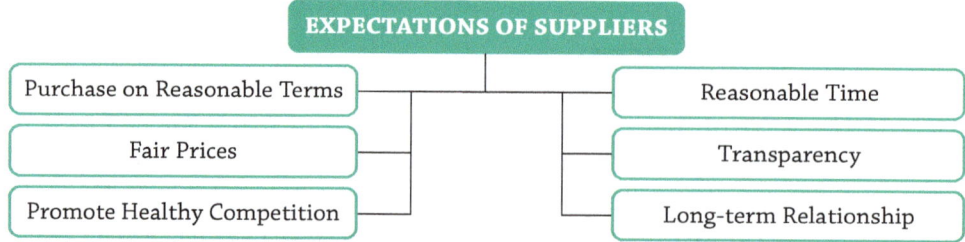

1. Purchase on Reasonable Terms:
Suppliers expect that the organisation is going to make purchases from them on reasonable terms, *i.e.*, if the supplier is new to the organisation he would not be exploited in terms of prices, proper time will be given to him to deliver the goods and favorable treatment will be given to the supplier during period of shortages.

2. Fair Prices:
Seller always expect cost plus profit from the buyer, same is the case with suppliers. They expect that any organisation purchasing goods from them will pay fair price and will not take any undue advantage due to the competition prevailing in the market amongst suppliers.

3. Promote Healthy Competition:
The primary objective of any business organisation is to earn profit. Profit can be increased either by cutting down the costs or by increasing the selling price. Later is not possible in today's competitive environment, thus, every business organisation wants to purchase at minimum price. To buy at the lowest price, every organisation negotiates with the different suppliers available in the market and opts for the one who supplies the required quality and quantity of goods at minimum price and on reasonable terms. At the same time, the suppliers expect that the organisation is going to promote healthy competition amongst different suppliers and does not mislead any supplier for their own advantage.

4. Reasonable Time:
The processing of order consumes time as the goods have to be given finishing touch and packed, before they are delivered to the buyer. Sometimes, in period of shortages, supplier has to arrange for the goods too. Thus, supplier expects that reasonable time should be given to them by the organisation for the supply of goods.

5. Transparency:
Suppliers want that the dealings between them and the organisation should be clear in terms of payment, time of the delivery of goods, quality of goods, quantity of goods and treatment of defective material, etc., so that no dispute arises later at the time of payment.

6. Long-term Relationship:
Suppliers expect long term relationship with the organization, so that they can have business for the longer period with them. Good relations with the organisation also help suppliers in avoiding any disputes regarding defective goods, financial matters or otherwise.

(D) Expectations of Creditors or Financial Institutions
Expectations of creditors or financial institutions from the organisation are discussed below:

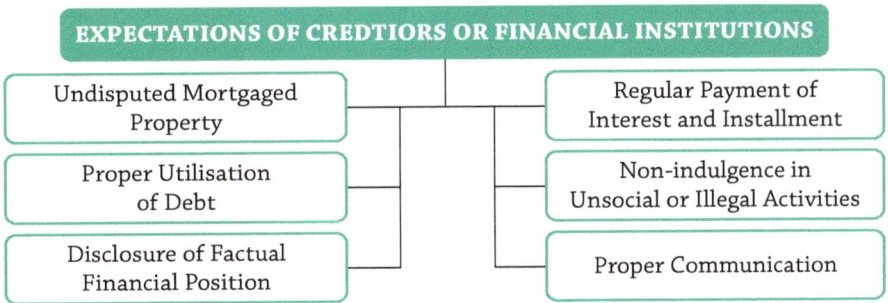

1. Undisputed Mortgaged Property:
Loan or credit given by the creditors or financial institutions is secured by some asset of the organisation. In other words, if organisation is unable to repay the loan to the creditor, creditor can sell out the pledged property and recover the dues. Thus, creditors expect that the property or assets pledged with them by the organisation does not have any dispute regarding its ownership.

2. Proper Utilisation of Debt:
Creditors or financial institutions expect that the debts raised by them will be used for the purpose stated. If it is misutilised, *i.e.*, it is used for some other or personal purposes, it would have an adverse impact on the business of organisation which would in turn affect the repayment schedule, which is not in favour of creditors or financial institutions.

3. Disclosure of Factual Financial Position:
Creditors expect that any organisation approaching them for credit, is going to disclose its factual financial position and is not going to portray fake image with the help of vague documents for the purpose of obtaining loan or credit. Thus, the documents or account statements submitted by the organisation should be real and not manipulated.

4. Regular Payment of Interest and Installment:
Creditors expect that the organisation to whom they have given credit, will make payment of interest and installment on due date so that regularity of cash inflows is maintained and they can further rotate that money.

5. Non-indulgence in Unsocial or Illegal Activities:
Creditors or financial institutions who lend the money to the organisation expect that the organisation is not going to engage in any unsocial or illegal activities because if it does so, it will have an adverse impact on business and it will not be in favour of creditors and financial institutions.

6. Proper Communication:
Financial institutions and creditors expect that the financial position of the organisation will be communicated to them periodically so that they can plan for the future credits and repayments accordingly.

(E) Expectations of Society
Expectations of society from the organisation are discussed below:

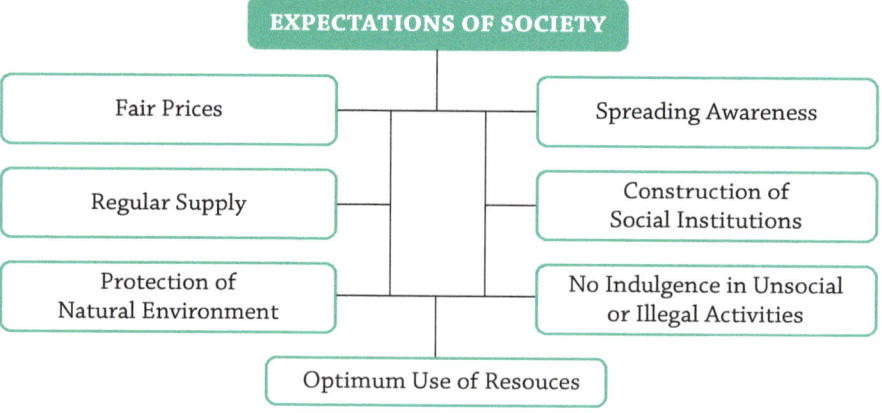

1. Fair Prices:
Society expects that goods will be supplied to them at fair prices. They expect that organisations producing the same product will not make a pool and charge higher prices from the customers.

2. Regular Supply:
Hoarding of goods leads to black marketing. Thus, public expects that the goods will be supplied to them regularly and no artificial shortage will be created in the market.

3. Protection of Natural Environment:
Profit maximisation is the primary objective of any organisation but public expects that during the attainment of their primary objectives, organisations do not destroy the natural environment and rather work for the protection of the environment.

4. Spreading Awareness:
Society expects that the organisation should spread awareness about its product amongst public and also inform public about the advantages and disadvantages of using that particular product. They should also inform public for whom their product is useful and for whom it is not.

5. Construction of Social Institutions:
Although profit maximisation is the primary objective of any business organisation but the society expects that organisations who are earning heavy profits will construct social institutions, such as old age homes, orphanages and rehabilitation centers for the use of public.

6. No Indulgence in Unsocial or Illegal Activities:
Unsocial or illegal products and activities will have negative impact on the growth of nation and its citizen. Thus, society expects that business organisations do not manufacture such products which are harmful for the society and refrain from engaging themselves in such activities which are detrimental to the health and image of society, for example, drug trafficking.

7. Optimum Use of Resources:
Society expects that the organisation is going to make optimum use of resources and will promote the research environment so that better quality goods at cheaper rates will be made available to the public.

(F) Expectations of Government
Expectations of government from the organisation are discussed below:

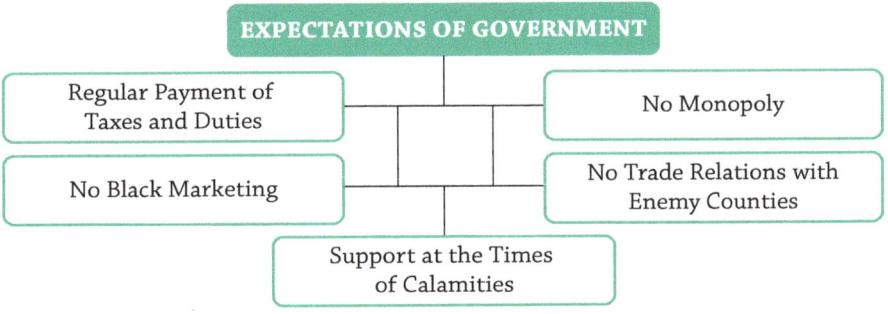

1. Regular Payment of Taxes and Duties:
Revenue generated by the government in form of taxes and duties is spent by it on the social welfare and defence of the country. Thus, government expects that business organisations pay the taxes and duties regularly and do not try to evade them.

2. No Black Marketing:
Many organisations stock the goods and do not supply to the public at normal prices, due to which an artificial shortage is created in the market. These goods are supplied to consumers at higher prices through black markets, which is an illegal activity. Thus, government expects that organisations do not themselves indulge in such black marketing of goods.

3. No Monopoly:
Government expects that any business organisation in the course of its business should not gain monopoly and exploit the customers. Although government has established Competition Commission of India to check unfair and monopolistic trade practices, it expects organisations not to concentrate economic powers which are detrimental to social interests.

4. No Trade Relations with Enemy Countries:
Government expects that business organisation should not engage themselves in trade with the enemy countries through any channel. Developing trade relations with enemy countries is neither desirable nor expected.

5. Support at the Times of Calamities:
At the time of natural calamities, government expects organisation to join hands with it and help the residents of the affected area to overcome the disaster. Earthquake of Gujarat is a recent example where many business and social organisations joined hands with the government and helped the people of affected areas.

Lesson at a Glance

- **Stakeholders:** Stakeholders are the individuals or groups that are directly or indirectly affected by an organisation's decisions and actions. They include owners/shareholders, employees, suppliers, distributors, general public, labour union, creditors, financial institutions and government.
- **Internal and External Stakeholders:** Internal stakeholders are the individuals or groups which themselves form the organisation and include (i) Employers (shareholders, owners, managers); (ii) Employees, (iii) Shareholders. The external stakeholders are the individuals or groups which are outside the organisation and include : (i) Suppliers; (ii) Creditors and Financial institutions; (iii) Distributors / Retailers; (iv) Society; (v) Government.
- **Distinction between Internal and External Stakeholders:** (i) Nature; (ii) Nature of Impact; (iii) Who are they ?; (iv) Employed by the entity; (v) Responsibility of the company towards them; (vi) Examples.

Stakeholders in Commercial Organisations

- **Expectations of Stakeholders:**
  - ***Expectations of Employers:*** (i) Profit; (ii) Growth; (iii) Market leadership; (iv) Expectations from suppliers; (v) Expectations from employees; (vi) Expectations from government; (vii) Expectations from creditors.
  - ***Expectations of Employees:*** (i) Fair wages; (ii) Good working conditions; (iii) Organisational culture; (iv) Participation in management; (v) Training and development; (vi) Retirement benefits; (vii) Settlement of grievances; (viii) Bonus, rewards and incentives.
  - ***Expectations of Suppliers :*** (i) Purchase on reasonable terms; (ii) Fair prices; (iii) Promote healthy competition; (iv) Reasonable time; (v) Transparency; (vi) Long-term relationship.
  - ***Expectations of Creditors or Financial Institutions:*** (i) Undisputed mortgaged property; (ii) Proper utilisation of debt; (iii) Disclosure of factual financial position; (iv) Regular payment of interest and installments; (v) Non-indulgence in unsocial or illegal activities; (vi) Proper communication.
  - ***Expectations of Society:*** (i) Fair prices; (ii) Regular supply; (iii) Protection of natural environment; (iv) Spreading awareness; (v) Construction of social institutions; (vi) No indulgence in unsocial or illegal activities; (vii) Optimum use of resources.
  - ***Expectations of Government:*** (i) Regular payment of taxes and duties; (ii) No black marketing; (iii) No monopoly; (iv) No trade relations with enemy countries; (v) Support at the times of calamities.

Project Work

Visit a manufacturing organisation in your nearby area. Choose two persons each from employers, employees, suppliers, creditors, general public and taxation authorities and find out their expectations from the organisation. Prepare a report and justify whether their expectations are worth consideration or otherwise. Give suitable reasons to explain, how these expectations are beneficial to organization, if same are duly cared for.

Assignments

1. Your friend was absent on the day when your teacher taught you the meaning of term stakeholder and its importance. Now your friend is asking you to explain the same to him. How are you going to do it?
2. Your neighbour argues on the point that customer is also a stakeholder. How will you explain to him the basic difference between stakeholder and customer?
3. You have studied the various expectations of internal and external stakeholders. How will you explain the same in the class?

A. **Short Answer Type Questions:**
   1. Distinguish between internal and external stakeholders.
   2. What do you mean by stakeholders?
   3. Name two types of internal stakeholders.
   4. State any two types of external stakeholders.
   5. Give any three expectations of employers from the organisation.
   6. Give any three expectations of employees from the organisation.
   7. Give any three expectations of creditors from the organisation.
   8. State any three expectations of society from the organisation.
   9. Give any three expectations of government from the organisation.
   10. Distinguish between stakeholders and customers.
   11. Mention any two expectations of suppliers from a business organisation.
   12. State any two expectations of shareholders from a business concern. [ICSE 2017]
   13. Distinguish between internal and external stakeholders. [ICSE 2020]

B. **Essay Type Questions:**
   1. Discuss the various types of Internal and External stakeholders.
   2. State any five expectations of employers from a business enterprises. [ICSE 2019]
   3. State any five expectations of employees from a business organisation. [ICSE 2020]
   4. Explain the various expectations which creditors have from the organisation.
   5. "With profits, social welfare should also be considered." Enumerate this statement with reference to the expectations of society.
   6. Describe in detail the difference between the internal and external stakeholder.
   7. Explain the conflicting needs of the stakeholders of a company.
   8. Explain any five expectations of Suppliers from a business organisation. [ICSE 2018]
   9. Explain expectations of the Government from a business organisation. [ICSE 2017]

CHAPTER-02
Marketing: Meaning and Objectives

MARKET

The term market appears to have its origin from the Latin word 'Marcatus', which means a place where business is conducted, buyers and sellers come together to facilitate exchange and by means of which the prices of goods tend to be equalized easily and quickly.

Traditionally market has been expressed from the point of view of a specific place, but with time the concept of market has evolved. Following are the various concepts on which, a market can be defined:

- Meaning of Market
- Meaning of Marketing
- Definitions of Marketing
- Traditional and Modern View of Marketing
- Features of Marketing
- Objectives of Marketing
- Meaning of Sales
- Difference between Marketing and Sales.

Place Concept:
To any common person a market means a specific place where buyers and sellers meet and complete the transactions of goods and services in exchange of a certain price. The buyer gets both ownership and physical possession of the products once the payment is being made to the seller.

Area Concept:
A market may be viewed as a geographical region where buyers and sellers can establish continuous business relations for the exchange of goods and services through various means of communication. It is because of the availability of fast means of communication that the price of a commodity tends to be same throughout the entire area or region.

There is free interplay of the forces of demand and supply throughout the region leading to almost the same price in all places in the particular region. The region may be small or large. For instance, the entire world is a market for BMW cars, whereas India is the market for Tata Nano.

Demand Concept:
According to the demand concept the mere existence of demand for a product or service constitutes a market. This viewpoint emphasizes the demand of consumers. The size of the market is determined by consumers' demand and their willingness to pay. The greater the demand for a product, the larger will be its market. Consequently if the demand, for certain product, shrinks, then the market also shrinks.

- *"A market means any body of persons who are in intimate business relations and can carry extensive transactions in any commodity."* —Prof. Jevons
- *"In fact the market must be thought of not as a geographical meeting place but as any getting together of buyers and sellers in person by Mail, Telephone, Telegraph or any other means of communication."* —H.E. Mitchell

- *"It is a center about which, or an area in which the forces leading to exchanges of titles to a particular product operate and towards which and from which the actual goods tend to travel."* —Clark and Clark
- *"A market is the set of all actual and potential buyers of a product."* —Philip Kotler

Thus, based on these definitions, it can be said that, market is the sum total of the situation or environment in which the resources, activities and attitudes of buyers and sellers affect the demand for products in a given area. It should be clearly understood that the term market means a place where buyers and sellers come together in person by mail, telephone, telegraph, cable, fax or any other means of communication.

MARKETING

Marketing is a process of buying and selling of products and services in exchange of consideration to satisfy the consumer's needs. It consists of all those activities that a seller undertakes, in order to ensure that a company is able to sell the product at a price that gives them adequate profit in returns.

Today, marketing is regarded as the most important of all management functions in any business organisation. Goods and Services cannot be sold by merely producing them, but they have to move from place of production to customers for consumption. In the modern world, producers are bound to be consumer oriented because customers have a wide range of products and brands to which they can switch which gives them the utmost satisfaction, *i.e.*, the product has to be developed according to the needs and wants of the customer. Thus, marketing involves development of products or services according to the needs of the customer and then moving them from place of production to place of consumption profitably, to satisfy customer wants.

- *"Marketing includes all activities involved in the creation of place, time and possession utility."* —Converse, Huegey and Mitchell
- *"Marketing consists of those activities which effect transfers in ownership of goods and care for their physical distribution."* —F.E. Clark
- *"Marketing is the performance of business activities that direct the flow of goods and services from producer to consumer or user".* —American Marketing Association
- *"Marketing is the economic process by means of which goods and services are exchanged and their values are determined in terms of money prices."* —Dudhey and Reizan

There are two approaches to marketing–traditional (product oriented) and modern (consumer oriented).

TRADITIONAL AND MODERN VIEW OF MARKETING

Traditional View

In olden time, marketing was defined as the flow of goods from the producers to the consumers. This is a product-oriented definition of marketing. The process of marketing began after the process of production. The producers concentrated on what they could produce and sell. The needs of the customers were not taken into consideration. The product-oriented definition is based on the assumption that whatever is produced is bound to be sold.

Modern View

Consumer-Orientation is the modern concept of marketing. It analyses the needs of the customers and then produce goods that strive to meet their needs. According to J.F. Pyle,"Marketing is that phase of business activity through which human wants are satisfied by the exchange of goods and services." This definition takes into consideration the satisfaction of human wants. It emphasises the determination and the satisfaction of the requirements of potential customers which take precedence over production.

The customer oriented marketing involves 'selling of satisfaction' rather than 'selling a product'.

Business must produce what the consumers want, in the quantity and quality they desire, at a price they are willing to pay, at the time they need and through the channels most convenient to them.

- *"Marketing is a total system of interacting business activities designed to plan, price, promote and distribute wants satisfying products and services to present and potential customers."* —Stanton

FEATURES OF MARKETING

1. Customer Oriented:
Marketing is a customer oriented activity. Every business depends on human needs. It identifies the need of the customers and then produce accordingly. In a competitive market, the goods that are best suited to the customer are the ones that are well-accepted. Hence, marketing focuses on customer-orientation.

2. Consumer Satisfaction:
Customer satisfaction is one of the main features of marketing. The aim should be maximization of profit through customer satisfaction. The consumers get pleased when product performance matches with customer expectation. When product performance is below customer expectation, the customers are dissatisfied. When product performance exceeds customer expectation, the customers are delighted.

3. Marketing is both Art and Science:
Science is the systematic body of knowledge, based on fact and principles and Art is the application of that knowledge. The concept of marketing includes both. The principles of marketing are based on certain facts and the application of those principles is an art.

4. Objective-Oriented:
All marketing activities are objective-oriented. The main objective is to earn profit through satisfaction of consumers' needs and wants.

5. Continuous and Regular Activity:
Marketing is a continuous and regular activity which starts with identification of human wants. It does not merely end on sales. Its demand to be continued after the selling process in the form of after sales services. It addresses both the actual and potential consumers. Thus, it is a continuous process.

6. Exchange Process:
Marketing is an exchange process. Exchange takes place between sellers and buyers. Buyer gets goods and services in exchange of money and seller gets money in exchange of goods and services.

7. Marketing Mix:

A marketing mix is a combination of 4 Ps *i.e.*, product, price, place and promotion. It is the flexible combination of variables influenced by consumer behavior, trade cycle, government and other important factors.

OBJECTIVES OF MARKETING

The objectives of marketing can be discussed as below:

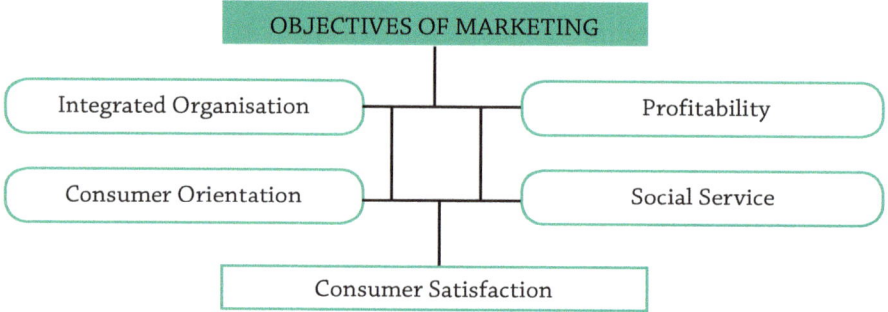

1. Integrated Organisation:

Integrated organisation means that all the different departments of organisation, *i.e.*, production, finance, purchase and planning must be tightly integrated with each other, keeping marketing at the centre. This is important because every function of organisation has an impact on customer and the objective should be to see that all the functions lead to a favourable impression on customer. For this to happen, all the departments have to be integrated and consequently orient themselves towards customer satisfaction.

2. Consumer Orientation:

In the words of Peter F. Drucker, "The purpose of any business is to create a customer. It is the customer who determines what a business is. It is the customer and he alone, who being willing to pay for a good or service, converts economic resources into wealth and things into goods. What a business thinks it produces is not of first importance—especially not to the future of the business and to its success. What the customer thinks he is buying–what he considers value, is decisive; it determines what a business is, what it produces and whether it will prosper." Thus, it can be concluded that a customer does not buy whatever the producer produces but the producer produces whatever the consumer needs. Therefore, the first objective of marketing is consumer orientation.

3. Profitability:

Business organisation is an economic institution which is set up for earning profits and not for charity. Thus, one of the main objectives of marketing is to maximise profits with minimum investment but it should not be carried out at the expense of consumer satisfaction. Therefore, marketing seeks both–obtaining commitment and building relationships.

4. Social Service:

The other objective of marketing is social orientation. Only those goods and services should be marketed which are environment friendly, useful to the consumer and enhance the standard of living. Reasonable prices should be charged for qualitative goods and services. Marketing should also provide opportunities for employment and should not deceive by carrying restrictive, monopolistic and unfair trade practices.

5. Consumer Satisfaction:

Mere consumer orientation does not fulfill the objective of marketing. Consumer orientation along with an integrated organisation leads to consumer satisfaction. This is also one of the most important objectives of marketing. In today's market, no organisation can even think to ignore the satisfaction of consumers.

SALES

'Sale' is a direct transaction happening between two parties–the buyer and the seller. The buyer receives the goods, which can be either tangible or intangible (in case of a service) and in exchange he/she offers the seller an agreed price. Sale is nothing but a contract between the buyer and the seller.

While both sales and marketing are aimed at increasing the revenue of the firm, there are certain basic differences which demarcate the concepts. In certain small or medium scale companies, it is usually the same group of employees who manage sales and marketing functions. However, the underlying concepts of both marketing and sales are quite different.

Selling Concept

According to the selling concept, customers would not act upon by themselves if not persuaded to purchase. The idea behind the concept is that the companies, no matter how much marketing they do, need to give the final push of sales to make the customers buy the product or the service. Despite producing good quality of products and providing good service many companies fail to generate substantial profit. For that reason selling concept is being created. The concept believes that the customers will only buy the products by means of sales promotion efforts. Or to put it simply, consumers will not make the final purchase with their own initiative. The company needs to make the final push to convince the customers to buy the products or services.

Features of Selling

1. Selling Orientation:
Here the focus is not on the consumers but rather on the seller. It believes that the product or service should be sold at any cost.

2. Aggressive Selling and Promotion:
The selling concept encourages the use of aggressive selling strategies to encourage the customers to buy the product.

3. Not Focused on Consumers:
The selling concept is not focused on the consumers' needs and wants and rather they concentrate on the number of products that needs to be sold.

4. Consumer Persuasion:
The selling concept only focuses on persuading the customers to make the purchase. It does not necessarily take into account customer's needs and wants.

Difference Between Marketing and Sales

Basis of Difference	Marketing	Sales
Definition	Marketing is the process of systematic planning and implementation of the business activities aimed at increasing sales.	Sales is just the transaction happening between two parties in the form of buyer and seller.
Approach	Marketing encompasses a wide range of approaches including product design, pricing, sales promotion, advertising, understanding consumer need and many more.	Sales include the interactions and the transactions happening at the end of the marketing cycle.
Focus	The entire focus of marketing is to deliver the product or service in demand at a competitive price and generate maximum revenue from it.	The focus of sales is to achieve as many transactions as possible, in a given time period.
Process	The process of marketing involves the analysis of market needs, understanding the consumer behaviour, and setting up price for the product along with many other things.	It only involves a one-to-one interaction between the sales person and the buyer.
Scope	Scope of marketing is very wide which includes, Market research; Advertising; Sales; Public relations; Customer service and satisfaction.	Persuading the customers to buy the product or service and help them fulfill their requirements.
Horizon	Long Term	Short Term
Strategy	Pull	Push
Priority	Priority of marketing is to reach out to more and more consumers and maintain a healthy relationship.	Sales is the ultimate result of marketing.
Creations	Marketing creates specific brand identity for the product/service or for the company as a whole.	Sales does not necessarily create brand identity but it focuses on meeting the customer requirement at a given point of time.

Lesson at a Glance

- **Market:** Market is the whole or any region in which buyers and sellers are brought into contact with one another and by means of which the prices of goods tend to be equalized easily and quickly.

Marketing: Meaning and Objectives

- **Marketing:** Marketing involves development of products or services according to the needs of the customer and then moving them from the place of production to the place of consumption profitably to satisfy the wants of the customer. According to William J. Stanton, "Marketing is a total system of interacting business activities designed to plan, price, promote and distribute want satisfying products and services to present and potential customer."

There are two approaches to marketing–traditional approach (product-oriented) and modern approach (consumer oriented).

- **Features of Marketing:** (i) Customer oriented; (ii) Consumer satisfaction; (iii) Marketing is both art and science; (iv) Objective oriented; (v) Continuous and regular activity; (vi) Exchange Process; (vii) Marketing Mix.
- **Objectives of Marketing:** (i) Integrated organisation; (ii) Consumer orientation; (iii) Profitability; (iv) Social service; (v) Consumer satisfaction.
- **Sale:** Sale is any transaction taking place between two parties the buyer and the seller, where the buyer receives the goods or services in exchange for money.
- **Difference between Marketing and Sales:** (i) Definition; (ii) Approach; (iii) Focus; (iv) Process; (iv) Scope; (vi) Horizon; (vii) Strategy; (viii) Priority; (ix) Creations.

Select a company of your own choice and find out the marketing activities performed by that company to promote its products.

Your friend was absent in class when your teacher taught objectives of marketing. Explain to him/her the same.

A. **Short Answer Type Questions:**
   1. Define marketing.
   2. Give any three objectives of marketing.
   3. State any four features of marketing.
   4. How does marketing ensure consumer satisfaction?
   5. State two differences between marketing and sales?
   6. Define the word 'Sales'.
   7. How are Marketing and Sales related?
   8. Distinguish between marketing and sales. [ICSE 2019]

B. **Essay Type Questions:**
   1. What do you mean by marketing? Give its definitions.
   2. Define marketing and state its main objectives.
   3. Discuss social service as one of the main objectives of marketing.
   4. Give at least six points of difference between marketing and sales.
   5. Explain any five objectives of marketing. [ICSE 2020]
   6. Briefly explain the importance of marketing. [ICSE 2018]

CHAPTER-03
Product and Service

PRODUCT AND ITS CLASSIFICATION

The term "product" refers to any object or service that is capable of being created and sold at a price and which serves human need or satisfies a want. In short, a product is any commodity or service, offered for sale. It can be in physical or virtual form. Thus, a product has a combination of tangible and intangible benefits, features, functions, and uses. It is because of these attributes that the customer buys the product. Examples of tangible products are bathing soap, shirt, a can of soft-drink, etc. Intangible products or better known as "services" can be in the form of medical advice from a doctor, or legal advice from a lawyer.

- Meaning of Product
- Classification of Products
- Characteristics of Product
- Meaning of Service
- Classification of Services
- Characteristics of Service
- Difference between Product and Service

A product can range from being a high-end customized offer like Ferrari Cars to very generic merchandise like detergent soap. From the sophisticated patio furniture set to the toothpaste you use–everything falls under the definition of a product. Services are also sometimes highly customized to individual needs, like a legal service or a doctor treating a patient. But just like products, in many other occasions it is generic and catering to the need of the mass. Movies shown in a movie theatre is a good example of generic services or for that matter, electric supply provided at your home.

The products can broadly be classified on the basis of three factors which are as follows:
(A) Durability, (B) Consumer Products, (C) Industrial Products.

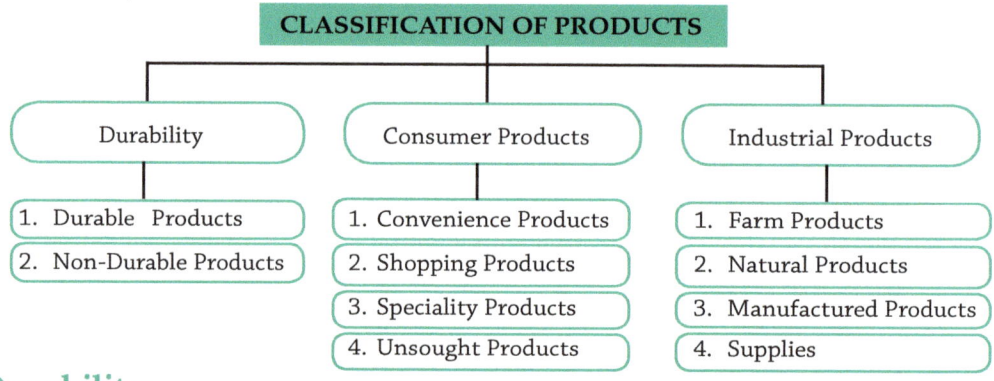

(A) Durability

According to durability, products can be classified into two categories:

1. Durable Products:
The products which are tangible and can be used repeatedly many a times, are termed as durable goods. For example, television, refrigerator, clothes, machines etc.

2. Non-Durable Products:
The products which are tangible and perish within one or few uses, are termed as non-durable products. For example, salt, pepper, soap etc.

(B) Consumer Products
According to consumer's shopping habits, products can be classified into following categories:

1. Convenience Products:
These products which are purchased frequently, and immediately and with minimum efforts, are known as convenience products. For example, newspaper, toothpaste, washing detergent, cigarette, tobacco etc.

2. Shopping Products:
The products which customer purchases less frequently and after careful comparison, on the basis of suitability, quality, price and style, are known as shopping products. For example, major appliances, clothing, furniture, cars etc.

3. Speciality Products:
Those products that have brand identification or unique characteristics are known as specialty products. Buyers for these goods generally spend more time seeking the product they want than on comparing brands. For examples, cars, stereos, television etc.

4. Unsought Products:
Those consumer products that are either not known to the consumers or even if they are known, customers generally do not have compelling impulse to buy them, are known as unsought products. For example–Life insurance, blood donation etc.

(C) Industrial Products
Those products that are purchased for further processing or for use in operating a business are called industrial products. They can be classified as:

1. Farm Products:
Products which are produced on farms and supplied as raw material to different organisations, are termed as farm products. For example, wheat, cotton, livestock, vegetables, fruits etc.

2. Natural Products:
Products which are gift of nature, are termed as natural products. For example, crude oil, fish, timber, iron-ore etc.

3. Manufactured Products:
The products which have been manufactured but still, are used as products for further industrial use, are known as manufactured products. For example, pig-iron is converted in steel and then steel is further used for making bars, utensils etc.

4. Supplies:
Any short-term good or material which is necessary for the day-to-day operations of a business is termed as supplies. Supplies are of two types–operating (*e.g.*, lubricants, coal, typing paper, etc.) and maintenance (*e.g.*, paint, nails, brooms etc.).

CHARACTERISTICS OF PRODUCT

From the categories mentioned above, we now know that the products can be of different shapes and sizes, catering to the different needs of the consumers. However, some of the features are generic for all the products and are listed below:

Physical configuration | Mobility | Associated Services | Packaging and Branding | Life-Cycle | Storability | Medium of Communication | Exchange Value

1. Physical Configuration:
A product can be seen, has bulk or mass and can be felt. These features define the dimension of a product and it is one of the most basic features all products have, irrespective of the usage it possesses.

2. Mobility:
A product has to be manufactured, can be stored and physically transported from the point of production to the point of sale. Thus it acquires utility of place.

3. Associated Services:
Products are often associated with certain services. Starting from simpler services like providing a "user manual" (before-sale service) to the consumer to actual installation of the product, (after-sale service) all fall under the concept of associated service. For instance the periodical and maintenance service of a water purifier can be cited as a good example.

4. Packaging and Branding:
The packaging is considered as a part of a product. It is packaging and branding that differentiates a product from its competing products. The packaging also determines the size of each unit to be sold along with the price of the product. We can determine and differentiate the price of a 500 gm Amul butter packet from a 500 gm of Britania butter packet on the basis of packaging and branding.

5. Life-Cycle:
Every product has its life cycle, which can be determined at some stage of its existence. The life-cyle of a product consists of introduction in the market, growth, maturity and decline (*i.e.*, a fall in its sales). Life-cycle has its own importance for the manufacturers and customers.

6. Storability:
All tangible goods can be stored over a period of time. However, this feature is only applicable for non-perishable products. Though perishable products can also be stored but only for a limited time period.

7. Medium of Communication:
Every product speaks about itself, what it is made up of, what uses it can be put to, who has manufactured it, where it is available etc. Thus, a product is a medium of communication also.

8. Exchange Value:
Each product has a exchange value, which means its value can be measured in terms of money.

SERVICE AND ITS CLASSIFICATION

A service is any act or performance that one party can offer to another. It is essentially intangible and does not result in the ownership of anything. Its production may or may not be tied to any physical product. Products themselves sometime do not satisfy customer's need but it is the service which they render that provides satisfaction to the customer. For instance, if you have to go to school by bicycle, bicycle, being a product, does not provide you the desired satisfaction by itself. Rather, it is the service of transportation, which it renders, provides satisfaction to you.

Services can be broadly classified into four categories, which are as follows:

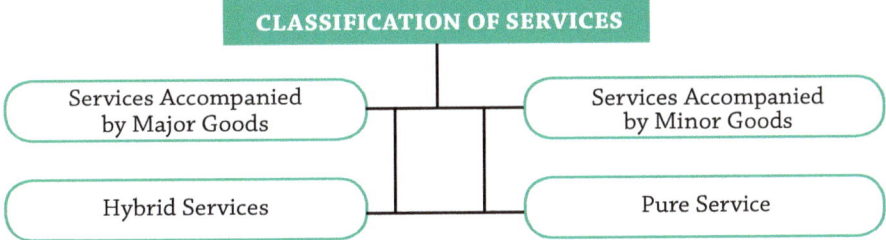

1. Service Accompanied by Major Goods:
When tangible product is accompanied by one or more services to enhance its consumer appeal, it is known as service accompanied by major goods. For example, when Maruti Ltd., along with the car, promises three free services and one year warranty, these free services and one year warranty are the services which are accompanied by the major product, *i.e.*, car.

2. Hybrid Services:
These types of services are not separable from the product itself, *i.e.*, they consist of equal part of goods as well as the services. For example, if one goes to the Restaurant, he gets both product (food) and service (waiters etc.).

3. Service Accompanied by Minor Goods:
When tangible minor product is supplied along with the service, it is known as service accompanied by minor goods. For example, when a passenger travels through aeroplane, he buys transportation services but the service include provision of food, drinks and magazines which are the minor products.

4. Pure Service:
A service in which no tangible product is given along with, is known as pure service. For example, in psychotherapy, the psycho-analyst only provides service, no product is accompanied along with it.

Characteristics of Service

Following are the characteristics of service:

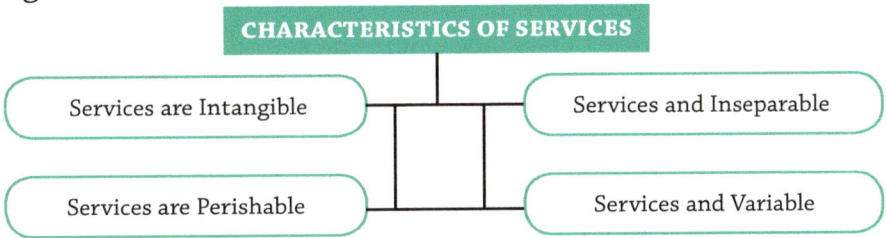

1. Services are Intangible:
This means they cannot be felt, seen, or heard before they are purchased. They are abstract and invisible.

2. Services are Perishable:
Services cannot be produced and kept in inventory. Thus, they are perishable, they cannot be produced ahead of time and stocked for the periods of peak load of demand. They can only be delivered at the time of consumption.

3. Services are Inseparable:
With customer participation in the process, services are typically produced and consumed at the time of its production. That means services are produced and consumed at the same time. Products are first produced and then they are sold, whereas, services are generally first sold and then they are produced and consumed at the same time.

4. Services are Variable:
Services are not always standardised and uniform in very clear terms. It is often impossible to assure consistencies in the services provided by a seller or to standardise offerings among the sellers of the same service while it is possible to offer consistencies and uniformities in case of products.

DIFFERENCE BETWEEN PRODUCT AND SERVICE

Product can be differentiated from services on the following grounds:

1. Tangibility:
Products are tangible, *i.e.*, they can be felt, seen, tasted, heard or smelled before they are purchased, whereas, services are intangible, *i.e.*, they cannot be felt, seen, tasted or smelled before they are purchased. For example, a person wants to purchase a car. He/she can feel, and see the car before purchase but a person going for a massage to the parlour, cannot feel the result before getting the massage done.

2. Separability:
Products are separable, *i.e.*, products are manufactured, put into inventory, then through channel of distribution they reach the ultimate consumer. Thus, product is separable but this is not true in case of services, they are produced and consumed simultaneously. For example, a car is manufactured, put into inventory, distributed through their showrooms and then it is purchased by the customer but when a person travels by aeroplane, services of aeroplane (transportation) can only be taken while it is flying, thus, it is inseparable.

3. Variability:
Services are highly variable but products are not. Quality of service depends on the quality of the service provider, the place where the service is provided and the time. These factors cause variation in the quality of service provided. This, however, is not the case with tangible products. For example, if a patient wants to get his liver transplanted, the services given by a hospital situated in Delhi, which is equipped with all modern amenities for doing so, will be quite different from a hospital situated in rural areas of India.

4. Perishability:

Products can be stored whereas, services cannot be stored. Thus, products are not immediately perishable but services are. If a showroom keeps twenty scooters for sale during one month and they are not sold, they don't perish. But if a passenger bus has to carry fifty passengers at one time and it carries only 30 then the service meant for 20 passengers perishes, for the single ride.

5. Homogeneity:

Products are homogeneous in many respects. In case of standardized products, a product is a perfect substitute for another where it is impossible for an individual to distinguish one from another. Thus, if a person has to buy a Gillette shaving gel, he can pick any one lying at the store. But services are not homogeneous, they are heterogeneous. For example, when you go to a same restaurant every time and order a snack then you will find the difference in the taste each time you visit, even the cook is same which suggests that services are heterogeneous in nature.

6. Participation:

Customers do not participate in the production of a product. But in case of service, service cannot be performed in absence of the customer's active participation. For example, when a car is manufactured, customer does not stand there when the production process is on, but when a person goes for a hair cut or massage, he has to participate in the process.

7. Transferability:

When a transaction of a product takes place, the title of ownership moves from the seller to the buyer. In case of services, there is no transfer of title of ownership from the seller to the buyer. For example, if a person purchases a car the ownership of car is transferred from the seller to the purchaser. When a patient goes to doctor for treatment, he has to pay fees every time he visits the doctor. He cannot take the doctor for granted after paying the doctor's fees only once. Next time when he goes for treatment, he will have to pay the fees again.

Difference between product and Service

	Product	Service
Tangibility	Products are tangible: (a) They can be felt and seen. (b) They can be fully standardised.	Services are Intangible: (a) They cannot be touched. (b) They cannot be standardised.
Separability	Products are separable.	Services are inseparable.
Variability	Products are not variable.	Services are highly variable.
Perishability	Products are not perishable.	Services are perishable.
Homogeneity	Products are homogeneous in many respects.	Services are heterogeneous.
Participation	While manufacturing a product customers do not participate.	Customers participate in the process of production to consume a service.

| Transferability | When a transaction of a product takes place, the title of owner moves from the seller to the buyer. | In case of services, there is no transfer of title of ownership from the seller to the buyer. |

LESSON AT A GLANCE

- **Product:** A product is any object or service, that is offered for sale in the market and can satisfy human needs and wants.
- **Classification of Products:** Products can be classified on the basis of:
  - **(A) Durability:** (i) Durable products; (ii) Non-durable products.
  - (B) Consumer Products: (i) Convenience products; (ii) Shopping products; (iii) Speciality products, (iv) Unsought products.
  - **(C) Industrial products:** (i) Farm products; (ii) Natural products; (iii) Manufactured products; (iv) Supplies.
- **Characteristics of Product:** (i) Physical configuration; (ii) Mobility; (iii) Associated service; (iv) Packaging and branding; (v) Life-cycle; (vi) Storability; (vii) Media of communication; (viii) Exchange value.
- **Service:** A service is any act or performance that one party can offer to another. It is intangible and does not result in ownership of any thing.
- **Classification of Services:** (i) Services accompanied by major goods; (ii) Hybrid;
  (iii) Services accompanied by minor goods; (iv) Pure services.
- **Characteristics of Services:** (i) Services are intangible; (ii) Services are perishable,
  (iii) Services are inseparable; (iv) Services are variable.
- **Difference between Product and Service:** Product can be differentiated from services on the grounds of : (i) Tangibility; (ii) Separability; (iii) Variability; (iv) Perishability; (v) Homogeneity; (vi) Participation; (vii) Transferability.

Find out five types of consumer products and industrial products. Give their names, company's name and use/uses of those products to their customers.

You have to explain to your class the difference between product and service. How would you do the same with the help of examples ?

QUESTIONS

A. **Short Answer Type Questions:**
   1. Define product.
   2. Name different types of products.
   3. Give four examples of durable products.
   4. Give four examples of non-durable products.
   5. Give four types of consumer products. Give two examples of each.
   6. Give four types of industrial products. Give two examples of each.
   7. Give four main characteristics of products.
   8. Define service.
   9. Give four types of services. Also give two examples of each.
   10. Give four differences between product and service.
   11. Distinguish between a product and a service. [ICSE 2019]
   12. Distinguish between a consumer goods and an industrial goods. [ICSE 2018]
   13. What are convenience products? Give any two examples. [ICSE 2017]

B. **Essay Type Questions:**
   1. Define product and discuss different types of products.
   2. Discuss the characteristics of product.
   3. Define services and discuss different types of services.
   4. Discuss the main types of consumer products.
   5. Discuss the main types of industrial products.
   6. Discuss the characteristics of services.
   7. State the differences between product and service.

CHAPTER-04
Pricing

- Meaning of Pricing
- Objectives of Pricing

Pricing is a mechanism by means of which a business sets a specific price for a unit of its product or servicing sold in the market. The price of the product or service is a predefined agreement between the seller and the buyer. Once the company or the business sets a price of a unit of the product or the service sold, it cannot alter it without informing the buyers in advance. This is part of the overall marketing strategy of a company where they determine the cost of manufacturing a product or delivering a particular service to the customers. In order to determine the price of the product, a profit margin is added to the cost of producting the product.

For example, the manufacturing cost of a tube of toothpaste is INR 30 and the company wants to sell 10,000 units of toothpaste tubes at a certain price INR 200,000. In order to achieve this goal, they will determine the profit they earn from one tube of toothpaste. In this case it would be 200000/10000= INR 20. Hence, the price of the product will be set to INR (30 + 20) = INR 50. Where INR 30 is the manufacturing cost of the product and INR 20 is the profit margin per unit. Several other factors such a machinery expenses, factory expenses, electricity expenses, labour cost, are also taken into account while determining the price of a product.

The price of the product is depending on the cost of raw materials, cost of manufacturing the product, demand for the product, purchasing power of the consumers, price of the competing firms, government regulations, intended profit margin of the business etc. Price is also influenced by the marketing method used by the company *e.g.*, commission, which is to be paid to the middlemen for sale of the goods.

OBJECTIVES OF PRICING

The objectives of pricing can be classified into five major segments, *i.e.*, profit-related objectives, sales-related objectives, competition-related objectives, customer-related objectives, and other objectives.

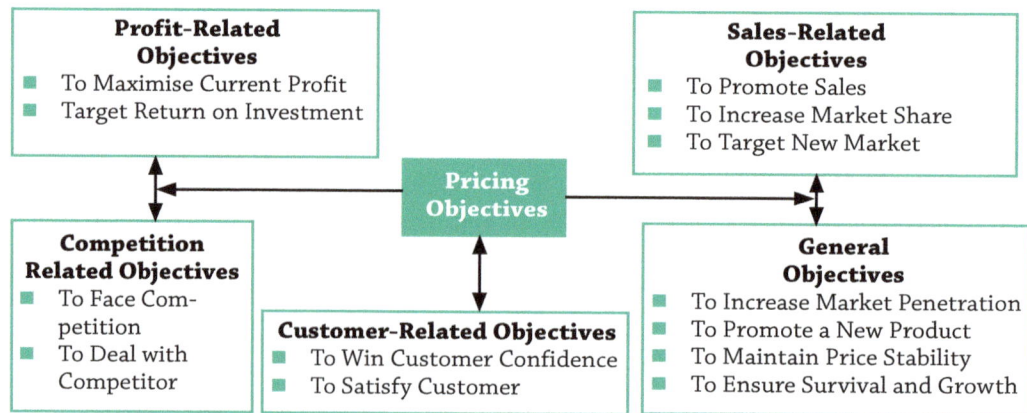

Profit Related Objectives

As aforementioned one of the major objectives of pricing is to gain profit. A company fulfills several profit related objectives by setting up a price for its product.

(a) To Maximise Current Profit:
One of the core objectives of setting up a price is to maximize profit. Companies set that price for their product or service that will maximize their current profit margin.

(b) Target Return on Investment:
Pricing is also set with an objective of gaining a specific return on the investment made in the production of product or service.

Sales Related Objectives

At times, a company sets up that price for its product that will boost its sale. Offering discounted pricing is one example of how companies try and achieve their sales related objectives. Below are the sales related objectives of setting up a price.

(a) To Promote Sales:
Companies tend to set up price in a way that more sales occur in the long run. In this way the pricing strategy also involves an objective of increasing sales volume for the organization.

(b) To Increase Market Share:
Increasing the market share of the firm is also a major objective of determining the price of a product. The company captures more share in the market when a consumer gets attracted to purchase a product because of its pricing.

(c) To Target New Market:
Sometimes innovative pricing enables a company to target unexplored markets. In that way, one of the objectives of pricing is to attract new customers and earn more profit from them.

Competition-related Objectives

Competition is a powerful factor which determines how companies price their products. Competitive brands like Pepsi or Coke always price their products in a similar manner to negate the chances of any competitive advantage to their competitors.

(a) To Face Competition:
One of the major objectives of pricing is to make the product or service competitive in the market. Pricing provides major competitive advantage to the companies.

(b) To Deal with Competitors:
Pricing often keeps competition away. Especially for a bigger company it is easier to achieve a price leadership which would help them to differentiate itself from local competitors. Price leadership can be gained when a firm produces the same quality and quantity of a product at a much lesser price. For example potato chips company Lay's achieved price leadership by introducing INR 5/pack offer thereby keeping the local and unbranded potato chips company out of competition.

Customer-related Objectives

Pricing also helps companies attract more customers. The customer related objectives of pricing are given below:

(a) To win Consumer Confidence:
Good pricing strategy often helps in winning customer's confidence. Appropriate pricing, keeps the customers happy and satisfied. The customers should be satisfied with the benefits they get from the product or the service at a particular price set by the company. The company should also be satisfied with the profit they earn from selling its product.

(b) To satisfy the Customers:
One of the prime objectives of pricing is to satisfy the customers. That is why pricing is such an important part of the entire marketing strategy of a company. The companies aim to design pricing in such a way that the customer satisfaction level remains maximum.

General Objectives

Apart from the specific objectives of pricing there are also some general objectives which are as follows:

(a) To increase Market Penetration:
Companies adopt competitive pricing strategies to penetrate unexplored markets. Reliance Communication's 'Jio' offer is a recent example of how the company ventured into untapped markets through a competitive pricing policy.

(b) To promote a New Product:
Whilst introducing a new product in the market the company must price the product very carefully. One of the major objectives of pricing is to make the new product attractive to the customers.

(c) To maintain Price Stability:
Companies who offer a stable price throughout the year are preferred by the customers. Seasonal variation of prices sometimes confuses and irritates the customers when they suddenly have to pay a higher price for the same product. To avoid annoying consumers, Supermarkets selling vegetables often maintain similar prices throughout the year, unlike the local markets.

(d) To ensure Survival and Growth:
Finally, pricing also aims to ensure survival of the company. Throughout the entire life cycle of the product, the company must alter the pricing strategy so that profit is earned at every stage of the cycle.

Lesson at a Glance

- **Pricing:** Pricing is a mechanism by means of which a business sets a specific price for a unit of its product or service being sold in the market.
- **Objectives of Pricing:**
  (1) Profit-Related Objectives: (a) To Maximise Current Profit, (b) Target Return on Investment.

(2) **Sales-Related Objectives:** (a) To Promote Sales, (b) Increase Market Share, (c) To Target New Market.
(3) **Competition-Related Objectives:** (a) To Face Competition, (b) To Deal with Competitors.
(4) **Customer-Related Objectives:** (a) To Win Customer Confidence, (b) To Satisfy the Customers
(5) **General Objectives:** (a) To Increase Market Penetration, (b) To Promote a New Product, (c) To Maintain Price Stability, (d) To Ensure Survival and Growth.

Find out how pricing of different packages of Coke is made differently. Compare it with Pepsi and write a report on that.

With the help of proper examples explain Customer-Related Pricing objective of few companies. Cite examples of firms who give heavy discounts and promotions to win consumer confidence.

A. **Short Answer Type Questions:**
   1. Define Pricing.
   2. State the five segments of pricing objectives.
   3. State two Profit-related Objectives.
   4. State two Sales-related pricing objectives.
   5. Mention two competition-related pricing objectives.
   6. Mention two customer-related pricing objectives.
   7. How is market penetration a pricing objective?
   8. Describe how maintaining price stability is a pricing objective.
   9. Mention any two objectives of Pricing. [ICSE 2019]

B. **Essay Type Questions:**
   1. What is pricing? Describe with examples.
   2. What are the major categories of pricing objectives? Explain with examples.
   3. What are the profit-related objectives of Pricing?
   4. What are the sales-related objectives of pricing?
   5. How can pricing aid in giving competitive advantage to a firm?
   6. What are the customer-related pricing objectives?
   7. 'Pricing helps in gaining customer confidence.' Explain the statement.
   8. Describe how pricing can help a company to penetrate new markets.

CHAPTER-05
Advertising

Advertising is a combination of actions taken in order to draw public attention towards any particular product or service. It is a kind of 'paid announcement' which the company creates in order to inform, educate and tempt the public to purchase their products or services.

- Meaning of Advertising
- Features of Advertising
- Importance of Advertising
- Merits and Demerits of Advertising
- Meaning and Definition of Publicity
- Distinction between Advertising and Publicity
- Advertising Agency
- Functions of Advertising Agency
- Social Media Advertising

The word 'advertising' has been derived from the Latin term 'advertere' which means 'turn to' or turning the attention towards the product. Goods are always produced in anticipation of demand. Success of a business depends upon fast sales and repeated orders. Every businessman, therefore, tries to increase the sales. In order to obtain high turnover, business enterprises now use various methods of persuading the people to buy their products. Advertisement is the art of making yourself and your product known to the world in such a way that a desire for buying that product is created in the hearts of the people. It has been rightly pointed out that in order to fly the aeroplane of sales, advertisement acts as fuel. Advertising in fact, is a salesmanship in print. It is inevitable for increasing the volume of sales.

- "Advertising is a means of communicating information pertaining to product or ideas by other than direct personal contact and on an openly paid basis with an intent to sell or otherwise obtain favourable consideration." —R. V. Zacher
- "Advertising consists of all the activities involved in presenting to a group, a non-personal, oral or visual, openly sponsored message regarding a product, service or idea; this message called an advertisement, is disseminated through one or more media and is paid for by the identified sponsor." —William J. Stanton
- "Advertising is any paid form of non-personal presentation or promotion of ideas, goods or services of an identified sponsor." —American Marketing Association

FEATURES OF ADVERTISING

1. Non-personal Form of Presentation:

Advertising is non-personal because no face to face contact is involved between the advertiser and customers. The messages that are disseminated are for public at large. It is often described as non-personal selling by creating awareness among the prospective customers.

2. Paid Form of Communication:
Advertisement can be made through any medium, but the advertiser has to pay for the use of space or time utilized by him to convey his message to the prospective customers.

3. Presence of Sponsor:
Advertising is issued by an identified sponsor. The name of the advertiser is mentioned in the advertisement itself. Its sponsor can either be the seller or the producer of that product or service.

4. Presence of Medium:
Advertising takes place through some media or medium. For example, newspaper, radio, television, etc.

5. Variety to Consumers:
Advertising provides the consumers with a wide range of products to choose from. This enables them to make an informed choice and enhances their knowledge about various products available in a specific product line.

IMPORTANCE OF ADVERTISING

Advertising has become inevitable in the contemporary business environment. It is necessary for producers, consumers as well as the society.

(A) Importance of Advertising to Producers:

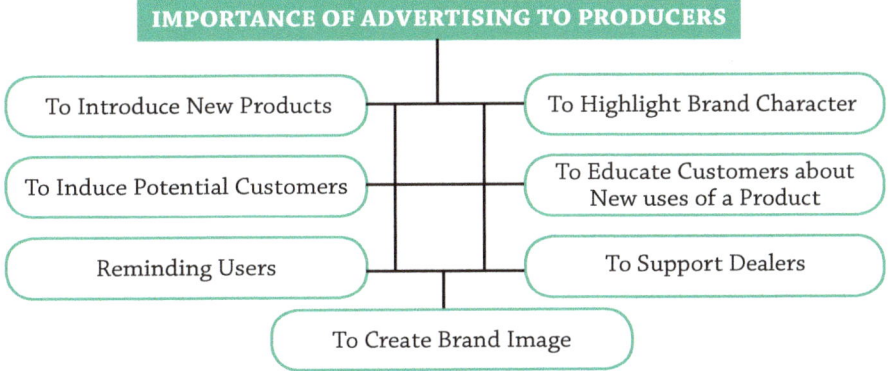

1. To Introduce New Products:
Advertisement of the new product is necessary so that consumers become aware about the product, its availability, its utility, its price etc., thus, advertising is crucial to promote the sale of a new product.

2. To Induce Potential Customers:
Advertising is one of the best means by which the sale of an existing product can be increased. For this purpose, the advertisement should emphasize the usefulness of the product, its quality, price advantages, etc., so as to win over the potential buyers and make them actual buyers.

3. Reminding Users:
In a competitive market, new products are introduced frequently. All these products are advertised in the market. As a result, old brands are likely to be forgotten by

the consumers. To offset this possibility, manufacturers continue to advertise their products to maintain the buyers' interest. Thus, advertisements are also designed to serve as a reminder to existing customers.

4. To Create Brand Image:
Business firms very often advertise for establishing an image for the product and creating customers' loyalty for that product. When customers develop brand loyalty, they are unlikely to switch to other brands easily.

5. To Highlight Brand Character:
For certain products, consumers feel that a particular characteristic is very important. Its existence determines the buyer's choice of a particular brand out of several brands. If the product has that feature, advertising is used to stress it and demonstrate its advantages.

6. To Educate Customers about New Uses of a Product:
Advertising is sometimes, used to convey new uses of an existing product to the customers or to draw their attention to some new features of the product. The basic objective of advertising in this case is to convince the customers about the superiority of a product in comparison with other products in the same line.

7. To Support Dealers:
Sometimes, the aim of advertisement is to provide support to dealers and distributors. Thus, there are many advertisements in newspapers in which the list of dealers and distributors is given along with the particulars of the product.

(B) Importance of Advertising to Consumers

1. Improved Quality of the Product:
It is absolutely essential to improve the quality of the product to maintain confidence of the customers and ensure brand loyalty. Hence, advertised goods are usually of good quality.

2. Protect Consumers from Exploitation:
Advertising also acts as an information service and educates the consumer. It enables him to know exactly what he wants and where to get it.

3. Reduction in Price:
Advertising stimulates production and reduces the cost per unit. This reduction in the cost is generally passed on to the consumer and that is why price of well-advertised goods is found to be generally lower than other goods of the same quality which are not so well advertised.

4. Facilitates Direct Selling:
Advertising also makes it possible to sell direct to the consumer by Mail Order Business. Thus, consumers from remote areas can also enjoy the comforts and luxuries available only in the cities or towns. In this way advertising improves social welfare.

5. Improved Consumer Satisfaction:
As manufacturers control the price of well-advertised goods, price-cutting is not available to the retailers and the shopkeepers as they try to attract customers by giving better and more satisfactory service.

6. Enables Comparison:
Advertising helps consumers find best product for themselves by facilitating comparison among various products available in the market. When consumers are aware about the range of products, they are able to compare the price, quality and characteristics and pick up the best from among them.

(C) Importance of Advertising to Society

1. Advertising helps in increasing awareness among people. Advertising dealing with social issues such as child labour, liquor consumption, female foeticide, smoking, family planning etc. and promotes social welfare.
2. Advertising provides direct employment to large number of people engaged in designing, writing and issuing advertisements. Indirectly, advertising increases employment opportunities by increasing the volume of production and distribution.
3. Advertising helps in improving the standard of living of people by promoting variety and quality in consumption. It educates people about new uses of a product and provides information for developing better ways of leading life.

MERITS OF ADVERTISING

Advertising is beneficial to manufacturers, traders, consumers and society as a whole:

1. Promotion of Sales:
Advertising helps the producer to increase his sales. A form attempts to increase the demand for its product, either by reducing the price or by inducing buyers to purchase more of its product; even at the constant price. The latter involves the use of sales promotion and hence advertising.

2. Expansion of Production:
Increased demand brought about by advertising has to be met by a corresponding increase in production. In this way, advertising causes production to expand in order to cater to an increased demand.

3. Enhances Goodwill:
Advertising is instrumental in increasing the goodwill of the company (advertises). It introduces the manufacturer and his product to the people. Repeated advertising and better quality of products strengthens manufacturers reputation and enhances his goodwill.

4. Large Turnover and Huge Profits:
An increased demand, generated through advertisements can create a larger turnover for the company and eventually resulting in more profits.

5. Information about Different Options and Comparative Prices:
Advertisement keeps the buyers well informed by providing information about the different products and their relative prices. This helps the consumer to take adequate decision regarding the features they want and the amount they want to spend, even before physically going to the shops.

6. Creates Employment Opportunities:

Advertising is capable of providing employment to large section of the society including the professionals like painters, photographers, singers, cartoonist, musicians, models and people working in different advertising agencies.

7. Higher Standard of Living:

Advertisement promotes larger consumption, increased production and greater employment. This further reflect on lower prices, better quality and greater variety of goods to the consumers. Advertising, thus, ensures better and happier living.

DEMERITS OF ADVERTISING

Despite of being regarded as the life-blood of modern business advertising has the following disadvantages:

1. Adds to the Cost of Production and Product:

Advertising increases the cost of the advertised product, as the expenses on advertisement add to the total cost of the product. To mitigate the cost incurred during advertising of the product or the service, the advertiser adds the cost of advertisement to the total price of the product or the service. So, the advertising cost is actually being borne by the consumers.

2. Leads to Price War:

Large scale competitive advertising by prominent competing firms can possibly lead to advertising wars with the consumers being made to pay for it. It leads to a situation of price war and that makes the production activity unduly wasteful. The entire industry has to suffer a setback.

3. Deceptive Advertising:

Sometimes, advertising is used as an instrument of cheating. Unscrupulous firms defraud the consumers by misrepresenting their products through advertising. In order to induce people to purchase their product, firms issue false statements with regard to different virtues of a products; this undermines public confidence in advertising. As a result we have the Advertising Code of Conduct that regulates advertising and ensures commercial honesty.

4. Leads to Unequal Competition:

The producers spend a huge amount of money for the advertisement of their products and services. Small local firms cannot match the big advertising budgets of multinational companies. Therefore, the scales are always tilted in favour of the bigger producers leading to unequal competition.

5. Creates a Monopolistic Market:

Larger firms by virtue of their larger advertising budgets drive the smaller firms out of the market. This leaves the market open to just a few large producers. In this way the bigger firms win competition and monopolize the market.

6. Promotes Unnecessary Consumption:

Advertising promotes the consumption of goods and services which are not even required by the people. Hence it is wastage of national resources.

7. Decline in Moral Values:

In order to attract attention of the people, many times advertisers use indecent, vulgar language and obscene photographs.

All these reasons together justify the statement that "Advertising is Social Waste", because it does not add any real value to the society.

PUBLICITY

Publicity, in its simplest form, means conveying information to the general public through the media. The information being publicised could be news, awareness about a product and service etc. Publicity is not paid for by the organisation. According to Definition Committee (1948) of the American Marketing Association, "Publicity can be defined as any form of commercially significant news about a product, an institution, a service or a person published in space or radio time that is not paid for by the sponsor." Publicity media include posters, pamphlets, films, radio, television, direct mailing demonstrations, fairs and exhibitions, meetings, conferences, social media like Face book, Twitter and blogs etc. These may be arranged all together or one by one as the case may be.

The words 'Advertising' and 'Ability' are often used interchangeably. But following distinctions must be kept in mind:

Basis of Distinction	Advertising	Publicity
Nature of Communication	Communication of only commercial information to the public.	Publicity may or may not be related with the communication of commercial information.
Decisions Regarding Format	The content, style, format, etc. of the advertising message are decided by the sponsor, i.e., the advertiser.	The content, style, and other matters, such as space and timings of dissemination of the message, are controlled by the media owners.
Payment	The advertisers have to pay to the advertising agencies and media owners for conveying message to the public.	Sponsor does not pay for the use of space or time to convey the message to the public.
Inter-dependability	Advertising is just a part of publicity.	Publicity includes advertising.
Identity and Purpose	The identity and purpose of the sponsors of an advertisement are clearly known.	The identity and purpose of the sender of the message are unknown in many cases.
Party which Suffers	The sponsor of the advertisement suffers the loss.	The public which ignore or disregard the message, suffers.

ADVERTISING AGENCY

Advertising agencies are third-party vendors who conceptualize, design and actually make the advertisement on behalf of the company. Thus an advertising agency is involved in various forms of activities like planning, preparing the adverts and choosing when and on which media should the advertisement appear. These agencies take all the efforts for promoting the product of the clients (Advertisers). For this purpose, they have a team of different people for difference functions like copywriters, art directors, planners etc. The agencies make optimum use of these people, their experience and their knowledge.

Functions of Advertising Agency

Functions of an Advertising agency are listed below:

1. Advertising Planning:

One of the primary functions of the advertising agencies is to plan for the advertising. After analysing the clients' products or the service, the prevailing competition and the market conditions the agency makes the entire advertising plan and executes the plans after obtaining clients' approval.

2. Creative Function:

An advertising agency also performs creative functions. The creative functions include copy writing, drawing photographs, preparing illustrations and layouts and write effective advertisement taglines and dialogues. These functions are performed by copywriters, artists, designers, who are highly skilled in their respective fields. This function makes an advertisement more appealing and helps increase sales of a product.

3. Media Selection:

Advertising agency assists an advertiser in selecting a proper media (advertising platform) to promote his advertisement. Media selection is the most critical function of an advertising agency as it must select the most suitable media for its client's advertisement which has the potential to give best results at lowest costs. It must also select more than one media for the advertisement. This function determines the effectiveness of the advertisement and the impact it will have on the targeted audience.

4. Determining Advertising Budget:

The advertising agencies also help the advertisers to decide on the advertising budget. That is the entire cost of advertising. The advertising agencies need to give a proper estimation of the cost of the plan and wait for the advertiser to approve it.

5. Coordination and Connection:

Advertising agency maintains close coordination among the Advertiser itself, media houses and distributors. This is a crucial function because proper coordination helps in boosting the sales of a product.

6. Market Research:

Many advertising agencies conduct market research on behalf of their clients (advertisers) and consult them on the kind of advertising that needs to be done.

7. Non-Advertising Functions:
Advertising agencies often provide consultations regarding the pricing and design of the products. They also help the companies in designing the packaging, trade marks, tables etc.

SOCIAL MEDIA ADVERTISING
Social Media's Advertising often create and deliver messages with an aim to educate the public about certain social issues including the impact of global warming, stopping child abuse, the importance of vaccinating your child, ill effects of smoking, curbing female foeticide etc. Social advertisements contain strong and direct messages and they do not generally talk about any particular product or service but the message itself is paramount to any other objective.

For example :
1. Tata Tea "Jago re" campaign was a kind of social advertisement.
2. Havell's: "Hawa Badlegi" ad is also a social advertisement campaign which has gained popularity in India.
3. Fastrack: The Closet-based on theme of queer rights.
4. Kaun Banega Crorepatis' Kohima ad highlights racial discrimination faced by people from North-Eastern states of India.

Social Issues like child marriage, dowry, corruption etc. are being highlighted by means of these adverts.

LESSON AT A GLANCE

- **Advertising:** According to William J. Stanton. "Advertising consists of all the activities involved in presenting to a group, a non-personal, oral or visual, openly sponsored message regarding a product, service or idea. This message called an advertisement, is disseminated through one or more media and is paid for by the identified sponsor."
- **Features of Advertising:** (i) Non-personal form of presentation; (ii) Paid form of communication; (iii) Presence of sponsor; (iv) Presence of medium, (v) Variety to consumers.
- **Importance of Advertising:**
  - *(A) To Producers:* (i) To introduce new products; (ii) To induce potential customers; (iii) Reminding users; (iv) To create brand image; (v) To highlight brand character; (vi) To educate customers about new uses of a product; (vii) To support dealers.
  - *(B) To Consumers:* (i) Improved quality of the product, (ii) Protects consumers from exploitation; (iii) Reduction in price; (iv) Facilitates direct selling; (v) Improved consumer satisfaction; (vi) Enables comparison.
  - *(C) To Society:* (i) Helps in increasing awareness in public; (ii) Provide direct employment; (iii) Helps in improving standard of living.
- **Merits of Advertising:** (i) Promotion of sales; (ii) Expansion of production; (iii) Enhances goodwill; (iv) Larger turnover and huge profits; (v) Information about different options and their comparative prices; (vi) Creates employment opportunities, (vii) Higher standard of living.

- **Demerits of Advertising:** (i) Adds to the cost of production and product; (ii) Leads to price war; (iii) Deceptive advertising; (iv) Leads to unequal competition; (v) Creates a monopolistic market; (vi) Promotes unnecessary consumption; (vii) Decline in moral values.
- **Publicity:** Publicity can be defined as any form of commercially significant news about a product; an institution, a service or a person published in space or radio time that is not paid for by the sponsor.
- **Distinction between Advertising and Publicity:** Basis of distinction are: (i) Nature of communication; (ii) Decisions regarding format; (iii) Payment; (iv) Inter-dependability; (v) Identity and Purpose; (vi) Party which suffers.
- **Advertising Agency:** Advertising agency is a third party vendor who conceptualise, design and actually makes the advertisement on behalf of the advertiser.
- **Function of an Advertising Agency:** (i) Advertising planning; (ii) Creative function; (iii) Media selection, (iv) Determining advertising budget; (v) Coordination and connection; (vi) Market Research, (vii) Non-advertising functions.
- **Social Media Advertising:** Social Media Advertising often create and deliver messages with an aim to educate the public about social issues.

Collect 20 punch lines of various advertisements and explain what they convey to public.

If a head of advertising agency has to give a speech on the advantages of advertising, how and what he will tell people about these concepts.

A. **Short Answer Type Questions:**
   1. Define advertising.
   2. Mention two importance of advertising.
   3. Give two differences between advertising and publicity.
   4. Write two disadvantages of advertising.
   5. What is an advertising agency?
   6. State two functions of an advertising agency.
   7. What is social media advertising? [ICSE 2019]
   8. "Advertising encourages unhealthy consumption." Explain.
   9. Advertising is a social waste.
   10. Distinguish between Advertising and Publicity. [ICSE 2020]

B. Essay Type Questions:
1. What is advertisement? Explain briefly its features and importance.
2. "It pays to advertise." Do you agree? Give reasons.
3. Explain the importance of advertising.
4. Discuss the role of advertising in modern business.
5. What is an advertising agency? Explain any two of its functions. [ICSE 2019]
6. What is a Social Media Advertising? Provide examples of Social Advertising in India.
7. "Advertising encourages artificial living." Do you agree with this statement? Why?
8. Briefly explain any five benefits of advertising to producers. [ICSE 2020]
9. Advertisement is a social waste. In this context explain the demerits of advertisement. [ICSE 2017]

CHAPTER-06
Sales Promotion

Sales promotion is a set of marketing activities under-taken to boost sales of a product or service, by persuading or giving incentive to a potential customer, to buy that product or service.

- Meaning of Sales Promotion
- Techniques of Sales Promotion
- Difference between Advertising and Sales Promotion

According to American Marketing Association (AMA) sales promotion can be defined as, "sales activities that supplement both personal selling and advertising and coordinate them and help them effectively, through displays, shows and expositions, demonstrations and other non-recurrent selling efforts not in the ordinary routine." The definition implies that sales promotions are different from advertising, personal selling and publicity but complement personal selling and advertising. For instance, advertising and personal selling can be used to inform potential customers about the incentives offered for sales promotion. Thus, sales promotion consists of all activities other than advertising and personal selling that helps to boost sales of a particular commodity.

Sales promotion adopt short term, non-recurring methods to increase sales. These offers are not available to the customers throughout the year and are generally found during festivals, end of the seasons and some other occasion.

Sales promotion is important for producers and manufacturers because it helps to increase sales in a competitive market and thus, increases profits. It also helps to introduce new products and to communicate new uses of an existing product to the customers. It is often used to maintain sale of seasonal products like air conditioners, refrigerators, cooler etc. by offering off-season discount. Sales promotion measures have also become essential to retain the market share of the seller, in the era of intense competition.

Sales promotion is important for consumers as well because they get the product at a cheaper rate. Sales promotion also enables the consumers to get all information about the quality, features and uses of different products, helping them to raise their standard of living. By exchanging their old items, they can use latest items available in the market.

TECHNIQUES OF SALES PROMOTION

To increase sales of any product, producers adopt different measures like distributing samples, gifts, coupons, bonus, etc. They are known as techniques of sales promotion. Some of the commonly used tools of sales promotion are as follows:

1. Coupons:
Coupons are issued by producers of packaged goods or by retailers that enables customers to buy the product next time at a reduced price. These coupons are either

advertised by producers/retailers in newspapers or distributed in weekly flyers via mail across households. For examples, Big Bazaar issues coupons for selected items in their weekly flyers that are distributed via mail or along with newspapers.

2. Free Samples:
Free samples are small and packaged portion of the (main) merchandise distributed for free. Free samples are developed for introducing new products. These samples may be distributed door-to-door (through personal selling) or retail stores. For examples, Sensodyne Toothpaste meant for relieving tooth sensitivity is unique product introduced in India.The manufacturer of Sensodyne has been reaching out to local dentists of Mumbai who have been distributing free sample of these toothpastes to create awareness among their patients.

3. Price-off offer:
This involves offering products to consumers at discounted or reduced prices by a certain percentage from the regular price of the product. This activity aims at attracting consumers to other or newer brands, seasonal and unseasonal goods. For example, a 15 to 60 percent off on clothes before some festive season in retail shops are examples of sales or sales promotion.

4. Fairs and Exhibitions:
Fairs and exhibitions may be organised at local, regional, national or international level to introduce new products, demonstrate the products and to explain special features and usefulness of the products. For example, 'International Trade Fair' held in New Delhi in November every year.

5. Free Gifts:
Producers may distribute a free gift along with their product as a incentive to the consumers for purchasing the product. For example, milkshaker along with Nescafe, toothbrush along with a toothpaste.

6. Competitions or Contests:
Producers can organise competitions or contests among salespersons to encourage them to generate more sales from new customers. Companies can offer a car or consumer durables for generating a certain percentage sales in a particular month or quarter.

7. Free Service:
Producers/retailers may promise free service to consumers for a specified period of time after sales. For example, few car retailers offer free servicing for the first 6 months if certain car components are damaged or are under performing.

8. Special Rebate:
Rebate is a partial refund to someone who has paid more or extra on purchase of a specified quantity or value of goods within a specified period. Unlike, price cut off or discounts, rebates are provided after the full payment of full invoice amount.

9. Full Finance @ 0%:
Under this method, the product is sold and money is received on installment basis at 0% or without interest rate. The seller determines the number of installments in which the price of the product will be recovered from the customers.

10. Scratch and Win Offer:
Under this scheme, a customer scratches a specific marked area on the package of the product and gets the benefit according to the message written therein.

11. Money-back Offer:
Under this scheme customers are given assurance that full value of the product will be returned to them if they are not satisfied after using the product. This creates confidence among the customers with regard to the quality of the product.

12. Exchange Schemes:
It refers to exchange of old product for a new product at a price less than the original price of the product. This is useful for drawing attention to product improvement.
Example : "Exchange your black and white television with a colour television."

Difference Between Advertising and Sales Promotion

Basis of Difference	Advertising	Sales Promotion
Meaning	One-way communication of a persuasive message by an identified sponsor, whose purpose is non-personal promotion of product/services to potential customers.	Sales Promotion involves an immediate incentive for a buyer (intermediate distributors or end consumer). It can also involve disseminating information about a product, product line, brand or a company.
Objective	It is done to build brand image and boost sales.	It is done to push short term sales.
Time-Frame	Long term.	Short term.
Nature of Appeal	Emotional in nature.	Unemotional and rational in nature.
Directness	Advertising uses indirect and subtle methods to create a brand image.	Sales promotions are more direct.
Results	Slow, can be seen over time.	Instant.
Cost Involved	Expensive.	Cost-effective (Less expressive)
Frequency	Recurrent.	Mostly non-recurrent.
Contribution to Profit	Moderate.	Medium to high.
Focused Ideas/ Products	Current and new.	Current.
Suitable for	Medium to large companies.	Small to large companies.
Communication	One way process.	To way process.
Strategy	Promotional.	Marketing.

| Employed Tools for Interaction | Mass media such as television, hoarding, newspapers, social media handles like facebook, twitter etc. and Retail stores. | Free gifts, coupons, exhibitions and fairs, price-off offers, exchange offers etc. |

LESSON AT A GLANCE

- **Sales Promotion:** It is a set of marketing activities undertaken to boost sales of a product or service, by persuading or giving incentive to a potential customer, to buy that product or service.
- **Techniques of Sales Promotion:** (i) Coupons; (ii) Free Samples; (iii) Price-off Offer; (iv) Fairs and Exhibitions; (v) Free Gifts; (vi) Competitions or Contests; (vii) Free Service; (viii) Special Rebate; (ix) Full Finance @ 0%; (x) Scratch and Win Offer; (xi) Money-back Offer; (xii) Exchange Schemes.
- **Difference between Advertising and Sales Promotion:** (i) Meaning; (ii) Objective; (iii) Time-Frame; (iv) Nature of Appeal; (v) Directness; (vi) Results; (vii) Cost involved; (viii) Frequency; (ix) Contribution to Profit; (x) Focused Ideas/Products; (xi) Suitable for; (xii) Communication; (xiii) Strategy; (xiv) Employed Tools for Interaction.

Make a visit to any departmental store and consult with its marketing manager or sales manager. Ask him the techniques adopted for sales promotion of his products in different departments. Also, ask him the results of methods adopted and evaluate which one is the best for boosting sales.

You have to explain, to the class, the importance of sales, promotion from the point of view of the manufacturer.

A. **Short Answer Type Questions:**
   1. What do you mean by sales promotion?
   2. Name two methods of sales promotion.
   3. What do you mean by coupons?
   4. Distinguish between advertising and sales promotion.

B. **Essay Type Questions:**
   1. What do you mean by sales promotion?
   2. Describe in detail the difference between sales promotion and advertising.
   3. Suggest five techniques used in sales promotion.   [ICSE 2018]

CHAPTER-07
Consumer Protection

CONSUMER (UNDER CONSUMER PROTECTION ACT 2019)

A person who has indicated his or her willingness to obtain goods and/or services from a supplier with the intention of paying for them is termed as consumer.

The word "consumer" has been defined under Consumer Protection Act of 2019 as follows:

"consumer" means any person who:

- Meaning of Consumer
- Consumer Exploitation
- Meaning and Types
- Consumer Awareness
- Importance of Consumer Awareness
- Consumer Protection Act (COPRA), 2019—Features of the Act
- Consumer Rights

1. Buys any goods for a consideration which has been paid or promised or partly paid and partly promised, or under any system of deferred payment and includes any user of such goods other than the person who buys such goods for consideration paid or promised or partly paid or partly promised, or under any system of deferred payment, when such use is made with the approval of such person, but does not include a person who obtains such goods for resale or for any commercial purpose, or

2. Hires or avails of any service for a consideration which has been paid or promised or partly paid and partly promised, or under any system of deferred payment and includes any beneficiary of such service other than the persons who hires or avails of the services for consideration paid or promised, or partly paid and partly promised, or under any system of deferred payment, when such services are availed of with the approveal of the first mentioned person, but does not include a person who avails of such service for any commercial purpose. It should be noted that:

    (a) The expression "commercial purpose" does not include use by a person of goods bought and used by him exclusively for the purpose of earning his livelihood, by means of self-employment;

    (b) The expressions "buys any goods" and "hires or avails any services" includes offline or online transactions through electronic means or by teleshopping or direct selling or multi-level marketing;

Thus, a person is not a consumer if he purchases goods for commercial or resale purposes. However, the word "commercial" does not include use by consumer of goods bought and used by him exclusively for the purpose of earning his livelihood, by means of self-employment and his purchase (goods or services) Includes both offline and online transactions.

A consumer is supposed to be the 'king of the market' *i.e.* all the production brought about by the producers should be carried keeping the needs of the consumers in mind and consumer satisfaction should be of prime importance in all these activities, but in practical scenario it has been witnessed that the needs of most important component of business, the consumer, are actually neglected and the obligation every business holds towards the consumer remains unfulfilled. This results in exploitation of the consumers.

CONSUMER EXPLOITATION

Consumer exploitation is a process by which business intentionally cheat or deceive consumers in order to gain profit. This takes place either because of limited information on the part of consumers about the product, such as guarantees and terms of purchase, quality and price, or because of lack of awareness about consumer rights. Illiterate consumers are especially vulnerable; consequently they are likely to be cheated into paying more and even purchasing a counterfeit product. Also, it is very difficult for an ordinary consumer to distinguish between a genuine product and its imitations. Since consumers are large in numbers and are segregated, they often find themselves in a weak position, when there is a complaint regarding goods and services. Sellers, on the other hand, leverage this situation and never accept responsibility of selling bad quality goods or any other misappropriation.

Consumers have to act responsibly to avoid getting exploited. They should beware of misleading advertisements. They should be quality conscious and inspect a variety of goods before making selection. A Consumer should insist on a valid documentary evidence (cash memo/invoice) relating to purchase of goods or availing of any service. They should be aware of their rights and exercise them while buying goods and services. Most importantly, a consumer should complaint for genuine grievances in the redressal forums and consumer protection councils.

Ways In Which A Consumer Gets Exploited

Some common ways by which consumers are exploited by manufacturers and traders are given below:

1. Underweight and Under-measurements:
The goods being sold in the market are sometimes not measured or weighed correctly.

2. Sub-standard Quality:
The goods sold are sometimes of sub-standard quality. Selling of consumable beyond their expiry dates and supply of deficient or defective home appliances are generally the regular grievances of consumers. This also includes the sales of medicines after expiry date, and selling spurious drugs (sub-standard drugs).

3. High Prices:
Very often the traders charge a price higher than the prescribed retail price.

4. Duplicate Articles:
In the name of genuine parts or goods, fake or duplicate items are being sold to the consumers.

5. Adulteration and Impurity:

Costly edible items such as oil, *ghee* and spices are adulterated in order to earn higher profits. Adulteration of foods causes heavy loss to the customers; they suffer from monetary loss as well as spoil their health.

6. Lack of Safety Devices:

Electronic goods, electrical devices or other appliances produced locally, lack the required inbuilt safeguards. This poses health risks to the consumers.

7. Artificial Scarcity:

In order to make illegitimate profit, businessmen often create artificial scarcity by hoarding. They sell the products at a later stage at higher prices.

8. False or Incomplete Information:

Sellers easily mislead consumers by giving wrong information about a product, its price, quality, reliability, life cycle, expiry date, durability, its effect on health, environment, safety and security, maintenance costs involved, and terms and conditions of purchase. Cosmetics, drugs and electronic goods are common examples where consumers face such problems.

9. Unsatisfactory After-sale Service:

Many of the high cost durable items, such as electrical or electronic equipments, home appliances and cars, need adequate after-sale care. The suppliers do not provide the satisfactory after-sale services despite the necessary payments made by the consumer.

10. Rough Behaviour and Undue Conditions:

In matters related to procuring LPG gas connection, fixing of a new telephone line, procurement of licensed items etc. consumers are often harassed and subjected to undue conditions in order to obtain the desired service.

11. Hidden Price Component:

A lot of companies give offers that invites the consumers to buy products at very low prices or make exchange offers or offers like buy one get one, which are good enough to lure the innocent consumers initially but have some or the other hidden price component attached to it which the consumer is forced to fulfill later, leading to his exploitation.

12. Environmental Hazards:

The producers may cause ecological and environ-mental hazards for the consumers and society by causing water, air and noise pollution.

13. Other Ways:

There are few other ways by which consumers are cheated, like:

(a) Variations in the content filled in the packaged goods.

(b) Illegal fixation of maximum retail price (MRP) and selling above MRP.

(c) Non-compliance with the terms and conditions of sales and services.

Reasons or Factors Causing Exploitation of Consumers

Limited Information:

Producers provide incomplete and incorrect information about various products.

Limited Supplies:
When goods and services are hoarded by producers/suppliers with an intention to create short supply, then prices shoot up.

Limited Competition:
Single producer may manipulate the market in terms of price and stocks *i.e.*, when seller enjoys monopoly in the market.

Low Literacy:
Illiteracy leads to exploitation. Lack of consumer awareness is the root cause for exploitation.

Lack of Bargaining Power:
This results among consumers due to lack of market information.

Irregular Prices Offered:
Sellers often manipulate the pricing of the product in absence of government control and there is price discrimination by the seller.

Misleading Advertisements:
Form a basic reason causing exploitation of a consumer. They have been designed and projected in such a way that the consumer gets carried off and gets trapped in the mesh of hidden costs, etc.

For example:
The producers may advertise a low price for the goods on offer. But when one goes to purchase the goods, he ends up paying more than the advertised price because it did not include the price of accessories or other things that are necessary to use the goods.

Lack of Unity:
Consumers lack courage and unity to voice against the exploitation, irrespective of the rights issued to them by our government.

Cumbersome and Time Taking Legal Proceedings:
Our legal procedures are critical and cumbersome. This puts off the courage in people to file any complaint against exploitation.

According to the Consumer Protection Act 2019, a consumer can complaint against any exploitation by seller. Here, "complaint" means any allegation in writing, made by a complainant for obtaining any relief provided by or under this Act, that:

(i) An unfair contract or unfair trade practice or a restrictive trade practice has been adopted by any trader or service provider;

(ii) The goods bought by him or agreed to be bought by him suffer from one or more defects;

(iii) The services hired or availed of or agreed to be hired or availed of by him suffer from any deficiency;

(iv) A trader or a service provider, as the case may be, has charged for the goods or for the services mentioned in the complaint, a price in excess of the price:

    (a) Fixed by or under any law for the time being in force;

(b) Displayed on the goods or any package containing such goods; or

(c) Displayed on the price list exhibited by him by or under any law for the time being in force; or

(d) Agreed between the parties;

(v) The goods, which are hazardous to life and safety when used, are being offered for sale to the public:

(a) In contravention of standards relating to safety of such goods as required to be complied with, by or under any law for the time being in force;

(b) Where the trader knows that the goods so offered are unsafe to the public;

(vi) The services which are hazardous or likely to be hazardous to life and safety of the public when used, are being offered by a person who provides any service and who knows it to be injurious to life and safety;

(vii) A claim for product liability action lies against the product manufacturer, product seller or product service provider, as the case may be.

CONSUMER AWARENESS

Consumer awareness is the knowledge that a consumer should have about his/her legal rights and duties.

Broadly, it refers to the combination of the following:

(1) The knowledge of the product purchased by the consumers in terms of its quality and its impact on their lives.

(2) The education about the bad effects of an advertisement and its contents.

(3) The knowledge about the consumer rights. A consumer should know that he/she has the right to get the right kind of product and he/she also has the right to claim compensation, if the product is found out to be faulty.

(4) The knowledge about consumers' responsibilities: This implies that consumers should not indulge in wasteful and unnecessary consumption.

Importance of Consumer Awareness

Following facts list the need of making consumers aware:

(1) To Achieve Maximum Satisfaction:
A consumer wants to buy maximum goods and services with his limited income. Therefore, it is necessary that he should get the goods which are measured appropriately and he is not cheated in any way, to maximise his satisfaction. For this, he should be made aware.

(2) Protect Against Exploitation:
Producers and sellers exploit the consumers through under weighing, charging more price than the market price, selling duplicate goods, misleading advertisement etc. Consumer awareness shields the buyer from getting exploited.

(3) Control over Consumption of Harmful Goods:
There are several goods available in the market which cause harm to consumers, for example—Cigarette, tobacco, liquor etc. Consumer education and awareness inspire people not to purchase such goods which are injurious to their health.

(4) Motivation for Saving:
Consumer awareness motivates people to keep away from wastage of money and extravagancy and inspire them to take the right decision. Such consumers are not attracted by sale, concession, free gifts, attractive packing etc. which means, people can use their saved income in a productive manner.

(5) Knowledge Regarding Solution of Problems:
Consumers are cheated due to illiteracy, innocence and lack of information. Therefore, it is important that consumers are made aware of their rights and the procedure for claiming compensation in the grievance redressal forums and the consumer court.

(6) Construction of healthy society:
Every member of the society is a consumer. So, if a consumer is aware and rational, then the complete society becomes alert towards their rights.

CONSUMER PROTECTION ACT, 2019 (COPRA)

The Consumer Protection Act was passed in 2019 and it came into force on 20 July, 2020. The main objectives of the Act are to provide better protection of the interests of the consumers and effective safeguards against different types of exploitation such as defective goods, deficient services and unfair trade practices. It also lays down the provisions for a simple, speedy and inexpensive machinery for redressal for consumers' grievances.

Objectives of the Consumer Protection Act, 2019

1. To conduct investigations into violations of consumer rights and institute complaints/prosecution.
2. Order recall of unsafe goods and services.
3. Order discontinuance of unfair trade practices and misleading advertisements.
4. Impose penalties on manufacturers/endorsers/publishers of misleading advertisements.
5. Act includes trade carried out through e-commerce and direct selling under its ambit. It defines e-commerce as buying or selling of goods or services including digital products over digital or electronic network and online market place or online auction sites
6. The CPA 2019 also provides for the settlement of disputes by way of mediation in case there is a likelihood of compromise at the acceptance point of the complaint or at some further date, provided the parties consent. For accelerated settlement, a mediation cell would be attached to each city, state, and national commission and its regional benches.

Scope of the Act

1. The Consumer Protection Act extends to the whole of India except the state of Jammu & Kashmir.
2. Unless otherwise provided by the Central Government by notification, this Act shall apply to all goods and services.

3. It covers all sectors whether private, public or cooperative.
4. The provisions of this Act are compensatory in nature.

Salient Features Of Consumer Protection Act, 2019

The salient features of Consumer Protection Act (COPRA) 2019 are as follows:

(1) It applies to all goods, services and unfair trade practices, unless specifically exempted by the Central Government.

The term 'goods', under this Act, covers all types of movable property other than money and includes stocks and shares, growing crops, etc. The term 'service' means service of any description made available to potential users and includes banking, financing, housing construction, insurance, entertainment, transport, supply of electrical and other energy, boarding and lodging, amusement, etc. It also includes the services of doctors, engineers, architects, lawyers etc.

(2) It covers all sectors whether private or public.

(3) It provides for establishment of consumer disputes redressal agencies at the district, state and national levels for resolution of consumer grievances and complaints. These are know as District commission, State Commission and National Commission.

CONSUMER PROTECTION COUNCILS

The Act provides for the establishment of a Central Protection Council by the Central Government and a State Consumer Protection Council in each state by the respective State Governments.

The Central Consumer Protection Council/Central Council:

This council will be established by the Central Government by notification and it will consist of the following members:

(a) The Minister-in-charge of the Department of Consumer Affairs in the Central Government, who shall be the Chairperson; and

(b) Such number of other official or non-official members representing such interests as may be prescribed.

The Central Council shall meet as and when necessary, but at least one meeting of the Council shall be held every year.

The objects of the Central Council shall be to render advice on promotion and protection of the consumers' rights under this Act.

The State Consumers Protection Council / State Council:

This council will be established by the State Government by notification. The State Council shall consist of the following:

(a) The Minister-in-charge of Consumer Affairs in the State Government who shall be the Chairperson;

(b) Such number of other official or non-official members representing such interests as may be prescribed;

(c) Such number of other official or non-official members, not exceeding ten, as may be nominated by the Central Government.

The State Council shall meet as and when necessary but not less than two meetings shall be held every year.

The objects of every State Council shall be to render advice on promotion and protection of consumer rights under this Act within the State.

District Consumer Protection Council /District Council:
The State Government establish by notification, for every District, a District Consumer Protection Council or the District Council.

The District Council shall be an advisory council and consist of the following members, namely:

(a) The Collector of the district (by whatever name called), who shall be the Chairperson; and

(b) Such number of other official and non-official members representing such interests as may be prescribed.

The District Council shall meet as and when necessary but not less than two meetings shall be held every year.

The objects of every District Council shall be to render advice on promotion and protection of consumer rights under this Act within the district.

CONSUMER DISPUTES REDRESSAL AGENCIES

The Consumer Protection Act provides for a three tier redressal system comprising of the following:

There is a proper method which has to be followed by a consumer to produce his complaint to the consumer protection council.

Where to file the complaint (depends upon the cost of the goods or services or the compensation)

A. **District Commission:** If any of the above is less than ₹ 1 Crore.

B. **State Commission:** If any of the above more than ₹ 1 Crore but less than ₹ 10 crore.

C. **National Commission:** If any of the above more than ₹ 10 crore.

A. District Commission:

The State Government shall, by notification, establish a District Consumer Disputes Redressal Commission, to be known as the District Commission, in each district of the State:

The State Government may establish more than one District Commission in a district, if it deems fit.

Each District Commission shall consist of:

(a) A President; and

(b) Not less than two and not more than such number of members as may be prescribed, in consultation with the Central Government.

Jurisdiction:

Subject to the provisions of this Act, the District Forum will have Jurisdiction to entertain complaints where the value of goods or services and the compensation of any claim does not exceed ₹ 1 Crore.

(B) The State Commission (Consumer disputes redressal agency at state level)

Composition:

Each state commission shall consist of:

(a) A President; and (b) not less than four or not more than such number of members as may be prescribed in consultation with the Central Government.

Jurisdiction:

Subject to the provision of the Act, the State Commission has the jurisdiction:

- To entertain complaints where the value of goods or services or compensation claimed is between ₹ 1 Crore and ₹ 10 crore.
- To entertain appeals against the orders of any District Forum within the state, and
- To call for the records and pass appropriate orders in any consumer dispute that is pending before or has been decided by any District Forum within the State, where it appears to the State Commission that such District Forum has exercised jurisdiction not vested in it by law or has failed to exercise a jurisdiction so vested or has acted in exercise of its jurisdiction illegally or with material irregularity.

(C) The National Commission (Redressal commission at the national level)

Composition:

The National Commission will consist of:

(a) A President; and (b) Not less than four and not more than such number of members as may be prescribed.

Jurisdiction:

The National Commission shall have Jurisdiction:

- To entertain complaints where value of the goods or services and the compensation if any claimed exceeds ₹ 10 crore.
- To entertain appeals against the orders of any State Commission, and
- To call for the records and pass appropriate orders in any consumer dispute which is pending before or has been decided by any State Commission where it appears to the National Commission that such State Commission has exercised a jurisdiction not vested in it by the law, or has failed to exercise a jurisdiction so vested or has acted in the exercise of its jurisdiction illegally or with material irregularity.

COMPLAINTS BEFORE THE DISTRICT FORUM AND STATE COMMISSION

A complaint in relation to any goods sold or delivered or any service provided may be filed with a District Forum or State Commission as the case may be, by:

- The consumer to whom such goods are sold or delivered or such service provided.
- Any recognised consumer association, whether the aggrieved consumer is a member of such association or not, or
- The Central or State Government.
- One or more consumers on behalf of consumers having same interest, and
- A legal heir or representative of a deceased consumer.

Remedial Action:
If after the conduction of the proceedings any of the consumer redressal agencies is satisfied that the goods complained against suffer from any of the defects specified in the complaint or that any of the allegations contained in the complaint about the services provided, it will issue an order to the opposite party directing him to take any or more of the following actions namely:

- To remove the defects and deficiencies pointed out by the appropriate laboratory from the goods and services in question.
- To replace the goods with new goods of similar description which should be free from any defect.
- To return to the complainant the price or as the case may be, the charges paid by the complainant.
- To pay such amount as may be rewarded by it as compensation to the consumer for any loss or injury suffered by the consumer due to the negligence of the opposite party.
- To withdraw hazardous goods.
- To take steps to discontinue unfair or restrictive trade practices.

If a trader or person against whom a complaint is made, fails or omits to comply with any order made by a redressal agency, he shall be punishable with imprisonment upto three years or with fine not less than 25,000 extendable to 1 lakh, or both.

CONSUMER RIGHTS

To deal with cases of consumer exploitation, government of India has provided the following rights to all the consumers under the Consumer Protection Act, 2019:

1. Right to Safety:
Means right to be protected against the marketing of goods and services, which are hazardous to life and the property. This right not only meets their immediate needs but also fulfills their long term interest. Before purchasing, consumers should be informed of the products and services. They should preferably purchase quality marked products, such as ISI, AGMARK etc.

2. Right to be Informed:
Means the consumer has the right to be informed about the quality, quantity, potency, purity, standard and price of goods or services so as to protect the consumer against the abusive and unfair practices. The consumer should insist on getting all the information about the product or services before making a choice or a decision. This will enable the consumer to desist from falling prey to high pressure selling techniques.

3. Right to Choose:

Means right to be assured, wherever possible, of access to variety of goods and services at competitive price, of satisfactory quality and service at a fair price. It also includes right to basic goods and services. This is because of denial to the majority of their fair share. This right can be better exercised in a competitive market where a vast variety of choices are available to the consumer at competitive prices.

4. Right to be Heard:

Means that consumer interests will receive due consideration at appropriate forums. It also includes the right to be represented in various forums formed to consider the consumers' welfare. The consumers should form non-political and non-commercial consumer organisations and other bodies to give them unity and a platform to voice their problems.

5. Right to Seek Redressal:

Means right to be redressed against unfair trade practices or unscrupulous exploitation of consumers. Consumers must make complaint for their genuine grievances. Many a times their complaint may be of small value but its impact on the society as a whole may be very large. They can also take the help of consumer organisations for getting redressed of their grievances.

6. Right to Consumer Awareness:

Means the right to acquire the knowledge and skill to be an informed consumer throughout life. Ignorance of the rights is responsible for their exploitation. They should know their rights and must exercise them. Only then consumer exploitation will be prevented.

Thus, the concern of consumer protection is to ensure fair trade practices; maintain quality of goods and efficient service quantity, potency of the product, composition and price for their choice of purchase. Such a consumer protection policy would enable satisfaction from the delivery of goods and services needed by them.

Lesson at a Glance

- **Consumer:** Is a person who has indicated his/her willingness to obtain goods or services from a supplier with the intention of paying for them.
- **Consumer Exploitation:** When producers cheat consumers of their hard earned money and hurt them physically, mentally or financially, it is called consumer exploitation.
- **Ways in Which a Consumers gets Exploited:** (i) Under-weight and under-measurements; (ii) Sub-standard quality; (iii) High prices; (iv) Duplicate articles; (v) Adulteration and Impurity; (vi) Lack of safety devices; (vii) Artificial scarcity; (viii) False or incomplete information; (ix) Unsatisfactory after sale services; (x) Rough behaviour and undue conditions; (xi) Hidden price component; (xii) Environmental hazards; (xiii) Other ways.
- **Consumer Awareness:** It is the knowledge of rights and duties of a consumer; so that he/she does not get exploited. Consumer awareness can be promoted through consumer education.

- **Importance of Consumer Awareness:** (i) To achieve maximum satisfaction; (ii) Protect against exploitation; (iii) Control over consumption of harmful goods; (iv) Motivation for saving; (v) Knowledge regarding solution of problems; (vi) Construction of healthy society.
- **Consumer Protection Act, 2019:** The consumer protection act, 2019 was enacted to promote and protect the rights of the consumer. The Act provides for simple, speedy and inexpensive redressal of grievances and is compensatory in nature.
- **Consumer Rights:** (i) Rights to safety; (ii) Right to be informed; (iii) Right to choose; (iv) Right to be heard; (v) Right to seek redressal; (vi) Right to consumer awareness.

Your mother intends to purchase an automatic washing machine. Explain her the ways by which she may be exploited by the sellers/ manufacturers. Also explain her the rights which she enjoys as a consumer. In case, she is exploited, educate her where she should appeal for redressal of grievances and ways by which she may be protected.

Explain to your class the importance of consumer protection and why it is necessary.

A. Short Answer Type Questions:
1. Who is a consumer?
2. What is consumer exploitation?
3. How does false and incomplete information be a way for exploiting the consumers?
4. What is meant by hidden price component?
5. How do advertisement cause consumer exploitation?
6. Write a short note on consumer awareness.
7. "Consumer education is an important method to eliminate consumer exploitation." Explain.
8. What is COPRA 2019 and when did it come into force?
9. What are the two features of Consumer Protection Act 2019?
10. Explain the Right to Consumer Awareness under the Indian Consumer Protection Act 2019.

B. Essay Type Questions:
1. 'Consumer is the king of market', still he is exploited. Discuss the reasons.
2. What are the various ways by which consumers are exploited.   [ICSE 2020]
3. Explain the factors causing 'consumer exploitation'.
4. What is consumer awareness and how has it grown in recent times?
5. What is the need for consumer awareness in the modern days world?
6. Enumerate six consumer rights conferred upon the consumers by COPRA, 2019.

CHAPTER-08
E-Commerce

E-commerce is a means of conducting business, where the buying or selling of goods and services or the transmitting of funds or data, occur via electronic medium. There is no physical market place and the entire process of marketing and selling of goods, takes place on-line or electronically. This means, the buyer and the seller do not often meet face to face. It is a replica of a physical market place in the virtual world.

E-commerce, also called e-trading, operates in all four major market segments: Business to Business, Business to Consumer, Consumer to Consumer and Consumer to Business. Examples of E-commerce include on-line shopping, electronic payments, on-line auctions, Internet banking, on-line ticketing, etc.

- Meaning of E-Commerce
- Benefits over traditional means of transactions
- E-Tailing
- E-Advertising
- E-Marketing
- E-Security
- ERP and its Modules

BENEFITS OF E-COMMERCE OVER TRADITIONAL MEANS OF TRANSACTIONS

The key benefits of e-commerce revolve around the fact that it eliminates limitations of time and geographical distance, encountered while conducting business in a conventional manner. The advantages of e-commerce over traditional commerce are listed below:

(1) Overcomes Geographical Boundaries:
The reach of a physical store is limited to the area of its location. Even if it has several branches throughout the city or the country, the constraints of the physical space remains. However, an e-commerce web site can reach to customers beyond borders. This enables it to expand its market to national and international level with minimum capital investment.

(2) Wider Customer Reach:
E-commerce businesses can get new customers more easily than traditional businesses. This is due to the fact that e-commerce has a wider reach than traditional marketing networks. They can promote their business on the Internet, on various social networking sites as well as on television, newspapers etc., to reach their target audience.

(3) Lowers Cost:
Setting up an e-commerce network is cheaper as compared to a traditional business set-up. The cost of labour, personnel management, infrastructure, advertising and marketing is comparatively less. A part of these lowered costs is passed on to customers in the form of discounted prices.

E-commerce also lowers the cost for consumers by eliminating travel time and costs incurred in commuting to the physical store. E-commerce allows them to access desired products and services, with just a few mouse clicks.

(4) Remains Open all the Time:
E-commerce provides the option for the consumers to shop any time, as per their convenience. Unlike traditional shops, the e-commerce sites never shut down and that allows the businesses to thrive.

(5) Enables Comparative Shopping:
E-commerce facilitates comparison shopping. A customers can compare between various brands and prices, which helps him in making the best choice.

(6) Customer Care and Feedback:
E-commerce facilitates quick redressal of consumer's grievances. These web sites provide users an opportunity to write down their feedback through which they can identify needs and demands of customers. Most of the traditional and local form of businesses have failed to establish good relationship with consumers and customer service is slow.

E-TAILING

E-Tailing is the abbreviation of electronic retailing. It is the sale of goods and services through the Internet. E-tailing involves business-to-business or business-to-customers transactions. It can be regarded as the Internet front of any traditional retailer.

E-tailing shops believe in building strong brands. The web sites they create are easily understood by the visitors. They also provide discounts and offers to engage the customers. The pricing, in E-tailing shops, is generally lower than that of a traditional shop. In this way the e-tailing shops lure the customers to make purchases on-line. The customers also get benefited from the fact that he/she does not need to physically visit the shop for making the purchase. The customers are free to make their own decisions regarding the purchase, at their own leisure time.

However, e-tailing shops need to have a strong distribution network in order to secure the delivery of the products. Otherwise, the purpose of the e-tailing site will be defeated. Big e-tailing sites like Ebay.com and Amazon.com are making great business in this country.

Advantages of E-Tailing
1. No requirement of physical infrastructure.
2. Order completion is smoother than that of physical shops.
3. Customers might get addicted to on-line shopping, which in turn boost sales and increase revenue.
4. It is easy to review the product before, actually, purchasing it.
5. Most items available on-line are cheaper with quick and easy shipping and returns.

Disadvantages of E-Tailing

1. Creating and maintaining an e-tailing web site is an expensive process.
2. Customers do not often get to check the actual dimensions of the products and the quality displayed there.
3. Customers may have trust issues before providing their personal details and credit card details.

E-ADVERTISING

E-Advertising is the mechanism of promoting products or services on-line. It is the process of gaining attention of the customers, through the digital media.

The main purpose of e-advertising is to reach out to a wider range of customers. It is more cost effective when compared to the traditional forms of advertising. E-advertising also enables you to target the specific customers.

On safeguard to be taken regarding E-advertising is that advertisements have to be consistently monitored and controlled because if it is done poorly, it can severely damage the image of the company.

Features

1. E-advertising will only be published on the Internet.
2. Sometimes e-advertising will provide hyper links to the company's web site.
3. Can include image, texts, and even animations within the advertisements.

Types of E-Advertising

There are various types of e-advertising.

(a) Wallpaper Advertising:
It changes the background of the web site to the chosen promotion.

(b) Pop Up Advertising:
It pops up a new screen upon clicking on a certain link on the web site, that itself advertises the product.

(c) Floating Advertising:
The floating e-advertising is a kind of a floating banner on the web site, which tempts the visitor to click on it.

(d) Ad Sense Advertising:
This refers to companies' paying major search engines (such as Google) to promote their business within the first three links that appear when a search is entered.

E-MARKETING

Electronic Marketing (e-marketing) is also known as Internet marketing, web marketing, digital marketing on on-line marketing. It is the process of marketing a product or service using the Internet, e-mail and wireless media. Unlike e-advertising, e-marketing is very subtle. It is not always a direct message of persuasion but rather it is something which will educate the customers and convince them to buy the product or service.

Digital marketing techniques include Search Engine optimization (SEO), Search Engine Marketing (SEM), content marketing, e-commerce marketing, social media marketing, display advertisement, marketing through SMS and on-hold mobile ring tones, etc.

When compared to the means of traditional marketing, e-marketing offers several advantages.

Advantages of E-Marketing

1. E-marketing provides much better return on the investment made by the marketer.
2. It reduces the cost of marketing campaign.
3. The marketer can easily monitor and track the results of the campaign.
4. The results are often easily measurable and quickly obtained.
5. E-marketing allows marketers to create viral content, allowing viral marketing.

Disadvantages of E-Marketing

1. Devising a strong online marketing campaign involves spending money, the cost of which is ultimately borne by the customer. The cost of website design, software, hardware, maintenance of website, online distribution cost and invested time, are also factored in, while deciding the cost of providing a service or a product online.
2. Website of the company has to be constantly updated, which required research and skills and thus timing of updates is also critical.
3. Digital marketing is not suitable for marketing of industrial goods and pharmaceutical products making it useful for only specific categories of products, namely consumer goods.

Types of E-Marketing

There are several options through which the e-marketers can promote their product and services:

1. Article Marketing:
Writing articles about products and services often helps in the process of educating the customers.

2. Affiliate Marketing:
It is a kind of referral marketing where reference of any product will be provided on the other websites and when the customer buy's the product based on the recommendation this website owner with gets commission.

3. Video Marketing:
In this kind of e-marketing, a video will be shared describing the usage and benefits of the product or a service. It is often similar to television commercials.

4. Email Marketing:
Direct emails are being sent to potential customers describing benefits of the product or service.

5. Blogging:
Publishing blogs about similar products is also a very subtle way of marketing some business.

6. Social Media Marketing:
This form of marketing means promoting company's products and service on social media handles like facebook, Twitter and instragram. It is cost-effective because these platforms allow business to create profiles for free.

E-SECURITY

E-security is the process of securing the data and information, adopted by a website, from the external attacks. It involves protection of e-commerce assets from unauthorized access, use, alteration or destruction. Various e-marketing and e-tailing websites follow strict e-security measures in order to protect their sensitive information, from getting hacked.

Many customers provide their personal and financial information on these sites, which makes e-security crucial for the e-shopping websites.

Harms Caused by the Lack of E-Security

1. Data about customers being stolen.
2. Bank account details can be hacked and used for malicious purposes.
3. Blocking of real time financial transactions between the customer and the website and steal the customer's money.
4. Steal business information.
5. Hack and modify the website.

Ways to Minimize E-Security Threats

1. Preventing unauthorized data modification.
2. Protection against unauthorized data disclosure.
3. Authentication of data source.
4. Developing security policy, listing what data has to be protected, from whom and by whom.
5. Creating a security organisation to implement and administer security policy.
6. Performing a security audit regularly.

ENTERPRISE RESOURCE PLANNING AND ITS MODULES

Enterprise Resource Planning or ERP is a kind of software which is used to manage various functions of an organization. Right from the inventory management to payment done to the employees, every aspect of the business can be monitored and managed by the system.

ERP manages business processes of various departments and functions and helps the top management to have a better sense and control over the business. The centralized software system is divided into some basic modules, based on which the performance of the various departments can be checked. The following are the basic modules of ERP:

1. Human Resource:
This module helps in managing and tracking employees' performance. It also helps the management to decide on the pay hike and performance bonus.

2. Inventory:
This module helps the inventory system to keep track of the items and trace their current location in organization.

3. Sales & Marketing:
It tracks the sales process starting from the queries made by the customers to the dispatch of the orders.

4. Purchase:
It keeps track of all the purchases made by the organization.

5. Finance & Accounting:
Whole inflow & outflow of money/capital is managed by the finance module.

6. Customer Relationship Management (CRM):
CRM module helps to manage and track detailed information of the customer.

7. Engineering/Production:
This module consists of functionalities like production planning, machine scheduling, raw material usage, Bill of material preparation, track daily production progress, production forecasting and actual production reporting.

8. Supply Chain Management (SCM):
SCM module manages the flow of product items from manufacturer to consumer and consumer to manufacturer.

LESSON AT A GLANCE

- **E-Commerce:** E-Commerce is the means of conducting business where the buying or selling of goods and services occur via electronic medium.
- **Benefits:** (i) Overcomes geographical boundaries, (ii) Wider customer reach, (iii) Lowers Cost, (iv) Remains Open all Time, (v) Enables comparative shopping, (vi) Customer care and feedback.
- **E-Tailing:** E-Tailing is the abbreviation of E-Retailing. E-tailing can involve business-to-business or business-to-customers transactions. It can be regarded as the Internet front of any traditional retailer.
- **E-Advertising:** E-Advertising is the mechanism of promoting products or services online. It is the process of gaining the attention of the customers through the digital media.
- **E-Marketing:** E-Marketing is also known as Internet Marketing and it comprises of a whole array of activities on the Internet in order to create awareness about a certain product or a service.
- **E-Security:** E-Security is the process of securing the data and information, adopted by a website, from the external attacks.

- **ERP:** Enterprise Resource Planning or ERP is a kind of software which is used to manage the various functions of an organization.
- **ERP Modules:** (i) Human Resource, (ii) Inventory, (iii) Sales and Marketing, (iv) Purchase, (v) Finance and Accounting, (vi) CRM, (vii) Engineering (Supply chain management) Production, (viii) SCM.

Project Work

Study the promotional offers given in a e-shopping website and write a report on the kind of discounts and offers they provide.

Assignment

Explain to your class the concept of e-security in online shopping and why it is necessary.

Questions

A. **Short Answer Type Questions:**
1. What is e-commerce?
2. State two advantages of e-commerce.
3. State one disadvantage of e-tailing.
4. What is e-advertising?
5. State two features of e-advertising.
6. State two types of e-advertising.
7. What is e-marketing?
8. State and describe one form of e-marketing.
9. What is e-security?
10. State one reason for ensuring e-security.
11. What is ERP?
12. What does the production module of ERP do?
13. What is the function of the SCM module of ERP?
14. What is e-tailing? [ICSE 2020]
15. What do you mean by e-security? [ICSE 2020]

B. **Essay Type Questions:**
1. What is e-tailing? What are the advantages of e-tailing?
2. Describe in details the shortcomings of e-tailing.
3. What is e-advertising? What are the different types of e-advertising?
4. What is e-marketing? What are the different forms of e-marketing?
5. What is e-security? What are the downsides of not having e-security?
6. What is ERP? Explain any three modules of ERP system. [ICSE 2020]
7. Briefly discuss any five advantages of e-commerce over traditional methods of transactions. [ICSE 2019]

CHAPTER-09
Capital and Revenue

CAPITAL RECEIPTS

Capital receipts are the receipts which are not received in the ordinary course of business. These are non-recurring receipts and their benefit is enjoyed over a long period of time.

Examples of capital receipts include:
(i) Money obtained from the sale of fixed assets or investments.
(ii) issue of shares or debentures
(iii) Loans raised
(iv) Additional capital introduced the proprietor etc.

Capital receipts are shown on the liabilities side of the Balance Sheet.

REVENUE RECEIPTS

Revenue receipts are the receipts which are obtained in the normal course of business. They are a receipt against supply of goods or services. These receipts help a business to carry out its day-to-day activities and are recurring in nature.

- Meaning of Capital Receipts
- Meaning of Revenue Receipts
- Difference between Capital and Revenue Receipts
- Meaning of Capital Expenditure
- Meaning of Revenue Expenditure
- Difference between Capital and Revenue Expenditure
- Deferred Revenue Expenditure

Examples of revenue receipts include:
(i) income received from sale of goods
(ii) interest earned on investments,
(iii) rent received from leasing out business property,
(iv) commission received,
(v) dividend received from shares etc.

Revenue receipts are credited to profit and loss account.

Difference Between Capital and Revenue Receipts

Basis of Difference	Revenue Receipts	Capital Receipts
Meaning	Revenue Receipts are the incomes that are generated from the operating activities of the business.	Capital Receipts are the incomes that are generated from investment and financing activities of the business.
Effect	They have a short term effect. The benefit of these receipts is derived for one accounting period only.	It has a long term effect. The benefit of these receipts is derived over many accounting periods.

Basis of Difference	Revenue Receipts	Capital Receipts
Nature	They are obtained repeatedly over the course of business, *i.e.*, they are recurring in nature.	They are non-repetitive and non-recurring in nature.
Generation of Capital and Revenue Receipts	Revenue receipts do not generate capital receipts.	Capital receipts generate revenue receipts when capital is invested by the owner of the business.
Value of Asset or Liability	These receipts increase the value of assets and decrease the value of liabilities.	These receipts increase the value of liability and decrease the value of asset.
Shown in	These receipts are shown in the Profit and Loss account.	These receipts get reflected in the Balance Sheet.
Nature of Expenses Incurred to Generate Receipts	Sometimes, expenses of capital nature have to be incurred to gene-rate revenue receipts, *e.g.*, purchase of shares of a company is capital expenditure but dividend received on shares is a revenue receipt.	Sometimes, expenses of revenue nature have to be incurred to generate capital receipts, *e.g.*, on obtaining loan (which is a capital receipt), interest is paid until its repayment which is a revenue expenditure.
Received in exchange of	Income	Source of income

CAPITAL EXPENDITURE

The expenditure incurred for acquiring a fixed asset or which results in increasing the earning capacity of the business is called capital expenditure. These expenditures are 'non-recurring' in nature and the assets which are acquired by incurring capital expenditure are used in the business and are not for sale. The benefit of these expenditures is derived over several accounting periods.

Capital expenditures aid the process of production of goods and services and helps in reducing costs and in increasing the profits of a business.

Examples of capital expenditure include:
(i) Purchase of land, building, machinery or furniture
(ii) Cost of acquisition of long term rights and benefits (*e.g.*, Patents, copyrights),
(iii) Cost of addition or extensions to existing asset.
(iv) Cost of overhauling second hand machine.
(v) Preliminary expenses incurred before the commencement of business such as legal charges paid for drafting the memorandum and articles of association of a company or brokerage paid to brokers, or commission paid to underwriters for raising capital.

REVENUE EXPENDITURE

The expenditure incurred for conducting the day-to-day business of a firm is called the revenue expenditure. These expenditures are incurred on a regular basis and the benefits from these expenditures are obtained over a relatively short period of time. These expenditures are also known as "expired costs".

These expenditures are incurred on items or services which are useful to the business but are used up in less than one year. Therefore, they amount to temporary increase in profit.

Examples of revenue expenditure include:
(i) Salaries and wages paid to employees.
(ii) Rent paid for the factory or office premises.
(iii) Depreciation on plant and machinery.
(iv) Expenditure on consumable items, on goods and services for resale either in their original or improved form such as on purchase of raw material.
(v) Expenditure incurred on purchase of goods meant for sale such as carriage inwards, octroi, import duty etc.

Difference Between Capital Expenditure and Revenue Expenditure

Basis of Difference	Revenue Expenditure	Capital Expenditure
Purpose	This expenditure is incurred in acquiring a fixed asset or improving the capacity of an existing one, resulting in the extension of its life years.	This expenditure is incurred in regulating day to day activities of the business.
Effect	The effect is temporary and the benefits are derived during one accounting year only.	The effect is long term. The benefits are availed over many accounting periods.
Acquisition of Assets	No assets are acquired.	An asset is acquired or the value of an existing asset is increased.
Occurrence of Expenditure	It is a recurring expense	It is a non-recurring expense.
Nature of Expense	This expense is incurred in order to maintain the business.	This expense is incurred in order to improve the position of the business.
Earning Capacity	It does not increase the earning capacity of a business.	It increases the earning capacity of a business.
Placement in Financial Statements	It appears in the trading or profit and loss account and is shown on the debit side of the either of the two accounts.	It appears in the balance sheet on the asset side.

| Amount Involved | The amount involved in revenue expenditure is relatively small. | Capital expenditures tend to involve larger monetary amounts than revenue expenditures. |

DEFERRED REVENUE EXPENDITURE

Deferred Revenue Expenditures are those expenditures which are incurred in one accounting period and they do not create any assets but their benefit is spread over more than one accounting period. It is a kind of revenue expenditure and is incurred during a particular accounting period but is applicable either wholly or in part to future accounting periods. These expenses are usually large in amount.

A proportionate amount is charged to profit and loss account of each year and the balance is carried forward to subsequent years as deferred revenue expenditure. It is shown as an asset in the balance sheet.

Examples of Deferred Revenue Expenditure include:
(i) Discount on issue of shares and debentures,
(ii) Heavy initial advertising expenditure incurred for introducing a new product in the market,
(iii) Expenditure incurred on research and development,
(iv) Repairing and painting of building,
(v) Expenditure incurred in shifting business to more convenient premises.

LESSON AT A GLANCE

- **Capital Receipt:** Capital receipts are the receipts which are not received in the ordinary course of business. These are non-recurring receipts and their benefit is enjoyed over a long period of time.
- **Revenue Receipt:** Revenue receipts are the receipts which are obtained in the normal course of business. They are receipts against supply of goods or services.
- **Capital Expenditure:** The expenditure incurred for acquiring a fixed asset or which results in increasing the earning capacity of the business is called capital expenditure.
- **Revenue Expenditure:** The expenditure incurred for conducting the day-to-day business of a firm is called the revenue expenditure.
- **Deferred Revenue Expenditure:** Deferred Revenue Expenditures are those expenditures which are incurred in one accounting period and they do not create any assets but their benefit is spread over more than one accounting period.

Analyze balance sheets of a firm for 5 consecutive years and find out the change in the capital investments made. Try and find out the reasons for the change in capital investments.

Capital and Revenue

 **ASSIGNMENT**

Try and find out 10 examples of deferred revenue expenditure of a business firm and explain the benefits derived from those expenditures.

 **QUESTIONS**

A. **Short Answer Type Questions:**
   1. Define Capital Receipt.
   2. What is revenue receipt?
   3. State two differences between capital and revenue receipt.
   4. What is capital expenditure?
   5. What is meant by revenue expenditure? [ICSE 2017]
   6. State two differences between capital and revenue expenditure.
   7. What is meant by deferred revenue expenditure? [ICSE 2019]
   8. Distinguish between capital and revenue expenditure. [ICSE 2020]
   9. What is meant by 'Capital Receipt'?

B. **Essay Type Questions:**
   1. What is capital receipt? Describe with examples.
   2. What is revenue receipt? Describe with examples.
   3. State the differences between capital and revenue receipts.
   4. What is capital expenditure? Describe with examples.
   5. What is revenue expenditure? Describe with examples.
   6. What are the differences between capital and revenue expenditure?
   7. Explain the concept of deferred revenue expenditure and how it is entered in the books of accounts.

CHAPTER-10
Final Accounts of a Sole Trader

FINAL ACCOUNTS

Mathematical accuracy of account books is ascertained by trial balance. After ascertaining mathematical accuracy of account books, every businessman wants to know whether he has earned a profit or suffered a loss during the accounting period and what is the financial position of his business at the end of the said accounting period. To obtain this information, final accounts are prepared with the help of the trial balance which include the following:

(A) Trading Account; (B) Profit and Loss Account; and (C) Balance Sheet.

Trading account reveals gross profit or gross loss for the accounting period while profit and loss account portrays net profit or net loss. Balance Sheet discloses financial position of the business on the last day of the accounting period. Since these accounts or statements are prepared at the end of the accounting period and in the last stage of accounting process and books of the business are closed after the preparation of these, so they are known as 'Final Accounts'. These are also termed as 'Financial Statements'.

- *Meaning of Final Accounts*
- *Meaning of Sole Proprietorship*
- *Preparation of Final Accounts*
- *Trial Balance*
- *Trading Account*
- *Main Items of Trading Account on Debit and Credit Side*
- *Determining Gross Profit or Gross Loss on Trading*
- *Profit and Loss Account*
- *Main Items of Profit and Loss Account on Debit and Credit Side*
- *Some specific items which are not shown in Profit and Loss Account*
- *Balance Sheet*
- *Preparation of Balance Sheet*
- *Items included in Balance Sheet on Liability Side and Asset Side*
- *Format of a Balance Sheet*

Final accounts are of great need and importance, not only for the owner of the business but also for other parties related to the business, such as creditors, lenders, employees, etc. On the basis of final accounts, creditors and lenders take decisions relating to credit sales and loan facility, respectively. Employees estimate the stability of their employment, increments in salary and promotions on the basis of profit/loss and financial position of the business. Final accounts of large companies are also important for Government, investors and public at large. Government receives revenue from these companies, in form of taxes while investors receive return on their investment. Public at large is also affected by these companies because their failure causes loss to national property.

SOLE PROPRIETORSHIP

A sole proprietor, also known as a sole trader, is a person who owns the business and is personally responsible for its debts. He can conduct a business under his own name or under a fictitious name. He pays personal income tax, based on the profit he earns. He typically signs contracts in his own name because sole proprietorship has no separate legal entity.

PREPARATION OF FINAL ACCOUNTS

For the preparation of final accounts of a business, it is essential that proper accounts of transactions during the accounting period should be maintained and while maintaining these accounts, adherence to basic concepts, conventions and assumptions of accounting be ensured. From this point of view, the following points are worth mentioning :

1. Since business and businessman are separate entities and final accounts are prepared to disclose profit or loss and financial position of business, personal incomes and expenses of the businessman should be separated from business incomes and expenses.
2. Capital and revenue incomes and expenses should be differentiated.
3. Incomes and expenses of the accounting period should be separated from the incomes and expenses related to other period.

(A) Trial Balance

The starting point for preparing final accounts is the trial balance prepared by the book-keeper. It is a list of all balances standing in the ledger accounts and cash book of a firm, at any given time. It is the shortest method of verifying the arithmetical accuracy of entries made in the ledger. If the trial balance agrees, it is an indication that the accounts are correctly written up but it is not a conclusive proof. All the figures recorded in the trial balance helps to prepare the, Trading A/c, Profit & Loss A/c and Balance Sheet.

Preparation:

There are two methods for preparing the trial balance:

First Method:

In this method, ledger accounts are not balanced, they are totaled. The debit totals of and the credit side are entered in a separate sheet. The grand total of debit column will be equal to the grand total of the credit column.

Second Method:

This method is more widely used. In this method, ledger accounts are balanced. The brought down balances are then brought to a sheet as given below:

Firm's Books

Trial Balance as on.........20.........

S. No.	Name of Account	L.F.	Debit Balance (in rupees)	Credit Balance (in rupees)

Assets, Sundry Debtors, Losses, Expenses and Drawings are debit balances. Capital, Liabilities, Sundry Creditors, Gains, Incomes and Capital, Revenues are credit balances. Debit and credit balances should match, which would be an indication that accounts have been correctly prepared.

(B) Trading Account

Trading account, in nature, is a nominal account. It is also called Goods A/c. It provides information about the gross result of trade (*i.e.* purchase and sale of finished goods) during the accounting period which is known as gross profit or loss. For this, net sale value of goods sold, generally known as 'net sales', during the accounting period is compared with the cost of goods sold. If the former exceeds the later, excess is termed as 'gross profit'. In the reverse case, *i.e.*, if the former is less than the later, the deficit is known as gross loss. This gross profit or loss is transferred to profit and loss account. Net sales means the amount derived by subtracting sales return from the total of cash and credit sales while cost of goods sold is calculated as follows :

Cost of Goods Sold = Opening Stock + Net Purchases – Closing Stock + Direct Expenses

Direct expenses are all those expenses which are incurred in bringing the purchased goods to the godown or trading place of the trader.

For example, if the opening stock of the year is ₹ 50,000, net purchases during the year is ₹ 4,00,000 and closing stock at the end of the year is ₹ 30,000, then cost of goods sold will be ₹ 50,000 + ₹ 4,00,000 – ₹ 30,000 = ₹ 4,20,000. If net sales during the year is ₹ 6,00,000, amount of gross profit will be ₹ 6,00,000 – ₹ 4,20,000 = ₹ 1,80,000.

Format of Trading Account

Trading Account

Dr. For the year ended............ Cr.

Particulars	Amount (₹)	Particulars	Amount (₹)
To Opening Stock	....	By Sales	
To Purchases		Cash	
Less: Purchases Returns		Credit	
on Return Outwards		*Less:* Sales Returns	
Less: Goods used as :		or Return Inwards	....
Charity		By Closing Stock	....
Drawings		By Profit & Loss A/c	....
Donation		(Gross Loss transferred to	
Loss by fire theft		P & L A/c)	
Free Sample			
To Wages/Wages on Purchases	....		

To Wages and Salaries	....		
To Carriage/Carriage Inward	....		
To Inward Expenses	....		
To Custom Duty	....		
To Import Duty	....		
To Freight/Freight on Purchases	....		
To Railways Freight	....		
To Dock Charges	....		
To Brokerage & Commission on Purchases	....		
To Cartage/Cartage on Purchases	....		
To Royalty on Purchases	....		
To Other Direct Expenses	....		
To Profit & Loss A/c (Gross Profit transferred to P & L A/c)			
	....		....

Main Items to be shown on debit side of trading account

1. Opening Stock:
Closing stock of the previous accounting year is opening stock for the current year, which is shown on the debit side of the trading account. There is no opening stock in the first year of a business. Opening stock includes opening stock of raw material, opening stock of semi-finished goods and opening stock of finished goods.

2. Purchases:
It includes purchases of goods during the accounting year in cash and on credit for the purpose of sale. It is shown on the debit side of trading account. But assets purchased during the year and goods received on consignment are not included in purchases. Amount of net purchases is shown on the debit side of the trading account for which the following items are subtracted from the total purchases: (i) Purchases return, (ii) Donation of goods, (iii) Drawings of goods by the owner of the business, (iv) Theft of goods, (v) Loss of goods by fire, (vi) Goods distributed as free sample, and (vii) Goods used as advertisement material etc.

3. Direct Expenses:
All the expenses incurred in bringing the purchased goods to the godown of the trader or trading place are known as direct expenses, *e.g.*, carriage inward, brokerage and commission on purchases, wages, import duty, octroi, etc. If such expenses are related to the purchase of an asset, then these will not be debited to trading account. Rather, these will be added to the cost of that asset.

Main items to be shown on credit side of trading account

1. Sales:

Aggregate of cash and credit sales of goods during the accounting year is termed as total sales. Net sales is ascertained by deducting the amount of sales return from total sales which is shown on the credit side of trading account. Here, it is pertinent to note that sale of assets is not shown in trading account.

2. Closing Stock:

Goods remaining unsold at the end of the accounting year are known as closing stock. A single account is not sufficient to open in account books to show inflow and outflow of goods, rather several accounts are opened for this purpose, viz. opening stock account, purchases account, purchases return account, sales account, sales return account, etc. Therefore, closing stock account generally does not exist in trial balance. To ascertain the amount of closing stock, goods remaining unsold at the end of the year are physically counted and evaluated. The amount thus ascertained is shown on the credit side of trading account and on the assets side of balance sheet. If closing stock already exists in the trial balance, it is shown only on the assets side of balance sheet and not on the credit side of trading account.

3. Sales Returns:

Sales returns must be deducted from total sales and to be shown on the credit side of the trading account. Sales returned are the sold goods which are returned by the customers.

Determining Gross Profit or Gross Loss on Trading account

When all the necessary balances have been transferred to the Trading Account, the balance of this account will represent Gross Profit (if it is a credit balance, *i.e.*, if the credit total of Trading Account exceeds its debit total) or Gross Loss (if it is a debit balance, *i.e.*, if the debit total of the Trading Account exceeds its credit total). If there is no balance, it would mean the absence of Gross Profit or Gross Loss. The balance of the Trading Account will then be transferred to the Profit and Loss Account.

If the Trading Account has a credit balance implying Gross Profit, Profit and Loss Account would be credited and Trading Account will be debited. If the Trading Account has a debit balance implying Gross Loss, Profit and Loss Account would be debited and the Trading Account credited with the amount thereof.

(C) Profit and Loss Account

After ascertaining the Gross Profit, the next stage is to prepare the Profit and Loss Account. Besides the normal purpose for helping the management in understanding the performance of business, this Profit and Loss Account is necessary for two other purposes also.

Firstly, the profits can be distributed to the owners only out of net profit. Secondly, the tax liability is computed after ascertaining the net profit. The profit and Loss Account is an account which shows the net result of the operations of the enterprise during the financial year. The main feature of a Profit and Loss Account is that it contains indirect gains (*i.e.*, gains or incomes not directly connected with the routine business activities *e.g.*, rent received, sale of old newspapers, commission from agency etc.) and indirect expenses (connected with selling or distribution of goods, administration like salaries, etc.)

Final Accounts of a Sole Trader

Need:

The purpose of preparing the Profit and Loss Account is to ascertain the net profit or net loss from business operations. The net income of the current year can be compared with that of previous years, and deviation in incomes of different periods may be analysed to ascertain the causes of such deviations. Such an analysis will be helpful in controlling expenses that are incurred in running the business enterprise in selling the goods and in eliminating wastage.

Format of Profit and Loss Account

Profit and Loss Account

Dr. For the year ending………… Cr.

Particulars	Amount (₹)	Particulars	Amount (₹)
To Trading a/c (Gross Loss)	…………	By Trading A/c (Gross Profit)	…………
To Salaries & Wages	…………	By Interest Earned	…………
To Rent, Rates & Taxes	…………	By Commission Earned	…………
To Fire Insurance Premium	…………	By Rent Earned	…………
To Repairs & Maintenance	…………	By Profit on Sale of Fixed Assets	…………
To Royalty on Sales	…………	By Income from Investments	…………
To Depreciation	…………	By Sale of Scrap	…………
To Audit Fees	…………	By Miscellaneous Incomes	…………
To Bank Charges	…………	By Discount Received	…………
To Legal Charges	…………	By Dividends Received	…………
To Miscellaneous Expenses	…………	By Apprentice Premium	…………
To Discount Allowed	…………	By Bad Debts Recovered	…………
To Interest/Interest on Loans	…………	By Capital a/c (Net Loss transferred to Capital Account)	…………
To Carriage Outward	…………		
To Freight Outward	…………		
To Commission on Sales	…………		
To Trade Expenses	…………		
To Travelling Expenses	…………		
To Entertainment Expenses	…………		
To Sales Promotion Expenses	…………		
To Advertising and Publicity	…………		
To Bad Debts	…………		
To Packing Expenses	…………		
To Loss on Sale of Fixed Asset	…………		
To Loss by Theft	…………		
To Loss by Fire	…………		

To Loss by Embezzlement	....		
To Printing & Stationery	....		
To Postage & Telephone Expense	....		
To Office Expenses	....		
To Other Indirect Expenses	....		
To Capital A/c (Net Profit transferred to Capital A/c)	....		
	....		....

Main Items to be Shown on the Debit Side of Profit and Loss Account

1. Gross Loss:
If trading account discloses gross loss, it is shown on the debit side of profit and loss account, first of all.

2. Indirect Expenses:
All expenses other than direct expenses are known as indirect expenses. Such expenses have no relationship with purchase of goods. These include administrative expenses (such as; salary of employees, officers employed in general office, rent and taxes of office building, printing and stationery, postage, telegrams, fax and telephone expenses, etc.), selling and distribution expenses (such as; godown expenses, advertisement expenses, commission of sales representative, freight and cartage on sales, packing expenses, etc.), finance expenses (such as; interest on loan, interest on capital, interest on bank overdraft, etc.) and other miscellaneous expenses (such as; donation, subscription, etc.).

3. Losses:
Loss on sale of fixed assets and all other losses related to business are shown on the debit side of profit and loss account. Depreciation on fixed assets, bad debts, loss of goods by theft, fire or any natural calamity etc., are some examples of these losses.

Main Items to be Shown on the Credit Side of Profit and Loss Account

1. Gross Profit:
If trading account reveals gross profit, it is shown on the credit side of profit and loss account.

2. Incomes and Gains:
All incomes and gains except those which are credited to trading account, are shown on the credit side of profit and loss account. Example of such incomes and gains are; discount received, rent received, commission received, interest received on investment, interest received from debtors, recovery of bad debts, profit on sale of fixed assets, etc.

Some Specific Items Which Are Not Shown In Profit And Loss Account

1. Drawings:
Drawings from the business by the businessman whether these are in the form of cash or goods or payment of his personal expenses (such as; life insurance premium, club membership fees, etc.) are not business expenses. Therefore, these

should not be debited to profit and loss account, rather, these should be debited to businessman's capital account.

2. Income Tax:
In case of single entrepreneurship, income tax is the personal expense of a businessman. Therefore, it is treated as drawings and debited to capital account and not to profit and loss account. In case of partnership firms and companies, payable income tax is a business expense. Therefore, it is debited to profit and loss account just like other expenses.

3. Sales Tax:
It is a tax which the businessman collects from the customers and then deposits in the Government treasury. Therefore, sales tax should not be shown in profit and loss account. If the amount of sales tax, though collected but has not been deposited with the Government treasury by the time of preparation of final accounts, it should be shown on the liabilities side of balance sheet.

4. Ascertaining Net Profit or Loss:
Net profit or net loss is ascertained by comparing the totals of debit and credit sides of profit and loss account. If the total of credit side is more than that of debit side, the excess will be net profit. In the reverse case, there will be net loss. This net profit or loss is transferred to capital account.

(D) Balance Sheet

The information conveyed by the Trading and Profit and Loss Account is no doubt very valuable to the owner of a business, as it enables him to determine the Gross and Net Profit and loss resulting from his dealings during a fiscal period. This, however, is not the only point on which a businessman wants to be enlightened. As his assets and liabilities change from day to day, as a result of business transactions, he also wants to find out what his true financial position is at the end of each trading period. In the first place, he would like to know whether the net profit as is disclosed by the Profit and Loss Account is correctly arrived at, if so, his capital at the end of the period must be necessarily increased by that amount. He is equally anxious to see for himself as to how such capital is locked up, *i.e.*, what the components, assets and liabilities are, of which this capital is made up. In order, to obtain this information at the end of the trading period, he has to set out his Assets and Liabilities in the shape of a statement and this statement is called the Balance Sheet.

- A Balance Sheet may, therefore, be defined as *"A statement prepared with a view to measure the exact financial position of a business on a certain fixed date."*
- *"Balance Sheet is a screen picture of the financial position of a going business at a certain moment."*
  —Francis R. Stead

It is prepared from the Trial Balance, after all the balances on nominal accounts are transferred to the Trading and Profit and Loss Account and the corresponding accounts in the Ledger are closed. The balances now left in the Trial Balance and remaining open in the Ledger represent either Personal Accounts or Real Accounts. In other words, they represent either Assets or Liabilities existing at the date of the financial close.

All such assets and liabilities are set out in the Balance Sheet in a classified form. On the right-hand side are shown the various assets or possessions of the business and on the left-hand side, the various liabilities, *i.e.*, the amounts owing by the business. The excess of assets over liabilities represents the capital of the owner. This figure of capital must tally with the closing balance of the Capital Account in the Ledger after the net profit or loss has been transferred thereto. As the balance of Profit and Loss Account is transferred to the Capital Account and as the closing balance on the Capital Account is shown in the Balance Sheet, it is clear that the Balance Sheet shows the financial position, inclusion of the profit or loss made during the trading period. It is called a Balance Sheet because it is a sheet of balances of ledger accounts which are still open after the preparation of the Trading and Profit and Loss Account.

The Balance Sheet is prepared on a particular date and, therefore, the information contained in it is valid only for that date. In a Balance Sheet, the total of all assets and all liabilities must be equal to the total of all liabilities and capital at a given date, *i.e.*,

Total Assets = Capital + Liabilities
or
Capital = Total Assets – Liabilities

In preparing the Balance Sheet, the accounting equation serves as the base. The accounting equation states that Total Assets = Capital + Liabilities or Capital = Total Assets – Liabilities. It becomes convenient and logical that there should be two sides—the Assets and the Liabilities. thus, both the sides should tally.

Preparation of Balance Sheet

As the purpose of Balance Sheet is to show the financial position of the business, it follows that it should be drawn out in some intelligible form or order.

The Assets and Liabilities should be grouped together and properly classified under appropriate heads so as to convey the information in a summarized form. The Debtors and Creditors need not be shown in the shape of individual balances, but must be set out in total. Further, the balance owing by customers must be shown separately under the heading of "Trade Debtors" or "Book Debts" and must not be mixed up with Debtors for Loans or Prepaid Expenses. Similarly, Trade Creditors must be distinguished from Creditors for Loans, or from Liabilities for Expenses. In fact, the whole of the Assets and Liabilities must be disclosed in a manner as would present a clear view of the true state of affairs to anyone reading the Balance Sheet.

No definite rules can be laid down as to the correct order in which the Assets and Liabilities shall appear in the Balance Sheet. It is usual, however, to start with the Fixed Assets, and follow it with the Floating Assets in the order of realization. Similarly, the Fixed Liabilities are stated first and are followed by Floating Liabilities. There are concerns, however, which prefer to reverse this order and in Partnership Accounts, usually the assets are shown in the natural order of their reliability and the liabilities in the order in which they are payable.

Again, banks usually prefer to state assets in order of their realisability. Thus, the most liquid assets are set out first and are followed by assets which are more difficult in realisation.

Items included on the Liability side of the Balance Sheet

1. Current Liabilities:
Current Liabilities are those liabilities which are expected to be paid within a year and which are usually to be paid out of Current Assets.

2. Bank Overdraft:
When an undertaking withdraws from the bank more than the amount deposited in its account, it is known as overdraft.

3. Outstanding Expenses:
Those expenses which have become due for payment but have not yet been paid, are known as outstanding expenses.

4. Bills Payable:
Bills of exchange accepted in favour of creditors, are known as bills payable. They represent the amount of bills which have not yet become due for payment.

5. Sundry Creditors:
This represents the sum total of credit balances appearing in the accounts of creditors.

6. Long-term Liabilities:
Those liabilities which matures for payment after a period of one year, are known as long-term liabilities.

7. Contingent Liabilities:
Those liabilities which are not liability on the date of Balance Sheet, but may or may not turn out to be a liability in future, are called contingent liabilities. Such liabilities are only 'noted' in the particulars column of the Balance Sheet and no record is made in the books of account. Guarantees in respect of loans, liability on bills discounted, disputed claims, etc., are examples of contingent liabilities.

8. Capital:
It is the excess of assets over liabilities due to outsiders. It represents the amount originally contributed by the proprietor or partner, which is increased by profits and decreased by losses and drawings.

9. Drawings:
Drawings by the proprietor has the effect of reducing the balance on his Capital Account. Therefore, the Drawings Account is closed by transferring its balance to his Capital Account. However, it is shown by way of deduction from the capital in the Balance Sheet.

Items included on the Asset side of the Balance Sheet

1. Current Assets:
These assets are those which are either in the form of cash or can be converted into cash very easily.

2. Cash at Bank:
It represents the balance of cash in the account of the enterprise with a bank.

3. Bills Receivable:
Bills of exchange received from customers are termed as 'bills receivable'. Bills receivable shown under this heading are those bills of exchange which have not

yet matured for payment and which have not been discounted or endorsed to third parties.

4. Sundry Debtors:
This represents the sum total of debit balances appearing in the customer's accounts.

5. Prepaid Expenses:
This represents the amount which have been paid in advance for services to be received in the future. It is shown as an asset in the Balance Sheet.

6. Accrued Income:
This represents the income which has been earned but has not yet been received or has become due.

7. Closing Stock:
Goods remaining unsold at the end of the accounting year.

8. Fixed Assets:
Fixed assets are those assets which are of permanent nature and which the proprietor of a business purchases because these are helpful in the operation of the business for a number of years. They are not intended for resale but are purchased for permanent use. These include plant, machinery, furniture, buildings, motor lorries, land, patent, leasehold land, etc. Fixed assets are also known as 'Capital Assets' or 'Long-term Assets'. Some accountants consider them as Block Assets.

9. Fictitious Assets:
Those assets that are not assets in reality but are shown in the Balance Sheet on the asset side are known as Fictitious Assets. These include debit balance of expenses or losses carried forward from an accounting period to the next, *e.g.*, Suspense Account. Debit balance of Profit and Loss Account is also included in the fictitious assets.

10. Intangible Assets:
Such assets have no material existence, they cannot be touched or seen, and they exist merely in form of a book entry, *e.g.*, goodwill, patent, copyright, etc. Goodwill is the value, in terms of money, attached to the good name of an established concern. It is the amount which the potential buyer would pay for a well established business over and above its net worth. Copyright refers to the exclusive right of the author of a book on its publication. The right of an inventor of a new process or machinery is called patent right.

11. Wasting Assets:
Some of the Fixed Assets may also be Wasting Assets. These are the assets which are exhausted or consumed in the course of time for example, mines, quarries, etc. The Fixed Assets depreciate in value through wear and tear and with the passage of time, whereas Wasting Assets get reduced in value through being worked.

Format of Balance Sheet

Assets and liabilities are displayed in balance sheet in a specific order. From this point of view, the orders are of two types: 1. Liquidity Order and 2. Permanence Order.

Final Accounts of a Sole Trader

1. Liquidity Order:

This order is also known as realisation order. According to this order, in assets side, first of all cash in hand is shown. Then other assets are arranged in order of their being easily converted into cash. Similarly, in liabilities side, liabilities are shown according to their payment priorities. Format of balance sheet in liquidity order is as follows:

Specimen
Balance Sheet as on......

Liabilities	Amount (₹)	Assets	Amount (₹)
Current Liabilities:		**Current Assets:**	
Bank Overdraft	......	Cash in Hand	......
Bills Payable	......	Cash at Bank	......
Outstanding Expenses	......	Bills Receivable	......
Sundry Creditors	......	Sundry Debtors	......
Income rec. in advance	......	Accrued Income	......
Long Term Liabilities:		Stock: Finished Stock	
Bank Loan	......	Work-in-progress	
Loan on Mortgage	......	Raw Material	......
Capital		Prepaid Expenses	......
Add: Net Profit		**Investment**	......
or		**Fixed Assets:**	......
Less: Net Loss		Furniture	
Less: Drawings		Plant & Machinery	......
Less: Income-tax	......	Building	......
		Patents	......
		Goodwill	......
	......		......

2. Permanence Order:

This order is just reverse of the liquidity order. According to this order, on assets side, first of all intangible and fixed assets, such as goodwill, patent, building etc., are shown. After fixed assets, investments are shown and at the end, current assets, such as bank balance, cash in hand, etc., are shown. In liabilities side, first of all, capital is shown and then long term liabilities, such as bank loan and at the end, current liabilities, such as bills payable, bank overdraft, etc., are shown. Format of balance sheet in permanence order is as follows:

Specimen
Balance Sheet as on......

Liabilities	Amount (₹)	Assets	Amount (₹)
Capital:		**Fixed Assets:**	
Add : Net Profit		Goodwill	......
or		Patents	......
Less :Net Loss		Building	......
Less : Drawings		Plant & Machinery	......
Less : Income Tax	......	Furniture	......
Long-term Liabilities:		**Investments**	
Loan on Mortgage	......	**Current Assets:**	
Bank Loan	......	Prepaid Expenses	......
Current Liabilities:		Stock: Raw Material	
Income received in advance	......	Work-in-progress	
Sundry Creditors	......	Finished Goods	......
Outstanding Expenses	......	Accrued Income	......
Bills Payable	......	Sundry Debtors	......
Bank Overdraft	......	Bill Receivable	......
	...	Cash at Bank	......
		Cash in Hand	......
	......		......

Sole traders and partnership firms generally prepare balance sheet in liquidity order though it is not compulsory for them to do so. According to the Companies Act, 1956, it is mandatory for companies to prepare their balance sheet in permanence order.

Illustration 1: The following is the Trial Balance of a Trading Co. as on 31st March, 2018.

Trial Balance

Particulars	L.F.	Debit (₹)	Credit (₹)
Machinery		98,000	
Land and Buildings		8,60,000	
Investments		70,000	
Bad debts		3,000	
Sundry Debtors		40,000	
Purchases		3,09,800	
Stock on 1st April, 2017		23,000	
Interest		3,500	
Bills Payable			6,750
Sundry Creditors			76,000
Travelling Expenses		700	

Final Accounts of a Sole Trader

Trade Expenses	5,000	
Discount	1,250	2,625
Purchases Returns		9,850
Sales Returns	6,775	
Bills Receivable	2,275	
Capital		10,25,000
Sales		3,75,775
Mobile Phone Bills (Official)	6,000	
Postage	1,200	
Wages and Salaries	12,000	
Salaries and wages	51,000	
Carriage	2,500	
	14,96,000	14,96,000

The closing stock was valued at ₹ 9,000. Prepare a Trading and Profit and Loss Account and the Balance Sheet as on 31st March, 2018.

Trading Account
for the year ending 31st March, 2018

Particulars	Amount (₹)	Particulars	Amount (₹)
To Opening Stock	23,000	By Sales 3,75,775	
To Purchases 3,09,800		Less : S. Return 6,775	3,69,000
Less : P. Return 850	2,99,950	By Closing Stock	9,000
To Wages & Salaries	12,000		
To Carriage	2,500		
To Gross Profit transferred to P & L A/c	40,550		
	3,78,000		3,78,000

Profit & Loss A/c
for the year ended 31st March, 2018

Particulars	Amount (₹)	Particulars	Amount (₹)
To Bad debts	3,000	By Gross Profit transferred from Trading A/c	40,550
To Interest	3,500		
To Travelling Expenses	700	By Discount	2,625
To Trade Expenses	5,000	By Net Loss transferred to Capital A/c	28,475
To Discount	1,250		
To Mobile Phone bills	6,000		
To Postage	1,200		
To Salaries & Wages	51,000		
	71,650		71,650

Balance Sheet
as on 31st March, 2018

Liabilities	Amount (₹)	Assets	Amount (₹)
Bills Payable	6,750	Bills Receivable	2,275
Sundry Creditors	76,000	Sundry Debtors	40,000
Capital 10,25,000		Investments	70,000
Less: Net Loss 28,475	9,96,525	Closing Stock	9,000
		Land & Buildings	8,60,000
		Machinery	98,000
	10,79,275		10,79,275

Prepare a Trading, Profit & Loss Account and Balance Sheet of Krishna Enterprises for the year ended 31st March, 2019 from the following Trial Balance.

Illustration 2: The Closing Stock on 31st March was valued at ₹ 32,000.

Trial Balance

Heads of Accounts	Dr. (₹)	Cr. (₹)
Capital		29,000
Drawings	1,500	
Cash at Bank	1,450	
Purchases & Sales	22,000	39,000
Returns	2,000	1,000
Discount	200	
Carriage Outwards	600	
Salaries	6,000	
Trade Expenses	1,200	
Opening Stock	5,000	
Bad Debts	600	
Rent	1,500	
Machinery	36,000	
Furniture	8,000	
Debtors & Creditors	4,000	10,000
Stationery	2,500	
Commission		150
Bank Loan		13,400
	92,550	92,550

Trading A/c
for the year ended on 31st March, 2019

Particulars	Amount (₹)	Particulars	Amount (₹)
To Opening Stock	5,000	By Sales 39,000	37,000
To Purchases 22,000		Less: Returns 2,000	32,000
Less: Purchase Returns 1,000	21,000	By Closing Stock	
To Gross Profit transferred to Profit & Loss A/c	43,000		
	69,000		69,000

Profit & Loss A/c
for the year ended on 31st March, 2019

Particulars	Amount (₹)	Particulars	Amount (₹)
To Discount	200	By Gross Profit transferred from Trading A/c	43,000
To Carriage Outwards	600	By Commission	150
To Salaries	6,000		
To Trade Expenses	1,200		
To Bad Debts	600		
To Rent	1,500		
To Stationery	2,500		
To Net Profit transferred to Capital A/c	30,550		
	43,150		43,150

Balance Sheet
as on 31st March, 2019

Liabilities	Amount (₹)	Assets	Amount (₹)
Creditors	10,000	Cash at Bank	1,450
Bank Loan	13,400	Debtors	4,000
Capital 29,000		Closing Stock	32,000
Add: Net Profit 30,550		Furniture	8,000
59,550		Machinery	36,000
Less: Drawings 1,500	58,050		
	81,450		81,450

Difference Between Trial Balance and Balance Sheet

Basis of Difference	Trial Balance	Balance Sheet
Objectives	Trial balance is prepared with an objective to check mathematical accuracy of ledger.	Objective of balance sheet preparation is to ascertain financial position of the business.
Necessity	To prepare a trial balance is not necessary.	Preparation of balance sheet is essential to complete the accounting process.
Sides	It has debit and credit columns to show the amounts.	It has assets and liabilities sides.
Information of Profit or Loss	Trial balance does not provide any Information about profit or loss.	Information about net profit or loss can be obtained from the details of capital account shown in balance sheet.
Types of Accounts	It discloses balances of all types of accounts.	Balance of personal accounts and asset accounts are shown in it.
Display of Closing Stock	Generally, closing stock is not shown in it.	Closing stock is always shown in it.
Part of Final Accounts	Trial Balance is not a part of final accounts.	Balance sheet is a part of final accounts.
Closure of Accounts	Closure of accounts is not necessary for its preparation.	Closure of accounts is essential for its preparation.
Authenticity	Trial balance is not accepted as a proof in a court of law.	Balance sheet has got an authenticity from legal point of view.
Period	Trial balance can be prepared by trader a number of times during a year.	Balance sheet is generally prepared only at the end of the financial year.

Difference Between Trading and Profit & Loss Account and Balance Sheet

Basis of Difference	Trading and Profit & Loss Account	Balance Sheet
Objectives	Objective of preparation of trading and profit & loss account is to ascertain gross profit or loss and net profit or loss for a specific period.	Objective of preparation of balance sheet is to ascertain financial position of business on a particular date.

Sides	It has debit and credit sides.	It has assets and liabilities sides.
Nature	It is normal account.	It is a statement.
Use of 'To' and 'By'	Words 'To' and 'By' are used in it just as in other accounts.	Words 'To' and 'By' are not used in it.
Types of Accounts	Nominal accounts are shown in it.	Personal accounts and asset account are shown in it.
Order of Entry	There is no specific order to show the accounts in it.	It has two specific orders for dis-closure of assets and liabilities-liquidity order and permanence order.
Transfer of Balance	Balance of trading account is transferred to profit and loss account and that of profit & loss account is transferred to capital account.	Balance sheet does not have a balance. Totals of its both sides are equal.

Lesson at a Glance

- **Final Accounts:** Every businessman wants to know whether he has earned a profit or suffered a loss during the accounting period and what is the financial position of business at the end of said accounting period. To obtain this information, final accounts are prepared which include (i) Trading account (ii) Profit and loss account (iii) Balance sheet.
- **Sole Proprietor:** Single owner of an unincorporated business.
- **Trading Account:** It is a summarised form of all transactions occurring during a trading period which have direct relation to the goods dealt in by the business. It is prepared for ascertaining the gross profit or gross loss.
- **Profit and Loss Account:** It is an account which shows the net result of the operations of an enterprise during the financial period. The main feature of a Profit and Loss Account is that it contains indirect gains and indirect expenses. It helps in ascertaining net profit or net loss from business operations, in an accounting year.
- **Balance Sheet:** It is a statement prepared with a view to measure the exact financial position of a business on a certain date. It is prepared from the Trial balance. In a Balance Sheet, the total of all assets and all liabilities must be equal.

Visit a trading organisation and record their process of accounting and preparation of final accounts.

You are a Chief Accountant of a company. How will you explain the importance of Trading and Profit and Loss Account and Balance Sheet to your colleagues of other departments?

A. Short Answer Type Questions:
1. What is trading account?
2. What is profit and loss account?
3. What is a balance sheet?
4. What are the characteristics of balance sheet?
5. Distinguish between liquidity preference and permanence preference.
6. What are fictitious assets?
7. Who is a sole trader?
8. What tax does a sole trader pay?
9. What are contingent liabilities?
10. What is current assets?
11. Distinguish between trading account and profit and loss account.
12. Distinguish between profit and loss account and a balance sheet.

B. Essay Type Questions:
1. Give the format of profit and loss account and trading account.
2. Give the format of a balance sheet.
3. Distinguish between profit and loss account and balance sheet.
4. Who is a sole proprietor?
5. Write a short note on trading account.
6. Explain the purpose of preparing final accounts.

C. Numerical Problems:
1. The following is the Trial Balance of A.B. Chandra as on 31st December 2019.

Trial Balance of A.B. Chandra
as on 31.12.2019

Particulars	Amount (Dr.)	Particulars	Amount (Cr.)
Cash in Hand	2,000	Discount Received	750
Drawings	2,800	Capital	40,000
Opening Stock (1-1-2018)	4,000	Purchases Returns	1,250
Wages	2,000	Sales	83,000
Cash at Bank	3,500	Creditors	15,000
Insurance	700	Bank Loan	10,000
Trade Expenses	1,200		

Furniture	20,000		
Buildings	61,000		
Salaries	5,000		
Discount Allowed	750		
Sales Returns	3,000		
Purchases	31,250		
Debtors	10,000		
Telephone Charges	1,000		
Bills Receivable	1,800		
Total	1,50,000		1,50,000

The closing stock was valued at ₹ 12,000.

You are required to prepare a Trading Account and a Profit and Loss Account for the year ending 31st December, 2019 and a Balance Sheet as on 31st December, 2019. [ICSE 2020]

2. The following is the Trial Balance of ABC Industries as on 31st December 2015.

Trial Balance of ABC Industries
as on 31.12.2015

Particulars	Amount (Dr.)	Particulars	Amount (Cr.)
Salaries	4,000·00	Sales	83,000·00
Cash Balance	2,000·00	Rent Received	2,000·00
Bank Balance	3,000·00	Purchases Returns	1,000·00
Wages	1,500·00	Creditors	7,000·00
Insurance	500·00	Capital Account	25,000·00
Trade Expenses	7,000·00		
Discount Allowed	750·00		
Opening Stock (1.1.2015)	5,000·00		
Buildings	40,000·00		
Furniture	15,000·00		
Sales Returns	250·00		
Drawings	1,000·00		
Debtors	5,000·00		
Purchases	30,000·00		
Legal Charges	1,000·00		
Advertisement Expenses	2,000·00		
Total	1,18,000·00		1,18,000·00

The closing stock was valued at ₹ 9,000.

You are required to prepare a Trading Account and a Profit and Loss Account for the year ending 31st December 2015 and a Balance Sheet as on 31st December, 2015. [ICSE 2019]

3. The Trial Balance given below was prepared by Pratim Pal on 31st December, 2000.

   Prepare a Trading Account and a Profit and Loss Account for the year ending 31st December, 2000 and Balance Sheet as on 31st December, 2000.

   Trial Balance

	Dr. (₹)		Cr. (₹)
Drawings Account	1,000·00	Capital Account	14,400·00
Premises	7,500·00	Sales	23,120·00
Fixtures and Fittings	1,560·00	Discount Received	330·00
Opening Stock (1.1.2000)	2,730·00	Purchase Returns	730·00
Purchases	15,410·00	Sundry Creditors	1,700·00
Discount Allowed	580·00		
Sales Returns	1,020·00		
Rates	750·00		
Insurance	210·00		
Wages	1,250·00		
Trade Expenses	960·00		
Sundry Debtors	2,310·00		
Cash in Hand	650·00		
Cash at Bank	2,350·00		
Salaries	2,000·00		
	40,280·00		40,280·00

   Closing stock was valued at ₹ 3,140.00 on 31st December, 2000.

4. The value of stock on 31st December, 2014 was ₹ 14,920. [ICSE 2018]

   Prepare a Trading Account and a Profit and Loss Account for the year ended 31st December, 2014 and a Balance Sheet as at that date in the books of ABC enterprises.

   Trial Balance

	Dr. (₹)		Cr. (₹)
Drawings Account	7,000.00	Capital Account	90,000.00
Purchases	82,210.00	Purchase Return	4,240.00
Sales Return	1,820.00	Sales	1,49,840.00
Opening Stock	11,460.00	Discount	180.00
Salaries	6,280.00	Sundry Creditors	16,980.00
Wages	8,560.00		
Leasehold Premises	25,000.00		
Rent, Rates and Insurance	6,940.00		
Carriage Inward	2,310.00		

Office Expenses	9,520.00		
Plant and Machinery	24,000.00		
Light and Water	7,950.00		
Bills Receivable	1,240.00		
Sundry Debtors	38,970.00		
Cash at Bank	12,400.00		
Cash in Hand	2,210.00		
Office Furniture	3,500.00		
Travelling Expenses	9,870.00		
	2,61,240.00		2,61,240.00

[ICSE 2017]

5. Prepare a Trading, Profit & Loss A/c and Balance Sheet of Mr. A. Haridas for the year ended 31st March, 1980 from the following Trial Balance.
   The Closing Stock on 31.03.80 was valued at ₹ 40,000.

Trial Balance

	Dr. (₹)	Cr. (₹)
Capital		1,55,000
Drawings	9,000	
Trade Expenses	12,000	
Cash in Hand	750	
Cash at Bank	22,700	
Land & Buildings	1,30,000	
Stock as on 1-4-79	35,000	
Purchases & Sales	75,000	2,50,000
Returns	2,800	2,000
Carriage Inwards	1,500	
Carriage Outwards	3,500	
Debtors & Creditors	48,000	25,000
Bills Receivables & Bills Payables	22,000	10,500
Furniture & Fixtures	15,400	
Discount Allowed	1,500	
Wages	25,000	
Salaries	19,850	
Advertisement	15,000	
Rent, Rates & Taxes	3,500	
	4,42,500	4,42,500

[ICSE 2016]

CHAPTER-11
Fundamental Concept of Costs

COST

'Cost' means the money expenditure incurred by the producer to purchase (or hire) factors of production and raw materials to produce goods and service.

Cost, in a way, is a sacrifice made by the producer, *i.e.*, sacrifice in terms of making payments such as wages to labourers, rent for use of land etc.

In broad terms, cost has been defined by AICPA as, "*Cost is the amount measured in money or cash expended or other property transferred, capital stock issued, services performed or a liability incurred in consideration of goods or services received or to be received.*"

- *Meaning of Cost*
- *Elements of Cost*
- *Elements of Total Cost*
- *Classification of Costs*
- *Expenses excluded from Costs*
- *Cost Centre*
- *Cost Unit*

Thus, cost is the aggregate amount spent in producing a product or rendering a service; taking together all elements of it.

The accounting 'cost' figures are useful to meet the legal, financial and tax needs of the firm but are not directly helpful to the management in the decision making process. Normally, the management uses the concept of cost :

1. To fix the price of a product for a prospective buyer;
2. To find out whether a particular investment should or should not be made;
3. To determine the profit of the firm;
4. To estimate the amount of dividend, a firm would like to pay to the shareholders; and
5. To estimate additional cost that would be incurred if the firm accepts a large order for its products.

Elements of Cost

Cost of production consists of various expenses incurred on production of goods or services. These are the elements of cost, which can be divided into three groups (i) Material (ii) Labour and (iii) Expenses. All the three elements are further divided into two categories: (a) Direct and (b) Indirect. The direct cost is also known as Prime Cost which is a sum of Direct Material, Direct Labour and Direct Expenses. Indirect cost is known as Overheads.

The elements of cost may be depicted as:

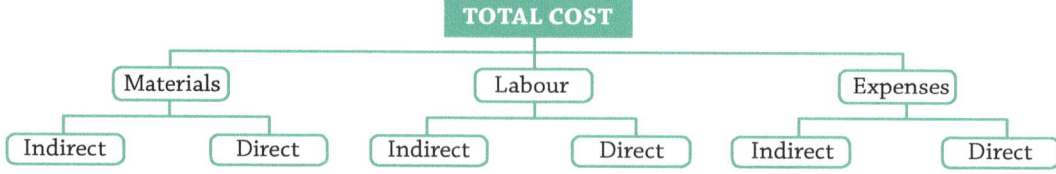

The terms given above are discussed below:

1. Material Cost:

Substances which can be identified in the product and can be conveniently measured and directly charged to the product, are called materials. In simple terms, substances from which the products are made are known as materials. The cost of commodities purchased by an organisation to manufacture or finish the product, is known as Material Cost.

Thus, materials directly enter into the process of production in a raw state or in a manufactured state and form a part of the finished product. For example, timber in furniture making, bricks in building a house are materials.

(a) **Direct Materials:** Direct materials are those materials which can be easily identified and related with specific product, job and process. The following are included in direct materials:

   (i) Any material specially purchased for manufacturing a particular item.
   (ii) Any material, semi-finished goods or components used in manufacturing a particular item.
   (iii) The primary packing materials. For example the bottle used in Pepsi or Coke is a direct material.

(b) **Indirect Materials:** Indirect materials are those materials which cannot be easily and conveniently identified and related with a particular product, job and process. For example, grease, oil, stationery, nails, small tools, brushes, etc.

2. Labour Cost:

Human efforts expended in altering the construction, composition, and condition of the product, is called labour. In simple words, it is that labour which can be conveniently identified or attributed wholly to a particular job, product or process. That is, human resources needed for conversion of raw materials into finished goods is termed as labour. Wages of such labour are known as direct wages.

The cost of remuneration paid to the workers, supervisors, factory manager of an organisation comes under this head.

(a) **Direct Labour:** Direct labour is referred to as one which can be easily identified and related to a specific product, job and process. Direct labour is easily traceable to specific products and varies directly with the volume of output. Wages paid to the carpenter in furniture industry is the example of direct labour. The following are included in direct labour:

   (i) Labour engaged in actual production of the product.
   (ii) Labour engaged in aiding manufacturing by supervision, maintenance, etc.
   (iii) Inspectors, analysts, etc. specially required for such production.

(b) **Indirect Labour:** Indirect labour refers to the one which cannot be easily identified and related with specific product, job and process. It includes all labour not directly engaged in converting raw material into finished product. It may or may not vary directly with the volume of output. The salaries paid to storekeeper, foremen, time-keeper, inspectors, etc., are the examples of indirect labour.

3. Expenses:

Expenses refer to all the cost incurred in the production of finished goods and services, other than the material cost and labour cost. It also refers to the cost of services provided to an organisation.

(a) Direct Expenses: Direct expenses are those expenses which can be identified with and allocated to cost centers or cost units. In simple terms, all direct costs, other than direct material and direct labour, are termed as direct expenses. Direct expenses are also called chargeable expenses. For example, hire charges of a special machinery or plant, experimental expenses, cost of patents, royalties, etc.

(b) Indirect Expenses: Indirect expenses are those which cannot be directly and wholly allocated to specific cost centre or cost units. In simple terms, all indirect costs, other than indirect material and indirect labour, are termed as indirect expenses. Indirect expenses are treated as part of overheads. They fall under three heads :

(i) Factory overheads: Indirect Material: For example, grease, oil, consumable stores, etc. Indirect Wages: For example, salary of storekeeper, etc., and Indirect Expenses : For example, power and fuel, carriage inwards, etc.

(ii) Office and Administrative Overheads: Indirect Material: For example, printing and stationery, postage, etc. Indirect Labour : For example, salaries of office managers, clerks, etc. Indirect Expenses: For example, office rent, legal expenses, etc.

(iii) Selling and Distribution overheads: Indirect Materials : For example, samples, catalogues, price list, etc. Indirect labour : For example, sales commission, etc. Indirect Expenses: For example, advertising, rent, bad debts, etc.

Elements of Total Cost—the alternate method

The total cost may be expressed in two terms :

(i) Total cost of production, or total cost of goods produced, and

(ii) Total cost of sales or total cost of goods sold.

The major components of total cost are as follows :

(1) Prime Cost:

It consists of three items:

(i) Direct Material, (ii) Direct Labour, and (iii) Direct Expenses.

All the three direct costs combined together make what is known as Prime Cost or Direct Cost or First Cost.

(2) Factory Cost:

It comprises the prime cost plus factory (or works) overheads or expenses. Factory expenses include indirect material, indirect labour and indirect factory expenses. This cost is also known as Works Cost or Manufacturing Cost or Production Cost.

(3) Office Cost:

It comprises factory cost plus office and administrative overheads or expenses. This is also called total cost of production or total cost of goods produced.

(4) Selling and Distribution Cost:

It comprises office cost plus selling and distribution overheads or expenses. This is also called total cost or total cost of sales, or total cost of goods sold.

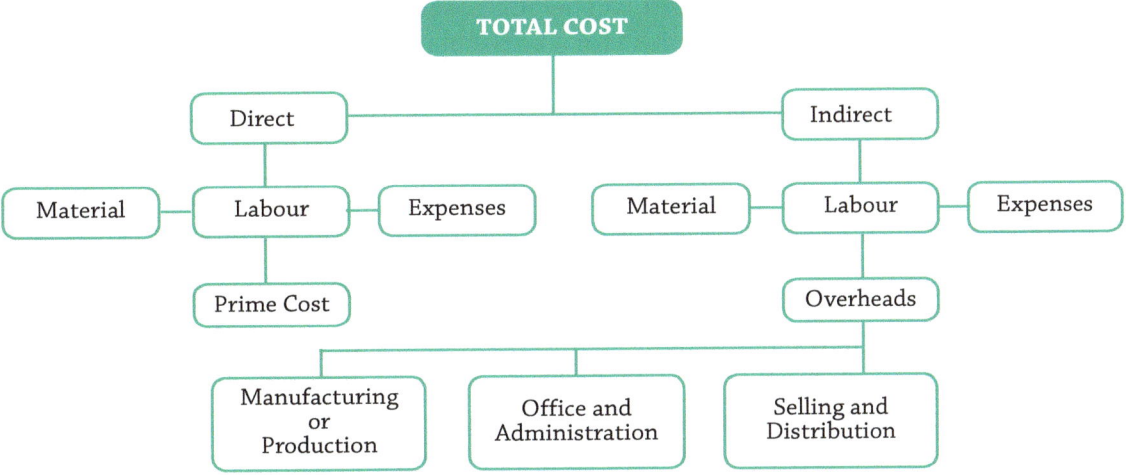

Classification of Costs

Apart from elements of cost, the costs can be classified by grouping them according to the following features :

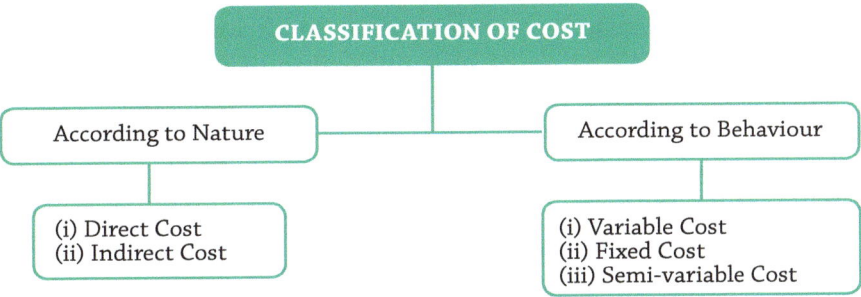

1. According to Nature

(A) Direct Costs:

Material, labour and other expenses which are directly or easily traceable to a product, service or job are known as direct cost. In the production of an article, materials are purchased, wages are paid to workers and certain other expenses are incurred directly. All these take an active and direct part in the manufacturing of a product and are, therefore, called direct cost. These costs have a direct relationship with a product, process or department of the firm and can be directly identified with a particular unit of output. For example, the cost of gravel, sand, cement and wages incured on the production of concrete.

Direct Costs include:

(i) Direct Material: All material which becomes an integral part of the finished product and which can be conveniently assigned to specific physical units of the finished product is known as direct material or process material.

(ii) Direct Labour: Labour which takes an active and direct part in the production of a particular commodity is known as direct labour. Direct labour costs are specifically and conveniently traceable to specific products. Direct labour is also known as productive or operating labour.

(iii) Direct Productive Expenses: These are the expenses which can be directly, conveniently and wholly allocated to specific cost centers or cost units. Rent paid for hire of a special machine required for a particular contract, cost of defective work incurred in connection with a particular job, etc., are examples of direct expenses. These are also known as chargeable expenses.

(B) Indirect Costs:

Indirect costs refer to the expenses incurred on those items which are not directly chargeable to production. Salaries of timekeeper, storekeeper, foremen are examples of indirect costs. In the running of a particular train, cost of railway station and railway staff are indirect costs.

Indirect costs include:

(i) Indirect Material: All material which is used for ancillary purposes and which cannot be conveniently assigned to specific physical units is known as indirect material. Consumable stores, oil and waste, printing and stationery material, etc., are a few examples of indirect material. Such material may be used in the factory, office or selling and distribution division.

(ii) Indirect Labour: Labour employed for the purpose of carrying out tasks incidental to goods produced or services provided is indirect labour. Such labour does not alter the composition, construction or condition of the product. It cannot be easily traced to specific units of output. Wages of storekeepers, timekeepers, foremen, salesmen's salaries, directors' fees, etc., are examples of indirect labour costs.

(iii) Indirect Expenses: These are the expenses which cannot be directly, conveniently and wholly traced to a particular product. Rent, lighting, insurance charges, etc., are examples of indirect expenses.

The distinction between the direct costs and the indirect costs is important. Modern big firms are often multi product firms. Any decision to expand output or change the product mix affects the total costs in many ways. A producer will like to know the effect of his decision on costs so as to minimise costs and maximize profits. Different processes involved in production may have some common costs and changes in these processes may affect costs. Thus, traceability of costs is important to management for making decisions concerning pricing, marketing, addition and deletion of product lines, expansion of output, etc.

Distinction between Direct Costs and Indirect Costs

Basis of Distinction	Direct Costs	Indirect Costs
Meaning	Costs that are easily attributed to a cost object are called direct costs.	Costs that cannot be allocated to a particular cost object are called indirect costs.
Benefits	Specific projects.	Multiple projects.

Classification	Direct material, direct labour, direct expenses.	Indirect material, indirect labour, indirect expenses.
Aggregate	When all the direct costs are taken together, they are known as prime costs.	Total of all the indirect costs is called as overheads.
Traceable	Yes	No.
Behaviour	Direct costs tend to be variable costs.	Indirect costs are more likely to be either fixed costs or period costs.

Note : A cost object is something for which a cost is compiled, such as a product, service, customer, project, or activity.

2. According to Behaviour

(A) Variable Costs:

The costs which vary or change with change in the size of output are called variable costs. These are attributable to the use of variable inputs. Such costs increase or decrease in the same proportion in which the output changes *i.e.*, these costs increase, when output increases and decrease when output falls. That is why they are called direct cost, since they vary directly with the change in the level of output. In other words, variable costs are incurred so long as production continues but the moment production stops, variable costs also cease to exist. The costs incurred on raw material, power, fuel, wages of temporary labour, wear and tear of machines, etc., are examples of variable cost. For instance, when sugar mill is working, the mill owner has to incur costs on sugarcane, power, wages of temporary labour, etc. If production of sugar has to be increased, these costs will also increase and if production has to be decreased, these costs will also decrease. And if sugar mill closes, variable costs will also fall to zero.

Thus, Total Cost = Total Fixed cost + Total Variable Cost

TC = TFC + TVC

(B) Fixed Costs:

Costs which are generally attributed to fixed factors of production, are called fixed costs. *These are the costs which do not change with the change in the size of output during short period.* These are primarily incurred on fixed factors like machines, building, etc. These are not related to the level or quantity of output in the short run. Production may come down to zero or be doubled, but fixed costs remain the same. These have to be borne even if no output is produced. For instance, a sugar mill usually remains closed for about 3 months during a year for want of raw material (sugarcane) but still the mill owner has to incur certain costs like rent of building, interest on past borrowings, salaries of permanent employees, municipal taxes, insurance premium etc. These costs are called fixed costs or *supplementary costs or overhead costs.* They remain the same during short period whether quantity of production is less or more or nil.

(C) Semi-variable Costs:

The costs which vary with every increase or decrease in the volume of production but do not vary proportionately are called as semi-variable costs. They also do not remain stationary at all times. Such costs contain fixed and variable elements. Because of the variable element, they fluctuate with volume and because of the fixed element they do not change in direct proportion to output. Semi- variable or semi-fixed costs change in the same direction as that of the output but not in the same proportion. Depreciation, repairs,, etc. are the examples of semi-variable costs.

EXPENSES EXCLUDED FROM COSTS

The total cost of a product should include only those items of expenses which are charge, against profit. Items of expenses, which relate to capital assets, capital losses, payments by way of distribution of profits, payments made for arranging finances, should not form a part of the costs. Examples of such expenses which are excluded from the costs are : interest paid on loans, depreciation, discounts, income tax, dividends, abnormal wastage, loss on sale of assets, discount on shares or debentures, interest on capital, expenses on raising of capital, preliminary expenses, underwriting commission, etc.

COST CENTRE

A cost centre is a location, person or item of equipment or group of these, for which costs may be ascertained and used for the purpose of cost control. A cost centre is the smallest organizational sub-unit for which separate cost allocation is sought or attempted. It is an individual activity or group of similar activities for which costs are accumulated or collected. Thus, cost centre refers to one of the convenient sub-units into which the whole company has been appropriately divided for costing purpose. Typically, cost centres are division, departments, sections, a machine, or a group of persons in a company. Thus if we identify all costs relating to marketing department and accumulate them to know its total cost, then marketing department is said to be a cost centre in this case. Similarly, the Production Manager or the Automatic Polythene Bags Machine can be cost centres.

COST UNIT

In preparing cost accounts, it becomes necessary to select a unit of measurement in terms of which expenditure may be identified. The quantity in terms of which cost can be conveniently allocated, is known as a cost unit or unit of cost. Thus, a cost unit may be defined as a unit of quantity of product or service or time in relation to which costs may be ascertained or expressed. Some examples of cost unit may be given as follows:

(a) Textile companies	–	Per metre of cloth manufactured or yarn spun
(b) Steel companies	–	Per tonne of steel manufactured
(c) Transport companies	–	Per passenger kilometer, or per tonne kilometer
(d) Electricity companies	–	Per unit of electricity generated
(e) Coal mines	–	Per tonne of coal extracted
(f) Brick fields	–	Per 1,000 bricks made

(g) Machines   –   Per hour of use
(h) Labour   –   Per hour of employment.

LESSON AT A GLANCE

- **Cost:** Cost, in common terminology, means the 'price paid for something'. According to AICPA, "Cost is the amount measured in money or cash expended or other property transferred, capital stock issued, services performed or a liability incurred, in consideration of goods or services received or to be received." Thus, cost is the aggregate amount spent in producing a product or rendering a service taking together all elements of it.
- **Elements of Cost:** There are basically three elements of cost: (i) Material (ii) Labour (iii) Expenses. All these three elements are further divided into two categories : (a) Direct (b) Indirect.
- **Material Cost:** (i) Direct Materials; (ii) Indirect Materials.
- **Labour Cost:** The cost of human efforts expended in altering the construction, composition, confirmation or condition of the product, is called labour cost. The cost of remuneration paid to the workers, supervisors and factory manager of an organisation, comes under this head. It includes : (i) Direct Labour; (ii) Indirect Labour.
- **Expenses:** All costs incurred other than the material and labour costs for a particular product or process, are called expenses. This includes: (i) Direct Expenses; (ii) Indirect Expenses.
- **Elements of Total cost:** (i) Prime cost; (ii) Factory Cost; (iii) Office cost; (iv) Selling and distribution cost.
- **Classification of Costs:**
  - *According to Nature:* (i) Direct Costs; (ii) Indirect Costs.
  - *According to Behaviour:* (i) Variable Costs; (ii) Fixed Costs; (iii) Semi-Variable Costs.

Visit an organisation which is into manufacturing business and find out the components of the total cost of one of its products. For this you will require the details about raw materials being used, the method and cost of procurement, consumption pattern and labour employed, besides cost of fuel, electricity, rent of building, etc. Please take necessary guidance from your subject teacher and prepare cost sheet for that product. Compare with its selling price and find out margin of profit.

Explain to your friend who does not have Commercial Studies as his subject, the various types of costs.

A. Short Answer Type Questions:
1. Define the term 'Cost'.
2. Define fixed costs of a firm. Give examples.
3. What are overheads?
4. Name the elements of cost.
5. Define variable costs of a firm. Give examples.
6. What is direct cost?
7. What do you understand by indirect cost?
8. What is meant by cost centre?
9. Name the expenses which are excluded from costs.
10. What is meant by labour costs?
11. Distinguish between Direct costs and Indirect costs. [ICSE 2017]
12. Distinguish between variable cost and semi-variable costs.
13. What do you mean by 'Indirect Material'? Give two examples. [ICSE 2018]
14. What is fixed cost? [ICSE 2020]
15. What do you mean understand by 'semi variable cost'? [ICSE 2019]
    OR
    What is semi-variable cost? Give one example. [ICSE 2017]

B. Essay Type Questions:
1. Discuss the various elements of cost.
2. "The term 'cost' must be qualified according to its context." Discuss this statement referring to important concepts of cost.
3. Explain different components of direct costs and indirect costs.
4. Write notes on:
   (i)   Variable costs
   (ii) Fixed costs
   (iii) Semi-variable costs
5. What is cost? Discuss the components of total cost.
6. Differentiate between direct cost and indirect cost.
7. Explain with an example for each, the meaning of fixed costs and variable costs.

CHAPTER-12
Budgeting

BUDGET

Budget is a forecast of the financial activities of the business to achieve certain specific purpose, over a specified time period. In short, budget is an estimate of the future receipts and payments. It is compiled and re-evaluated on a periodic basis. Budgets can be prepared for a person, a family, a group of people, a business, a government, a country, a multinational organisation etc.

- Budget
- Forecast
- Comparison between Budgeting and Forecasting
- Types of Budget
- Utility of Budget
- Limitations of Budget

Kotler defines budget as:

(i) Any financial plan serving as an estimate of and a control over future operations.

(ii) Hence, any estimate of future costs.

(iii) Any systematic plan for the utilisation of manpower, material or other resources.

According to Chartered Institute of Management Accountants, London, Budget can be defined as:

- *"A financial and/or quantitative statement, prepared prior to a defined period of time, of the policy to be pursued during that period for the purpose of attaining a given objective."*

A budget, thus, is an estimate of expenditure, revenue and resources, over a specified time period, providing a reading of future financial conditions and goals.

The essential features of a budget are as follows:

1. It is a statement expressed in monetary and/or physical units prepared for the implementation of policy formulated by the management.
2. It is laid down prior to the budget period during which it is followed.
3. It is prepared for the definite future period.
4. The policy to be followed to attain the given objective must be laid before the budget is prepared.

FORECAST

A forecast is an assessment of probable future events. That is, it is an act of predicting business activity for a future period of time, based upon specific assumptions. At planning stage, it is necessary to prepare forecasts of probable course of action for the business in future. Budget is a sort of commitment or a target which the management seeks to attain on the basis of the forecasts made. Forecasts are made regarding sales, production cost and financial requirements of the business. A forecast denotes some degree of flexibility while a budget denotes a definite target.

Difference Between Budgeting and Forecasting

Basis of Comparison	Budget	Forecast
Meaning	It shows the policy and program to be followed in future period under planned conditions.	It is a mere estimate of what is likely to happen. It is a statement of probable events which are likely to happen under anticipated conditions during a specified period of time.
Time Period	It is usually planned separately for each accounting period.	It may cover a long period or years.
Functional Area Covered	It comprises the whole business unit. Sectional budgets are coordinated into a logical whole.	It may cover a limited function or activity of business as sales forecast.
Target	Budget sets target.	There are no targets.
Control	It acts as an instrument of control by providing standards for evaluating performance.	Forecasting, being statements of future events, do not connote any sense of control.
Updation	Annual basis	At regular intervals.
Estimates	What business wants to achieve.	What business will achieve.
Order	It begins when forecasting ends. Forecasts are converted into budgets.	Forecasting is a preliminary step for budgeting. It ends with the forecast of likely events.
Scope	It has limited scope. It can only be made of phenomenon capable of being expressed quantitatively.	It has a wider scope, since it can be made in those spheres also where budgets cannot interfere.
Variance Analysis	The budget is compared to actual results to determine variances from expected performance.	There is no variance analysis that compares the forecast to actual results.

TYPES OF BUDGET

1. Sales Budget

The sales budget is the most important budget and forms the base of all other budgets. The sales budget is a forecast of total sales, expressed in terms of money and quantity. The first step in the preparation of the sales budget is to forecast as accurately as possible the sales anticipated during the budget period. The sales budget is based on sales forecasting which is the responsibility of the sales manager and market research staff. The sales budget is regarded as the pivotal point of budgeting.

Sales forecasts are influenced by a variety of factors, external as well as internal. They are:

(a) Past Sales Figures and Trends:
As the past performance is based on actual business conditions, the record of previous year's sales and their trend is the most reliable basis of the future sales.

(b) Salesmen's Estimates:
The estimates of the sales received from salesmen should be considered while preparing sales budget because being in direct contact with customers, their estimates are more accurate.

(c) Availability of Raw Materials and Other Supplies:
Adequate supply of raw materials and other supplies should be ensured before preparing the sales estimates. Sales estimates should be adjusted according to the availability of raw material, if the raw materials are in short supply.

(d) General Trade Prospects:
General prospects of trade or industry affects the sales probability of the firm. Trade journals, papers or magazines can provide valuable information in this regard.

(e) Orders in Hand:
Value of orders in hand and booked, have considerable influence on the amount of sales to be budgeted.

(f) Seasonal Fluctuations:
Special concessions and off-season discounts should be used as measures to minimise the effects of seasonal fluctuations on sales.

(g) Competition:
To have a realistic sales budget the nature and degree of competition prevailing in the industry should be taken into consideration while preparing sales budget.

(h) Miscellaneous Considerations:
Other considerations, such as advertising, production, government intervention, import possibility, product profitability etc., should also be kept in view.

2. Production Cost Budget

The production cost budget is a forecast of the production for the budget period. It is prepared in two parts, viz., production volume budget for the physical units of the products to be manufactured and the cost of manufacturing budget detailing the budgeted costs. The main steps involved in the preparation of a production budget are production planning; consideration of capacity; integration with sales forecasts; inventory-policies; management's overall policies. The operation of a production budget results in various advantages, major being optimum utilisation of productive resources of the enterprise, production of goods according to schedule enabling the firm to adhere to delivery dates, proper scheduling of factors of production. The Works Manager is responsible for the total production budget and the Departmental

Managers are responsible for the departmental production budget. While preparing the production budget, the following five questions are to be answered:

(i) What is to be produced?
(ii) When is to be produced?
(iii) How is to be produced?
(iv) Where is to be produced?
(v) How much is to be produced?

The material, labour and plant requirements should be ascertained to have the desired production to meet the sales programme.

Production cost budget is prepared to answer the above questions, to plan and organise production programme and to prepare a cash forecast.

Production forecasts are influenced by a variety of factors, which are as follows:

(a) Sales Requirements:
The quantity of goods to be produced will depend mainly on the quantity of goods to be sold in the market. Therefore, sales requirements will mainly decide the production budget.

(b) Inventory Policy:
Inventory levels influence the output. Therefore, inventory levels should be decided in advance so that neither there is shortage of goods nor overstocking of goods.

(c) Plant Capacity:
The maximum quantity of goods that can be produced depends upon the available plant capacity. Production should be evenly distributed throughout the year so as to ensure better utilisation of plant facilities and to reduce costs.

(d) Time Taken in Production Process:
Production process should be started well in time, keeping in view the time taken in the factory to convert the raw materials into finished goods.

3. Cash Budget

Cash budget is an estimate of cash receipts and payments. Working capital is required to meet the day-to-day requirements of the business. These cash requirements are met out of cash sales, amount collected from debtors and from other receipts. Cash is also received from non-trading receipts, such as sales of fixed assets, issue of shares and debentures, increase in loans and from other non-regular sources. These cash proceeds are used to meet various trading expenses which include cash purchases of goods, payment to creditors and payment of manufacturing, selling and distribution expenses. Non-trading expenses include purchase of fixed assets, redemption of debentures, payment of loans and payment of taxes and dividend. Cash budget may be both short-term and long-term. Cash budget in this way anticipates future cash requirements and makes arrangement of the requisite cash. It is a recorded plan of the financial operations of the business expressed in quantitative terms.

Objectives of Cash Budget: The main objectives of preparing cash budget are as follows:

(a) The probable cash position as a result of planned operation is indicated and thus, the excess or shortage of cash is known. This helps in arranging short-term borrowings in advance to meet the situations of shortage of cash or making investments in times of cash in excess.

- (b) Cash can be coordinated in relation to total working capital, sales investment and debt.
- (c) The effect of sudden and seasonal requirements, large stocks, delay in collection of receipts etc., on the cash position of the organisation is revealed.

4. Purchase Budget

A purchase budget is an estimate of the amount of inventory that a company must purchase during each budget period. The amount stated in the budget is the amount needed to ensure that there is sufficient inventory on hand to meet customer orders for products. Therefore, the amount stated in the budget should match the exact number of units expected to be sold in the budget period.

The budget outlines the cost of inventory in terms of current and future inventory levels. Determining the value of the company inventory enables the business owners to allocate the cash required to purchase materials. It also enables the company to prepare for increase or change in product lines or for new product launches.

Purchase forecasts are influenced by a variety of factors, which are as follows:

(a) Inventory Levels:

If there are considerable number of units on hand at the beginning of the budget period, the number of units to be purchased will have to be reduced. Therefore, inventory levels should be known in advance so that neither there is shortage of goods nor overstocking of goods.

(b) Service Levels:

If management wants to keep more units on hand to meet short-term customer needs, it may be necessary to increase the number of units purchased. A purchase budget should take this into account.

(c) Product Termination:

If a product line has to be terminated, a purchase budget should reflect the number of units needed through the termination date.

5. Master Budget

Master budget is a consolidated summary of the various functional budgets. According to C.I.M.A. London, a master budget is "the summary budget incorporating its component functional budgets and which is finally approved, adopted and employed". It is the culmination of the preparation of all other budgets, like the sales budget, production budget, purchase budget etc. It consists in reality the budgeted profit and loss account, the balance sheet and the budgeted funds flow statement.

The master budget is prepared by the budget committee on the basis of coordinated functional budgets and becomes the target of the company during the budget period when it is finally approved. This budget acts as the company's individualised key to successful financial planning and control. It provides the basis of computing the effect of any changes in any phase of operations, such as sales volume, product mix, prices, labour costs, material costs or change in facilities. It segregates income, costs and profits by areas of responsibility. Master budget presents all this information to the depth appropriate for the top management action.

In the master budget, costs are classified and summarised by types of expenses as well as by departments. This information extends the range of usefulness of the master budget. It is considered as the best mode of understanding the company's micro-economic position relating to the forthcoming budget period. The figures, that it contains, are the reflection of the actual intentions of the company relating to different areas for the forthcoming budget period.

UTILITY OF BUDGET

Budget expresses plans in terms of physical units or monetary units, and provides target to be achieved. It is not only essential for large business undertakings or Government of the country but also for a very small business unit or a family, to ensure long term financial security, Planning and foresight. Thus, budget is the integral part of planning strategy.

The following points enumerate the utility of a budget:

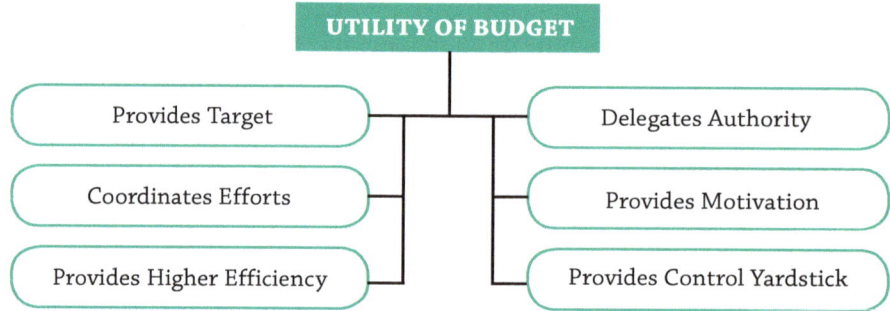

1. Provides Target:
A budget fixes the target in physical and financial terms. This helps the managers to understand their responsibilities precisely, by which they can take decisions to attain the set targets. This prevents the use of discretionary power by which the managers would have wasted resources and time.

2. Coordinates Efforts:
A budget helps to coordinate the efforts of various divisions and departments. It is possible to fix the divisional or departmental targets so that all divisions or departments may work harmoniously.

3. Provides Higher Efficiency:
A budget brings efficiency and economy in the working of an enterprise. It helps the management to achieve the most profitable combination of different factors of production. Budget also establishes divisional and departmental responsibility.

4. Delegates Authority:
A budget allows delegation of authority without loss of control. It permits participation of employees at all levels. According to KOONTZ and O' DONNELL,"reduction of plans to definite numbers, forces a kind of orderliness that permits the managers to see clearly what capital will be spent by whom, and where, and what expense, revenue or units of physical input or output his plans will involve. Having ascertained this, the manager can more freely delegate authority to effect the plan within the limits of the budget. Budget is somewhat a democratic way of managing."

5. Provides Motivation:
A budget represents the goals to be achieved. It tells the management what efforts and results are expected out of them. It motivates them to work hard in order to achieve the target represented by the budget. Budget works as a source of motivation to people.

6. Provides Control Yardstick:
A budget fixes control yardsticks. Performance of various managers, divisions and departments is evaluated, against the budget. This is done by finding out the difference between the budgets and actuals and analysing the results thereof.

LIMITATIONS OF BUDGET
Although Budget offers multiple advantages, it has few limitations, which are listed below:

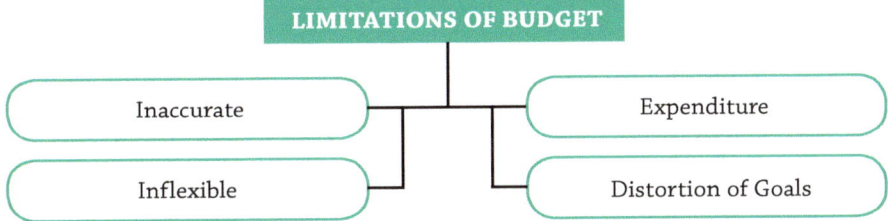

1. Inaccurate:
Forecasts, projections and historical trends form the base of budget making. But as forecasts may not be absolutely correct and trends may not repeat, budgets may prove to be inaccurate. The budgets estimates may become meaningless in the state of inflation or depression in the market.

2. Inflexible:
Many-a-times budgets are prepared in such a detailed way that their flexibility ends and they become cumbersome. Rigidity is caused by over-budgeting and managers are deprived of the freedom and flexibility in dealing and managing their departments.

3. Expenditure:
Budget-making process involves a lot of expenditure in terms of time, money and efforts. Preparation of various kinds of budgets is a difficult task for the management.

4. Distortion of Goals:
Sometimes, the limits in budgets are treated as hard marked lines by the management. People become extra cautious to function within the boundaries of budget figures. As such goals of the organisation may be overlooked.

LESSON AT A GLANCE

- **Meaning of Budget:** Budget is a forecast of the financial activities of the business to achieve certain specific purpose. It is an estimate of the future receipts and payments.
- **Classification or Types of Budget:** (i) Sales Budget; (ii) Production Cost Budget; (iii) Cash Budget; (iv) Purchase Budget, (v) Master Budget.

- **Utility of Budgets:** (i) Provides Target; (ii) Co-ordinates Efforts; (iii) Provides Higher Efficiency; (iv) Delegates Authority; (v) Provides Motivation; (vi) Provides Control Yardstick.
- **Limitations of Budgets:** (i) Inaccurate; (ii) Inflexible; (iii) Expenditure; (iv) Distortion of goals.

Project Work

1. Prepare a Budget for expenditure on your studies in the coming year.
2. Prepare a Budget for the month, in respect of your family. Based on the monthly salary of your parent, find out likely expenditures of various items—quantity and cost of each.

Assignment

Explain to your family members (other than father) about the relevance of Budgets and their utility in planning.

Questions

A. Short Answer Type Questions:

1. Define the term 'Budget'.
2. What is a master budget?
3. Give any three benefits of budgets.
4. State two limitations of budgets.
5. Give a list of any four functional budgets.
6. Distinguish between production budget and master budget.
7. Distinguish between Budget and Forecast.
8. What is a Budget? [ICSE 2020]
9. Explain 'Sales Budget'. [ICSE 2019]
10. Why is 'Master Budget' also known as summary budget? [ICSE 2019]
11. Mention any two utilities of a budget. [ICSE 2018]

B. Essay Type Questions:

1. Explain the main types of budgets used in business enterprises.
2. Discuss the advantages and limitations of budget.
3. What do you understand by master budget?
4. What is a Budget? Discuss any six uses of a Budget to a business enterprise.
5. Describe any five utilities of a budget.
6. Briefly explain any five types of budget.
7. "Budgets are useful for management". Justify.

CHAPTER-13
Sources of Finance

Economic development of any country depends upon the existence of a well organized financial market. It is the financial market which supplies necessary financial inputs for the production of goods and services in a country, which in turn, promotes the well being and standard of living of the people.

- Financial Market
- Capital Market
- Functions of Capital Market
- Sources of Raising Capital
- Difference between Shares & Debentures

FINANCIAL MARKET

A financial market is a market where financial assets and financial liabilities are bought and sold. Financial markets perform the essential economic function of channelising funds from savers, who have an excess of funds to business firms and governments, who have shortage of funds.

Financial markets may be classified into two types: Capital Market and Money Market.

(i) Capital Market:
Capital market deals in the lending and borrowing of long term finance. Thus, capital market is a market for financial assets which have a maturity period of more than one year. Capital Market caters to the long-term credit needs of the industrialists and provides fixed capital to buy land, machinery, etc. The main instruments used in capital market are Stocks, Shares, Debentures, Bonds etc and the important institutions operating in a capital market are stock exchanges, commercial banks and non-banking institutions, such as insurance companies, mortgage banks, etc.

(ii) Money Market:
Money market deals in the lending and borrowing of short-term finance. Thus, money market is a market for financial assets of short term nature, that is, which have a maturity period of upto one year. Money market meets the short-term credit needs of businesses by providing working capital to the industrialists. Main credit instruments used in Money Market are commercial bills, commercial papers and bills of exchange. Money Market instruments have the characteristics of liquidity (quick conversion into money), minimum transaction cost and no loss in value. Important institutions operating in the Money Market are central banks, commercial banks, acceptance houses, non-banking financial institutions etc.

CAPITAL MARKET

Capital market is a financial market where buyers and sellers engage in trade of financial securities of long term nature like shares, debentures etc. A capital market comprises of a number of institutions and mechanisms through which medium term funds and long term funds are pooled and are made available to individuals, businesses, and governments for use in productive ventures. An efficient and well organised capital market is essential for raising capital by the corporate sector of the economy and for the protection of the interest of investors in financial securities.

The capital market has two interdependent and inseparable segments, namely, the primary market and the secondary market.

1. Primary Market:

It refers to a market where new securities are bought and sold for the first time. In other words, the market wherein resources are mobilised by companies through issue of new securities is called the primary market. These resources are required for new projects as well as for existing projects for expansion, modernisation, diversification and upgradation. Thus, primary market is the market where companies issue their Initial Public Offerings (IPOs). First public offering of equity shares and other securities by a company followed by the listing of the company's shares on a stock exchange is known as initial public offering (IPO).

It is through the primary market that funds flow for productive purposes from savers (lenders) to entrepreneurs and business firms (borrowers). The latter use the funds for creating new products and rendering services to the customers.

2. Secondary Market:

Secondary Market refers to a market where securities are traded after being initially offered to the public in the primary market and/or listed on the stock exchange. Majority of the trading is done in the Secondary Market. It can be stated that secondary markets consist of stock exchanges and over the counter markets. In the secondary markets, securities are traded, cleared and settled within the regulatory framework prescribed by the Securities and Exchange Board of India (SEBI).

Functions of Capital Market

1. Acts as a link between Savers and Investors:

Capital Market is composed of those who demand funds (borrowers) and those who supply funds (savers and lenders). Transfer of resources from those with surplus funds (that is, households and individuals) to others with deficiency of funds (that is, investors and entrpreneurs) and in productive need for them, is perhaps the most crucial function of capital market. Thus, capital markets acts as a linking pin between savers and investors. Healthy, efficient and transparent functioning of the capital market is therefore imperative for industrialisation and economic development of a country.

2. Encouragement to Saving:

Efficient and well functioning capital markets provide good returns and enhance profitability of the investments. This encourages people to save and invest more. In the absence of a capital market, there are very little savings and those who save often invest their savings in unproductive activities, for example, in buying gold, land, luxury items etc.

3. Encouragement to Investment:
Capital markets facilitate lending to the business firms and the Government and thus encourage investment. They provide an investment avenue to people who wish to invest resources for a long period of time. Instruments such as bond, equities, mutual funds, insurance policies, etc. provide diverse investment avenues and suitable interest rate returns to the public. With the development of capital markets, funds become more accessible and therefore, investment increases.

4. Promotes Economic Growth:
Capital Market not only reflects the general condition of the economy, but also smoothens and accelerates the process of economic growth. Various institutions of the capital market allocate resources rationally in accordance with the development needs of the country. Proper allocation of resources results in the expansion of trade and industry in both public and private sectors, thus promoting balanced economic growth in the country.

5. Stability in Security Prices:
Capital Market tends to stabilise the values of stocks and securities and reduce the fluctuations in the prices to the minimum. The process of stabilisation is facilitated by providing capital to the borrowers at a lower interest rate and reducing the speculative and unproductive activities.

6. Benefits the Investors:
Capital markets bring together buyers and sellers of securities and thus ensure the marketability of investments. By advertising security prices, they enable the investors to keep track of their investments and channelise them into most profitable lines. It is also responsible for safeguarding the interests of the investors by compensating them from the Stock Exchange Compensating Fund in the event of fraud and default.

SOURCES OF RAISING CAPITAL
Sources of raising capital refer to the mediums through which an organization raises funds for its long-term capital requirements and for meeting working capital needs. Capital can be raised in two ways, namely, through long-term sources of finance and through short- term sources of finance.

1. Long-term Sources of Finance:
Long-term financing means capital requirements for a period of more than 5 years. Capital expenditures of a business in fixed assets like plant and machinery, land and building etc. are generally funded using long-term sources of finance. Part of working capital which permanently stays with the business is also financed through long-term sources of finance. Long-term financing sources can be in the form of Shares, Debentures, Term Loans from Financial Institutions and Commercial Banks ,Venture Funding , etc.

(a) Shares:
The total capital of a company is divided into convenient units of equal value and each unit is called a share. Shares represent the interest of a shareholder in the company and attach various rights and liabilities to the shareholder. It is an

invisible unit of capital which expresses the relationship of ownership between each shareholder and the company. The shareholders are also part owners of the company. There are two types of shares–Equity Shares and Preference Shares.

(i) Equity Shares:

Equity shares, commonly referred to as ordinary shares, represents the form of fractional ownership in which a shareholder, as a fractional owner, undertakes the maximum entrepreneurial risk associated with a business venture. Equity shareholders get dividend only after the holders of preference shares receive their share of profit because of which the rate of dividend received by the equity shareholders is not fixed. The holders of such shares are the members of the company and have voting rights.

(ii) Preference Shares:

Preference shares are those shares which carry a preferential right over equity shares in the case of distribution of dividend and repayment of capital in the event of winding up of a company. They generally carry a fixed rate of dividend and are redeemable after specific period of time. However, preference shareholders do not have voting rights in a company.

(b) Debentures:

Debentures are medium to long term debt instruments, used to borrow money at a fixed rate of interest. They are issued by a company as a certificate of its indebtedness and they establish the fact that the company has to pay a specified amount with interest to the debentureholder. Debentures usually indicate the date of redemption and also provides for the repayment of principal and payment of interest at specified dates. They, however, create a charge on the assets of the company. If the company does not pay interest or if it does not repay the principal amount, the lenders may take action against the company to realise their dues by sale of the assets earmarked as security for the debt.

Difference Between Shares and Debentures

Basis of Difference	Shares	Debentures
Meaning	Shares are the owned funds of the company and represent the capital of the company.	Debentures are the borrowed funds of the company and rep-resent the debt of the company.
Holder	The holder of shares is known as shareholder.	The holder of debentures is known as debentureholder.
Status of Holders	Owners	Creditors
Form of Return	Shareholders get dividend	Debentureholders get interest.
Payment of Return	Dividend can be paid to shareholders only out of profits	Interest has to be paid to debentureholders even if there is no profit.

Voting Rights	The holders of shares have voting rights.	The holders of debentures do not have any voting rights.
Repayment of Capital in the Event of Winding up.	Shareholders are repaid after the payment of all the liabilities and debt.	Debentureholders get priority over shares, so they are repaid before shareholders.
Conversion	Shares can never be converted into debentures.	Debentures can be converted into shares.

2. Short-term Sources of Finance:

Short-term financing means financing for a period of less than one year. Short-term finance may be needed to finance the working capital requirements of a business like for buying inventory of raw material and finished goods, for paying debtors, to maintain minimum cash and bank balance etc. Thus, short term financing is also termed as working capital financing. Short term finances are available in the form of cash credit, overdraft facilities from commercial banks, discounting of bills etc., Fixed Deposits for a period of 1 year or less, Advances received from customers etc.

(a) Cash Credit:

Cash Credit is an arrangement by which a bank advances cash loans of a specified limit to the customers against a bond or other securities. When the cash loan is granted, the borrower opens a current account with that amount in the bank. The borrower has the right to withdraw the full amount of loan. Interest is charged on the amount actually utilised by the borrower and not on the whole amount granted to him.

(b) Credit Draft or Overdraft:

A Commercial Bank allows the facility of overdraft only to its depositors who have current accounts in the bank. Under this arrangement, a depositor is allowed to withdraw more than what he has deposited. But, this extra withdrawal has to be repaid by the customer within a short period, along with the interest charged by the bank on the extra amount withdrawn. The rate of this interest may be somewhat more than the interest rate charged on loans. Banks, however, give overdraft facility only on the security of some assets or on the personal security of the customer.

(c) Discounting of Bills:

Banks provide financial help to their customers (the business-men, the merchants, the exporters etc.) by way of discounting their bills of exchange.

A bill of exchange is an instrument in writing containing an unconditional order, signed by the maker, directing a certain person to pay a certain sum of money only to the bearer of the instrument.

When a customer (say, an exporter) comes to the bank with a bill of exchange, the bank pays him the amount of the bill after deducting the usual discount (interest) charges. The bank, thus assists its merchant customers considerably by accepting their bills of exchange and by providing them cash in return to meet their short term capital requirements. After a few months or weeks, when the bill matures (a bill generally matures in 90 days), the bank presents it to the Acceptor (say, an importer) and gets back its full amount. In this case, a bill of exchange is of great benefit, both to the importer and the exporter. By using bill of exchange, the exporter gets the amount from the bank and the importer does not have to pay anything to the exporter immediately. Importer pays the amount only when he has funds in his hands. In case the payment is not received on due date, the bank recovers this amount from the customers (that is, the exporter in this case).

LESSON AT A GLANCE

- **Capital Market:** Capital market is a financial market where buyers and sellers engage in trade of financial securities of long term nature like shares, debentures etc.
- **Functions of Capital Market:** (i) Acts as a link between Savers and Investors; (ii) Encouragement to Savings; (iii) Encouragement to Investment; (iv) Promotes Economic Growth; (v) Stability in Security Prices; (vi) Benefits the Investors.
- **Sources of Raising Capital:**
  - **Long-term Sources of Finance:** (i) Shares-Equity Shares, Preference Shares (ii) Debentures
  - **Short-term Sources of Finance:** (i) Cash Credit (ii) Credit Draft or Overdraft (iii) Discounting of Bills.

PROJECT WORK

Find out and list the different financial regulators functioning in India.

ASSIGNMENT

With the help of proper examples show how the absence or the presence of a proper capital market has an impact on an economy.

QUESTIONS

A. **Short Answer Type Questions:**
   1. Define Capital Market.
   2. List the six functions of a Capital Market.
   3. State two sources of raising capital.
   4. What is Long-term source of financing?
   5. What is Short-term source of financing?
   6. Define Shares.
   7. What are equity shares?
   8. What are preference shares?
   9. Define Debentures.

10. Give examples of two different short-term sources of financing.

B. **Essay Type Questions:**
1. Describe the functions of Capital Market in detail.
2. Explain the various sources of raising capital.
3. State the differences between Shares and Debentures.
4. Write short notes on:
    (i) Equity shares
    (ii) Preference shares
    (iii) Overdraft
    (iv) Cash credit
    (v) Discounting of bills

CHAPTER-14
Recruitment and Selection

Human element is undoubtedly an essential, active and sensitive factor of production. Without human factor, all other physical factors are useless. working force does not only initiate and sustain work but it also activates other factors of production. It is rightly said that, an organisation without workers is an unproductive shell. It clearly stresses on the fact that recruitment and selection of employees should be done very carefully.

- *Meaning of Recruitment*
- *Sources of Recruitment*
- *Internal Sources of Recruitment and their Evaluation*
- *External Sources of Recruitment and their Evaluation*
- *Meaning of Selection*
- *Steps in Selection of Employees*
- *Importance of Selection*
- *Difference between Recruitment and Selection*

RECRUITMENT

Without employees the enterprise would have been a collection of materials and equipments. While efficient employees are assets of the enterprise, inefficient employees prove to be a liability. Therefore, every organisation should recruit the most suitable and competent employees on the basis of the needs and nature of the job. The process of identification of different sources of personnel is known as recruitment. It is the process of attracting potential candidates to the business concern. In other words, recruitment implies locating, maintaining and contacting the sources of manpower. A logical sequence of events would be: Identifying the different sources of labour supply–Assessing their validity–Choosing the most suitable source–Inviting applications from the prospective candidates.

In this way, recruitment is an activity of establishing a contact between an employer an applicant. The most important objective of any recruitment policy is to keep the labour turnover ratio as low as possible. It is the positive activity in the sense that it aims at reaching as many job seekers as possible for jobs in the enterprise. Recruitment process is the first step towards creating the competitive strength and the strategic advantage for the organisation. The process begins when new recruits are sought and ends when their applications are submitted. The result is a pool of applications from which new employees are selected.

- *"Recruitment as process of searching for prospective employees and stimulating them to apply for jobs in the organisation."* —Edwin B. Flippo
- *"Recruitment is the development and maintenance of adequate manpower resources. It involves the creation of a pool of available labour force upon whom the organisation can draw when it needs additional employees."* —Dale S. Beach

Thus, recruitment is a continuous process by which an organisation seeks to develop a pool of qualified applicants for the future human resource needs, even though specific vacancies do not exist at present.

The main objective of the recruitment process is to expedite the selection process.

Sources of recruitment

The sources of recruitment of personnel may be classified into two broad categories:
1. Internal sources (recruitment from within the enterprise); and
2. External sources (recruitment from outside).

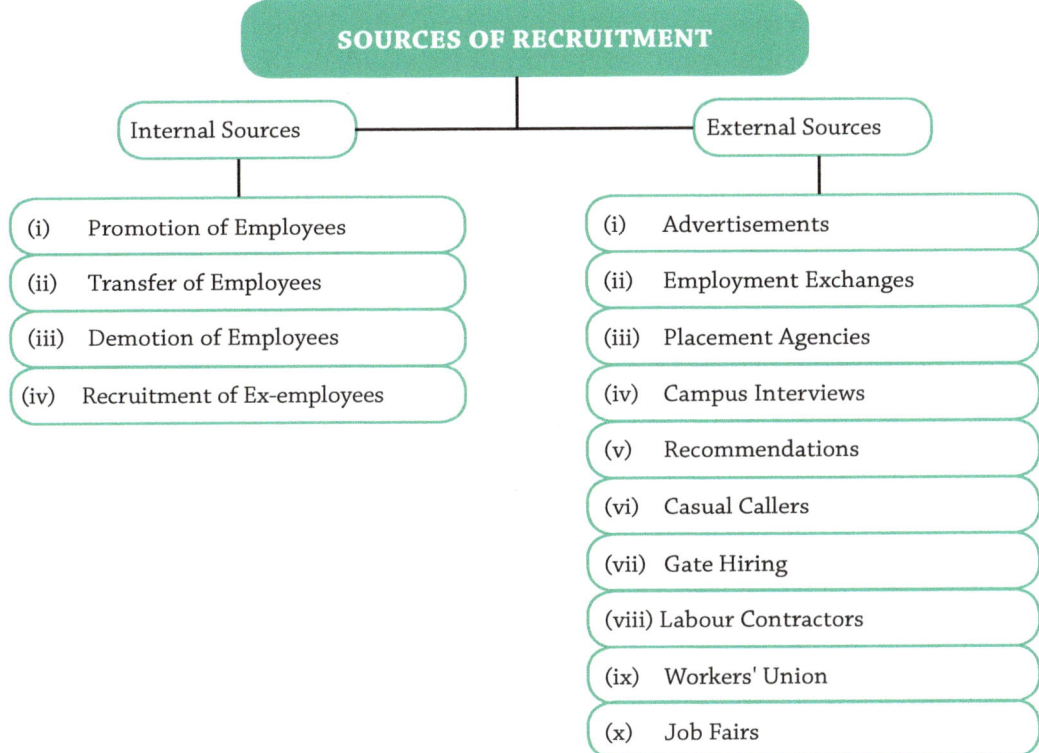

1. Internal Sources

Internal sources of recruitment means shifting of the existing employees of the organisation from one department to another department and from one post to another post. The sources of internal recruitment are as under:

(i) Promotion of Employees:
Promotion implies vertical movement or advancement of an employee from a lower position to a higher one. Positions falling vacant in higher ranks may conveniently be filled up by promoting suitable employees from below. This promotion may be based upon both, the seniority and merit. In a good promotion policy, employees should know what will be the contribution of their seniority in merit for their promotion. The employee has the privilege of working in the real situations of the business, so he does not feel any difficulty in case of promotion. Thus, promotion leads to shifting an employee to a higher position carrying higher responsibilities, facilities, status and pay.

(ii) Transfer of Employees:
Transfer involves the shifting of an employee from one job to another without special reference to change in responsibility, rank or compensation. Transfer is the

change in a job equal to the old one in terms of pay, status and responsibilities. If the management finds that a person is misfit or he will be more useful at some other place, he is shifted. However, it may significantly affect the efficiency and morale of the employee, depending on the type of environment where he has been transferred.

(iii) Demotion of Employees:
Employees may be demoted back to their original jobs. Demotion shakes the morale and self-respect of employees, so it should be avoided. Demotions are generally made, when the promotion is conditional or the court has dis-approved or vacancy was temporarily caused by the leave of a senior employee.

(iv) Recruitment of Ex-employees:
This source of internal recruitment is adopted to re-employ the ex-employees of the organisation. It may happen when employees who have left the organisation are willing to rejoin it. In such a case, the organisation accords them priority and enterprise too gets trusted, competent and experienced employees.

Advantages:

(i) Upgradation of Several Employees:
The existing employees of the organisation get an opportunity for promotion. When a certain person is promoted, several other persons below his rank are automatically promoted. In this way, one vacancy filled from within, results in upgradation of several employees.

(ii) Familiarity with Policies:
The Existing employees are aware of policies, plans and the actual working conditions of the enterprise, so they are not required to waste time and energy in learning it.

(iii) Economical:
Internal source is economical because the enterprise is not required to incur expenses on recruitment from outside the organisation. There are lesser number of candidates and the most suitable candidate is selected according to merit or seniority or both.

(iv) Availability of Experienced Employees:
Promoted employees have already been performing the job in the organisation before their promotion, so they do not have any difficulty. The organisation is also benefitted because employees are efficient and experienced and they start working without any formal training.

(v) Increase in employees' Morale:
Promotion from within the organisation increases employees' morale. The policy of internal promotions makes them enthusiastic and optimistic and they contribute their best efforts and energies.

(vi) References not Required:
The service records of employees are available in the organisation. It knows the abilities and loyalties of its employees. Therefore, any outside reference about their ability, integrity and moral character is not required.

Disadvantages:

(i) No Opportunity for Fresh Talent:
The major drawback of this source is that the enterprise may deprive competent, talented and deserving candidates from outside to get an opportunity to take up challenging jobs.

(ii) Promotion of Inefficient Employees:
Sometimes, unsuitable persons use their influence to get promotions. They are promoted from within the organisation without giving any importance to their merit simply because they are working in that organisation.

(iii) Not a Complete solution:
Internal source of recruitment is not capable to meet entire requirement of the organisation. The management has to knock at the doors of external sources also.

Evaluation of Internal Sources of Recruitment

Advantages	Disadvantages
(i) Upgrading of several employees	(i) No opportunity for fresh talent
(ii) Familiarity with policies	(ii) Promotion of inefficient employees
(iii) Economical	(iii) Not a complete solution
(iv) Availability of experienced employees	
(v) Increase in Employees, Morale	
(vi) References not required	

2. External Sources

All the vacancies at all the levels, cannot be filled up through internal sources of recruitment only. Therefore, use of external sources is also necessary for all organisations. External recruitment means the sources through which the suitable candidates are sourced from outside the concern. The recruitment at lower levels is made from external sources only. Main external sources of recruitment are as under:

(i) Advertisements:
Recruitment through advertising in local or national newspapers or trade or professional journals is one of the most common methods of attracting personnel of all types — skilled workers, clerical staff and higher staff. It is very convenient and economical also. The vacancies are advertised in newspapers and the interested candidates submit their applications, on the basis of such advertisements. Sometimes, an enterprise may not disclose its name in the advertisement and ask candidates to reply to a Post Box Number, or to a consulting firm. This may be because the enterprise does not want to reveal its identity for some reasons, or because the advertisement relates to a vacancy that is to be filled internally.

(ii) Employment Exchanges:

The Government has set up employment exchanges throughout the country. Anyone seeking employment can get himself registered at the employment exchange. Employees notify the vacancies and the various exchanges refer suitable candidates for recruitment. Employment exchanges are a useful source of semi-skilled and unskilled personnel. But skilled personnel may not be available. Persons with specialised skills and experience do not prefer registration at the employment exchange because they consider it below their dignity. Employers too have a feeling that employment exchanges cannot provide personnel having specialised skills and experience.

(iii) Placement Agencies:

Several recruitment agencies, like ABC consultants, A. F. Ferguson Associates, etc., provide recruitment and selection services. The employer can hire such an agency to payon the complete task of recruitment. The agency will advertise the job, receive and screen applications and shortlist suitable persons them. The employer saves his time and effort and gets the benefit of the agency's expertise. His identity is also kept secret. But the agency charges a substantial fee for this task. This source of recruitment is employed for recruitment of senior positions (technical as well as managerial).

(iv) Campus Interviews:

Managers, officers, technicians; like engineers, electricians, mechanics and skilled workmen are often recruited from institutions, like Indian Institute of Management (IIM), Indian Institute of Technology (IIT), Engineering Colleges, Industrial Training Institutes, Polytechnics, etc. Companies send their managers to such institutions where there are suitable candidates recommended by the institutes. These candidates are interviewed for selection by the managers.

(v) Recommendations:

Many organisations have a structured system where the current employees of the organisation can refer their friends and relatives for some position in the organisation. when a present employee recommends a person, a type of preliminary screening takes place. Indeed, many employers prefer to take such persons because something about their background is known.

(vi) Casual Callers:

These are the persons who either gather at the factory gate to serve as casual workers or reach the employer by letter, telephone or in person, with request for appointment against a real or presumed vacancy. Applicants apply on their own initiative assuming that certain vacancies are likely to be filled up. Managers keep record of such applications and contact suitable ones when they need them.

(vii) Gate Hiring:

This type of recruitment is made by labour officers. Generally, workers gather at factory gate or they are called through a notice. The suitable candidates are recruited. This method is applied to meet the casual needs of the employees. These casual workers having once served in the factory for sometime, are considered for regular employment.

(viii) Labour Contractors:

It is quite common to engage jobbers and contractors to supply workers for vacancies which are of casual nature, or which may be filled at the factory gate itself. In fact, where the workers have to be hired on a short notice and without going through the usual selection procedure, jobbers and contractors serve as an ideal and economical source. Jobbers and contractors maintain close links with small towns and villages which offer a ready and plentiful supply of unskilled workers. They, also, sometimes at their own expense, bring workers to the place of work.

(ix) Workers' Union:
In order to keep workers and their union satisfied, employers can recruit through workers' union also. The unions have agreement with the managements, whereby managers are required to consider their recommendations on a priority basis.

(x) Job Fairs:
Job fairs are conducted by different companies to attract candidates for entry level jobs.

Advantages:

(i) Wider Choice:
Selection from external sources facilitates the choice of personnel from among a large number of applicants. The enterprise can carefully weigh the plus and minus points of all the candidates and then select the best.

(ii) Fresh Outlook:
The enterprise greatly benefits from the freshness of outlook and approach of personnel chosen from external sources. This is because they are without any in-built preferences and prejudices, so common in the case of personnel promoted or transferred to fill the vacancies internally.

Disadvantages:

(i) Heart-Burning Among Old Employees:
Personnel chosen from external sources may cause heart-burning and demoralisation among old employees, for whom any outsider is unwanted, especially so if he deprives them of a coveted job.

(ii) Expensive:
Recruitment of staff from outside sources may sometimes, be quite expensive. Beginning with advertisements in the press, which itself is a costly affair, then the holding of written tests and personal interviews may involve substantial expenditure. A new employee learns after a considerable expense and waste in terms of time and material.

(iii) Chances of Maladjustment:
If a person chosen from an external source fails to adjust himself to working in the enterprise, or is an idler or otherwise undesirable, he may have to be shunted out. This means there will be yet more expenditure on finding his replacement.

Evaluation of External Sources of Recruitment

Advantages	Disadvantages
(i) Wider Choice	(i) Heart-Burning among Old employees
(ii) Fresh Outlook	(ii) Expensive
	(iii) Chances of Maladjustment

SELECTION

Selection means going through the qualifications and experience of the candidates to decide whether the candidates fulfill the requirements of the job or not. It involves evaluation of the applicants. It is the process of dividing the applicants into two categories: (i) those who are to be employed; and (ii) those who are to be rejected. Selection is a very important activity because it helps to minimize labour turnover and absenteeism. The process of selection starts with comparing the requirements of a job with the qualifications of the applicants. The purpose of selecting the right person for the right job also helps to improve the quantity and quality of performance. Selection is said to be a negative process, because the number of candidates rejected is much more than that of selected persons. There are some stages of selection. At every stage, the qualities of candidates are tested. Number of candidates goes on reducing at each subsequent stage. it eliminates the unsuitable candidates at every step. It is the process of picking up the most competent and suitable candidates.

- *"Selection is the process in which candidates for employment are divided in two classes, those who are to be offered employment and those who are not."* —Dale Yoder
- *"Selection means making a choice by preference. This choice by preference is based on comparison between two factors: (i) What the job requires for successful execution, and (ii) What the applicant has to offer. For the most part, the better the balance between these two factors, the better the selection work and more likely the attainment of a satisfactory working force."* —George Terry

Steps in the Process of Selection of Employees

The basic principle for the recruitment and selection is, the "right man for the right job." Presuming that all the requirements that are necessary for inviting applications have been fulfilled and the applications have been received in the office, the following steps are generally performed for the selection of employees:

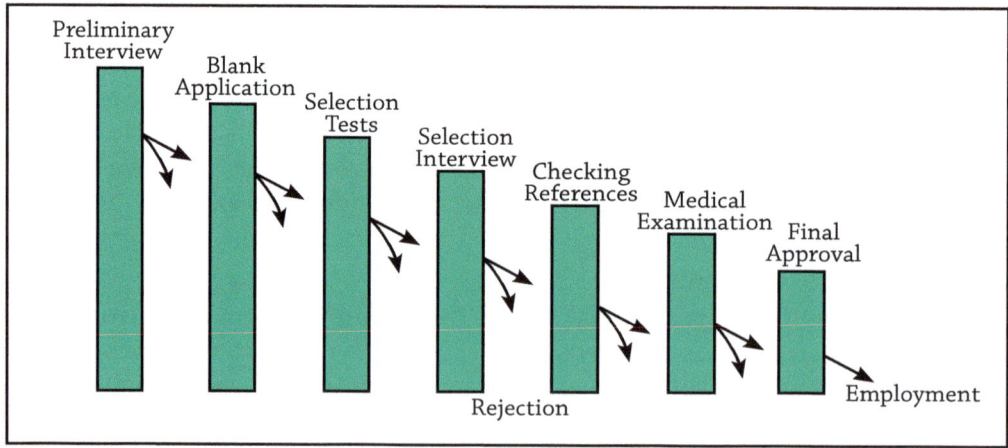

1. Preliminary Interview

The Executive of the organisation conduct a brief interview of the candidates to determine whether it is worthwhile for the candidate to fill up the blank application. Minimum qualifications and experience of the candidate, his age, etc., are ascertained. Preliminary interview helps to eliminate those candidates who are obviously unfit for the job.

2. Blank Application

The candidates who succeed in preliminary interviews are required to fill in a specially drafted blank application form. It provides a written record of the qualifications, experience age, etc., of candidates. It can be used as a good test device for the expression, handwriting and other abilities of the candidates. Therefore, it should be designed carefully so as to secure all relevant information about the candidate. There is no standard form of blank application for all firms. As far as possible, it should be simple and brief.

3. Selection Tests

Candidates may have to undertake selection tests to establish their claim for the job. These tests are based on the assumption that, human behaviour in an actual work situation can be predicted by sampling it.

Selection tests are classified into six types. They are as follow :

(i) Aptitude Tests.

(ii) Achievement Tests.

(iii) Situational Tests.

(iv) Proficiency Tests.

(v) Interest Tests.

(vi) Personality Tests.

(i) Aptitude Tests:

Aptitude means the potential which an individual has for learning the skills required to do a job efficiently. Aptitude tests measures an applicant's capacity and his ability to learn a given job if given adequate training. These tests are the most promising indices for predicting employee's success. Aptitude tests can be divided into general and mental ability or intelligence tests and specific aptitude tests such as mechanical aptitude tests, clerical aptitude tests, etc.

(A) Intelligence Tests: These tests are used to measure a person's capacity for reasoning and comprehension in terms of his memory, mental alertness, vocabulary, and grasping capacity. A candidate's IQ or mental alertness can be estimated through intelligence tests. The tests consists of logical reasoning ability, data interpretation, comprehension skills and basic language skills. Though these tests are accepted as useful ones, they are criticized to be against deprived sections of the community.

(B) Mechanical Aptitude Tests: These tests deal with the ability of the candidate to do mechanical work. They are used to judge and measure the specialised knowledge, perceptual speed and problem solving ability. These tests are useful for selecting apprentices, skilled mechanical employees, technicians, etc.

(C) Psychomotor Tests: These tests judge abilities like manual dexterity, motor ability and eye-hand coordination of candidates. These tests are useful to select semi-skilled workers and workers for repetitive operations like packing, watch assembly, quality inspection, etc.

(D) Clerical Aptitude Tests: These tests measure specific capacities involved in office work, like spelling, computation, comprehension, copying, word measuring, etc.

(ii) Achievement Tests:

The candidate's achievement in his career is tested regarding his knowledge about the job and actual work experience. These tests are more useful to measure the value of specific achievement when an organization wishes to employ experienced candidates. These test are classified into:

(A) Job Knowledge Tests: Under this test, a candidate's knowledge is tested for a particular job. For example, if a junior lecturer applies for the job of a senior lecturer in Economics, he may be tested in job knowledge where he is asked questions about microeconomics, macroeconomics, central bank, etc.

(B) Work Sample Test: Under this test a portion of the actual work is given to the candidate as a test and the candidate is asked to do it. If a candidate applies for a post of a lecturer in Management, he may be asked to deliver a lecture on Management Information System as work sample test.

(iii) Situational Tests:

These tests evaluate a candidate in a similar real life situation. In these tests, the candidate is asked either to cope with the situation or to solve critical situations of the job. Situational tests are classified into:

(A) Group Discussion: Under this test, candidates are observed in the areas of leadership, proposing valuable ideas, conciliating skills, oral communicating skills, coordinating and concluding skills.

(B) In Basket: Situational test is also administered through 'in basket'. The candidate, in this test, is supplied with actual letters, telephone and telegraphic message, reports and requirements by various officers of the organization. The candidate is asked to take decisions on various items based on the in basket information. The candidate is then evaluated by the decisions he took, during the test.

(iv) Proficiency Tests:

Proficiency tests seek to measure the skill and abilities which the candidate already possesses at the time of testing. Trade tests or skill tests are examples of proficiency tests. They determine whether the claims made by the candidate about his skills and abilities are proved by his actual test performance.

(v) Interest Tests:

Interest tests identify patterns of interest, that is, areas in which the individual shows special concern, fascination and involvement. These tests will suggest what types of jobs may be satisfying to the employees.

(vi) Personality Tests:

Personality tests are aimed at finding out emotional balance, maturity, temperament, etc., of the candidate. It is very difficult to design and use these tests as they are concerned with discovering clues to an individual's emotional reactions, maturity, etc. Personality tests have disadvantage in the sense that they can be faked by sophisticated candidates and most candidates give socially acceptable answers. Further, personality tests may not successfully predict job success.

4. Selection Interview

Interview serves as a means of checking the information given in the application forms and the tests results. It also provides an opportunity to the candidates to enquire about the job during interview. Managers get an opportunity to take a decision about their suitability for employment. Selection interview should be conducted in an atmosphere which is free from disturbance, noise and interruption. Interview should be conducted in great depth to judge the suitability of the candidates.

There are no hard and fast rules of interviewing candidates. Interviews, in general, can be conducted in the following ways:

(A) Structured or Patterned Interview:
In such an interview different sets of questions, having the same pattern and with the same difficulty level, are framed in advance. Different candidates are asked different series of questions. Each series, having the same pattern and the same difficulty level, bring about objectivity in the interview.

(B) Unstructured or Non-directive Interview:
In this interview, questions to be asked are not planned in advance. Questions pertaining to the job are asked and candidates are asked to respond freely to show their ability for the job.

(C) Stress Interview:
This interview is held to note how thick-skinned the candidate is. The candidates are asked awkward questions and it is seen how they react to such questions. If they do not lose their balance of mind, they prove their worth as suitable candidates.

(D) Group Interview:
In this interview, a number of candidates face the interview committee together. The candidates are asked to give their opinion on an issue or they are asked to discuss on a topic. When the candidates respond and give reasons and counter-reasons, their ability to communicate, presence of mind, expression, etc., are judged by the inter-viewers.

5. Checking References

References are generally required to enquire about the conduct of those candidates who have been found suitable in the interviews and tests. References can be collected from the previous employers, colleges last attended or from any other reliable source. Before forming a balanced opinion, it is necessary to enquire from three to five persons about the conduct of the prospective candidate. However, this exercise may not always produce the desired results because (i) no candidate will cite the name of a referee who might speak unfavourably about him; (ii) the referee may not always respond; and (iii) due to a prejudice the referee may deliberately speak against the candidate.

6. Medical Examination

A physical examination of the potential employee is necessary for the company, to protect itself against the risk of claims for compensation from individuals who are afflicted with disabilities. The medical examination should be both general and thorough. The findings, should be carefully recorded so as to give a complete medical history, the scope of current physical capacities, and the nature of disabilities, if any. But, it need to be remembered that the medical examination is an aid to selecting employees who, besides fulfilling the requirements as to abilities and skills, also possess necessary physical characteristics. In other words, medical examination should not be used unfairly to reject an otherwise suitable candidate.

7. Final Approval
After a candidate has cleared all the hurdles in the selection procedure, he is formally appointed by issuing him an appointment letter or by making a service agreement with him. No selection procedure is foolproof and the best way to judge a person, is by observing him working on the job.

8. Employment
Candidates who give satisfactory performance during the probationary period are made permanent.

Importance of Selection

It is an accepted fact, that the efficient, competent and devoted employees are the most valuable asset of the business enterprise, whereas the incompetent workers are liability of the firm. It is, therefore, necessary that the selection of employees should be made very carefully, because any lapse or errors committed in the selection may prove fatal to the enterprise. Defective selection will lead to:

1. Absenteeism resulting in loss of work and reduction in labour turnover.
2. Decline in the efficiency of the organisation.
3. Shirking responsibility of the employees.
4. Suspension, retrenchment and termination of employees. Such practice will pollute the atmosphere.
5. Wastage of time, energy and money in hiring, training and developing unsuitable employees.

Effective selection of employees will result in:

1. Building up a suitable work force.
2. Low absenteeism and high labour turnover.
3. Boosting the morale of employees.
4. Higher efficiency and maximum production at minimum cost.

DIFFERENCE BETWEEN RECRUITMENT AND SELECTION

Recruitment and selection are closely inter-connected. Recruitment is inviting and procuring applications from various sources. Whereas selection starts after applications have been received, *i.e.*, where recruitment ends.

In the recruitment process, there is matching of the applicants with the requirements of the job and selection tasks place after that thus, recruitment facilitates the work of selection. Recruitment is a positive process as it seeks to persuade people to apply for vacant posts. Selection is a negative process in the sense that it eliminates the unsuitable candidates while retaining the suitable ones.

Both recruitment and selection are the two phases of the same process. Recruitment being the first phase envisages taking decisions on the choice of tapping the sources of labour supply. Selection is the second phase which involves giving various types of tests to the candidates and interviewing them in order to select the suitable candidates.

Basis of Comparison	Recruitment	Selection
Meaning	Searching prospective candidates and stimulating them to apply for jobs.	Choosing the candidates having necessary qualifications.
Nature	Positive process.	Negative process.
Aim	To create a large pool of candidates.	To eliminate all unsuitable candidates.
Process	Simple, as candidates are not required to cross many hurdles.	Complex, as the candidates are required to cross several hurdles.
Number	No restriction upon the number of candidates.	Only a limited number of candidates are selected.
Order	It is done prior to selection.	It is made only after recruitment.

LESSON AT A GLANCE

- **Recruitment:** It is the process of searching for prospective employees and stimulating and encouraging them to apply for jobs in an organisation. The process of identification of different sources of personnel is known as recruitment. According to DALE S. BEACH, "Recruitment is the development and maintenance of adequate manpower resources. It involves the creation of a pool of available labour force upon whom the organisation can draw when it needs additional employees."

Sources of Recruitment
- **Internal Sources:** (i) Promotion of employees; (ii) Transfer of employees; (iii) Demotion of employees; (iv) Recruitment of ex-employees.
- **Merits:** (i) Upgradation of several employees; (ii) Familiarity with policies; (iii) Economical; (iv) Availability of experienced employees; (v) Increase in employee's morale; (vi) References not required.
- **Demerits:** (i) No opportunity for fresh talent; (ii) Promotion of inefficient employees; (iii) Not a complete solution.
- **External Sources:** (i) Advertisements; (ii) Employment exchanges; (iii) Placement agencies; (iv) Campus interviews; (v) Recommendations; (vi) Casual callers; (vii) Gate hiring; (viii) Labour contractors; (ix) Worker's union; (x) Job fairs.
- **Merits:** (i) Wider choice; (ii) Fresh outlook.

- **Demerits:** (i) Heart-Burning among old employees; (ii) Expensive; (iii) Danger of maladjustment.
- **Selection:** Selection means going through the qualifications and experience of the candidates to decide whether the candidates fulfill the requirements of the job. It is the process of dividing the applicants into two categories : (i) those who are to be employed; (ii) those who are to be rejected.
- **Steps in Selection of Employees:** (i) Preliminary interview; (ii) Blank application; (iii) Selection tests : (a) Aptitude tests; (b) Achievement tests; (c) Situational tests; (d) Proficiency test; (e) Interest tests; (f) Personality tests; (iv) Selection interview : (a) Structured or patterned interview, (b) Unstructured or non-directive interview, (c) Stress interview, (d) Group interview; (v) Checking references; (vi) Medical examination; (vii) Final approval; (viii) Employment.
- **Difference between Recruitment and Selection:** (i) Meaning; (ii) Nature; (iii) Aim; (iv) Process; (v) Number; (vi) Order.

Visit any four big organisations and record their methods of recruitment and selection of the staff. Compare the methods and procedure adopted by different organisations.

You are the principal of a school. Which methods would you adopt for recruitment of teaching and non-teaching staff for school ? What procedure would you follow to make the final selection of the staff ?

A. **Short Answer Type Questions:**
   1. Define recruitment.
   2. Name any three methods of recruitment.
   3. State in brief the internal sources of recruitment.
   4. State the external sources of recruitment.
   5. Define selection.
   6. What is the significance of selection?
   7. Name any three methods of selection.
   8. What are the types of interviews?
   9. Distinguish between recruitment and selection. [ICSE 2017]
   10. Distinguish between internal recruitment and external recruitment.
   11. What is meant by Gate Hiring in recruitment?
   12. State two advantages of internal recruitment. [ICSE 2020]

13. State two advantages of campus recruitment as an external source of recruitment. [ICSE 2020]
14. Breifly explain any two types of selection tests. [ICSE 2020]
15. "Selection is a negative process'. Explain. [ICSE 2018]
16. State two disadvantage of internal recruitment. [ICSE 2017]

B. **Essay Type Questions:**
   1. What do you mean by recruitment of employees?
   2. Explain briefly merits and demerits of internal and external sources of recruitment.
   3. Explain in the external sources of recruitment.
   4. What is meant by selection? Explain the steps involved in the selection process.
   5. Discuss the various types of tests and interviews as a part of the selection process.
   6. An organisation has decided to follow a three tier selection process of appointing Executive Trainees: Aptitude Test (A.T.), Group Discussion (G.D.) and Final Interview (F.I.). Outline the details of this process stating clearly the tasks involved at each stage.
   7. Briefly discuss the various methods of recruitment.
   8. How would you recruit and select new sales representatives to persuade the dealers?

CHAPTER-15
Training of Employees

The most valuable asset of any business enterprise is its work force, gifted with understanding, competence and skill to accomplish their work faultlessly. In order to develop such proficiency in the work, proper training of employees is must. Training acquaints the workers with the intricacies of work and ensures greater efficiency and productivity.

- Meaning of Training
- Training and Development
- Training and Education
- Objectives of Training
- Importance of Training
- Levels of Training
- Types of Training
- Methods of Training

TRAINING

Training means imparting the knowledge, skills and aptitudes necessary to undertake the required jobs efficiently with a view to developing the worker to his fullest potential. As an organised activity, training is designed to create a change in the thinking and behaviour of people. Training is a two-way and continuous process because there is no end to learning and secondly, a person gets to learn new technology, new patterns etc. continuously. The training acquaints the employee with the requisite skill, real life situations at the work place and helps him in the faultless accomplishment of the work. Training, thus, involves the development of the manual and mental skills that are necessary for performing a specific work, through instruction, drill and discipline.

- *"Training is the act of increasing the knowledge and skill of an employee for doing a particular job."*
  —Edwin B. Flippo
- *"Training is a process by which the attitudes, skills and abilities of employees to perform specific jobs are increased."*
  —Michael J. Jucious
- *"Training is the organised procedure by which people learn knowledge and/or skill for a definite purpose."*
  —E. F. L. BReach

TRAINING AND DEVELOPMENT

Though no clear cut distinction can be made between the terms 'training' and 'development'; yet it is apparent that training always leads to the development and growth of workers. Further, the word 'training' is mostly used in relation to first level managers or non-managerial personnel, *i.e.*, the operative employees, while the term 'development' is applied to the growth of managerial personnel, *i.e.*, the second and third level managers. 'Training' is used to add to the skills and abilities of the workers, while 'development' involves improving the capacity and capability of the managerial personnel to take up more difficult and risky ventures with greater success besides increasing their skill and competency in their present jobs.

TRAINING AND EDUCATION

According to *Michael Jucious*, "training is any process by which the aptitudes, skills and abilities of employees to perform specific jobs are increased". On the other hand, "education is the process of increasing the general knowledge and understanding of employees." Education involves the general knowledge and developing overall understanding of the total environment. For example, a mechanic who is trained can bind an electric motor better than an engineer but, can not design a next generation advanced electrical device because he is uneducated and is not exposed to the basic principles and fundamentals of engineering. The scope of education is much wider than that of training. Secondly, the purpose of education is general development whereas, training has a specific and immediate purpose of making a person proficient in a particular job. Thirdly, education involves formal instruction in a school or college whereas, training can be given on the job itself. Fourthly, education is generally theoretical whereas, training is practical in nature. Finally, the cost of education is generally paid by the government and the student. On the other hand, the cost of training is generally borne by the employer.

OBJECTIVES OF TRAINING

The training objectives are laid down keeping in view the company's goals and objectives. The general objectives of a training programme are as follows:

(1) To Increase Productivity of Employees:
Training helps in developing the capacities and capabilities of the employees–both new and old, by upgrading their skills and knowledge so that the organization could gainfully avail their services for higher grade professional, technical, sales or production positions from within the organization. In case of new employees, training aims to provide them with basic knowledge and skill they need for an intelligent performance of their specific tasks.

(2) To Remain Competitive in the Market:
To tackle the immensely growing competition in the target market, it is important for an employer to increase the productivity of its workers while reducing the cost of production of the products. Training, therefore, aims to bring about efficiency and effectiveness in an organization to enable it to remain competitive in a highly competitive market situation and for the achievement of organizational goals.

(3) To Change Attitude of the Workers:
Training not only provides new knowledge and job skills to employees, but also brings about a change in their attitude towards fellow workers, supervisor and the organization. It increases job satisfaction among employees and keeps them motivated. It gives them security at the workplace and as a result, labour turnover and absenteeism rates are reduced. It also develops in them self consciousness and a greater awareness to recognize their responsibilities and contribute their very best to the organization.

(4) To Enable Workers to Adapt Quickly to Changes:
Technology is changing at a fast pace. Technological changes like automation and development of highly mechanized and computer oriented systems, threaten the survival of dynamic companies by creating new problems, new methods, new procedures, new equipments, new jobs, new skills and knowledge, new product and services etc. In such a situation, the employees may find themselves helpless to adapt to the changes and may feel frustrated and compelled to leave their jobs.

Thus, training acts as a continuous process to update the employees in the new methods and procedures and make them efficient in handling advanced technology.

(5) To Mitigate the Risk of Accidents:
Trained workers can handle the machines safely. They also know the use of various safety devices in the factory. Thus, they are less prone to industrial accidents.

(6) To Reduce Wastage of Time and Resources:
Training aims at making employees efficient in handling materials, machines and equipment and thus to avoid wastage of time and resources. It also helps in imparting new skills among the workers systematically so that they may learn quickly. If the workers learn through trial and error, they will take a longer time and even then, may not be able to learn right methods of doing work.

(7) To Provide Growth Opportunities to Existing Employees:
Sometimes, it may not be possible for the management to fill in higher work positions from outside. Under such conditions, the apprenticeship programmes aiming at improving the skills of the present employees come to the aid of the company by make available their requirements of the personnel from within the organization. This reduces the need for recruiting people from outside and also improves the morale of the existing employees.

(8) To Make the Management Effective:
One of the primary objectives of training and development process is to give rise to a new and improved management which is capable of handling the planning and control without any serious problem. Knowledge and experience gathered through training enables them to handle the tough situations and confusing realities, thus opening the way for bigger and better opportunities for business. It can also be used for strengthening values, building teams, improving inter-groups relations and quality of work life.

IMPORTANCE OF TRAINING

Training is useful for both employers and employees. A well-trained employee is an asset to the enterprise. Training enables the employee to get job security, higher earnings and promotion. It increases the productivity of the workers and the output for the organisation. The main advantages of training are as follows:

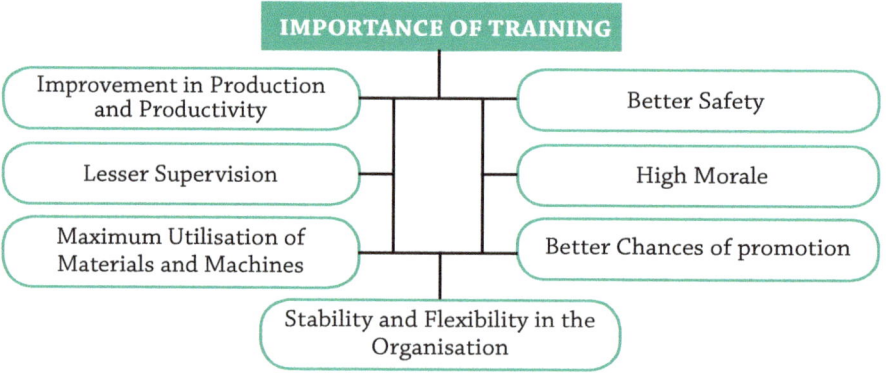

1. Improvement in Production and Productivity:
Training helps to improve the efficiency and productivity of employees. Well-trained employees make better use of materials and machinery. Wastage is reduced and as a result quality and quantity of production becomes higher.

2. Lesser Supervision:
Well-trained employees, have the knowledge about their jobs and equipments and can do their work efficiently. Thus, the training reduces the need of supervision to bare minimum.

3. Maximum Utilisation of Materials and Machines:
Training teaches the employees the method of doing their job in the best possible manner. They have knowledge of operating machines and equipments and handle them properly and methodically. As a result of it, they make the best possible utilisation of materials and machines.

4. Better Safety:
Human error or negligence is the major cause of accidents in the industry. Due to the operational efficiency of the trained workers and the complete knowledge about the working of the plants and machines, chances of accidents are reduced.

5. High Morale:
Effective training improves the self-confidence and job satisfaction of employees. Well-trained employees take greater interest in their job and derive a sense of security. By boosting the morale of employees, training helps to reduce absenteeism and improve labour turnover.

6. Better Chances of Promotion:
As the trained employees have the requisite qualification and training, they can be promoted to higher grades and position more easily than untrained workers.

7. Stability and Flexibility in the Organisation:
An enterprise, where trained personnel's are available, can expand and grow easily. Its survival is not threatened when a few key personnel's are lost because proper replacements are available. Well-trained employees can be transferred from one job to another in order to meet the requirements of other departments. Thus, training also lends flexibility to the organisation.

LEVELS OF TRAINING

Just as the distribution of administration at different levels is essential for the efficient management, similarly the training program may have its own levels for effective results. The following are some of the important levels of training of the employees:

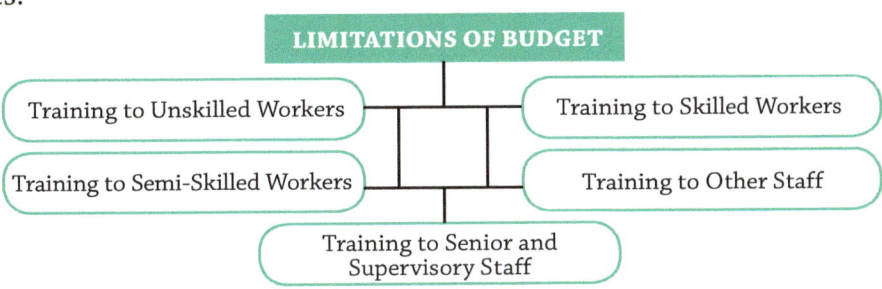

1. Training to Unskilled Workers:
Unskilled workers require training to acquaint themselves with improved methods of handling their work to reduce the cost of production and do the job in the most economical and efficient way. Such employees are given training on the job itself and the training is imparted either by their immediate superior officers, or foremen.

2. Training to Semi-Skilled Workers:
This category of employees requires training to cope with the requirements of the industry arising out of the adoption of mechanisation and rationalisation. These employees are given training either in the section or department itself, or in segregated training shops, where machines and other facilities are easily available. The training is usually imparted by more proficient workers and it lasts for a few hours or weeks, depending upon the number of operations and speed and accuracy required.

3. Training to Skilled Workers:
Skilled workers are given training through the system of apprenticeship, varying in length upto a period of 5 years. Crafts training is imparted through training centres and the industry itself.

4. Training to Other Staff:
Besides the above categories of unskilled, semi-skilled and skilled workers, other employees are also required to be trained, they are computer operators, typists, stenographers, accounts clerks, etc. They need training in their field but such training is usually not provided. Salesmen are also given training about the nature of the products; routine involved in putting through the deal and art of salesmanship, alongwith the latest knowledge of the products being developed in the organisation.

5. Training to Senior and Supervisory Staff:
Since the supervisors form a very important link in the chain of administration, therefore, they need advanced up-to-date training at frequent intervals. The training programmes for the supervisory staff must be specific and tailor-made to fit the need of the undertaking. They are generally given training in :

(a) Organisation and control of production, maintenance and materials handling at the departmental levels.

(b) Planning, allocation and control of work and personnel.

(c) Planning their own work and allocation of time to their various responsibilities.

(d) Effect of industrial legislation at the departmental level.

(e) Cost factors and costs control.

(f) Accident prevention.

(g) Training of subordinates.

(h) Communication, effective instructing, report-writing.

(i) Handling and settling human/labour problems.

(j) Leadership for effective working of the undertaking.

TYPES OF TRAINING

Following are the main types of training:

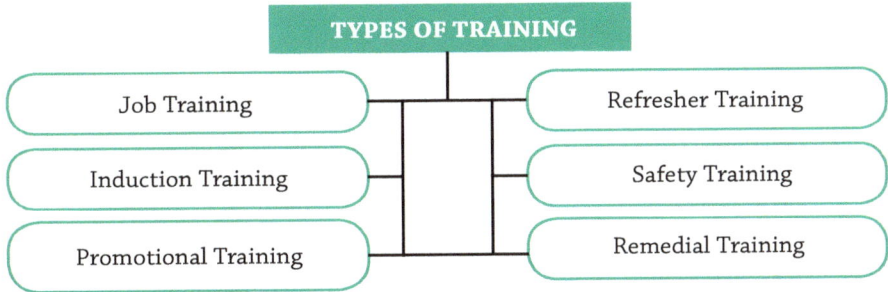

1. Job Training:
Such training is given to make the employees proficient in performing the operations of the job. The new entrants are trained to handle the equipments and raw-materials correctly and perform the job operations efficiently. Old employees are acquainted with the latest methods of executing the jobs.

2. Induction Training:
Induction or orientation training refers to the training given to the new employees. The training is imparted by a competent and experienced executive, who provides knowledge about the work, tools, equipments, techniques and situational problems. The object is to make the employee aware and believe in the ideologies of the working.

3. Promotional Training:
Promotions provide encouragement to employees, and in many organisations, senior posts are filled by promotions. Promotion carries with it new responsibilities for which the incumbent must be prepared. The purpose of this type of training is to meet this demand.

4. Refresher Training:
Such training is designed to revive the earlier learning and to train employees in the use of new tools and work equipments. Short-term refresher courses are organised for this purpose. Such training helps to avoid personnel obsolescence.

5. Safety Training:
Under this type of training, employees are familiarised with safety devices, so that accidents may be prevented. The purpose of this training is to create safety consciousness among employees.

6. Remedial Training:
This type of training is designed to correct the mistakes and shortcomings in the work behaviour and job performance of employees.

METHODS OF TRAINING

Training is concerned with the development of the employees and impart the skills, knowledge and attitudes that are required for specific jobs. The nature of training method will depend on the nature of the job, the type of trainees and the purpose of training. Different methods are followed for providing training to its employees by different organisations. The main methods of training for workers are explained below:

METHODS OF TRAINING

On the Job training methods:
1. Coaching
2. Mentoring
3. Job Rotation
4. Job Instruction
5. Apprenticeship
6. Internship Training
7. Under Study

Off the job training methods:
1. Lectures and Conferences
2. Vestibule Training
3. Simulation Exercises
4. Sensitivity Training
5. Films and Videos
6. Learner Training

A. On the Job Training

On the job training involves assignment of the new employee to a specific job at a machine or work place in the shop, office or laboratory. The worker is trained while he is engaged in the work by utilising the actual work situation for the purpose. He is given the work straight away under the supervision of some senior employee and he learns the job at the hands of this experienced worker. He carries out his orders and instructions and follows the technique of operations advised to him. In this way, he is able to learn the work practically. Problems faced by him are immediately tackled; doubts if any removed and effective leadership offered. In this way, he goes on learning step by step by practically doing his job and reach mastery level. Thus, even during the course of his training, such worker contributes towards total production. There is no problem of adjustment to the actual job after the training. With competent instructor, this type of training may be most effective for rapid training of large number of unskilled and semi-skilled workers. But sometime, employees may cause damage to expensive equipment and the rate of accidents may be high. It is not a suitable method where the job is of complex nature. The success depends entirely on the trainee's own initiative and capabilities.

On the job training methods include the following:

1. Coaching:
Coaching is a one-to-one training. It helps in quickly identifying the weak areas and focus on them. It also offers the benefit of transferring theory learning to practice. The biggest problem is that it perpetrates the existing practices and styles.

2. Mentoring:
The focus of this training is the development of attitude. It is used for managerial employees. Mentoring is always done by a senior person. It involves one-to-one interaction, like coaching.

3. Job Rotation:
It is the process of training employees by rotating them through a series of related jobs. Rotation not only makes a person well acquainted with different jobs, but it also alleviates boredom and allows to develop rapport with a number of people. However, rotation must be logical.

4. Job Instruction:

It is a step by step (structured) on the job training method in which a suitable trainer (a) prepares a trainee with an overview of the job, its purpose, and the results desired, (b) demonstrates the task or the skill to the trainee, (c) allows the trainee to show the demonstration on his or her own, and (d) follows up to provide feedback and help. The trainees are presented the learning material in written or by learning machines through a series called 'frames'.

5. Apprenticeship Training:

This method of training is in vogue in those trades, crafts and technical fields in which a long period is required for gaining proficiency. Apprenticeship training aims at providing necessary background practical knowledge and necessary experience to the worker. Its purpose is to prepare employees for skilled occupations, like carpentry, plumbing, etc. It combines classroom instructions, demonstrations and on the job training. This method familiarises the trainee with the complications and intricacies of the job. A trainee, serving as an apprentice, has to work in direct association and under the direct supervision of his masters. Sometimes, workers are also placed as assistants to experienced workers to learn the process of work by imitation and experience. The apprentice works under his master. During the period of apprenticeship, the trainee may be given a stipend.

In India, apprenticeship training is governed by 'Apprenticeship Act, 1961'. According to this Act, a contract must be signed between the enterprise and the trainee regarding apprenticeship. A copy of the contract must be registered with Apprenticeship authorities. The maximum period of the contract is five years.

6. Internship Training:

This method of training refers to a joint programme of training in which the technical institutions and business houses cooperate. The objects of such cooperation is to provide such training which will bring about a balance between theory and practice. The trainees are given theoretical instructions in technical or professional institutions. After theoretical instructions, they get practical training in factories or offices. In medical, auditing, management and lawyer's profession, internship training is essential. The candidates while in institutions or sometimes, even after their theoretical education receive internship training in hospitals, courts, management institutions and auditing firms. Internship training is useful in the case of technical and professional employees who require advanced theoretical knowledge and practical experience on the job. The method makes them familiar with the complications and intricacies of the work. However, this method is time consuming.

7. Under Study:

In this method, a superior gives training to a subordinate as his understudy like an assistant to a manager or director (in a film). The subordinate learns through experience and observation by participating in handling day to day problems. Basic purpose is to prepare subordinate for assuming the full responsibilities and duties.

B. Off the Job Training

Off the job training is conducted separately from the job environment. Study material is supplied and there is full concentration on learning rather than performing. Importance of the off the job training method include:

1. Lectures and Conferences:

Lectures and conferences are the traditional and direct method of instruction. Every training programme starts with lecture and conference. It's a verbal presentation for a large audience. However, the lectures have to be motivating and interesting to the trainees. The speaker must have considerable knowledge in the subject. In the colleges and universities, lectures and seminars are the most common methods used for training.

2. Vestibule Training:

Under this method, new workers are trained with special machines or equipment in a separate location near the actual place of work under practical work situation. This place is called a vestibule and the actual work situation is duplicated here. An enterprise will arrange vestibule training when the number of workers to be trained is very large, and the line managers are not in a position to spare time for providing training. This type of training emphasis on teaching the best method of doing a task. Furthermore, trainees have an opportunity to get accustomed to the work routine and recover from their initial nervousness before going on the actual jobs. Workers are, thus, trained, without hampering the actual work of production, by qualified instructors. But vestibule training is comparatively expensive and trainees are not able to experience the actual work situations on the shop floor. It may be used as a supplement to 'on the job training.'.

3. Simulation Exercises:

Simulation is any artificial environment exactly similar to the actual situation. These are four basic simulation techniques used for imparting training : management games, case study, role playing, and in basket training.

(a) Management Games:

Properly designed games help to ingrain thinking habits, analytical, logical, and reasoning capabilities, importance of team work, time management, communication and leadership capabilities etc. Use of management games can encourage novel and innovative mechanisms for coping with stress. Management games orient a candidate with practical applicability of the subjects. Different games are used for training general managers and the middle management and functional heads.

Example: In a trucking business, managers could create games that teach truckers the impact of late deliveries, poor customer service or unsafe driving.

(b) Case Study:

Case studies are complex examples which give an insight into the context of a problem as well as illustrate the main point. Case studies are trainee centered activities based on topics that demonstrate theoretical concepts in an applied setting.

A case study allows the application of theoretical concepts to a situation, thus bridging the gap between theory and practice, encourage active learning, provides an opportunity for the development of key skills such as communication, group working and problem solving, and increases the trainees' confidence hence their desire to learn.

(c) Role Playing:

Each trainee takes the role of a person affected by an issue and studies the impact of the issues on human life and/or the effects of human activities from the perspective of that person.

In particular, role-playing presents the student a valuable opportunity to learn not just the course content, but other perspectives on it. The steps involved in role playing include defining objectives, choose context and roles, introducing the exercise, trainee preparation/research, the role-play, concluding discussion, and assessment. Types of role play may be multiple role play, single role play, role rotation, and spontaneous role play.

Role playing can be effective in connecting theory and practice, but may not be popular with people who don't feel comfortable performing in front of a group of people.

(d) In-basket Training:

In-basket exercise, also known as in-tray training, consists of a set of business papers which include e-mail, SMS, reports, memos, and other items. Now the trainer is asked to prioritise the decisions to be made immediately and the ones that can be delayed.

4. Sensitivity Training:

Sensitivity training is also know as laboratory or T-group training. This training is to make people understand about themselves and others reasonably, which is done by developing in them social sensitivity and behavioral flexibility. It is the ability of an individual to sense what others feel and think from their own point of view.

Sensitivity training program comprises of three steps–unfreezing the old values, development of new values and refreezing of new values. It reveals information about his or her own personal qualities, concerns, emotional issues and things that he or she has in common with other members of the group.

5. Films and Videos:

Films and videos can be used on their own or in conjunction with other training methods. To be truly effective, training films and videos should be geared towards a specific objective. They are also effective in stimulating discussion on specific issues after the film or video is finished.

Films and videos are good training tools, but have some of the same disadvantages as a lecture *i.e.*, there is no interaction with the trainees.

6. Learner Training:

This method is also known as vocational school training. This method combines training with education. Learners are those who join industry for semi-skilled jobs without any prior knowledge about the elements of industrial engineering. They have, therefore need to undergo a programme of educational training. For this purpose, it may become necessary to send them to vocational schools for some time for the study of workshop mathematics and learning operation of machines. After this, they may be assigned a regular production jobs.

Lesson at a Glance

- **Training:** Training means imparting the knowledge, skills and aptitudes necessary to undertake the required jobs efficiently with a view to develop the worker to his fullest potential.
- **Training and Development:** Training always leads to the development and growth of workers. Training adds to the skills and abilities of workers.
- **Training and Education:** Training is any process by which the aptitudes, skills and abilities of employees to perform specific jobs are increased. On the other hand, education is the process of increasing the general knowledge and understanding of the employees.
- **Objectives of Training:** The basic objective of training is to help develop capacities and capabilities of employees and improve their level of performance : (i) To increase productivity of empolyees; (ii) To remain competitive in the market; (iii) To change attitude of the workers; (iv) To enable workers to adopt quickly to changes; (v) To mitigate the risk of accidents; (vi) To reduce wastage of time and resources; (vii) To provide growth opportunities to existing employees; (viii) To make the management effective.
- **Importance of Training:** (i) Improvement in production and productivity; (ii) Lesser supervision; (iii) Maximum utilisation of materials and machines; (iv) Better safety; (v) High morale; (vi) Better chances of promotion; (vii) Stability and flexibility in the organisation.
- Levels of Training: (i) Training to unskilled workers; (ii) Training to semi-skilled workers; (iii) Training to skilled workers; (iv) Training to other staff; (v) Training to senior and supervisory staff.
- **Types of Training:** (i) Job training; (ii) Induction training, (iii) Promotional training; (iv) Refresher training; (v) Safety training; (vi) Remedial Training.
- **Methods of Training:** (i) On the Job Training method; (a) Coaching; (b) Mentoring; (c) Job Rotation; (d) Job instruction; (e) Apprenticeship Training; (f) Internship training; (g) Under study. (ii) Off the job training method : (a) Lectures and Conferences; (b) Vestibule Training; (c) Simulation exercise; (d) Sensitivity Training; (e) Films and Videos; (f) Learner Training.

Visit any four big organisations. Find out the methods of training used by each organisation to train their workers. How have training programmes helped the workers in increasing their working capacity? Compare the results of training programme of each organisation.

You are the Human Resource Manager in an organisation. How would you train the workers of your organisation ?

QUESTIONS

A. Short Answer Type Questions:

1. Define training.
2. What is the difference between training and development?
3. List two importance of training.
4. Name the different levels of training.
5. What are the different types of training?
6. State different methods of training.
7. What is on the job training?
8. What is meant by vestibule training?
9. Distinguish between training and education.
10. Explain the benefits of training.
11. List two main objectives of orientation training.
12. What do you mean by on-the-job training and off-the-job training? [ICSE 2019]
13. Name and explain the type of training designed to correct mistakes. [ICSE 2018]

B. Essay Type Questions:

1. What is training? Differentiate between training and development.
2. Explain the different levels of training.
3. Enumerate the various types of training.
4. What do you mean by: (i) On the job training; (ii) Vestibule training; (iii) Apprenticeship training; and (iv) Internship training.
5. What is training? How does it differ from education and development?
6. Suppose in a large modern organisation, you have been recruited as a staff training officer. Name and explain briefly different types of training programmes you would like to organise. Also indicate what should be your pre-training and post-training activities?
7. What is 'induction training'? Is it the same as on the job training?
8. Describe the importance of training.
9. Suggest on the job training by explaining its major techniques that would increase the level of productivity of employees.
10. Explain the two methods of 'off-the-job training'. [ICSE 2017]

CHAPTER-16
Industrial Relations and Trade Unions

Maintaining cordial industrial relations has been one of the several challenges faced by the modern industrial society. With growing prosperity and rising wages, workers have attained a higher standard of living; they have acquired education, sophistication and greater mobility. In such a scenario, to achieve the objectives of industrial development and of social justice simultaneously, the relations between labour and management must be cordial and harmonious. Such relations can be established and maintained in an industry only when both the workers and employers realise their duties and responsibilities towards each other. Factors such as poor working environment, automation and mechanization, computerization, nepotism, disproportionate wages, lay off, militancy of the trade unions etc. have become a cause of friction between the interests of workers and employers. As a result of such frictions, many industrial problems like—strikes, agitations, lock-outs etc., have become frequent. These have vitiated the industrial atmosphere, decreased the production and productivity of the enterprise, increased the costs of production, decreased the real income of the workers and hampered the industrial development of the country. Therefore, to avoid these consequences, it has become necessary that there must be harmonious relations between labour and management.

- Meaning of Industrial Relations
- Causes for Poor Industrial Relations
- Objectives of Industrial Relations
- Meaning of Trade Unions
- Functions of Trade Unions
- Advantages of Trade Union

INDUSTRIAL RELATIONS

The term 'industrial relations' refers to the complex set of human relationships which emerge in work situations. In other words, the relationships between employers and employees or trade unions are called Industrial Relation. Thus, Industrial Relations deals with the workers and employers relation in any industry. Industrial relations are also known as labour-management relations or employee-employers relations. Industrial relations involve attempts to arrive at workable solutions between the conflicting objectives of profit motive and social gains, of discipline and freedom, of authority and industrial democracy and of bargaining and cooperation.

Industrial Disputes Act, 1947 defines industrial relation as "a relation between employer and employees, employees and employees and employees and trade unions".

- *the term industrial relations "include recruitment, selection, and training of workers, personnel management as well as collective bargaining policies and practices".*

—Dale Yoder

- *"It is the complex of inter-relations among workers, managers and government."*

—Prof. Dunlop

On the basis of analytical study of above definitions, it may be concluded that industrial relations are the results of those mutual feelings and views of employers and employees which they adopted to get better results of planning, organising, supervision, direction, co-ordination and control of their industrial enterprise. It includes their efforts to minimise mutual frictions and to develop mutual co-operation and co-ordination. It also includes the laws passed by the Government for the settlement of industrial disputes and for the establishment of harmonious industrial relations. Thus, Industrial Relations are the inter-relations between employees, employers and Government. In other words, there are three parties to industrial relations:

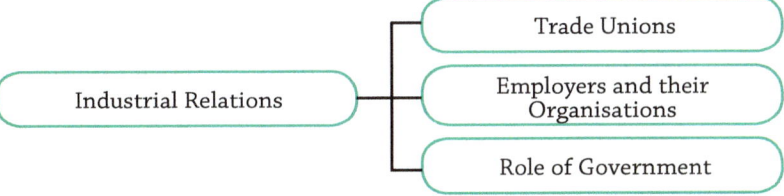

1. Trade Unions:
Trade Unions try to protect the interests of workers. These unions stress upon the development of cultural and educational qualities of their members.

2. Employers and their Organisations:
Employers and their organisations try to protect the interests of employers to create a healthy industrial atmosphere so that the organisational objectives may be achieved. They try to get full co-operation of workers in achieving this objective.

3. Role of Government:
Government also plays an important role in establishing better industrial relations. Government tries to protect the interests of both the employees and employers. For this purpose, the Government enforces various acts and laws.

Therefore, it can be said that industrial relations are the joint liability of labour unions, employers and the Government.

Causes For Poor Industrial Relations

Industrial Relations are characterised by both conflict and co-operations. This is the basis of adverse relationship. So the objective of Industrial Relations is to focus on the attitudes, relationships, practices and procedures developed by the contending parties (that is, by the workers and the employers) to resolve or at least minimize conflicts.

Major causes of rapid decline in the industrial relations and rising industrial disputes are:

1. Economic Causes:
Poor wages and poor working conditions are the main reason for unhealthy relations among management and labour. When employers deny equitable and fair remuneration and good working and living conditions to the working class, trade unions agitate and industrial peace is disturbed. Narrow mindedness of the employers and the employees is also the cause of straining industrial relations. Employers want to extract maximum work with minimum remuneration, while the workers try to avoid work and get more hike in wages.

2. Organisational Causes:

Among organisational causes responsible for poor industrial relations are : Faulty communication system, dilution of supervision and command, non-recognition of trade unions, rapid changes in the methods and techniques of production, nepotism, unequal work loads, disproportionate wage, and responsibilities, etc.

3. Social Causes:

Tensions and conflicts in society, break-up of joint family system, growing intolerance, cultural, religious and linguistic differences among workers have also led to poor industrial relations. Dissatisfaction with job and in personal life culminates in industrial conflicts.

4. Psychological Causes:

Psychological reasons for unsatisfactory employer-employee relations are : Lack of job security, poor organisational culture, non-recognition of merit and performance etc.

5. Political Causes:

Political nature of trade unions, multiple unions and inter-union rivalry weakens trade union movement. Attitude of the government and political parties who may indirectly control some the unions for their own gains or to get a hold on the industry may also strain industrial relations.

Objectives of Industrial Relations

Important objectives of industrial relations are as under:

1. To Create Mutual Faith and Trust between Workers and Management:

Most important objective of industrial relations is to create an atmosphere in the enterprise in which both the workers and management may have faith and trust upon each other. To achieve this object, it is necessary that both the parties should get proper opportunities to express their feelings and emotions.

2. To Settle Industrial Disputes:

Another important objective of industrial relations is to settle industrial disputes peacefully and, at the earliest, so that the harmonious atmosphere may be created and the production and productivity of the enterprise may be increased.

3. To Create Full Employment:

Industrial relations have to be maintained to enhance productivity of the workers and to ensure full employment by reducing the rate of labour turnover and absenteeism.

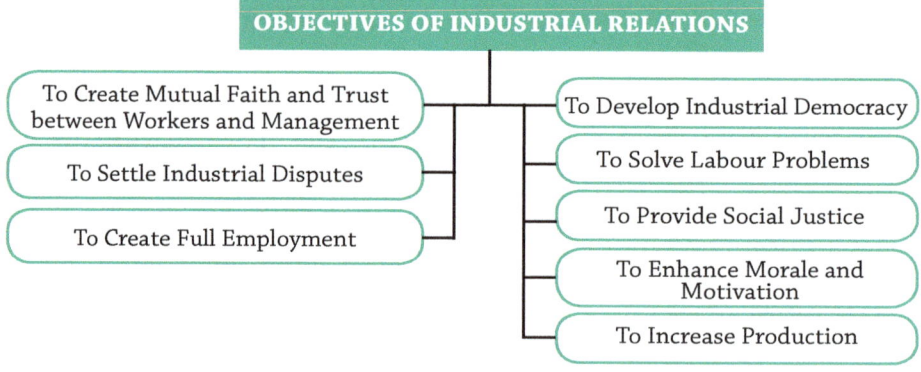

4. To Develop Industrial Democracy:
Industrial relations aims to establish good and harmonious labour-management relations which promote mutual understanding, mutual confidence and resolve the mutual differences. Workers get an opportunity of participation in management. It develops the feelings of responsibility among them and they direct their efforts for the achievement of organisational objectives.

5. To Solve Labour Problems:
Good industrial relations aim at minimising labour problems, such as strikes, lock-outs, gheraos etc. They strive to eliminate labour problems by providing reasonable wages, fringe benefits, improved living and working conditions, etc. Industrial relations also strive to change the traditional and contrary views of labour and management towards each other so that they may develop mutual understanding and co-operation and both may work in the best interests of the concern.

6. To Provide Social Justice:
Industrial relations help in providing social justice to the workers by ensuring fair and equitable wages and thus improving their standard of living.

7. To Enhance Morale and Motivation:
Good industrial relations increase the morale of the workers and motivate the workers to put in more efforts. Every problem is solved by mutual consent which increases worker's participation in management and profits of the firm and also provides job satisfaction to the workers.

8. To Increase Production:
Good industrial relations boost the production and improve both the quality and the quantity of the goods produced. It also increases labour efficiency. An increase in the morale of workers reduces per unit cost of production. Thus, industrial relations have far reaching impact on the production.

TRADE UNION

In every industrial community there are two distinct classes, the employees and the employers, without whom production at a large scale is not possible. Both these parties usually have contradictory motives, which create many problems. Individually, the labourers can do little to resolve their grievances against their employers and to prevent their exploitation. They are effective only when they act in union. This idea of joint action laid down the foundation of the instrument of struggle for security and advancement called "Trade Union".

Trade union is the association of the workers for maintaining and improving the conditions of their working lives and for securing them a better status in the industry and the society. Workers form unions in order to resist employers' exploitation and protect and safeguard their interests.

According to V.V Giri, *"Trade unions are voluntary organisations of workers founded to promote and protect their interests by collective action."*

Edwin B. Flippo defines trade union as *"an organisation of workers to promote, protect and improve, through collective action the social, economic and political interests of its members."*

It is apparent from the above definitions that trade unions are voluntary organisations of workers. The workers form an association in order to protect and safeguard their economic interests and to put up a united resistance against exploitation by the industrialists. The most outstanding feature of the trade unions is their own accord. Generally, all workers in a particular occupation are the members of the trade union representing their occupation. But there is no element of compulsion in membership. If a worker so desires he can stay away from the trade union.

Functions of Trade Union

All functions concerning the well being of workers are mostly regulated by trade unions. These functions may broadly be divided into three headings:

1. Intra-mural Activities:

Intra-mural activities refer to those efforts of trade unions which are mainly performed for the betterment of workers in relation to their employment. Through these activities, trade unions ensure adequate wages, better working conditions, better treatment and a reasonable share and control in the profits and management of industry.

2. Extra-mural Activities:

Extra-mural activities refer to those activities of the trade unions which are performed for providing help to workers in times of need. Therefore, trade unions help the workers in case of sickness and accident and give them financial support during the period of unemployment, strikes and lock-out. They also foster a spirit of co-operation and diffuse education among labourers.

3. Political Activities:

Trade unions, at present are not only confined to their intra-mural and extra-mural activities. They also contest elections and try to send their representatives in Parliament and State Legislatures. In India, such development is not yet significant and trade unions are politically unorganised.

Advantages of Trade Union

(A) Advantages to Workers

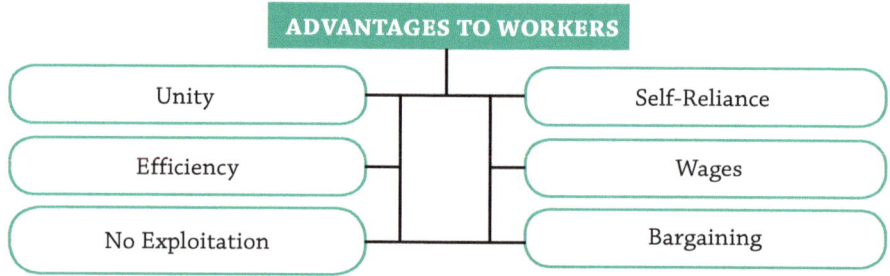

1. Unity:

It promotes unity among workers.

2. Efficiency:

Worker's efficiency is increased by improving their working conditions and by providing them with better welfare facilities.

3. No Exploitation:
Employer's attitude of exploiting workers changes.

4. Self-Reliance:
Trade unions induce self-reliance and self-respect among the workers. They are paid fair share of the profits based on the actual work done.

5. Wages:
Trade unions help to maintain the wages at a uniform level in terms of the actual economic value.

6. Bargaining:
Trade unions negotiate better with the employers through collective bargaining. Being an organised body, they may avoid strike and disputes by putting pressure on the employers to solve the problems amicably and mutually.

(B) Advantages to Employers/Producers

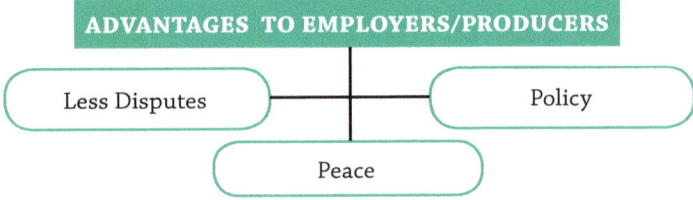

1. Less Disputes:
Industrial disputes can be avoided or may be solved amicably by developing mutual interests and thus, employers can maintain work flow.

2. Peace:
Trade unions may develop a sense of responsibility and loyalty among workers through counselling and collective bargaining. In this way, they help in maintaining industrial peace.

3. Policy:
Trade unions may associate with the employers in framing healthy labour policies which may weaken the chances of disputes in future.

In this way labour unions play an important role in developing labour-force, promoting industrial peace, increasing production and improving working conditions.

 LESSON AT A GLANCE

- **Industrial Relations:** Industrial Relations means the relations between employees and employers. According to Prof. Dunlop, "Industrial Relations may be defined as the complex of inter-relations among workers, managers and government." Thus, there are three parties to industrial relations: (i) Trade unions; (ii) Employers and their organisations; (iii) Government.
- **Causes for Poor Industrial Relations:** (i) Economic causes; (ii) Organisational causes; (iii) Social causes; (iv) Psychological causes; (v) Political causes.
- **Objectives of Industrial Relations:** (i) To create mutual faith and trust between workers and management; (ii) To settle industrial disputes; (iii) To create full-

employment; (iv) To develop industrial democracy; (v) To solve labour problems; (vi) To provide social justice, (vii) To enhance morose a motivation; (viii) To increase production.

- **Trade Union:** Trade union is the association of the workers for maintaining and improving the conditions of their working lives and securing them a better status in the industry and society.
- **Role/Functions of Trade Unions:** (i) Intra-mural activities; (ii) Extra-mural activities; (iii) Political activities.

  Advantages of Trade Unions
- **Advantages to Workers:** (i) Unity; (ii) Efficiency; (iii) No exploitation; (iv) Self-reliance; (v) Wages; (vi) Bargaining.
- **Advantages to Employers/Producers:** (i) Less disputes; (ii) Peace; (iii) Policy.

Visit a big organisation and talk to the President/Secretary of its trade union about the reasons of its formation, benefits which workers are getting etc. Thereafter, make a brief report on the working of the trade union in that organisation.

Explain to your friend the importance of trade unions in an organisation.

A. **Short Answer Type Questions:**
   1. What do you mean by industrial relations? [ICSE 2020]
   2. What are objectives of industrial relations?
   3. What is a trade union?
   4. What is the role of trade unions in relation to its members?
   5. What is the role of a trade union in relation to the industrial organisation in which it has been established?
   6. What are the advantages of trade union to workers?
   7. Explain the extra-mural function of trade unions.
   8. Mention two objectives of industrial relations.

B. **Essay Type Questions:**
   1. What do you mean by industrial relations? Explain the objectives of industrial relations.
   2. Discuss the causes of poor industrial relations in India.
   3. Define trade union. Discuss the objectives of trade unions.
   4. Point out the advantages of trade unions.
   5. Discuss the functions of trade unions.
   6. Discuss the role of trade unions in a business concern. [ICSE 2018]
   7. Explain any five objectives of Industrial Relations. [ICSE 2019]

CHAPTER-17
Social Security

Social security is a dynamic concept which is considered as an indispensable chapter of the national programme in all advanced countries of the world. With the development of the idea of the welfare state, it has been considered to be most essential for the industrial workers, though it includes all sections of the society. Social security refers to the protection provided by the society to its members against providential mishaps over which a person has no control. As the name stands for the general well being of the people, it is the duty of the state to promote social security which may provide the citizens with benefits designed to prevent or cure disease, to support him when he is not able to earn and to restore him to gainful activity. To enjoy security one must be confident that benefits will be available as and when required.

- Evolution of Social Security
- Characteristics of Social Security
- Scope of Social Security
- Social Security in India
- New Pension Scheme

EVOLUTION OF SOCIAL SECURITY

The term 'Social Security' originated in U.S.A. in 1935. The Social Security Act was passed there and the Social Security Board was established to govern and administer the scheme of unemployment, sickness and old age insurance. In 1938, social security was adopted by New Zealand, when it created for the first time, a comprehensive social security system—a measure of income security for all citizens. Later on, the term was adopted in various countries in various forms conveying different meanings.

- *According to the International Labour Organisation, "Social security is the security that society furnishes through appropriate organisation against certain risks to which its members are exposed. These risks are essentially contingencies against which the individual of small means and meager resources cannot effectively provide by his own ability or foresight alone or even in private combination with his fellows. These risks being sickness, maternity, invalidity, old age and death. It is the characteristic of these contingencies that they impair the ability of the working man to support himself and his dependents in health and decency."*
- *According to WIlliam Beveridge, "Social security means the security of an income to take the place of earnings when they are interrupted by unemployment, sickness or accident, to provide for the retirement through old age, to provide against loss of support by death of another person and to meet exceptional expenditure connected with birth, death or marriage. The purpose of social security is to provide an income upto a minimum and also medical treatment to bring the interruption of earnings to an end as soon as possible."*
- *Encyclopedia of social work defines social security as the endeavour of community as a whole, to afford itself to the utmost extent possible to any individual during periods of*

physical distress consequent on illness or injury and from the economic distress consequent on reduction or loss of earnings due to illness, disablement, maternity, unemployment, old age or death of the working members."

The concept of social security is primarily an instrument of social and economic justice. It is essentially related to the high ideals of human dignity. The social security system of a country consists of its social insurance and social assistance schemes and a clear cut demarcation cannot be made between these two.

CHARACTERISTICS OF SOCIAL SECURITY

On the basis of the above mentioned definitions, the following characteristics of social security can be listed:

(a) Social security is an instrument of ensuring social and economic justice.

(b) In a welfare state, social security is an essential part of public policy.

(c) Social security is not static; it is a dynamic concept which changes with the change in social and economic conditions prevailing in a country at a particular point of time.

(d) The basic aim of social security is to provide protection to people of small means against risks or contingencies.

(e) The contingencies which may impair a person's ability to support himself and his family may include sickness, old age, invalidity, unemployment, death etc.

(f) Social security measures are generally guided by social legislation.

(g) Social security measures provide for cash payment to affected persons to partly compensate them for the loss of income due to any of the contingencies mentioned above.

(h) Social security is a must for the protection and stability of the labour force Social security is a wise investment made by the state which yields good social dividends in the long run.

SCOPE OF SOCIAL SECURITY

The scope of social security is very wide. Even though the social security measures differ from country to country, they have some basic features in common. Generally, the social security schemes are of the following types:

(1) Social Insurance:
Under social insurance, workers and employers make periodical contribution to a fund, with or without a subsidy from the Government. Out of these contributions, benefits are provided to the contributors necessary for satisfying wants during old age, sickness, unemployment and other contingencies of life.

(2) Social Assistance:
Social assistance includes non-contributory benefits towards the maintenance of children, mothers, invalids, the aged, the disabled and others like the unemployed. Under this scheme, the Government provides benefits to persons of small means in sufficient quantity so that their minimum standards of needs could be satisfied.

The social security (Minimum standards) convention of the International Labour Organisation prescribes the following components of social security:

(a) Medical care
(b) Sickness benefit
(c) Old age or retirement benefits
(d) Employment injury benefit
(e) Family benefit
(f) Maternity benefit
(g) Invalidity benefit
(h) Survivor's benefit

(3) Public Service:
Public service programmes are usually financed directly by the Government from its general revenue in the form of cash payments or services to every member of the community falling within a defined category.

SOCIAL SECURITY IN INDIA

Although social security measures had been introduced in many countries decades ago, in India, they were introduced only after the independence of the country. It was partly due to lack of official sympathy and the comparative weakness of the trade unions in pressing their demands for such measures. After independence, India declared itself a welfare state under the constitution and as such, several social security measures were introduced.

According to Article 41 of the Constitution of India, *"The state shall within the limits of its economic capacity and development make effective provision securing the right to work, to education and to public assistance in case of unemployment, old age, sickness and disablement and other cases of unserved wants."*

Social security is an important step towards the goal of welfare state. Many State Governments have introduced old age assistance schemes and other types of social assistance benefits. Several laws have been enacted since independence in the country to provide for social security to the workers. Some of the important social security laws are given below:

(1) The Workmen's Compensation Act, 1923

In 1923, the Government of India passed the Workmen's Compensation Act. This Act, marked the beginning of social security system in India. The main objective of this Act is to impose upon the employers an obligation to pay compensation to workers for accidents arising out of and in the course of employment. It also helps to reduce the number of accidents, to give workers greater freedom from anxiety and to make industry more attractive to workers. The Act has been amended several times. The last amendment was made in April 2017 by which the government specified that this Act may now be called as 'Employees' Compensation (Amendment) Act 2017. The government by this amendment has made it mandatory for employees to inform the employee of his rights to compensation under this Act, at the time of his employment. The Act applies to all permanent employees employed in railways, factories, mines, plantations, mechanically propelled vehicles, construction work and certain other hazardous operations. It does not apply to members of armed forces, casual workers and workers covered under the Employee's State Insurance Act, 1948. The State Governments administer this Act and are empowered to extend the application of this Act to other classes of persons or diseases not covered by the Act. The State Governments have appointed labour compensation commissioners for the settlement of disputed cases.

Under this Act, the employer is liable to pay, the compensation in case of personal injury caused by accident arising out of and in the course of employment. No compensation is, however, payable if the incapacity does not last for more than 3 days or if it is caused by the default of the worker, not resulting in death. Besides, body injuries, compensation is also payable in the case of certain occupational diseases.

The amount of compensation payable depends upon the nature of injury and the average monthly wages of the worker concerned. For this purpose injury has been divided under three categories: (i) causing death; (ii) total or partial permanent disablement; and (iii) temporary disablement.

In order to protect the interest of dependents in case of fatal accidents, it is provided in the Act that all cases of fatal accidents are to be brought into the notice of commissioner of labour. In case of admission of liabilities by the employer, the amount of compensation is to be deposited with the commissioner. If the employer denies his liability, the commissioner must decide whether or not there is a ground for claim. The commissioner may inform the dependents and it is open to them for accepting a claim, if they feel so.

(2) The Employee's State Insurance Act, 1948

The Employee's State Insurance Act was passed in 1948 to provide medical facilities and unemployment insurance to industrial workers during their illness. This Act provides medical benefits in the form of medical attendance, treatment, drugs and injections to insured persons and to members of their families, where the facility has been extended to the families also. The ESI Act is applicable to all non-seasonal factories run with power and employing 20 or more persons. It covers all types of employees—manual, clerical, supervisory and technical. This Act is a land mark in the history of social security in India and its object is to introduce social insurance for workers.

The Employees State Insurance Scheme introduced under this Act is compulsory and contributory. Compulsory in the sense that all workers covered under this Act must be insured and contributory in the sense that it is financed by the contributions from both the employees and the employers.

The administration of the Act has been entrusted to an autonomous body called the Employees State Insurance Corporation. The corporation is managed by a governing body representing the Union and the State Governments, Parliament, employers and employees organisations and the medical professionals. This body elects a Standing Committee. A third body called the Medical Benefit Council, advises the corporation on matters relating to medical benefits. State-wise regional boards have also been constituted.

The scheme is financed by the Employees State Insurance Fund which consists of contributions from employers and employees, grants, donations and gifts from Central and State Governments, local authorities or any individual or body. The rate of contribution of employees depends upon the daily wages.

The Scheme provides for five types of benefits to the injured workers and their dependents. These benefits are:

(i) Sickness Benefit:
Sickness benefit consists of cash payment for a maximum period of 91 days per year to the sick worker. The daily rate of sickness benefit is calculated at half of average daily wages. The Insured worker who is getting this benefit must be under the medical treatment at a dispensary or hospital maintained by the Corporation. The benefit is useful to a worker who is unable to attend his work due to sickness.

Workers suffering from long term diseases like T.B., leprosy etc. are entitled for extended sickness benefit at 62·5% of average wage for a period of 309 days.

(ii) Maternity Benefit:
An insured women is entitled to receive cash benefit for confinement, miscarriage or sickness arising out of pregnancy. The benefit is paid at double the sickness benefit rate for a period of 12 weeks of which not more than 6 weeks shall precede the expected date of confinement. If the insured woman dies during the period of confinement, her nominee will receive the benefit for the entire period.

(iii) Disablement Benefit:
Disablement benefit is given in case of temporary as well as permanent disablement. An insured person is entitled to receive disablement benefit for any injury arising out of and in the course of employment which lasts for not less than 3 days excluding the date of accident. In case of temporary disablement, full pay is paid in addition to free medical treatment. In case of permanent partial disablement, the insured worker is entitled for cash benefit for life to be paid at a percentage of the full rate on the basis of percentage of disability. In case of permanent total disablement, the cash benefit will be paid at full rate for the whole life.

(iv) Dependent Benefit:
This benefit is given to the dependents of an insured deceased person. If a person dies as a result of employment accidents, his widow and children are entitled to pension. The widow get it throughout her life or till remarriage. The sons get it upto the age of 18 years while the daughters get it upto the age of 18 years or marriage whichever is earlier.

(v) Medical Benefit:
This benefit is given to a worker claiming sickness benefit, maternity benefit or disablement benefit. This benefit is also available to the family members of the worker. It consists of free medical treatment at dispensary or hospital run by the corporation or at home of the sick.

The ESI Act has provided much needed protection to workers. However, the ESI scheme is criticised on the grounds that the medical treatment given is not satisfactory and there is delay in providing benefits to insured workers. The Act needs to be enforced more effectively. However, in general, the scheme is working in a satisfactory manner.

(3) The Maternity Benefits act, 1961

The Maternity Benefits Act, 1961 was enacted to provide uniform standards for maternity protection. It applied in the first instance to all factories, mines and plantations except those to which the Employee's State Insurance Act applied. This

Act was amended in 1976 to extend the benefit to all women workers covered by the ESI Act. The main purposes of this Act are :

(i) To regulate the employment of women in certain establishments for certain specified periods before and after child birth.

(ii) To provide for the payment of maternity benefits to women workers.

(iii) To provide for certain benefits in case of miscarriage, premature birth or illness arising out of pregnancy.

Under this Act, a women worker can get paid maternity leave upto 26 weeks. Out of this 8 weeks could be availed prior to the delivery of the child and remaining 18 weeks can be availed post childbirth. However, for woman expecting their third child, the duration of paid maternity leave shall be 12 weeks. During the period of leave, the employee is entitled to full wage/salary. In addition, a medical bonus of ₹ 25 per day is payable if the employer provides no free medical care. In order to avail of these benefits, the employee must have worked for at least 100 days in the 12 months immediately preceding the date of expected delivery. The maternity claim will be forfeited if the employees works in any other establishment during the period of leave.

(4) The Employee's Provident Fund Act, 1952

Retirement benefits in the form of provident fund, family pension and deposit linked insurance are available to the employees under the Employees' Provident Fund (and Miscellaneous Provisions) Act, 1952. The Act is applicable to a factory in any industry in which 20 or more persons are employed or which the Central Government notifies in the official Gazette. The Act does not apply to cooperative societies employing less than 50 persons and working without the aid of power. It also does not apply to new establishments for 3 years from the date of establishment. The Government is empowered to grant exemption from the operation of this Act to any class of establishments under certain conditions.

The schemes under this Act are administered by a Tripartite Central Board of Trustees, consisting of representatives of employers, employees and the Government. The Act provides the following benefits:

(i) Provident Fund Scheme:

Under the contributory provident fund scheme, monthly deductions from the employee's salary are made. The employer contributes an equivalent amount. The total contributions are deposited with the provident fund commissioner or invested in the prescribed manner. An employee can obtain advances, and permanent withdrawals (after 15 years of service) for construction of house, higher education/ marriage of children, purchase of car etc. On retirement, death, migration, leaving service etc. the full balance at his credit with interest is payable.

(ii) Employee's Family Pension Scheme, 1971:

Under the Employee's Family Pension Scheme, pension is paid to the widow/ children of the employee who dies while in service. Under the new pension scheme, pension is payable to the employee after his retirement in place of provident fund. According to the new regulations all new employee will have to opt for pension scheme. Persons already employed can switch over from provident fund to pension scheme.

(iii) Employee's Deposit Linked Insurance Scheme, 1976:

The Employee's Deposit linked Insurance Scheme, 1976 was introduced for the members of the Employee Provident Fund with effect from August 1976. On the death of the member, the person entitled to receive the provident fund accumulations would be paid an additional amount equal to average balance in the provident fund account of the deceased during the preceding three years, if such average balance was not below ₹ 10,000 during the said period. The maximum amount of benefit payable under this scheme is ₹ 35,000 and the employees do not have to make any contribution for it.

(5) The Payment of Gratuity Act, 1972

This Act is applicable to all factories, mines, oil fields, plantations, ports, railways, ships or establishments in which 10 or more workers are employed. All persons employed in these establishments are entitled to receive gratuity irrespective of the amount of their wages. The Central Government is empowered under the Act to extend this Act to any establishment.

Gratuity is payable on retirement, death, disablement or termination, subject to the condition that the employee has rendered five years of continuous service with the same employer. Gratuity is payable at the rate of 15 days wages for each year of completed service or part there of subject to a maximum of 20 months wages or ₹ 3,50,000 whichever is lower.

(6) Group Life Insurance

Group life insurance may be defined as a plan which provides coverage for the risks on the lives of a number of persons under one contract. The basic feature of this scheme is the coverage of a number of persons under one contract. Group insurance facility is provided to the employees working with one employer. The important features of this scheme are as follows:

(a) Insurance is provided to all employees working under one employer without any evidence of insurability.

(b) This scheme provides risk coverage to the employees so long as they remain in the service of the employer.

(c) Group life insurance is a contract between the employer and the insurance company. The policy issued to the employer is called Master contract.

(d) The premium is paid jointly by the employer and the employees.

(e) The amount of premium is payable at a flat rate without any regard of the age and the salary of the employees.

(f) In case of injury or death of an employee, the claim received by the employer is paid to the employee or his nominee.

Group insurance proves to be very cheap because of economy in mass administration. It is a welcome relief for the employees as they get insurance cover by paying a very small amount of premium. High salaried people can use group insurance as a supplement to the individual life insurance. For the insurance company, the cost of administration is low as only one policy is issued for several persons. The employer can provide security cover for the employees at very low cost. Because of these reasons, Group life insurance is becoming very popular nowadays.

PENSION

Today, major retirement schemes in India include provident fund, gratuity, and pension plus. The first two plans provide lump sum retirement benefit while the last one makes payment in the form of a monthly annuity. A pension is a type of retirement plan that provides monthly income in retirement. It has the following objectives :

(a) To provide old age income.

(b) To provide reasonable market based return over long run.

(c) To extend old age security coverage to all citizens.

National Pension Scheme:

Government of India establishment Pension Fund Regulatory and Development Authority (PFRDA) on 10th October, 2003 to develop and regulate pension sector in the country. The National Pension System (NPS) was launched on 1st January, 2004 with the objective of providing retirement income to all the citizens. It is a voluntary defined contribution pension system, launched in 2004 by the Government of India. It is administered and regulated by Pension Fund Regulatory and Development Authority of India. NPS aims to institute pension reforms and to inculcate the habit of saving for retirement amongst the citizens. It can be regarded as the most economical pension scheme in India. It is a market linked retirement plan and it is till date the cheapest. The minimum yearly contribution is INR 6000. This can be paid either in one go or in monthly installments of INR 500. The age of the applicant should be between 18 to 60 years. NPS offers following important features to help subscriber save for retirement:

- The subscriber will be allotted a unique Permanent Retirement Account Number (PRAN). This unique account number will remain the same for the rest of subscriber's life. This unique PRAN can be used from any location in India.

Types of account under National Pension Scheme:

- **Tier I Account:** This is a non-withdrawable account meant for savings for retirement. The applicant can claim tax benefits against the contribution made to this account, subject to income tax rules applicable.
- **Tier II Account:** This is simply a voluntary savings facility. The subscriber is free to withdraw savings from this account whenever subscriber wishes. No tax benefit is available on this account. PRAN provides the subscriber an access to Tier I account and Tier II Account.

New Pension Scheme:

The New Pension Scheme was initiated by the government in 2009, to enable people to receive a pension after they retire. Government employees already receive pension as per the National Pension Scheme (NPS) and this new schemes was introduced under NPS to provide pension for all citizens of the country including the unorganised sector workers on a voluntary basis.

A contribution of a certain amount is made every month during the years when an individual is actively working. This amount is invested as per the individual's preference. There are a couple of options for investment to choose from based on the individual's preference of asset allocation and withdrawal. The money can then be withdrawn at a minimum age of 60 years.

Eligibility creteria and contribution requirements for New Pension Scheme is as follows:
- The applicant for the scheme should be an Indian citizen.
- The applicant should be of atleast 18 years of age.
- The applicant should be a maximum of 60 years of age.
- The minimum contribution to be paid is INR 500.
- The contribution has to be made at least once a year.
- The minimum annual contribution should be INR 6,000.
- The maximum contribution to the scheme should not exceed INR 12,000 per annum.

Benefits of the New Pension Scheme:

The following are the major benefits of the New Pension Scheme:

1. Tax Benefits:
There is no direct tax exemption mentioned except that during the time of withdrawal, the amount is free from tax as per the Income Tax Act, 1961.

2. Options of Investment:
There are two options for investments under this scheme, Tier I account restricts withdrawal before the individual reaches the age of withdrawal *i.e.*, 60 years, while Tier 2 account allows the facility of withdrawal before the maturity age which is 60 years.

3. Low Investment Charges:
NPS has a low investment charge, which is 0·0001% of the total amount of investment and hence is a relief in the savings effort for senior citizens.

4. Minimum Requirements:
The investor can deposit a minimum of ₹ 500 per month and the minimum amount to be deposited per year is only ₹ 6,000, making it extremely convenient for common Indian citizens.

5. Government Initiative:
Since this is an initiative of the Indian Government, there is a guarantee of receiving the pension on retirement, without any potential risk of default.

Lesson at a Glance

- **Concept of Social Security:** Social security is that security which the society furnishes through appropriate organisation against certain risks or contingencies to which its members are exposed.
- **Evolution of Social Security:** The term 'Social Security' originated in U.S.A. in 1935. Later on the term was adopted in various countries in different forms conveying different meanings.

- **Scope of Social Security:** (i) Social insurance, (ii) Social assistance; (iii) Public service.
- **Social Security in India:** India became a welfare state after independence under the constitution, and as such, several social security measures were introduced.
  - *(a) The Workmen's Compensation Act, 1923:* Under the Act, the employer is liable to pay the compensation, in case of personal injury caused by accident arising out of and in the course of employment.
  - *(b) The Employee's State Insurance Act, 1948:* The object of the Act is to introduce social insurance for workers in the form of (i) Sickness benefit; (ii) Maternity benefit; (iii) Disablement benefit; (iv) Dependent benefit; (v) Medical benefits.
  - *(c) The Maternity Benefits Act, 1961:* The Act was enacted to provide uniform standards for maternity protection.
  - *(d) The Employees Provident Fund Act, 1952:* The Act provides retirement benefits in the form of (i) provident fund; (ii) family pension; (iii) deposit linked insurance.
  - *(e) The Payment of Gratuity Act, 1972:* Gratuity is payable on retirement, death, disablement or termination subject to the condition that the employee has rendered five years of continuous service with the same employer.
  - *(f) Group Life Insurance:* It provides coverage for the risks on the lives of a number of persons under one contract.
- **National Pension Scheme:** National Pension Scheme is a voluntary defined contribution pension system administered and regulated by the Pension Fund Regulatory and Development Authority (PFRDA).

Visit a big organisation and talk to Labour Welfare Officer about the social security facilities available in the organisation. Make a brief report of each facility available and the persons benefitted from it.

Explain to your friend the social security measures available in India.

A. **Short Answer Type Questions:**
   1. What do you mean by social security?
   2. Give one definition of social security.
   3. Give two characteristics of social security.
   4. List the scope of social security.
   5. What is Workmen's Compensation Act?
   6. List two benefits which are available under Employee's State Insurance Act.

7. Mention purpose of maternity benefit Act.
8. What do you understand by provident fund scheme?
9. List two benefits of group insurance to employees and employers.
10. Briefly explain provident fund. [ICSE 2020]
11. Distinguish between Gratuity and Provident Fund. [ICSE 2017]

B. **Essay Type Questions:**
1. Explain the concept and scope of social security.
2. What social security measures have been initiated by the Government of India?
3. Discuss in brief the social security measures available to the workers under the workmen's compensation Act.
4. Discuss the role of Employee's State Insurance Scheme.
5. Explain the retirement benefits available to employees in India.
6. Write a note on Group Life Insurance.
7. What is National Pension Scheme? What are the types of accounts under it?

CHAPTER-18
Logistics : An Overview

LOGISTICS

In ancient times, logistics management was mostly confined to military science. In today's industrial and commercial age, this term has attained a broader significance. It covers a variety of business activities for the material flow from the various sources to the processing facilities and the consecutive distribution of finished products to the ultimate users.

> - Meaning of Logistics
> - Features of Logistics
> - Classifications of Logistics

Logistics refers to that part of supply chain management that plans, implements and controls the flow and storage of goods, services and related information between the point of origin and the point of consumption in order to meet customers' requirements.

In other words, logistics refers to designing, developing, producing and operating an integrated system, which responds to customer expectations by making available the essential quantity and quality of products as and when required in order to provide best customer service at the least possible costs.

Logistics is an internal combination of inter-related managerial functions that ensures a smooth flow of raw materials, semi-finished goods and finished goods from the first point of production to the point of consumption. Thus, the range of logistics includes a set of activities like procurement, material handling, transportation, warehousing, insurance etc.

Logistics create value for customers, suppliers and stakeholders of an organisation. Here, value is expressed in terms of time and place. Products and services have no value unless they are in possession of the customers at the right place and at the right time. An efficient logistics system creates both time utility and place utility for both, the customers and the producers. Thus, good logistics management looks at the overall activity of the supply chain as contributing to the process of adding value to the products and services. If an activity adds very less value to the product, the need for its existence should be scrutinised. In case customers are ready to pay more than the actual cost for a product or a service as a result of pursuing a particular activity, then it means that the concerned activity has added value to the product.

Features of Logistics

A close scrutiny of the definitions of logistics can help us to enlist the following salient features of Logistics:

1. Logistics ensures an uninterrupted and uniform flow of goods such as raw materials, semi-finished and finished goods.

2. It possesses the ability of meeting customers' expectations and customers' requirements of goods and services.
3. It ensures delivery of quality products on time.
4. It provides the best possible customer service at the lowest possible cost.
5. It is an integration of various managerial functions for the optimum utilisation of resources.
6. It deals with the movement and storage of goods in appropriate quantity.
7. Logistics enhances productivity and profitability of business enterprises.

Classification of Logistics

Logistics can be classified into the following categories:

(i) Transportation:
Transportation means the movement of goods from the point of production to the place where they are required for consumption. It is an important part of commerce as it creates time utility and place utility. Geographical and climate factors force certain industries to be located in particular places. These places are far away from the markets and places where production takes place may not have any demand for their products. As such transport bridges the gap between production and consumption centres.

(ii) Warehousing:
Warehousing is the practice of storing goods in properly constructed buildings with the main objective of protecting them from fire, dust, theft, weather, heat, cold and moisture etc. and thus preventing deterioration in quality of materials. In other words, warehousing involves the making of proper arrangements for retaining the goods in perfect state till they are needed by the consumers and are to be taken to market.

(iii) Insurance:
Insurance is a contract by which a person or an organisation, in consideration of a sum of money, undertakes to make good the loss of another person or organisation against a specified risk, *e.g.*, fire, or to compensate him or his estate on the happening of a specified event such as accident or death.

Lesson at a Glance

- **Definition of Logistics:** Logistics refers to that part of supply chain management that plans, implements, and controls the flow and storage of goods, services and related information between the point of origin and the point of consumption in order to meet customers' requirements.
- **Features of Logistics:** (i) Ensures uniform flow of goods; (ii) Meet customer expectations; (iii) ensures delivery of quality products on time; (iv) provides the best possible customer service at the lowest possible cost; (v) Integrate various managerial functions; (vi) Deals with the movement and storage of goods; (vii) Enhances productivity and profitability.
- **Classification of Logistics:** (i) transportation, (ii) warehousing, (iii) insurance.

 **Project Work**

Study the logistics operations of swiggy and write a report on their delivery network.

 **Assignment**

Explain to your Class the concept third party logistics and how it affects the retailer market.

 **Questions**

A. Short Answer Type Questions:
   1. Define the term 'Logistics'. [ICSE 2019]
   2. What do you mean by warehousing?
   3. What is insurance?
   4. What are the classifications of logistics?

B. Essay Type Questions:
   1. Explain the meaning of logistics.
   2. List the features of logistics.
   3. Explain the various classifications of logistics.

CHAPTER-19
Transportation

If agriculture and industry are regarded as the body and the bones of the Indian economy, transportation and communication constitute its nerves, which help in the circulation of men and materials. The transportation system helps to broaden the market for goods and by doing so, it makes possible large-scale production through division of labour. Regions may have abundant agricultural, forest and mineral resources but they cannot be developed if they continue to be remote and inaccessible. By linking the backward regions with the relatively more advanced, transportation development helps in the better and fuller utilisation of resources. Finally, expansion of transport facilities, in turn, helps industrialisation directly. Expansion of transportation is thus of fundamental importance for a developing country like India.

- *Meaning of Transportation*
- *Functions of Transportation*
- *Advantages and Importance of Transportation*
- *Modes of Transportation: Land; Water; and Air*
- *Merits and Demerits of Road Transportation*
- *Merits and Demerits of Rail Transportation*
- *Types of Water Transportation : Inland and Ocean*
- *Merits and Demerits of Water Transportation*
- *Merits and Demerits of Air Transportation*
- *Suitability of Different means of Transportation*

Transportation means the movement of goods and persons from one place to another. Transportation is the physical means whereby goods are moved from the point of production to the place where they are required for consumption. Assembling and dispersion of goods are done with the help of one or the other mode of transportation. It is an important part of commerce as it helps in removing the hindrance of distance. The road, rail, river, canal, ocean and air transport, all contribute to commerce by enabling goods to be sent where and when they are required.

No country can progress without efficient and sufficient facilities of the transport. It has been rightly said that, *"If agriculture and industry are the body and bones of national organism, transport and communications are its nerves."*

- *"The transport industries, which undertake nothing more than movement of persons and things from one place to another, have constituted one of the most important activities of men in every stage of advanced civilization."* —Professor Marshall

FUNCTIONS OF TRANSPORTATION

1. It helps in the growth of industries whose products require quick marketing. Articles like fish, green vegetables are carried to various consumers quickly, even in distant markets.

2. It increases the demand for goods. Newer customers in newer places can be easily contacted and products can be introduced to them. Today, markets have acquired national and international dimensions only because of transport.
3. It creates place utility. Geographical and climate factors force certain industries to be located at particular place. These places are far away from the markets and places where production takes place and there, they may not have any demand for their products. As such transport bridges the gap between production and consumption centres.
4. Of late it has started creating the time utility also. This has been made possible mainly by virtue of the improvements in the speed of transport. It now helps the product to be distributed in the minimum possible time.
5. Transportation exerts considerable influence upon the stabilisation of the prices of several commodities. This is achieved by moving commodities from surplus to deficit areas. This maintains the balance of supply and demand factors and keeps the price of commodities stable as well as equal.
6. It ensures even flow of commodities into the hands of the consumers throughout the period of consumption.
7. It enables the consumers to enjoy the benefits of many goods not produced locally. This increases the standard of living, an essential factor for further development of the economy.
8. Transportation intensifies competition which, in turn, reduces prices. Prices are also reduced because of the facilities offered by it for large-scale production. Thus, advantages of large scale production are possible only due to transportation.
9. Transportation increases the mobility of labour and capital. It makes people of one place to migrate to other places in search of jobs. Import of capital machinery and equipment from foreign countries is only possible due to availability of proper means of transportation.

ADVANTAGES AND IMPORTANCE OF TRANSPORTATION

The advantages provided by transportation are as follows:
1. Transportation helps in the distribution of goods in wider market and thus creates greater demand for the goods.
2. It helps in bringing the stability in the price level by transporting the goods from the surplus areas to the deficit areas.
3. It helps those industries which produce perishable goods like meat, fishing, dairy farming, etc.
4. Transportation helps in reducing the cost and increases the purchasing power of the consumers.
5. Improved means of transport benefit the consumers in many ways. The consumers can enjoy the benefits of many goods (which are not produced locally by transporting such goods from other distant places.
6. It has also helped the growth of cities and urban areas by facilitating mobility of labour and capital.

7. It helps in increasing the production and thereby raising the standard of living of the people.
8. Transportation helps the people of different regions to come in contact with each other. It encourages exchange of ideas and promotes cooperation, cordial relations and understanding amongst the people of the world.
9. It helps in increasing the wealth and income of a nation. It is also a source of revenue to the government.
10. It provides employment to millions of people throughout the world.

MODES OF TRANSPORTATION

Broadly, the various modes of transportation fall into three categories—Land, water and Air. These can further be classified on the basis of vehicle used. A detailed classification of various modes of transportation is given below:

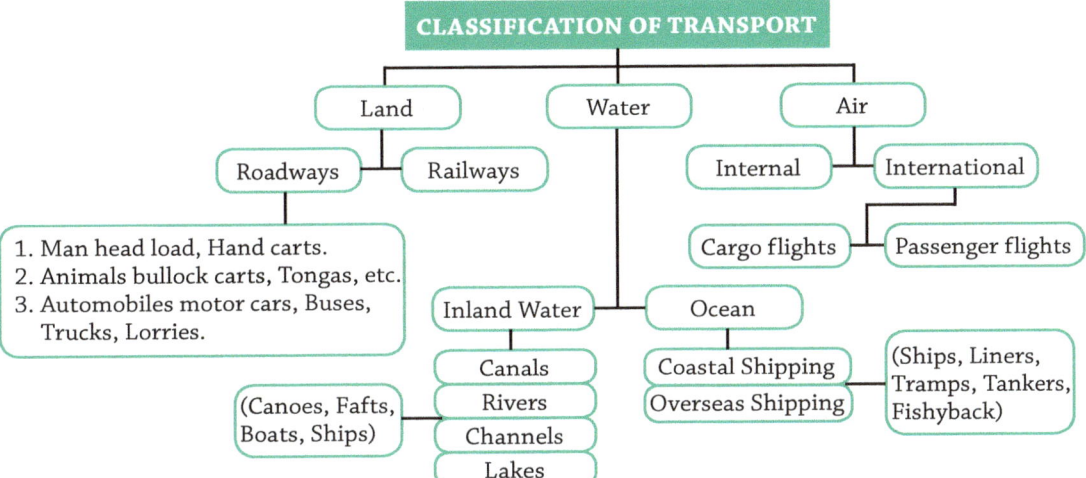

(A) Land Transportation

In land transportation, we include, Road transportation, Rail transportation, Tram-ways and Pipe lines.

(a) Road Transportation:

Road transportation is the most ancient and one of the most widely used means of transportation. Originally, man and animals used roads to carry goods and people. In remote areas or villages, animal transportation (cart, bullock cart) is used even today. The animals used in transportation are Camels, Donkey, Oxen, Mules, Buffalo, Horse etc. These are known as beasts of burden.

Motor cars and other kind of modern vehicles are the result of Industrial Revolution. They needed some regular paths and thus came modern roads—surfaced or unsurfaced, metalled or unmetalled. This is a mechanised form of transportation and has overtaken earlier modes of transportation.

Merits of Road Transportation

1. Cheapest Mode of Transportation:
All forms of road transportation—man driven, animal driven and motor driven are the cheapest form of transportation as the laying and maintenance cost of roads is the responsibility of the State and not of the owners of the vehicles.

2. Flexibility:

This is the one advantage available only to the user of road transportation. It collects goods from the point of production and delivers the goods at the place of user. Door to door service is the most attractive feature of road transportation.

3. Safety:

Damage due to handling of goods is lesser in this form of transportation, because, it unloads the goods directly at the door of the user.

4. Quick:

It is a very quick means of transportation over short distances.

5. Less Time Consuming:

It takes less time for carrying goods from one place to another and thus it helps the businessmen in increasing their turnover.

6. Frequent Service:

Bus and truck services can be as frequent as one may like. This is not possible in other means of transportation. It provides complete service to the businessmen.

Demerits of Road Transportation

1. Irregularities:

The road transportation is most irregular and uncoordinated. It plies according to its own convenience. It reduces regularity and affects the regular and continuous flow of goods.

2. Limited Carrying Capacity:

The load carrying capacity of the road transportation is limited. In case, bulky goods are to be transported, road transportation cannot be effective and also costlier. Moreover, its capacity of undertaking continuous long journey is also limited.

3. Slow Speed:

Speed of road transportation is very slow.

4. Rates:

The rate structure often is oscillating in character. Hence, it creates problems to companies that consider permanency of physical distribution a prestige.

(b) Rail Transportation:

The development and expansion of railways has revolutionised the transportation system the world over. It is a convenient mode of transportation for long distances and is most suitable for carrying heavy and bulky goods like iron ore, iron and steel, heavy machinery, minerals, etc. Railways carry raw materials from the mines and the quarries and other interior areas of the country to the industrial centres. They link up the various regions of the economy and increase the occupational mobility of people. In short, they play a crucial role in economic development.

Railways occupies a dominant role in the transportation system of a country. Rapid industrialisation took place only after the development of rail transportation system. In India also, rail transportation has played a commendable role in the development of trade. It is considered as the life line of the nation.

Merits of Rail transportation

1. Most Suitable for Heavy and Bulky Commodities:
Railways can carry the heavy and bulky goods like engineering and other industrial raw materials etc. Since, they could carry the heavy quantities, the rates are cheaper.

2. Long Distance Travel:
Railways can carry goods and people for long distance. It has now become easier to carry goods to a longer distance with the introduction of diesel and electric power. Speed has also increased considerably.

3. Cheap Rates:
Railways are cheaper than road transportation. It is because, it handles large volume of goods in a single go.

4. No Effect of Weather:
Changes in weather do not affect railways. This advantage is not found in other means of transportation.

5. Safe:
This means of transportation is safer as compared to other means of transportation. Also this means of transportation is more regular.

Demerits of Rail transportation

1. Lesser Accessibility:
It cannot serve rural areas. They can serve only those places which are connected by rails.

2. Inflexibility:
Railways cannot offer door to door service. Goods are carried to terminals (railway stations) resulting in unavoidable additional transportation cost and loading and unloading charges.

3. Not Suitable for Local Transportation:
Local or short distance transportation cannot be imagined through railways. They are profitable only for long distance transportation.

4. Huge Maintenance Expenditure:
Railways involve huge capital and maintenance cost. The low cost of transportation in most cases is, therefore only theoretically valid.

(B) Water Transportation

Water transportation is the primitive mode of transportation. In past it was the only means of transportation available for moving bulky goods. It is the cheapest mode of transportation.

Types of Water Transportation
Water transportation may be classified into two types : (a) Inland, and (b) Ocean transportation.

(a) Inland Water Transportation:
When rivers, canals, channels or even lakes within the national boundaries of a country are used for transporting goods, it is known as inland water transportation. Early civilisation and trade and commerce developed only through this mode of

transportation. The primitive societies used rafts, canoes, and boats made of wood for transporting goods. Later, mechanised boats, and even steamships appeared on the scene. Now, its popularity has diminished because of the development of rail and road transports and its own inherent limitations.

(b) Ocean Transportation:
This is further classified as coastal and overseas shipping:

(i) Coastal Shipping:
Countries having long sea-coasts, use this type of water transportation. It is a dignified form of inland water transportation and serves only the coastal areas within a country with the means of modern and well equipped ships.

(ii) Overseas Shipping:
This is mainly used in international trade. In international trade, its importance grew because the road and rail transportation are purely national in character and cannot move beyond national boundaries. Quantitatively, even today shipping predominates the international transportation scene.

Shipping on the basis of purpose may be divided into Merchant ship and Navy. The former is used for commercial purposes while the latter one is meant for national defence.

According to regularity of service, the Ships are classified into Liners, tankers, tramps, and industrial carriers. Liners provide a regular service from one port to another on specified routes and move only on the basis of pre-determined schedule. Tankers are exclusively meant for transporting crude petroleum or petroleum products. Tramps are handy sized vessels and are not restricted by routes and schedules. They go wherever they find trade. Industrial Carriers are private ships owned and operated for the exclusive use of manufacturers. They transport own finished products and bring back raw materials for their own use.

Merits of Water Transportation
1. It is the cheapest mode of transportation.
2. Water ways are the gift of nature and investment required in maintenance is practically nil.
3. Its operating cost is very low when compared to others means of transportation.
4. Its load carrying capacity is much more and it can carry the heaviest load of goods.
5. It helps all nations in engaging effectively in international trade.
6. In areas, where other modes of transportation cannot be operated, water transportation is best suited.

Demerits of Water transportation
1. Its speed is very slow and so it cannot create time utilities.
2. This form of transportation is seasonal. Some rivers or seas freeze during winter and some are not navigable due to falls or shallowness.
3. Zigzag and circuitous movements required due to meandering of rivers, create inordinate delays in transportation.

4. It is fully dependent on climatic conditions. Storms, high tides and undercurrents are the usual enemies of ocean going ships.
5. It can move only where there is a route. The route cannot be constructed artificially except for a very short distance like Suez canals or Panama canals.

(C) Air Transportation

With the advent of airways, the distance is now measured not in miles but in hours. Air transportation has contributed a lot to commercial activities in international field. It has created time utility even in international markets.

Air transportation has a significant role to play. It offers saving in time that cannot be matched by surface transportation over long distances. Air transportation helps optimise technological, managerial and administrative skills in a resource scarce economy. Transportation of high value light goods and perishable goods is increasingly being done by air transportation.

Merits of Air Transport
1. It is most suitable for carrying goods of perishable nature which require quick delivery.
2. It is also suitable for light goods of high value such as gold, diamonds, jewellery, etc.
3. It provides a regular, convenient, efficient and quick service.
4. It helps in transporting goods to areas inaccessible by any other means of transportation.
5. In the event of stoppage of other means of transportation due to flood, earthquake or other natural calamities, air transportation is the only means of transportation which provides articles of necessities.

Demerits of Air Transportation
1. It is uncertain and unreliable means of transportation as it is controlled to a great extent by weather conditions.
2. The cost of operation of air transportation is higher as compared to other means of transportation.
3. Due to greater degree of possibility of accident, this means of transportation is considered to be dangerous.
4. The fares of air transportation are the highest and it is beyond the reach of a common man.
5. This means of transportation is unsuitable to carry cheap and bulky goods.
6. The construction and maintenance of aerodromes require a large amount of capital investment.

SUITABILITY OF DIFFERENT MEANS OF TRANSPORTATION

The following factors should be taken into consideration while choosing a particular means of transportation:

1. Cost:
Water transportation is comparatively a cheaper means of transportation for carrying heavy and bulky goods over long distances, particularly when time is not

an essential element. Rail transportation ranks second in terms of cost of service. It is cheaper than road transportation for carrying bulky goods over long distances. Road transportation is the cheapest means of transportation for small goods which are to be carried over short distance. Air transportation is the most costly means of transportation and its capacity is limited. It is suitable only for carrying perishable, light and valuable goods.

2. Speed:
Air transportation is the quickest means of transportation while water transportation is the slowest means of transportation. Road transportation is quicker than the rail transportation over short distances. Goods can be loaded directly into a road vehicle and transported straight to their destination. Rail transportation is faster than road transportation over long distances.

3. Flexibility:
Road transportation has the great advantage over all other means of transportation for its flexible service. Road transportation is capable of providing door-to-door services. Its routes and timing can be adjusted to individual requirements. Other means of transportation like water, rail and air transportation are not flexible and cannot provide door-to-door service. Road transportation also acts as a complementary service to other means of transportation.

4. Regularity:
Rail transportation is most certain, regular and uniform as compared to other means of transportation. It is not influenced by weather conditions. Other means of transportation like water, road and air transportation are influenced by weather conditions and are not dependable means of transportation. The effect of weather on road transportation is comparatively less as compared to water transportation and air transportation. Air transportation is most uncertain and unreliable means of transportation. Unfavourable weather may cause cancellation of scheduled flights.

5. Safety:
- Road transportation is the safest means of transportation. Rail transportation also provide sufficient safety to goods. Water transportation and air transportation are the most risky means of transportation.

From the above discussion, it can be concluded that:
(a) Road transportation is particularly suited for carrying goods which are not very cheap or bulky and over short distances. It is also suited for carrying perishable goods such as vegetables, fruits, eggs, milk, etc.
(b) Rail transportation is suited for carrying heavy and bulky goods over long distances.
(c) Water transportation is the best means of transportation for carrying heavy and bulky goods of low price which do not require quick delivery.
(d) Air transportation is suited for carrying perishable, valuable and light articles of high value such as gold, jewellery, etc., which require quicker delivery.

LESSON AT A GLANCE

- **Transportation:** Transportation means the movement of goods and persons from one place to another.
- **Functions of Transportation:** (i) It helps in the growth of industries whose products require quick marketing; (ii) It increases the demand for goods; (iii) it creates place utility; (iv) it creates time utility; (v) helps stabilisation of prices; (vi) Regularity in consumption; (vii) Enjoyment of goods not produced locally; (viii) Intensifies competition; (ix) Increases mobility of labour and capital.
- **Modes of Transportation:** (A) Land; (B) Water; (C) Air.
- **Land Transportation:** (a) Road Transportation; (b) Rail Transportation
- **Merits of Road Transportation:** (i) Cheapest mode of transport; (ii) flexibility; (iii) Safety; (iv) Quick; (v) Less time consuming; (vi) frequent service.
- Demerits of Road Transportation: (i) Irregularities; (ii) Limited Carrying capacity; (iii) Slow speed; (iv) Rates.
- **Merits of Rail Transportation:** (i) Most suitable for heavy and bulky commodities; (ii) Long Distance Travel; (iii) Cheap Rates; (iv) No effect of weather; (v) Safe.
- **Demerits of Rail Transportation:** (i) Lesser Accessibility; (ii) Inflexibility; (iii) Not suitable for local transportation; (iv) Huge maintenance expenditure.
- **Water Transportation:** (a) Inland Water Transportation; (b) Ocean Transportation: (i) Coastal Shipping; (ii) Overseas Shipping.
- **Merits of Water Transportation:** (i) Cheap; (ii) Low maintenance; (iii) Low operating cost; (iv) High carrying capacity; (v) Helps international trade; (vi) Best suited.
- **Demerits of Water Transportation:** (i) Slow speed ; (ii) Seasonal ; (iii) Zigzag; (iv) Dependent on climatic conditions; (v) Requires route.

  Air Transportation:
- **Merits of Air Transportation:** (i) Suitable for Perishable goods; (ii) Suitable for light goods of high value; (iii) Quick service; (iv) Transportation of goods to inaccessible areas; (v) Regular supply in case of natural calamities.
- **Demerits of Air Transportation:** (i) Unreliable; (ii) Cost of operation is high; (iii) Dangerous; (iv) High fare; (v) Unsuitable to carry cheap and bulky goods; (vi) High maintenance cost.
- **Suitability of Different Means of Transportation:** (i) Cost; (ii) Speed; (iii) Flexibility; (iv) Regularity; (v) Safety.

Visit a nearby store and collect the information about the different modes of transportation through which they collect the majority of goods available for sale. Ask the logistics manager about the problems and advantage of each mode they use.

Explain to your class the different modes of water transportation.

A. Short Answer Type Questions:
1. Explain the meaning of transportation.
2. Write three functions of transportation.
3. Write two benefits of transportation.
4. List the modes of transportation.
5. Give three merits of road transportation.
6. Give three demerits of road transportation.
7. Write two advantages of rail transportation. [ICSE 2018]
8. List three demerits of rail transportation.
9. List two kinds of water transportation.
10. Write two merits of water transportation.
11. Write two demerits of water transportation.
12. List two merits of air transportation.
13. List two demerits of air transportation.

B. Essay Type Questions:
1. "Transportation is the life blood of commerce." Discuss and explain the importance of transportation.
2. Discuss the merits and demerits of road transportation
   OR
   Explain any five merits of road transport.
3. Discuss the merits and demerits of rail transportation.
4. Discuss the merits and demerits of air transportation.
   OR
   Explain any five disadvantages of Air Transport. [ICSE 2019]
   OR
   Explain any five advantages of Air transport over water transport.
   [ICSE 2018]
5. Discuss the merits and demerits of water transportation.
6. What factors should be taken into consideration in selecting a means of transportation?

CHAPTER-20
Warehousing

All the goods produced or manufactured are not consumed at the time of their production. This means that the goods are first produced and then consumed. Most of the products are produced seasonally, *i.e.*, their supply is seasonal in nature. But the demand for these products is year-round. This means that the goods are to be stored to ensure their year round supply. The goods may therefore, be stored by the producers, the middleman or by the consumers themselves. Generally, it is the middleman, who stocks the produce because they possess facilities of warehousing.

- Meaning of Warehouse
- Characteristics of a Warehouse
- Objectives of Warehousing
- Functions of Warehouses
- Importance of Warehouse
- Types of Warehouses

Warehousing is the practice of storing goods in properly constructed buildings with the main objects of protecting them from fire, rust and corrosion, dust, theft, weather, heat, cold and moisture etc. and to prevent deterioration in quality of materials. In modern business, a warehouse is as essential as the bank. At present, warehouse is an essential function of the marketing process. In other words, warehousing involves the making of proper arrangements for retaining the goods in perfect state till they are needed by the consumers and are to be taken to the market.

WAREHOUSE

A warehouse is a properly constructed place where surplus goods can be kept safely for future use. Modern warehouse are equipped with latest equipments and facilities for safety of goods as per the requirements of different kinds of goods. Rubber goods, leather goods, textiles, metals, etc., require their own kind of care. Cold storage further enables many perishables such as butter, eggs and fruits, to be stored for regular supplies.

Warehousing is an important function of commerce. It creates time utility and removes the hindrance of time. Warehousing may be defined as the assumption of responsibility for the storage of goods. A warehouse is a place used for the storage or accumulation of goods in proper condition from the time they are produced until they are needed by consumers.

- *The importance of warehousing can be gauged from the statement of S.S. Chatterjee, who remarked that "If transporting and advertising are designed to widen the market, then storage must be taken for deepening the market."* —S.S. Chatterjee
- *"A warehouse is an establishment for the storage or accumulation of goods. It is one of the most important auxiliaries in the service of trader, since by its means the necessity for delay in availing the arrivals of goods from the producers is avoided."*
—James Stephenson

From the above meaning and definitions of warehousing we may conclude that "Warehousing refers to the arrangement by which goods are stored when they are not immediately needed and are kept in such a manner that they are protected from deterioration." Storage of goods is necessary throughout the marketing processes. By preserving goods from the time of production to the time of consumption, it ensures the continuous flow of goods to the market.

Characteristics of A Warehouse

1. Sufficient Space:
Warehouse is a place used for the storage or accumulation of goods. Thus it requires a sufficient space to store maximum goods. Insufficient space is a hindrance in the future development of trade.

2. Safety:
Warehouse should be established at that place where there is no possibility of deterioration of goods. In other words, they should be built strong enough to be safe from pilferage's, theft, dacoities, rain, dust, sun and natural calamities.

3. Proper Supervision:
Warehouse should be properly supervised to avoid the possibility of deterioration of the goods.

4. Near to the Means of Transport:
Warehouses should be established at that place where there is a facility of means of transport.

5. Easy Approach:
Warehouses should be established at that place where buyers and sellers and other related persons (such as a middlemen) may reach conveniently.

6. Economy:
Warehouses should be properly managed so that goods may be stored economically. This is possible only if there is a full utilisation of space.

Objectives of Warehousing

There are four main objectives of warehousing:
1. To protect all goods in warehouse against losses.
2. To provide maximum warehousing service at a minimum cost.
3. To provide prompt delivery of goods.
4. To provide variety of goods of different grades, throughout the year.

Functions of Warehouses

Warehouses thus aid in making an adjustment between production, on the one hand, and demand, on the other. The following are the main functions of the warehouses:

1. Storage of Goods:
The primary function of a warehouse is the storage of surplus goods.

2. Sharing the Risk:
When a storekeeper receives goods for storage he accepts the responsibility for returning them in as good a condition as he receives them. He thus takes over from

the owner the risks attached with the goods and becomes responsible if the goods while in storage, are lost or damaged.

3. Sorting, Packing and Labelling:
Modern warehouses provide the services of sorting the commodities, packing and placing labels on them.

4. Incidental Services for Marketing:
Modern warehouses clean, dry and prepare goods for the market.

5. Exhibiting and Selling of Goods:
Some warehouses provide the facilities of exhibiting and even selling of goods on behalf of the depositor.

6. Economy in Time:
Goods produced by the producers are stored in warehouses which are situated in the central place of the towns, thus the time which ordinarily is to be spent for collecting the goods from the producers scattered far away in the industrial units is saved.

7. Provision of Market:
It performs the most important function of facilitating the retailers to examine the variety of goods at different grades.

8. Regulation of Supply:
By storing goods during periods of excess supply and releasing them during the time of excess demand, warehouses help in regulating the supply of goods.

9. Handling of Exports and Imports:
An efficient system of warehousing is essential for the export of goods. The owners of warehouses sometimes take upon themselves the function of shipping goods on behalf of their clients. They, thus, work as forwarding agents for the exporters.

10. Miscellaneous Functions:
The owner of warehouse is a businessman. In a competitive environment, he wants to get more business by rendering miscellaneous services such as facility of cold storage, purchasing goods on behalf of his clients, collecting market information etc.

Advantages and Importance of Warehouse

1. Seasonal Production:
Goods which are produced seasonally (like wheat, rice, etc.) must be stored so that they are supplied to the consumers throughout the year. In order to supply such commodities to the consumers, their storage is of utmost importance.

2. Seasonal Demand:
Many goods (like woollen cloth, umbrella, rain coats, fans, etc.) are produced throughout the year but their demands are seasonal. Such goods must be stored and preserved until the beginning of the next season. To enable the producers producing such goods to work throughout the year, goods produced by them in off-season must be stored in warehouse.

3. Storage of Perishable Goods:
Perishable goods like vegetables, fruits, eggs, etc. are stored in cold storage to enable the consumers to consume them regularly throughout the year. In the absence of warehouses, the market for the sale of perishable goods will be limited.

4. Production at One Place but Demand at Various Places:
When goods are produced at a distance from the consumers, they must be stored safely in the warehouses near the market as a protection against delays in supply. It enables goods to be made available to the consumers whenever and wherever they are required by them.

5. Stabilisation of Prices:
Prices of goods may oscillate in periods of excess demand and excess supply. During periods of excess supply, if the goods are allowed to flood the markets, the prices would reduce drastically, causing loss to the producers and the farmers. Alternatively during periods of excess demand, warehouses release the goods stored in them to bridge the supply gap, preventing the prices of goods from rising. It is, therefore, necessary to store the goods in the warehouses to avoid violent fluctuations in their prices, especially those goods which are produced during a particular season.

6. Storage of Raw Materials:
It is necessary to store raw materials to ensure continuous largescale production.

7. Production in Anticipation of Demand:
Most of the goods are not produced to meet ready orders but in anticipation of their demand. Therefore, such goods have to be stored until they are demanded.

8. Grading, Packing and Processing:
Warehouses these days provide the facilities of processing, packing and grading of goods. Goods can be graded and packed in convenient sizes as per the instructions of the owner.

9. Financing:
Loans can be raised from the warehouse keeper against the goods stored by the owner. Goods act as security for the warehouse keeper. Similarly, banks and other financial institutions also advance loans against warehouse receipts. In this manner, warehousing acts as a source of finance for the businessmen for meeting business operations.

Types of Warehouses

1. Private Warehouses
These warehouses are owned by the traders or manufacturers to store goods manufactured or bought by them until they are sold out. Since these warehouses are operated for own purposes, their services are not available to other manufacturers. Wholesalers also find it more convenient to deliver goods directly from their own warehouses.

2. Public Warehouses
A public warehouse is the one which operates to store goods of any member of the public in consideration of charges. Public warehouses are held to be public

utilities. They are organised to provide storage service and facilities to the retailers, wholesalers, stockist or even general public in return for a storage fee or charge. In order to provide proper storing facilities to the farmers, *General Warehousing Corporation* and *State Warehousing Corporation* have been set up under the Second Five-Year Plan.

The purpose of public warehouses may be enumerated as under:

(a) They provide full safety to the goods and take all possible precautions to prevent them from damage.

(b) They provide transport facility for receiving and shipping the goods both on rail and ship.

(c) They also provide useful services to the businessmen for the sale of products such as packing, branding, etc.

(d) Purchasers can be taken to the warehouse to inspect the goods.

(e) Manufacturers or traders can easily borrow on the security of warehouse receipts.

3. Cold Storages

These warehouses are established and organised for providing storage services and facilities to perishable goods such as, vegetables, fruits, eggs, fishes, etc. They charge storage fee from the traders. In India more and more cold storages are coming into existence.

Advantages of Cold Storages:

(a) They use scientific method for preserving the perishable goods.

(b) They help in preserving the quality of goods.

(c) Because of cold storages, perishable goods are available throughout the year for consumption to public.

(d) They ensure regular and smooth supply of perishable goods.

(e) They also ensure better prices to the farmers.

4. Bank Warehouses or Godowns

Goods pledged to banks against loans advanced by them are kept in such godowns. They are controlled by banks.

5. Railway Warehouses

Railway authorities establish railway warehouses. Goods received by railways are kept in such warehouses till they are loaded in the wagons. Similarly, goods unloaded at the destination are kept in such warehouses till the owners claim them by submitting the railway receipt (R/R).

6. Warehouses of Food Corporation of India

There is a chain of warehouses established under the direct or indirect control of Food Corporation of India, where the food grains procured from farmers are stored for either to be distributed under public distribution system or for exigencies such as natural calamity, which may reduce agricultural supply.

7. Bonded Warehouses

Bonded warehouses are those warehouses which are licensed by the Government to accept imported goods for storage before the payment of custom duties by importers of such goods. These warehouses are situated near the ports. The goods are delivered by the warehouse-keepers only after the payment of import duty. Such warehouses are called 'Bonded Warehouses' and goods stored therein are said to be 'in a bond'.

By storing their goods in such warehouses, importers gain some control over their goods even before they have paid duty on them. Goods which are meant for re-export are also kept in such warehouses.

These warehouses may be owned by the dock authorities or may be privately owned. They have to work under the control and supervision of the custom authorities. A strict watch is kept on these warehouses by custom authorities.

Some Benefits and Services of Bonded Warehouses are as Follows:
(a) The importers are given the facility to keep their goods in such warehouses till they are able to arrange for the payment of import duty.
(b) The goods stored in such warehouses may be taken in parts by paying the proportionate duty.
(c) The warehouse authorities allow the owners of goods to take their customers in the warehouse for the inspection of goods.
(d) The owners of imported goods are allowed to get their goods branded, blended, labelled, etc. in the warehouse.
(e) Goods stored in such warehouses are quite safe and there is no fear of their being damaged.
(f) For the goods imported for re-export, the importer need not first pay the custom duty and later claim it back after exporting the goods. This saves him from a lot of botheration and considerable expenses.

8. Field Warehousing (Custodian Warehousing)

These are centrally-located warehouses from where goods are further distributed to wholesalers and retailers. This is necessary where products from different plants have to be mixed together.

9. Cooperative Warehouses

The ownership of these warehouses is vested in the hands of a few primary Cooperative Societies. They have not been very popular so far in India but if properly organised they will be a boon to the agriculturists.

Lesson at a Glance

- **Warehouse:** A warehouse is an establishment for the storage or accumulation of goods.
- Characteristics of a warehouse: (i) Sufficient space; (ii) Safety; (iii) Proper Supervision; (iv) Near to the Means of Transport; (v) Easy Approach; (vi) Economy.
- **Functions of Warehouses:** (i) Storage of goods; (ii) Sharing the Risk; (iii) Sorting, Packing and Labelling; (iv) Incidental Services for Marketing; (v) Exhibiting and selling

of goods; (vi) Economy in time; (vii) Provision of Market; (viii) Regulation of Supply; (ix) Handling of Exports and Imports; (x) Miscellaneous functions.

- **Advantages/Importance of Warehouse:** (i) Seasonal Production; (ii) Seasonal Demand; (iii) Storage of Perishable Goods; (iv) Production at One Place but Demand at Various Places; (v) Stabilisation of Prices; (vi) Storage of Raw materials; (vii) Production in Anticipation of Demand, (viii) Grading, Packing and Processing; (ix) Financing.
- **Kinds of Warehouses:** (i) Private Warehouses; (ii) Public Warehouses; (iii) Cold Storages; (iv) Bank Warehouses or Godowns; (v) Railway Warehouses; (vi) Warehouses of Food Corporation of India; (vii) Bonded Warehouses.

Visit a cold storage or a Bonded warehouse near your town. Prepare a list of commodities that are stored in the warehouse. Ask the warehouse manager about the working of warehouse and the services provided by the warehouse to the traders. Also find out whether that warehouse is managed by a private individual or a Cooperative society.

Explain to your class the different forms of warehousing and their benefits.

A. Short Answer Type Questions:
1. What is a warehouse?
2. Give one definition of warehouse.
3. Write two characteristics of a warehouse.
4. Give three functions of warehouse.
5. List three advantages of warehouse.
6. Write three kinds of warehouses.
7. What is public warehouse?
8. What are bonded warehouses? [ICSE 2020]
   OR
   What is a bonded warehouse? [ICSE 2017]
9. List two benefits of bonded warehouse.
10. How do warehouses helps in price stabilisation? [ICSE 2019]
11. Distinguish between private warehouse and public warehouse. [ICSE 2017]

B. Essay Type Questions:
1. What do you mean by warehousing? What are its characteristics?
2. What do you mean by Bonded warehouse? Describe its importance in trade.
3. Describe the advantages of warehousing.
4. Describe the different types of warehouses.
5. Describe any two kinds of warehouses.
6. Discuss six reasons for the increasing necessity of storage in business.
7. Explain any five importance of warehousing. [ICSE 2017]

CHAPTER-21
Insurance

INSURANCE

- Meaning of Insurance
- Objectives of Insurance
- Common Terminology used in Insurance
- Business Risks
- Fundamental Principles of an Insurance Contract
- Advantages and Importance of Insurance
- Types of Insurance

Risk and uncertainty are incidental to life. These risk and uncertainties are increasing day by day due to increase in the pace of life. Man may meet an untimely death. He may also suffer from accident, destruction of property from fire, sea, floods, earthquakes etc. Whenever there is uncertainty, there is risk as well as insecurity. It provides a coverage against risk and insecurity.

Insurance is a contract between two parties by which one of them undertakes to indemnify the other against a loss which may arise on the happening of some event. The document containing the contract is called the Policy of Insurance, the person insured is called the Assured or Insured, and the party which insures is known as the Assurer, Insurer or Underwriter. In return for the insurer's guarantee to make good a specific loss, the insured undertakes to pay the insurer regularly a sum of money known as the premium. The contingency or happening against which insurance is effected is called the risk.

- *"Insurance is a device for the transfer of risks of individual entities to an insurer, who agrees, for a consideration (called the premium), to assume, to a specified extent, losses suffered by the insured."*
  —W.A. Dinsdale
- *"Insurance is a social device providing financial compensation for the effects of misfortune, the payments being made from the accumulated contributions of all parties participating in the scheme."*
  —D. S. Hansel
- *"Insurance is a contract in which a sum of money is paid by the assured in consideration of insurers incurring the risk of paying a large sum upon a given contingency."*
  —Justice Tindal

To conclude, a contract of insurance is a contract by which a person, in consideration of a sum of money, undertakes to make good the loss of another person, against a specified risk, *e.g.*, fire, or to compensate him or his estate on the happening of a specified event such as accident or death.

Objectives of Insurance

Human life and property are subject to the risk of loss or damage from numerous events. The earning member of a family may die, leaving the family in poverty. The house of a person may catch fire and may be reduced to ashes in no time. The ship of a merchant may be upturned by high waves, lost or damaged. The persons who incur such losses suffer financially and in several cases they are practically ruined.

Common Terminology used in Insurance

1. Insured:
One who is covered by an Insurance Company (Individual, Company, Firm, Corporate body etc., with legal status)

2. Insurer:
Party granting the protection under an insurance policy.

3. Policy:
A written contract of insurance between the insurer and the insured, containing all the terms, conditions and warranties of the insurance cover, and as well as the amount of premium, sum insured and the expiry date of the contract among others.

4. Premium:
Non-refundable, small amount of money contributed to the Insurance Company in return for insurance cover.

5. Risk:
It can be defined as the unforeseen element which may impede a person's progress in achieving an objective.

There are two types of risks namely: Insurable risks and Non-Insurable risks.

Insurable risks are those risks that;
(a) can easily be assessed and whose frequency of occurrence can be estimated
(b) can have premiums fairly calculated
(c) have past statistical records
(d) can be accepted for coverage by the insurance company

Examples of Insurable risks include; fire, theft, death, accidents, claims from third parties, damage to property, burglary, bad debts, etc.

Non-Insurable risks are those risks that;
(a) can not be easily assessed and their frequency of occurrence can not be estimated
(b) whose premium can not be fairly calculated
(c) do not have any past statistical record of occurrence
(d) can not be accepted to be covered by the insurance company

Examples of Non-Insurable risks include : bad management, illegal acts such as theft, losses due to change of fashion, natural calamities such as earthquakes, etc.

BUSINESS RISKS

There are multifarious risks in business. The business property is subject to loss by fire, theft, burglary and fraud. The goods are subject to loss by natural causes such as storms, earthquakes, floods, etc. In times of war, the risk is multiplied manifold.

At present, due to industrial revolution and technological changes, risks in business have increased. Business risks can be classified into the following categories:

1. Natural Factors:
Loss by natural causes such as floods, fire, storms, earthquakes, lightening etc., are included in this category.

2. Human Factors:
Losses due to human factors like negligence, incompetence, strikes, riots and civil commotion, lockouts, embezzlement are included in this category.

3. Economic Factors:
Decline in demand or a fall in prices due to changes in economic policy are included in this category.

4. Miscellaneous:
There are so many other factors due to which, risks arise such as changes in government policy, damage caused by insects, pests, rodents, etc., such risks are included in this category.

FUNDAMENTAL PRINCIPLES OF AN INSURANCE CONTRACT

Insurance contracts are governed by Indian contract act, 1872 which states that to be legally valid, following elements should be in order :

(a) Offer and acceptance

(b) Consideration

(c) Agreement between the parties

(d) Capacity of the parties

(e) Legality of the contract

The following are the principles of Insurance:

1. Principle of Utmost Good Faith or Uberrimae Fidei Contract:
Uberrimae Fidei Contract refers to an insurance contract signed on the foundation of utmost good faith on the part of both the insurer and the insured. It is the duty of the person who wants the insurance policy to share all the material facts about the subject to be insured. These facts affect the judgment of an insurance company in assessing the degree of risk and it is imperative that the insured discloses any information or details in good faith to the insurance company. The insurance company assumes that the facts disclosed on the proposal form are reliable and accurate. Consequently, as any loss occurs, the insurance company will check the facts and materials provided by the insured. In case the details provided were inaccurate, then the insured shall not be compensated. For example, a person driving in a drunken state may meet with a car accident, and then claim compensation from his or her insurance company. However, instead of revealing the truth, the insured may fabricate the facts and say that the accident occurred due to the negligence of other driver. In such a case, the insurance company has full rights to reject the contract of insurance on grounds of fabricating the truth and insured will not be entitled for any compensation.

2. Principle of Insurable Interest:

Insurable interest is said to exist when the insured person obtains some benefit from the existence of an insured object or living persons in case of life insurance. The person having insurable interest in an object or person will be subjected to a financial loss by its destruction. For example, a businessman has insurable interest in his shop, and the bank has insurable interest in the life of the businessman till the loan given to him has been repaid.

In case of life insurance policy, the presence of insurable interest must be at the time of taking up the policy. However, it is not necessary that the insurable interest must be present at the time of death also. In marine insurance, insurable interest must exist at the time of loss; it may or may not exist at the time of contract. In case of fire insurance, insurable interest must exist at the time of death as well as loss. In the absence of insurable interest, a contract of insurance becomes a wager or gambling contract; hence, null and void and unenforceable by law.

3. Principle of Indemnity:

The literal meaning of indemnity is 'protection against a loss or other financial burden.' The objective of insurance policy is to restore the insured to the same financial position after incurring the loss as he/she was before facing the loss. The insured is entitled to receive only the amount of the claim or compensation in accordance to the actual loss. Under the principle of indemnity, the insured is not allowed to earn profit out of insurance because the objective of insurance is to cover the perils, and not to be the means for profit-making. For example, Y has insured his factory for ₹ 1,00,00,000. One day, a fire engulfs the property and destroys it. However, Y succeeds in recovering goods worth ₹ 10,00,000 stored in the factory.

Now, Y will be compensated up to ₹ 90,00,000 (*i.e.*, 1,00,00,000-10,00,000). The principle of indemnity is applicable to all types of insurance except life insurance because no amount of compensation is sufficient to make up for the loss of life. The sum insured in case of life insurance is fixed and is payable either on the expiry of the policy or after death of the insured. Therefore, the contract of life insurance could be called a contingent contract, not a contract of indemnity.

4. Principle of Causa Proxima:

Causa Proxima or Proximate Cause means 'that the insurer will consider the immediate and not the remote cause of the loss or liability.' Under this principle, the insurance company pays the claim only if there is a loss of property as per the terms mentioned in the insurance policy. In other words, the insured can claim damages when the loss has been caused due to insured perils (risks), and the cause has been proximate or nearest to the loss. For instance, if sacks of grains kept in a warehouse are destroyed in the rain due to the holes created in them by the rats, then the insurers will ascertain if the cause of loss were the rats or the rain water. If rain water is the primary cause of the loss, then the insurance company will pay the claim even if it all happened due to the holes created by the rats. The losses incurred due to the negligence of the workmen of the warehouse are not covered under insurance.

5. Principle of Subrogation:

According to this principle, after the compensation of losses suffered by the insured, the insurer gets all the rights in the damaged property and the rights of claiming the losses are shifted to the insurer. This principle allows the insurer to pursue legal actions to recover the amount of loss. Suppose an insurance company insures a four-wheeler and the vehicle gets damaged in an accident. If the insurance gives full claim to the insurer for the vehicle, the insurer will become the new owner of the damaged property. The insurer may also choose to sell the scrap of the vehicle to recover money but the insured cannot sell the damaged vehicle to the scrap dealer and earn profit.

Another crucial facet of this principle is that after paying the compensation for the insured loss, the insurance company can rightfully recover the amount from the insured which he or she has received from the third parties for the damage done. For example, A insures his shop against fire for ₹ 70,000. If the shop is set on fire by a jealous rival of A; A will be entitled to receive a claim of ₹ 70,000 from the insurance company. However, if A has recovered a sum of ₹ 40,000 from his rival, he will have to hold this sum as a trustee and return it to the insurance company. The principle of subrogation is applicable to all contracts of indemnity except to life insurance.

The characteristics of this principle are:

(i) The insurance company cannot sue third party in its own name; it can sue them only in the name of the insured.
(ii) The insurance company receives all those rights in property against third parties which were enjoyed by the insured.
(iii) The insured cooperates with the insurance company by taking the side of insurance company.
(iv) The claim recovered by the insured goes to the insurers.

6. Principle of Contribution:

According to this principle, an insurer who paid the insurance claim may rightfully ask other insurers to contribute to the claim he has paid to the insured. If an insured has taken more than one policy on the same subject matter, he will not be getting claim from each insurer more than the proportion of loss for which they are liable. Put together his total claim from all the insurers cannot be more than the total loss suffered by him. The amount of claim is contributed by the insurance companies in the ratio of insured amounts.

This principle is applicable only if four conditions are met, which are :

(i) The insured must be the same person.
(ii) All the policies must cover the same risk.
(iii) All the policies must be in force at the time of loss of property.
(iv) The total amount of compensation under all policies must not exceed the amount of loss.

7. Mitigation of Loss:

This principle implies that the insured should dutifully take measures to minimize the losses in the event of an accident or mishap. The insured should not act under the impression that the insured assets were anyway protected by the insurance cover, and hence, fail to make attempts to protect them from loss. He should take all preventive steps to ensure that the damage is curbed or minimized as much as possible.

ADVANTAGES AND IMPORTANCE OF INSURANCE

Immense are the benefits of insurance to the modern business. The goods may be destroyed due to fire, theft or in transit. The workers are also exposed to various risks which can cause death or permanent disability. Insurance has been helpful in solving these problems of business and private life. Following are the advantages of insurance :

1. Mitigating Fear and Ensuring Employee Welfare:
There is always a fear of sudden loss. Insurance helps to mitigate various types of fear from the mind of the people. Insurance provides security against losses to both individuals and businessmen. The insured feels secured because of the protection of the insurance policy, in the event of some financial loss. It thus creates confidence and eliminates worries which are difficult to evaluate, but the benefit is very real. These days insurance also assures social security by providing unemployment insurance, health insurance, accident insurance, old age insurance etc. These insurance schemes are beneficial to the poor and help in establishing social justice.

2. Protection Against Risks:
The fundamental principle of insurance is to spread risk among a large number of people. Insurance helps in reducing risks by suggesting precautionary measures on one hand and by sharing the losses to a group of people who have agreed to join the common pool on the other hand. Whenever a loss occurs, it is compensated out of funds of a large number of insurers, thus, the loss is spread among multiple policyholders.

3. Removal of Uncertainties:
Insurance company takes the risks of large but uncertain losses. in exchange for a small premium, it relieves the businessman and gives him a sense of security. If all uncertainty could be removed from business, income would be sure. Insurance removes many of these uncertainties and to that extent, is profitable. It improves the efficiency of business operations.

4. Promotion of Saving:
Insurance not only provides protection against risks but it is also a good form of investment. Saving is a device of preparing for the bad consequences of the future. Insurance helps is developing habit of saving money by making regular premium payments mandatory. In case of fixed time policies, the insured gets a lump-sum amount after the maturity of the policy.

5. Capital Formation and Economic Development:
Insurance helps in capital formation and economic development of the nation. Large funds are collected by way of premiums. These funds can be gainfully employed in industrial development of the country. The employment opportunities also increase

because of the large investments made by insurance companies. So insurance has become an important source of capital formation.

Insurer accumulates large resources from the various insurance funds. Such resources are generally invested in the country, either in the public or private sector. This facilitates considerably the over all development of the economy.

6. Promotion of International trade:
Insurance has helped the development of international trade on a large scale. Marine insurance provides protection against all types of sea-risks.

7. Insurance as an Investment:
A life policy is a combination of protection and investment which helps in diminishing the impact of financial losses. These days large variety of policies have been designed for different purposes. Persons, by taking different types of life insurance policies provide for their social and business obligation. The premium that the insured pays go on accumulating in a fund every year. The sum so accumulated by the insurance company earns interest. Under life assurance a person may also invest his capital in a annuity which will pay him an income every year till death. Therefore, insurance may be regarded as an investment.

TYPES OF INSURANCE

There are a number of insurances, but the following types stand out as being of special importance:

1. Life Insurance:
Everyone born on this planet has to die one day but how and when is not known. It is life insurance that covers the risk of loss of life, and offers a sense of security to the insured and his family. Life insurance is not a contract of indemnity as the sum assured is payable to the insured either on his death or maturity of Life Insurance Policy whichever is earlier. Thus, it is also known as 'Life Assurance'. Life insurance is a contract whereby the insurer, in consideration of a premium, undertakes to pay a sum of money or an annuity, either at the death of the insured or on the expiry of a specified period, whichever is earlier. The premium is payable annually or half yearly on a regular basis during the period of the policy. Failure to pay the installment of premium renders the insurance contract as null and void. Once the policy period expires, the insurance company pays the sum assured to the insured. In case the insured dies before the expiry of the policy period, the sum assured is given to the nominated representatives (like the spouse or children) of the policy holder.

The Insurance Act 1938 defines *"Life Insurance as a contract to which the insurer, in consideration of a premium either in gross sum or by periodical payment, undertakes to pay to the person for whose benefit insurance is effected, a sum of money or annuity on the death of the person whose life is insured or upon his attaining a certain age."*

The Life Insurance Corporation of India is the largest Indian state-owned insurance group and investment company, headquartered in Mumbai. Several private sector players like ICICI Prudential Life Insurance, ING Vyasa Life Insurance, Birla Sunlife Insurance, Max HDFC Life Insurance, and Aviva Life Insurance are doing well in the business of life insurance.

Importance of Life Insurance

Life insurance is the most important form of insurance for the numerous benefits it offers. These are:

(a) Protection Against Risk:
Life insurance policy offers protection to the family of the insured from several uncertainties after his demise. If the policyholder dies a premature death, the sum assured could be given to his or her nominees or the dependents of the insured.

(b) Provision for Old Age:
After retirement from work, a person can still remain financially independent by taking a life insurance policy offering pension benefits. Once the policy period gets over, the sum assured goes to the policyholder. Thus, life insurance helps the insured to lead a graceful, independent life even after retirement.

(c) Encourages Saving:
Life insurance helps people develop the good habit of saving money because the premium is paid in installments, which covers the risk and also leads to capital formation. It also enables the policyholder to raise loan against policy, if required.

(d) Tax Savings:
The amount paid as premium of the life insurance policy is allowed as a deduction from income for calculating incomes tax under Income Tax Act. Thus, people can save their taxes by taking a life insurance policy.

(e) Capital Formation:
The funds collected by life insurance firms are channelized into developmental and other industrial projects. It helps in capital formation, which in turn, leads to the economic growth of the country.

(f) Employment Generation:
Life insurance companies offer self-employment opportunities to a large number of people. People from several walks of life such as retired persons, college students, homemakers etc. can work as insurance agents to earn their livelihood, provided they are self-motivated and satisfy the minimum eligibility requirements.

2. Health Insurance:

Health insurance is an insurance risk hedged against the probability that if and when someone, unexpectedly becomes sick, requires expensive treatments, or is at the mercy of a chronic condition, which requires long-term care, will not fall into dire financial state. It is an effective tool to cover the costs of diseases or accident, thereby saving people from financial hazards resulting from illness or accident. The financial loss from diseases or accidents arises from loss of income and medical expenditure. Individual and group health insurance helps in dealing with these losses. The medical expenses up to a certain amount are paid by the insurance company to the hospital. In case of health insurance, insurable interest must be present at the time of taking the policy. Health insurance mostly covers the consultation fee of the doctor, cost of medicines and hospitalization expenses. There are various types of health insurance policies such as:

(a) Mediclaim Insurance:
Mediclaim is the most preferred insurance policy these days. Under this policy, the insured can even get cashless treatment from the specified hospital which means

that the bills are directly paid to the hospital or the insured can pay the bills in the specified hospital and get a reimbursement after submission of bills to the insurance company.

(b) Disability Insurance:

This insurance provides periodic payment if the insured becomes disabled or incapable of working as a result of an illness or accident. The insured is compensated on the basis of the kind and level of disability.

(c) Long-term Hospitalisation:

It covers the treatment expenses of specified serious illnesses like heart problems, cancer, and kidney failure among many others. This insurance policy asks for heavy premium to be paid by the insured.

(d) Maternity Health Insurance:

It covers the expenses associated with maternity and other additional expenses .The policy covers pre and post-natal care, delivery of babies (normal/cesarean), physician fees, hospitalisation, etc.

Importance of Health Insurance

Health insurance is important for the following reasons:

(a) Huge Coverage at Small Cost:

Health insurance helps the insured in avoiding significant expenses involved in hospitalization for serious conditions like heart ailments, cancer, kidney problems etc. By paying regular premium in small amounts, the insured can get beneficial coverage against health risks.

(b) Tax Savings:

The premium paid for health insurance is allowed as a deduction up to a certain amount from taxable income under the Income Tax Act.

(c) Controls Emergency Hospitalisation Expenses:

If the insured is hospitalised urgently, his or her family does not need to bear the expenses of unexpected hospitalisation.

(d) Economic Development and Social Welfare:

Health insurance contributes remarkably to the economic and social development of the people by making the people healthy.

3. Fire Insurance:

Fire insurance is a contract of indemnity under which the insurer undertakes to indemnify any loss of insured on the event of the subject matter getting destroyed by accidental fire. Generally, a fire insurance policy is taken for a year.

As per the Fire Insurance Act, 1938, *"In addition to other insurances, fire insurance is that insurance which takes place against fire and such other risks which are mentioned in the fire insurance contract."*

Fire insurance is a contract of indemnity. The policyholder has the right to get compensation of actual loss due to fire, not the insured sum. Fire insurance is only meant for safety and not as a means of earning money. In order to claim, the insured must compulsorily assure the damage of insured property. The claim is not paid more than the actual loss suffered. The insurable interest in goods must exist at the time of taking the policy as well as at the time of loss by fire.

An insurance company is liable to pay for compensation of loss caused to insured due to fire only if the following conditions are satisfied:

(a) There must be fire or ignition in reality. Loss of property due to smoke or heat is not covered under fire insurance. Loss by electricity, lightning or explosion is not covered unless it results in fire which damages the property.

(b) The fire should be accidental, not intentional or planned. Loss resulting solely by the negligence of the insured person is covered. However, if the loss is caused due to the malicious intentions of someone it is not covered.

Importance of Fire Insurance
Fire can cause major losses to the property of a person. It may gut down the office or warehouse of a business person, thereby destroying the source of income of the victim and the staff. Fire insurance comes to bailout people by providing the impenetrable and protective shield against fire, and placing the insured person in the same financial position as he or she was before the loss by fire had occurred.

4. Marine Insurance:

Marine insurance is a contract of indemnity under which the insurance company promises to compensate for the loss or damage to the ship or cargo or freight on account of marine travel. The risks covered under marine insurance are sea storms, fraud by ship captain, collusion of ships, fire, sea piracy, political upheavals, natural disasters etc. Marine insurance provides protection against these risks to importers, exporters and shipping companies.

Section 3(IA) of Marine Insurance Act, 1963 defines marine insurance as, *"The business of affecting contracts of insurance upon the vessels and items of any description including cargo, freights and other interests which may be legally insured."*

Marine insurance policy can be taken either for a particular time period or for a particular trip. The insurable interest must exist at the time of signing the policy as well as at the time of marine loss. In marine insurance, there are mainly three implied warranties–(a) seaworthiness of the vessel, (b) non-deviation from the route, and (c) legality of the venture.

Importance of Marine Insurance
Marine insurance plays a key role in decreasing sea perils (risks) and thus supporting foreign trade. It protects the insurer against Jettison or throwing off the good over board in the middle of the sea to avoid sinking of the ship. It also safeguards the insurer against breach of duty on part of the captain or staff. As the time taken for goods to reach the destination is long, the chances of their damage are also high. The owners of ship usually take hull insurance policies to insure the ship against the risk of loss or damage during voyage. Similarly, cargo insurance provides security cover to the shipment freight (or bulk goods) against possible perils. In addition, when freight is supposed to be paid at the port of destination, the shipping company may not receive the freight if the goods are lost in transit. Therefore, the shipping company may choose to insure the freight to be received. This is known as freight insurance.

Lesson at a Glance

- **Insurance:** Insurance is a contract between two parties by which one of them undertakes to indemnify the other, against a loss, which may arise on the happening of some event. Insurance in its technical sense is a social device which employs the use of pooling technique to eliminate uncertainty.
- **Objectives of Insurance:** Insurance is a useful commercial device for protecting people from financial losses.
- **Common Terminology used in Insurance:** (i) Insured; (ii) Insurer; (iii) Policy; (iv) Premium; (v) Risk. Risks are of two types: (a) Insurable risks; (b) Non-Insurable risks.
- **Business Risks:** (i) Natural factors; (ii) Human factors; (iii) Economic factors; (iv) Miscellaneous.
- **Principles of an Insurance Contract:** (i) Principle of utmost good faith; (ii) Principle of Insurable Interest; (iii) Principle of Indemnity; (iv) Principle of Causa Proxima or Proximate Cause; (v) Principle of Subrogation; (vi) Principle of Contribution; (vii) Mitigation of Loss.
- **Importance of Insurance:** (i) Mitigating Fear and Ensuring Employee Welfare; (ii) Protection against risks; (iii) Removal of uncertainties; (iv) Promotion of saving; (v) Capital formation and economic development; (vi) Promotion of international trade; (vii) Insurance as an investment.
- **Types of Insurance:** (i) Life Insurance; (ii) Health Insurance, (iii) Fire Insurance; (iv) Marine Insurance.

Project Work

Students are advised to ask their parents about the Insurance cover they have chosen for themselves and their family. Also try to find out the objectives for the choice of particular type of insurance.

Assignment

Explain to your class the different forms of business risks and the importance of insurance.

Questions

A. Short Answer Type Questions:

1. What do you mean by Insurance? [ICSE 2020]
2. List two principles of Insurance.
3. What do you mean by Insurable interest?
4. What do you mean by indemnity?
5. Write two importances of Insurance.
6. Give a proper definition of Insurance.

7. Briefly explain the principle of utmost good faith of insurance. [ICSE 2020]
8. What do you understand by 'Health Insurance'? [ICSE 2019]
9. Explain 'Contribution' as a principle of insurance. [ICSE 2018]
10. Mention any two main advantages of group life insurance to employees and employers. [ICSE 2017]

B. **Essay Type Questions:**
   1. What do you mean by Insurance? Give proper definition of insurance.
   2. Discuss briefly the principles of an insurance contract.
   3. "Insurance is a contract of indemnity." Explain
   4. Differentiate between insurable and non-insurable risks.
   5. What are the advantages of insurance?
   6. Explain the Principles of Insurance:
      (i) Doctrine of subrogation.
      (ii) Mitigation of loss.
   7. What do you mean by Group Life Insurance? Explain three main features of Gorup Life Insurance.
   8. Explain any five Principles of Insurance.

CHAPTER-22
Banking

Banking is an important aid to business. Banks facilitate trade, mobilise savings and provide much needed finance to businesses and industries. Finance is the foundation of every business activity which is provided by banks of different types. Banks are thus, regarded as indispensable spokes of the wheels of commerce.

- Meaning of Bank
- Kinds of Bank
- Central Bank or Reserve Bank of India
- Functions of Reserve Bank of India or Central Bank
- Commercial Banking in India
- Functions of Commercial Banks
- Difference between Central Bank and Commercial Bank
- Internet Banking

BANK

Bank is an institution which deals in money and credit. It is often described as a credit institution which accepts deposits from the public and lends money. On deposits, the bank pays interest and for lending money, it charges higher rate of interest. The difference between these two rates of interest is the profit of the bank.

According to Banking Regulation Act, 1949, *"Banking means the accepting, for the purpose of lending or investment, of deposits of money from the public repayable on demand or otherwise, and withdrawal by cheque, draft, order or otherwise."*

Thus, a bank is an institution which accepts deposits from the public and in turn advances loans by creating credit. It is different from other financial institutions in the sense that they cannot create credit though they may be accepting deposits and making advances. Hence, it may as such be defined as an institution which purchases and sells money, and transacts other businesses of like nature.

Kinds of Bank

1. Commercial Banks:
Commercial Banks are those banks which perform all kinds of banking functions, such as accepting deposits, advancing loans, credit creation, and agency functions. They are also called joint-stock banks because they are organised in the same manner as joint-stock companies. They are meant to finance the internal trade of a country. Some of the commercial banks in India are Andhra Bank, Canara Bank, Indian Bank, Punjab National Bank, Axis Bank, HDFC Bank, Yes Bank, etc.

2. Exchange Banks:
Exchange Banks are a type of commercial banks whose main function is financing foreign trade. They are also called foreign exchange banks. They are incorporated

outside India but conduct foreign exchange business in India. Exchange banks work under the direct guidance of Reserve Bank of India.

They provide services such as discounting of foreign bills of exchange, facilitating foreign remittances, financing internal trade through regular banking methods, etc.

3. Industrial Banks:

Industrial Banks are those banks which provide medium-term and long-term finance to industries for the purchase of land, machinery, etc. They underwrite debentures and shares of industrial undertakings and also subscribe to them.

Functions of these banks may be summarised as follows:

(a) Providing long-term loans to industries requiring block capital for their schemes of expansion, modernisation, etc.;

(b) Subscribing directly to shares and debentures of industrial undertakings;

(c) Underwriting of shares and debentures issued by industrial concerns;

(d) Promoting new industrial ventures;

(e) Providing technical guidance in the management of industries;

In India, there are a number of financial institutions which perform the functions of Industrial Banks, such as Industrial Development Bank of India (IDBI), Industrial Finance Corporation of India (IFCI), Industrial Credit and Investment Corporation of India (ICICI), etc. Each State in India has its own State Financial Corporation. These institutions are also known as Development Banks. The loans provided by these institutions are both in Indian and foreign currency.

Agricultural Banks Or Land Mortgage Banks: Agricultural Banks are those banks which provide credit to farmers for short-term, medium-term and long-term needs. In India, commercial banks, regional rural banks and agricultural co-operative banks provide short-term loans to farmers. Land Development Banks give long-term loans to farmers on the mortgage of their land. The National Bank for Agriculture and Rural Development (NABARD) provides refinance facilities to all types of banks which give loans to agriculturists.

4. Co-operative Banks:

Co-operative Banks are those financial institutions which are organised on the principle of co-operation. They provide short-term finance to farmers and small-scale industrial units. They also encourage thrift among their members. In rural areas, there are agricultural co-operative banks which accept deposits and give loans to agriculturists, rural artisans, etc. In urban areas, co-operative bank perform the functions of ordinary commercial banks but give loans to their members only.

5. Indigenous Bankers:

Indigenous bankers in India play a very significant role in financing trade and industry. They carry on banking business as a hereditary occupation. They are known as Mahajans, Seths, Sahukars, etc. They carry on the business of financing along with their usual commercial activities. They issue, negotiate and discount hundies, etc., as commission agents. However, they charge a higher rate of interest on loans advanced by them than what is charged by the commercial banks.

6. Export-Import Bank (EXIM):
The Export Import Bank of India (Exim) was launched on 1st January, 1982, with a view to promote, finance and facilitate export and import of goods and services so as to promote the country's international trade and commerce by way of expert advice, viability studies, coordination with bankers of the world, and quick supply of information.

7. Central Bank:
Central Bank of a country is an institution which acts as the leader of the banking system and the money market. It regulates money and credit in close cooperation with the Government. It also controls and regulates all the commercial banks of the country. It occupies a central position in the banking structure, but its operations are not guided by profit motive. In our country, the Reserve Bank of India acts as the Central Bank.

THE CENTRAL BANK OR RESERVE BANK OF INDIA

The bank that controls the operations of the banking system in a country and carries out its monetary policies, is referred to as the Central Bank. Central Bank is the apex institution of the banking system.

According to Vera Smith, *"The primary definition of Central Banking is a banking system in which a single bank has either a complete or a residuary monopoly in the note-issue. It was out of monopoly in the note-issue that were derived the secondary functions and characteristics of modern Central Banking."*

R.S Sayer has differentiated the central bank from a commercial bank by remarking that, *"The business of a Central Bank as distinguished from a Commercial Bank is to control the commercial banks in such a way, as to promote the general monetary policy of the state."*

Thus, the Central Bank may be defined as the apex banking and monetary institution whose main function is to control, regulate and stabilize the banking and the monetary system of the country in the national interests.

The Central Bank in our country is called the Reserve Bank of India. It was established in the year 1935 under the Reserve Bank of India Act of 1934. In the beginning it was a shareholders' bank with a share capital of ₹ 5 crores, divided into 5 lakh shares of ₹ 100 each. The Reserve Bank of India was nationalized in the year 1949 and its entire share capital was acquired by the Government of India.

Functions of Reserve Bank of India or Central Bank

The functions of Reserve Bank of India are the same as performed by the Central Banks of various countries of the world. But these functions are basically different from those performed by the Commercial Banks. It is because like other Central Banks, the Reserve Bank of India also plans and acts particularly to promote and stabilize the economy of the country. It also tries to solve the balance of payments and foreign exchange problems.

The main functions of Reserve Bank of India have been described below:

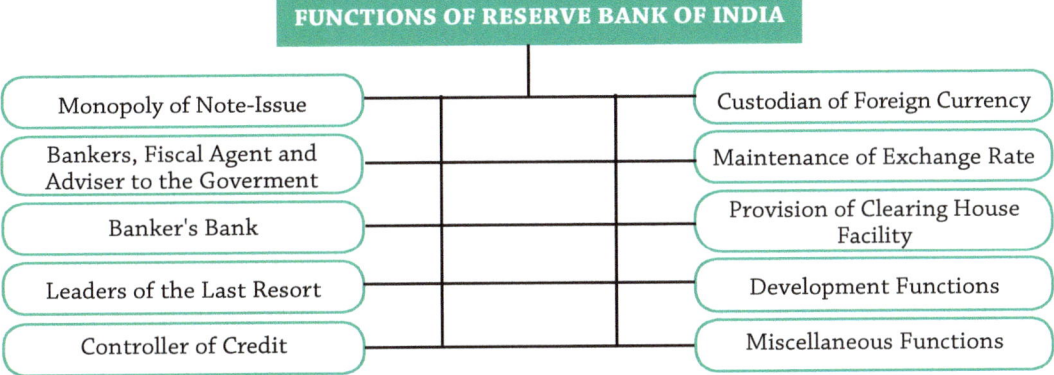

1. Monopoly of Note-Issue:
The Central Bank has the monopoly to issue currency notes. For issuing notes, the Central Bank keeps reserves of gold, silver and foreign securities in fixed proportions to inspire confidence among the people in the paper currency. The Reserve Bank of India issues all the currency notes from ₹ 2 to ₹ 5, ₹ 10, ₹ 20, ₹ 50, ₹ 100, ₹ 200, ₹ 500 and ₹ 2,000.

2. Banker, Fiscal Agent and Adviser to the Government:
The Central Bank is the Government's bank. It acts as a banker, agent and adviser to the Government. The Central Bank makes and receives payments on behalf of the Government. It floats and manages public debts for the Government. It acts as the fiscal agent of the Government in matters relating to monetary and banking policies. The Central Bank also acts as a representative of the government in international conferences on monetary and economic matters.

3. Bankers' Bank:
The Central Bank is the bank for all the commercial banks of the country. Legally or conventionally, commercial banks have to keep a certain proportion of their deposits in the form of cash, as reserve with the Central Bank. These reserves facilitate the Central Bank to control the issue of credit by commercial banks and, thus, keep the credit system elastic. As a bankers' bank, the Central Bank also provides the facilities of short-term loans, discounting bills, etc., to commercial banks. Further, the Central Bank also advises commercial banks on various matters concerning their business.

4. Lender of the Last Resort:
In times of emergency, Commercial Banks may have to borrow from other banks. But other banks, sometimes, may not be in a position to help the bank in trouble. In such situations, the Central Bank is the lender of the last resort. Central Bank helps Commercial Banks either by granting loans or by buying their securities. The RBI extends this facility to protect the interest of the depositors also.

5. Controller of Credit:
Credit control is the most important function of the Central Bank. A country can have a stabilized economy only when the Central Bank of the country exercises its

strict control on the credit granting capacity of the banking structure. Fluctuations in the level of credit available cause fluctuations in the price level, business and level of employment which destabilizes an economy. The Central Bank, therefore, exercises control, qualitatively as well as quantitatively on the credit-granting capacity of Commercial Banks.

6. Custodian of Foreign Currency:

This is one of the most important functions of the Central Bank. The Central Bank is the sole custodian of gold and reserves of foreign exchange of a country. It collects and preserves the gold and foreign currency reserves of the country, in order to utilize them for making payments to foreign countries. If the country's balance of payment is favourable (exports of goods, services and capital > imports of goods, services and capital), then it will earn foreign exchange. However, if the balance of payment is unfavourable (exports of goods, services and capital < imports of goods, services and capital), then foreign exchange goes out of the country. RBI keeps a close watch on external value of its currency and undertakes exchange management control. It also buys and sells foreign currencies at international prices. Further, it fixes the exchange rates of the domestics currency in terms of foreign currencies.

7. Maintenance of Exchange Rate:

The Central Bank keeps a watch on the exchange rate of the home currency in relation to foreign currencies. An exchange rate of two currencies is the rate at which one currency will be exchanged for another. The Central Bank makes every effort to maintain a stable exchange rate by buying and selling foreign currencies at the rates fixed by it.

8. Provision of Clearing House Facility:

The Central Bank performs 'The-Clearing-House Function' for the commercial banks. This means, it settles the claims of commercial banks and enable them to clear their dues by a process of book entries. as such, the daily balances between the commercial banks can be adjusted conveniently by means of debit and credit entries in their respective accounts in the Central Bank. This can be explained by an example; Suppose, the Union Bank of India has to pay an amount of ₹ 5 lakhs to the Syndicate Bank. In this case, the only thing the Union Bank of India has to do is to issue a cheque of this amount to the Syndicate Bank. By means of this cheque, the Union Bank of India's account will be debited by ₹ 5 lakhs, and the account of the Syndicate Bank will be credited by ₹ 5 lakhs. This process has several advantages. Firstly, it facilitates settlement between different commercial banks by a very simple operation, *i.e.*, making entries in the book. Secondly, it eliminates the use of money in these operations. Finally, it helps to stabilise the banking system of the country, as it reduces the possibilities of cash withdrawals during the period of economic crisis. Here, it is important to mention that the Reserve Bank offices are not at all places in India. As such, in those places, where there is no branch of the Reserve Bank, the State Bank of India has been empowered to conduct these settlements.

9. Development Functions:
The above mentioned functions are performed by the Central Banks of all the countries, whether they are developed or underdeveloped. These are known as the traditional functions of the Central Bank. These functions, as such have become regulatory in nature. But in underdeveloped countries, the Central Bank also performs many developmental and promotional functions. For example, it creates special financial institutions for promoting economic developments in different sectors of the economy. In our country, the Reserve Bank of India has a special department of agricultural credit. This department provides long-term credit for agriculture to the farmers and coordinates the activities of the cooperative societies, cooperative banks, and land mortgage banks in rural areas. The Reserve Bank also provides loan facilities to special agencies, like Industrial Finance Corporation, Industrial Development Bank of India, etc., for financing various kinds of industries. Thus, in underdeveloped and developing countries, the main task of Central Bank is to make adequate funds available to finance developmental programmes in respect of agriculture, industry, transport and trade.

10. Miscellaneous Functions:
Besides the above functions, the Central Bank also performs several optional functions. These are called optional functions because they are not regulatory and the Central Bank may or may not perform them. Some of these functions are as follows:

(a) The Central Bank studies different economic problems of the country and compiles data and information, and publishes reports and periodicals for the use of banks and the public. The Reserve Bank of India bulletin is one of them.

(b) It acts as an agent to international institutions, like the International Monetary Fund, the World Bank, etc., on behalf of the Government.

COMMERCIAL BANKING IN INDIA

Progress of Commercial Banking in India: After Independence, the Indian banking system has recorded a rapid progress. This was due to planned economic growth, increase in money supply, growth of banking habits, control and guidance by the Reserve Bank of India and above all, nationalisation of banks in July 1969. After the economic reforms of 1991, a number of private banks and foreign banks have started their operations in India. Recently, Reserve Bank of India has approved the setting up of payments bank and small finance banks for financial inclusion of the poor people as well as of the people living in rural and unbanked areas.

Payments banks are expected to reach its customers mainly through their mobile phones rather than traditional bank branches. These banks can accept a restricted deposit, which is currently limited to ₹ 1 lakh per customer. These banks, however, cannot issue loans and credit cards and cannot accept term deposits. Examples of payment banks are Airtel Payment Bank and India Post Payment Bank.

Small Finance Banks can accept deposits and lend to people who typically won't be served by commercial banks. These people include small farmers, unorganised workers, small business units, etc. They were set up with the twin objectives of providing an institutional mechanism for promoting rural and semi-urban savings and for providing credit for viable economic activities in the local areas.

FUNCTIONS OF COMMERCIAL BANKS

Banks perform numerous functions which throw light on the variety of services they render to the modern society. They have been termed as the 'nerve centre' of the modern world.

Some of the most important functions of Commercial Banks have been discussed below:

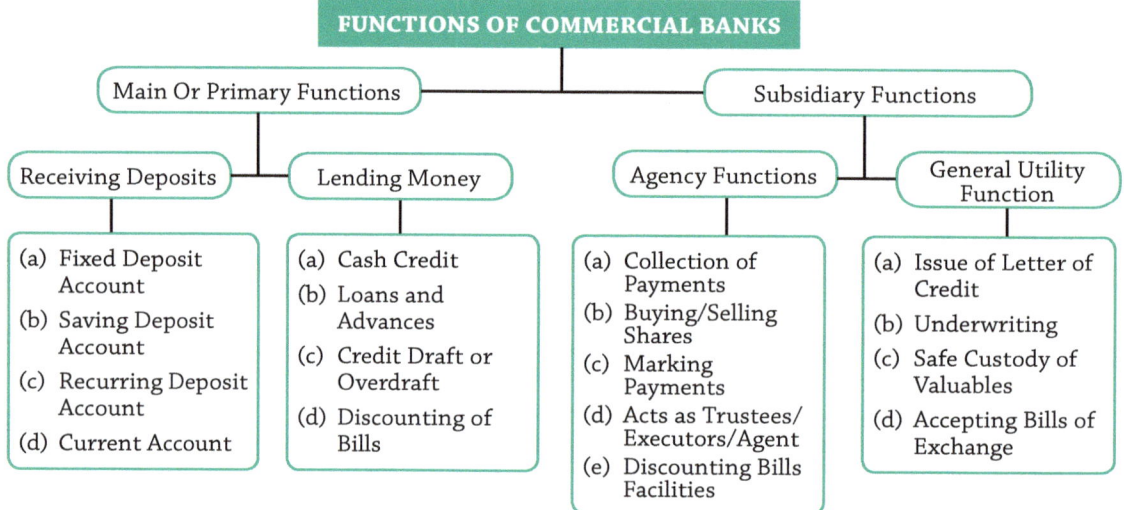

(A) Main or Primary Functions

(i) Receiving Deposits:

Receiving deposits is the primary function of a Commercial Bank. A Commercial Bank accepts deposits from the people for the purpose of making investments and providing loans. People deposit their money for the sake of safety and also for the sake of interest, which is paid by the bank. Commercial banks accept deposits from individuals, firms, industries and institutions. As borrowers, Commercial Banks pay interest on the balance of deposits and undertake to repay them in full legal tender money as and when demanded by the depositors. The banks by accepting the deposits become indebted to the depositholders to the extent of the credit balance indicated by the depositholders' accounts.

Deposits are accepted by these banks in the form of Fixed Deposits, Saving Deposits, Recurring Deposits and Current Deposits.

(a) Fixed Deposit Account: Fixed deposits are made for a specified period and cannot be withdrawn before the expiry of the period for which they have been deposited in the bank. These deposits are repayable after the expiry of the fixed period. It is also known as Time Deposit or long term deposits. Higher rate of interest is offered to attract such deposits. However the interest varies with the duration of the deposits.

(b) Saving Deposit Account: Saving deposits are those deposits an which bank pays a contains rate of interest to the depositors but places certain restriction on their withdrawals. This account is opened with the small amount. The main aim of the saving account is to develop the habit of saving among the common people.

(c) Recurring Deposits Account: This deposit account has been started to encourage those people to save who cannot give large deposit in lump sum. This account can be opened with small amount and the depositor keeps on depositing a certain amount of money every month for a specified period of time. After the expiry of the specific period the depositor get back his money along with interest.

(d) Current Account: It is generally operated by business houses under this account the depositor can withdraw money from this account by cheque at any time during the working hours of the bank. There is no restriction to limit the number of withdrawals subjected to minimum credit balance to be kept on per rules of the bank.

(ii) Lending Money:

Lending money is the most important function of a Commercial Bank. The bank lends out the money which it gets as deposits from the public. A Commercial Bank lends money to traders, businessmen, agriculturists, artisans, etc., to finance their need for capital. Commercial Banks usually lend money in the following ways:

(a) Cash Credit: Cash Credit is an arrangement by which the bank advances cash loans of a specified limit to the customers against a bond or other securities. When the cash loan is granted, the borrower opens a cash credit account which is similar to current account, with that amount in the bank. The borrower has the right to withdraw the full amount of loan. Interest is charged on the amount actually utilised by the borrower and not on the whole amount granted to him.

(b) Loans and Advances: A loan is a lump sum advance repayable wholly after an agreed period or in installments. The borrower may withdraw the whole amount at once or draw as and when he needs. Interest, however, is charged on the entire amount of the loan. When the loan is granted for a period not exceeding one year, it is known as short-term loan. When the period of the loan ranges from 5 to 7 years, it is called medium-term loan. Loans for more than 7 years are called long-term loans. Usually a loan is granted against the securities of assets or the personal security of the borrower.

(c) Credit Draft or Overdraft: A Commercial Bank allows the facility of overdraft only to its depositors who have current accounts in the bank. Under this arrangement, a depositor is allowed to withdraw more than what he has deposited. But, this extra withdrawal has to be repaid by the customer within a short period, along with the interest charged by the bank on the extra amount withdrawn. The rate of this interest may be somewhat more than the interest rate charged on loans. Banks, however, give overdraft facility only on the security of some assets or on the personal security of the customer.

(d) Discounting of Bills: Banks provide financial help to their customers (the businessmen, the merchants, the exporters, etc.) by way of discounting their bills of exchange.

A bill of exchange is an instrument in writing containing an unconditional order, signed by the maker, directing a certain person to pay a certain sum of money only to the bearer of the instrument.

When a customer (say, an exporter) comes to the bank with a bill of exchange, the bank pays him the amount of the bill after deducting the usual discount (interest) charges. The bank, thus assists its merchant customers considerably by accepting their bills of exchange and by providing them cash in return to meet their short term capital requirements. After a few months or weeks, when the bill matures (a bill generally matures in 90 days), the bank presents it to the acceptor (say, an importer) and gets back its full amount. In this case, a bill of exchange is of great benefit, both to the importer and the exporter. By using bill of exchange, the exporter gets the amount from the bank and the importer does not have to pay anything to the exporter immediately. Importer pays the amount only when he has funds in his hands. In case the payment is not received on due date, the bank recovers this amount from the customers (that is, the exporter in this case).

(B) Subsidiary Functions

(i) Agency Functions:

Commercial Banks render several services as the agents of their customers. These services are known as their agency functions. Some of the most important agency functions are as follows:

(a) Collection of Payments: Commercial Banks collect the payment of the bills of exchange, promissory notes, cheques, etc., on behalf of their customers. They also collect dividends, interest on shares, debentures, rent, etc., on behalf of their customers.

(b) Buying/Selling Shares: Commercial Banks buy and sell shares and securities on behalf of the customers as per their instructions.

(c) Making Payments: They transfer funds from one branch of the bank to another and from one place to another as per the instructions of their customers. They make payments of loan installments, interest, insurance premiums, taxes, etc., on behalf of their customers.

(d) Act as Trustees/Executors/Agents: Commercial Banks act as trustees or executors and deal with the financial matters, relating to other institutions, for their customers. They act as the agents or representatives of their customers for other banks and financial institutions, inside the country and abroad.

(e) Discounting Bills Facilities: Commercial Banks offer discounting facilities in respect of foreign and local bills of their customers.

(ii) General Utility Functions:

Besides the above mentioned functions, Commercial Banks also perform several general utility and miscellaneous services not only to their customers but to the public in general as well. These are described below:

(a) Issue of Letter of Credit: Commercial Banks issue letters of credit like circular notes, drafts and provide credit card services and travellers cheques which facilitate the customers in purchasing goods in distant places.

(b) Underwriting: They give references about the financial position of their customers, when it is so required. The banks also undertake to sell shares and debentures of companies on behalf of their customers for which they charge a specified commission.

(c) Safe Custody of Valuables: They provide safety vaults or lockers for the safe custody of jewellery, valuable documents and other precious possessions of their customers.

(d) Accepting Bills of Exchange: Letter of credit represents an undertaking by the banker that bills drawn by the exporter will be duly honoured as per terms of credit specified in the letter. Letter of credit opened by a bank at the request of the importer authorises its branch or correspondent bank in the exporter's country to pay the Bills of Exchange drawn by the exporter relating to specified transactions.

Differences between Central Bank and Commercial Bank

Basis of Comparison	Central Bank (Reserve Bank)	Commercial Bank
Meaning	The Central Bank is the apex institution of the monetary and banking structure of the country.	The Commercial Bank is one of the organs of the money market. It accepts deposits and lends money to individuals, firms and industries.
Status	It is a banker to the Government and does not engage itself in ordinary banking activities.	It is a banker to the general public.
Profit Motive	It is non-profit institution which implements the economic policies of the Government.	It is a profit-making institution.
Ownership	It is owned by the Government.	It is owned by shareholders.
Monetary Authority	It has the monopoly of issuing note.	It can issue only cheques.
Advancement of Loans	The Central Bank is the banker's bank. As such, it grants assistance to commercial banks in the form of rediscount facilities, keeps their cash reserves, and clears their balances.	It advances loans and accepts deposits from the public.
Credit Control	It controls credit in accordance with the needs of business and economy.	It creates credit to meet the requirements of business.
Number of Banks	Every country has only one Central Bank with its offices at important cities of the country.	There are a number of Commercial Banks with hundreds of branches within and outside the country.
Foreign Currency	It is the custodian of the foreign currency reserve of the country.	It is the dealer of foreign currencies.

Designation	The chief executive of the Central Bank is designated as "Governor".	The chief executive of the Commercial Bank is called "Chairman".
Governing Statute	Reserve Bank of India Act, 1934.	Banking Regulation Act, 1949.
Deals With	Banks and government	General public

INTERNET BANKING

Internet banking or on-line banking is basically virtual banking which is done through the use of Internet. Internet banking refers to systems that enable bank customers to access accounts and general information on bank products and services through a personal computer (PC) or other intelligent devices.

Internet banking products and services can include wholesale products for corporates and businesses as well as retail products for consumers. The products and services obtained through Internet banking is same as offered by banks through physical delivery channels.

Some examples of wholesale products and services include: Cash management, Wire transfer, Automated clearing house (ACH) transactions, Bill presentation and payment. Examples of retail products and services include: Balance inquiry, Funds transfer, Downloading transaction information, Loan applications, etc.

Numerous factors such as competitive cost, customer service, and demographic considerations are motivating banks to provide Internet banking facilities to their customers. Competitive pressure is the chief driving force behind increasing use of Internet banking technology. Banks see Internet banking as a way to keep existing customers and attract new ones to the bank. Internet banking technology and products can provide a means for banks to develop and maintain an ongoing relationship with their customers by offering easy access to a broad array of products and services. Banks can deliver banking services on the Internet at transaction costs far lower than traditional brick-and-mortar branches. Internet banking also allows expanded customer contact through increased geographical reach. In fact, some banks are doing business exclusively via the Internet, that is, they do not have traditional banking offices and only reach their customers on-line.

Modes of Transferring Money:

1. NEFT:

NEFT stands for National Electronic Funds Transfer. NEFT is a nation-wide payment system facilitating one-to-one funds transfer. It is one of the most prominent ways of transferring money since its inception in the year 2005.

Under this scheme, individuals, firms and corporates can electronically transfer funds from any bank branch to any individual, firm or corporate having an account with any other bank branch in the country participating in the scheme. There is no limit – either minimum or maximum – on the amount of funds that could be transferred using NEFT. However, maximum amount per transaction is limited to ₹ 50,000/- for cash based remittances within India.

The NEFT system takes advantage of the core banking system in banks. Accordingly, the settlement of funds between originating and receiving banks takes places centrally at Mumbai, whereas the branches participating in NEFT can be located anywhere across the length and breadth of the country.

Presently, NEFT operates in hourly batches - there are twelve settlements from 8 am to 7 pm on week days (Monday through Friday) and six settlements from 8 am to 1 pm on Saturdays.

2. RTGS:

The acronym 'RTGS' stands for Real Time Gross Settlement, which can be defined as the continuous settlement of funds transfers individually on an order by order basis. 'Real Time' means the processing of instructions at the time they are received rather than at some later time; 'Gross Settlement' means the settlement of funds transfer instructions occurs individually (on an instruction by instruction basis). Therefore, under RTGS, the funds transfer takes place on a real time basis, or in other words, at the time the request is received. It is one of the fastest inter bank money transfer facility available through banking channels in India.

The RTGS service window for customer's transactions is available to banks from 9:00 hours to 16:30 hours on week days and from 9:00 hours to 14:00 hours on Saturdays.

The RTGS system is primarily meant for large value transactions. The minimum amount to be remitted through RTGS is ₹ 2 lakh. There is no upper ceiling for RTGS transactions.

The difference between NEFT and RTGS is that NEFT is an electronic funds transfer system that operates on a Deferred Net Settlement (DNS) basis which settles transactions in batches whereas in RTGS, the transactions are settled individually and beneficiaries are expected to receive the funds in real time as soon as funds are transferred by the sender.

Both NEFT and RTGS systems are maintained by the Reserve Bank of India and they can be used for transferring money only within the country.

3. IMPS:

Immediate Payment Service (IMPS) is an instant interbank electronic fund transfer service which is carried out through mobile phones. It was launched in the year 2010. Unlike NEFT and RTGS, the service is available 24 × 7 throughout the year including bank holidays. Thus, IMPS is an emphatic tool to transfer money instantly within banks across India through mobile, which is not only safe but also economical both in financial and non-financial perspectives. It is managed by the National Payments Corporation of India (NPCI) and is built upon the existing National Financial Switch network.

4. Mobile Wallets:

Mobile wallets are digital wallets which act as the user's real wallet. Mobile wallets help the users to store their payment card information on the application and to pay or receive payments through their smartphones.

How mobile wallets work

1. Download the mobile wallet application on your smartphone.
2. Add your credit card or debit card information to the mobile wallet.
3. When making purchases at participating merchants, access the mobile wallet and choose your card. If you're making an in-store purchase, just hold your mobile device at the terminal to make payment. Paytm, MobiKwik, Oxigen are a well known mobile wallets in India.

LESSON AT A GLANCE

- **Bank:** Bank is an institution which deals in money and credit. It accepts deposits from the public and lends money to individuals, firms and governments.
- **Various Kinds of Bank:** (i) Commercial Banks; (ii) Exchange Banks; (iii) Industrial Banks; (iv) Agricultural Banks; (v) Cooperative Banks; (vi) Indigenous Bankers; (vii) Export-Import Bank (EXIM); (viii) Central Bank.
- **Central Bank:** Central Bank in our country is called the Reserve Bank of India. It is the apex institution whose main function is to control, regulate and stabilise the banking and the monetary system of the country.
- **Functions of Reserve Bank:** (i) Monopoly of note-issue; (ii) Banker, fiscal agent and adviser to the government; (iii) Banker's bank; (iv) Lender of the last resort; (v) Controller of credit; (vi) Custodian of foreign currency; (vii) Maintenance of exchange rate; (viii) Provision of clearing house facility; (ix) Development functions; (x) Miscellaneous functions.
- **Functions of Commercial Banks:** (i) Receiving Deposits; (ii) Lending Money; (iii) Agency functions; (iv) General utility functions.
- **Internet Banking:** Internet banking refers to systems that enable bank customers to access accounts and general information on bank products and services through a personal computer (PC) or other intelligent devices.

Prepare a list of banks located in your city/town and categorise them into public sector banks and private sector banks.

You have to explain to your class the relationship of central bank and commercial banks.

A. **Short Answer Type Questions:**

1. What is a Bank?
2. Explain Industrial Banks.

3. Explain Exchange Banks.
4. Name two types of banks.
5. Explain Commercial Banks.
6. Give the meaning of Central Bank.
7. State two functions of the Reserve Bank of India.
8. Name the Central Bank of our country.
9. Give two major functions of the Central Bank of our country.
10. "A Central Bank is a banker's bank." Explain in brief. [ICSE 2020]
11. State two agency functions performed by commercial banks.
12. What are the two main functions of a commercial bank?
13. What is 'National Electronic Fund Transfer'? [ICSE 2019]
14. What is RTGS?
15. What is IMPS?
16. What is a Mobile Wallet?
17. What are indigenous banks?
18. Mention any two agency functions of commercial banks.
19. A Commercial Bank serves as an agent for its customers. Justify.
20. The Central Bank is the lender of the last resort. Explain.
21. Distinguish between Central Bank and Commercial Bank. [ICSE 2020]
22. Explain:
    (i) NEFT   (ii) RTGS [ICSE 2020]
23. Distinguish between Central Bank and Commercial Bank. [ICSE 2019]

B. Essay Type Questions:
1. Define Bank. Explain different types of banks.
2. What is a Central Bank? What are its important functions? Which of these functions are more important in a country like India?
3. What is meant by the term 'commercial bank'? Explain the functions of a commercial bank.
4. Give in detail the functions of a Bank in modern time.
5. Explain the five functions of the Central Bank of India.
6. What is Internet Banking? What are the different modes of Internet Banking?
7. Explain five differences between a central bank and a commercial bank.
8. What do you understand by Agency services of a commercial bank? Explain any four agency services of a commercial bank.
9. Explain the 'Clearing House Function' of the Central Bank. [ICSE 2019]

CHAPTER-23
Banking Transactions

A bank is an institution which accepts deposits from the public and in turn advances loans by creating credit. Banks create credit by advancing loans on cash credit basis or by an overdraft arrangement and by purchasing securities and paying for them with its own cheques. Banks are different from other financial institutions in the sense that other financial institutions cannot create credit though they may be accepting deposits and making advances. Hence, a bank may as such be defined as an institution which purchases and sells money, and transacts other businesses of like nature.

TYPES OF DEPOSIT ACCOUNTS

Banks receive deposits in various forms. the different types of Bank Deposits or Bank Accounts are as follows:

(i) Fixed Deposit Account
(ii) Savings Deposit Account
(iii) Recurring Deposit Account
(iv) Current Deposit Account.

- *Types of Deposit Accounts*
- *Cheque*
- *Parties to a Cheque*
- *Advantages and Disadvantages of Payment by Cheque*
- *Pass Book*
- *Bank Drafts*
- *Traveller's Cheque*
- *Bill of Exchange*
- *Promissory Note*
- *Hundies*
- *ATM*
- *Advantages and Disadvantages of ATMs to Customers and Bankers*
- *Credit Card*
- *Debit Card*
- *Types of Debit Card*
- *Difference between Debit Card and Credit Card*
- *Cautions to Be Taken While Using Debit Card and Credit Card.*

(i) Fixed Deposit Account:
Deposits are made in this account for a specified period and cannot be withdrawn before the expiry of the period for which they have been deposited in the bank. These deposits are repayable after the expiry of a fixed period, *e.g.*, one year, five years or any other period. These are also known as 'Time Deposit' or 'Long-Term Deposit'. Higher rate of interest is offered to attract such deposits. However, the rate of interest varies with the period of deposit. The longer the period of deposit, the higher will be the rate of interest. No Pass Book or Cheque Book is issued for fixed deposits. Only a fixed deposit receipt is issued containing the name and address of the depositor, the amount and period of deposit etc. This receipt is signed by the Bank Manager. The depositor is entitled to claim back his money on producing the receipt on the due date.

(ii) Savings Deposit Account:
Savings deposits are those deposits on which the bank pays a certain rate of interest to the depositors but places certain restrictions on their withdrawals. For savings

deposits, an account is opened with the bank which is called savings account. This account is opened with small amounts. The main aim of these accounts is to develop the habit of saving among common people. Such an account can also be opened by two persons in joint names. Overdraft facilities are generally not allowed to the operators of these accounts. The accountholders are allowed to withdraw money by cheque or by withdrawal form subject to the condition that they maintain a minimum balance in their accounts. Withdrawals are limited to two or three times a week to discourage the habit of frequent withdrawals. In order to deposit the money, a pay-in-slip is filled in. A Pass Book is also issued in which transactions relating to the account are recorded from time to time. Interest is paid on minimum monthly balances and credited to the respective accounts on a yearly or half yearly basis. In order to tap small savings, banks have introduced various schemes, such as daily home collection scheme or door-to-door collection scheme, to encourage the habit of thrift to mobilise savings.

(iii) Recurring Deposit Account:
This deposit account has been started to encourage those people to save who cannot give large deposit in lump sum. Recurring deposit account can be opened with small amount and the depositor keeps on depositing a certain sum of money every month for a specified time period. The number of monthly installments may be 12, 24, 36, 48, 60 and so on. After the expiry of the specified period, the depositor gets back his money along with interest thereon. A Pass Book is issued to the depositor showing the installments deposited by him from time to time. Cheques cannot be drawn to withdraw money from a recurring deposit account.

(iv) Current Deposit Account:
Current Account is one into which money may be deposited and withdrawn at any time. Current account is generally operated by the business houses. Most banks agree to open current account with a minimum deposit of ₹ 5000. Under this account, the depositor can withdraw money from his account by cheque at any time during the working hours of the bank or any working day. There are no restrictions to limit the number of withdrawals, subject to the minimum credit balance to be kept as per the rules of the bank. The bank does not pay any interest on current deposits but infact makes a small charge (bank charge) from the operators of this account according to the number of transactions. The bank also grants overdraft facilities in case of need to the operator of this account.

Distinction Among Different Types of Bank Accounts

Basis of Distinction	Current Deposit Account	Fixed Deposit Account	Savings Deposit Account	Recurring Deposit Account
Objective of the Banks	To provide facilities to account-holder to deposit and with-draw the money as and when they need.	To attract savings for a longer period of time.	To cultivate habit of saving and thrift.	To accumulate small savings.

Period of deposit	No fixed period.	Fixed period.	No fixed period.	One year to five years.
Number of deposits	No limit to the number of deposits that can be made.	Deposit can only be made once at the time of opening Fixed deposit account.	No limit to the number of deposits that can be made.	Deposits are made every month
Time and number of withdrawals	Withdrawals can be made as many times in a day as one pleases.	Withdrawal can be made only after the expiry of the fixed period.	Withdrawals can be made once or twice a week according to the rules of the banks.	No withdrawals are allowed before the due date.
Rate of interest	No interest or a very low rate of interest is allowed.	A high rate of interest is allowed as compared to other accounts.	Small rate of interest is allowed.	A comparatively low rate of interest is allowed.
Operation by cheques	It is normally operated by cheques.	Cheques are not used.	It is normally operated by cheques and withdrawal form	Cheque facility is not allowed.

CHEQUE

The most important negotiable instrument is the Cheque. Payment by issue of cheques is a easy and convenient method of making payments. It avoids the risk of carrying cash from one place to another. The cost involved is very small and it is a documentary evidence for payment made.

It can be defined as a signed document by which money is transferred from the account of one person to the account of another person. A cheque can be said to be an instrument in writing containing an unconditional order signed by the maker, directing a banker to pay on demand, a certain sum of money to the bearer of the instrument. Cheques are printed by banks on a special type of paper.

Parties to a Cheque

There are three parties to a cheque:
  (i) The first one is a drawer or maker who is the person or depositor who writes it.
  (ii) Second comes the drawee or banker on whom the cheque is drawn. In other words, drawee is the bank of the drawer which pays money to the payee.

(iii) Last comes the payee. Payee means the person named in the cheque to whom the money is to be paid. Sometimes, the drawer makes the cheque in his own favour by writing the word 'self' in place of writing any name. In such a condition, he is both a drawer and payee. In case the payee is a fictitious person, the cheque may be treated as payable to its bearer.

Advantages and Disadvantages of Payment by Cheque

Advantages:
1. The cheque provides an easy and inexpensive means of transferring money. It may be drawn for any sum within the limit of the drawer's current account balance. The cost of transmission is the same for any amount, namely the cost of postage.
2. Payment by cheque eliminates the need for counting and checking bank notes.
3. The cheque, excepting the bearer cheque, acts like a receipt. It is a proof once it has been cleared, that the money has been received.
4. The cheques avoids risks involved in carrying cash from one place to another.
5. It increases the credit worthiness of a business concern.
6. There is no need to keep large amounts of cash in office or at resident.
7. It saves frequent use and handling of government currency.

Disadvantages:
1. Cheques are not legal tender and a creditor may refuse to take a cheque in payment.
2. Unless a cheque is carefully drawn, it may be altered by a dishonest person.
3. A cheque for a big sum is of the same dimensions as a cheque for a small sum and can be just as easily mislaid or lost without the loss being noticed immediately. Such a risk in the use of cheques makes it necessary to handle them with great care.
4. Receiving payment by cheque may be inconvenient for those who have no bank account.

PASS BOOK

A pass book is a book issued by the banker to customer to record the entries simultaneously in the bank account and in the book, to tell about the position of the account on any given date or at any point of time. This book contains only the true copy of the entries made in the bank account. It acts as an information card to the customer to know the position of his account maintained with the banker. When the cheques are credited, a credit entry will be made in the pass book and when the debit is made for payment or withdrawal of cash, the debit entry in the pass book is also made. The balance is shown for the information of the customer. As the book passes from banker to customer, it is called pass book.

BANK DRAFTS

A bank draft is a type of cheque, drawn by a bank either on its own branch or on another bank. It is the most convenient and the cheapest method of remitting money from one place to another. For remitting money by a bank draft, a person first obtains the bank draft from the bank by paying the amount he wants to remit and the prescribed commission. He, then, sends the bank draft to the receiver by post. When the receiver receives the bank draft, he goes to the concerned bank and gets it encashed. The draft is payable only at demand. In many respects bank drafts are similar to cheques as both are dated and both can be crossed.

TRAVELLER'S CHEQUE

The tourists and travellers have to carry adequate money with them. It is always risky to carry large sums of money while travelling from one place to another. There are possibilities of theft, pick pocketing, misplacement or overspending. Ordinary cheques may be carried out but they are not accepted everywhere as they may even get dishonoured. To avoid these difficulties, traveller's cheques are issued by the State Bank of India or leading commercial banks for the convenience of the travelling public.

Traveller's cheques are issued in different denominations printed thereon, *e.g.*, 50, ₹ 100 or ₹ 500. A person can buy any number of traveller's cheques. However, he will have to deposit equivalent amount of money with the issuing bank. A person without a bank account may also purchase it. The purchaser will have to sign on the traveller's cheque at the prescribed place. To convert the cheques into cash, he has to sign again in the presence of the authorised officer of the State Bank of India or some leading Commercial Banks. The cheques are valid until use, unused cheques can be returned and the cash is received from the issuing bank. Thus, traveller's cheques make the journey safe and comfortable.

Specimen of A Traveller's Cheque

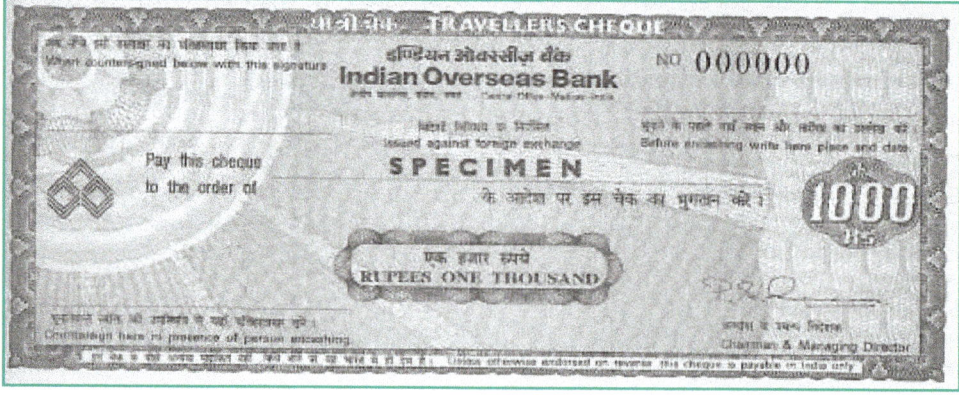

BILL OF EXCHANGE

A bill of exchange is an instrument in writing containing an unconditional order, signed by the maker, directing a certain person to pay a certain sum of money only to, or to the order of, a certain person, or to the bearer of the instrument. The important characteristics of a bill of exchange are:

1. It must be an unconditional order to pay.
2. It must be in writing.
3. It must be signed by the maker.
4. The maker must direct a certain person to pay money.

5. The payment must be of a certain sum of money only.

Bill of Exchange

₹ 500/-   Mumbai
                                                            January 19, 2008

Stamp

    Three months after date please pay to me or my order a sum of Rupees Five Hundred only, for value received.

                                                              Miss Liza Rey
                                 18, Villey Parle Scheme, Mumbai

To,
Mr. Merry Desouza
4300 Crooked Tree , SW- 6, Wyoming,
Michigan - 49509

Parties to the Bill of Exchange

A bill of exchange has three parties to it:

1. The drawer, *i.e.*, the person who makes the order,
2. The drawee, *i.e.*, the person on whom the order is made, and
3. The payee, *i.e.*, the person who will collect the money on the due date.

The bill may be issued by an exporter of goods (or an inland seller) upon the buyer, requiring the buyer to pay the stated amount, that is, the price of the goods through a named banker.

PROMISSORY NOTE

A promissory note can be said to be an instrument in writing with unconditional undertaking signed by the maker to pay a certain sum of money only to, or to the order of a certain person, or to the person having the possession of the promissory note.

Following are the essentials of promissory note:

1. It must be in writing.
2. It should contain an unconditional promise to pay, *i.e.*, the promise to pay must not depend upon the happening of a certain event.
3. The amount promised to be paid must be a certain sum of money only and not shoes or clothes or any other thing.
4. It must be signed by the maker.
5. It must be payable to the bearer of the instrument.

Essential Parties to a Promissory Note: There are two parties to a promissory note:

1. Maker, *i.e.*, the person who signs the note and thereby undertakes to pay.
2. Payee, *i.e.*, the person to whom money is to be paid.

Specimen of Promissory Note

> ₹ 700/-
>
>   Mumbai
>
>   March 1, 2008
>
> Stamp
>
>   Three months after date, I promise to pay Mr. S. Henry or order the sum of Rupees Seven Hundred only, for value received.
>
>   For Smith & Co.
>
>   Liza Rey
>
>   Manager

A promissory note contains a promise to pay money either on demand when it is called a demand promissory note, or after a fixed period, when it is known as a time promissory note.

A promissory note may be made by an individual or by two or more persons. The Promissory Note made by a single individual is called Single Promissory Note. The Promissory Note made by two or more persons may be either Joint Promissory Note or Joint and Several Promissory Notes.

A promissory note is prepared on stamped paper.

Distinction between Promissory Note and Bill of Exchange

Promissory Note	Bill of Exchange
A promissory note has two parties *i.e.*, maker and payee.	A Bill of Exchange has three parties, *i.e.*, Drawer, Acceptor or Drawee and Payee.
In a promissory note, the debtor himself creates the instrument.	In a bill, the creditor usually originates it by directing the debtor to pay.
The liability of a maker of promissory note is primary and absolute because he himself is the main debtor.	The liability of the drawer of a bill is secondary and conditional, *i.e.*, drawer will be liable only if the bill is presented to the drawee and is dishonoured by the drawee.
It does not need any acceptance for its legal validity.	It has to be accepted by the drawee to enforce his liability on it.
Notice of dishonour need not be given to the maker of a promissory note.	Notice of dishonour has to be given to the drawer of the bill to make him liable.

HUNDIES

A hundi is an Indian bill of exchange which has been in use in our country from time immemorial. It is indeed the oldest surviving form of credit instrument in this country. It may be defined as a written order, usually unconditional, drawn by one person on another for payment, on demand or after a specified time, of a certain sum of money, to a person named therein. A bill of exchange, is always unconditional. But a hundi is sometimes, conditional, *e.g.*, a Jokhami Hundi. Such a conditional hundi is not, strictly speaking, a bill of exchange.

AUTOMATED TELLER MACHINE (ATM)

An ATM is a device located on or off the bank's premises to receive and give out cash round the clock and to provide, other banking services. It is a specialized terminal connected to a bank's central computer via public telephone network. ATMs allow access to a range of banking transactions by inserting a magnetic strip plastic card called ATM card containing account details and keying in a personal identification number (PIN).

Various useful services provided by an ATM are as follows:

1. ATMs allow round the clock cash withdrawal.
2. Mini statements can be issued using ATMs.
3. ATMs allows one to request for a cheque book.
4. To ensure safety, ATMs allows one to change his PIN whenever needed.
5. Pay credit card bills: Credit card bills can be paid through the ATM using a debit card. However, this facility can be availed only if the customer's credit card and debit card are of the same bank.
6. Pay utility bills: Electricity bills, telephone bills, insurance premium etc. can be paid through ATMs. This helps in saving both time and money.
7. Recharging mobiles: Prepaid services of most mobile operators can be recharged from at ATM.
8. Transfer funds: Banks allows you to transfer funds from one bank account to another bank account using an ATM. These accounts should however be linked to your ATM/Debit card.
9. Income tax payment: Some banks offer the convenience of paying income tax using ATMs. This includes advance tax, self-assessment tax as well as tax due after regular assessment. However, to avoid this service, one needs to register for the facility on the bank's web site or branch first.
10. Book air and railway tickets: Air and railway tickets can be booked using an ATM only if one's banks ATM has this option or has a tie up with a particular airline company or the Railways. At present, SBI, PNB and Bank of Baroda and Karur Vysya Bank offer this facility.
11. Open or withdraw a fixed deposit: Fixed deposit can be made in one's bank using an ATM. For this, one has to select the option 'Open Fixed Deposit' on the ATM menu, select the duration, enter the amount and confirm the other necessary details.

Advantages of ATMs to customers

1. It gives round the clock service and thereby banking time is saved.
2. Service is quick and efficient and free from errors.
3. The cardholder can access cash and services at any place, where an ATM is located.
4. Funds can be transferred easily to any branch of the banks.
5. Withdrawals can be made at any time and hence it can be called as anywhere banking facility.

Advantages of ATMs to Bankers

1. Crowd at the bank counter is considerably reduced.
2. It is an alternative to extend banking hours and new branches and therefore the operating expenses are reduced.
3. Help bank employees to focus on the analytical and innovative work.
4. It increases the volume of banking business by placing ATMs at the central places.
5. It avoids the cash transportation and cash handling.

Disadvantages of ATMs to Customers

1. Presence of Various Constraints:
Banks have a very few or no branches in rural areas in India and even if banks make some efforts to introduce ATM services in the country side, various constraints like illiteracy of the villagers, security concern, lack of commuting facilities etc., may obstruct smooth functionality of ATMs.

2. Limitation on Cash Withdrawals:
There is a limitation on the amount of cash that can be withdrawn from the ATMs in one transaction and also in a day. For example, many banks do not permit withdrawal of more than ₹ 10,000 at a time.

3. Possibility of Fraud:
ATM card, if misplaced, lost or stolen, may be misused by unscrupulous persons. Criminals can fit skimming devices and small cameras inside ATMs. These machines record account details and personal identification numbers of the customers using the ATMs. These criminals can later use these details to withdraw amount from the customers' accounts.

4. Loss of Personnel Touch With the Banks:
Customers lose personal touch with their bankers when they start using ATMs for nearly all transactions.

5. Operational Issues:
ATMs located in busy locations may not have adequate funds for busy holiday weekends when large numbers of people are taking out cash.

6. Fees:
Banks and machine owners draw a huge source of revenue from ATM fees. Cardholders can usually withdraw cash for free from ATMs owned by their bank, but typically have to pay to use machines owned by other banks.

CREDIT CARD

A Credit card, issued by the customers' bank, is a small plastic card entitling the holder to buy goods and services on credit. The name, account number of the holder and the validity period are marked on the card. The specimen signature of the cardholder are given on the reverse of the card. The cardholder is sanctioned a limit by the bank. The cardholder can buy products and services at specified outlets by swiping the card, within the limit sanctioned by the bank.

The seller of goods or services, at the specified outlets verify the validity of card, cardholder's identity and credit limit before selling the goods or services to the customers.

Thereafter a credit card voucher showing the details of purchases is prepared. The image of card is transferred on the voucher by means of an imprinter and signatures of the cardholder are obtained on the voucher.

The card issuing bank release payment to the seller on the basis of these vouchers. The cardholder is required to make payment to the bank in due course of time.

Some banks also allow cash withdrawal facility to the cardholders. For this cardholder has to pay service fees/interest.

DEBIT CARD

A debit card (also known as a bank card) is also a plastic card that provides an alternative payment method to cash when making purchases. Functionally, it can be called an electronic cheque, as the funds are withdrawn directly from either the bank account, or from the remaining balance on the card. In some cases, the cards are designed exclusively for use on the Internet, and so there is no physical card.

The use of debit cards has become widespread in many countries and has overtaken the cheque, and in some instances, cash transactions by volume. Like credit cards, debit cards are used widely for making purchase on telephone and Internet.

A point of sale terminal electronically tied to the bank computer automatically transfers the money from customer's account to seller's account.

The debit cardholder can make purchases only to the extent of availability of funds in his account.

Types of debit card

Debit cards can also be used as ATM card for withdrawing cash. Merchants can also offer "cashback"/"cashout" facilities to customers, where a customer can withdraw cash along with their purchase.

There are currently three ways in which debit card transactions are processed: (i) On-line Debit Card (also known as PIN Debit); (ii) Off-line Debit Card (also known as Signature Debit) and (iii) Electronic Purse Card.

(i) On-line Debit Card:
On-line debit cards require electronic authorization of every transaction and the debits are reflected in the user's account immediately. The transaction may be additionally secured with the personal identification number (PIN) authentication system and some on-line cards require such authentication for every transaction, essentially becoming enhanced automated teller machine (ATM) cards. One difficulty in using on-line debit cards is the necessity of an electronic authorization device at the point of sale (POS) and sometimes also a separate PIN pad to enter the PIN, although this is becoming common place for all card transactions in many countries. Overall, the on-line debit card is generally viewed as superior to the off-line debit card because of its more secure authentication system and live status, which alleviates problems with processing lag on transactions that may have been forgotten or not authorized by the owner of the card. Banks in some countries, such as Canada and Brazil, only issue on-line debit cards.

(ii) Off-line Debit Card:

Off-line debit cards have the logos of major credit cards (*e.g.* Visa or Master Card) or major debit cards (*e.g.* Maestro in the United Kingdom and other countries, but not the United States) and are used at the point of sale like a credit card (with payer's signature). This type of debit card may be subject to a daily limit, and/or a maximum limit equal to the current account balance in the account from which it draws funds. Transactions conducted with off-line debit cards require 2-3 days to be reflected on users' account balances. In some countries and with some banks and merchant service organizations, a "credit" or off-line debit transaction is without cost to the purchaser beyond the face value of the transaction, while a small fee may be charged for a "debit" or on-line debit transaction (although it is often absorbed by the retailer). Other differences are that on-line debit purchasers may opt to withdraw cash in addition to the amount of the debit purchase (if the merchant supports that functionally); also, from the merchant's standpoint, the merchant pays lower fees on on-line debit transaction as compared to off-line debit transaction.

(iii) Electronic Purse Card:

Smart-card-based electronic purse systems are those in which value is stored on the card chip, not in an externally recorded account, so that machines accepting the card need no network connectivity. These are in use throughout Europe since the mid-1990s.

The Differences between Debit Card and Credit Card

Debit card	Credit card
Transactions are made with the available funds in the current or savings account of a customer.	Transactions are made on credit even when there are no available funds in the customers' account. The payment is made by the bank to the seller on behalf of the customer.
Interest is earned on the deposits in the account.	Interest is charged on the amount taken on credit by the customer from the bank.
Need to be connected to a savings or checking account.	Need not to be connected to any savings or checking accounts.
Nothing to repay as no money is borrowed.	Repayment is required by the borrower to the bank with the interest within the due period.

CAUTIONS TO BE TAKEN WHILE USING DEBIT CARD

1. Memorise your PIN and do not write it down anywhere. Also, do not share your PIN with anyone.
2. You may receive fake calls asking for your bank details. Do not share any such information on calls as the bank will never ask for your bank details as they already have them.
3. After completing your transaction in the ATM, always press the cancel key.
4. If you lose your debit card, report to the bank immediately and get your card blocked.

5. Change your PIN numbers as often as possible.

CAUTIONS TO BE TAKEN WHILE USING CREDIT CARD
1. Always keep your card private and do not reveal your credit card number to anyone.
2. Do not give your credit card details over phone unless you get the call from the trusted bank.
3. Keep a regular track of your credit card statements and reports.
4. Contact your bank immediately when you lose your credit card or when you suspect a deceptive activity.
5. Make your passwords complex using with both letters and numbers.

Lesson at a Glance

- **Types of Deposit Accounts:** (i) Fixed Deposit Account; (ii) Saving Deposit Account; (iii) Recurring Deposit Account; (iv) Current Deposit Account.
- **Cheque:** The most important negotiable instrument is the cheque. It is a signed document by which money is transferred from the account of one person to the account of another person.
- **Pass Book:** A pass book is a book issued by the banker to customer to record the entries simultaneously in the bank account and in the book, to tell about the position of the account on any given date or at any point of time.
- **Bank Drafts:** A bank draft is a type of cheque, drawn by a bank either on its own branch or on another bank. It is the most convenient and the cheapest method of remitting money from one place to another.
- **Traveller's Cheque:** Traveller's cheques are issued in different denominations printed thereon, *e.g.*, ₹ 50, ₹ 100, or ₹ 500. A person can buy any number of travellers' cheques. However, he will have to deposit equivalent amount of money with the issuing bank.
- **Bill of Exchange:** A bill of exchange is an instrument in writing containing an unconditional order, signed by the maker, directing a certain person to pay a certain sum of money only to, or to the order of, a certain person, or to the bearer of the instrument.
- **Parties to the Bill of Exchange:** (i) The drawer; (ii) The drawee; (iii) The payee.
- **Promissory Note:** It is an instrument in writing with unconditional undertaking signed by the maker to pay a certain sum of money only to or to the order of a certain person, or to the person having the possession of the promissory note.
- **Hundies:** Hundi is a written order, usually unconditional, drawn by one person on another for payment, on demand or after a specified time, of a certain sum of money, to a person named therein.
- **Automated Teller Machines (ATM):** An ATM is a device located on or off the bank's premises to receive and give out cash round the clock and to provide other banking services.
- **Credit Card:** It is a card entitling its holder to buy goods and services on credit based on the holders promise to the bank to pay for these goods and services on a later date.

- **Debit Card:** A debit card is a plastic card that provides an alternative payment method to cash when making purchases.
- **Types of Debit Card:** (i) On-line debit card; (ii) Off-line debit card; (iii) Electronic purse card.

Project Work

Visit a nearby bank and record the formalities which are to be fulfilled for opening a savings account and a current account.

Assignment

Explain to your friend the various types of bank accounts that can be opened in a bank

Questions

A. **Short Answer Type Questions:**
   1. What do you mean by bank deposits?
   2. Name the accounts that can be opened in a bank.
   3. What is Fixed Deposit Account?
   4. What is Current Account?
   5. What is Recurring Deposit Account?
   6. What is Hundi?
   7. What is Pass Book?
   8. What do you understand by Bank draft?
   9. What do you understand by a Cheque?
   10. What is traveller's cheque?
   11. What purpose is served by a Bank draft?
   12. What is a Savings Account?
   13. What are the different parties of a cheque?
   14. What is the Bill of exchange?
   15. Write any two advantages and disadvantages of a cheque.
   16. Who is the drawee on a bill of exchange?
   17. What is a promissory note?
   18. Differentiate between promissory note and bill of exchange.
   19. What is a bank account called in which a depositor can deposit and withdraw amount at will?
   20. State two features of current account.
   21. What is credit card?

22. What is debit card?
23. Name two types of debit card.
24. Distinguish between debit card and credit card.
25. What is an ATM?
26. Distinguish between a bill of exchange and a promissory note.
27. What is 'Discounting of bills of exchange'? [ICSE 2019]
28. State any two precautions while using an 'ATM'. [ICSE 2019]
29. Distinguish between Saving Account and Current Account. [ICSE 2018]
30. State any two advantages of Traveller's Cheques. [ICSE 2018]
31. Distinguish between Over Draft and Cash Credit. [ICSE 2017]

B. Essay Type Questions:

1. What are the different types of deposit accounts that can be opened in a commercial bank? Briefly explain them.
2. What is the bill of exchange? Distinguish between a Bill of Exchange and a Promissory Note.
3. Define a promissory note. What are the essential parties to a promissory note?
4. What do you mean by a cheque? List down the various parties to a cheque.
5. What is credit card? Differentiate between credit card and debit card.
6. "Your journey becomes safe and comfortable by taking traveller's cheque." Explain clearly.
7. What is a cheque? What are the advantages of a cheque?
8. Differentiate between:
   (i) Savings Deposit and Current Deposit.
   (ii) Fixed Deposit and Recurring Deposit.
9. What are the precautions to be taken while using Debit card and Credit card?
10. Write short note on:
    (i) Bank draft; (ii) Traveller's cheque; (iii) Recurring Deposit Account; and (iv) The importance of a cheque.

CHAPTER-24
Financial Fraudulent Practices

FRAUDULENT PRACTICES

Fraudulent practices are any act or omission, including a misrepresentation, that knowingly or recklessly misleads, or attempts to mislead, a party to obtain a financial or other benefit or to avoid an obligation. The example of fraudulent act is forging a document or signature or altering a document.

- Fraudulent Practices
- Types of Fraudulent Practices
- Credit card Frauds
- Insurance Fraud
- Intellectual Property Fraud
- Internet and Cyber fraud
- False Accounting

Omission

An "omission" is the act of knowingly and deliberately failing to disclose any fact to take the advantage, for example, that a contractor has been debarred, to obtain an improper benefit or avoid an obligation.

Misrepresentation

A misrepresentation is the act of giving a false statement of facts or manipulating some fact to get undue advantage.

Generally, a fraudulent practice relates itself with illegal methods to obtain financial gain. This can happen in various ways. Sometimes the motto behind the frauds can be simple hatred for the individual or company but mostly it is because of the next level financial gain that it would bring.

Types of Fraudulent Practices

Since the main motive of fraudulent practices is financial gain, fraudsters can commit fraud in many ways. Some of the ways are discussed below in detail:

1. Credit Card Fraud
2. Insurance Fraud
3. Intellectual Property Fraud
4. Internet and Cyber Fraud
5. False Accounting

Credit Card Fraud:
This type of fraud is most common in recent times due to ease of access makes it one of the most committed fraud of recent times. A wide range for theft and fraud has been committed involving a credit card or a debit card which is the source of funds in a particular transaction. The main motto for this type of fraud can be to purchase goods without paying through on-line payments, or to obtain unauthorized funds from an account of any person.

One can access the account and retrieve cash from the account at any point if he or she has the PIN number of the debit or credit card. This particular type of fraud can also be termed as cyber fraud where fraudsters call up a consumer at random claiming to be from the bank and take their details, withdrawing cash from them at a later point. The fraudsters can also make clone of the card to withdraw money.

Insurance Fraud:

Any act that is committed keeping a fraudulent outcome from an insurance process in mind falls under this category. If the claimant attempts to obtain some benefit or advantage for which the claimant is not entitled or when the insurer denies the due benefit, an insurance fraud is committed.

Fake insurance agents visit the houses of the consumers to commit these frauds. Enticing the consumer with lucrative options, they take the deposit cheque and then pick up the money from the bank.

Intellectual Property Fraud:

This type of fraud is committed when the fake counterfeit products and pirated products which are no longer original, are passed to customers as being original. The industries that usually fall under this category of frauds are–health, fashion, films and music where piracy and theft are very common.

Counterfeit goods have lower safety standards, which can pose health and safety risks to the consumers. They also damage the reputation of the companies who produce the legitimate products as it creates negative perception about the company.

Piracy is one of the best examples that can be given for this type of fraud. Original design or work is copied and then a fake product made based on the design for selling it at a cheap rate. Piracy is punishable and a person who is caught with a pirated version of any good is also punishable under the law.

Internet and Cyber Fraud:

Cyber fraud is one of the most committed frauds which are gaining fast recognition in today's time. As per the FBI statistics of Internet Crime Complaint Centre, 2014's, there were around 2,69,422 complaints were filed. The numbers of complaints are increasing in recent times. This fraud is a threat to people across the world as everything is managed by computers. In today's world, it is mandatory to increase the awareness among the people so that they can be careful against these frauds. Hacking, is the example of the most common cyber frauds.

An experienced unethical hacker can actually hack the on-line account and commit frauds. Sometimes frauds are committed if we click on a link while browsing which turns out to be a spam and downloads malware into the system, gaining access to every data in your computer. This not only affects the Internet security but also increases the chances of having access to an individual's banking details. The main motto of this fraud can be harassing the individual or financial gain.

False Accounting:

Deception is common in today's world. The easiest way of deception now-a-days has to be through the accounting. False accounting is done by changing the figures of the accounts books, records or presenting false information in the accounts of a company is a punishable offence. All this is done to gain money through unfair means.

It is, thus, advised to be very careful while handling the finance or accounting statements of any company or entity and every person should be aware of the types of frauds committed.

Raising awareness also helps in decreasing the rate of frauds happening in the country.

Lesson at a Glance

- **Fraudulent Practices:** Fraudulent practices are any act or omission, including a misrepresentation, that knowingly or recklessly misleads, or attempts to mislead, a party to obtain a financial or other benefit or to avoid an obligation.
- **Types of Frauds:**
  1. **Credit Card Fraud:** Done through the misuse of the financial transaction cards
  2. **Insurance Fraud:** Done through fake agents on the phone or by visiting the house
  3. **Intellectual Property Fraud:** The major medium being Piracy
  4. **Internet and Cyber Fraud:** Some through dangerous malware, spam links, Hacking
  5. **False Accounting:** Done through false digits in the financial account statements

Project Work

Find out the different types of frauds that are happening in your locality, citing examples of each.

Assignment

Write a report of 1000 words on the most committed fraud in 2017 with proper statistics.

Questions

A. **Short Answer Type Questions:**
   1. Define Fraudulent Practices.
   2. State the different types of frauds that take place.
   3. Explain in brief a credit card fraud? [ICSE 2020]
   4. What do you mean by Internet and cyber fraud? [ICSE 2019]
   5. What is False Accounting?

B. **Essay Type Questions:**
   1. Mention the different types of financial Fraudulent Practices with examples of each.
   2. What are the ways that one can commit false accounting fraud and how do you think it can harm a company?
   3. State examples of intellectual property frauds along with its definition.

CHAPTER-25
Government Initiatives in Environment Protection

ENVIRONMENT PROTECTION

- Environment Protection Act, 1986
- Central Pollution Control Board and its functions

We live within the walls of our environment. The environment is our mother and it supports the life of each and every living thing on earth. We depend on our environment to sustain our life. If we protect our environment we can get better health, better food, and better quality of air to breath. The environment protection is the steps taken to protect and preserve the natural environment by reducing the overuse of natural resources and reducing the pollutants that can degrade the quality of the environment. Individuals and organisations have to play their part to conserve the environment for the benefit and existence of the human life.

Over consumption, technology advancement, population exceeding the permissible limit is some of the reasons which have adverse effect on our environment. The degradation of the environment has been acknowledged by the government and a lot of steps have been taken to protect the environment from further degradation. The major step that has been taken by government in this direction is the implementation of Environment Protection Act, 1986.

ENVIRONMENT PROTECTION ACT, 1986

Government of India enacted the Environment Protection Act of 1986 under Article 253 of the Constitution. This Act was passed in March 1986 and comes into force on 19 November 1986 for the protection and the improvement of the environment and for matters connected there with.

Under this Act "environment" includes water, air and land and the inter-relationship which exists among and between water, air and land, and human beings, other living creatures, plants, micro-organism and property.

Features of the Environment Protection Act, 1986:

The Act gives the powers to the Central Government for controlling environmental pollution:

1. Take all necessary steps to protect the quality of the environment.
2. Coordinate the actions of States, officers and other authorities under the Act.
3. To make the list of standards to be maintained for the discharge of the pollutants in the environment.
4. Plan and execute a nationwide programme to prevent and control the environmental pollution.

5. Empower any person to inspect, take samples and perform any kind of tests to find out the level of pollution.
6. Appoint any kind of government analysts.
7. Restrict areas under which any industry, operation may not be carried out without safeguards.
8. Lay down safeguards for prevention of accidents and take remedial measures in case of such accidents.
9. Lay down procedures for handling hazardous substances.
10. Form a committee of people having the right to exercise powers and control.
11. Issue directions to any person, officer or authority including the power to direct closure, prohibition or regulation of any industry, operation or process.
12. Delegate powers to any officer, authority or state.
    - The Act makes it compulsory for any person who is in charge to inform the authorities with regards to any accidental discharge of the pollutant when there's an excess of prescribed standards.
    - The Act makes sure of charging penalties in case of violation of the provisions of it.
    - The Jurisdiction of civil courts is barred under the policies of the Environment Protection Act, 1986.

CENTRAL POLLUTION CONTROL BOARD

The Central Pollution Control Board (CPCB) of India is a statutory body established in 1974 under the Ministry of Environment, Forest and Climate Change (MoEF&CC). It coordinates and control the activities of the State Pollution Control Boards by providing technical assistance to them. It is the apex organisation in country in the field of pollution control, and works as a technical wing of MoEF.

It is responsible for maintaining and monitoring of water and air quality in the country. It advises the Central Government and assist in the formulation of strategies to prevent and control water and air pollution. CPCB along with the State Pollution Control Boards (SPCBs) are responsible for implementation of legislation relating to prevention and control of environmental pollution.

Functions of the Central Pollution Control Board

CPCB functions fall under both national level and as State Boards. CPCB, under the Water (Prevention and Control of Pollution) Act, 1974, and the Air (Prevention and Control of Pollution) Act, 1981, aims for prevention, control and abatement of water pollution, and to improve the quality of air in the country by controlling air pollution.

1. Air Pollution Check:
The Central Pollution Control Board ensures that the vehicles run at a proper speed and do not emit the harmful smoke in case of overheating or over speeding. Regular monitoring of the four pollutants (Sulphur Dioxide, Nitrogen Oxide, Suspended Particulate Matter and Respirable Suspended Particulate Matter) is done by the CPCB.

2. Water Pollution Check:
Fresh water is a warehouse for agriculture, propagation of fisheries etc. Water quality monitoring is done on a quarterly basis so as to make sure that there is no pollutant in the water and it remains fresh for consumption.

3. Noise Pollution Check:
Places where sound is high is kept under the monitoring system so that the sound limit doesn't exceed the decibel level for the safe and protected living of the elderly, children and the animals.

4. Urban Area Programs:
Various programs have been set up in urban areas as those areas have been identified as the major problem areas.

5. Municipal Solid Waste Rules:
MSW rules, 2000 is taken into consideration for the collection, storage, transportation, disposition of the solid municipal waste. The necessary information collection is CPCB's duty.

6. Environment Data Statistics:
The maintenance of the data related to air, water and noise pollution is also one of the main functions of the CPCB.

Lesson at a Glance

- **Environment Protection:** The environment protection is the steps taken to protect and preserve the natural environment by reducing the overuse of natural resources and reducing the pollutants that can degrade the quality of the environment.
- **Environment Protection Act, 1986:** The Environment Protection Act, 1986 was set up by the government as an act to provide for the protection and the improvement of t he environment and for matters connected there with.
- **Central Pollution Control Board:** The Central Pollution Control Board (CPCB) of India is a statutory body established in 1974 under the Ministry of Environment, Forest and Climate Change (MoEF&CC). It is responsible for maintaining and monitoring of water and air quality in the country. It advises the Central Government and assist in the formulation of strategies to prevent and control water and air pollution.
- **Functions of the CPCB:** (i) Air Pollution check (ii) Water Pollution check (iii) Noise Pollution check (iv) Urban Area Programs (v) Municipal Solid Waste Rules (vi) Environment Data Statistics.

Find out the sources which are creating environment pollution in your society. Implement at least one activity that helps to improve the quality of environment. Note your observations from it with proper pictures.

Write an essay stating how would you control and change the system and what steps would you have taken as the Chairman of the Central Pollution Control Board to control the pollution.

A. Short Answer Type Questions:
   1. What do you mean by Environment Protection?
   2. Define the Environment Protection Act, 1986.
      OR
      Explain any two feature of Environment (Protection) Act, 1986.   [ICSE 2019]
   3. What are the ways by which the environment gets degraded?
   4. What is the Central Pollution Control Board?

B. Essay Type Questions:
   1. State the features of the Environment Protection Act, 1986.
      OR
      Explain any five features of Environment Protection Act.   [ICSE 2020]
   2. What are the functions of the Central Pollution Control Board?   [ICSE 2019]
      OR
      Explain briefly any five functions of 'Central Pollution Central Board.
   3. Explain any five rights enjoyed by consumers as per the Consumer Protection Act, 1986.   [ICSE 2019]

www.ingramcontent.com/pod-product-compliance
Ingram Content Group UK Ltd.
Pitfield, Milton Keynes, MK11 3LW, UK
UKHW050418240426
12048UKWH00014B/692

ISC
CONCEPTS
OF
COMMERCE

In accordance with the latest syllabus prescribed by the Council for the Indian School Certificate Examination, New Delhi.

ISC

CONCEPTS OF COMMERCE

CLASS XII

Najmi Salim
Former Principal, St. Xavier's School, Pratapgarh
Coordinator, Aga Khan Education Service, Tanzania
Ex-Vice Principal, Al-Rayyan National (Pvt.) School, Abu Dhabi, UAE
Ex-Headmaster, Devprayag School, Allahabad

Swarup Biswas
M.Com., B.Ed.
St. Joseph's School, North Point,
Darjeeling

OSWAL PUBLISHERS
1/12, Sahitya Kunj, M. G. Road, Agra-282 002

No part of this book can be reproduced in any form or by any means without the prior written permission of the publisher.

Edition : 2019

ISBN : 978-93-87660-82-3

OSWAL PUBLISHERS

Head office : 1/12, Sahitya Kunj, M.G. Road, Agra-282 002
Phone : (0562) 2527771– 4, +91 75340 77222
E-mail : contact@oswalpublishers.com, sales@oswalpublishers.com
Website : www.oswalpublishers.com
Facebook link : https://www.facebook.com/oswalpublishersindia
Available at : amazon.in, Flipkart, snapdeal

Preface

We are absolutely delighted to place this excellent book in the hands of teachers and students. The content of this book is customized to meet the academic needs of the students based on the latest ISC syllabus. Considerable time has been invested and meticulous care taken in ensuring that the content of this book, while in line with the Council's syllabus, is also in sync with today's globalised business conditions so as to enable Commerce students to keep in tune with time. Dynamics of modern marketing has been kept in mind, and societal marketing has been duly given its rightful place. Our objective is to draw out students from the shadows of knowledge to the daylight of learning. End of chapter questions have been framed with the specific purpose of ensuring students put on their thinking caps, catalyze their understanding and come up with carefully thought out original answers.

Progress will come to a grinding halt if we cease efforts to improve. We welcome all critical comments which will be of immense help to us to improve this book.

Author

SYLLABUS

*There will be **two** papers in the subject.*

Paper I :	Theory	3 hours	(80 Marks)
Paper II :	Project Work		(20 Marks)

PAPER–I (THEORY)–80 Marks

Part I (20 marks) will consist of **compulsory** short answer questions testing knowledge, application and skills relating to elementary/fundamental aspects of the entire syllabus.

Part II (60 marks) will consist of **eight** questions out of which candidates will be required to answer **five** questions, each carrying 12 marks.

1. Business Environment

Concept and importance of Business Environment.

Meaning, features and importance of Business Environment.

Dimensions of Business Environment– Micro (Internal and External factors) and Macro (Economic, social, technological, political and legal)– meaning and components.

S.W.O.T. Analysis– A basic understanding of S.W.O.T. (Strength, Weakness, Opportunity and Threat) Analysis.

2. Financing

(i) Capital : Sources of finance for sole trader; partnership; joint stock company; financial planning.

Importance of finance for business. Sources of finance for different types of business firms. Meaning, features and importance of financial planning. Factors affecting capital structure. Fixed capital– meaning, factors affecting fixed capital. Working capital– meaning, types, factors affecting working capital. Comparison between fixed and working capital.

(ii) Sources of finance for a Joint Stock Company.

　(a) Different types of shares : equity, preference.

　　Bonus shares, Rights issue, ESOP, Sweat equity shares, Retained earnings.
　　Long-term sources of funds.
　　Equity shares– features, advantages and disadvantages.
　　Preference shares– features, types, advantages and disadvantages; distinction between equity shares and preference shares.
　　Bonus and rights issue, ESOP and Sweat equity shares– meaning. Distinction between bonus shares and right shares.
　　Retained earnings– meaning, merits and demerits.

　(b) Loan capital : debentures.

　　Debentures– meaning, kinds of debentures, advantages and disadvantages of debentures. Distinction between shares and debentures.

　(c) Loans from Commercial Banks and Financial Institutions.

　　Loans from Commercial Banks and Financial Institutions– meaning, advantages and disadvantages.

　(d) Short-term sources of funds.

　　Short-term sources of funds– different types of short-term financial assistance by Commercial Banks; public deposits, trade credit, customer advances, factoring, inter corporate deposits and installment credit. Meaning, advantages and disadvantages of various sources of funds.

(iii) Banking– latest trends.

Online services– transfer of funds through Real Time Gross Settlement (RTGS), National Electronic Funds Transfer (NEFT), issue of demand drafts online meaning and features.

Online payments, e-Banking– meaning and features, advantages and disadvantages.

Mobile Banking– SMS alerts, transfer of funds, making payments– advantages and disadvant-ages.

Debit Cards v/s Credit Cards, ATM (Automated Teller Machine)– Meaning; Debit card and Credit card : features and differences.

3. Management

(i) Management : Meaning, objectives and characteristics of management.

Meaning of Management : as an activity; as a group; as a discipline; as a process. Objectives and characteristics of management.

(ii) Nature of Management : Science, Art and Profession.

Self explanatory.

(iii) Importance of Management.

Self explanatory.

(iv) Principles of Management : Nature of principles; need for principles.

Nature of principles of management; need for principles of management; Taylor's 5 scientific principles of management; Fayol's 14 principles of management; Relevance of the principles of management in today's business scenario. Comparison of Taylor's and Fayol's principles.

(v) Functions of Management : Planning; Organising; Staffing; Directing; Controlling and Coordinating.

  (a) Planning :

  Meaning, steps, importance and limitation; Types of plans; objectives, policy, procedures, method, rule, budget, program– meaning, features and differences.

  (b) Organising :

  Meaning, importance, steps; Structure of organisation (line, line and staff; functional and divisional; formal and informal organisation)– Meaning, features, merits, demerits and differences between line and line and staff, functional and divisional, formal and informal; Meaning and importance of delegation of authority; Decentralisation v/s Centralisation, comparison between delegation and decentralisation, merits and demerits.

  (c) Staffing :

  Meaning, steps and importance; Recruitment– Meaning and sources; Selection– Meaning and procedure; Training and development– Meaning, types of training, difference between selection and recruitment, Training and Development.

  (d) Directing :

  Meaning and importance; Supervision– Meaning, functions and span of control;
  Motivation– Meaning and Maslow's theory; Leadership– Meaning and qualities of a good leader;
  Communication– Meaning, objectives and process. Barriers to communication and overcoming barriers to communication.

  (e) Controlling :

  Meaning, steps and importance; Relationship between Planning and Controlling; Management by Exception.

  (f) Coordination :

  Meaning of Coordination; Coordination as an essence of management.

4. Marketing

(i) Marketing : Concept and functions.

Meaning of markets and marketing. Concept of marketing : traditional v/s modern. Comparison between marketing and selling. Objectives of marketing, importance of marketing; functions of marketing.

(ii) Marketing Mix.

Product– Goods and services, branding, labeling and packaging (meaning only).
Price– Meaning, factors determining price.
Place– Channel of distribution (direct and indirect : meaning only) and physical distribution (meaning only). Factors affecting choice of channel of distribution.
Promotion– Meaning and elements; promotion mix.
Elements– Advertising, sales promotion, personal selling and publicity– meaning, features, objectives and differences.

(iii) Consumer protection : Rights of consumers, methods of consumer protection.

Need for consumer protection; rights of consumers; methods of consumer protection– self help, legislative measures and consumer associations, Consumer Protection Act, 1986.

PAPER–II (PROJECT WORK)–20 Marks

*Candidates will be expected to have completed **two** projects from any topic covered in Theory.*

The project work will be assessed by the teacher and a Visiting Examiner appointed locally and approved by the Council.

Mark allocation for **each** Project [10 Marks] :

Overall format	1 mark
Content	4 marks
Findings	2 marks
Viva-voce based on the Project	3 marks

A list of suggested Projects is given below :

1. Compare marketing strategies adopted by two different companies of the same industry (FMCG/Telecommunication/Media/Education industry, etc.) keeping in mind the follow-ing :
   - Product Mix
   - Price Mix
   - Place Mix
   - Promotion Mix

2. Collect newspaper/magazine clippings of five cases filed by consumers in the Consumer Court.
   Find out the rights violated, and the redressal mechanism used.
   What was the outcome of each case ?

3. Visit a Commercial Bank. Find out the procedure to open a savings account.
   Find out the details of various Agency and General utility services provided by the bank.

4. Compare the interest rates offered by five different commercial banks on fixed deposits under various categories (general and senior citizens) and various time durations.
   Find out the procedure and formalities for opening a fixed deposit account.
   What is the procedure for closing the account on maturity and before maturity period ?

5. Select five different companies across varying industries such as I.T., Textiles, FMCG, Health Care, etc., included in the SENSEX. Keeping a hypothetical base money of Rupees one lakh, invest in the shares of the selected companies. The movement of share prices selected by you should be monitored over a period of one month on a daily basis. A uniform/standard practice of either using the opening price or the closing price on a particular day of the week should be used by all students in the class.
   At the end of the month, analyse your invetment in a spread sheet and give reasons for your choice of scripts.

6. Find out the names of companies under various sectors (FMCG, Pharma, Automobile, etc.) included in the NIFTY and the SENSEX.
   Make a chart of the same and track its movements over a period of one week.

7. (a) Study the sources of recruitment and steps involved in the selection procedure adopted by two companies of the same industry.
   (b) Compare and evaluate the sources of recruitment and the selection process adopted by the selected companies.

8. Formulate a capital plan for a hypothetical business organisation.
   Justify your formulated plan.

9. Choose two companies of the same industry. Study their organisational structure. Also give information with regard to :
   (i) Hierarchy
   (ii) Centralisation and delegation of authority
   (iii) Flow of information (scalar chain)
   (iv) Span of control
   (v) Channel of communication

10. Select any business undertaking. Study the selected business in terms of ownership, capital and profitability.
    Make a S.W.O.T. analysis and present it in a tabular form.

NOTE : No question paper for Practical work will be set by the Council.

Scanner Table

Based on questions set in ISC Councils Examination (2006 to 2015)

Unit	Contents	Ch. No.	Short	Long
Unit-I Business Environment	Business Environment	1		
Unit-II Financing	Financing : Fixed & Working Capital	2		
	Sources of Finance for a Joint Stock Company	3		
	Banking : Latest Trends	4		
Unit-III Management	Management : Meaning & Nature	5		
	Principles of Management	6		
	Functions of Management & Coordination	7		
	Planning	8		
	Organising	9		
	Staffing	10		
	Directing	11		
	Controlling	12		
Unit-IV Marketing	Marketing : Concepts & Functions	13		
	Marketing Mix	14		
	Consumer Protection	15		

Data Table (Short / Long per chapter)

Year	1 S	1 L	2 S	2 L	3 S	3 L	4 S	4 L	5 S	5 L	6 S	6 L	7 S	7 L	8 S	8 L	9 S	9 L	10 S	10 L	11 S	11 L	12 S	12 L	13 S	13 L	14 S	14 L	15 S	15 L
2015	2	6	4	4	8	20	4	6		4	2		8	5		5		7	2	4		9	2		2	19	2	9		8
2014	2	5	2	8	8	7	4	6	4		2		8	2		7		12	2	5		16			2	4	2	8		4
Total	4	11	6	12		27	10		4	4	4	4	15	7		12		19	4	9		25	2		4	23	4	17	12	12

Ranking

	Short	Long	Overall
Ch 1	4	9	7
Ch 2	3	7	6
Ch 3	1	1	1
Ch 4	4	12	12
Ch 5		13	13
Ch 6		4	
Ch 7		11	7
Ch 8		7	10
Ch 9		4	5
Ch 10		10	9
Ch 11		2	3
Ch 12		7	15
Ch 13		3	2
Ch 14		5	4
Ch 15		7	10

Old Syllabus

Year	1 S	1 L	2 S	2 L	3 S	3 L	4 S	4 L	5 S	5 L	6 S	6 L	7 S	7 L	8 S	8 L	9 S	9 L	10 S	10 L	11 S	12 S	12 L	13 S	13 L	14 S	14 L
2013	2	3			4	24	4		2	6	2	10		3		4	2							2		6	19
2012				6	6	4			2	4	4	6		4							2			2	8	2	10
2011					4	24				16	10	6												4	4	4	6
2010				4	8	16		2			2				2			4	2					2	3	2	16
2009			4	6	13		10		2	2	2	6		3									4		4	6	9
2008				6	8	12			2			10						5		5						6	14
2007			5	4	20						2													4		6	10
2006			2		6	20	2		2	4		4		6											6	6	20

CONTENTS

UNIT–I : BUSINESS ENVIRONMENT

1.	BUSINESS ENVIRONMENT	11–22

UNIT–II : FINANCING

2.	FINANCING : FIXED AND WORKING CAPITAL	23–36
3.	SOURCES OF FINANCE FOR A JOINT STOCK COMPANY	37–59
4.	BANKING : LATEST TRENDS	60–71

UNIT–III : MANAGEMENT

5.	MANAGEMENT : MEANING AND NATURE	72–85
6.	PRINCIPLES OF MANAGEMENT	86–94
7.	FUNCTIONS OF MANAGEMENT AND COORDINATION	95–107
8.	PLANNING	108–123
9.	ORGANISING	124–146
10.	STAFFING	147–160
11.	DIRECTING	161–177
12.	CONTROLLING	178–187

UNIT–IV : MARKETING

13.	MARKETING : CONCEPT AND FUNCTIONS	188–202
14.	MARKETING MIX	203–230
15.	CONSUMER PROTECTION	231–238
	PROJECT WORK	239–248

1   Business Environment

LEARNING RESULT

After reading this chapter, you should be able to :
- Understand the concept and importance of Business Environment.
- Identify the dimensions of Business Environment.
- Comprehend Micro and Macro Environment.
- Evaluate the importance of using of SWOT Analysis.

The business environment is a set of factors having an impact on a business organisation. The business organisation has to interact with these influences on a continuing basis. Thus, its performance is subject to these influences.

> Business Environment is the climate in which business activities are conducted.

CONCEPT OF BUSINESS ENVIRONMENT

According to Arthur Weimer, business environment *"encompasses the climate or set of conditions, economic, social, political, or institutional in which business operations are conducted."*

We can say that business environment is the aggregate effect of all forces that influence a business, adversely, or favourably. These can be the competitors, government, suppliers of raw material or the consumers. As a result the business environment comes to posses certain features or characteristics. These features are listed below :

1. Correlation– One characteristic of business environment is that the forces in a business environment are correlated. One factor influences another factor. For example, a change in the political environment will bring about economic changes which will impact the different firms in an industry.

2. Specific and general influences– Business environment has influences that are specific to an industry. These will affect all firms in the industry, but with varying intensity. The general influences exert equal influence on all firms within the industry or business. The specific influences can be in the form of customers, suppliers, investors, competing firms while general influences are political, legal, technological forces.

3. Dynamic– It is the affect of continuous changes that imparts dynamism to the business environment. Consumer likes and preference may change. What is considered in fashion today may get out of fashion the next month. New technology may bring radical changes in methods of production. These factors make the nature to the business environment ever changing.

> The competent and successful management must be capable of adapting to the business environment.

4. **Complexity**– The interrelation of factors lends a great complexity to the business environment. Changes in one factor may cause changes in not just one but many other interrelated areas of business. The difficulty lies in not being able to know the impact as well as how intensive the impact of these changes is.

5. **Relativity**– Business environment is a concept of relativity. Changes in one country or a part of the market leave impact on the business located in another country. If the raw materials are being imported from country X, political disturbances in the country X will hamper the supply of raw materials to the business based in country Y. Similarly, the demand for goods in both countries X & Y will be influenced.

6. **Unpredictability**– There is always an element of uncertainty attached with the business environment. It cannot be predicted with any degree of accuracy, what changes might come and when.

IMPORTANCE OF BUSINESS ENVIRONMENT

We are in an environment which is subject to great and continual changes. These changes could be political, environmental, social and cultural. Changes can be technological as well. The nature of these changes is subject to the dynamics of a fast-paced world. The business unit has to strive to survive in such a dynamic environment. The survival and subsequent growth of an organisation is dependent on how well it can anticipate the changes in an environment, readapt itself and its strategies to those changes. The organisation has to continually scan the horizon for signs of changes, be in a state of flux and ready to bring about changes. These changes could be a change in strategy or tactics, adjustments in size of plant and machinery, or realignment of its objectives and goals. It could also be a change in the attitude and culture of its workforce.

The points listed below will help to understand the importance of business environment better.

1. **Gives direction for growth**– Business environment gives a direction for growth to the organisation. By scanning the business environment, the organisation can identify new areas for its growth and expansion. It can exploit new business opportunities.

2. **Helps business identify its weakness and strength**– The business environment can help the organisation identify its areas of strength and weakness to take steps for plugging those loopholes and benefit from the advantages it enjoys over its competitors. By continually scanning the business environment, it can go from strength to strength.

3. **Helps to identify hindrances and opportunities**– Opportunities and threats can be identified early if the organisation pays attention to its business environment. Then it can place itself in a better position to make the best use of opportunities while fortifying its position to take care of situations that could represent potential threats to its survival.

4. **Lends flexibility and adaptability**– The business environment provides flexibility and dynamism to a business entity because is it necessary for a company to keep adjusting itself to changing trends. The management remains alive and proactive to rapid changes required.

5. **Helps build strategy for growth**– Business environment is the basis of strategy building. By careful observation of the environment, a company can devise a long term business strategy for growth and expansion. The business strategy can also be used by

the company to stay ahead in the market and for coping up with the dynamics of the changing business environment.

6. Image building– The business environment helps in image building. By observing the changes in the environment and its likely impact on the organisation's image, the organisation can create a favourable public image which helps it in furthering its goals.

DIMENSIONS OF BUSINESS ENVIRONMENT

We can divide the business environment into two parts, namely, the micro and the macro environment. The micro environment consists of factors that are beyond or within the control of the organisation to varying extent. These factors may be internal or external to the business organisation. The macro environment consists of general factors such as the political or technological environment that are completely beyond the influence of business and affect all business organisations equally.

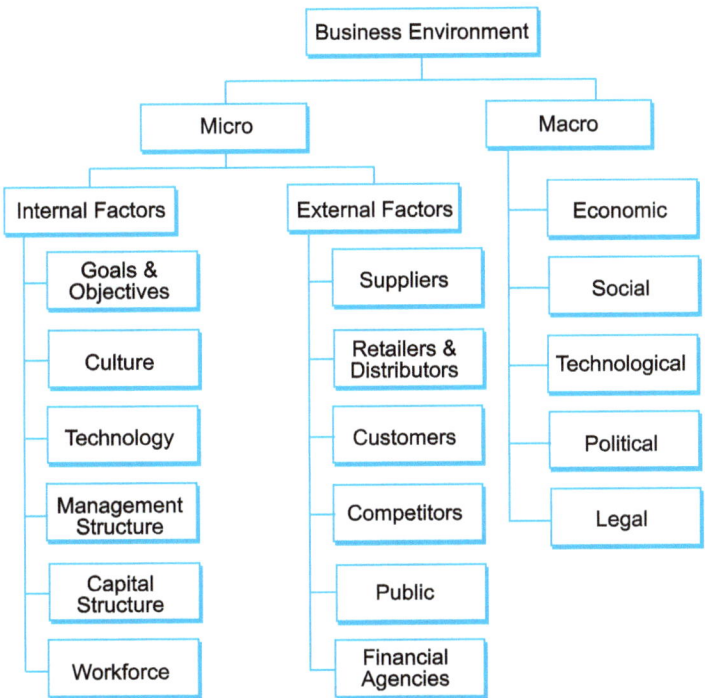

Fig. 1.1 Dimensions of Business Environment

Micro Environment

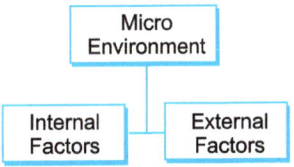

Fig. 1.2 Components of Micro Environment

Micro environment consists of all those factors that directly influence the working of the business organisation. It is also known as the Direct Task Environment. These factors may be internal or external to the business organisation. Micro environment will include those factors that are in very close touch with the business organisation and influence the organisational functioning. Micro environmental factors do not affect all firms within an industry in the same way; their impact varies from firm to firm.

Internal Factors

The internal factors are all those elements that are internal to a business organisation. In other words, all those influences that operate within an individual business unit, and which are considered controllable by the business organisation will be internal factors or the internal environment for that business unit. We do not take into account the extent or degree of control by the business organisation over these factors. The business unit may have complete control or partial control over these factors. For better understanding, let us take the example of the size of the workforce of an organisation. The business unit can increase or decrease the size of this workforce. Thus, it will be considered an internal factor.

The major internal factors that affect the working of a business unit are listed and explained below.

1. **Organisational culture–** The organisational culture needs to be in tune with time. When business organisations realise that their work culture does not match with the changed circumstances, they employ outside agencies to bring about a cultural change across the entire organisation and make it fit to match prevailing culture. Some business units resort to major overhaul of their management in case it fails to embrace the required new organisational culture.

2. **Management structure–** A business unit can alter its management structure for adjusting to changed conditions. This practice has become common now-a-days considering the frequent upheavals in the economy.

3. **Organisational goals and objectives–** An organisation has the power to bring about a change of direction in its organisational objectives and goals keeping in view new business dynamics prevailing in the market.

4. **Technology–** High-octane technology is being increasingly used in plant and machinery in all types of industry these days. The plant and machinery tend to become outdated if the company continues using old technology. If companies do not adapt themselves to the changing technological environment, they may get beaten down by the competitors. They may also find their production capacity declining compared to that of the firms that deploy comparatively better technology available in that industry. Technology has become a very important internal factor that influences the firm.

5. **Workforce–** The size of organisational workforce can be increased or cut down as per the requirements of the company. This trend of downsizing is very common now-a-days even in India. The objective is to retain the position of the business in the market. The workforce can also be retrained to learn new technology that the firm may use in view of changed business environment.

6. **Capital structure–** Capital is a set of resources with which a business organisation seeks to achieve its objectives doing business and earning profit. This capital consists of the plant and machinery, infrastructure, and the finances required to conduct the organisation's business. The efficiency and quality of the plant and machinery affects the production and subsequently the profitability of the organisation. Similarly, the timely availability or non-availability of adequate funds also affects the daily working of the firm. The infrastructure is the physical and organisational structure that is required

for the firm to accomplish its daily working. Thus, capital is an important internal factor for a business firm.

External Factors

The external factors of the micro environment are those groups or bodies with which the business organisation will have direct interaction in the course of its business activity.

> The external environment creates both risks and opportunities for a business entity.

They are also called as stakeholders because of their direct interest in the business. These stakeholders or factors, as we may choose to call them may not affect all firms in the industry equally. In other words, they affect business units differently, depending upon how the business organisations interact with them.

The external factors of the micro environment are listed and explained below :

1. Competitors– Competitors are persons or business units producing similar goods, can impact a firm by reducing its market share and cut down its profitability. This directly influences the firm's revenue and profitability. For example, Samsung mobiles face direct competition from other leading brands like LG, Sony, Micromax and Microsoft to name a few. Likewise, a cinema house faces indirect competition from other entertainment entities.

2. Public– Public include all those groups who have a real or latent interest in or impact on a company's ability to achieve its objectives. Entities like social organisations, vigilante groups and media groups can affect a business. They can put social as well as legal pressure and compel businesses to adhere to certain morals and code of conduct. They can also have financial implications for business. Union Carbide India Ltd., the pesticide company based in Bhopal, closed down due to immense legal and social pressure brought about by social and political organisations, after the leakage of poisonous gas killed lakhs of people.

3. Distribution channels– The distribution channel or the middlemen are very important functionaries that ensure the firm's products reach the buyers at the right time. They move the products from the point of production to the point of sale. They also store the products to create time utility. Thus, the distribution channels are very important factor influencing the business environment. They are categorized as external factor because the business firm has very little or almost no control over them.

4. Suppliers– These are the sources who supply the raw materials to the producer. The producer turns these raw materials into finished goods ready for consumption by the consumer. The suppliers control the price and supply of the raw materials and thus they are in a position to influence the business. An increase in price of raw materials can resultantly increase the price of the finished goods. It can also decrease the profit level of the firm by eating into his profits. Thus, the suppliers are together an important factor externally in the business environment.

5. Customers– The focus of all business activities - the consumer - can make or break even the biggest business organisation of the world. It is the consumer's demand, preference, likes and wishes that keep the producer's plant and machinery working. The customer will buy only if the producer's goods are satisfactory. The company has to sell products at a price acceptable to the customer. The customer is the most important factor to be taken into account by the company. If the customers lose interest in the company's product, the business will incur losses and will be forced to shut operations.

6. Financial agencies– The changing policies and practices along with the lending capacity of financial agencies such as commercial banks and specialised financial institutions impact the business environment of any company. Liberal financial market assists in promoting business.

Macro Environment

This is the overall environment that envelopes the business organisation. The micro environment factors such as competing business firms, suppliers, financiers, etc. also work within this macro environment. This means the macro environment influences all other factors, which in turn, influence the business firm. However, the business firm is not influenced directly by the micro environment. It is indirectly influenced.

For example, the Reserve Bank of India raises the interest rate charged by the banks as a result of change in economic policy. Thus, the cost of finance will go up. Now, this increased cost of financing will indirectly influence the business firm when suppliers of raw materials increase their prices to adjust for the higher interest they may have to pay. The economic cause cited here indirectly affects the business firm.

The macro environment is also known as the Indirect Action Environment as it does not interact directly with the business organisation. This environment creates opportunities for some business organisation and it may also create threats for others.

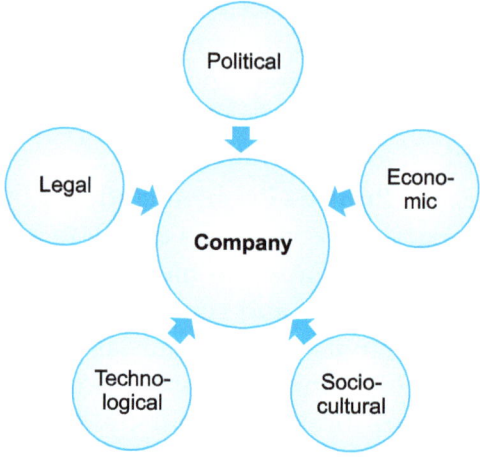

Fig. 1.3 Components of Macro Environment

The macro environment factors are more uncontrollable by the business organisations. Business firms have no option but to adapt themselves to the environmental changes to suit the demands of the macro environment factors. When a business adapts itself to the macro environment, it finds it easier to do business and make profit. Its success depends on its adapting ability to any change in the macro environment.

The macro environmental factors are listed and explained below :

Political Factors

Political environment consists of those factors that affect public administration and affairs and have an impact on business organisations. The political factors affect the business in a big way. Political factors also affect the government.

Example 1: With the rise of globalisation, India invited foreign companies to invest in India under the leadership of Rajiv Gandhi. Earlier, foreign companies could not do business in India because foreign firms were not allowed entry in the country. However, due to the change in political vision, the Indian economy witnessed entry of foreign banks, car manufacturers, two-wheeler manufacturers and a host of similar companies.

Example 2: Coca-Cola left the Indian market in the mid-seventies because then Indian government decided not to allow foreign soft drink companies to do business in India. Instead, it wanted Indian companies to produce soft drinks. Coca-Cola had to wait till the late eighties or early nineties when the era of globalisation dawned on India and foreign companies were again allowed to do business in the Indian market.

Mentioned below are some components of the political environment :
1. Political system– Nature and ideologies of political parties.
2. Political structure– Nature of relations between the center and the state governments.
3. Stability of the government– How strong a government and how long can it be expected to remain in power.
4. Foreign policy of the country– This could be tilted towards or against foreign investments, etc.
5. Degree of politicisation of the economy and business.

Economic Factors

The success of any business depends on how much money or purchasing power the consumer has, whether he wants to buy things, or prefers saving the money. If a business firm needs funds to invest, then at what rate of interest can receive the funds, are the banks and financial institutions readily willing to advance loans to business units, etc. These elements together constitute economic factors. If the economy is flourishing, the business firm grows at a fast rate. But in a stagnant economy or during an economic depression, the business operates at a low level of profitability. Economic factors are very important as they can either make or mar a business.

Example : The increased globalisation in the 1990's resulted in foreign companies investing in India. This led to increased opportunities for jobs and employment and more money was pumped into the economy. Consequently, the younger generation came in possession of more purchasing power. In turn, it resulted in increased demand for goods such as ready-made clothing, cosmetics, cars and two-wheelers and music appliances.

Components of economic environment are listed below :
1. Income and wealth in the country.
2. Employment levels.
3. Productivity.
4. Inflation and deflation.
5. Interest rates.

Socio-Cultural Factors

This is a very important factor which focuses on the behavioural characteristics of the people. It consists of the social and cultural factors. These factors determine how people make choice and how they behave as consumers. These factors are the prevailing culture, and life style, attitude, the demographic profile, religion, the sociability of the consumers, their standard of living, and all such related aspects.

Example : The spread of education and the growing population migration from the small town to big cities has contributed to popularity of events like Valentine's Day,

Father's Day and Friendship Day. In turn, this presents a growth opportunity to certain sectors of the Indian business.

The factors that together create the socio-cultural environment are listed below :
1. Demographic trends– This includes the size and distribution of the consumer population, their age, gender ratio, income, purchasing power, etc.
2. Social attitudes, customs, traditions, life styles and mores.
3. Social concerns as honesty or corruption, status of minorities, level of media interaction, etc.
4. Education levels, awareness of rights, etc.
5. Family structures and their values.

Technological Factors

Technology has become a very important factor in business environment. Technology in the business context means its application in daily use and in the workings of business. The level of technology depends on innovation and creativity, education, research and development, etc. Methods of production now involve the extensive use of technology. This leads to efficiency and lowers the cost of production.

Example 1: The widespread use of internet has contributed to the emergence and subsequent growth of a new sector in business, the online shopping. More and more people are now using the internet to shop online. This is one example of technology as a factor impacting the business environment.

Example 2: Technology has enabled the banking sector to come up with innovative methods that were unimaginable earlier. The wide spread network of ATM machines, the facility of online payment, net banking, mobile banking, etc. are all because of access of technology.

The factors that create the technological environment are listed below :
1. Facilities of research and development.
2. Spirit of invention and innovation among people.
3. Incentives and concessions for expansion and application of new technology.
4. Access to foreign technology, etc.

Legal Factors

The legal environment includes the framework of all the laws and regulations of a country in which the business firm operate. Every country has its own laws relating to various aspects of business. There could be laws relating to joint stock companies, private limited companies, foreign investments, consumer protection laws or the laws relating to import and export of finished products and raw material. All business units have to comply with the legal laws that are in force in the economy where their operations are. These legal factors have a significant impact on business firms.

Example 1: With the enactment of Minimum Wages Act, it has become mandatory for every organisation to pay a certain minimum wage to its employees. The minimum wage has been fixed by the government.

Example 2: Consumer Protection Act passed by the Indian government has made it compulsory for business organisations to have the price, date of manufacture, date of expiry (where required), contents, etc. printed on the packaging. The absence of this information makes the organisation liable for legal action.

The components of the legal environment are listed below :
1. The judicial system of the country.
2. Rights and duties of the citizens.
3. Laws relating to business.
4. Elasticity and adaptability of laws.

THE SWOT ANALYSIS

This business analysis tool is the brainchild of Albert Humphrey who came up with it in the 1960's. It has become a popular technique for analysing and diagnosing the environment that a business unit operates in and in estimating the strengths and weaknesses of the business unit and its capabilities to survive, grow and expand.

SWOT is an acronym for Strengths, Weaknesses, Opportunities and Threats. The SWOT analysis is a business tool that helps a businessman in examining his business in terms of the above parameters. The ultimate objective being bringing about appropriate changes in its approach, in its way of functioning so that it can reposition itself in a better way in the market. The business unit has to scan its internal and external environment in terms of the above parameters as part of a planning process designed to ensure that it stays in the market and continues to earn increasing sales revenue. According to Bonnie Taylor, a renowned management professional, "SWOT is the cornerstone of any strategic business plan."

The SWOT analysis helps a business organisation identify all positive and the negative influences that impact it from outside as well as inside. It makes the management aware of all the factors that may affect decision making. It compels the business unit in leveraging its strength and resources on its weak areas while focusing on opportunities. It is very necessary to evaluate a business from all possible angles for the management to formulate a strategy to move ahead in business. This is made possible by the SWOT analysis into four simple steps. It is a simple assessment technique that lends itself as an invaluable business analysis tool which, if done correctly, will help the business organisation in sound decision-making.

The SWOT analysis can be used when the business organisation plans to embark in a new direction, like entering a new market, putting a new product into the market and revamping its distribution channels. It is used in strategic planning when the business organisation needs a strategy to quickly capitalise on a profitable opportunity that may have come its way. It can also be used to counter the threat that may come up as a result of actions by competitors. The SWOT analysis organises meaningful information, identifies possible hindrances while highlighting the opportunities for growth. It successfully identifies key areas where the firm enjoys advantages over its rivals while highlighting areas where the firm is at a disadvantage. It helps capitalise the organisational strength while helping remove weak and blind spots which could be detrimental to business if left undiscovered.

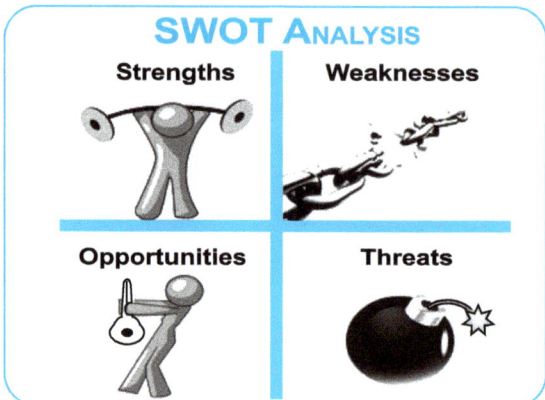

The SWOT analysis is typically conducted using a four-square analysis template as shown in the diagram above. The relative strengths and weaknesses, opportunities and threats in context of a business unit are explained below :

Strengths

It is used to assess the business unit's resources worthy of giving a greater competitive advantage over existing or future competitors. Such resources may include any price advantage the unit has over its competitors, the loyalty its existing customers may have towards it (brand loyalty), access to or easy availability of raw material at lower prices, efficient workforce, access to technology, good network of distributors or retailers to state a few. The below given attributes can be generally considered as areas of strength of a company.

Strengths

- Technological skills
- Leading brands
- Distribution channels
- Customer loyalty/relationships
- Production quality
- Scale
- Management

1. Manufacturing, research and development advantages.
2. Tangible assets.
3. Skills, experience and reputation.

Weaknesses

Weakness may be seen as lack of strength in any area that it could possibly impact a business unit's competitive abilities and undermine its profitability. The company's weakness is its competitor's advantage. For a company, the following weaknesses can prove detrimental to its operations :

Weaknesses

- Absence of important skills
- Weak brands
- Poor access to distribution
- Low customer retention
- Unreliable product/service
- Sub-scale
- Management

1. Absence of good network of distributors or retailers.
2. Weak brand loyalty especially in fast moving consumer goods (FMCG) units.
3. High operating costs.
4. Poor access to raw materials.
5. Inefficient workforce.
6. Lack of up-to-date production technology.

Inability to make efficient use of existing resources or technology can also be a point of weakness for a business unit. If the unit has accumulated inventory, it means working capital is kept locked up. Similarly, inability to put plant and machinery to optimum use despite having a large working capacity will be construed as a weakness.

Opportunities

These are prospects worth exploring by the business unit to derive more profits. Such conditions could have existed from before but may have gone overlooked by the business unit. Or such conditions could be the result of some new environmental dynamics.

Opportunities
- Changing customer tastes
- Technological advances
- Changes in government politics
- Lower personal taxes
- Change in population age
- New distribution channels

Removal or reduction of import duties, excise duties, easing of import or export formalities and reduction of costs of raw material are some examples of opportunities. Other examples of opportunities are change in consumer demand or taste to benefit the manufacturer or business unit and availability of new technology of production that could increase the output and company turnover.

Threats

Threats can be defined as any change in the external environment that can adversely impact the business unit's interest. It is an uncontrollable and unfavourable condition in the external environment which places the business at risk. Some possible threats to a business are :

Threats
- Changing customer base
- Closing of geographic markets
- Technological advances
- Changes in government politics
- Tax increases
- Change in population age
- New distribution channels

1. New rules restricting business operations.
2. Entry of new or substitute goods in the market.
3. Shift in the taste and likes of consumers.
4. Adverse effect of political changes.

SUMMARY

Business Environment– It is the atmosphere in which a business organisation operates. It impacts and affects the way business is carried out.

Micro Environment– Micro environment consists of all those factors that directly influence the working of the business organisation.

External Factors– The external factors are the firm's customers, competitors, suppliers, financiers and middlemen and all those that have a financial interest in the business of the firm.

Internal Factors– Internal factors consist of the factors that impact the business unit from within and are controlled by it. These can be the objectives and goals, style of management, power structure and work culture of the business. The firm can modify or alter these to suit changing conditions.

Macro Environment– Macro environment is the overall environment that envelopes the business organisation.

SWOT Analysis– A scan of the business organisation within the context of its operating business environment which reflects its areas of strength, weakness, opportunities and threats. It is carried out to develop a business strategy, assess a changing business environment and respond proactively.

QUESTIONS FOR PRACTICE

Very Short Answer Type Questions
1. Write a short note on business environment.
2. List one dimension of the business environment.
3. List one component of the internal factors of business environment.
4. What is the meaning of business environment?
5. Write a short note on the concept of business environment.
6. Write short note on technological environment of business concern.
7. List one difference between the external and internal factors of a business organisation?
8. Expand the term SWOT.

Short Answer Type Questions
1. Define the term 'business environment'.
2. Name two factors influencing a business environment.
3. Why is environment important for a business firm?
4. What do you mean by the internal environment of a business?
5. Explain one internal factors of a business environment.
6. List and explain any two elements of the macro environment of a business firm.
7. What is SWOT analysis?
8. Outline the utility of the SWOT analysis for a business unit.

Essay Type Questions
1. How can the business environment prove helpful for growth of a business unit?
2. Explain the internal and external factors of the micro environment.
3. Briefly explain any five external factors of a business's micro environment.
4. List the factors that a business firm can control to achieve its goals and objectives.
5. Explain two ways in which economic factors impact the business unit.
6. Explain how social factors can help in creating a market for a new product.
7. Explain two utilities of SWOT analysis.
8. What do you understand by the term 'Opportunity' in a SWOT analysis?

2 | Financing : Fixed and Working Capital

> **LEARNING RESULT**
>
> After reading this chapter, you should be able to :
> ◆ Understand the nature of finance, its importance and sources.
> ◆ Define Financial Planning–meaning, features, objectives, importance and implications.
> ◆ Assess the factors affecting capital structure of a company.
> ◆ Define Fixed Capital– meaning, factor affecting fixed capital.
> ◆ Discuss the meaning and types of Working Capital and factors affecting it.
> ◆ Differentiate between Fixed Capital and Working Capital.

MEANING AND ROLE OF FINANCING

Finance is the art and science of managing various available sources of money such as securities, assets, investments, etc. and using them for profit making in business.

According to Ferrel and Geoffrey Hirt, finance is, *"all activities related to obtaining money and related use."* Bodie and Merton define finance as the *"study how scarce resources are allocated over time."* Simon Andrade defines finance as *"area of economic activity in which money is the basis of various embodiments."*

Finance is the management of money and other valuables which can be easily converted into cash. It is the procurement and utilisation of funds for furthering of business objectives. The businessman needs funds for buying land and plant and machinery, for buying regularly the stock of raw material. He needs money to pay the labour force, to pay for meeting the expenses of marketing his products or services, for advertising and for physical distribution of the goods. He may need money for any contingency in future. It is the function of financing that makes money available as and when it is needed by business and industry.

> **Sourcing/Financing**
>
> The issue of where to acquire the funds required for starting and developing a business organisation.

NATURE OF BUSINESS FINANCE

Listed below are some important characteristics of finance.
1. Finance is the life blood without which business cannot exist.
2. It facilitates the smooth flow of goods and services from the point of production to the ultimate consumer and circulation of money, generation of revenue and the creation of profit. Finance or revenues generated through sales are used to create more goods which are again sold to bring in more revenue.
3. In the absence of finance no revenue can be generated.

4. Scale of finance needed by a business is directly proportional to the size and nature of the business.
5. Finance required by any business unit varies from time to time and is dependent on a number of factors.

IMPORTANCE OF FINANCE

Finance is as essential to business as breath is for sustaining life. In any business enterprise, workers have to be employed, raw material or trading goods have to be bought for manufacturing or reselling, certain costs are incurred in all these activities before the finished goods (or services) reach the final consumer. As the business progresses, the monetary needs of the business unit also undergo a change. Larger amount of money is continuously required to meet the growing business needs. Funds may be required for promoting sales, increasing production in the short or long run, for adding more plant and machinery. Money or finance is needed for all these activities.

The importance of finance is underlined by the fact that not only it should be available easily and at affordable rates, but it should be available readily at the time it is required and needed. Timely availability or non-availability can make or break a business enterprise in today's dynamic business environment.

The importance of finance and its significance for a business organisation is listed below :

1. Helps in taking advantage of business opportunities– The ability to secure business finance is a deciding factor in making or breaking a business firm in this age of globalisation. The firm must have a ready availability of finance to take advantage of opportunities in this dynamic business environment. Waiting for finance means the possible losing of a business opportunity.

2. Helps to meet short term business liabilities– A business firm needs finance to cover its short-term costs and expenses. Creditors have to be paid for services and raw materials they may have supplied to the producer. Failure to cover these recurring expenses can result in production cycle getting disturbed, with a subsequent loss of sales, besides souring of business relations.

3. Helps in meeting long term liabilities– Long term financial obligations have to be met by a business firm. Generally, these require heavy funding for which sources of finance have to be identified much beforehand. Capital budgeting has to be done with a reliance on long-term financing that will finance long term projects and expansion plans. Finance and financing assume very significant importance in such cases because the need here is for huge sum of money that has to be invested and the return on which will be received only in the long run.

4. Invaluable role in achieving business objectives– Every business firm has its own financial plans, and prioritises the financial resources according to its planning. It has to manage its finances and meet its long and short term finance obligations from its resources. At times it may see the need to expand short-term production or invest extra amount of money in any other business related activity. During such times finance assumes a greater significance because of the need to obtain funds from external sources within a stipulated time and at terms and conditions that do not exert pressure on the firm's profitability.

5. Helps in achieving business efficiency– Lastly, the great importance of finance arises from the fact that it adds to the efficiency of a business. Effective utilisation of financial resources leads to good financial and business health of a company. However, if the financial health is not good, if there is improper utilisation of valuable financial resources which can make the firm bankrupt.

SOURCES OF FINANCE

When we talk of sources of finance we are in fact referring to the sources that are available to a business organisation for its capital. Capital is the finance or money needed for continuing business operations. Listed below are the sources of finance open to different types of business.

1. Sole trader– A sole trader has the option of approaching a bank for financing his needs for money. Banks have now simplified their procedures for providing finance, especially to the small traders and village units. There are nationalised banks, private banks, *grameen* banks that can be approached by the sole trader or proprietor for his commercial needs. Personal and family savings can also be an easy source of finance for a sole trader. In fact, a village moneylender too is a good source of finance.

2. Partnership firm– A partnership firm differs from a sole proprietorship concern in the number of co-owners that exist. While, a sole trader is the only owner of the business, the business partners in a partnership firm are the joint owners and are jointly as well as individually responsible for the firm's debt. These partners have to look for finance to run the business. All the sources of finance listed in 'sole trader' are open to become business partners if the business owner is borrowing from them. If all sources of finance get exhausted, a partnership firm can bring in new partners and thus open a new source of funds to be injected into the partnership.

3. Joint stock company– A joint stock company has a number of sources to obtain finance. There are commercial banks, specialised financial institutions, industrial banks and share markets that can be approached for getting various types of finance ranging from short-term to long-term funds. Joint stock companies also have the option of approaching venture capitalists and they have the option to choose franchising as a means of obtaining funds for business growth.

FINANCIAL PLANNING

Planning always refers to making or formulation of a program for a particular course of action for the future. Without a sound financial roadmap a business unit cannot hope to survive in the long run. Since finance is the life of business, the finances of a company have to be very carefully and meticulously planned.

Financial planning formulates a set of statements that clarify the current financial position and earnings of a company along with outlining the destination it has to reach in financial terms in a given period of time. This includes :

1. The current resources of the company set out in financial or monetary terms.
2. Its financial requirements *i.e.,* the amount of money required for a given future period.
3. The sources of finance.

4. The anticipated sales revenue the company is expected to generate.
5. Profit margin or operating profit margin.

In other words, in a financial plan all statements are broken down into financial denominators in such a way that the management can get a fairly good idea of how much the company will earn during the period planned for.

> **Financing –Making the Right Choice**
> **Need–** Long-term or short-term?
> **Sources–** What are available?
> **Quantity–** Amount required?

Features of Financial Planning

Financial planning is concerned with raising, providing and managing the funds used in business planning. The major features or characteristics of financial planning are listed below :

1. **Estimates the amount of capital required–** The financial planning involves estimating very accurately the amount of capital that a business will need in order to attain its goals and objectives. It keeps the organisational objectives in mind while making the estimates. It keeps in the future in mind and ensures that any future adjustment required can be incorporated with ease. It anticipates various contingencies that could possibly arise in the future and makes provisions for unforeseen situations.

2. **Determines the capital structure–** It is financial planning that determines the capital structure of a business firm. It strikes a proper balance between the fixed and working capital so that the daily working of the firm goes on smoothly.

3. **Administering the capital–** It provides policies and procedures for coordinating different departments of a business. It also makes sure that available funds are used properly. It introduces flexibility so that the organisation can adapt itself to a changing environment. Thus, it helps avoid situations of shortage or surplus of funds.

4. **Formulates programs–** While financial planning programs are formulated to ensure intensive and effective use of the capital of the organisation. It ensures a balance between equity and debt funds and helps develop a sound capital structure. It facilitates smooth flow of funds and helps avoid blockage of capital. This gives optimum output while making intensive use of the capital.

5. **Safeguards the firm's profitability–** Financial planning is a mechanism for safeguarding the firm's profitability. By seeking to minimise the dependence on external funding and by placing reliance on the most economic self generation of funds financial planning seeks to maximise the firm's long term profitability.

Objectives of Financial Planning

Financial planning is of paramount importance to every business firm if it intends to achieve its goals and objectives. The company must prepare a blueprint of how it will acquire the financial resources required to carry out its long-term and short-term operations, from where it will derive funds for its expenses and how it will utilise its financial resources to get the optimum returns.

The objectives of financial planning are listed below :

1. **To determine the capital needs of the organisation–** Financial planning is done keeping in view the financial requirements of the organisation. In other words, it is done to determine the long and short term requirements of the capital. It looks into what will

be required in terms of assets, working capital, fixed capital, etc. In fact, it looks into all aspects of needs and requirements and converting them into monetary denominator for easy comparison.

2. To compute the capital structure– The financial plan determines the funds required by the organisation and breaks it into different types of capital and the proportion in which it may be required. For example, a joint stock company must decide through its financial planning the amount of capital it will require through equity and preference shares and the types of preference shares it can have in its capital structure.

3. To frame the financial policies and related time frames– During the normal working an organisation may have to resort to borrowing from banks and financial institutions. It will have to monitor and control cash flows. All these and other cash and credit transactions will be subject to financial planning. They will have to support the long term goals and objectives of the organisation.

4. To ensure optimum utilisation of available funds– The financial plans of an organisation are meant to ensure that the funds of the business unit are spent in such a way that they optimise the output of the organisation and progressively increase the profitability of the unit. Financial plans enable monitoring of the expenditure of company's resources. They also enable distortions and deviations to be rectified, thereby, minimising the gaps between actual performance and the standard decided by the management.

Importance of Financial Planning

The importance of financial planning is outlined below :

1. Ensures collection of optimum funds– Financial planning looks after the availability of adequate funds for carrying out the day-to-day operations and long-term management of the business. It helps avoiding wastage and over-capitalisation.

2. Ensures wise deployment of funds– Financial planning taps various resources at different times. There are different sources for long-term, medium-term, and short-term funds. These funds are contributed by different sources at different times. It is financial planning that determines the appropriate time for tapping various sources for varying financial needs.

3. Helps in proper utilisation of finance– Funds have to be properly utilised so that each rupee invested yields the optimum return. The soundness of financial planning determines the profitability of the business organisation.

4. Determines the success of operational activities– The financial planning and decision making is the determinant of production success and distribution aspect of the business. Efficient flow of production, distribution and resultant flow of funds will be possible only if sound financial decisions are taken in a well-planned financial environment.

5. Link between investment and financing– Financial planning is responsible for creating the link between investment and financing decisions. It optimises investment decisions by helping identify areas to invest the organisation's available funds.

From the above points we see that a company's finance plan starts from calculating the cost of the project planned, the sources from where the businessman will get his finance, the cost of getting the finance (in terms of interest and other costs) the revenue and the profit that he intends his business to give him. This includes the costs of producing the goods too.

A financial plan can also be for a period of 12 months and it may also be for more than a year. It will depend on the organisation and its objectives. A good example of a year-long financial plan is the annual budget made by the government.

The following areas must be covered when formulating a financial plan.

(a) Capital market dynamics– Since the business depends on the capital market for finance any plan must take into account the nature and attitude of various sources of funds, the prevailing interest rates, the ease or difficulties in financing, and all such related aspects.

(b) Nature of business– Many industries are more capital intensive than others, and require very heavy investment of funds. The stage of a business, whether it is in a growth, or a maturity stage is also a factor that will have to be taken into account when making a financial plan. Nature of financial needs varies from company to company and needs to be considered during planning.

(c) Degree of risk in particular business– Financial planning has to take into account the degree of risk the management is willing to take. Excessive dependence on the share market may cause a dilution of control. Withholding of dividend to compensate financing may damage the image of the company.

(d) Organisational goals and objectives– Financial Planning is a tool to help achieve organisational goals and objectives. The goals may fix a certain margin of profit for the company. In such a scenario, a financial plan must make sure that the funds are utilised to allow the stated profit margin.

FACTORS AFFECTING CAPITAL STRUCTURE OF A COMPANY

The capital structure of a joint stock company is affected by any or all of the factors that are listed below :

1. Promoters' control– The capital structure will be affected by the degree of control the promoters wish to have over the company. They may not issue equity shares beyond a certain number to prevent control by the shareholders. Thus, they may opt for either debenture issue or an issue of preferential shares.

2. Capital market conditions– The capital market has great influence on the capital structure of a company. During economic prosperity investors will readily take up shares. But during times of depressions the equity market may be sluggish as investors may not be willing to invest in shares that may give them more of loss than return. They will instead prefer to invest in debentures and preference shares which will carry fixed returns.

> **Important Factors Influencing Capital Requirements**
> - Manufacturing units– Large investment, Trading units– Comparatively smaller investment.
> - Larger scale of operation– More the need of capital, Smaller scale operation– Lesser the need of capital.
> - Greater the growth prospect– More the need of capital, Smaller the growth prospect– Lesser the need of capital.
> - Greater the involvement of technology– More use of capital, Less involvement of technology– Less capital.

3. **Nature of business–** If a business firm deals in goods that are subject to wide fluctuation in demand, its capital structure will weigh in favour of equity capital. On the other hand, well established and entrenched companies will have high gearing, *i.e.,* high debt funds. The newly established companies may not find investors willing to invest in their debentures and preferential shares. They may have to look elsewhere to satisfy their capital needs.

4. **Objective of financing–** The capital structure is affected by the purpose of financing. Fixed investment requires equity financing but medium term capital needs can be fulfilled by debentures and preferential shares.

5. **Flexibility–** Flexibility in capital structure is a great advantage to a firm. A business organisation should be able to shed off its debt capital as and when it feels the need. A company can pay off its debentureholders, and thus get rid of its debts according to its needs. Of course it has to adhere to statutory requirements; but then a debenture or preferential share is not a lifetime debt or investment unlike equity shares.

6. **Legal requirements–** Countries have their rules and regulations regarding fund raising by companies and these rules have to be adhered to. There are rules and regulations regarding debt-equity ratio and ceilings in public deposits. These have their impact on the capital structure of a company.

7. **Cost of financing–** The company has to take into consideration the cost of capital financing. Prevailing rate of interest, return on investment expected, issue costs, etc. have to be taken into account to arrive at the cost of financing. The cost of alternative finance must be taken into account. If there is high rate of tax then debt financing can be considered.

8. **Cash flow–** A company has to consider its cash flow position before deciding on the type of financing because in the case of debentures or long term debt it will have to pay out interest along with installments at fixed time intervals.

9. **Needs of investors–** The capital structure of a company is designed keeping in mind the potential investors. Equity shares will attract investors that prefer risks along with a say in the management. However, if investors choose to avoid risks, the company will prefer preferential shares and debentures instead.

10. **Objectives of financing–** This also influences the capital structure of a company. For medium term finance to serve the purpose of modernisation or expansion, companies prefer raising debentures and preferential shares as these do not give voting rights. But for permanent investment, companies always prefer equity shares.

MEANING OF FIXED CAPITAL

Fixed capital is that part of the company's assets that is in the form of plant and machinery, land and buildings, furniture and fixtures. It is of permanent nature and generates revenue or income for the company. We can call it blocked capital because it can be disposed off only in the eventuality of the company's liquidation.

A company raises fixed capital through long-term sources of finance as shares, debentures and long-term loans. It may also invest retained earnings in its fixed capital. Fixed assets serve strategic or long-term plans of the organisation and its benefits are spread over a number of years.

According to Wheeler, *"Fixed capital is invested in the fixed or long-run assets. The amount of fixed capital need, therefore, varies directly with the amount of fixed assets owned or used by a business."*

Factors Affecting Fixed Capital Structure

The factors that influence decisions regarding fixed capital are listed below :

1. **Nature of business–** The nature of an organisation's business affects the size of its fixed capital. The nature of business will decide the type of plant and machinery required, the extent of the land needed for business purpose, the sources of power required to work the machineries, etc. To serve this purpose, heavy and long term investment is needed.

2. **Size of the company's operations–** A large business house will require big scale operations. And big scale operations will give birth to the need to have a greater amount of fixed capital to run the business. The size of a business unit's operation depends on a number of factors such as the overall market size for the product or service and the profitability level of the business in the industry.

3. **Future growth–** The fixed capital is an instrument to meet not only the current growth but also the future growth requirements of an organisation. The management takes a long-term view of the business scenario before deciding the extent and size of the business. It makes sure the benefits derived from the fixed capital are long-term and not just immediate short-term.

The amount of fixed investment will depend on the management plans. If the growth prospects seem good, the organisation may see it wise to have a large fixed capital base. It could also plan for diversification. It could be quite opposite where the organisation does not expect future growth beyond a certain period.

4. **Nature of products–** The nature of products decides the type of plant and machinery that will be used to produce them. In turn, the cost of the plant and machinery determines the amount of fixed capital that needs to be invested in the business. Thus, the investment in fixed capital is dependent upon what is required to be produced by the business. Refineries, for example, are very cost intensive and require large amount of fixed capital. On the other hand, a business unit selling packaged drinking water will work with a comparatively smaller amount of fixed capital.

5. **Production methods/techniques–** The production methods and technologies employed by a business organisation plays a very important role in shaping the structure and base of the fixed capital. Modern production demands latest tools and machineries that are technology-driven and more expensive to run. They also require skilled manpower to run them and this manpower does not come cheap. Naturally, if an organisation goes in for technology-based production methods it will need larger capital as compared to one that relies on manual labour, or where the dependency is not so much on latest technology machines.

6. **Diversity of production lines–** If a business firm is engaged in the production of a single commodity, it will require certain amount of fixed capital. But if it engages in producing a diversified product line, it will need more of fixed capital than in the earlier case. In the same way, if a firm produces each and every part of a finished product by itself, it will require more of fixed capital investment than if it were to outsource some of the parts.

7. Mode of acquiring assets– Many organisations, instead of outright purchase, may go in for long-term leasing of plant and machinery and other equipment. It can also buy on an installment basis. What is common in both the cases in that the business unit is spared from the pain of making an immediate investment in fixed capital terms. In other words, the business unit can pay slowly and can use the precious capital thus saved in ways that can bring it more returns.

MEANING OF WORKING CAPITAL

The working capital of a company is the amount of capital that is deployed in the day-to-day working of the company in its stated business. If we add up the current assets of the company, deduct current liabilities from it, we arrive at the working capital. It is used to pay for the recurring expenses that must occur in the course of the daily business of the company. For the purpose of accounting we can say that the total amount of funds required by a company to run its operations for one accounting year will be regarded as its working capital. A company must have adequate funds to cover its day-to-day working. It is also known as *revolving capital* or *circulating capital* as it keeps on revolving or circulating in business.

All resources that can be used in the short-term to cover the costs of running the company will be regarded as 'working capital'. The below given list shows the assets the company has at its disposal to help it in covering the running cost.

- Liquid cash
- Bills receivable
- Inventories

Liquid cash– The money collected by the organisation's sales force from dealers and retailers by selling the company's products. This is called liquid cash because it is either in hard cash, cheques and drafts, which are again as good as hard cash.

Bills receivable– Some of the goods may be sold on credit, or on a deferred payment basis. The company gets post-dated checks that will mature by a certain date. These are known as bills receivable. These bills are converted into cash and enter the cash flow.

Inventories– It consists of finished goods that are awaiting sale and those semi-finished goods which will be converted into finished goods in due course and will be sold out.

Different types of Working Capital

The working capital is broadly divided into two types, namely, Concept-based or Balance Sheet View and Time-based or Operating Cycle View.

The Concept Based or Balance Sheet View

This divides the working capital into (1) Gross working capital, and (2) Net working capital.

Types of Working Capital
- Gross Working Capital– Short term assets that can be converted into cash within a period of a year.
- Net Working Capital– Difference between the current assets and the current liabilities.

1. The **Gross Working Capital** will be the total capital invested in the current assets of the company, which means, the assets which could be converted into liquid cash within an accounting period, or one year. It represents the liquidity position of the organisation.

Gross Working Capital = Book value of Current Assets

2. The **Net Working Capital** is the difference between the current assets and the current liabilities. It is used to evaluate the short-term financial position of the organisation. Net working capital means excess of current assets over current liabilities.

Net Working Capital = Current Assets – Current Liabilities

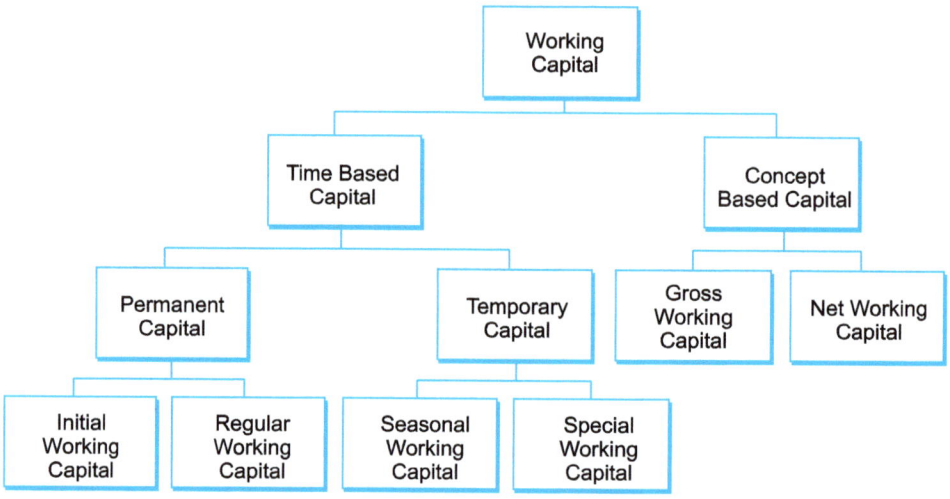

Fig. 2.1 Types of Working Capital

The Time Based or Operating Cycle View

This concept divides the working capital into Permanent and Temporary working capital. The different types of working capital on the basis of time are :

1. **Permanent working capital–** It is the minimum amount of working capital that a business organisation requires at all time to be able to operate its business operations at a minimum level. It is part of the current assets of the company. The permanent working capital is of two kinds as listed below :

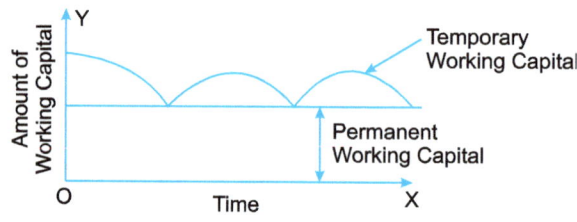

Fig. 2.2 Time-based view

(a) **Initial working capital–** This is the working capital with which the company initially starts the business. It is part of the permanent working capital needed for commencement of business. The initial capital is intended to meet all operating expenses. Suppliers do not give credit to new companies and these expenses have to be paid for in cash.

(b) **Regular working capital**– It is also a part of the permanent working capital. The company requires it for its continuous business operations. It is required to build inventories, stock finished goods, which will be sold in due time, and for short term business expenses.

2. **Temporary working capital**– It is also called variable working capital, and is in addition to the permanent working capital. The need for it and the amount of temporary working capital needed may vary from time to time. It is used to satisfy the seasonal and occasional needs of the company. For example, it is used to cope with extra production to meet sales demands of a temporary nature. The company raises this capital from short-term sources of funds. Temporary working capital is classified into two types, namely seasonal and special working capital.

(a) **Seasonal working capital**– It is that extra working capital required by a company for a particular season. When a business deals in seasonal products such as woollen garments, it required extra working capital, beyond the regular working capital, during particular season when the demand goes up. To meet increased demand in products, the company has to buy more raw materials and incur more expenses in terms of wages, etc. That is how the need for seasonal working capital can be defined.

(b) **Special working capital**– Special working capital is the additional capital required to meet contingency expenses that may arise in the course of business. It is a sort of reserve capital set aside and is meant to serve as support during times when a sudden and unforeseen need arises for funds. Such contingent needs must be as listed below :

(i) Extra working capital to meet a sudden spike in demand.
(ii) Need for extra capital to tide over stagnancy or unexpected drop in demand. During such period the sales and cash inflow slows but the expenses keep on mounting and have to be paid for.
(iii) During periods of strikes, lockouts and natural calamities.

Factors Affecting the Working Capital

The factors that affect the working capital of a company are below :

1. **Nature of business**– The nature of business of any organisation affects its working capital. If the organisation is in a trading business it will require comparatively smaller amount of capital than a unit engaged in manufacturing goods. Manufacturing units have to keep larger inventories and hence, will require larger capital.

2. **Size of business**– The bigger the size of the business unit, the greater the working capital. A larger business organisation will have to keep more inventories; its market will be more widespread and will have to incur more distribution costs. The bottom line is that it will need larger capital to ensure its smooth functioning. But a small firm will have a smaller market and will have lower expenses.

3. **Inventory time**– Long inventory period also affects working capital. Inventory period means the waiting period for the raw material to be processed into finished product and sold off. In other words, having to keep more working capital to offset that

amount which remains blocked as work-in-progress or in the company warehouses awaiting sale.

4. **Credit limit to customers–** Every organisation allows certain time limit to its distributors or retailers to pay for the goods or services that they buy from the producer. Longer credit limit results in delay in the conversion of bills to cash. Thus, a liberal credit policy increases the need for capital.

5. **Raw material availability–** If the nature of raw materials is such that a producer can acquire it as and when needed at reasonable rates, then they need not stock raw material in large quantities. This means the company would need a small amount of capital for purchase of raw material for any production cycle. If raw materials are subject to fluctuation in price or availability, it means the company ought to invest more in working capital.

6. **Growth and expansion plans–** The working capital of an organisation is also affected by its expansion and growth projections. When a company plans to increase its production in order to cater to an expanding market, it requires more working capital. If the expansion plans are more, the company will have to set aside more amount of working capital for expenditures such as purchase of raw materials, paying large-sized workforce, spending money on bigger advertising and public relations, etc. On the other hand, an organisation with little or no expansion plan will feel no need for going in for an increase in its working capital.

7. **Ease of accessibility to capital market–** If an organisation has quick and easy access to the capital market, it can approach it for any short-term loan. The source of working capital generally is through short-term borrowing where needed and this part is reflected as current liabilities in the balance sheet. When in need the business can easily approach banks for overdrafts or it may also dispose of bills receivable to raise liquidity for working capital at short notice.

8. **Production and sales efficiency–** A very important factor that affects a unit's working capital is the efficiency with which the organisation converts raw material into finished goods and affects sales. The shorter the time span required by a production cycle, the lesser will be the need for a large working capital. Faster sale of products will stabilise the organisation's cash flow and shorten the expected time for liquid cash to reach the organisation. Thus, waiting time is reduced, and consequently there is lesser need for a larger working capital.

9. **Cyclical fluctuation–** Certain products are subject to cyclical fluctuation in demand. In seasons of high demand, the company has to come up with a higher output to satisfy the teeming buyers. During such boom periods he will require a larger working capital.

10. **Price fluctuations–** When price of raw materials and related inputs is unstable, a company will have to keep a large working capital. It will need to buy in large quantities in order to get benefit of economies of scale and keep its production cost within budgeted limits.

Distinction between Fixed Capital and Working Capital

	Fixed Capital		Working Capital
1.	Fixed capital is the fund invested in the plant and machinery, land and buildings, etc.	1.	This is the fund invested in current assets, such as cash, stock, raw materials, debtors, etc.
2.	Objective is to help establish the business	2.	Objective is day-to-day running of the business
3.	The value of assets changes over a period of time	3.	When working capital in the form of raw material changes into finished goods, its value changes rapidly over a period of time
4.	Fixed capital is in the form of fixed assets of the company.	4.	Working capital can be in the form of raw materials, finished goods, cash, etc.
5.	Fixed capital cannot be disposed off without breaking up the business.	5.	Working capital is continuously undergoing change as cash is converted into raw material, and converted into finished products disposed off and converted into cash. It needs quick conversion and disposal.
6.	Fixed capital is represented by fixed assets.	6.	Working capital is represented by liquidity.
7.	It is raised through long-term sources of finance, such as shares and debentures.	7.	It is raised through short-term sources of finance, such as short-term bank credit.
8.	Fixed capital is unaffected by seasonal or cyclical variation in demand.	8.	Working capital is affected by both seasonal variations and cyclical fluctuation of demand.

SUMMARY

Finance– It denotes all aspects of funding, planning for fund acquisition, ensuring that funds are utilised to bring optimum benefits to the business firm.

Financial Planning– It makes possible to achieve goals and objectives by putting guidelines, checks and balances to ensure optimum utilisation of available financial resources.

Fixed Capital– It is the large scale investment of a business firm in its plant and machinery, land and such acquisitions and depends on the nature and size of the business.

Working Capital– Is that part of the capital that is used to cover the working expenses of the firm on a period to period basis. It can be subdivided into permanent and temporary working capital.

QUESTIONS FOR PRACTICE

Very Short Answer Type Questions

1. Write a short note on financial planning.
2. Write about two sources of finance for a sole trader.
3. List two sources of finance open to a partnership firm.

4. What is meant by working capital?
5. Distinguish between fixed capital and working capital.
6. Differentiate between temporary and permanent working capital.

Short Answer Type Questions

1. Explain briefly the factors affecting fixed capital of a joint stock company.
2. Explain briefly your understanding of working capital.
3. Explain any four factors that determine the working capital requirement of a business.
4. Identify any two differences between gross working capital and net working capital.
5. List any two objectives of a financial plan of a business firm.
6. Explain the meaning of financial planning.
7. Name the broad parameters covered in a financial plan of a business firm.
8. List one reason a business unit may have to increase its fixed capital.

Essay Type Questions

1. "Finance is the life blood of a business organisation." Give your opinion.
2. List and explain any two objectives of a financial plan of a joint stock company.
3. Explain the factors affecting the capital structure of a company.
4. What is fixed capital? Discuss any four factors affecting fixed capital requirement of Joint Stock Company.
5. How does the size of a business firm affect its fixed capital?
6. Briefly discuss any five factors affecting the fixed capital requirements of an organisation.
7. Examine any four dominant factors determining the amount of fixed capital requirements for a business.
8. Does technique of production affect the fixed capital of a business unit? Explain.
9. In how many ways can you classify the working capital of a joint stock company?
10. Under what circumstances may a business firm require additional working capital? Briefly explain two situations.

3. Sources of Finance for a Joint Stock Company

> **LEARNING RESULT**
> After reading this chapter, you should be able to :
> ◆ Understand and identify the long-term sources of funds for a joint stock company.
> ◆ Comprehend the meaning, advantages and disadvantages of Equity Shares.
> ◆ Grasp the meaning, advantages and disadvantages of Preference Shares.
> ◆ Define Bonus Shares, Right Shares, ESOP and Sweat Equity Shares.
> ◆ Describe meaning, advantages and disadvantages of Retained Earnings.
> ◆ Understand the meaning, types, advantages and disadvantages of Debentures.
> ◆ Differentiate between Shares and Debentures.
> ◆ Identify the role of Commercial Banks and Financial Institutes in providing business finance and their associated pros and cons.
> ◆ Understand short-term sources of funds for companies.

SOURCES OF FINANCE

A joint stock company requires two kinds of funds, namely short-term finance and long-term finance. Short-term finance is raised through commercial banks, public deposits, trade credit, customer advances, factoring, etc. and the long-term credit is raised by issuing shares and debentures, raising loans through financial institutions and commercial banks and by way of retained earnings, etc.

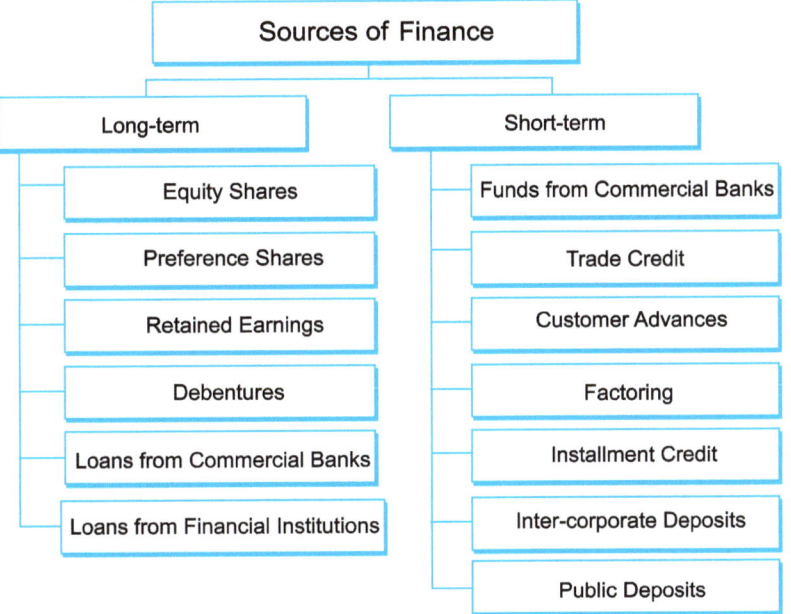

Fig. 3.1 Sources of Finance

LONG-TERM SOURCES OF FUNDS

Joint stock companies may face the need of funds from time to time in order to effectively carry out their business operations. These funds may be borrowed for varying periods of time. Depending on the payback period, these funds are classified either as short-term or long-term. Long-term funds are those that a company may need for long-term expansion of the business, *e.g.* purchase of land, plant and machinery. Generally, a business unit outsources its long-term finance not just from a single source, but a number of sources. Sometimes the magnitude of finance needed may make it necessary for the business unit to tap more than one source. Business organisations need large amount of money because they need to operate on a large scale. They compete against both national and international business firms. This increases the need of large corpus of fund to finance business operations. Given below are some sources of long-term funds for a joint stock company.

Equity Shares

Equity shares are those shares that carry voting rights and provide capital on a permanent basis. They are also known as *ordinary shares* for being the most common type of shares. The people holding these shares can be called the shareholders of the company. Generally the ordinary shares have a low nominal value. However, their market value may be many times over and above the nominal value. A company can raise funds by selling ordinary shares in the open market. It could be offered to the general public and existing shareholders alike.

Features of Equity Shares

1. The equity or ordinary shares of a listed company are registered on the stock exchange and can be readily bought or sold. Thus, for a joint stock company it represents a quick means of raising capital.
2. The equity or ordinary shares carry voting rights at the annual general meeting of the company. Thus, the equity shareholders have a voice in the management of the company that they have chosen to invest in. They have the right to be informed about the date and time of the annual general meetings of the company.
3. The equity share by virtue of its rights guaranteed by law enables the equity shareholder to elect, or dismiss the directors and auditor of the company.
4. The equity shares grants to its holders the right to enjoy residual profits of the company.

Advantages of Equity Shares

Advantages accrue to both holders and the business organisation. Some of them are given below :

From Shareholder's Perspective :

The equity shares confer certain rights and advantages to their holders that are listed below :

1. Give shareholders voice in the management– Shareholders have the right to approve the final dividend payable to them by the company. If they feel the company is withholding what is rightly due to them as dividend, the equity shareholders can withhold approval at the annual general meeting of the company. They have the authority to dismiss the directors. However, these powers can be exercised by following stipulated procedures.

    2. **Limits their liability**– Shareholders' liability is limited to the face value of the shares held by them.

    3. **Share in the prosperity**– If the company mints more profit than usual, the equity shareholders reap the benefit. The percentage of dividend is not subject to any ceiling. More profit will give greater dividend to the equity shareholders unlike preference shares where the annual rate of dividend is fixed.

    4. **Capital gains**– The value of equity shares may increase. Consequently, the capital gains for the shareholder also increase.

From Management's Perspective:

    1. **Imparts strength**– Large equity capital imparts prestige and respect for a company both in business and financial circles. Thus, its credit worthiness goes up.

    2. **Assets remain free**– Equity shares, unlike debentures, do not create any charge on the assets of the company. The company remains free to raise loans on its assets.

    3. **Permanency of capital**– The equity share becomes a lifetime capital to be refunded only if the company decides to close down.

    4. **No burden on the company**– The dividend to be paid on the equity share is decided by the company and is only payable if the company is making profit. If there is no profit there is no dividend.

Disadvantages of Equity Shares

From Shareholder's Perspective:

> Equity share is a high-risk investment; Returns are fluctuating and unguaranteed.

    1. **Low priority in return of capital**– A very serious drawback of equity share is that equity shareholders are the last to get their investments back in case the joint stock company goes into liquidation. This is a big disadvantage that ordinary shares carry. In case no fund is left after other shareholders, creditors and employees have been paid, the equity shareholders may not get back their investment.

    2. **Dividend not guaranteed**– The equity shareholders get dividend only after the preference shareholders have been given their dividend. In case the profits fall short, or shrink after the payment of dividend to preferential shareholders, the board can decide to declare no dividend or very low dividend to equity shareholders. Thus, there is no guarantee on the dividend of equity shareholders.

    3. **Fluctuating return**– The quantum of dividend accruing to the ordinary shareholder may change from year to year depending upon the profitability of the business organisation. Thus, the ordinary shareholder may not get expected return on his investment.

    4. **At the management's pleasure**– The management of the company may not declare dividends in any particular year if it feels that adequate profit has not been

made. In such circumstances, ordinary shareholders are deprived of their dividend for that year. Dividends are declared only if the management feels pleased.

From Management's Perspective:

1. Reflects inflexibility– The company is legally barred from issuing shares in excess of its authorised capital. This is a reflection of inflexibility.

2. May be costly– At times the cost of issuing equity share can be higher than issuing other types of securities.

3. Over-capitalisation risk– It is possible that a company could err in estimating its financial requirement and may over–capitalise. Since the equity shares are a permanent investment for the company, it will have to pay dividends for its lifetime, thus, causing valuable profits to be drained out.

4 Chances of loss of company control– Equity shares carry voting rights. Institutions and people may subscribe and hold onto major chunks of equity shares and thus gain control of the company for their own motives.

Preference Shares

Preference shares are those shares that enjoy certain privileges regarding the payment of dividends and the return of capital. Dividend at a fixed rate is payable on preference shares and this is to be paid before dividend is paid on equity shares. In the event of the liquidation of the company, the preference shareholders are to be paid back their capital before the equity shareholders.

Features of Preference Shares

1. The preference shares do not give voting right to their holders.
2. Preference shares enjoy priority over ordinary shares in terms of repayment. They will get their capital paid back before the ordinary shareholders in case of the company going into bankruptcy.

> **Preference Shareholders**
> - Receive their dividend distribution first.
> - Receive their capital before the equity shareholders.
> - Receive constant rate of dividends.

3. Preference shares carry a regular and fixed rate of dividend.
4. Preference shares are of different types, like cumulative and non-cumulative, participating or non-participating. They carry different rights with regard to payment of dividend and profit.

Types of Preference Shares

Preference shares are further subdivided into the following types of shares.

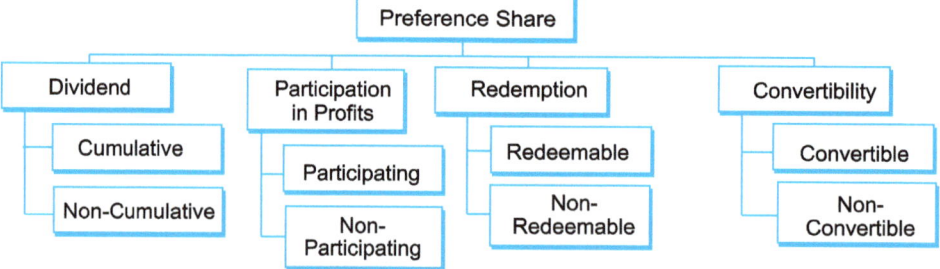

Sources of Finance for a Joint Stock Company | 41

1. **Cumulative preference shares**– This type of share entitles the holder to get accumulated dividends in case no dividend is given in any particular year due to reasons whatsoever.

2. **Non-cumulative preference shares**– Non-cumulative shareholders do not get any dividends if no profit is declared any year. Unlike cumulative preference shares, the non-cumulative shareholders dividend is not carried forward to or payable in the next year.

3. **Redeemable preference shares**– Redeemable preference shares are those shares that have to be paid back by the company after the completion of their maturity period. In other words, they are for a specified period of time.

4. **Non-redeemable preference shares**– These shares need not be repaid except upon the liquidation of the company. However, under the Indian Companies Act, a joint stock company cannot issue preference shares redeemable after a period exceeding ten years.

5. **Participating preference shares**– Such shares enable the shareholder to get his dividend on the preference share and then allow the holder to receive another portion of the dividend, in case, the remainder dividend is left over after ordinary shareholders have been paid their portion of the dividend.

6. **Non-participating preference shares**– The non-participating preference shareholders are not entitled to any extra dividend after the distribution of dividend to ordinary shareholders.

7. **Convertible preference shares**– The shareholders of convertible preference shares can get their shares converted into equity shares after a fixed time period.

8. **Non-convertible preference shares** – Such shares cannot be converted into equity shares.

Advantages of Preference Shares

Advantages accrue to both holders and the business organisation. They are as follows :

From Shareholder's Perspective:

1. **Fixed rate of dividend**– The preference shareholders get a fixed rate of dividend every year. The shareholders know what percentage of dividend per share they are entitled to and can calculate the approximate amount of dividend they will get. This is an advantage to them when compared to equity shareholders who do not know what rate of dividend their shares will bring for them.

> Preference shareholders enjoy priority over equity shareholders in payment of dividend and return of capital in case of liquidation.

2. **Cumulative**– Cumulative preference shareholders are entitled to profits for each year. If the company is unable to pay them for any particular year when it has declared a profit that unpaid dividend will have to be paid for in the future to them. As soon as the company gets in a position to make the payment, the outstanding amount of unpaid dividend will have to be ultimately paid to the shareholders.

3. **Preferential treatment–** The preference shareholders are paid their dividend before the ordinary shareholders get their dividend. Thus, preferential treatment is given to preference shareholders.

4. **Low risk investment–** In case of liquidation of a company, the capital of the preference shareholders is paid before that of the ordinary shareholders. This guarantees safety to their investment.

From Management's Perspective:

1. **Allows flexibility–** The company can redeem the redeemable preference shares and rid itself of debt. Thus the company has the flexibility and the choice of issuing preference shares to suit its requirements and needs.

2. **No interference in management–** Since preference shares do not carry voting rights, preference shareholders cannot interfere in the company management.

3. **No charge on assets–** Preference shares do not carry a charge on the company's assets which remain freely available for the company to take loans against.

4. **No burden on annual profit–** Since the dividends are paid out of the profits, it does not put any unnecessary burden on the company's financial resources.

Disadvantages of Preference Shares

The disadvantages of preference shares are listed below :

From Shareholder's Perspective:

1. **No share in higher than normal prosperity–** The dividend to be paid to the preference shareholders is fixed, hence they cannot be paid higher dividend in the event of a higher than normal performance by a company in terms of profit. They do not stand a chance to derive benefit when the company prospers extraordinarily.

- Preference shareholders lack a voice in the management.
- They have no share in above normal prosperity of the company.
- In the case of return of investment during liquidation they come after creditors have been.

2. **Dividend accumulation restricted to cumulative preference shares–** Ordinary preference shareholders will lose dividend if the company did not earn enough profit but the cumulative preference shareholders will get accumulated dividend if profits permit in the following year. This advantage is restricted to the cumulative preference shareholders and does not extend to ordinary preference shareholders.

3. **Lack of voting rights–** Preference shareholders do not have the right to vote at the annual general meetings of the company. They have no right to take part in the company's annual meetings where they can exercise their right to change the directors and auditors as the ordinary shareholders can do. Hence, preference shareholders have no say in the management of the company.

4. **Order of refund lower after creditors–** Preference shareholders are entitled, over and above ordinary shareholders, to get their investments back in the unlikely case of liquidation of the company. The priority, however, is given to the creditors of the company over the preference shareholders in such matter. The preference shareholders may not get back their investment if nothing remains after the claims of the creditors have been settled.

From Management's Perspective:

1. **Permanent burden–** Unlike equity shares, preference shares have to be paid fixed rates of dividend. This may prove costly for a company when profitability is low.
2. **High cost–** As compared to debentures, the cost of financing through preference shares is high. Dividend paid on preference shares is not deductible as expenditure. Thus, it raises the tax liability of the company.
3. **Not very attractive to investors–** Preference shares do not represent an attractive option to shareholders. They are not popular and not very effective as a means of raising capital.
4. **Legal formalities–** The redemption of preference shares is a lengthy procedure and involves a number of legal formalities. There are a number of conditions laid down by the Companies Act for redemption of preferential shares.

Distinction between Equity Shares and Preference Shares

Equity Shares	Preference Shares
1. Forms a comparatively larger portion of a company's share capital in terms of type of shares.	1. Forms a comparatively smaller part of the company's share capital in terms of type of shares.
2. Bestows voting rights.	2. Imparts no voting right.
3. Nominal value of equity shares is generally low.	3. Nominal value of preference shares is generally high.
4. Ordinary or equity shareholders are the last to receive dividends.	4. Preference shareholders are the first to receive their dividends.
5. Equity shareholders will be the last to receive their share of the company's residual value.	5. Preference shareholders are entitled to get their funds back before equity shareholders.
6. Ordinary shareholders' dividends vary with company profit.	6. Preference shares carry fixed rate of dividends.
7. Equity share is not redeemable during the lifetime of the company.	7. Preference share can be redeemed during the life time of the company.
8. In case of liquidation, if there is residual, equity shareholders are entitled to the residual too.	8. Preference shareholders are not entitled to the residual.

Bonus Shares (Bonus Issue)

Bonus shares are a company's 'gift' to its current shareholders, paid to them in the form of shares. They represent the accumulated earnings of the company over a span of time. The company could have paid these profits in the form of dividend to shareholders, but it chooses to give it in the form of shares. As

- Bonus share is dividend being paid to the shareholders in the form of shares.
- It is the capitalisation of the reserve funds into share capital.
- Bonus shares are fully paid-up shares.

mentioned above, these are not charged for, and are gifts from the company. These bonus shares are given out on a proportion basis, *i.e.,* shareholders get bonus shares on the basis of the number of shares they already hold in the company. Bonus share can be rightly assumed to be the capitalisation of the company reserve funds into share capital.

The conditions to be fulfilled before the issuance of bonus shares are :

1. A joint stock company can issue bonus shares only if authorised by its articles of association.
2. In the absence of such a provision in the articles board of directors of the company must pass a special resolution to the effect at the annual general meeting.
3. In case this issue causes the total share capital to exceed the authorised share capital, the capital clause of the memorandum of association can be amended to the effect.
4. The relevant stock exchange must be informed of the board's decision to issue bonus shares as soon as the resolution is passed in the company.
5. The issue of bonus shares must be supported by adequate undistributed profit.

Rights Share (Rights Issues)

In an issue of rights, a company gives its existing shareholders the right to buy a specific number of shares at a specific rate in the company within a specific time period. The shares are often offered at a discounted price and shareholders can buy in proportion to their current holding. The objective is to give employees the opportunity to maintain their proportionate ownership of the business unit. They resort to rights issue when companies have a problem in raising equity capital from the general public. Rights issue is offered to all shareholders, and may or may not be transferable. Since the company receives money in exchange for the shares, it is a source of capital for a company.

There are certain procedures to be followed with rights issue. When the company decides to issue shares after a period of at least two years from its formation or after one year from its first allotment of shares, it must first offer these shares to its existing shareholders. A notice of at least fifteen days is to be given for acceptance of the offer, after which it is considered to have been declined.

A company need not offer rights issue to its shareholders in the following cases :

1. Where the company passes an ordinary resolution for not offering further shares to existing shareholders, and gets it approved by the central government.
2. When an issue is made within two years of formation of the company, or within one year of the first allotment of shares, whichever is earlier.
3. When a special resolution is passed by the company stating that existing equity shareholders need not be offered such shares.
4. Where all existing shareholders decline the offer.

Distinction between Bonus Shares and Right Shares

Bonus Shares	Rights Shares
1. Bonus shares are new shares given free of cost to company's existing shareholders.	1. Rights shares are shares offered to existing shareholders at a discounted price through a letter of offer. It is a time bound offer.

2. The bonus share is the distribution and capitalisation of undistributed profits.	2. A rights share is used for raising of capital for growth needs of the company.
3. The Companies Act, 1956 does not regulate the issue of bonus shares.	3. The Companies Act, 1956 through its Section 81 regulates the issue of rights shares.
4. No minimum subscription requirement for issuing bonus shares.	4. 90% of the minimum subscription must be received within 60 days of the closure of bonus issue, failing which, the money has to be returned.
5. Bonus shares are always fully paid shares.	5. Rights shares may be partly paid-up.

Employee Stock Ownership Plan (ESOP)

ESOP's or Employee Stock Option Plans provide employees the right to purchase a certain number of shares of the company at a predetermined price. This right is awarded to outstanding employees *i.e.*, the employees who fulfilled the specified eligibility conditions (*e.g.* minimum period of service) and is meant to serve as a reward for their performance and to motivate others to improve their performance.

An ESOP is an option to buy the company's share at a certain price which could be the market price or a preferential price, *i.e.*, a lower than market price. If the company's shares are not listed on the stock exchange the management fixes the price of the shares.

Sweat Equity Shares

Sometimes a joint stock company may wish to acknowledge the special role of an employee or a director towards the better performance of the company. It could also be that an employee may have provided technical know-how or made available to the company some intellectual property rights without any consideration. Generally, what the company does is issue equity shares, under Section 79A of the Companies Act of 1956, to the employee in lieu of, *i.e.*, as a gift or acknowledgment.

However, a company has to follow the below given set of rules and procedures in issuing sweat equity shares.

1. At least a year must have passed since the company was issued the license to commence business.
2. A special resolution authorising the sweat equity share issue must have been moved and passed at the annual general meeting. The resolution should specify the name of the employee(s) to whom the sweat shares are intended to be issued, the number of shares the company intends to issue their type and value in the stock market.

- Sweat issue is thanks giving by the company to its employee(s).
- It can be given free or at discounted rate.
- A special resolution for sweat issue must be passed at the annual general meeting.

3. If the company issuing the sweat shares is listed with the stock exchange, the sweat equity shares are to be listed with the exchange.
4. The shares must be issued as per SEBI Regulations, 2002 (in case of listed companies) and as per Unlisted Companies Rules, 2003 (in case of unlisted companies).

5. These shares are issued subject to the condition that they cannot be sold off during a three-year lock-in period. In other words, they can be sold by their holders only after at least three years from the date of issue.
6. The employees have the option to receive the value of the sweat shares in cash in case they don't want the shares.

Retained Earnings

Normally, the profit that the company earns during any financial period is paid off as dividends to its various shareholders. However, sometimes it so happens that a part of the profit generated by the company is withheld, *i.e.*, not distributed as dividend. It is reinvested into the business. This is known as retained earnings or ploughing back of profit. It is practiced more by capital-intensive and growing industries. These industries require comparatively more funds to operate. Earnings may also be retained to pay off liabilities. We need to understand that retained earnings do not represent surplus funds subsequent to payment of dividends. Retained earnings indicate what a company did with its profits; it is an indicator of its dividend policy. It reflects a company's decision to either reinvest profits or pay them out to shareholders. However it remains a form of financing.

> **Calculating Retained Earnings**
> Starting Retained Earnings + Net Income during the period – Dividends paid = Retained Earnings.

Merits of Retained Earnings

From Management's Perspective:

1. Surplus with the company gives it greater strength of capital, especially in capital-intensive and growing industries.
2. It will not have look to external or bank borrowing in times of trouble, thus saving funds that would have been otherwise given away as interest to the lending source.
3. In industries which require large scale investment into research and development, it is a good way for small companies of finding the financial resource for such requirements.
4. In bad times when the company is not making enough profits, yet when it has to maintain a positive image of a profitable company, it can use the undistributed earnings to declare dividends and maintain its image.
5. Ploughing back of profit represents injection of additional fund into the company without any legal hassle and botheration. It represents an economical financing.
6. Extra fund in the form of retained earnings enables the company to go in for debt redemption and replacement of obsolete assets and programs of modernisation.
7. Retained earnings when re-invested represent tax benefits for the company.

From Shareholder's Perspective:

1. In capital-intensive industries retained earnings represent a good avenue of ploughing back the profit into reinvestment, thus giving the shareholders the maximum on their investments. The return on the ploughed back profit represents a very good investment of the shareholder's earnings.

2. Shareholders stand to receive regular dividends as shortfalls as made up from retained earnings.

3. Shareholders know their investment is safe when the company has large reserves to be used in times of need.

4. Retained profits add to the profitability and business capacity of the business organisation.

Demerits of Retained Earnings

1. **Wastage of resources–** If retained earnings are allowed to accumulate over a longer period of time and no constructive or wise use is made of that corpus; it amounts to waste of precious resources. The company, by not distributing that profit, withholds it from those to whom it should have been distributed. Logically speaking the retained earnings should be re-invested in such a manner that it generates the highest returns for the shareholders. What happens sometimes is that the retained earnings may be invested in assets that may fail to generate good returns for the company, and by extension, for the shareholders. In such a case it defeats the very purpose of retained earnings. That is why analysis of retained earnings is done with a focus on evaluating which action generated or would generate the highest return for the shareholders.

2. **Loss of company's image–** A company cannot go on keeping back profits which are ideally supposed to be distributed to the shareholders. It will lose its goodwill, and confidence of shareholders. Such companies could be seen as those with serious financial problems. Thus, financial institutions and banks may stay away from them causing the company to lose out in the long run.

3. **Possibility of manipulation–** Reinvesting of profit can be used to manipulate share price on the stock exchange. Investors may be duped and defrauded.

4. **Lopsided industrial growth–** Generally, a company invests its retained earnings in either expanding itself or in the same industry as itself. When many companies within the same industry follow suit, it may lead to the growth of one and the same industry at the cost of other industries. Had the profits been distributed to the shareholders they may have invested it in industries other than the one in which their company invested. The investment may have earned more growth in other industries. Thus, there is a danger of unbalanced industrial growth when companies use retained earnings to invest within the same industry.

5. **Unstable source of finance–** Retained earnings cannot be regarded as a stable source of finance for an organisation as profits may not turn out to be the same each year. The profits may fluctuate. In such case, the company may have to look somewhere else for funds.

Debentures

Debenture, a type of loan stock, is a medium or long-term debt instrument used by a company to borrow money from the holder at a fixed interest rate. The interest rate is subject to change depending on the prevailing credit market conditions. Basically, a debenture is a bond or certificate issued by a company to the holder of the debenture and is an acknowledgment of debt incurred by the company. It contains printed terms and conditions for the payment of interest there upon and the repayment of debenture amount by the company.

Debentures are for a specified period of time after which they have to be redeemed by the company. In the event of liquidation or bankruptcy, the debentureholders have a secured fixed or floating charge on the assets of the company and will have to be compensated or paid back the debenture amount and any interest thereupon by the company. The Debentureholders don't receive any voting rights in the company's general meetings of shareholders, but they may have separate meetings or have a say in the changes to the rights related to the debentures. The interest paid to debenture holders is a charge against profit reflected in the company's financial records.

Types of Debentures

1. **Redeemable and irredeemable debentures**– Redeemable debentures are those debentures that have to be paid back or redeemed after a certain time period. Irredeemable debentures are redeemed at the time of winding up of the company.

2. **Secured and unsecured debentures**– Secured debentures have a charge on the assets of the company; the charge may be specific or floating. In the case of liquidation of the company, the charged assets cannot be disposed-off without the permission of debentureholders. In case of their disposal, the debentureholders will have to be paid from the proceeds of the asset disposed. Unsecured debentures are free of charge on the company's assets. However, now all debentures are secured.

3. **Registered and bearer debentures**– Registered debentures are registered with the company and the holder must re-registered them under the new holder's name in case of sale or transfer of debentures. The bearer debentures are neither registered nor require any registration, and are easily transferable by delivery.

4. **Convertible and non-convertible debentures**– Convertible debentureholders are given an option to convert their debentures into shares after a time period specified at the time of issuance of debentures or later. The non-convertible debentures cannot be converted into shares.

Advantages of Debentures

From Management's Perspective:

1. **No dilution of control**– For a joint stock company, the debenture represents the advantage of raising loan capital or debentures without affecting any dilution of its control over capital. Its management remains undisturbed while it gets access to required funds for business.

- Debenture is an acknowledgement of debt by a company to its holder.
- Debentureholders have a charge on the assets of the company.
- Debentures are serial numbered.

2. **Low cost and economical source**– The rate of interest payable on the debenture raised by a company is fixed and does not fluctuate unlike the bank interest rate. The bank may raise its interest rate on its loans but the debenture interest rate is fixed and does not vary for the term of the debenture. Thus, debentures represent low and economical cost of finance.

3. **Tax saving**– The interest paid by the company to debentureholders is regarded as an expense by the government. The interest is thus a saving for the company in terms of tax on its income or profit.

4. **Flexibility**– Debenture represents flexibility because a debenture is repaid at the end of the redemption period when the company is no longer in need of funds. Thus, the company becomes free of the debt and regains its financial independence.

From Debentureholder's Perspective:

1. **Assured return**– The debentureholder enjoys his advantage in that he gets his interest on the debenture irrespective of whether the company makes a profit or not. Thus, his income is assured. He knows what sum of money his debentures will fetch him at the end of a fixed period of time.

2. **Safety of investment**– The debenture is guaranteed in terms of payment of interest as well as return of money invested in the debenture. Thus, for the investor debenture represents a secured form of investment.

3. **Priority in event of liquidation**– When the question of debt payment arises in time of liquidation, the debentureholder enjoys priority over other unsecured creditors. The fact that debentures represent secured loans relieves the debentureholder from worry of losing his investment. In the event of liquidation, the debentureholders are entitled to repayment on a priority higher than equity or preference shareholders.

Disadvantages of Debentures

From Management's Perspective:

1. **Charge on assets**– Assets of the company that are held as security against the debentures cannot be used as guarantee against any other loans or borrowings. This limits the company's borrowing capacity. Thus, debentures represent a limiting factor for borrowing purposes.

2. **Reduces creditworthiness**– If a company issues a large number of debentures, its creditworthiness is reduced in the financial market. Banks and financial institutions are reluctant to give loans to such companies.

3. **Drain on financial resources**– For a company that has fluctuating and unpredictable earning, issuance of debentures represents a very difficult proposition. The company will have to pay interest on debentures, and at the end of the redemption period will have to pay back the principal. This will strip the company of its resources.

4. **Reduces dividends**– The interest on debentures has to be paid from the company profit before the dividends are declared. In case of less revenue generations, the company may be compelled to pay low dividends to its shareholders. Consequently, this may show the company in poor light for its inability to pay good dividends to its shareholders. As a result, the market value of its shares may go down.

From Debentureholder's Perspective:

1. **No voting rights**– The debentureholder is not entitled to vote in the company from which he buys debentures. The debentureholder has no say in the management unlike the equity shareholders. This is disadvantageous for the investor who is not considered as a co-owner in the company.

2. No participation in prosperity– The debentureholder is entitled to just the amount due on the debenture irrespective of how much profit the company makes or how much dividend the shareholders get. This works to the disadvantage of the debentureholder especially when bank lending interest rates go up while the rate of return on the debenture remains static.

3. High unit price– Debenture is always priced higher than the share. This uneven pricing makes it difficult for small investors to invest in debentures.

Distinction between Shares and Debentures

1. A share represents the ownership of a company whereas debenture signifies creditorship. The shareholder is a part owner of the company whereas the debenture confers no such right upon its holder. In the eyes of the law the debentureholder is only a creditor of the company.
2. Share is a lifelong relationship with the company and will end with the liquidation of the company. But debentures are for a fixed period of time.
3. Shares confer voting rights to the holder. The shareholder can vote out the directors in their company and elect new directors. No such rights are vested in the debentures.

- Shares denote ownership in the company whereas debentures are an acknowledgment of debt.
- A debenture is for a certain period of time but a share is for the lifetime of the company.

4. The shareholder is paid out of the profits of the company. But the interest on the debenture represents an 'expense' to be paid whether or not the company makes a profit. If it cannot be paid from the profit, the debentureholder has to be paid from the capital of the company.
5. Shareholders get dividend which is fluctuating by nature, is not fixed, and depends on the profits of the company. However, debentureholders are entitled to a fixed rate of interest on the amount of the debentures.
6. Shareholders are entitled to have their voice in the management, they elect the board, decide policies. They attend the annual general meetings of the company. However no such rights are vested in the debentureholders.
7. Shares carry the risk of not getting any dividend if no dividend is declared a year, or of the company incurs a loss that financial year. Debentureholders are free of such risk; they are assured of interest irrespective whether the company makes a profit or loss.
8. In the case of liquidation of the company, the debentureholders are to be paid their amount before shareholders as they enjoy a priority in repayment.

The below given tabular representation will provide a more thorough understanding of the differences between shares and debentures.

Shares	Debentures
1. Shareholders are owners of the company.	1. Debentureholders are mere creditors of the company.
2. Dividend paid on shares is not fixed and depends upon the company's profit.	2. Interest is paid on debentures at a fixed rate. It cannot vary with the company's profitability.

3. Shareholders being the 'owners' have to bear maximum risk.	3. Debentures are usually secured by a fixed or floating charge till the time its holders are lenders.
4. Shareholders have a right to participate in the affairs of the company, vote and elect the directors.	4. Debentureholders can't participate in the affairs of the company.
5. Shares are not convertible into debentures.	5. Debentures may be convertible into shares.
6. Certain restrictions are levied on the issue of shares.	6. No restrictions on the issue of debentures.
7. Except for redeemable preference shares, shares are not redeemable.	7. Debentures are redeemed after a certain time period.

Loans from Commercial Banks

Borrowing from banks remains an important source of finance when the joint stock company is in need of funds. Both short-term and medium-term loans can be arranged through the banks. *Short-term* loans are for a period of up to three years while *medium-term* loans are for a period of three to ten years. Borrowing from the bank can also be in the form of *overdraft*. This means the company can overdraw its account with the bank within the limit mutually agreed upon. The bank charges interest on the amount of the overdraft facility availed by the business unit.

The bank charges interest on all borrowings. Before fixing the bank rate the bank will examine the credit worthiness of the business unit and take into account its size and scale of operations. The rate of interest to a large company may be variable or fixed. The banks are at liberty to adjust the rate of interest in accordance with changes in the Base Lending Rate.

When smaller companies require loan, it can be at a margin slightly above the bank's base rate. It can be either at an affixed rate of interest or a variable rate. Companies looking forward to purchase of property for business purposes can approach a bank and such a loan will be in the form of a mortgage.

Advantages of Loans from Commercial Banks

Raising loan capital through banks is advantageous in certain ways for a business organisation. Banks give loans depending on the value of business and its perceived ability to pay back the loan within the stipulated time. The loans from commercial banks have the following advantages :

1. The business organisations can tackle any obstacles that may come their way in the form of funds requirement when they have ready access to commercial bank financial help.
2. The business organisation gets the required loan for a fixed duration as and when it requires the need of capital. The timely availability is of utmost importance to the business unit.
3. Business ownership is in the hands of existing owners because banks do not interfere or takeover the management as in the case of equity investors.

4. A business organisation has the option of choosing the bank that offers it the most attractive terms and conditions for the loan. The quantum of the loan is never a hindrance for large business organisations.

Disadvantages of Loans from Commercial Banks

1. Loans have to be repaid to the bank under any condition. The bank will ultimately recover the principle along with the interest from the borrower. In extreme situation of financial difficulty, a business unit may even have to sell off some of its assets in order to pay back the loan. In case the firm is unable to pay back the loan, a bank can take legal recourse, thereby, causing a business unit to be liquidated to recover the principle and interest from the sale of its assets.
2. Interest has to be paid from the profits of the company which affects the distributable profit for the year. At times high rate of interest may have to be paid which can have a serious impact on the profitability of the business unit.
3. The loans taken by the business unit affects its credit ratings.
4. Collaterals may be required by the bank before it finally disburses the loan. Banks make sure the business unit can repay the loan which may sometimes be a time-consuming job.

Loans from Financial Institutions

Financial institutions have been set up by the government to facilitate loans to the business sector and have become a major source of finance for business. The modernisation and development of business had largely been through the assistance of these institutions. Besides giving financial services, financial institutions also provide managerial, technical and other assistance to business organisations.

Some of the popular financial institutions are :
- Industrial Development Bank of India (IDBI)
- Industrial Finance Corporation of India (IFCI)
- Small Industries Development Bank of India (SIDBI)
- Industrial Credit and Investment Corporation of India (ICICI)
- Life Insurance Corporation of India (LIC)
- General Insurance Corporation of India (GIC)
- State Financial Corporation(s) (as a group) (SFCs)

Advantages of Loans from Financial Institutions

The main advantages of institutional finance are given as under :

1. Ready source of finance– If a business organisation experiences difficulty in raising finance from the sale of its shares there are financial institutions ready to give it the necessary finance. If they need funds for expansion of business and modernisation of their plant and machinery financial institutions are willing and ready to give quick and timely loans when needed. Thus, we find that financial institutions are a ready source of timely finance for business firms.

2. **Give loans in foreign exchange–** If a business organisation needs loans for importing plant and machinery, or buying raw materials from abroad the financial institutions give timely loans in foreign exchange so that their business continues uninterrupted.

3. **Economical–** Reasonable and low rates of interest and convenience in repayments are an advantage when availing loans from financial institutions.

4. **Give business guidance–** The financial institutions guide the company in setting up and managing new business units.

5. **Underwriting and insurance facilities–** Besides offering loans, the financial institutions also provide underwriting or business insurance facilities to business units.

Disadvantages of Loans from Financial Institutions

The disadvantages of institutional finance are as follows :

1. **Need security for loans–** Financial institutions require security and fulfillment of stringent conditions for loans which many business units find difficult to fulfill.

2. **Insist on their nominee in borrower's management–** Financial institutions at times insist on having their nominees in the borrower's management, which proves to be a hindrance to loan disbursement.

3. **Red tape–** Borrowing companies have to pass through a number of formalities to get loans. At times red tape and lengthy procedures delay the process of raising loans.

SHORT-TERM SOURCES OF FUNDS

Short-term funds enable an organisation to react quickly in making the best use of a business opportunity that may have arisen at short notice. Short-term loans or funds are required by a business unit from time to time for the following reason(s) :

(a) Purchase of raw materials.
(b) Increasing the working capital urgently.
(c) For contingencies such as making payments to workforce and getting plant and machinery repaired without delay.

The sources of short-term funds for a joint stock company are given below :

Funds from Commercial Banks (Bank Credit)

Commercial Banks are a source of quick and convenient short-term loans and advances for companies. The primary function of commercial banks is to accept loans and advance funds on regular basis. These banks provide funds in the following forms :

1. **Loans and advances–** Loans are direct advances in lump sum to the borrowing firm that can draw the entire amount in one go. It can be paid back in agreed installments or as a onetime full payment. The bank charges interest on the entire amount from the date of sanction. Loans may be secured or unsecured.

2. **Bank overdrafts–** The overdraft is an amount a business organisation is allowed to overdraw from its bank account. The bank decides the amount the customer is allowed to overdraw and it charges an interest on the amount actually overdrawn. This facility enables the business firm to tide over working capital shortage for a few days.

3. **Cash credits**– Under the cash credit arrangement, a business firm is allowed to borrow upto an agreed limit. It is like a current account from which funds can be withdrawn and put back on time and again. The banks generally give this facility to firms that have good creditworthiness. They give secured cash credit where the borrower gives sureties or securities in the form of assets or guarantees. Banks can also give cash credit without asking for any security or guarantee. However, they insist on the borrowing firm submitting a promissory note signed by at least two sureties. This is known as clean cash credit.

4. **Discounting of bills**– Banks give the facilities of discounting or paying cash in exchange for credit instruments forwarded by the business firm. Promissory notes, bills of exchange and hundies are instruments bought by the bank from business units at a discount. When these instruments attain maturity, it is the bank that gets the value mentioned on the instruments. Thus, banks provide finance to the firms by timely buying their bills and taking upon themselves the burden of collecting payment on their maturity.

Advantages of Bank Credit

1. **Variety in choices**– Banks provide different kinds of funds and assistance. Thus, the borrower enjoys a range of options.

2. **Flexibility**– The credit facilities are flexible and the borrowed amount can be repaid in installments as per the customer's convenience.

3. **No meddling in borrower's business**– Another advantage is that banks do not interfere in the management of the borrower's business affairs.

Disadvantages of Bank Credit

1. Banks require a number of legal formalities before they advance loans and credit.
2. The banks grant loans against securities and a charge is created on the business unit's assets.
3. Commercial bank loans are for a short period of time and renewal is not guaranteed.
4. Commercial banks charge a comparatively high rate of interest which eats into the profit of the business unit.

Trade Credit

Trade credit is the window period granted by the suppliers to producers when the former supply the latter with raw material, components and other things for business operations. The credit period may vary from 30 days to 90 days depending on the terms, conditions and relationship between the two parties. The producer does not have to make payment immediately on the receipt of raw material or other goods. Therefore, it is a win-win option for the producer. In other words, this enables the producer to continue production and defer the payment for raw materials or other inputs. In effect, trade credit serves as getting a loan from the supplier without having to pay interest.

Advantages of Trade Credit

1. **Simplicity**– It represents a very simple and easy way of raising short term finance.

2. **Interest absent**– There is an absence of interest and the provision of security for credit.
3. **No charge on assets**– No charge is created upon the company assets.
4. **Deferred payment**– It is simply paying later for goods and services availed now.

Disadvantages of Trade Credit

1. **Requires larger working capital**– The business units charge a higher amount for credit sale. Hence, large working capital is required to supply goods on credit.
2. **Possibility of bad debt**– Certain cost is incurred for administering the credit accounts. There is a danger of buyers or debtors not paying back and the subsequent possibility of bad debts.
3. **No cash discount for buyer**– The buyer is at risk of losing the cash discount that he would have got in case of cash sales.

Customer Advance

Generally, all business units decide beforehand the terms and conditions with their distributors or retailers regarding payment terms for goods supplied by the business unit. Some organisations make it compulsory for their distributors or retailers to pay a certain sum as advance when ordering sales from them. This is generally a set percentage of the ordered volume. The organisation, when in need of funds, can readjust this margin and thus get much needed funds this way.

Advantages of Customer Advance

1. **Adds to the working capital**– The advance amount received at the time of booking orders provides good and timely working capital to business units.
2. **Require production target becomes known**– This enables the business firm to know beforehand the approximate demand and required output. This way it can adjust its resources to match the demand. The customer advance considerably reduces the quantum of bad debts or loss through order cancellations.

Disadvantages of Customer Advance

1. **Working capital locked up**– Many times, wholesalers and stockists don't like paying in advance for goods that will be delivered later. They prefer dealing with business units where their capital will not be locked-up by way of advance against goods ordered.
2. **Production orders difficult to cancel**– Once a firm has advanced payment against an order and wishes to cancel the order, it cannot easily do so without paying a penalty or forfeiting its advance.

Factoring (Accounts Receivable Financing)

Factoring is a process through which a company in direct need of funds can sell or mortgage its accounts receivable to a commercial finance company, known as a 'factor' in commercial terms. The factor buys the accounts receivable at a discount, immediately makes payment to the company and advances up to 60 per cent of the accounts receivable pledged with them. Thus, the organisation is saved from waiting for the payment to attain maturity. Factoring must not be confused with loan. It is not a form of loan, nor does it have any ceiling. It can be considered as a service by the factor to the organisation.

Advantages of Factoring

Factoring enables the business firm to encash its bills receivable when it needs working capital rather than wasting time waiting for their maturity. Thus, it enables the raising of finance through sale or mortgage of book debts. Another advantage is that factoring saves the business firms a lot of time and money that would otherwise have been spent in collecting the debts.

Disadvantages of Factoring

Factoring involves selling off the accounts receivable. A big disadvantage of factoring is that the accounts receivable have to be sold off at a huge discount. In other words it means that the business unit stands the chance of losing valuable profit when it gets rid of its accounts receivable. It has to sell off at a heavy discount because then the finance company takes upon itself the cost and effort of collecting the debts of the business firm. If any bad debts occur the business firm is no longer responsible. The loss has to be borne by the finance company.

Installment Credit

Installment credit is the system whereby a customer is given possession of goods upon part payment of the price and signs a contract to pay the balance amount in an agreed number of installments. It should be noted here that though possession is given to the purchaser, the title remains with the seller till all installments are fully paid. In case the purchaser defaults on payment, the seller has legal rights to take back the goods without making good the amount already paid by the purchaser. Banks and specialised finance companies are involved in installment credit sales and purchase. They pay on behalf of the purchaser and collect the amount in installments.

Advantages of Installment Credit

The big advantage of installment credit is that it enables the business firm to make use of the items bought (*i.e.* plant and machinery, heavy equipment, etc.) without having to pay in full at the time of initial purchase. The firm is able to make use of the asset and pay its cost from the earning generated by the asset.

Disadvantages of Installment Credit

The disadvantage of installment credit is that each installment paid by the purchaser or buyer conceals a huge amount of concealed interest which is charged by the seller.

Inter-corporate Deposits

These are deposits made by one company in another company ranging from a period of three to six months. A business firm having surplus funds may choose to deposit the funds with another company. This serves as a source of finance to the company with whom the funds are deposited. These deposits are arranged by financiers in the financial market and do not involve any legal formalities.

Advantages of Inter-corporate Deposits

The prime advantage of Inter-corporate deposit is that no legal formalities are involved. Second, there can be no public disclosure of the identity of the borrower. Third, the interest rate charged on inter-corporate deposits is lower than that charged by commercial banks.

Disadvantages of Inter-corporate Deposits

The availability of Inter-corporate deposits depends on the personal connections and relationships between the lenders and borrowers. The size of the company determines its contacts in the corporate world. A large company would have better contacts. In other words, smaller companies are not suitable for taking advantage of such deposits.

Public Deposits

Public deposits are deposits of money made by the public with non-banking institutions. These deposits represent loan from the public which could include employees and shareholders of the company. The non-banking institutions offer a higher rate of interest than banks which makes them popular with the general public.

Advantages of Public Deposits

1. The interest payable on public deposits is lower than that charged by the commercial banks.
2. The administrative cost of deposits is comparatively lower than that incurred on the issuance of debentures and shares.
3. Since the rate of interest is fixed, the company can derive the benefit of trading on equity.
4. Public deposits do not hold any charge on the company's assets. Therefore, the company's assets are free to be used as security for loans.
5. The company can return the deposits when it no longer requires its need.
6. The deposit holders cannot interfere in the company's management as they do not have any voting rights.

Disadvantages of Public Deposits

1. Newly formed business organisations may find it challenging to attract public deposits.
2. The borrowing company may find it difficult to pay back deposits when it has invested the same in fixed assets. Moreover, at the time of payback it may not have funds ready.
3. Public deposits are not a dependable form of financing. During economic turbulences, public deposits may be hard to get.
4. Depositors do not enjoy any security on their deposits.
5. The growth capital market can get restricted by the widespread use of public deposits.

SUMMARY

Long-term Funds – These are needed for expansion and growth of the business on a long-term basis. Its returns are spread over a period of several years.

Equity Shares – These confer ownership and voting rights to its holders and are very risky. Equity shareholders may not get any dividend if there is no profit and they also stand to lose their capital if a business unit becomes bankrupt. Equity shares are also known as ordinary shares.

Preference Shares – These get priority in matters of dividend payment but do not carry any voting rights for their holders. They are classified into different types, each type having varying rights and privileges.

Debentures – This is the public borrowing by the company through issue of certificates known as debentures which carry an indicated rate of interest. It is an acknowledgement of debt.

Finance from Commercial Banks/Institutions – Banks provide invaluable funds, both long and short-term to business, thereby, injecting life breath into business units. They provide other services like bills discounting, short-term credit and overdrafts.

Trade Credit – This is the extra time duration given to the organisation by its various suppliers to settle bills for raw materials or supplies purchased.

Customer Advance – It is the advance payment received by a producer or business unit from the reseller for the delivery of goods.

Factoring – This means raising funds through the sale of account receivable.

Installment Credit – A source of short-term funding whereby customers are given possession of goods upon part payment and the balance is paid in installments.

Inter-corporate Deposits – Short-term deposits done by one company in another company usually for periods of three to six months.

Public Deposits – Public deposit money with non-banking companies instead of banks. These non-banking companies give higher interest on deposits compared to banks.

QUESTIONS FOR PRACTICE

Very Short Answer Type Questions

1. List two sources of long-term fund for a joint stock company.
2. What is a Participating Preference Share?
3. What is meant by Cumulative Preference Shares?
4. What do you mean by issue of Bonus Shares?
5. Outline one advantage of issuing Debentures.
6. Give two differences between 'Shares' and 'Debentures'.
7. Differentiate between Bearer Debentures and Registered Debentures.
8. State any four sources of short-term finance for a joint stock company.
9. Write about two features of Bank Overdraft.
10. What is meant by Trade Credit?
11. Write a short note on Cash Credit.
12. What is factoring?

Sources of Finance for a Joint Stock Company | 59

Short Answer Type Questions

1. Can the organisation make a gift of shares to its employees at will?
2. What are Preference Shares? Explain the advantages of issuing these shares.
3. What are participating Preference Shares?
4. How flexible is a redeemable preference share from the management's perspective?
5. What are Equity Shares? Explain any three advantages of issuing Equity Shares from the standpoint of a company.
6. State three merits and three demerits of raising finance by issuing Equity Shares.
7. What are sweat equity shares?
8. Explain the meaning of Employees Stock Option Plan (ESOP).
9. Write short note on Retained Earnings.
10. Discuss five merits of Retained Earnings.
11. Distinguish between Bonus Shares and Right Shares.
12. Define Debentures. Describe any four types of Debentures.
13. Write a short note on customer advance as a short-term source of funds.
14. What is installment credit?

Essay Type Questions

1. Compare the rights of an Equity Shareholder with those of a Preference Shareholder.
2. Is Retained Earning beneficial for the long-term growth of a business organisation?
3. Under what circumstances does a company require short-term loans?
4. What are the advantages of obtaining funds from special financial institutions?
5. Throw light on the comparative advantages and disadvantages of Equity Shares.
6. What are Public Deposits? Discuss the merits and demerits of Public Deposits.
7. What is a Debenture? Explain any two advantages and any two disadvantages of Debentures from the company's perspective.
8. What are the drawbacks of issuing Debentures?
9. Discuss any four advantages of "Ploughing back of profits" from the company's standpoint.
10. State any six differences between a Share and a Debenture.

4   Banking : Latest Trends

> **LEARNING RESULT**
>
> After reading this chapter, you should be able to :
> - Understand the importance of online banking services.
> - Electronic fund transfer systems.
> - Electronic banking (e-banking).
> - Credit and Debit cards.
> - Automated Teller Machine (ATM).
> - Mobile Banking.

LATEST TRENDS IN BANKING

With the upward mobilisation of technology and its widespread and far-reaching footprints, the banking sector has been quick in harnessing the opportunity to provide better services to its customers. Bankers have progressively changed the very face of banking through the wide use of technology, and have been able to bridge the gap between rural and urban system of banking. Now all banks have a technology department that makes sure technology is readily available for day-to-day banking operations. When the bankers saw that the use of technology could give a quantum jump to their volume of operations, they began to work on new and hitherto unexplored areas, explore new market opportunities and expand the areas of banking. They diversified into new branches open to banking. Investments, insurance and under-writing of securities are a few areas they have been able to enter.

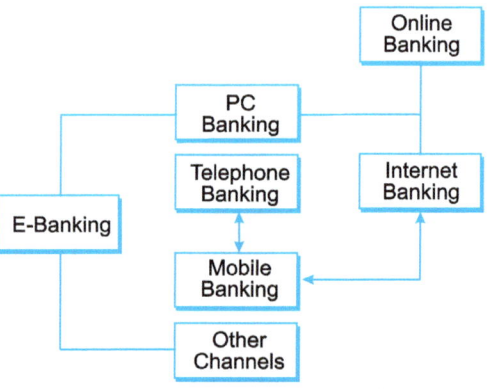

Fig. 4.1 Banking Latest Trends

Due to the subsequent availability of technology, banks have been able to provide new amenities to customers and have come up with customised services to suit different classes of clients or customers. The market for banks has expanded many times over as a result of rapid globalisation and easing of rules and regulations that in the past restricted the growth of the banking sector. Mobile banking, internet banking and widespread network of ATMs across the length and breadth of the country has been possible through the progressive advancement of communication technology, and its availability at a gradually decreasing cost.

With the increasingly widespread use of technology-driven gadgets such as the smart phone, there has been a marked progress in the evolution of mobile banking and its popularity. Banks are using innovative methods and programs to enhance their outreach and engage increasingly large number of prospective and existing customers. It is predicted by bankers that as the comfort level of the customers grows, the use of cheques will be rendered redundant as more and more customers will prefer making mobile payments rather than writing cheques.

ONLINE BANKING SERVICES

Online banking is a gift of information technology and communication to the modern mankind. The fast spread of online banking has been possible because of advancement in technology and its increased usage by the masses. Online banking is an electronic payment system that enables the customers to conduct financial transactions on a website securely operated by the bank.

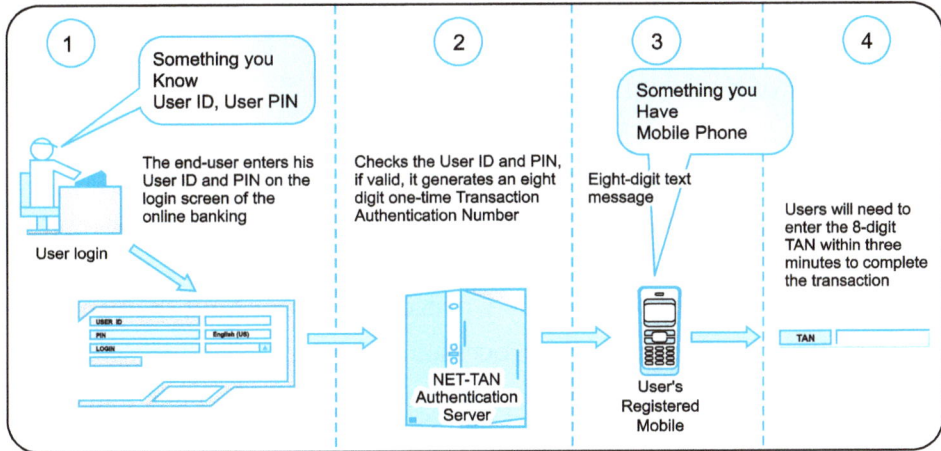

Online Banking was initiated by Chase Manhattan Bank in the early eighties. We can also call it electronic banking or just e-banking. Online banking offers various banking services that can be availed from the comfort of the customer's home or office anywhere and anytime without any hassle.

To use online banking facilities an account holder with internet access needs to sign up for free on the bank's website. The customer will be sent a password for customer verification. That's how the customer gains access to the bank's secured website through the username and password. After getting done with the formalities, the customer can avail all services offered by the bank in its online menu. Some of the services banks provide for online banking are mentioned below:

1. Fund transfer
2. Paying third parties
3. Investment purchase or sale
4. Credit card applications
5. Utility bill payments

Real Time Gross Settlement (RTGS)

The Reserve Bank of India started this scheme to allow bank customers to transfer money intra-bank via electronic medium. It is a continuous transfer of funds on an order basis. We can define RTGS as "the continuous settlement of funds individually on an order by order basis (without netting) by processing instructions as soon as they are received." We can consider RTGS as a system of fund transfer between two banks on a real-time basis. This means that the moment one bank transfers an amount to the other bank, the transfer gets completed. The bank which receives the fund must actually credit the amount to the beneficiary's account within a time period of two hours. These transfers or payments are irrevocable for they gain entry in the RBI books. The least amount allowed to be transferred through the RTGS transaction is ₹ 2 lakhs. This facility is available only at core banking solution-enables bank branches.

Information Needed for RTGS Transfer

1. Amount to be remitted.
2. Remitting customer's account number which is to be debited.
3. Name of the beneficiary bank and branch.
4. Name of the beneficiary customer.
5. Account number of the beneficiary customer.
6. IFSC code of the destination bank branch.

Features of RTGS

1. RTGS facility is available only at Centralised Banking System (CBS) enabled bank branches in the country.
2. The RTGS transactions are continuously processed throughout the banking hours.
3. RTGS transactions are individually processed.
4. The minimum amount that can be transferred through RTGS is ₹ 2 lakh. There is no maximum limit.
5. The beneficiary bank is required to credit the RTGS transacted amount to the beneficiary's account within two hours of receiving the transfer message.

National Electronic Funds Transfer (NEFT)

National Electronic Funds Transfer (NEFT) is a nationwide payment system facilitating one-to-one funds transfer under which people or firms can electronically transfer funds from any bank branch to any person, firm or corporate having an account with any other bank branch in the country participating in the system. There is no ceiling on the least or greatest amount allowed to be transferred through NEFT. Even the persons that do not have a bank account can deposit cash at the NEFT-enabled branches with the help of instructions for the NEFT transfer. However, only a sum up to ₹ 49,999 per transaction is allowed to be remitted. Such customers have to give full details including complete address, telephone number, etc.

Individuals or firms maintaining accounts with a bank branch can receive funds through the NEFT system. It is, therefore, necessary for the beneficiary to have an account with the NEFT-enabled destination bank branch in the country. The funds transfer takes place at a particular time. As NEFT operates in hourly batches, there are twelve settlements from 8 a.m. to 7 p.m. on weekly days and six settlements from 8 a.m. to 1 p.m. on Saturdays.

Process of Funds Transfer through NEFT

Any person who wants to transfer funds through NEFT has to fill an application form providing details of the beneficiary such as name of the beneficiary, name of the bank branch where the beneficiary has an account, IFSC of the beneficiary bank branch, account type and account number and the amount to be remitted. The application form will be available at the originating bank branch. The one who remits funds authorises the branch of the bank in which he holds an account to transfer the specified amount to the beneficiary. Customers enjoying net banking facility offered by their bankers can also make funds transfer request online. Some banks offer the NEFT facility even through the ATMs. However, people who don't have an account are supposed to give their contact details (complete address and telephone number, etc.) to the branch. This helps the branch to refund the money to the customer for when the beneficiary's bank account does not get credited with the remitter's money or the transaction gets rejected or cancelled for any reason.

Features of NEFT

1. NEFT transactions cannot be used for receiving foreign remittances.
2. NEFT is not free of cost; charges have to be paid for using the facility by the remitter. But no charges are to be paid by the beneficiary.
3. In order to receive funds through the NEFT system, the receiver must have an account with an NEFT-enabled bank branch.
4. The remitter is free to transfer funds despite not having an active account with the NEFT-enabled bank branch.
5. Non-account holders can transfer an amount of ₹ 49,999 only per transaction via NEFT system.
6. There is no limit on fund transfer for an account holder of a bank having the NEFT facility.
7. NEFT transactions can be done six times a day on working days and three times a day on saturdays.

Benefits of NEFT

1. The remitter need not send the physical cheque or Demand Draft to the beneficiary.
2. The beneficiary need not visit the bank for depositing the paper instruments.
3. The beneficiary need not be apprehensive of the loss or theft of physical instruments or the likelihood of fraudulent encashment afterwards.
4. It is cost-effective.
5. Credit confirmation of the remittances are sent by SMS or email.
6. Remitter can remit from his home or work place using internet banking.
7. Real time transfer of funds to the beneficiary's account in a secure manner.

Online Issuance of Demand Draft

A Demand Draft or DD, are also called Sight Drafts as they are payable when produced before the bank or its branch to pay a certain amount to the specified party. In case of a DD, the issuing bank charges a fee for preparing the draft. Demand Drafts are a secure mode of payment as they can't be dishonoured. Gone are the days when customers had to stand in a bank queue awaiting their turn to get the bank draft made. Now-a-days, demand drafts can be made even if the account holder is located in a foreign country and can be issue online as well.

Another interesting feature of DDs is that there is no need for a customer to have a bank account in the bank from where the bank account is being prepared. Demand Draft can be made by paying the bank in cash too.

Demand Drafts are often compared to cheques. But, the subtle differences between the two modes of payments should be noted. DDs are pay to order *i.e.,* they can be made payable to specified recipients only. Cheques, on the other hand, can be made payable to the bearer. Also, DDs are orders of payments by one bank to another, whereas cheques are orders of payment from an account holder to a bank.

Features of Issue of Demand Drafts

1. Money can be securely and safely remitted from one place to another through the demand draft.
2. The demand draft is irrevocable, hence cannot be dishonoured.
3. The issuing bank charges some commission for a demand draft.

Online Payments

Online payment is the electronic exchange of money. It involves use of computer network, internet and digital stored value systems. When a seller collects payment through the internet, he is in effect accepting an online payment. Online payment is the transfer of money from the customer's bank or credit card account to the seller's bank account. The online payment can be done from a debit card, credit card or other clearing house like paypal.

Features of Online Payment

1. **Speedy of fund transfer–** The speed of fund transfer is one defining feature of online payment. There is an immediate transfer of funds which greatly benefits businesses. Purchasing becomes easier.

2. **Flexibility in payment mode(s)–** Many payment schedules allow deferred and installment payments using a third party vendor. Purchasers can directly transfer money from their banks and enjoy the option of using either credit or debit card for making the payment.

3. **Convenience–** Payments can be done by the customer at any time of the day or night from anywhere.

Advantages of Online Payment

1. Online payment is a fast and convenient method of transferring funds and making payments. It suits the current lifestyle and working needs of the customers.
2. Fund transfer can be initiated online which is an easy task for the customer.
3. Transactions made online can be done even after normal business hours.
4. For people making regular business payments online there is automated billing facility to save time.

5. Security tools installed by online merchants and websites have now reduced chances of frauds, thus, making online payments comparatively safer.

Disadvantages of Online Payment

Online payments can be risky because hackers and cheaters still commit online frauds though on a very small scale due to tight measures employed by banks to check phishing and online thefts. However, there have been several instances when bank's official websites have been tampered with and customer accounts accessed illegally. This is the sole disadvantage of online payments.

Some websites may not be user-friendly and cause inconvenience and discomfort to online users. Novice users generally may find it hard to figure out the technique of online payments. That is why the mode of online payment is taking some time to percolate down the masses.

Many users still prefer traditional mode of payment as they find the online system technically off-putting. Illiterate people and those with humble upbringing still prefer visiting their preferred bank's nearest branch for doing transactions. Many people still prefer a face-to-face interaction with the bank staff for help and assistance.

E-Banking

E-Banking stands for Electronic Banking. It simply means performing banking transactions over the internet with the help of a computer or laptop. The customer accesses the bank's website using a username and password. Thereafter, the customer can transfer funds, make payments, make business transactions and safely avail other banking services. The customer using e-banking is absolved from the need of visiting the branch to execute his transactions.

Features of E-Banking

1. E-banking services are available 24 × 7 and 365 days in a year.
2. The bank is virtually at the fingertips of the customer.
3. It saves the customers from the hassle of carrying cash.
4. Each transaction detail is available to customers.
5. Instant records of all transactions made by the customer are available.
6. E-banking reduces the expenses incurred by the bank in maintaining its branches.
7. Through e-banking the bank is able to connect to far more number of customers through the mobile devices that it can ever do with its traditional method of banking.
8. E-banking reduces the load of the bank branches.

Advantages of E-Banking

1. E-banking is very convenient. One can make a transaction or do online shopping and make payment for it any time of the day. There is no close down time for the bank as far as e-banking is concerned. All that is needed is a computer and internet access to enjoy e-banking.

2. Geographical boundaries do not matter in e-banking. One can be abroad in a foreign country and can still do transactions with the bank located in home country. Therefore, physical barriers become irrelevant.
3. Electronic banking is very fast, efficient and effective. Transactions are executed instantly. Several bank accounts can be handled from just one e-banking site.
4. E-banking enables very effective asset management. This is provided through a number of programs like Microsoft Money and Quicken that most online banking sites have for the convenience of their customers.

Disadvantages of E-Banking

E-banking is difficult for those who are not familiar with the use of computer and the internet. Learning the intricacies of e-banking may prove difficult for a beginner. It may look intimidating and complex, thus forcing the customer with no other option but to switch to traditional banking. For safety and security, an e-banking customer may be asked for photo identification by the bank's website to enroll for an account. This may appear inconvenient to the customer.

1. Having a computer or a mobile in hand with internet facility is indispensable for a person wishing to transact via e-banking. Some users may take it as an added cost.
2. E-banking is boon for literate and tech-savvy users. Illiterate people or the ones living in rural areas with no internet access derive no advantage from the modern banking facility.

Debit Cards

A Debit card is a small-sized electronic plastic card issued by a bank to its account holders to get access to their accounts. Debit cards are a convenient way of making payment without carrying hard cash. They are linked to customer's account and come with a microchip that has information embedded related to his account and is readable read by an ATM, or an electronic reader. The account holder can use the Debit card to withdraw money from an ATM. As soon as that transaction is done, the machine makes entries in the customer's ledger and updates the account. The customer can also make purchases using the debit card at retail outlets that accept debit cards. The electronic reader available with the seller reads the debit card, forwards the transacted amount details to the customer's bank via internet and the amount gets debited. It eliminates the need for a cash transaction. Here it must be noted that the customer can make transaction within the limit of the amount that he has in his account.

Features of Debit Card

1. Debit card is issued by the bank to a bank account holder at the time of opening a savings or current account.
2. The debit card is meant to facilitate the withdrawal of money through an ATM machine.
3. It is also used to check on the account balance, get the account statement, transfer money, etc.
4. The debit card can be used for shopping and making online payments too. The amount being paid out is deducted by the bank from the holder's account balance.

5. It can be used to the extent the customer has balance in his/her bank account. Once the customer exhausts the bank balance the debit card cannot be used to effect payments till the account is replenished.

Credit Cards

A Credit Card is a legal instrument that authorises the user to make transactions, take ownership of the goods and avail services by paying through the credit card. The credit card in effect offers a type of credit to its holder. When the holder does a transaction through the credit card, the issuing bank, *i.e.,* the bank that issues the credit card, makes payment on behalf of the card holder. The card holder repays the money to the issuing bank at a later date. A credit card is different from a debit card in the sense that it is not connected to the customer's bank account. The total transacted amount along with a small service charge is debited from the customer's account at the end of each month payable by the card holder.

Features of Credit Card

1. Credit cards are issued by a finance company or a bank.
2. The credit cards are issued at the issuer's discretion. The issuer issues the cards after a potential customer requests for it and the issuer satisfies himself with the applicant's credit worthiness. Each credit card carries a specific serial number. It may also show the card holder's name embossed on it.
3. The credit card allows its holder to buy merchandise or service without actually paying for it at the time of the sale. The money for the transaction is paid for by the issuer bank or financial institution. The holder of the credit card then goes into the issuer's debt to the extent of the transaction.
4. The user of the credit card has to pay a monthly bill which includes the transacted amount along with a fee for use of the card. If the credit card holder fails to pay his credit card bills in time the issuer can take legal action against him or her.

Difference between a Debit Card and a Credit Card

Debit Card	Credit Card
1. Debit cards are like digitised pass books linked to an account holder's bank account.	1. Credit card is connected to the financial institution or bank that issues the card.
2. Debit cards can be used to withdraw money from an ATM.	2. Money cannot be withdrawn through a credit card.
3. Every transaction done using a debit card results in the card holder's account being deducted with the transaction amount.	3. Use of credit card makes the user indebted as credit cards offer a line of credit. No interest is charged if the monthly credit card bill is paid on time.

4. Debit card becomes redundant if the holder's account does not have the required balance. Putting money into the account is the responsibility of the account holder.	4. Credit card is an extension of credit for the holder. It is not linked to his bank account. When the holder uses the credit card, the issuer puts money towards the transaction and the user goes into debt.
5. The debit card holder does not get any monthly bill but e-statements are sent regularly.	5. The credit card holder gets a monthly bill for its use.
6. The debit card is issued to an account holder on opening an account with a bank.	6. Issue of credit card is at the discretion of the issuer and is subject to a person's credit worthiness and occupation.

Automated Teller Machine (ATM)

Automated Teller Machine or ATM is an automated machine that dispenses cash to the bank's customers, thereby, eliminating the need to stand before a cashier with a cheque in hand at the branch of the bank. The customer has to insert his debit or ATM card into the machine which then reads out the customer details and dispenses the desired amount of cash as per the information that the customer keys into the machine. An ATM is also capable of other related transactions, like deposition of cash into a customer's account, printing and furnishing mini statement of the customer's account. Bill payments and funds transfer are done through ATM machines. Mobile talktime is purchased and cheque books are requested through ATM machines.

MOBILE BANKING

With the advancement in information, communication and digital technology, banking services are expanding like never before. The gap between the rural and the urban customer is now being swiftly reduced as far as the reach of banking services is concerned. Mobile banking has come to the fore and it is now rendering traditional methods of banking out of date. It may grow in popularity with the increased penetration of internet. A number of banking functions can now be accomplished without going to the bank. High-tech devices such as smart phones make banking easy. In fact, we can call it 'anywhere banking' for it can be done from any place and at any given time. The person can ring up the bank and communicate the desired instructions or give instructions online or even use an application specific to the bank. Mobile banking services are classified as either 'push' or 'pull' depending on the nature of the service. When the bank conveys a message to the customer, it is known as a 'push'. When the customer requests some information from the bank and the bank complies, the process will be called as that of a 'pull' nature. Mobile banking services are either transaction-based or enquiry-based depending upon the nature of the service required by the customer.

Given below are some advantages of mobile banking :

1. Available 24 hours a day, a very convenient way of conducting financial transactions. It saves on time and the need to visit the bank.

2. It is secure, comparatively free of frauds that are associated with internet banking. It keeps the customer informed of all transactions on a real time basis through instant SMS alerts.
3. Fund transfer, bill payment, cheque payments, investment management, currency exchange and all other banking transactions can be conveniently done through mobile banking.
4. Cuts down the cost of banking. Thus, it is a cost-saving facility for the bank.
5. Renders the task of contacting potential customers easy and cost effective.
6. It is a novel way of enabling banks to sell their other banking and service products, *e.g.* bank loans.

SMS Alerts

SMS alerts is a service of mobile banking, a technology-enabled service from banks to their customers, permitting them to run selected banking services through their mobile phones using SMS messaging. It is a text messaging service through which text messages are exchanged between a bank and its customer electronically. The banks may send messages like marketing messages or messages alerting an event which happens in the customer's bank account, such as a large withdrawal of funds from the ATM, a large payment using the customer's credit card or amount paid into the customer's account, etc.

Depending on the selected extent of SMS banking transactions offered by a bank, the customer is authorised to carry out either non-financial transactions, or both financial and non-financial transactions.

The below given transactions can be done by the customer through SMS banking :
1. Account balance enquiry.
2. Mini statement request.
3. Electronic bill payment.
4. Transfers between the customer's bank accounts.
5. Stop payment instruction on a cheque.
6. Requesting for an ATM card or credit card to be suspended.
7. De-activating a credit or debit card when it is lost or the PIN is leaked.

Transfer of Funds through Mobile Banking

Mobile banking is a system that allows bank customers to conduct financial transactions through a mobile device such as a mobile phone or tablet. It can involve funds transfer between a customer's linked account. The customer can also make third party payments and check his bank statements.

Making Payments through Mobile Banking

All payments through mobile banking are facilitated by the Inter-Bank Mobile Payment Service (IMPS), a platform for making payments created by NPCI (National Payments Corporation of India) in collaboration with its member banks.

Bank customers can make payments instantly 24 × 7 from any location through mobile phones for various transactions like railway ticket booking through IRCTC, mobile/DTH recharge, mutual funds, credit card bill payments, insurance premium, online shopping, donations, electricity bills, gas, airlines ticketing, etc.

SUMMARY

Online Banking is the facility of carrying out banking functions using the internet.

RTGS or Real Time gross Settlement is the electronic fund transfer system available to bank customers during fixed hours daily. Money is transferred into beneficiary account within two hours. Minimum transfer amount is two lakh.

NEFT or National Electronic Funds Transfer is used to transfer funds from one bank to another entity or individual having an account with any other bank across the country.

Online Issuance of Demand Draft is carried out upon online request by the customer to the bank. The customer is charged by the bank and his bank account is debited with the amount to be paid to the specified party.

E-Banking is done by using the internet. All banking transactions can be carried out 24 hours in a day.

Credit/Debit Cards are forms of plastic money also known as electronic cards to enable the customer of a bank to withdraw money from ATM machines, make payments at retail shops and pay during online shopping.

Automated Teller Machine is installed by banks to facilitate money withdrawal from customer account by inserting debit or ATM card into the machine.

Mobile Banking is about performing banking transactions through the mobile phone.

SMS Alerts are used by banks to keep in touch with customers regarding their account transactions. Banks send information to the customers on their registered mobile numbers to keep them updated about their bank transactions.

QUESTIONS FOR PRACTICE

Very Short Answer Type Questions

1. What is RTGS?
2. What is NEFT?
3. List two benefits of NEFT transfer.
4. What is online bank draft?
5. What is E-Banking?
6. State any two services provided by a bank ATM.

Short Answer Type Questions

1. Explain any four features of RTGS.
2. List any four features of NEFT.
3. What do you understand by Online Payments?
4. List the different types of electronic banking facilities.
5. How is mobile banking advantageous to business? Explain by giving two examples.

6. Explain the purpose of Debit Card.
7. Explain the meaning of SMS alert.
8. List three utilities of SMS alerts to a bank customer.

Essay Type Questions

1. Explain how commercial banks have adjusted themselves to the fast changing commercial environment.
2. What are the useful features of online banking services? Explain.
3. Write a short note on the latest trends in banking.
4. Define Mobile banking and explain the services provided by mobile banking.
5. Write short notes on the following :
    (i) ATM
    (ii) Issue of demand draft online
    (iii) Credit card
    (iv) Debit card

5. Management : Meaning and Nature

> **LEARNING RESULT**
>
> After reading this chapter, you should be able to :
> - Understand the concept and definition of Management.
> - Identify the characteristics of Management.
> - Understand the nature of Management as an Art, Science and Profession.
> - Comprehend the objectives and importance of Management.
> - Define the functions of Management.

BASIC CONCEPT OF MANAGEMENT

In any business organisation, there are a number of people in a workforce doing different work at a time. For example, some people are engaged in producing a product, others are busy packing the finished products. Another section of people are engaged in checking that suppliers are getting paid, while another group is busy making salary slips for the employees. All these people are engaged in seemingly different work. However, their goals are the same, *i.e.* the goal of the organisation. Whenever any organised group of people works towards a common cause, there is a need to watch the activities to make sure that everyone is working in the right direction. If there is any deviation, it is corrected and the group's activities are coordinated to get the desired result. This continuous monitoring of the activities and ensuring that things are moving in the right direction is the function of management.

Management is defined as *"the process of achieving pre-stated goals by people who work jointly and individually putting together concerted efforts towards the agreed goals for an organisation."*

- It is a joint accomplishment. This means it requires joint and concerted efforts.
- More than one person is involved. Therefore, it is an activity.
- The goals of the work are pre-stated and understood by all.

As an activity the functions of management includes making a plan of what work is to be done, how it is to be done and then overseeing the work by directing, guiding and integrating the resources so that everyone works towards the organisational goals.

Management has been defined in various ways.

Henri Fayol states, *"To manage is to forecast and to plan, to organise, to command, to coordinate, and to control."*

Harold Koontz says it differently. He says *"Management is the art of getting things done through and with people in formally organised groups."*

Peter Drucker, the father of management says *"Management is a multi-purpose organ that manages business, manages managers and manages workers and their work."*

Thus, we see that management has been given different meaning and definitions by different people at different point of time. Some refer it as a process while some prefer calling it as resource coordination. Others have talked of management as a joint effort towards goal achievement.

In order to understand the objectives of management one needs to understand the general objectives of business. The basic objective of any business is to use humans and machines to produce goods and services that give value to its customers, sell these at a price that exceeds the input costs and gives an acceptable profit to the investor. It is the management that brings into process the sequence followed in achieving the just stated business objectives. The management is in charge of using different inputs in the right proportion to help the organisation meet its stated goals and objectives.

The resources that management has at its disposal are listed below :

1. Human Resource or Labour
3. Raw Materials
3. Finance or Money
4. Plant and Machinery

The management directs these resources through agreed process and methods. The end result is dependent upon the efficiency of the management in using its resources. In other words, management is the unit of an organisation that is responsible for running the business unit objectively and achieving organisational goals and objectives.

DIFFERENT ASPECTS OF MANAGEMENT

Management is a multifaceted activity. It has different roles, and can be viewed in different ways. These are listed below :

Management as an Activity

As any activity that requires the participation of human beings, we need to direct the efforts of the workforce in order to impel them on the course to achieving objectives. We must have chosen a few personnel at different levels of the organisational hierarchy who are required to direct the activities of all others subordinate to them, or responsible to them. Efforts have to be coordinated. Management coordinates the efforts of all engaged in an organisation. It ensures that activities are planned and executed instead of being haphazard. Management as a joint activity ensures that plans are being executed the way they are meant to be executed. This results in optimised use of resources and achievement of organisational objectives.

Since management is an activity in which people are supposed to be directed towards a stated mission or goals; there is a need to constantly give formal or informal and written or oral directions. There has to be a constant flow of information back and forth, so that corrective measures, if required, can be taken timely. That means decisions have to be taken from time to time in the light of current situation. These decisions involve human beings, moving them as and when required, putting them in positions where they can contribute constructively to the joint organisational efforts towards goal achievement, rewarding them as and when required and also penalising or ensuring that corrective measures to help regain lost ground are taken.

Secondly, management has to provide an environment for motivating employees to greater efforts and optimum output. It has to deal with humans not robots. Managers have to appraise the efforts of employees. Positioning and repositioning of employees has to be done on a continuing basis. Monitoring of their efforts has to be carried out on a regular basis.

Looking at management as an activity, we find the following three attributes :

(a) Involves the constant flow of information both upwards and downwards.

(b) Involves human beings and hence continuing interaction on the human plane.

(c) Involves decision making which must be based on the points listed above.

Management as a Discipline

Discipline can be defined as a branch of knowledge. We can also look at discipline as a system of rules and regulations for conducting any activity, or a method that regulates practice. Management is also a discipline. People working as managers are expected to perform certain duties in the lines of company policies. They have to follow certain codes of conduct which others in a different field of work are not expected to. In order to become a professionally qualified manager one has to invest certain years studying the subject matter. After gaining the qualification, the prospective manager has to produce evidence to certify his reception of knowledge and experience of management principles so that he gets hired to carry out the company's work.

The fact that management is a discipline is further propounded by sub-division of it into branches and sub-branches like marketing, human relations, accounting, finance, etc. It is being taught at university level, and its depth is increasing by the day. One can study for a diploma, a bachelor's or a master's program in various branches of management. Research into different aspects of management is being conducted and new ways and methods are being put into practice.

These evidences prove that management has its own place and position as an important discipline of study.

Management as a Process

We can also look at management as a 'process'. Process is a chosen course of action for the accomplishment of any task. To achieve any desired result we need to go about in a certain system that holds the promise of giving us our desired result or output. Management has shown us certain ways that can help us to achieve our goals. For example, the system of rewarding human efforts helps a manager get sustained and increasing efforts from employees. These rewards are given only after evidence of employee putting in greater efforts manifest themselves. It is not given before the employee puts in efforts. So, it is a process. This is just one example. We live and work in a society wherein the human and social factor will have to be taken into consideration by a manager. Results can be achieved only upon directing unified human efforts. Managers will require support and cooperation of all working as subordinates.

Management as a function is not a collection of mere activities. It is a process because all management activities have to follow a set sequence. Only by following a set pattern of sequence each activity lends credence to what went before it and what will come after it. When a sequence is followed, each activity supports the one that preceded it thereby giving meaningful results. This is what a process is all about.

The fact that management is a process is ratified by the fact that just like a process consists of certain sequence of events or actions wherein the sequence is of prime importance; similarly successful management also consists of certain sequences in controlling or directing human efforts wherein the following of the sequence is of great importance. If the sequential efforts are not followed, management may not get the desired result.

Management, as a continuous process, can be applied in both profit-making and not-for-profit units with equal finesse.

Management as a Group

It includes all those persons who manage a business organisation. When we refer to management of a particular organisation as good or bad, we are actually referring to the group of people who are managing the organisation. Management includes all managers from the CEO to the frontline managers. However, in management parlance, management includes only the top management because only they make important decisions, have the authority to use resources to accomplish organisational objectives and also bear the responsibility for their efficient utilisation.

DIFFERENT CONCEPTS OF MANAGEMENT

1. **Classical concept–** According to this concept, management is entrusted with planning, executing and controlling. It includes directing human energy towards the goal. This concept focuses on goal achievement but overlooks the social and human obligations.

2. **Productivity concept–** The productivity concept focuses on achieving the maximum output but sadly overlooks the human and other aspects of management which are so essential for goal achievement.

3. **Human Relation concept–** It focuses on human resources and getting goals accomplished through organising human resources. It aims at developing the workforce and optimising its efficiency.

4. **Leadership concept–** Here the focus is on developing leadership qualities and accomplishing stated goals through sound decision-making.

5. **Modern concept–** This concept breaks down management into different areas of operation leading to effective and efficient attainment of objectives. It takes into account both human and non-human resources that play their role in goal attainment.

NATURE OF MANAGEMENT

It is hard to define the nature of management. Different people look at management differently. While a mathematician defines management as a logical process, a psychologist considers it as an art of understanding human behaviour. However, such approaches are narrow as they look at a particular aspect of management, thereby, missing to see the subject as a whole.

Management as a Science

If we look at the literary meaning of science, it means a "study of the physical and natural world using theoretical models and data from experiments and observations." Many writers claim that management qualifies to be called a science. The advancements made in various areas of management, knowledge derived through research in behavioural sciences, etc. can be claimed as evidence to advance the claim of management as a science. Any branch of knowledge, if it claims to be a science, must fulfill the following criteria :

1. **Laws must be constant**– Scientifically established laws are constant. They do not change. Laws of gravitation, Newton's laws, etc. are some of the examples because such laws should be capable of being applied anywhere and anytime.

2. **Show a clear cause-effect relationship**– Scientific laws clearly show what happens under certain set of conditions. It clearly shows what can be the result when certain conditions are changed. It explicitly mentions what can be obtained by changing the inputs.

3. **Capable of withstanding the test of time**– A scientific law must be capable of proving itself any number of times. It must give constant result each and every time it is put to test.

The various functions and sub-functions of management have been studied in-depth; models and experiments have led to acceptable deductions and writers have hailed management as an applied science. But we have to accept the fact that management cannot claim to be a science like physics, biology or any other branch of scientific subjects. Science is subject to physical laws that hold good in all conditions and are constant. However, management is not subject to any such laws. It is true that management has a systematised body of knowledge; it works on concepts and certain principles that may be using scientific techniques. Although management uses scientific methods in many areas, like decision-making, it does not amount to being a complete branch of science.

Management as an Art

Likewise certain writers are of the opinion that management is an art. We may see 'art' as a skill that can be perfected through practice. This means that theoretical learning is not enough by itself; it must be backed up by constant practice that will enable the practitioner to overcome hurdles and reach goals. Here we see that though theoretical knowledge is useful, the practical experience is of great importance. It arms the practitioner with the wherewithal to accomplish what he or she sets out to do. Management as an art has the following characteristics :

1. **Practical knowledge**– Mastery over any art requires delving into its theoretical aspect as well as practicing it. Hence, simply gaining theoretical knowledge is not sufficient. It is very essential to know the practical use of theoretical principles. For example, to operate the computer, the user must know the purpose of the keyboard, CPU, mouse and some main computer programs. Likewise, a manager can never become an efficient employee just by graduating from a Business school. To excel, he

must learn the art of applying management principles in real life situations and gaining first-hand experience to validate his theoretical knowledge.

   2. **Personal skill–** Every manager gains the same theoretical knowledge as others in the business do. Yet, every manager has his or her own style of managing. That is why the quality of performance and success of every manager varies. For example, India is populated with many good playback singers. But Lata Mangeshkar has a distinct voice which no one has. Similarly, the art of management is also distinct because every manager does work on the basis of his nature, knowledge, notions, experience, etc. This distinctness makes someone a good manager and others bad.

   3. **Creativity–** Just like a good artist dreams to produce something authentic and new by using his creativity, management too aims to come up with a different product by making judicious use of its human and non-human resources. For example, Snapdeal.com is the first online retailer to put luxury yachts on sale for the customers.

   4. **Perfection through practice–** As the saying goes, "Practice makes a man perfect." In the same way, managers also learn and excel by way of trial and error. By applying management principles in their workplace, over a period of time they become well-honed in their roles.

   5. **Goal-oriented–** Even when we learn and practice an art, we look ahead to achieve concrete results. For example, a classical dancer may aim at performing for international audience. In like manner, management is also focused on accomplishing pre-set goals. Managers make use of men, money, machinery, raw material and management methods to materialise the goals.

In this way, we can conclude that management is an art of studying human nature and activities. And the success of the enterprise lies in proper interpretation of the human nature.

Management as a Profession

In general sense, profession means occupation. An occupation requires certain specialised education, training and skills which should be used in the interest of society as a whole. Management fulfills the requirements and manages to qualify as a profession on the basis of the below given criteria :

1. It is a **specialised body of knowledge** and capable of being transferred. In the current age, management as branched out into specialised areas like Human Resource Management, Financial Management, Marketing and Sales, etc.
2. Management, like any other profession, requires formal **education and training**. For example, a person becomes a qualified manager only after he has fulfilled the basic educational requirements of the profession.
3. Management professionals are expected to **serve the society** like other professionals.
4. Like all other professionals, management professionals also have a **code of conduct** which they adhere to.

GOALS AND OBJECTIVES OF MANAGEMENT

All or any organisation will have certain sets of values that it hopes to achieve. The higher the values set by the management, while each succeeding level of management sets out to break these objectives down into achievable goals. These values could be represented by all or any of the below given objectives set in clearer terms :

1. **Optimum utilisation of organisational resources**– The efficiency of any management is reflected in its optimum utilisation of available resources so that the costs can be progressively reduced and profitability increased.

2. **Profitability**– This is the basic objective and purpose of business. Naturally, it becomes the basic objective of any management. All activities of the management have their sights on this basic goal.

Fig. 5.1 Goals and Objectives of Management

3. **Improve quality of work**– The salability and subsequent profitability depends on the quality of manufactured product. Good workmanship and quality creates avenues for revenue. Greater the revenue, greater the profitability and by extension, more efficient the management.

4. **Well developed and trained workforce**– Every management seeks to train and develop its workforce so that production efficiency remains optimised. A motivated work force, capable of delivering beyond what is required is the dream goal of every management.

5. **Positive company image**– This is an important objective of the management which seeks to develop a positive corporate image that will help gain loyalty and goodwill in the market and society.

6. **Reducing cost of production**– More the management succeeds in reducing the cost of production, greater will be the resultant profit for the company. This is an important goal of the management.

7. **Sound decision-making**– Sound decision making lies at the very heart of success. Good decision making is what every management seeks and works towards. This ensures efficiency and better control.

CHARACTERISTICS OF MANAGEMENT

Management is not visible by itself. It is just similar to a government that cannot be seen yet its presence is felt through good governance. Likewise an effective and efficient management's presence is felt through the managed body. A characteristic of good management is that it gets work done through the concerted and coordinated efforts of the entire organisation. The basic characteristics of management are listed below :

1. **Goal-oriented, focuses on stated objectives**– The basic task of management lies in the attainment of certain objectives that are set by the higher management. The success or failure of the management is judged by the level of achievement of stated goals and objectives of the organisation. The management has to apply its collective experience and skills to stay focused on the organisational goals and objectives.

2. **Human-focused activity**– All management activities focus on human beings. Management has to work with people. It is the people who will help and contribute towards achievement of the organisational goals and objectives. Their skills and abilities have to be harnessed for the benefit of the organisation. Work and responsibilities have to be delegated to get results. The management has to motivate its employees to impel them to greater efforts and output. Employees have to be transformed into a close-knit, pro-active and cohesive group that is capable of reacting fast to a dynamic environment.

3. **Unrelated to proprietorship**– Modern trends and requirements in business require that the management is apart from proprietorship. The owners must not interfere in the day-to-day running of the business as there may be a clash of interest leading to under-achievement of desired objectives. Requirements of today's dynamics demand greater professionalism and dedication on part of management personnel which makes it all the more imperative that management be divorced from proprietorship.

4. **Continuous process**– Management is an integrated and continuous process that has to take inputs from different departments of the organisation. The successful implementation of organisational plans depends on the management. The management does not function in isolation. It receives informational inputs, both written and oral on an ongoing basis. In turn it has to establish and maintain open channels of communication. These are its eyes and ears. On the basis of received inputs depends its decision making functions. Judgement by one manager becomes the basis of decision by other members of the management. Management involves getting work done by the people. Therefore, the management has to constantly interact with the workforce. The managers have to be in contact with one another, both up and down the management hierarchy. Problems need to be resolved as and when they arise. All these functions are not a one-off function, but they are part of a never ending cycle. That is why management is called a continuous process.

5. **Involves decision-making**– One of the most important characteristic of management is that it involves decision-making. Managers have to make choices in order to optimise the use of resources while keeping the end result in mind. This requires an element of evaluation on part of the management. The level and accuracy of decision-making based on available data and evidence can make or break a business organisation. The quality of decision-making has a direct bearing on the profitability of the business unit.

6. Strongly integrates organisational resources– The basic characteristic of management is that it is required to make the best use of the available workforce, raw material, plant, machinery and finance. These are the basic resources of a business organisation, and a correct mix of these and some other inputs is needed to propel the organisation in the right direction. Strong integration is required, both on the horizontal as well as vertical plane in order to convert the organisation into a viable, well-oiled machine capable of meeting organisational long-term and short-term objectives.

IMPORTANCE OF MANAGEMENT

Management is that dynamic ability of a business organisation that brings together various resources of production, converts the raw materials into goods and generates revenue. The importance of management is brought forth in the below mentioned points :

1. Helps in achieving group goals– Management arranges the various factors of production, assembles and organises the resources and integrates the resources in order to achieve goals. It directs group efforts towards achievement of pre-determined goals. Management converts resource like men, machines, money, etc. into useful enterprise and coordinates as well as directs these in such a manner that result is attainment of business goals.

2. Optimum utilisation of resources– Management utilises all physical and human resources productively, thereby, leading to efficiency. It provides maximum utilisation of scarce resources by selecting their best possible alternate use.

3. Reduces costs – It aims at getting maximum benefits, though minimum input to get maximum output by proper planning. Management uses physical, human and financial resources in such a combination that minimizes the cost.

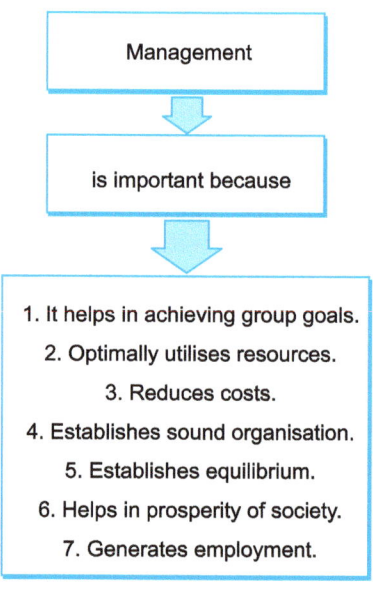

Fig. 5.2 Importance of Management

4. Establishes sound organisation– Establishing sound organisational structure is one of the main objective of management. It establishes effective authority and responsibility relationship *i.e.,* who is accountable to whom, who can give instructions to whom, who are superiors and who are subordinates. Management fills up various positions with right persons, having right skills, training and qualification. This streamlines the functioning of a business organisation.

5. Establishes equilibrium– It enables the organisation's survival in a changing environment. It keeps in touch with the changing environment. So, it enables the organisation to adapt the changing demand of market/changing needs of societies. It is responsible for growth and survival of organisation.

6. Prosperity of society– Efficient management leads to better economical production following which the welfare of people increases. Good management makes a difficult task easier by avoiding wastage of scarce resources. It also improves standard of living and profit which is beneficial to business.

7. Employment generation– By expanding business and contributing to the growth of business management creates employment opportunities, which in turn, generate income in hands and lead to satisfaction of human wants and needs.

LEVELS OF MANAGEMENT

This refers to the different tiers of management positions in an organisation. The levels in management are proportionate to the size of the business and workforce in the organisation. It is the chain of command, the level of authority and status of a managerial position.

The levels of management can be classified in three broad categories :

1. Top level   2. Middle rung   3. Supervisory or Frontline managers

Fig. 5.3 Levels of Management

Top Level Management

It comprises the board of directors, chief executive officer or the managing director. It is the ultimate source of authority and is saddled with managing the goals and policies for the business enterprise.

The role of the Top Management includes :
1. Framing the objectives and broad policies of the organisation.
2. Overseeing the preparation of department budgets, procedures, schedules, etc.
3. Strategic planning for the enterprise.
4. Appointing the middle rung management.
5. Controlling and coordinating the activities of the organisation.
6. Handling public relations.

Middle Level Management

The Middle Level looks after the functioning of their various departments on a daily basis. They focus on organisational and directional functions. They are answerable to the top management. The size of the Middle Level Management is determined by the size of the organisation.

Generally, they are assigned the following roles :
1. Ensuring implementation of organisational plans.
2. Making plans for the various departments of the organisation.
3. Training lower level management.
4. Interpreting and communicating policies from top level management to the lower level.
5. Coordinating the divisional activities.
6. Reporting to senior management.
7. Performance evaluation of junior managers.

Lower Level Management

Lower Level Management is also known as supervisory or the operative level of management. According to R. C. Davis, *"Supervisory management refers to those executives, whose work has to be largely with personal oversight and direction of operative employees."*

Their activities include the following :
1. Assigning of jobs and tasks and responsibilities to workers.
2. Issuing guidance and instructions to workers on a daily basis.
3. Ensuring quality control.
4. They communicate workers' issues to the higher management.
5. Provide on the job training to the workers.
6. Ensure necessary materials, machines, tools, etc. for getting the things done.
7. Evaluate performance of the workers.

MANAGEMENT AND ADMINISTRATION

Administration is different from management. According to Theo Haimann, *"Administration means overall determination of policies, setting of major objectives, the identification of general purposes and laying down of broad programs and projects."* It refers to the activities of higher level. It lays down basic principles of the enterprise. According to Newman, *"Administration means guidance, leadership & control of the efforts of the groups towards some common goals."*

On the other hand, management goes much beyond the mere setting of objectives and policies. It involves getting work done through joint human efforts. It is a group activity and its success depends chiefly on cooperation and human motivation towards efficient utilisation of organisational resources.

Difference between Management and Administration

Management	Administration
1. Management is the art of getting things done through the efforts of others by channelising their efforts towards organisational goals and objectives.	1. Administration is responsible for formulation of broad organisational objectives, plans and policies.
2. Management is an executing function. The level of success depends how well and efficiently various functions of management are executed.	2. Administration is a decision-making function. It ensures implementation of decisions.
3. Management decides who should do what and how he should do it.	3. Administration decides what is to be done and when it is to be done.
4. Management is a part supervisory function.	4. Administration is a higher level thinking function. It frames plans and policies.
5. Management requires technical and human skills to get work done.	5. Administration relies on human and conceptual skills, but not on technical skills.

FUNCTIONS OF MANAGEMENT

The actions or steps devised to be taken for achieving the goals of business are called as Management Functions. Management can be classified into the following six functions (Fig. 5.4) :

(i) Planning   (ii) Organising   (iii) Staffing
(iv) Directing   (v) Controlling   (vi) Coordinating

It is important to note that these functions are interdependent and inter-related and together they compose the entire process of management. They are overlapping and needed to be carried concurrently and not in any fixed manner.

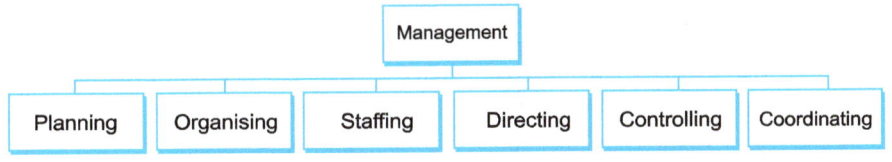

Fig. 5.4 Functions of Management

Planning is a primary management function that determines the course of action to achieve organisational objectives and goals. It calls for foresight, imagination and sound decision making. It is deciding what activity it to be done, where it is to be done, when it is to be done, how it is to be done and by whom it is to be done. Planning determines the direction in which the organisational ship has to sail.

Organising is the very essence of management. It creates organisational structure, distributes responsibilities and authority. It brings all members of the organisation together, binds them and creates a relationship, thereby, giving life and strength to the organisation and motivation to work towards the organisational goals.

Staffing ensures that all organisational positions are adequately manned by persons fit for the job. It selects, trains and assigns them a well-defined role, designed as per organisational needs. It also makes sure to provide enough opportunities for promotion to higher roles. In the last many years, staffing has grown into a full-fledged function known as Personnel or Human Resource Management. In simple words, Human Resource Management means finding the right candidate for the right job across all the departments of the organisation.

Directing focuses on the execution of plans. It motivates and leads the workforce towards the fulfillment of organisational objectives. A manager ought to develop the skill of issuing impactful orders and directions to get the work done by acquiring conscious obedience of the subordinates without hampering their productivity. A proper system of communication and ace leadership skills come in handy to feed the workers with the right information required to do the assigned work.

Controlling and Coordinating are connected with the function of production. They focus on producing the right goods at the right time and right quantity incurring the most cost-effective cost of production. They ensure quality control and the correction of deviations in performance.

SUMMARY

Concept of Management– Management can be seen as an activity or a process. It can also be understood as a discipline. We can classify it on the basis of classical concept, productivity concept, human relations concept, leadership or the modern concept.

Characteristics– It is goal-oriented activity, multi-disciplinary in nature and carried out with or without the use of human resources to achieve goals. It claims to be a science and an art, both.

Objectives– Major management objectives include profitability, optimum utilisation of resources, improving the corporate image, long-term growth and organisational expansion.

Functions of Management– Management is divided into different functional areas like planning, organising, staffing, directing, controlling and coordinating.

Planning– This function consists of setting the goals and objectives. It is future-oriented and focuses on what is to be done in the future. It formulates budgets, lays down policies and procedures and standards of performance to be followed by the organisation.

Organising– It is that function which organises and provides all required infrastructure and raw materials to the organisation so that it can achieve its objectives on a continuous basis. It assigns authority, duties and responsibilities and benchmarks for evaluating performance.

Staffing– This function ensures various organisational positions are occupied by competent employees having the right experience to discharge the given duties.

Directing– This functions aims at supervising and leading the employees in the direction of achieving organisational goals. Leadership is a very important component of this function. It translates plans into performance and aims at ensuring that employees are working efficiently.

Controlling– Ensures that goals are achieved in accordance with pre-planned and benchmarked standards. It checks deviations from the established parameters, analyses and ensures corrective action is taken.

QUESTIONS FOR PRACTICE

Very Short Answer Type Questions
1. Define the term 'Management'.
2. Give definition of Management by Henri Fayol.
3. Give two objectives of Management.
4. State two characteristics of Management.
5. Define Management as a process.

Short Answer Type Questions
1. Explain two aspects of Management.
2. Why Management is considered a discipline?
3. Identify any three goals and objectives of Management. Explain any two briefly.
4. List any three characteristics of Management according to your priority.
5. Write a short note on Management Science or Art?
6. Outline two reasons for considering Management as an Art.
7. "Management is all-pervading." Explain.
8. List two differences between Administration and Management.

Essay Type Questions
1. Illustrate what you understand by the term 'Management'?
2. Explain five characteristics of Management.
3. Explain the importance of Management in modern times.
4. Is Management more than just a mere activity? Support your opinion with relevant examples?
5. State the importance of Management for the successful functioning of an organisation.
6. "Management is an all-pervading function." Comment.
7. Does management qualify as a discipline?
8. Evaluate the claim of management to be a science.
9. "Management is getting things done through people." Discuss.
10. "Management is both Science and an Art." Comment.
11. "To manage a business is to balance a variety of needs." Explain.

6   Principles of Management

> **LEARNING RESULT**
>
> After reading this chapter, you should be able to :
> - Understand the meaning and nature of Management Principles.
> - Identify the need for Principles of Management.
> - Explain Taylor's Principles of Scientific Management.
> - Explain Fayol's Principles of Management.
> - Evaluate the relevance of Management Principles.
> - Compare the Principles devised by Taylor and Fayol.

The word 'principle' signifies a set of rules, guiding facts and fundamental logic behind a process, or function. By inference, principles of management denote the fundamental rules, established set of tried and tested procedures that practitioners of management use, or must use in order to get desired results. In any discipline, we require a set of basic road signs that we must follow in order to reach the favoured destination.

MEANING OF PRINCIPLES OF MANAGEMENT

Principles of management are the established ways a manager or a management must apply, the process and procedures that must be followed in order to get things done through the efforts of others. We must remember that management is not the activity of just one person; it is a joint and concerted effort of formal or informal groups within the larger context of an organisation. We can define the term 'principles of management' as the guiding signs or lighthouses of management to be followed in order to get the desired results for an organisation.

CHARACTERISTICS OF PRINCIPLES OF MANAGEMENT

The main characteristics of management principles are defined below :

1. Universal applicability– All of the principles have universal application in the sense that they can be applied in all kinds of organisations, irrespective of the nature of the organisation. An organisation may be a non-profit making body, a religious body, a joint stock company; but the principles will be equally applicable in all cases.

2. Dynamism– The principles of management take into account the dynamic nature of the business environment. They are flexible, capable of being adapted to the size, nature and dynamics of the business. A very important aspect is that the principles have not been given any demarcating priority levels. This means that all are of equal importance.

3. Cause and effect relationship– These principles have a cause and effect relationship. In other words, the principles assume that certain things will result, or are likely to result if such and such situation is allowed to develop. For example, it assumes that environment unity will develop in the presence of peace and harmony. It also assumes that by influencing organisational behaviour, it can increase the output of the organisation. These are examples where the principles can be seen in a cause and effect relationship.

4. Influence human behaviour– The principles of management assume that by their proper application, the organisation can improve the area of decision-making. By division of labour and resultant specialisation, it is assumed, that with gradual passage of time, production can be increased.

5. Flexibility– The principles of management cannot and must not be applied blindly. We must remember that these are not absolute principles like those of applied sciences which will always hold good. They can be 'expected' to deliver only upon the happening of certain conditions.

6. Equal importance– All principles are given equal importance and are not prioritised.

NEED FOR PRINCIPLES OF MANAGEMENT

Principles of Management are needed for the following reasons :

1. To bring efficiency– Principles of management are designed to bring about greater efficiency to business. By providing guidelines to managers about how to function in different situations, these guidelines bring about greater efficiency. By resolving problems in an improved manner we can achieve better results.

2. To crystallise thinking– These principles help managers to look at situations with greater clarity. It systematises their thinking, making problem solving easier.

3. To develop management skills– Following the principles of management, managers can develop their managerial skills. The principles of management provide them the framework for a systematic and scientific training. It develops their skills and problem solving abilities.

4. To evaluate managerial performance– The approach to managerial problem solving by different managers when evaluated in the light of scientific principles of management helps evaluate their managerial skills.

5. Further business and social goals– Scientific principles help managers to direct human energy and motivation towards organisational goals. Reduction of waste, both of raw material and man-hours, helps in promoting the business goals. At the end of the day, it also means improving the social welfare which again works for the benefit of business.

TAYLOR'S PRINCIPLES OF SCIENTIFIC MANAGEMENT

According to Frederick Winslow Taylor, also known as the 'propounder of principles of scientific management', scientific management revolves around knowing exactly what it wants the workforce to do and subsequently ensuring that they do it in a way that is the best and the cheapest. Taylor advocated that the management should identify workers with the kind of jobs they were best suited to do and allocate them the tasks accordingly. He was of the view that cordial relations between the management and workers would provide an environment of progressively increasing output. That is why he called it a Mental Revolution.

Scientific management was meant to provide the management with a trained and efficient workforce that could accomplish standard work. It was expected that as this workforce became more and more familiar and trained with its recurring task at the production line, it would give increasing output, thereby, increasing the production and decreasing the costs of production. This was the basic idea behind the principles of scientific management. Taylor rooted for incentive or reward for enhanced output by the worker supplemented by cordial and amiable relations between the workforce and the management.

Frederick Winslow Taylor

Taylor's scientific management is based on careful observation and objective analysis. Its basic principles are discussed below :

1. **Cooperation, not individualism**–Taylor objective was that there should be an environment of cooperation in a business organisation. The workers should work as a unified and single workforce and not as individuals. He knew that if the employees saw themselves as individuals, then personal interests would stand in the way of organisational objectives.

> Scientific management is concerned with knowing exactly what you want your workforce to do and then seeing that they do it in the best and most economic way.

2. **Training and development of workers**– The productivity, according to Taylor, lies in a well-developed and well-trained workforce. Taylor suggested the workforce should be selected keeping in view the requirements and needs of the work environment.

3. **Science, not rule of thumb**– Taylor suggested that every job and the method of accomplishing it should be subjected to close scientific scrutiny and the production tasks should be scientific and well-planned. In fact, he suggested that all areas of the work right from the work place and its environment, to the plant and machinery should be standardised.

4. **Harmony, not discord**– Taylor advocated for cordial employer-employee relationship as a pre-condition for good industrial environment. He pleaded for a just and fair division of the gains of prosperity and profit between the workers and the management.

5. **Division of work and responsibility**– Taylor suggests that planning must be kept separate from all operations so that the management can focus on this function, and must not waste their time getting engaged in daily issues. The workers will be efficient if they focus on production.

FAYOL'S PRINCIPLES OF MANAGEMENT

Henri Fayol, a French industrialist, developed a general theory of management through his long practical experience. He classified all business activities into a set of six categories like :

(a) Manufacturing (b) Selling
(c) Financial (d) Accounting
(e) Security (f) Managing

He further sub-divided the managerial function into the following :

(a) Forecasting and planning (b) Organising
(c) Coordinating (d) Controlling
(e) Commanding

He went on to call for certain traits and characteristics in a managerial person such as technical and educational qualification, work experience, physical, moral and mental characteristics. He advocated not a few but fourteen principles of management which are defined below :

Henri Fayol

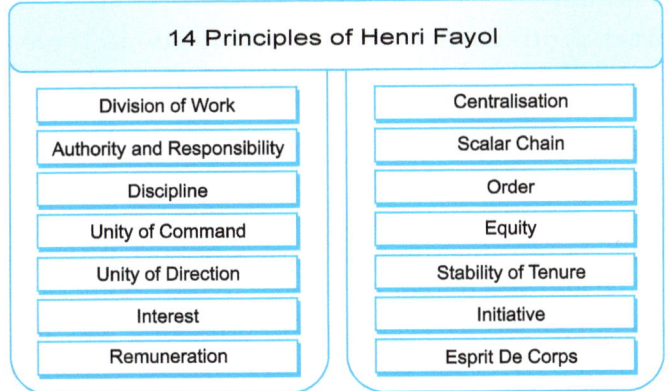

1. Division of work– Fayol was of the opinion that each worker should concentrate on one type of job. In this way he would gain skills and bring about efficiency in his work. He was not in favour of workers being transferred from one type of job to another.

2. Authority and responsibility– Both authority and responsibility go hand in hand. There should be parity between the two. People given authority must also be made accountable. There could be a lack of responsibility if the accountability part was missing. Taylor advocated a balance between responsibility and accountability.

3. Discipline– This is seen as responsible for the smooth running of the organisation. System of penalties should exist and rules and regulations must be observed for the smooth running of the organisation. There must be a healthy respect for rules and regulations in the entire organisation.

4. Unity of command– This implies that every employee must be accountable to just one superior from whom he must get all instructions. Man cannot take instructions from more than one master. Absence of the unity of command weakens the authority, divides loyalty and will create confusion in an otherwise disciplined organisation.

5. **Unity of direction–** This implies that one set of activities must have one plan, and just one head or superior to whom the group will look up for directions. In other words, it means that the instructions to perform a set of activities must come from one person only; there should be one plan for one activity or set of activities. This principle must not be confused with unity of command. Unity of command relates to the functioning of the workforce, whereas unity of direction refers to the way activities are to be performed.

6. **Prioritising organisational interest over personal interest–** The personal interests will have to be sacrificed for the sake of the larger organisational interest. Personal interests must not be promoted at the cost of organisational interest.

7. **Just and fair wages–** The workers must be fairly and justly compensated for their efforts in the process of production. This will motivate the workers to put in more efforts. They will feel rewarded for their efforts. The organisation will also benefit from the higher inputs by the workforce.

8. **Initiative–** All employees must be encouraged to take initiative in the implementation of the production plans. They must be made to feel that they are valuable and their suggestions are valued by the management. This initiative will be a source of strength for the organisation.

9. **Balance between centralisation and decentralisation–** There should be a careful balance between centralisation and decentralisation of authority and control. The right balance, according to Fayol, will be seen by the workers and lower management as increasing their importance in the organisation and it will boost their morale, thereby adding to the efficiency of the organisation.

10. **Equity–** Fair treatment to workers. Employees should be treated justly and fairly and there should be no discrimination of any sort. Favouritism, injustice and victimisation must not be allowed to rear their head in the organisation.

11. **Stability of tenure–** Service security will go a long way to promote loyalty to the organisation. The longevity of the tenure will help the worker acquire expertise in the work process. Where there is constant change in the workforce, workers do not get the opportunity to familiarise themselves with the methods of production, and thus, they cannot acquire skills. Inducting new workers means increasing training costs and more financial strain to the organisation and a loss.

12. **Order–** This principle is concerned with systematic arrangement of men, machinery and material. There should be a specific place for every employee in an organisation. Fayol explains that there is no fixed order of doing things; but any form of disorder is unacceptable. Disorder results in loss of time and increased mistakes, which in turn, hamper productivity and increased cost of production. Fayol believed that if the right person is doing the right job, the production would increase, as would the revenue of the organisation. Fayol also said that if employees are allotted tasks that maximize their skills, it would result in accomplished workers, more productivity and higher profit margins.

13. **Esprit de corps–** The management should promote team spirit to bring about harmony and good feelings among the employees.

14. Scalar chain– In management hierarchy, the managers are part of an invisible chain like authority scale. Right from the first line supervisor to the president, every member of the company has certain amount of authority. While the President possesses the most authority; the first line supervisor the least. Lower level managers should always keep upper level managers informed of their work activities. The existence of a scalar chain and obedience to it are necessary if the organisation aims to be successful.

This concept is explained as below. Suppose, in an organisation there are employees A, B, C, D, E, F, and G serving at various levels. If employee 'D' has to communicate with employee 'E' using the scalar chain, the route would be like D to C and all the way up to A and then all the way down to E. Thus, it will take a long time to communicate.

The drawback of this process is that it is too time consuming and thus ineffective where time is precious. To overcome this limitation of scalar chain, Fayol introduced the concept of 'Gang Plank'. This concept enables two executives of the organisation of different departments at the same level to communicate directly in case of emergency, so that speedy decisions and actions can be taken. In this case D can communicate directly with E using the "Gang Plank" denoted by the line at the bottom of the pyramid DE in the given figure.

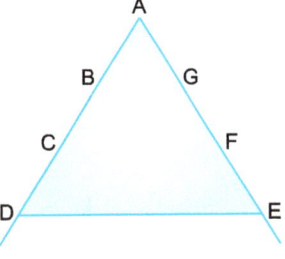

Fig. 6.1 Gang Plank

Taylor and Fayol – A Comparison of Doctrines

Let us compare the doctrines of Taylor and Fayol. Taylor propounded his theory in or around 1911, while Fayol came up with his version in 1914. Fayol looked at the issues dogging the management and tried addressing issues from the top to bottom, whereas Taylor looked at things from the shopfloor level. Taylor focused on increasing output by expecting the worker to perform better in the face of better training and intensive division of work. This was to be supplemented by an incentive system to reward and recognise increased output. Fayol believed in bolstering management to increase output by division of management on the basis of nature of managerial work.

Both Taylor and Fayol took a different approach. Fayol looked at things from a manager's point of view, whereas Taylor saw it as an engineer that he actually was. Both of them were accordingly affected and this can be seen in what they propounded. Though both emphasised on the division of work, they differed in their focus of action. Taylor advocated for differential payment to workers based on their output while Fayol favoured profit sharing.

Similarities

1. Objective of both the propounders are same. They strive to bring about an improvement in management practices.
2. Both stress upon the performance of human resource as very important.
3. Both stress upon the fact that an environment of mutual cooperation and understanding is essential.

Differences

1. Taylor's principles of scientific management advocate the maximisation of profit for the entrepreneur; but Fayol looks at management as comprising five distinct

functions which together constitute the process of management and stresses that the manager must receive feedback in order to be in a position to address issues.

2. Taylor's principles work themselves from the bottom, from the shopfloor, focus on the worker, and moves up the industrial hierarchy. This is in contrast to Fayol's principles that start from the top and move down the management hierarchy.

3. Fayol presents a theory of management that is universally applicable; whereas Taylor proceeds to address issues such as how to enhance worker productivity while reducing wastage. Taylor fails to take into consideration the fact that workers have social needs, they value recognition and they must be motivated in more than one way to put in more efforts.

Difference between Taylor and Fayol

Frederick Winslow Taylor	Henri Fayol
1. American Scientist.	1. French Industrialist.
2. Shopfloor level.	2. Managerial level.
3. Emphasised on time and motion study.	3. Gave importance to planning and controlling.
4. Recognised as an engineer's approach.	4. Recognised as a manager's approach.
5. Confined to production management.	5. Confined to overall managerial job.
6. Scientific based management.	6. Laid stress on administration.
7. Advocated differential payment system.	7. Emphasised on profit sharing for managers.
8. Scientific observation management.	8. Personal experience translated into universal truth.

RELEVANCE OF MANAGEMENT PRINCIPLES IN THE CONTEXT OF MODERN MANAGEMENT

The principles of management have universal applicability. As far as their application is concerned, it may vary from organisation to organisation, depending on the circumstances and conditions, such as the work culture and the needs of business. The general principles apply to all business organisations because all business houses share the common goals and objectives of profit maximisation and optimum utilisation of resources.

The principles of management are being implemented in all business organisations today. The work is divided among all employees in all business units. The division of functions and duties may differ from one organisation to another but the basic divisions are all-pervading in terms of work, authority and responsibility. The unity of command and unity of direction principle is also followed in by all companies. The order and equity principle is followed in all business units. The scalar chain of command is followed in most cases and above all, personal interest is not allowed to override corporate interest.

Thus, it can be concluded that principles of management are very much relevant in the context of modern management.

> **SUMMARY**
>
> ***Principles of Management–*** *The basic truth that establish relationship between cause and effect are derived from observation and experiments.*
>
> ***Characteristics of Principles–*** *They are universally applicable, capable of flexibility and are dynamic in nature. They effect human behaviour and establish a cause and effect relationship.*
>
> ***Need for Principles–*** *To increase management efficiency, help business organisations to attain goals and objectives.*
>
> ***Taylor's Principles–*** *Confined to production management advocating differential system of wages. It aims at increasing the productivity of workers.*
>
> ***Fayol's Principles–*** *Look at problems of managing an organisation from the top managements' point of view. Give importance to the controlling function. It aims at bringing about an improvement in efficiency of the administration.*

QUESTIONS FOR PRACTICE

Very Short Answer Type Questions

1. Who is known as the 'Father of Scientific Management'?
2. State one characteristic of the Principles of Management.
3. List two principles of management.

Short Answer Type Questions

1. What you understand by the term 'principle of management'?
2. Write any two features of principles of management.
3. Define the principle of equity as conceived by Henri Fayol?
4. State any two principles of management.
5. List any three principles that an organisation applies in managing its affairs.
6. What is meant by Unity of Direction?
7. What is 'Scalar Chain' in management?
8. Distinguish between Unity of Command and Unity of Direction.
9. What do you mean by 'Gang Plank'?
10. What is meant by 'Order' as one of the management principles framed by Henri Fayol?
11. Why are principles of management needed?
12. Write a short note on 'Authority and Responsibility'.

Essay Type Questions

1. Do you agree that the principles of management have universal applicability?
2. Why is management acquiring increasing importance in modern business?
3. Explain why principles in functional management are needed?
4. Summarise your understanding of Taylor's principles of scientific management.

5. Division of work contributes to efficient running of a business unit. Evaluate this statement in the context of today's business environment.
6. Explain the meaning and importance of Scalar Chain.
7. Describe the following principles of management:
   (a) Authority and Responsibility
   (b) Stability of tenure
   (c) Division of work
8. Describe any five principles of management formulated by Henri Fayol.
9. Bring out five basic differences between the principles of management formulated by both Taylor and Fayol.
10. Appraise the applicability of management principles in the current dynamic business scenario.
11. Why has management in modern business become very important?

7 Functions of Management and Coordination

> **LEARNING RESULT**
> After reading this chapter, you should be able to :
> ♦ Understand and define Management Functions such as Planning, Organising, Staffing, Directing, Coordination and Controlling.
> ♦ Assess their importance in management.
> ♦ Understand how coordination can be achieved through other management functions.

Management is a set of different functions that aim at ensuring optimum utilisation of the organisational resources to give continuing profit to the organisation. The functions of management are common to all business organisations. The management functions must be distinguished from business functions like sales, purchases, personnel, etc. These functions and its implementation may differ from organisation to organisation and from product to product. These are called as the operative functions.

CLASSIFICATION OF MANAGEMENT FUNCTIONS

The functions of management have been classified in various ways by different writers and practitioners of management. According to George and Jerry, the function of management consists of planning, organising, actuating and controlling; while according to Fayol, it is forecasting, planning, organising, commanding, coordinating and controlling. Koontz and O'Donnell are of the view that though management basically consists of planning, organising and controlling, it also includes the important functions of staffing and directing. The binding function is that of coordinating all the other functions and that is the very essence of management.

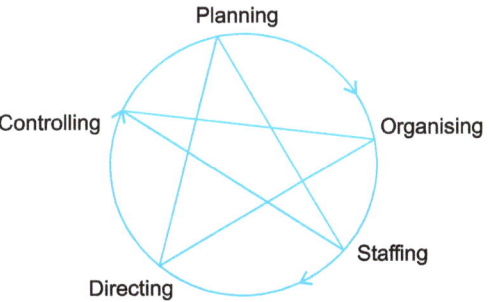

Fig. 7.1 Functions of Management

Managerial Functions and Sub-functions

The various functions and sub-functions of management are :

1. Planning– Policy-making and budgeting, forecasting and scheduling, strategy and decision-making, research and development.

2. Organising– Delegation of duties, task allocation, divisionalisation, span of management and functionalisation.

3. Staffing– Manpower planning, recruitment, selection and training of workforce; compensation and wage fixation, appraisal, promotion, etc.

4. **Directing**– Leadership, motivation, supervision, communication, etc.

5. **Controlling**– Reporting, setting up of benchmarks and standards, correction of deviations, etc.

Managerial Functions	Operative Functions
Planning	Framing of human resource policies
Organising	Manpower Procurement
Staffing	Human resources planning, Compensation of employees.
Directing	Training and Development, Motivation, Employee relations.
Controlling	Performance appraisal industrial relations.

Planning, organising and controlling remain the basic functions of management. Staffing has now become an important and separate function and is assuming increasing importance in today's environment. Along with staffing, directing is becoming increasingly important as the size and magnitude of business operations tend to increase with globalisation. There is an increasing need to support, guide and motivate the organisational workforce which may be physically located away from one another and away from the central management. There is also the need to communicate with them and this need grows depending on the expansion of business operations.

Many modern writers and practitioners of management argue that with the need for new products and their improvement, research and development should be considered as a function of management. The management must exercise creativity and bring out new and improved services and products that will make a difference to life and society. The ways and methods of production must stay in tune with changing times. Thus, business will be able to lower the cost of production. This will add to business revenues and further business goals.

Similarly, public relations are being considered as part of management functions whose objective is to present a good corporate image before the society. The business organisation must be seen as reaching out to the modern society that constitutes its customer base.

PLANNING

This is a very important function of management and deals with the anticipation of the future and of likely problems that may arise and their possible solution in order to provide a hindrance free environment for the business to carry on. It includes the framing of policies and procedures, objectives and strategies for the business. Planning function identifies the objectives of the business, it specifies the steps necessary to achieve those objectives and comes up with the time framework within which the objectives have to be achieved.

According to Koontz and O'Donnell, *"Planning is deciding in advance what to do, how to do it, when to do it, and who to do it."* According to these writers, planning bridges the gap from "where we are to where we want to go."

Another writer, Theo Haimann agrees with Koontz and O'Donnell in saying that *"planning is deciding in advance where we want to go."*

Characteristics of Planning

Planning function has certain features that are defined below :
1. **Future-oriented**– Planning is done with an eye on the future.
2. **Involves making choices**– Planners have to identify best options from the many available.
3. **Continuous process**– It cannot come to an end. Where one plan finishes, another starts.
4. **Take-off point for all other functions**– All other management functions take root in planning.
5. **Seeks to achieve business objectives**– Planning seeks fulfillment of organisational business objectives.

Steps in Planning

Listed below are the steps followed in the planning process :
1. Defining objectives.
2. Data collection.
3. Developing planning parameters.

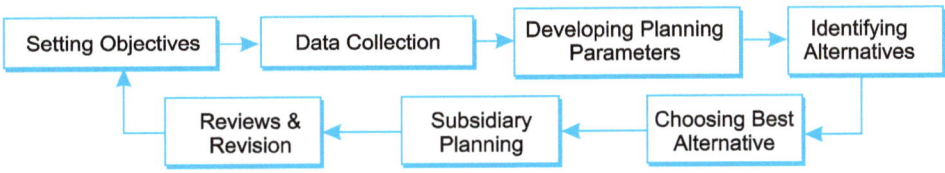

Fig. 7.2 Steps in Planning

4. Evaluating alternatives.
5. Choosing best alternative.
6. Subsidiary planning.
7. Reviews and revision.

Benefits of Planning

The planning function has the following benefits accruing to the business :
1. Helps overcome hindrances to business.
2. Improves business efficiency.
3. Serves as control and rectification of deviations.
4. Encourages innovation and creativity.

Limitations of Planning

Despite all advantages of planning, it has its own inherent weaknesses and limitations which are listed below :

1. **Lack of accuracy**– The future and expectations from the future are the very foundation of planning. If the actual picture of the future turns out to be very different from the anticipated picture, the plans can be a complete failure. The forecast about the future cannot be predicted with great accuracy. The planners may be biased, they may be prejudiced and thus reliable data may not be forthcoming. Planning can be rendered weak due to unreliable data supplied to planners.

2. Time consuming affair– Planning is a continuous and a time consuming affair. Data collection, analysis and interpretation require considerable time. Planning fails us when decisions have to be taken quickly and timely. If decision-makers wait for long, they stand the chance of losing business opportunities.

3. Potential barrier to creativity and initiative– This is a time of dynamic business environment wherein factors are fast changing in intensity and strength. Once plan are put into effect they have to be adhered to by all employees. However, the changed dynamics may have rendered the plans obsolete. But once they have been formulated, they cannot be abandoned even when they fail to help achieve the organisational goals. The policy of strictly sticking to plans may thus adversely impact the employees' creativity and initiative.

4. Human attitude– When plans are formulated to suit personal interests, they cannot fulfill organisational goals. Elaborate reporting procedures, or red tapism are all examples that are born out of human attitude and act as hindrances to smooth functioning of an organisation when incorporated into a plan. This human attitude is commonly visible in many organisational plans.

5. External barriers– Certain external factors severely restrict the degree of accuracy of planning. For example, we cannot predict with accuracy the way the economy will behave in the future. Changes in political, technological environment also cannot be predicted with any reliability. But these are important factors that need to be taken into consideration while planning. The unpredictability of these factors limits the accuracy of planning.

6. Costly affair– Planning is not without its expense in terms of money. Data collection, forecasting, analysis and all other related activities cost a lot of money. At times, the monetary cost surpasses the benefits that can be derived from the planning. This tends to discourage planning for the smaller business organisations.

ORGANISING

It is the function of determining the activities to be performed, allocating these activities to various administrative units and assigning managerial authority and responsibilities to people employed in the organisation.

According to Koontz and O'Donnell, "Organising is that part of management that involves establishing an intentional structure of roles for people in an enterprise to fill."

Henri Fayol says "to organise a business means to provide it with everything useful to its functioning such as raw materials, tools, capital and personnel."

According to Chester Barnard, "Organising is a function by which the concern is able to define the role positions, the jobs related and the co-ordination between authority and responsibility."

Steps in Organising

The organising function is performed by a manager by taking the following steps :

1. Identification of activities– First thing first. The activities to be carried out by the organisation have to be identified, grouped and classified into units.

Fig. 7.3 Steps in Organising

2. Departmentally organising the activities– This step requires the manager to combine and group similar and related activities of the company into units or departments. This process is called Departmentalisation.

3. Classifying the authority– The next step is about classifying the authority and how much of it is allocated to the managers in the hierarchy. The job of top management is to formulate the policies, the middle level staff is into departmental supervision and the lower level workers supervise the foremen. Clarifying the authority is useful in making the company's operations efficient. It also arrests the wastage of resources, prevents duplication or overlapping of efforts and aids smooth working of the company.

4. Coordination between authority and responsibility– Healthy relationships between various groups facilitates smooth interaction which assists the organisation in achievement of its goals. Every employee gets acquainted with the authority and gets heedful of the person they are supposed to report. A fair organisational structure is out in the open for all the employees.

Importance of Organising

The factors that make the Organising function helpful to a business organisation are mentioned as under :

1. Brings specialisation– Organisational structure is a network of relationships in which the work is divided into units and departments. The division of work assists in bringing specialisation in numerous activities of the company.

2. Clarifies authority– Organisational structure serves in defining every manager's role. This activity is performed by illuminating the manager about his powers and how they should be used. Well-defined jobs roles and responsibilities helps in making the managers work in a more skillful manner. The end result of this practice is increased productivity.

3. Well-defined jobs– Organising function allocates the right work to the right person by choosing them to work for various departments on the basis of their qualifications, skill and experience. This lends a helping hand in giving definition to the jobs and giving a clear picture to the employee about his role in the company.

4. Effective administration– Organisational structure specifies the role different managers are expected to perform. This division of work helps the managers specialise in their roles. The result of this system is an efficient and effective administration.

5. Coordination– Organising facilitates coordination among different departments of the business concern. Clear-cut relationships are formed among different posts and mutual cooperation develops among individuals. When top level managers exercise their authority over the inter-connected activities of the lower level managers, it results in harmony of work.

6. Scope for initiative and a new change– In a setting where every employee is allowed to perform a clear-cut role and enjoy independence at work; the manager gets a good platform to develop his talent base. The manager gets an environment conducive for taking independent decisions. This phenomenon gives way to more scope for introducing new changes in the business operations.

STAFFING

This management function looks after the human resources of the organisation. It recruits, trains, develops and places people in appropriate positions to harness their talent, experience and skills for achieving organisational objectives. According to Koontz and O'Donnell, *"the managerial function of staffing involves manning the organisational structure through effective and proper selection, appraisal, and development of personnel to fill the roles designed into the structure."*

In a newly launched business, staffing would come as a third step next to planning and organising. But in an old and operational business, staffing is a continuous process.

Nature of Staffing

1. People centric and concerned with all levels of workforce.
2. Human relation skills must be applied by every manager to provide guidance and training to the subordinates.
3. Responsibility of every manager.
4. A continuous function in a newly established as well as a running organisation.

Steps in Staffing

We can identify the following steps in the staffing function :
1. Manpower or human resources planning.
2. Recruitment, selection, placement and orientation.
3. Training and development.

Fig. 7.4 Steps in Staffing

4. Appraisal, promotion and transfer.
5. Remuneration.

Importance of Staffing

The staffing function is an important managerial function because of the following reasons :

1. Staffing is the chief function that ensures that all other functions are also performed well. If there is no competent staff in place in an organisation, other functions like planning, organising and control functions will not happen correctly.
2. Big organisations pay a good portion of their revenue to employees as salary. Moreover, the organisations also spend on recruitment, training and development of the employee. So, it gets important for the organisations to perform the staffing function properly so that optimum output could be obtained from the employees.
3. It is the management's responsibility to figure out the manpower requirements well in advance. It has also to train and develop the existing employees for career advancement. This will meet the requirements of the company in future.
4. By staffing in an efficient manner, the management can show to the employee how much importance it attaches to them. This way, the morale of the staff gets a good boost.
5. It is the human factor that is useful in the effective utilisation of latest technology, capital, material, etc. The management can hire the right employee by performing the staffing function.

DIRECTING

It is a very important function in the management of any enterprise and helps the managers in deriving quality performance from the employees, thus, propelling the organisation towards the right direction. It involves supervision, communication, good leadership and motivating the employees to contribute to the best of their capability.

According to Koontz and O'Donnell, *"Direction is a complex function that includes all those activities which are designed to encourage subordinates to work efficiently and effectively."*

Human says, *"Directing consists of process or technique by which instruction can be issued and operations can be carried out as originally planned."*

Directing is concerned with instructing, guiding, supervising and inspiring people in the organisation to achieve its objectives. It is the process of telling people what to do and making sure they do it in the best possible manner.

Characteristics of Directing

Directing as a management function has the following characteristics :

1. Pervasive function– Directing is required at all levels of organisation. Every manager provides guidance and inspiration to his subordinates.

2. Continuous activity– Direction is a continuous activity as it continuous throughout the lifetime of an organisation.

3. Human factor– Directing function is related to subordinates; therefore, it is related to human factor. Because human factor is complex and behavior unpredictable, direction function becomes important.

4. Creative activity– Direction function helps in converting plans into performance. Without this function, people would become inactive and physical resources meaningless.

5. Executive function– Direction function is carried out by all managers and executives at all levels of an enterprise.

Elements of Directing

Given below are the major elements of directing :
1. Supervision   2. Motivation   3. Communication   4. Leadership

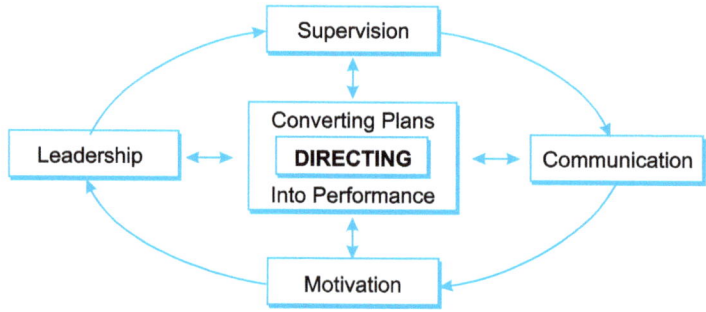

Fig. 7.5 Elements of Directing

Supervision

After the employees have been instructed regarding what they have to do and how to do, it is the duty of the manager to see that they perform the work as per instructions. This is known as supervision. Managers play the role of supervisors and ensure that the work is done as per the instructions and the plans. Functions performed by the supervisors :

1. Supervisors clarify all instructions and guide employees to work as a team. And also solve most of the routine job-related problems of subordinates.
2. Supervisors clarify orders and instructions issued to subordinates and ensure compliance.
3. They ensure that subordinates have the required facilities to perform their jobs.
4. Guide the activities of subordinates in performing their jobs.
5. Coordinate the work of the subordinates.
6. Detect errors & omissions and rectify them.

Motivation

Motivation is one of the important elements of directing. It requires a manager to inspire the employees to act and give the expected result. It is a driving force that pushes a person to work in the best way for achieving organisational objectives. Motivation may be in the form of financial incentives like bonus, commission and perks or non-financial rewards such as appreciation, recognition, etc. Basically, motivation is directed towards organisational goals and prompts people to act.

Importance of Motivation

1. Motivation makes possible the maximum utilisation of the factors of production like men, money, material, etc.

2. If employees are motivated, they are less likely to take frequent leaves.
3. Motivation fosters a sense of belonging among the employees towards the organisation and promotes loyalty.
4. Motivation helps in reducing the number of complaints and grievances.

Communication

Communication is a basic organisational function, which means the process by which a person (or the sender) transmits information or messages to another person (or the receiver). The purpose of communication is to convey orders, instructions or information so as to bring desired changes in the performance and the attitude of employees. Proper communication results in clarity and securing the cooperation of subordinates. Faulty communication can create problems due to misunderstanding between the sender and the receiver.

Communication in organisations is very important. It is the lifeblood of the organisation. Success of direction largely depends on how effectively the manager can communicate with his subordinates. Proper communication in organisations at all levels and between all levels improves both the quantity and quality of output.

Importance of Communication

1. Communication helps the employees to understand their role clearly and perform effectively.
2. It helps in achieving coordination and mutual understanding which in turn, leads to industrial harmony and increased productivity.
3. Communication improves managerial efficiency and ensures cooperation of the staff.
4. Effective communication helps in molding attitudes and building up employee morale.
5. Communication is the means through which delegation and decentralisation of authority is successfully accomplished in an organisation.

Leadership

Leadership is the process, which influences and inspires the people to willingly accomplish the organisational objectives. The main purpose of managerial leadership is to get willing cooperation of the workforce for accomplishing business goals. The person who is able to influence others and make them follow his instructions is called a leader. In practice, the managers have to effectively guide and lead the subordinates towards achievement of business goals; and to be effective, the manager has to be a good leader.

CONTROLLING

It is the function of measuring performance against pre-determined standards, looking at deviations, making certain that deviations are corrected and not allowed to recur.

According to Koontz and O'Donnell, *"controlling is measuring and correcting of actions performed by the subordinates so that the events conform to plans."*

According to Henri Fayol, *"control consists in verifying whether everything occurs in conformity with the plans adopted, the instructions issues and principles established."*

Steps in Controlling

The following steps are followed in the process of controlling :
1. Setting standards of performance.
2. Measurement of performance against predetermined goals.
3. Identification of deviations from these goals.
4. Taking corrective actions to rectify deviations.

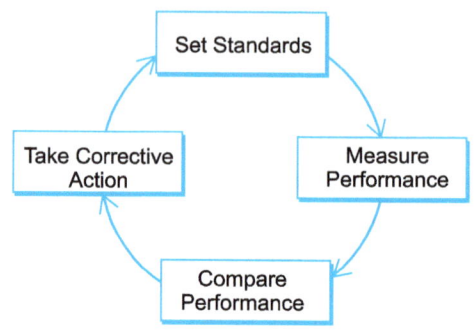

Fig. 7.6 Steps in Controlling

Controlling implies that objectives, goals and standards, benchmarks of performance exist and are known to employees and their superiors. It also implies a flexible and dynamic organisation which will permit changes in objectives, plans, programmes, strategies, policies, organisational design, staffing policies and practices, leadership style, communication system, etc. All this is to facilitate the achievement of goals and objectives. The satisfactory performance of the business organisation depends to a great extent on the controlling function.

Importance of Controlling

Controlling is a function that is of great importance in any organisation. The importance arises due to the following reasons :

1. To optimise resource utilisation– Every organisation must optimise the utilisation of its resources, including man-hours, so that profits can be maximised. Controlling cuts down operating costs and makes certain that quality products are produced within the stipulated time frame. Thus, it aims optimum usage of resources and prevents their wastage.

2. Facilitates decentralisation of authority– Controlling looks at checks and balances at all critical points in the various departments. It makes sure that procedures set in motion are implemented. It acts as a watchdog and sees to it that all decisions taken in the organisation are in agreement with the organisational policies.

3. Helps in attainment of organisational goals– The function of controlling makes sure that all plans are carried out and implemented within the general framework of the policies formulated by the top management. It constantly monitors performances, pinpointing deviations and ensuring they are rectified. In this way, it ensures the attainment of organisational goals.

4. Assists in coordination– Controlling ensures different departments work in harmony and close coordination. It sees to it that duplication and overlapping is avoided and everyone work towards attainment of organisational goals.

5. Improved planning– Controlling checks that plans are realistic by constantly monitoring their implementation and examining deviations. This way, it brings to notice any instance where plans may be not in consonance with ground realities. Thus, corrections are made and planning modified.

6. Ensures effective supervision– Controlling maintains effective supervision by constantly monitoring work and performance. Deviations are noted and resolved quickly.

COORDINATION

In management the term 'Coordination' means integration and the synchronisation of the different functions of management, its various activities into one unified, integrated unit that will work towards the organisational goals. Coordination is the integration of all the different activities going on in an organisation in a unified direction so that all contribute towards the achievement of the organisational goals. It is not a separate function of management. It pervades all aspects of management.

Coordinating is the function of establishing relationships among various parts of the organisation in such a way that they alltogether pull in the direction of organisational objectives. It is the process of tying together all the organisational decisions, operations, activities and efforts so as to achieve unity of action for the accomplishment of organisational objectives.

According to Dalton it is the *"process whereby an executive develops an orderly pattern of group efforts in the pursuit of common purpose."*

Coordination, as a management function, involves the following sub-functions :

1. Clear definition of authority-responsibility relationships.
2. Unity of direction.
3. Unity of command.
4. Effective communication.
5. Effective leadership.

Importance of Coordination

1. Unity of action– An enterprise has diverse resources, technique, activities, etc. and they all must be coordinated to achieve organisational goals.

2. Increase in efficiency and economy– Coordination brings efficiency because it is a concerted effort of all organisational members.

3. Survival of the organisation– Coordination helps in harmonising the work resources and physical facilities. Where activities are not harmonised, the organisation cannot achieve its goal and survive in the industry.

4. Differential perception– Different people have different perception. When all people are coordinated effectively, their efforts and power are focused to achieve organisational goals.

5. Accomplishment of objectives– When the employees, their task and the available resources are coordinated, the production will be increased and will lead to accomplishment of organisational objectives.

6. Basis of managerial function– All managerial functions such as planning, organising, directing and controlling cannot be conducted effectively without proper coordination.

7. Development of personnel– Coordination helps to obtain information about job, qualities of a job holder which helps to analyse about the potentialities of the job holder and improve coordination system.

Elements of Coordination

The elements of coordination are listed below :
1. Strong and effective leadership.
2. Well-defined organisational objectives.
3. Well-integrated organisational policies.
4. Effective system of communication.

COORDINATION AS THE ESSENCE OF MANAGEMENT

Coordination lies at the very core of all managerial functions. In fact, it is naturally integrated into each and every function of managerial nature and in every stage of any managerial function. Coordination is channelising efforts and constructive energy in a unified direction voluntarily or non-voluntarily to achieve organisational objectives and goals. It can be called as the very essence of management for the following reasons :

1. To plan, the planner has to coordinate through meetings and planning sessions with different functional departments at different levels of management so as to arrive at organisational goals.
2. In organising, coordination is required between the different resources of an organisation and also between authority, responsibility and accountability.
3. In staffing, coordination is required between the skill set of an employee and the job assigned to him.
4. In directing function, coordination is required between the superior and the subordinates.
5. In controlling function, coordination is required between the set standards and actual performance.

Fig. 7.7 Essential Nature of Coordination

DIFFERENCE BETWEEN COORDINATION AND COOPERATION

Coordination is the synchronisation of efforts from the stand-point of time in accordance with sequence of execution. It brings together the activities and resources of the organisation resulting in their mutual harmony. On the other hand, cooperation is the collective effort by the people who have a common goal to achieve. It signifies the willingness of people to work for a common purpose.

Coordination includes willful cooperation which is an essential element of it. Coordination can be achieved through both formal and informal relationships, but cooperation is the result of informal relationships.

Both coordination and cooperation are interlinked. One cannot exist without the other. If there is cooperation but no coordination the efforts will go waste. Vice-versa, if there is coordination unaccompanied by cooperation then the situation may lead to dissatisfaction in the business organisation.

SUMMARY

Functions of Management– Planning, Organising, Directing, Staffing and Controlling.

Planning– The process of framing objectives and how to achieve them. Planning promotes efficiency in the organisation.

Organising– Identifying what has to be done, how best it can be done, delegating authority and responsibility.

Directing– The function of directing starts with initiation of action that sets the organisational machinery into action. It includes issuing orders and instructions and supervising workers so as to ensure that all plans are implemented and the business organisation is moving towards targeted goals.

Staffing– Includes manpower planning, recruiting, selection, training and development of workforce and related activities.

Controlling– It is about setting standards, measuring performance, correcting deviations.

Coordination– It focuses on synchronising the efforts of different departments and focusing them to achieve goals.

QUESTIONS FOR PRACTICE

Very Short Answer Type Questions
1. List any two features of planning as a function of management.
2. Mention the steps involved in the organising function of management.
3. What is Staffing?
4. Define directing function of management.
5. Name the elements of directing function of management.

Short Answer Type Questions
1. List the main functions of management.
2. List any five features of planning as a function of management.
3. Explain two limitations of planning.
4. Explain three features of organising as a function of management.
5. Write a short note on staffing as a function of management.
6. Why is directing called Management in Action?
7. Briefly explain the role of Motivation.
8. What do you understand by Coordination?
9. "Planning provides the basis for control." Comment.

Essay Type Questions
1. "To manage is to forecast and plan, to organise, to command, to coordinate, and to control." Discuss.
2. Define the term 'Management'. Describe briefly the functions of management.
3. Explain the term 'Supervision'.
4. "Coordination is the essence of management." Comment.
5. What do you understand by elements of coordination?
6. What is the importance of cooperation in coordination?
7. What are the features of a well-coordinated organisation?
8. How can an organisation achieve good coordination through planning and organising?

8 Planning

> **LEARNING RESULT**
>
> After reading this chapter, you should be able to :
> ♦ Understand meaning of Planning.
> ♦ Identify the features of Planning.
> ♦ Define the importance of Planning.
> ♦ Assess the limitations of Planning.
> ♦ Evaluate the steps of Planning.
> ♦ Identify and understand different types of Plans.

Planning is the first and foremost function of management. All other functions are performed after planning. An organisation can achieve its objectives only with proper planning which is the key to business success.

MEANING OF PLANNING

Planning is a primary function wherein organisational objectives and goals are defined and strategy to achieve the identified goals and objectives is finalised. Planning formally marks the start of any business. It helps in giving direction to the people who are responsible for carrying out the implementation of the plan. Planning establishes organisational standards that are used to control the deviations or distortions in performance. It is a core action in the overall process and begins with defining the goals and objectives that have to be achieved.

According to Henri Fayol, *"Planning means to assess the future and make provisions for it."*

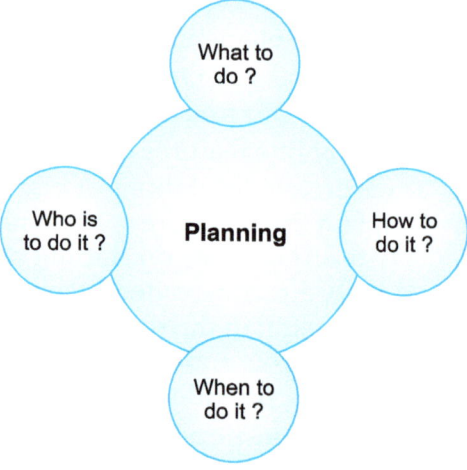

Fig. 8.1 Meaning of Planning

Koontz and O'Donnell believe that, *"Planning is deciding in advance what to do, how to do it, when to do it, and who is to do it."*

Theo Haimann says, *"Planning is deciding in advance what is to be done."*

FEATURES OF PLANNING

The main features of Planning are as under :

1. Planning is goal oriented– Planning seeks to achieve organisational goals. Therefore, plans are linked to overall organisational purpose and objectives. It seeks to identify actions that will lead to stated goals incurring minimum expenses.

2. Planning involves making choices– There would have not been any need of planning if the business organisation had only one choice. Since, there is more than one alternative before an organisation and the manager has to choose one from many available options, planning becomes all the more important. There are alternate ways of reaching the goals and the firm has to decide which one way to take. Thus, planning becomes a decision-making exercise.

3. Planning is future-oriented– Planning is always for the future. It is all about ensuring how the future can be managed to the best advantage of the business organisation. Planning commits an organisation to the future; since the past, present and future is tied in a chain. An organisation's objectives, strategies, policies and operating plans affect its future effectiveness. Decisions taken and activities performed in the present continue to impact the future.

4. Planning is a continuous process– Planning deals with the future, and future cannot be correctly predicted. The planner may base his plans on an informed and intelligent estimate of the future but the future events may not turn out to be exactly as predicted. This aspect of planning makes it a continuous process. Plans at best are a statement of future intentions relating to objectives and their means of attainment. They need revisions in response to changes taking place in the internal and external environment. Planning is therefore a continuous process.

5. Planning concerns all managers– Planning makes it necessary for every manager to set his goals and operating plans within the framework of the goals and plans of his superior. Planning is not the responsibility of the top management or the staff belonging to planning department only; all those who are responsible for the achievement of goals have an obligation to plan into the future. Managers at higher levels devote a large part of their time to planning and the time span of their plans also tends to be longer than that of managers at lower levels. Planning acquires greater importance and tends to be more complex at higher than at lower management levels.

6. Plans are hierarchical– Plans are first set for the entire organisation. Such plans are known as Corporate Plans. The Corporate Plan provides the framework for the formulation of divisional, departmental and sectional goals. Thereafter, each department sets its plans laying down the programs, projects, budgets, resource requirements, etc. The plans of each successively lower component are aggregated into the plans of successively higher component until the corporate plan integrates all component plans into a composite whole.

7. Planning aims at efficiency– The ultimate objective of planning is to achieve efficiency in the organisation. It will be irrelevant if it does not promote efficiency and optimised use of resources.

IMPORTANCE OF PLANNING

The importance of planning lies in the fact that it is the very foundation stone for all other management functions. Before any management function can be put into practice it must be planned out. If a management intends its plans to contribute in significant terms, it has to ensure the accuracy and relevancy of its plans. The importance of planning is listed below for better understanding.

1. **Planning is essential in modern business–** This is a world of rapidly changing environment where technology and socio-cultural factors impact the business very strongly. This is made more complex with the ever increasing competition in industry. All these factors make planning all the more important in modern business.

2. **Improves motivation–** A good planning system ensures participation of all managers, gives them recognition, thus improving their motivation. It improves the motivation of workers also because they know clearly what is expected of them.

3. **Identifies objectives–** The objective of planning is to make the organisational goals understandable and attainable. It breaks down the goals into quantifiable terms so that achievability becomes possible. These quantified terms, broken down into sub-objectives, serve as guides or benchmarks and indicate the levels to which goals are attained.

4. **Encourages innovation and creativity–** Planning is basically a decision-making function of management. It promotes innovative and creative thinking because many managers come up with several new ideas when they sit down to plan. It promotes a forward-looking attitude among the managers.

5. **Reduces uncertainty–** Planning helps in reducing uncertainties of future as it involves anticipation of future events. Effective planning is the result of focused thinking based on facts and figures. It involves forecasting also. Planning gives an opportunity to a manager to identify various uncertainties which may be caused by factors in the business environment. Plans are then made to offset these uncertainties.

6. **Facilitates control–** Planning helps the managers in controlling. Planning and control are inseparable in the sense that unplanned action cannot be controlled. Control means keeping activities on the pre-determined course by rectifying deviations from stated plans. Planning helps in controlling by laying down standards of control and performance which are essential for the performance of control function. It makes control meaningful and effective.

7. **Achieves better coordination–** Planning secures unity of direction towards the organisational objectives. When all the activities are directed towards a common goal there is an integrated effort throughout the enterprise. It helps in avoiding duplication of efforts. Coordination and cooperation inter-department becomes easier as all are involved in planning. It harmonises the efforts of all departments.

8. **Improves competitive strength–** Effective planning gives a competitive edge to a business organisation. This is because planning may involve expansion of capacity, changes in work method, improvement in quality, etc. Thus, new ideas and thinking can lead to an expansion and growth of a business firm.

9. **Relates activities to organisational goals–** Clearly defined goals help employees understand what is expected from them and why. They get a clear understanding of the objectives of their various activities and how it helps to achieve organisational goals. Thus, resources and efforts are aligned to corporate goals and objectives.

10. **Facilitates decision-making–** Effective planning lays down quantified objectives and alternate courses of action to achieve those objectives. Thus, it facilitates effective decision-making.

LIMITATIONS OF PLANNING

Sometimes, it so happens that companies fail due to faults in their plans. Discussed below are some weaknesses and limitations of planning.

1. **Lack of reliable data–** There may be a lack of reliable facts and figures on which plans may be based. Planning loses its relevance if reliable and accurate information is not available or if the planner fails to properly utilise the reliable information. To make planning successful, the planner must determine the reliability of facts and figures and must formulate the plans on accurate information only.

2. **High cost–** At times, the cost of data collection and processing, can be prohibitively high. This tends to push the cost of planning. Economic sense suggests that the cost of planning must not exceed the gains expected from planning. Secondly, cost can also be in terms of time. If planning is too time consuming, the plan loses its meaning and relevance.

3. **Non-acceptability of change–** Resistance to change is a very common factor that adversely affects planning. Often planners themselves do not like change. They have an adverse inclination to change. At times, the attitude and beliefs become a hindrance to effective planning. The resistance to change among executives also serves as a factor that creates limitations in planning. They try to escape or avoid changes.

4. **Rigidity in organisational working–** Internal inflexibility in many organisations may compel the planners to make rigid plans. They may tend to stick to long-held procedures and practice and hesitate from taking initiative and doing innovative thinking. Therefore, the planners must have sufficient discretion and flexibility in the enterprise. They should not always be encouraged to follow the procedures rigidly.

5. **External limitations–** The effectiveness of planning is sometimes limited because of external factors which are beyond the control of the planners. Changes in the economic, political and technological conditions, sudden break out of war, government control, natural havocs and many other factors are beyond the control of management. These can adversely affect the execution of plans. Plans may have to be frequently adjusted due to the ever changing dynamics of a turbulent business environment.

6. **Lack of initiative–** Planning is a forward looking process. A manager may have tendency to follow rather than lead his team. In such a condition, he will not be able to make good plans. Many a times planning fails because the managers do not take initiative. They must take the initiative. They should be proactive planners and should take adequate follow up measures to see that plans are understood and implemented properly.

STEPS IN PLANNING

Planning requires thoughtful and systematic thinking. Steps generally involved in planning are given as under :

1. **Establishing goals to be achieved–** The first and the foremost step in planning is to determine the organisational objectives which are often set by upper level or top managers, usually, after a number of possible objectives have been carefully considered. There are many types of objectives managers may select such as a desired sales volume or growth rate, the development of a new product or service, etc.

Objectives indicate the direction of efforts. The type of goal and objectives selected will depend on number of factors: the basic mission of the organisation, the values its managers hold and the actual and potential ability of the organisation. Objectives must be clear and in quantifiable terms which will make them understandable and achievable. They must be for each division and each department. They indicate the end result of planning.

2. **Establishing planning premises–** The second step in planning is to establish planning premises, *i.e.* certain assumptions about the future on the basis of which the plan will be based. Planning premises are vital to the success of planning as they furnish vital information as economic conditions, production costs and prices, probable competitive behaviour, capital and material availability, governmental control, etc. These are conditions that will influence the plan objectives.

The types of planning premises are listed below :

(a) **Internal and external premises–** Internal premises are factors that are within the control of the organisation. They can be the plant and machinery, workforce, its capital and such related factors. The external factors are those factors that are outside the organisation's control. These can be the government policies and regulations, the competition within the industry, demographic factors, technological factors, etc. They cannot be influenced by the company. Hence, these are external premises.

(b) **Tangible and intangible premises–** Tangible premises are those assumptions that are expressed in quantified terms. Examples of tangible premises are capital investment, annual production of goods, etc. Intangible premises are abstract assumptions and cannot be quantified. For example, goodwill of the business firm, employee motivation, consumer loyalty, etc.

(c) **Controllable and uncontrollable premises–** Controllable premises are those programs and policies of the company that can be controlled or influenced by it while the uncontrollable premises are those that are completely outside its control. These can be economic cycles, political changes, etc. We can also classify a third type, namely the semi-controllable premise. These are factors partly within the firm's control, like the firm's sales policy, etc.

3. **Deciding the planning period–** Once the top management has selected the basic long-term goals and the planning premises, the next task is to decide the period of the plan. Business firms vary considerably in their planning periods. In some, plans are made for a year only, while in others they span decades. In each case, however, there is always some logic in selecting a particular time range for planning. Companies generally base their period on a future that can reasonably be anticipated. Other factors which influence the choice of a period are lead time in development and commercialisation of a new product, time required to recover capital investments or the payback period and length of commitments already made.

4. **Finding alternative course of action–** The fourth step involves searching for and examining alternative courses of action that may be available for achieving the stated objectives. All possible alternatives are identified and various data regarding these alternatives are collected. For instance, technical know-how may be secured by engaging a foreign technician or by training staff abroad.

5. Evaluating and selecting a course of action– Having identified alternative courses, the fifth step is to evaluate them in the light of the premises and goals and to select the best course or courses of action. This is done with the help of quantitative techniques and operations research and involves evaluating them in terms of risks involved, expected return on investment, objectives for achievement, etc.

6. Developing derivative plans– Once the plan has been decided, its broad goals must be translated into day-to-day operations of the organisation. Middle and lower-level managers draw up the appropriate plans, programmes and budgets for their sub-units. These are called derivative plans. In developing these derivative plans, lower-level managers take steps similar to those taken by upper-level managers in selecting realistic goals, assessing their sub-units particular strength and weaknesses and analysing those parts of the environment that can affect them. Policies and procedures are laid down, programmes, schedules and budgets are finalised, financing is done, raw materials are procured, etc.

7. Monitoring and controlling the progress– A plan is always continuously monitored at regular intervals of time. The process of monitoring and controlling is a critical part of any plan. Managers need to check the progress of their plans so that they can take whatever remedial action is necessary to make the plan work.

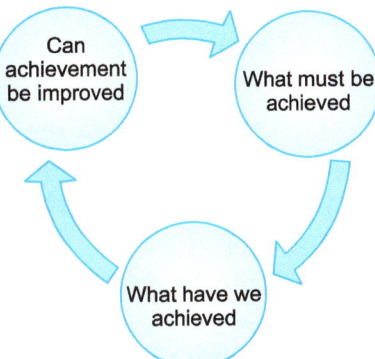

They can also change the original plan if it is unrealistic. This is contingency planning which must reflect how the organisation will bring damage control plans into play if some problems crop up unexpectedly and keep the organisation from advancing on its stated course. Contingency plans are specific but flexible. They are of a short duration.

Fig. 8.2 Monitoring and Controlling

TYPES OF PLANS

The management uses many types of plans. Plans can be repeat-use, or they can be single use. Repeat-use plans are also called Standing plans. Examples are objectives and strategies. Single-use plans are budgets and programmes.

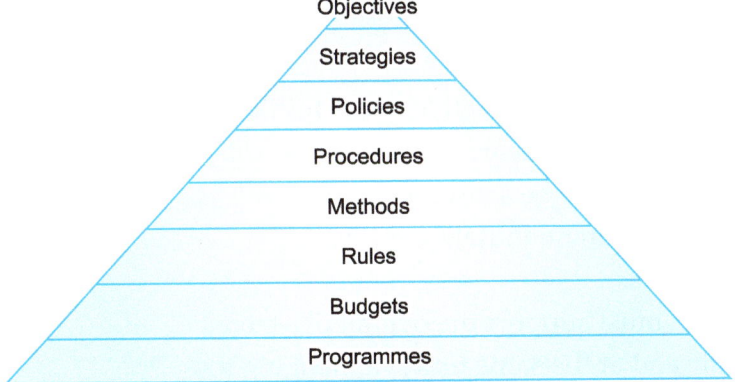

Fig. 8.3 The Hierarchy of Plans

Objectives

Objectives are the destination toward which organisational and individual activities are directed. They are the destination of the business organisation. Objective is the starting point of all planning. It is the goals that the organisation wants to achieve. A business organisation can have more than one objective. Where there is more than one objective, the objectives have to be prioritised. There can be different objectives at different levels of the organisation. Objectives indicate end results. The overall objectives need to be supported by sub-objectives. Objectives form a hierarchy as well as a network.

Importance of Objectives

1. **Justifies the organisation's existence**– The objectives spell out the reasons why the organisation is there in business. It lends it legitimacy.
2. **Gives it direction**– Organisational objectives define the course of the organisation. All business activities point towards the direction of objectives. Without objectives, employees would lose their sense of direction.
3. **Provide motivation**– The employees are better motivated when they know what the objectives of organisation are. This way they will know what they are expected to do They will be in better charge of their job role. Thus, they will be able to provide optimum inputs.
4. **Help in effective planning and decision-making**– Planning is effective when objectives are clear and unambiguous. Decision-making is rendered easier when there is clear communication of organisational objectives which are understandable to all.
5. **Essential for coordination**– The success of management lies on coordinated efforts on the part of all constituents of the organisation. In the absence of mutually agreed objectives all employees may not pull themselves in one common direction. Thus, the organisational efforts may go waste. Objectives provide the scaffolding that helps all organisational efforts into one concerted and coordinated effort.
6. **Yardstick for measuring performance**– Objectives are the standards against which the organisational performance is measured, be it the individual, departmental or the corporate performance.

Essentials of Objectives

All Objectives, in order to be effective, must fulfill the below given requirements :
1. Must be unambiguous and clear.
2. Must specify the results to be achieved.
3. Should be measurable in quantitative terms.
4. Must have a deadline.
5. All sub-objectives must support the overall objectives.
6. Must be realistic and at the same time, challenging too.
7. Must be flexible.

Strategy

The strategic plan is a very basic and a long-term plan which is based on the organisation's philosophy, long-range objectives, and is basically a bird's eye view of the entire business. Being the very basis of the organisation, it sets forth where the organisation sees itself on a long-standing basis, *i.e.,* ten or twenty years hence. All other plans get inspiration from the strategic plan. We can call it the 'mother of all other plans' for the organisation.

The origin of a strategic plan is in the top management and is meant to serve as the general framework for all other planning. Strategic plans may spell out such critical aspects as the goals and objectives of the organisation, the opportunities and threats faced by the organisation, or expected to face within the period of plan and how it perceives its areas of strength and weakness. It may also contain the policies and procedures for implementation for and carrying out its stated business. The strategic plan may also contain the estimate and the resource that the organisation sets forth for carrying out its business. Strategies, budgets, policies, procedures, marketing plans, etc. are to be derived here.

Characteristics of Strategy

Major characteristics of strategy are listed below :

1. Seeks deployment of key organisational resources to achieve organisational objectives.
2. Is long-term in nature.
3. Displays flexibility and dynamism.
4. Is arrived at after thoroughly considering all environmental factors.
5. Formulated by the top management and is based on organisational objectives.
6. Indicates the areas of major thrust of the organisation on a synchronised and sequential basis.

Policies

Policy is a general statement which guides as to how a particular situation or a problem should be handled by the managers at the micro level. Policy can relate to recruitment and lay-off, purchase, return of defective goods, channels of distribution, etc. It is general statement or understandings that guide or channel thinking into decision making. It defines an area within which a decision is to be made and makes sure that the decision will be consistent with and contribute to an objective. A policy helps to decide issues before they become problems.

Features of Policies

Following are the features of a policy :

1. It is a standing response to recurring problems.
2. Serves as broad guidelines for judgments.
3. Exists at all levels of the organisation.
4. Serves as a roadmap to achieving organisational objectives.
5. Helps in decision making by the executive.

Difference between Objectives and Policies

Objectives	Policies
1. Objectives are the end result towards which the organisation seeks.	1. Policies are the guidelines that help in achieving objectives.
2. Objectives indicate the organisation's destination.	2. Policies provide the way to get to the destination.
3. The top management determines the objectives.	3. The middle and the lower management contribute to policy making along with the top management.
4. Objectives determine what work is to be done.	4. Policy determines how the work is to be accomplished.
5. Objectives are essential for any organisation's existence.	5. Policies are not that essential for an organisation.

Difference between Policies and Strategies

Policies	Strategies
1. Policies provide guidelines to decision makers.	1. Strategies provide direction towards the effective use of resources.
2. Policies help to resolve problems which are foreseen.	2. Strategy helps overcome unforeseen problems where there can be no alternative possible in advance.
3. Implementation of policy can be delegated to middle or lower management.	3. Implementation of strategy cannot be delegated.
4. Policies are standing plans, they are generally not changed.	4. Strategies may change with conditions, situations and objectives.
5. Policy does not take competition into consideration when being framed.	5. Strategy takes into consideration the prevailing competition when being planned.

Types of Policies

The different types of policies are explained below :

1. Originated policy– An originated policy is formulated by the managers in the organisation for their subordinate's action as well as their own action. This policy may be broadly giving a general guidance for the action or may be spelled so completely as to leave little scope for definition and interpretation. An example of this type of policy can be the principle of recruiting only trained graduates for teaching.

2. Appealed policy– Appealed policy arises from an appeal made by a subordinate to his superior for deciding an important case. This may arise because the particular case hasn't been covered by earlier policies. The appeal is taken upward and decisions made on them set a kind of common law to be followed by others. For example, offering a discount on the sale price to company employees.

3. Imposed policy– Imposed policy arises from the influence of some outside forces like government, trade unions, and trade associations, etc. These factors may impose the specific policy or conditions may be created to adopt a particular policy. For example, giving priority in recruitment to weaker sections of the society.

4. Written policy– This is a policy that is written in the company records stating what is to be done in a particular situation. It gives specific directions to deal with a certain class of situation in a particular manner. For example, giving monetary incentives to outstanding workers.

5. Implied policy– It is always an unwritten policy. It is simply inference derived from the decisions of the management. For example, promoting employees to fill up middle management positions.

Importance of Policies

Policies provide the following benefits to a business organisation :

1. Help in delegation of authority– Policies make it easy to delegate authority because they set definite steps that are to be followed in dealing with recurring problems. When higher level of the management delegates some of its power to the lower level management, it makes it easier to resolve problems and issues.

2. Quick decision-making– Policies establish parameters within which decisions can be arrived at. Duplication of efforts is avoided because policies provide the framework for decision-making. They help to resolve an issue before it becomes a problem.

3. Ensures coordination– Policies tend to focus the organisational thinking on a common purpose which is consistent with the organisational objectives. Employees can easily understand why certain decisions are made. They can also predict what decisions will be made or are needed to be made under certain conditions. This facilitates better and quicker coordination.

4. Administrative control– Policies ensure that employees do not deviate from the company norms and guidelines. Decisions are made keeping the organisational interests and objectives in mind. Thus, administrative control on the employees remains intact.

5. Translate objectives into practice– Policies are the instruments through which the organisational objectives are attained. They set out the manner the organisation will function in order to reach the goals and objectives for which it is in business.

Limitations of Policies

A policy is a matter of protocol. It is a guide to decision making. Often it leads to friction and makes employees think that it is being imposed on them. Where there is a lack of clarity, a policy may create more confusion. If a policy is seen as inflexible and rigid it may throttle creativity in the organisation and may become a deterrent to employee's initiative and participation.

Essentials of Policies

A good policy must satisfy the below given conditions :

1. It should have clarity. It must be understandable to those for whom it is drawn. There must be no room for ambiguity otherwise the very purpose of the policy will be defeated.
2. For record purpose the policy must be put in writing so that there is no misunderstanding.

3. It must be realistic and capable of being implemented.
4. It should be flexible so that it can adjust to changing conditions and business environment.
5. The policy should be just, fair and equitable. It must not be discriminatory.
6. The policy must be capable of relating to the business environment. In other words, it should be capable of resolving the potential issues specific to the organisation.

Procedures

Procedures are sets of guides that lay down the exact steps that are to be followed in the resolution of problems and issues, settlement of industrial disputes, leaves, compensation to workers, etc. Procedures are plans that establish a required method of handling future activities. They are chronological sequences of required actions. They are guides to action, rather than to thinking and they detail the exact manner and steps in which certain activities must be accomplished.

Procedures often cut across departmental lines. They are in place to ensure that policies are carried out the way the management wants them to be carried out. The aim of procedure is to help achieve the organisational objectives. Procedures go along with policies. However, they display more rigidity than a policy. All functional areas of management have a procedure or procedures that have to be followed. A few examples are procedures for purchasing raw materials, procedures of sales, and procedures of selection, etc.

Importance of Procedures

Procedures play an important role in the daily functions of the business enterprise.
1. It is the benchmark that indicates that work is being done in the manner prescribed.
2. It serves as an instrument for routinizing recurring work, thus saving on cost and time.
3. Adds efficiency to the organisational working.
4. It saves the managers' considerable time because the details of how a work must be done are specified in the procedures. They don't have to explain the details thereof.
5. Brings about a consistency and uniformity of action in the working of the various departments of the business unit.
6. It promotes the concept of control by exception.

Limitations of Procedures

Procedures may have limitations such as :
1. Lack of review and inability to change can render them outdated and regressive.
2. May discourage creativity and initiative.
3. May contribute to rigidity in the working environment.

Essentials of Procedures

A sound procedure must be based on the following premises :
1. Should be capable of being adapted to a dynamic environment. At the same time it should be well balanced and reasonable.

2. Should be framed in such a way that it is capable of fixing responsibilities.
3. Should be broad based on facts of situations that it sets out to streamline.
4. The procedure must ensure that it helps in achieving the organisational goals and objectives.

Difference between Policy and Procedure

Policy	Procedure
1. Helps in decision making.	1. Helps in initiating action.
2. Policy indicates the management's attitude towards issues.	2. Is a method of handling future events.
3. It is a generalised statement.	3. It is an expressed and recorded methodology, more specific.
4. Drawn by top management.	4. Laid down by middle or lower management.
5. Policy is a derivation of organisational objectives.	5. Arises from policy.
6. Links purpose to performance.	6. Links performance and results.
7. Policy is an extension of strategy.	7. Procedure is a tool for organisational operation.
8. It has inbuilt flexibility.	8. Leaves no scope for deviation.

Methods

These are the standardised ways of doing routine jobs. Of the many ways of accomplishing a job available to an organisation it chooses one. The benefit of adopting one method or a set of methods is that it imparts uniformity and standardisation to day to day operations of the organisation and results in a systematized work. It saves on time, money and efforts. Members of the organisation know and become familiar with the prevailing method, thereby eliminating confusion, and bringing efficiency in the running of the organisational machinery.

Methods may revolve around the way production is carried out, or the way inventory is warehoused, or recorded. It may also relate to the system and the method of accounting, etc.

Rules

Rules are another form of plan. They are lines drawn between acceptable and non-acceptable behaviour. They help us in bringing order and discipline into the organisational working. They serve to channelize the organisational energy and behaviour towards the organisational objectives. They are instruments of enforcing discipline in the working environment of a business unit.

There are rules regarding the daily working hours, the timings and duration of the working hours, etc. All these are rules that have to be followed. If these rules are not followed, chaos and indiscipline will creep into the organisation and the business objectives will never be achieved. That is why rules are fixed and rigid.

At times rules may be seen by members of an organisation as being restrictive. This can be one potential cause of unrest and hostility towards the management. Rules need to be communicated to the organisation members clearly. There should be no ambiguity or chance of misunderstanding. They must be made to understand that rules are in place to bring about efficiency in the working and that it does not intend to curb initiative and creativity.

Difference between Rules and Methods

Rules	Methods
1. Rules govern organisational behaviour.	1. They are the best selected way of accomplishing a task.
2. Help in achieving discipline and order.	2. Help in achieving efficiency in operations.
3. Requires strict implementation.	3. Is the standardised way of doing a work.
4. Relate to behavioural aspects.	4. Relate to work aspects.
5. Rules are objective and value-based.	5. Methods are a result of research and observation.
6. Violators are penalised.	6. No penalisation in case of violation.
7. Rules can be authoritative.	7. Methods are always rational and logical.

Difference between Rules and Policies

Rules	Policies
1. Rules are very specific statements.	1. Policies are generalised statements.
2. Rules guide the organisational behaviour.	2. Policies guide the decision-making process.
3. No discretion possible in rules.	3. Have room for discretion.
4. Inflexible; very rigid.	4. Has flexibility.

Difference between Rules and Procedures

Rules	Procedures
1. These are very rigid plans with no scope for deviation.	1. Procedures are flexible plans.
2. Are impersonal, apply to all within the organisation.	2. Can be personal, may not apply to all.
3. Rules have no sequence.	3. Procedures are chronological.
4. Violations attract penalty.	4. Penalisation is absent here.

Budget

A budget is a statement of expected results expressed in numerical terms and can be called a "quantified" plan. A budget may be expressed in financial terms; in terms of labour-hours, units of product, machine-hours, or in any other numerically measurable terms. It may deal with operation, as the expense budget does; it may reflect capital outlays, as the capital expenditure budget does; or it may show cash flow, as the cash budget does.

A budget is a projection that defines the allocated costs and resources. It shows what the organisation sets out to achieve. There may be budgets for different departments. Budgets are instruments of both control and planning. The budget is necessary for control, but it cannot serve as a sensible standard of control unless it reflects the plans. They are standards for evaluation of performance of the organisation. Budgets are for duration of one year.

General Functions of a Budget

1. **Helps in business planning**– Budget is a plan laid down for the future. It shows the organisation's objectives in numerical or financial terms. It defines the anticipated costs and the results expected. It is an important tool for planning.

2. **Functions as a communication tool**– Budgets function as a communication tool as they are communicated down the line and helps managers familiarise themselves with the organisation's objectives broken down into figures to aid assimilation. Managers know what they have to accomplish and within what time period. Thus, they have more reaction time to plan for well in advance.

3. **Helps in evaluating performance**– Evaluation becomes easier because budgets contain the objectives and goals (broken down into understandable figures) which serve as criteria and parameters of evaluation. Managers know what they have to achieve within the stated time period, and thus they can evaluate their progress and correct deviations, if any. Fixing accountability also becomes easy when each department has its budget to adhere to.

4. **Control and coordination tool**– Budgets serve as sets of standardised tools within an organisation helping in controlling its working. All departments must adhere to the budgetary requirement pertaining to them. This helps in coordinating the working of all departments and confirming that they work in a coordinated manner to achieve the organisational objectives. The organisational resources can be controlled through a budget. It can also be monitored where the resources are being wrongly used or being wasted and corrective measures initiated. This helps bring about greater control over the working of the organisation, coordinating the efforts of the various departments and making sure that all efforts are in one and the same direction.

Types of Budgets

There are three types of budgets as mentioned below :

1. **Master budget**– It is the summary of the budgets for all the departments of the organisation. It shows the anticipated results along with the proposed activities for the entire organisation.

2. **Functional budget**– This budget shows the work allocation and the expected output for one department. It is also known as the operating budget for the particular department. Some important functional budgets are sales budget, production budget, materials budget, cash budget, marketing budget, etc.

3. **Capital and revenue budget**– The capital budget shows the estimated expenditure during the year on fixed assets such as plant and machinery, land and buildings. While, the revenue budget shows expected cash inflow and the expenditure for the year.

Programmes

A Programme is a complex of goals, policies, procedures, rules, task assignments, steps to be taken, resources to be employed and other elements necessary to carry out a given course of action. We can call it a scheme designed to achieve a certain objective of business. It clearly delineates what is to be done, how it is to be done, and by whom it is to be done.

Programmes may be used for different areas of the organisation. A business organisation may have a programme for developing a new product, training its work force, bringing about modernisation and automation of its plant and machinery, etc.

Programmes can be classified as Major and Minor. The Major programme is the basic plan, *e.g.* a programme to modernise the assembly area in the factory, or to introduce a new model into the market. The Minor programme comes out of the major programme. It is a derivative of the major programme. The minor plans are supporting plans without which the major plan may not succeed.

Features of Programmes

The features of programmes are recognised as under :
1. The programme is based on the organisation's stated goals and objectives.
2. Objective of a programme is to see that the organisational goals and objectives are being fulfilled through the smooth and efficient functioning of the organsational machinery.
3. The programme is an action plan that focuses on the activities to be performed within the given time frame.
4. The programme is a single use plan. It may consist sub-programmes to help achieve overall programme objectives.

SUMMARY

Planning– Deciding in advance what is to be done, how it is to be done, and who is to do it.

Importance– Focuses on objectives, facilitates control and decision making.

Limitations– May be inaccurate and rigid, may create a psychological barrier and be subject to external constraints.

Objectives– These are the aims and purpose of the organisation.

Policies– These are broad guidelines to assist in decision-making. They lay down guidelines for day-to-day operations, facilitate delegation of authority and ensure coordination.

Procedures– Sequential steps to be taken to implement organisational policies. Procedures are intended to help execute policies and achieve targeted objectives.

Methods– Methods are standardised ways of doing any work.

Rules– These are guidelines to ensure acceptable behaviour in an organisation.

Budget– An estimate of future cost, anticipated revenue and required resources for any business operation. It guides an organisation by reflecting on areas where the organisational strays from the pre-stated path. Budgets are of many types such as the sales budget, expense budget, production budget or administrative overhead budget.

Programmes– This is a complete plan that will help implement the organisational policies and attain the stated goals. It is very detailed and is time bound.

QUESTIONS FOR PRACTICE

Very Short Answer Type Questions
1. Define Planning.
2. List any two features of Planning as a function of management.
3. What is a Policy?
4. List two differences between Policy and Procedure.
5. Give one difference between a Rule and a Procedure.
6. What is a Budget?

Short Answer Type Questions
1. Define planning. Write any three limitations of Planning.
2. Does Planning facilitate control?
3. Outline the importance of Planning for a business organisation.
4. List three features of Planning.
5. List the essential steps in a Planning process.
6. Why planning is a mental exercise?
7. How does a Policy help in the attainment of objectives?
8. What do you mean by a Procedure?
9. What is a Programme?

Essay Type Questions
1. Define Planning. What priority would you give to Planning among all other management functions?
2. How many different types of Plans can you think of? Illustrate the importance of one in detail ?
3. Explain the differences between a Policy and a Plan.
4. 'Systematic planning is essential for any organisation to achieve its goals.' Comment.
5. Is Planning bound by external limitations? Please give your comments?
6. Outline the general functions of a Budget.
7. How does a Budget function as a tool for Control and Coordination in a business organisation?
8. What are the essential features of a sound policy?
9. What is the nature of a Budget?

9 Organising

> **LEARNING RESULT**
>
> After reading this chapter, you should be able to :
> ◆ Define the meaning and concept of Organising.
> ◆ Understand the importance of Organising.
> ◆ Identify the steps in Organising.
>
> In addition, the readers should be able to explain :
> ◆ Importance of Formal and Informal Organisation.
> ◆ Significance of Organisational structure– Line, Line and Staff.
> ◆ Relevance of Functional and Divisional structure.
> ◆ Difference between Formal and Informal organising.
> ◆ Importance of Centralisation and Decentralisation.
> ◆ Meaning of Delegation of authority and its importance.

MEANING OF ORGANISING

The term 'Organising' means to arrange anything by systematic planning and united efforts. It follows the 'Planning' function. In management terminology organising function seeks to synchronise human, financial and physical resources; and harness the same to achieve organisational goals and objectives. Through organising, a pattern of relationship is created among workers, their activities are identified and the job roles are defined. This enables the organisation to move ahead on its path to goal achievement. The various functions of organising include :

- Identifying and grouping the activities that the organisation must carry out.
- Establishing points of authority.
- Delegating authority wherever required.
- Giving responsibility while forming formal groupings so that activities can be carried out for attaining organisational goals.

According to Theo Haimann, *"Organising is the process of defining and grouping the activities of the enterprise and establishing the authority relationships among them."*

George R. Terry defines Organising as, *"the process of establishing effective authority relationships among selected works, persons and work places in order for the group to work together efficiently."*

Henri Fayol has stated the following *"to organise a business means to provide it everything useful for its functioning - raw materials, tools, capital and personnel."*

It is through the function of organising that a network of authority-responsibility relationships is created. This network enables the members of an organisation to combine their efforts for the achievement of common organisational goals and objectives.

IMPORTANCE OF ORGANISING

If a business organisation is well-organised there will be good coordination and understanding among the members, and the firm will function more efficiently. Organisation imparts the following attributes to an organisation :

1. Helps in effective administration– Organising contributes to the organisational goals by making clear the organisational structure, defining jobs, authorities and their limits. The role to be played by different people in the hierarchy is clearly outlined. People know what they have to do. Thus, division of work is carried out which leads to better functioning of the administrative machinery.

2. Helps in coordination– Organising creates relationships among the people whose jobs are interconnected. They work together in close coordination. Thus, an environment of cooperation among the employees is created. If the employees realise that they have a common goal, and that everyone must work towards fulfilling the common objectives, it helps in coordinating efforts to achieve the overall purpose of the business.

3. Brings specialisation across the organisation– By organising the company into units or departments according to the nature of the work done, a great deal of specialisation is introduced. Each department, then becomes skilled in the work or tasks, it supposed to perform.

4. Streamlines the organisation– Due to proper organising, job roles are clarified, work requirements are clearly delineated, coordination is established between authority and responsibility and organisational structures are defined. All these lead to the functioning of the organisation like a well-oiled and streamlined machine. This will help in goal achievement and growth.

5. Imparts adaptability– A well-organised business working towards a common goals becomes capable of reacting and adapting quickly to changes in the environment. This quality is of supreme importance in today's dynamic business environment. The changes in the business environment could relate to alternations in the markets, production technology, inputs, etc. In simple words, organising lends flexibility to the business.

6. Contributes to job satisfaction– When an organisation has well-defined roles and responsibilities, when people work in close cooperation, when the lines of communications are well-established, a sense of job security tends to set in. This phenomenon leads to job satisfaction among the workers. It has a long-term effect on the progress and well-being of the organisation.

STEPS IN ORGANISING

The important steps of organising are discussed as under :

1. Division of work– All the work cannot be done by a single man or machine. Therefore, the initial step will entail dividing the work into different and specific areas or jobs. The division of work enables people to acquire skills and experience in their particular area, and consequently brings efficiency into the organisation. The management has to identify all the different activities required to be done in order to achieve organisational objectives.

In a manufacturing organisation, production and sales are the two major activities. In a trading organisation, purchases and sales are the two main activities. Service organisations provide services such as transportation to their customers. In carrying out these major activities, business units have to perform many other activities such as producing, financing, marketing, accounting, recruiting employees, etc. Thus, the initial step is dividing the entire work into specific jobs. This is known as the division of work in management terms.

2. Departmentalisation– This is the step of grouping the work into specific departments, also known as departmentalisation. Once the activities have been identified, they have to be grouped into units and each group is placed under the charge of a manager. Thereafter, a number of groups will be combined and grouped into larger units or departments. After that, departments may be linked depending on their related activities or functions. Organising ensures all departments complement the activities of each other so that they support one another as far as the overall organisational objectives are concerned.

3. Assigning duties– In this step, the employees are assigned duties as per their qualifications, experience and suitability to a particular job. Areas such as production and maintenance require certain technical skills and qualifications, and as such, jobs in these areas are given too technically qualified people. People having good skills in communication are given jobs in sales department. People with an aptitude for figures and numbers may be seen fit for the accounts department.

Fig. 9.1 Organising Process

Managerial positions are defined and the extent of their power and authority is fixed. In short, who-is-who and who-will-do-what is decided. People are assigned their duties after matching their capabilities to the job requirements.

4. Delegation of authority– After assigning duties, authority is delegated to employees. Delegation of authority is very important as it gives a person the right to carry out his or her responsibilities. This creates the chain of command right from the top to the bottom and a hierarchy is thus created. In a hierarchy, the authority flows from the top to the bottom. The top has more authority than the lower levels. People are made aware of their responsibilities and authority. Lines of accountability are drawn in black and white. The delegation of authority is responsible for creating subordinate-superior relationship. Thus, channels of communications are also created.

5. Coordinating activities– This is where the activities of different individuals are carefully synchronised, and interrelationships clearly defined. It is at this stage that members of the organisation know from whom each has to take instructions and to whom one has to issue instructions. The effect of this coordination is that it lends a feeling of teamwork and an environment of efficiency within the organisation.

CLASSIFICATION OF ORGANISATIONS

The organisations can be classified on the basis of the kind of relationships prevailing in them. They are either formal or informal depending on the type of organisational structure.

Formal Organisation

An organisation or a relationship existing within the organisation will be considered to be a formal if the job and the nature thereof is well-defined as well as there is a well-grounded system of hierarchy and authority that is being followed. The employees have been delegated tasks and objectives and they endeavour to follow and achieve the goals, each person is held accountable for his or her job performance. In such a setting, rules and regulations are in place, and employees are supposed to follow them formally and unconditionally. The authority is well-rooted here. In fact, authority and hierarchy are the cornerstones of any formal organisation.

Characteristics of Formal Organisation

The characteristics of the formal organisation are listed below :
1. Created by the management.
2. Specialisation or the division of labour is the basis of the formal organisation.
3. The authority and responsibility of people in a formal organisation is very clearly defined.
4. There are formal rules and procedures.
5. There is a clear system of authority attached with each member.
6. There are clearly specified lines of communication.

Advantages of Formal Organisation

The advantages of a formal organisation are listed below :
1. Clear definition of roles and responsibilities of all members, helps in avoiding duplication of efforts.
2. Accountability is easy to fix.
3. Provides stability to the organisation.
4. Unity of command is maintained.
5. Tasks can be mastered with maximum skills in minimum time and with minimum efforts.

Disadvantages of Formal Organisation

Listed below are the disadvantages of formal organisation :
1. Decision making can be a time consuming exercise as formal communication follows established chain of command.
2. Established rules and policies can create organisational rigidity. Thus, creativity may suffer.
3. Formal organisation can create too narrow jobs that may cost dear as far as very close managerial supervision is concerned.
4. Formal organisation focuses on formal structure and work. Thus, it can contribute to creation of human problems.

Informal Organisation

An informal organisation exists within a formal organisation. It develops due to friendly relations that spring up when people work together and develop common interests. The common interests bring them together as a group.

It is to be kept in mind that it is not necessary that there is supposed to be just one informal group within an otherwise formal group. Any number of informal groups may spring up within a formal group. It is also not necessary that informal groupings may work against the interests of the organisation.

> **An Informal Group**
> - Can exist within a formal group.
> - Can work towards the same goals, but not necessarily together
> - It can also work against the formal group.

Characteristics of Informal Organisation

Given below are the features of the informal organisation :

1. It is the result of relationships developing on the basis of common characteristics, like race, religion, language, culture, etc.
2. It is marked by the absence of any written or formal rules and regulations.
3. It has no structure, nor is it shown on an organisational chart.
4. It fulfills the social and psychological needs of its members.
5. It is not bound by any departmental or functional barrier.

Advantages of Informal Organisation

The benefits of the informal organisation have been recognised as under :

1. Informal groupings can at times surpass the formal organisation in terms of effectiveness and the tendency to close ranks in the event of a perceived threat to the organisation.
2. The social relationships formed in informal groupings can strongly motivate the workers towards the organisational goals.
3. At times it can lead to better coordination as a result of friendly relations among the members.
4. The flexibility in an informal organisation helps in bridging the gaps in the shortcomings of the management.
5. Innovation and creativity is promoted by the informal grouping, which in turn, helps in personality development and leadership skills.
6. Work problems are solved through informal groupings and assistance of the group.

Disadvantages of Informal Organisation

The limitations of an informal organisation are defined below :

1. There may be constant conflicts between the formal and the informal role of the member which may impact the organisation adversely. At times the interest of the formal group may go against the interest of the organisation, *i.e.* the formal group.
2. The informal organisation sees changes as a threat to its interests. Thus, it may put up resistance to changes within the formal organisation, thereby, acting against the overall interest of the organisation.

Distinction between Formal Organisation and Informal Organisation

	Formal Organisation		Informal Organisation
1.	Formal organisation is management created, based upon the needs and requirements of the formal organisation.	1.	Informal organisation is created by people themselves not out of any organisational need, but by perceived personal needs and interest.
2.	Officially and formally managed by the organisation.	2.	Managed informally by members of the group. They may elect/select a group leader as their spokesman and representative to safeguard their interest.
3.	The formal group leader has formal authority backed by the organisation.	3.	No formal authority, strength of the informal representative depends on support extended by group members.
4.	Formal grouping is permanent in nature.	4.	Can be temporary. Even when they are permanent, lack the stability of the formal group.
5.	Emphasis is on goal-oriented activities.	5.	Objectives and goals are not defined, are often blurred and satisfy the needs of the group.
6.	Formal groups are easy to control and direct as they lie within the ambit of formal rules and regulations.	6.	Informal groups are not bound by formal rules and regulations; hence can be difficult to manage.
7.	Formal grouping is marked by a formal flow of communication based on authority and responsibility.	7.	In the informal group there is no formal flow of communication.
8.	The formal organisation enforced the members' behaviour through written rules and regulations.	8.	Since the grouping is informal there can be no formal enforcement of members' behaviour.
9.	The formal organisation is stable and organised.	9.	The informal group is subject to instability.

ORGANISATIONAL STRUCTURE

The organisational structure represents relationships between different positions in the organisation. It helps in streamlining the functions that help in attaining the organisational goals. The organisational structure depends on the size and the nature of the organisation. Much of organising depends on the size of the organisation. The larger the organisation, the more departments are created, or larger is the size of each department.

Departments denote the division of work into different categories. As the organisation grows in size the depth of specialised work and skills required also increases proportionately. The work continues to be divided and distributed among the people and the objective of this distribution is the need for a proper functioning of the various departments of the organisation so that organisational goals are achieved with the least distortion. The organisational structure is very important for every business organisation. The correct structure imparts strength and cohesiveness to an organisation, whereas the wrong structure may likely bring an organisation on its knees.

Types of Organisational Structures

The flow of formal authority is a criterion for classifying an organisation. Listed below are the ways of classifying an organisation on the basis of the chain of command :

Line Organisation

In this type of organisation, the flow of formal authority is from the top to bottom, following the natural gravity of flow from high to low. The flow of command and communication is from the top to bottom in an unbroken line, often referred as the Scalar Chain. Line organisations can also be called Hierarchical Organisation. It is signified by vertical relationships connecting the position and tasks of each level with those below and above it.

Fig. 9.2 Line Organisation

Line managers take independent decisions in their departments. The strength of the line organisation lies in its simplicity and one-pointed nature of command. All line managers have fixed and well-defined authority and accountability with the overall control lying in the hands of one person at the top. The flow of command is easy and without bottleneck; responsibility is easily fixed and corrective measures taken speedily. The reporting head has complete command over his immediate subordinate and the subordinate takes instructions from and is directly responsible to him only.

Features of Line Organisation

1. It is the simplest form of organisation.
2. Line of authority flows from the top to the bottom.
3. Line managers can take decisions independently. Therefore, there is unified control throughout the organisation.

Advantages of Line Organisation

Line organisation has the below mentioned advantages :

    1. Unity of command– Scalar chain of command flows from top to bottom. Hence, the organisation maintains the superior-subordinate chain of command.

    2. Better discipline– Because the control is unified and concentrated in one person, he is able to take independent decisions. Each employee is subordinated to his immediate superior who promotes better discipline throughout the organisation.

    3. Fixed responsibility– The authority of every line manager is fixed. Every employee knows from whom to take instructions, and to whom he is responsible. This helps in fixing responsibility. At the same time, it eliminates ambiguity and duplication of instructions.

    4. Speedy decision-making– Since all line managers know the extent of their authority, they can take quick decisions. Lines of communications are simple and effective and help in disseminating information.

    5. Economy– Line organisation dispenses with the need for specialists, thus, bringing about economy to the organisation.

6. Flexibility– The clear and unambiguous lines of authority introduce an element of flexibility into the organisation. Independent judgments can be arrived at and decisions taken by managers.

Disadvantages of Line Organisation

The possible drawbacks of line organisation are presented below :

1. Autocratic authority– Sometimes the line authority can become very authoritative and this can be a cause of dissatisfaction to the members of the department or the concerned organisation. In such cases, authority can be misused. Favoritism and red tape can kill the initiative.

2. Lack of specialisation– In a line organisation, a manager has to perform a number of operations during the course of his duty. His experience is varied, but he lacks specialisation. This reduces the depth of his effectiveness as a manager.

3. Over-reliance– Since the line manager has to do all the managerial work of his department, he often gets overburdened by the work. The departmental needs are diverse, while the skills of the manager are limited. In such a scenario, all problems areas may not receive proper attention and the manager, too, may become loaded with too much work at the same time.

4. One-way communication– The lines of communication are from the top to bottom. The views and opinions of the lower levels may not be reported to the top management. This at times can be prove costly to the organisation

Line and Staff Organisation

In this type of structure line authority is present, but there are specialists who are attached to the line authority because there is greater complexity and vastness in the organisation. The work of the line managers is well expanded, and to help them with more inputs, advice, information, etc. are put more staff whose job is to assist them with support service. We can say that line and staff relationships allows line managers to get specialised assistance and inputs when required, thus making possible for better decision-making and coordination. Examples can be of supervisors to assist line managers. The nature of their work could be advisory, with the final decision resting with the line managers.

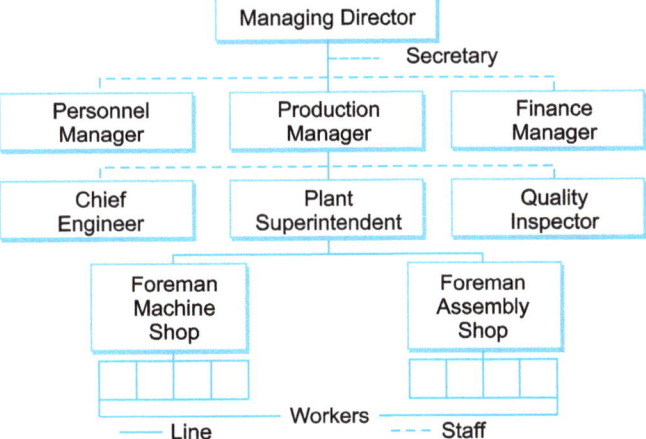

Fig. 9.3 Line and Staff Organisation

The line and staff combination addresses the issue of lack of specialisation in the line organisation. It brings in specialisation while maintaining the unity of command.

Features of Line and Staff Organisation

The major features are listed below :

1. Combination– It is a combination of line organisation that includes specialists. However, the specialists are in an advisory position rather than an authority position. This imparts a complexity to the organisation.

2. Division of work– Division of work and specialisation are elements of the line and staff organisation. There is now more scope for improved division of work.

3. Specialisation and efficiency– The specialisation brought in by staff experts promotes efficiency within the organisation.

Advantages of Line and Staff Organisation

The advantages of the line and staff organisation are shown below :

1. Specialisation– The line and staff organisation allows bifurcation of the line functions into conceptual and executive functions. This permits the line managers to concentrate on executive functions while the staff specialists concentrate on the conceptual functions.

2. Better co-ordination– A line and staff organisation facilitates better decision-making. However, the decision-making power rests in a few hands. This helps in coordinating the work as every employee concentrates on his own area.

3. Balanced decision-making– Now that the line managers have expert help to guide and counsel them they are able to take better decisions in the day-to-day management of the affairs of the organisation.

4. Scope for growth and expansion– A line and staff organisation presents more scope for the growth and expansion of the business. Additional staff experts can be brought in and activities of the company can be expanded without overburdening the line managers.

5. Expert advice– The staff executives are always available to give expert advice and help to the line managers during times of need. Line managers can focus on execution of plans while planning can be done by the staff personnel.

Disadvantages of Line and Staff Organisation

The main disadvantages of line and staff organisation are listed below :

1. Lack of understanding– In a line and staff organisation, two authoritative figures exists at the same time which may result in confusion between the employees. The staff members are not able to figure out exactly who is their commanding authority. Thus, problem could arise in effective running of the organisation.

2. Line and staff conflicts– This has been identified as the main problem of line and staff structure. The conflict between line and staff managers may be because of various reasons such as poor human relations, overlapping authority and responsibility and the misuse of staff personnel by top management. Sometimes, the organisational conflicts may be taken as personal conflicts resulting in interpersonal resentment.

3. Lack of sound advice– The line managers may be at times provided with erroneous facts and figures or unsound advice and they may make wrong choices. This can affect the efficient running of the enterprise. This becomes all the more possible when line managers become used to asking for expert advice and following it blindly.

4. Expensive– When the line and staff organisation is compared with the line organisation, it is seen that the former is more expensive because two sets of personnel have to be employed here. Thus, it can be a failure from the point of being economical.

5. Lack of creativity– There could be a lack of creativity if there is an over-dependence on staff for all sorts of help and advice. The judgment and initiative of the line managers may get affected. They may also lose creativity.

FUNCTIONAL AND DIVISIONAL ORGANISATION

The organisational structure of a business unit may also be based on the basis of its major functions, or on the basis of its products and services.

Functional Organisation

A Functional Organisation is one wherein different departments are created to take care of every day work related to carrying out the organisation's business. This system was suggested by F .W. Taylor and is signified by the fact that the organisation is divided into departments on the basis of the different business operations they perform. Each department is under the supervision or management of one person who is seen as qualified and experienced in that area of work. For example, the accounts department will be under the command of a formally qualified and trained accountant, while the production department will be headed by a person who has experience of the intricacies of producing that particular product.

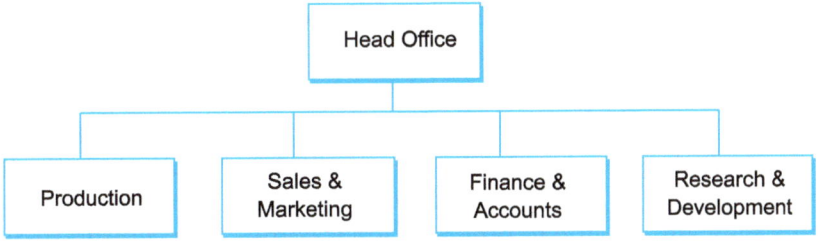

Fig. 9.4 Functional Organisation

Features of Functional Organisation

1. The organisational activities are divided into specific functions such as production, finance, marketing and personal relations.
2. Principle of unity of command does not apply as it applies in the case of line organisation.
3. It is a more complex form of administrative organisation compared to line organisation.
4. Three authorities exist– line, staff and function.
5. Each functional area is under the charge of functional specialists.

Advantages of Functional Organisation

The advantages accruing from Functional Organisations are shared below :

1. Specialisation– Better division of labour takes place that results in specialisation of function and its consequent benefits.

2. Efficiency– Since everyone performs a limited number of functions, they acquire increased experience with the passage of time. This results in a greater efficiency within the organisation and optimum utilisation of available manpower.

3. Effective control– Management control is simplified; checks and balances keep the authority within certain limits. Specialists evaluate the performance of various sections, thereby, exercising effective control.

4. Economical cost of production– In a functional organisation there is specialisation since each major function is organised as a separate department. This work arrangement promotes standardisation and facilitates maximum production at the most economical costs.

5. Ease of supervision and coordination– The managers quickly acquire familiarity with the process of production and related tasks and chain of commands. This facilitates easy supervision and coordination.

Disadvantages of Functional Organisation

Defined below are the disadvantages of the functional organisation :

1. Lack of coordination– Disciplinary control may become weak as a worker may have to report to not one but more than one person. Thus, at times there may be no unity of command.

2. Potentially conflicting– This could become a potentially conflicting situation when managers try to build up their individual areas of influence letting personal interest override the organisational interest. Disagreements may arise on different issues which may be contrary to interest of the company.

3. Inflexibility– Since the functional heads specialise in their specific functions, they may lack the required experience to take up responsibilities of higher management.

4. Difficulty in fixing responsibility–The presence of multiple authorities to whom a worker may be reporting makes it very difficult to pinpoint responsibilities. Managers and departments may shift blame to others when it comes to accepting responsibilities.

5. Delayed decision-making–As a functional organisation grows larger, the successive levels in the hierarchy also increase. As a result of departments growing large, time taken for formal communication may get delayed which may result in delayed decision-making.

Divisional Organisation

In a divisional organisation, the organisational activities are divided into a number of separate divisions created on the basis of the products. Each division looks after one complete product and including its sales. Such divisional organisations are common in products that are very complex and a considerable amount of capital is invested in them. Within each division there are different departments looking after different functions, but each department concentrating on just one divisional product.

Features of Divisional Organisation

1. Specialised product– The product range may be specialised to such an extent that every product may get the attention of an individual division. All the activities right from its production to product sales and after-sales service are looked after by an individual division.

2. Large investment– Divisional organisations are common where products are very complex and a remarkable capital is invested in them. Within each division there are different departments looking after different functions but each concentrating on just one divisional product. Such organisations are common in the electronics industry producing microprocessors and other microminiaturised electronic components.

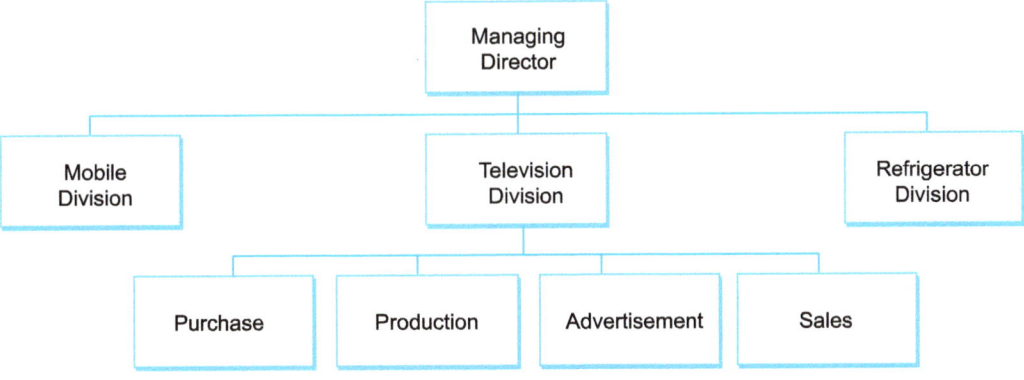

Fig. 9.5 Divisional Organisation

Advantages of Divisional Structure

The following are the advantages of a divisional structure :

1. Facilitates coordination– Since all activities of a particular product are concentrated at one point, coordination becomes easy.

2. Flexibility– It imparts flexibility and adaptability to the unit.

3. Specialised supervision– The top management can pay attention to each division as each represents one specific product line.

4. Ease of operation– It becomes easier for each division to expand its operations as expansion does not affect any other division.

5. Facilitates experience and skills– The divisional structure facilitates the growth of top managers of the future for its managers acquire different management skills under one roof.

Disadvantages of Divisional Structure

The disadvantages of the divisional structure are listed below :

1. Greater susceptibility to market fluctuation– One serious drawback is that the entire division suffers, if its product falls in demand. In such a case, the machinery and human resources will remain underutilised. Thus, the impact of loss is more serious in case of divisionally structured organisations.

2. High operating costs– Each division maintains its own facilities and workforce which may result in waste of resources because the divisional set up permits no sharing of resources. This pushes up the operating costs.

3. Potential conflict– Potential conflicts may arise between divisions with regards to sharing of corporate funds and other resources.

4. Overall organisational loyalty missing– The loyalty of employees may be restricted for a particular division when the need may actually require overall organisational loyalty.

5. Lack of centralised benefits– The divisions may suffer from lack of centralised activities, like corporate advertising, public relations, etc. Thus, the long-term benefits of centralised management may not be available to organisations with a decentralised structure.

AUTHORITY

Authority is the sum total of the rights entrusted to a manager or supervisor in order to achieve certain goals and objectives. In the business context, we can define authority as the power and right of a person to use and allocate the resources efficiently, to take decisions and to give orders so as to achieve the organisational objectives. Authority always flows from the top to bottom.

Features of Authority

1. It is the power and right of a person to use and allocate the resources efficiently and to take decisions.
2. It flows from the top to the bottom.
3. It is the determinant of superior-subordinate relationship.
4. Authority depends on the position of a person in the hierarchy.
5. Authority is always subject to limit.
6. Authority is separate and distinct from power.
7. It can be delegated to a subordinate.

Types of Authority

Authority can be classified into three categories. They are :

1. Formal authority– Formal authority is the authority given to an employee by virtue of the office held by him. Formal authority can be delegated to an employee by his superior through the chain of command. For example, authority is delegated to the Board of Directors by the shareholders.

2. Acceptance authority– This is type of authority is distinct from formal authority. It is the acceptance of an employee's authority because people accepting it, have faith in his capabilities.

3. Competence authority– This is the acceptance of an employee's expertise and knowledge within a certain circle, and the authority is due to this acceptance of his perceived superiority. Competence authority is distinct from formal authority; neither there is any formal backing nor is it delegated.

DELEGATION OF AUTHORITY

Authority represents the right, or the power to give orders and make decisions. It also carries the right to demand performance from the subordinate. Authority is vested in an 'office' as distinct from a 'person'. It is the office that carries authority. Authority is vested in an office so that necessary directions, orders and instructions can be issued there from. Such directions, orders and instructions are issued with the objective of ensuring that organisational goals and objectives are achieved by incorporating corrections and making good any deviations. The flow of authority follows a natural path, from the top to bottom, thus boosting performance.

According to Koontz and O'Donnell, *"Authority is delegated when enterprise discretion is vested in a subordinate by a superior."*

According to D. S. Hiner, *"Delegation takes place when one person gives another the right to perform work on his behalf and in his name and the second person accepts a corresponding duty or obligation to do what is required of him."*

> **Delegation of Authority**
> - Motivates employees.
> - Develops their skills.
> - Helps in effective management.
> - Improves coordination.

Theo Haimann defined delegation of authority as *"granting of authority to subordinates to operate within prescribed limits."*

According to F. G. Moore, *"Delegation means assigning work to others and gives them authority to do it."*

We can say that delegation (of authority) is sharing of certain 'power' or authority within an organisation that will enable it to ensure performance of all participants.

Characteristics of Delegation of Authority

The major characteristics of delegation of authority are identified below :

1. Delegation of authority means sharing authority to take important decisions, supervising and controlling activities of the subordinates.
2. One can delegate authority only when he has the authority.
3. Delegation of authority is from the manager to the subordinate. It is always systematic.
4. The delegated authority can be taken back, or its effect can be reduced.
5. The person who has delegated the authority remains responsible for the work assigned.
6. Delegation does not result in reduction of the powers or authority of the superior.

Importance of Delegation of Authority

Delegation of authority is an important function of management. Its benefits are elaborated as under :

1. Enables prioritising by senior managers– Helps allocate the work down the seniority ladder, thus, giving the senior manager much needed time to focus on other priority and critical areas.

2. Enables environment of trust and confidence– The flow of authority from the top to the bottom is through the process of delegation. It is a reflection of the confidence the senior management has in the lower rungs of the hierarchy. It gives life to the senior-junior relationship, thus, engendering a climate of trust.

3. Enables juniors to gain skill and experience– Through delegation of authority the skills and talent of the subordinates can be tested. By following this way, they acquire work experience and get groomed for shouldering more responsibility.

4. Motivates– Delegation provides motivation to the junior staff, and adds to their productivity.

5. Brings accountability– Delegation of authority puts accountability at the forefront. People cannot take unwarranted action, or use their whims and fancy in doing any job. The person delegated a task is answerable for its completion.

In this way, delegation of authority will enable better and effective functioning of the department as a unit, streamline the flow of information, thus, leading to overall efficiency in the working of the organisation.

Delegation enables the allocation of specific tasks and responsibilities to workers down the ladder while ensuring that they grasp the assignments they are required to carry out.

Elements of Delegation of Authority

The delegation of authority involves the following three basic elements :

1. Assignment of duty– The assignment of duty begins with a subordinate being instructed to discharge certain responsibilities on behalf of the superior. The duty or duties may consist of tasks to be performed, and the goals or objectives that are required to be achieved by the person to whom the task or duty is delegated. All these details are formally communicated to the assignee. A formal record is maintained of the subordinate having been duly communicated this.

2. Granting of authority– Sub-division of authority takes place when a superior divides and shares his authority with the subordinate with the objective of getting a task done. Delegation requires every subordinate be given enough independence to carry out the task given to him by his superiors. The sub-division of powers is very important to get the work done.

3. Fixing of responsibility and accountability– The person delegated the powers has to fulfill certain responsibilities. He is accountable to his superior for getting the delegated work done. At the same time, the person delegating the responsibility is also answerable to his superior.

Responsibility

Responsibility is the work or duty assigned to a person by virtue of his position in the organisation. It refers to the activities which must be performed to carry out the task or duty. It is an element of delegation. The duty must be expressed either in terms of function or in terms of objectives. If a subordinate is asked to control the operations of a machine, the duty is in terms of function. But if he is asked to produce a certain number of products, the duty is in terms of target or objective. Determination of duties in terms of objective will enable the subordinate to know by what standards his performance will be evaluated.

According to Alwin Brown, *"responsibility is capable of being understood in two senses. One, it denotes the definition of a part or role to be performed in administration. In the other sense, it denotes the obligation for the performance of that part."*

Difference between Authority and Responsibility

Authority	Responsibility
1. It is the legal right of a manager or a superior to command his subordinates.	1. It is the obligation of subordinate to perform the work assigned.
2. Authority is attached to the position of a superior in concern.	2. Responsibility arises out of superior-subordinate relationship in which subordinate agrees to carry out duty given to him.
3. Authority can be delegated by a superior to a subordinate.	3. Responsibility cannot be shifted and is absolute.
4. Authority flows from top to bottom.	4. Responsibility flows from bottom to top.
5. Authority has continuation.	5. Responsibility ends with the completion of the task.

Accountability

Accountability is the obligation of being answerable for the task that has been given to a person. It includes giving explanations for any deviation that may have occurred during the course of performance of the task. Thus, it amounts to being responsible for the end result. The person given a responsibility cannot escape being answerable and accountable. Accountability is different from responsibility. One can decline responsibility, but one cannot escape accountability.

1. The scope of accountability depends on the authority and responsibility delegated to a person. Greater the authority and responsibility, the more is the degree of accountability.
2. Accountability means the formalisation of reports by the subordinate to his superior showing how he has fulfilled the responsibility delegated to him.
3. Accountability moves from the lower to the higher. It cannot be delegated.
4. Accountability helps in controlling.

CENTRALISATION AND DECENTRALISATION

Centralisation of authority denotes the concentration of authority in a few hands, generally at the top of the organisational hierarchy. Decisions are taken at the top by a few, and communicated down to the lower rungs of the management. That's means that all operational and policy directions are given by a few at the top management level while those below have to carry out the instructions.

The concept of decentralisation refers to an extension of delegation of authority and responsibility by the senior management to the junior management in such a way that the latter can make decisions without the necessity of consulting the senior management. The senior management, however, remains in absolute charge of major decisions and policies concerning the organisation as a whole. The extent to which a junior manager can make decisions and the amount of authority that is vested in him denotes the greater the extent of decentralisation. On the opposite hand, if the decision-making and authority is mostly concentrated at the top level, it will denote centralisation of the authority.

According to Henri Fayol, *"Everything that goes to increase the importance of the subordinate's role is decentralisation, and everything that goes to reduce it is centralisation."* In other words, if decision-making and authority are evenly divided down the hierarchy, it shows decentralisation.

Concept of Centralisation

Centralisation of authority in an organisation can be said to be a management system wherein the concentration of decision-making is in a small group of the management. All important decisions, if taken at the middle management level are subject to the approval of top management before they can be implemented. According to Allen, *"Centralisation is the systematic and consistent reservation of authority at central points in the organisation"*. Thus, there is a dependency on the top management for all important decision-making. This top management strictly supervises the running of the organisation exercising strict control.

Centralisation is the concentration of authority at a certain point in the organisational hierarchy. Its effect is to reduce the role and decision-making authority of the subordinate. Inversely, it increases the role and authority of the superior authority or wherever there is a centralisation of authority. Centralisation can be either physical or functional. In physical centralisation, all staff and personnel are located in a centralised location. In functional centralisation, staff and personnel may be located far and wide but the authority is vested in few people and is exercised from a centralised point.

Merits of Centralisation

Listed below are the merits that result from a centralised system of management :

1. Reduced cost– Centralised authority means centralised decision-making and standardised procedures and methods. It doesn't require specialist staff at every level which, naturally results in economisation of the expenses incurred.

2. Uniformity of action– Since there is centralised administrative control supervision rests in the hands of a few chosen. This ensures uniformity of action.

3. Personal leadership– The centralised system of management is characterised by personal leadership which ensures quick and timely decision-making and implementation.

4. Flexibility and quick adaptability– Since decision-making is centralised, the organisation becomes more flexible. It is able to adapt itself to changed circumstances quickly and efficiently. It can react to changed environment with greater rapidity.

5. Better coordination– Centralisation leads to better coordination between the different departments in an organisation. Chances of conflict of authority are greatly reduced; duplication of work does not occur. Thus, efficiency sets in.

Demerits of Centralisation

1. Remote control– Since the employees are already loaded with extra work, better supervision becomes difficult. As a result, absence of better control and supervision leads to slackness in work.

2. Delay in communication and decision-making– Though centralised decision making is supposed to be free of red tape it is seen that at times decision-making is affected because of delay in information flow from multiple management layers to the centralised command. Quick decisions especially those at the ground level cannot be taken because decision-making authority does not rest with the subordinates. They can only communicate information and wait for the decision. This affects the working of the business organisation.

3. **Lack of loyalty–** In centralisation, the subordinate does not take any initiative at work because they are expected to perform only a given set of duties. They go on working like a machine in such case and lack any enthusiasm. These factors prove a roadblock in the development of employee loyalty towards the organisational work.

4. **No secrecy –** In a centralised set-up, orders flow freely from one place and reach all. Hence, there is no secrecy.

5. **Lack of specialisation–** Centralisation is marked by a lack of specialisation. In the absence of specialisation, the centralised leadership has to be very vigilant and extremely efficient regarding business decisions. This decision-making becomes all the more challenging when the power of centralised leadership rests in just one person. Chances of making the wrong decision are always present in such situations.

6. **Very heavy burden on central leadership–** In the centralised system, the responsibility of running the organisation rests solely at the top. This could be one body or just one person who has to outline the business vision and mission, set out business objectives and then after motivate the employees towards attaining these goals. These responsibilities place a very heavy burden on the centralised leadership.

Concept of Decentralisation

Decentralisation is a systematic distribution of decision-making and authority evenly starting from the top and percolating down to the bottom. In a decentralised organisation concern, the top management retains certain critical areas of decision-making for itself and delegates the rest of the authority to the middle and lower level of management. We can say that decentralisation is an extension of delegation.

Decentralisation is just the opposite of centralisation. Here the authority is diffused from the top to the middle and the lower level of management. Delegation of authority is a complete process and takes place from one person to another. Decentralisation increases the subordinate's responsibility and his accountability. It puts the decision-making responsibilities on the middle and the junior management, thus making them more accountable.

Centralisation is just the opposite of decentralisation. In centralisation authority is retained by the top management. The lower management has to follow instructions. It has no decision-making authority. The extent of centralisation or decentralisation will depend on the external factors facing an organisation. If the business environment is turbulent and complex it will be more favorable to decentralised management. Decentralisation is capable of raising the junior management's morale and motivation. On the other hand, centralised management may downplay the junior management's morale, giving them the notion that they have no role in the affairs of the company's management.

Some people are of the opinion that centralisation reduces the cost of management as it does not require specialists. There are fewer chances of conflicts and duplication of efforts. In fact there are chances of better coordination because of direct control and closer supervision. Decentralisation may require an increase in the number of line managers, and that may add to the costs of management. It may also lead to duplication of efforts.

Decentralisation has the effect of reducing the burden of the senior management; thus, giving opportunity to junior and middle level staff to contribute their creativity, expertise, and talent to take the organisation forward. In today's context, organisations are becoming huge in terms of their outreach and footprint; what they need is decentralisation. This enables coordination of efforts at a country-specific level for better functioning in case of multinationals. However, a flip side of decentralisation is that sometimes coordination may suffer in business concerns that are decentralised to a large extent.

However, what has been said above is not to suggest that one system is better than the other. In fact, both systems equally work well depending on the organisation. One system may be the best fit for one organisation, while it may not suit another. While going in for any system or level of centralisation, or decentralisation, the concern has to look within, asses its needs and requirements and culture before deciding the system it would like to choose.

Importance of Decentralisation

1. **Decision-making by middle and lower management–** In decentralisation, the subordinates get a chance to decide and act independently which develops their skills and capabilities.

2. **Effective communication–** The communication system becomes effective by way of a wider span of organisation and fewer levels of organisation. This increases the effectiveness of communication.

3. **Motivation of middle and lower level–** Decentralisation promotes independent thinking and innovation. It encourages employees to show initiative. It engages them with a sense of importance and social recognition. All these factors increase the productivity and helps in optimisation of employee output which generates revenue for the organisation.

- Where decision-making is dispersed, decentralisation is evident.
- Where decision-making is concentrated in few hands, centralisation is evident.

4. **Improved decision-making–** Decisions are faster and time is not wasted in decision-making. Decisions are made by those who execute the decisions. It cuts the red tape.

5. **Effective supervision and control–** This becomes possible because lower level managers and supervisors have the authority to control and bring about changes which they think will do good to the organisation. By controlling and supervising, the managers are able to evaluate performance of their units and by making necessary changes they are able to correct deviations. Thus, the performance of the organisation is improved.

6. Professional development of managers– The decentralised structure makes it possible for middle and lower level managers to exercise judgement and decision-making. This polishes their decision making and leadership skills. It provides them experience and prepares them for taking up bigger responsibilities.

7. Democratic environment– Comparatively more employees are involved in decision-making in a decentralised organisation. The decision-making is at all levels and all departments. This creates a democratic environment giving all people a feeling of contributing to the organisational goals.

Decentralisation denotes the percolation of decision-making to the junior management level of an organisation. In other words, it shows that the organisation has faith in the decision-making capabilities of the firm's junior functionaries. The functions of planning, organising, directing and controlling are spread down in a planned manner right from the top to the bottom. The decentralisation has its distinct advantages and disadvantages. They are discussed below :

Advantages of Decentralisation

   1. **Helps improve the quality of decision-making–** Decentralisation saves valuable time of the top management when it relieves them of the burden of having to take decision for every paltry and small management issue. The top management can spend more time on strategic and long-term planning safely leaving junior level employees look after day-to-day decision-making.

   2. **Develop management's talent–** Capability and decision-making can be developed only when organisational functionaries are exposed to it. When they are given the opportunities to exercise authority and decision-making, we can test their capabilities. Giving them exposure ensures that they grow and develop their managerial talents. Thus, they can be expected to contribute to decision-making and organisational growth at increasingly higher levels. Decentralisation gives them opportunities to showcase their talents. They become competent to take up greater responsibilities in this way.

   3. **Improves motivation and output–** People get satisfaction when they feel that they are contributors in the good performance of their organisation. By giving them decision-making authority the organisation makes them feel that they are an important part of the management. It raises their morale and motivates them to greater efforts. The all-round performance of the organisation increases manifold.

   4. **Speeds up decision-making–** In a decentralised management system, departmental decision-making authority rests with the individual departments and their heads. Hence, the decisions can be taken within the departments without the need to refer the problem to the top level. This saves time and speeds up the decision-making process.

   5. **Better control and supervision–** Decentralisation sees to it that subordinates are given responsibility for their units or departments and are made accountable. This ensures that they have knowledge of the departmental working under their control. They are given authority to supervise and take corrective action where necessary. As a result, it ensures a better supervised and controlled business organisation.

Disadvantages of Decentralisation

The limitations or disadvantages of decentralisation are listed below :

1. **Costly–** Decentralised management system requires greater financial resources because more trained and experienced employees are needed to ensure effective decentralisation, especially at the lower level, which grows up the administrative cost.

2. **Uniform policies not followed–** It has been seen that there is an inconsistency in the level of policies and procedures that are followed. Decentralisation fails to bring about uniformity when it comes to framing and following of policies and procedures. These are followed to varying extent by managerial personnel who work according to their talents and experience.

3. **Problem of coordination–** As an organisation expands and brings in greater degree of decentralisation, coordination across the organisation becomes an ever growing problem. As authority becomes more widely dispersed, controlling becomes unwieldy. Problems of coordination arise.

4. **Conflict of interest–** As decentralisation sets in and each department is required to function as an independent and profit making center there is increasing pressure on the departmental heads to make their department perform. This creates conflicts of interest between different departments.

5. **Not practicable for small organisations–** Decentralisation is expensive both in terms of manpower and administrative costs. It requires at times specialised staff. All this makes it impracticable for a small organisation with limited financial resources.

Difference between Delegation and Decentralisation

Major points of differences between delegation of authority and decentralisation are shown below :

1. Delegation is the creation of an authority-responsibility relationship between a superior and his subordinates, but decentralisation is the percolation of decision-making authority throughout the different levels of an organisation.

2. The purpose of delegation is to relieve the excessive burden of key managerial personnel, but decentralisation has a wider objective of bringing in a new concept of managing the organisation.

3. Delegation is a process whereby the superior assigns certain tasks and responsibilities within his control to his subordinates. But decentralisation involves dispersing decision-making authority down to the lower levels of the business organisation.

4. Delegation is a complete process between a superior and a subordinate. It comprises certain tasks alone and may be withdrawn. But decentralisation goes beyond and involves spreading out the decision-making powers throughout the organisation.

5. In case of delegation of authority, the supervisor has responsibility only in relation to his subordinates. It does not impart strength to the organisation. However, in a decentralised setting, direction is to a large extent substituted by control by the top management. The control mechanism in place is such that it ensures dispersal of authority strengthens the entire organisation.

6. Delegation can be a routine administrative activity involving only few managers and their subordinates. But decentralisation is a carefully planned and implemented organisational action to manage long-term growth and expansion.

Distinction between Delegation and Decentralisation

Delegation	Decentralisation
1. Delegation of duties takes place because one person cannot discharge all duties alone by himself.	1. Decentralisation is an option available to the management depending on the culture of the organisation.
2. It helps in reducing the burden of decision-making and supervision to subordinates.	2. Decentralisation helps in spreading and increasing the role of middle and lower levels of management.
3. The scope of delegation is narrow, confined to a few top managers and their immediate juniors.	3. Decentralisation has a very wide scope and it percolates down to the very low levels of management.
4. Initiative and decision-making is limited due to control by top management.	4. Initiative and decision-making is encouraged leading to acquisition of skills by junior managers.
5. It is a process for sharing of authority and decision-making.	5. It is a policy, decision brought about by the top management.

SUMMARY

Organising– It is the process of creating a structure or platform of human relationships for facilitating people to come and work together to achieve certain objectives for a business organisation. It denotes a network of relationships that constitutes a unit with certain goals and objectives to fulfill.

Formal and Informal Groups– Formal groups are created through formal organising process and their goal is the same as the organisational goal, decision-making power bring formally assigned to each member. In contrast, informal groups are created out of social interaction of formal group members, have no job or responsibility assignment and are created for social satisfaction.

Line and Staff Organisation– In a line organisation, the hierarchy is such that the top management has complete command over the organisation. But in a line-and-staff organisation, the line organisation is combined with staff departments that support line departments. The heads of staff department have authority over their employees by virtue of their relationship with the line department.

Delegation of Authority– It is the shifting of decision-making authority from a higher organisational level to a lower organisational level.

Centralisation and Decentralisation– Centralisation means decision-making has been confined to a few individuals at the top of the hierarchy, whereas decentralisation is the opposite wherein there is a systematic delegation of authority throughout the organisation.

Functional and Divisional Organisation– In a functional organisation, the departments are divided on the basis of common functions such as manufacturing, sales and marketing, R&D, etc. and is controlled from the top. The divisional organisation is divided into different divisions on the basis of the organisation's products and services. It is more skilled around product lines.

QUESTIONS FOR PRACTICE

Very Short Answer Type Questions
1. Define the term 'organising'.
2. Outline the steps in the organising process.
3. Define informal organisation.
4. What is line organisation?
5. Define delegation of authority.
6. Mention two benefits of decentralisation.

Short Answer Type Questions
1. Explain any five features of organising as a function of management.
2. Explain the steps involved in organising.
3. Explain the meaning of formal organisation.
4. Define three differences between Formal and Informal organisation.
5. Briefly explain the meaning of line and staff organisation.
6. What do you understand by responsibility?
7. What do you understand by the structure of an organisation?
8. State three differences between Centralisation and Decentralisation.
9. Write about any three principles to be followed while delegating authority.
10. What can be delegated - responsibility or authority? Or both? Give a brief opinion.

Essay Type Questions
1. What does organising denote?
2. Can both formal and informal organisation co-exist within one organisation?
3. Discuss the limitations of a Formal Organisation.
4. Is an informal organisation a hindrance in the efficient functioning of an organisation? If yes, explain how.
5. Does a line organisation have any disadvantages? If yes, explain them.
6. How is Line organisation different from a line and staff organisation? Mention any three differences.
7. Is Delegation of authority essential for effective organising?
8. What does accountability in management mean?
9. Explain centralisation of authority.
10. Describe how delegation is distinct from decentralisation.

10   Staffing

LEARNING RESULT

After reading this chapter, you should be able to :
- Understand the meaning and role of Staffing.
- Identify the importance of Staffing.
- Define the meaning and process of Recruitment.
- Understand the meaning and process of Selection.
- Difference between Recruitment and Selection.
- Discuss the meaning, need and importance of Training.
- Recognise the meaning and importance of Training and Development.
- Explain the difference between Training and Development.

MEANING OF STAFFING

Staffing is an important management function through which positions in an organisation are filled by qualified people. The function of staffing may be very simple in case of a sole proprietorship concern where the owners run it with help from a few hired hands. As the size of the concern goes up when the business expands, more and more people are required to run it efficiently. In a partnership firm, the partners help in running the firm. Operating a partnership firm may not require expertise beyond a certain level, and if the partners possess the required experience and expertise, they may need less staff which can be sourced locally.

However, when a business organisation grows in size due to the expansion of its market base, the complexity of running it increases manifold. This dynamic state requires more and more staff to look after each function and sub-function to enable the organisation maintain a steady pace of growth.

The responsibility of the management lies in identifying the nature of job or functions that exist within the organisation. Then after, it has to figure out the size of the manpower needed at each work station of every department. This process is called Manpower forecasting. After this, the management has to determine the required educational qualification, experience, and other attributes it may deem fit for a candidate to qualify as its employee.

NATURE OF STAFFING

The major characteristics of staffing are given below :

1. People centric– Staffing focuses on people irrespective of the size of the organisation. It deals with people, both individually and in groups, blue collared and white collared, managerial as well as non-managerial.

2. **Human relation skills–** Human skills are at the center of staffing. Human relationship skills are an integral part of training and guidance to subordinates, performance appraisal and transfer or promotion of employees.

3. **Common managerial responsibility–** In small companies, the top management generally performs this function. In medium and large-scale enterprises, it is performed especially by the personnel department or human resource department.

4. **Deals with active resource–** Staffing deals with the most important resource, the human resource that converts inactive resources *i.e.,* the raw materials, into productive outputs. It deals with the people without whose contribution the organisation's resources would remain raw.

5. **Continuous function–** Staffing is a continuous managerial function. As the organisation grows, the need for more and more staff also arises. Therefore, the managers have to unfailingly play their role by employing, training and compensating the staff.

IMPORTANCE OF STAFFING

Staffing is a very important function of the management. The reasons that make it vital are written below :

1. **Maximum and efficient utilisation of resources–** Staffing plays an important role in the maximum and efficient utilisation of resources. Resources like money, material and machine etc. can be utilised efficiently only through specialised manpower and specialised manpower can only be acquired through a good staffing system.

2. **Reduces cost of production–** Staffing plays an important role in reducing cost of production by bringing on-board the deserving candidate at the right time so that wastage and mistakes can be eliminated or reduced. Thus, it assists in reducing cost of production. When worthy personnel are selected through an established recruitment process, it is an assurance that the organisation is getting the right person for the job. This leads to efficient organisational performance.

3. **Provides job satisfaction–** Staffing contributes to an employee's job satisfaction. Staffing makes sure jobs are allocated to the personnel according to their inherent ability, talent, aptitude and acquired specialisation. As a result, the staff puts hundred percent effort to perform its duties.

4. **Long-term implications–** Staffing looks at the long-term human resource requirements of the organisation. By looking at organisational goals on a long-term basis, it gives a clear picture to the organisation as to its human resource requirement for the future. Thus, staffing fulfills the present and future human resource requirements of an organisation.

5. **Key management function–** Staffing is the function that infuses life into other departments of an organisation by providing the right man for every job and position. All other functions depend upon the effectiveness of staffing.

6. **Contributes to organisational efficiency–** Staffing improves employee output through in-house and continuous training and development programs.

7. **Promotes better working environment–** Careful and efficient staffing can lead to better employee bonding and relationships, effective supervision and leadership. Higher productivity can be achieved through better human relationships in an organisation.

Staffing is a very important managerial function and an ongoing process. It must be noted that staffing is not restricted to merely recruitment and selection; but also includes appraisal, professional development, training, performance evaluation, compensation, etc.

STAFFING AS RELATED TO HUMAN RESOURCE MANAGEMENT

The role of human resource management is to plan, develop and administer policies and programs designed to optimise the use of an organisation's human resources. It is that part of an organsation's management which is concerned with its employees and their role and relationship within the enterprise. Human resource management is involved in every department, whether it is planning, organising, production, controlling, etc.

The objectives of human resource management are :

1. Effective utilisation of human resources.
2. Desirable working relationships among all members of the organisation.
3. Maximum individual development.

Staffing is one of the very important functional areas of human resource management. It is responsible for recruiting, developing, integrating and maintaining the entire workforce in an organisation. Such a well-placed and maintained workforce works towards channelising its skills and know-how for the attainment of organisational goals.

STEPS INVOLVED IN STAFFING

The following steps are involved in the staffing process :

1. Manpower planning– The staffing process starts with an evaluation of the human resource requirement of the organisation, both in terms of number of personnel required along with the educational requirement and experience. The management has to identify the job responsibilities and define the expected output in terms of abilities and requirements from the required future staff. It is also known as Manpower Requirements Planning. When a company does manpower planning, it also considers the demand forecasts and pro-

Fig. 10.1 Steps in Staffing

duction schedule to get an overview of how much manpower it will require to meet the required production level.

2. Recruitment– Next is the recruitment stage. Recruitment can be defined as the process of finding and attracting candidates that have the potential to be the assets of the organisation. It simply means searching for suitable candidates.

3. Selection– Recruitment is followed by selection. This process involves assessment and evaluation, choosing the right candidate from a number of suitable ones. Certain processes and procedures go into making sure that the right candidate is selected. The process of selection begins by screening or vetting of applications received. Once the applications are vetted, the ones that are found to have potential are separated and these candidates may be shortlisted for a written test. However, not all organisers hold a written test. Some may call candidates for a formal preliminary interview. They may have more than one interview before the last and final one. After the last interview or just before the last interview, past work references may be looked into and medical tests may have to be undergone. In the last stage of selection, the candidate is given the appointment letter.

4. Placement– It is the process of putting the selected person at the right job or place. Once the chosen person is shown his place in the organisation, all the activities and duties to be performed are given to the new hire. The newly appointed candidate is then after asked to attend an orientation session by the human resource department to get acquainted with the organisation.

5. Orientation– The aim of orientation is to build up confidence, morale and trust of the employee in the new organisation with the main idea of so that he becomes a productive and an efficient employee of the organisation and contributes to the organisational success. The nature of orientation varies with the organisational size. A smaller organisation may have a more informal orientation session and a larger organisation may choose to go for a more formalised orientation program.

6. Training and development of employees– Training is a process which enhances the skills, capabilities and knowledge-base of the new employee for desired job performance. An employee is in a better position to discharge the allotted duties after getting trained. However, training is a continuous process and goes on throughout the employment span of the employee. The period of training may start after an employee gets done with the orientation programme. The objective is to change the perspective of the new hire towards the job and psychologically prepare the employee to work in tandem with organisational goals.

RECRUITMENT

Recruitment is the dissemination of information about a job vacancy and subsequent act of inducing prospective candidates to present themselves for appointment. It means searching suitable candidates for employment in the organisation. Recruitment aims at securing the largest possible number of applicants. After generating a large pool of potentially suitable candidates, the organisation examines them closely and the most suitable ones are selected from the lot for further scrutiny.

There are four important steps to be followed for proper recruitment :
1. Identifying the type of people required.
2. Identifying the sources of communication through which these people could be contacted.
3. Advertising the vacancies or requirements through the sources best suited for the task.
4. Securing the applications.

Sources of Recruitment

The sources of recruitment can be divided into two types– external and internal.

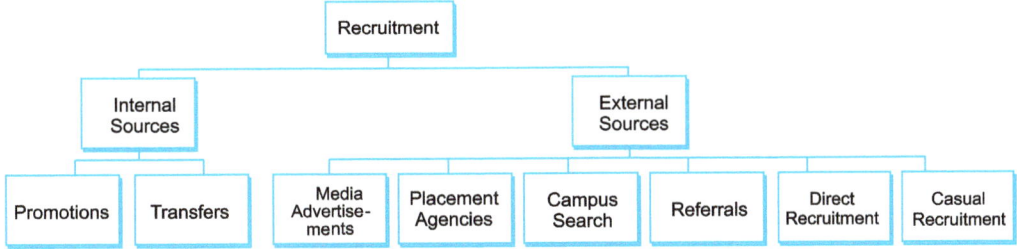

Fig. 10.2 Sources of Recruitment

External Sources

1. **Media advertisements**– In the present age, an organisation has a number of media sources at its disposal for advertising. There are newspapers and magazines which can be used for advertising vacancies. These are known as the print media. Beside them, we have trade journals and employment weeklies, which are part of the printed media. Television advertisements are also an option to invite job applications. Advertisements on online portals are another very popular effective way of advertising organisational vacancies. These days all organisations have their official website and they advertise job vacancies on the website too.

2. **Placement agencies**– An organisation has access to the services of a number of placement agencies that have ready databank of many job seekers. The agencies can share the database or simply contact the candidates on behalf of the recruiter at a short notice. They also serve the business firms by arranging interviews with the candidates. Of course, this service is rendered at a price.

3. **Campus search**– Organisations now-a-days maintain good relations with professional schools, colleges and universities. This relationship helps them in their recruitment drive. If there is a need, the organisation sends its recruitment staff to campus of prominent college in search of right candidates. Thus, institutes serve as recruitment centers. Today, many big players like Google, Facebook, Infosys, TCS and LinkedIn conduct campus interviews and recruit successfully.

4. **Referrals**– These days organisations are inviting 'referrals' by employees, trade unions, clients, and others that organisational people are familiar with. They communicate their requirements to these people and ask them to refer suitable candidates. In case the recruiter finds the candidates suitable and subsequently recruit them, they compensate the referrers very suitably. This process helps the recruiter save on recruitment costs.

5. **Direct recruitment**– The organisation can advertise for 'gate interviews'. It can hold interviews at the gate. It can also get applications informally which it can vet, and if found suitable, can recruit candidates.

6. **Casual applicants**– Many times, candidates in search of a suitable job forward their application directly to the employer. Their resume is saved by the company in case there is no vacancy or if the position gets filled by another deserving candidate. However, the company refers its database whenever there is a need to hire a new employee be fitting another vacant post.

Advantages of External Sources

An organisation derives the following advantages when it uses external sources of recruitment :

　　1. Greater choice– External sourcing has the advantage of the organisation getting access to a large number of potential candidates. Greater the number of candidates more the chances of the organisation getting better employees.

　　2. All under one roof sourcing– External sources fulfill all manpower requirements of the organisation, whether skilled, or unskilled, technical or non-technical, managerial or non-managerial.

　　3. Fresh blood– External sources have the added advantage of providing young and fresh blood that brings in new ideas to the table.

Disadvantages of External Sources

The following are the disadvantages of external sources of recruitment :

　　1. Expensive– The organisation has to pay for using the services of external sources like placement bureaus or agencies. The bigger the agency, the higher its fee. At times the charges for these services can be very high and small firms may find it hard to afford them.

　　2. Time consuming– Because of the long processes involved in using external sources, there may be delay in hiring the best candidate. Advertisements have to be published and adequate publicity has to be done regarding the job vacancy. All these factors make it a long-drawn-out procedure.

　　3. Desirable outcome not guaranteed– External sources cannot guarantee results in line with the company's needs and goals. Suitable candidates may apply or may not apply in adequate number.

Internal Sources

One way of using internal sources is through organisational promotions and transfers. It involves looking within the organisation for employees who are suitable and competent enough for vacant positions. Promotions and transfers are used to affect this. Promotion means shifting an employee to a higher position by hiking pay and increasing job responsibility, whereas transfer is shifting an employee to a similar job with no change in position, remuneration and responsibility.

This system has certain advantages. When positions are filled up from within, the person is familiar with the organisation's culture and work environment. They can practically do without orientation and can begin working in their new role in no time. Belonging to the same organisation makes it easy for the employee to gel with the rank and file of the department they have to work with, and they also stand greater chances of readily getting more cooperation from their subordinates.

Advantages of Internal Sources

An organisation enjoys four main advantages from internal sources of recruitment. They are presented below :

　　1. Utilisation of existing talent– Promotion and transfer enable the organisation to make the best utilisation of talents existing in-house.

2. Economy– It saves the organisation's considerable amount of money that would have been spent searching talents outside the organisation.

3. Familiarity– When the organisation fills vacancies by using internal resources, it bypasses the need for employee orientation. Similarly, because the employee is a familiar face and is well-acquainted with the organisational culture and working environment, he is able to settle quickly in his new surroundings.

4. Constitutes recognition of employees– Internal recruitment recognises an employee's contribution towards the organisation. It is a source of motivation and encouragement to the employees. Thus, the hardworking and motivated employees get the message that their loyalty to the organisation will not go unrecognised.

Disadvantages of Internal Recruitment

Internal recruitment has its disadvantages. The common ones are as defined as under :

1. Disgruntlement– The internal recruitment can lead to dissatisfaction among those employees who are not selected for promotion. This in turn can lead to infighting, jealousy, disturbances which can, in turn, impact the smooth working of the organisation.

2. Limited choice– By going for internal recruitment, the company limits its choice to its existing employees who may have lost their efficiency or may have outdated views. Thus, the company may be losing the chance to derive more benefits by hiring new candidates with the potential to infuse new energies by their fresh outlook and ideas. In simple words, new hires bring something new to the table.

3. Lethargy– The time bound system of promotion in a company induces the employees to become lazy and laid back. Becoming assured of time bound promotion makes them prone to old and outdated systems of working. This results in loss of efficiency and consequent loss of production and revenue.

4. Falls short of full requirement– All workforce requirement cannot be met from the internal sources. Ultimately, the organisation has to resort to external recruitment.

SELECTION

Selection is the process of carefully putting the right men on the right job. It is a procedure of matching organisational requirements with the skills and qualifications of people. Proper screening of candidates takes place during selection procedure. Their applications are vetted, qualifications scrutinised and undesirable applications are rejected at this stage. Only the best candidates for the job are shortlisted for further action and subsequent processes. Ultimately, the most suitable ones are identified, interviewed and finally selected.

Importance of Selection

Selection involves the cautious screening of candidates and subsequent identification of the most suitable person for the vacant position in an organisation. Hence, it is a very important function. A wrong selection can prove very expensive to the organisation. If a wrong person is selected, it may lead to his possible absenteeism, inefficiency and may ultimately cost the organisation a member of the staff. Moreover, the time and money spent by the organisation on the employee's selection and training will go waste.

Right selection is mandatory as it leads to increase in efficiency and output of the organisation. It also puts in place a competent and well-equipped workforce that works towards achieving organisational objectives. When right people are chosen to do the right work, the organisation moves forward in a coordinated and objective manner. The people understand what they need to do to achieve the organisational objectives. Their job satisfaction is high. Consequently, the employees become an asset to the organisation.

Distinction between Recruitment and Selection

Recruitment	Selection
1. It is the process that brings suitable candidates to the employer.	1. It is the process that brings candidates fulfilling the job requirement.
2. It creates a large pool of candidates, both good and the not-so-good ones.	2. Selection identifies the most suitable among the good ones.
3. This is a positive and all-embracing process as it aims at the largest number possible.	3. It has a negative side for it selects only those who are most suitable while eliminating the others.
4. Candidates are not required to qualify in recruitment.	4. Selection happens after qualifying many interview rounds.
5. Recruitment is an exercise done prior to selection.	5. Selection is the final step of staffing and is done after recruitment.

Steps in Selection Process

It should be noted that different organisations follow different steps in the selection procedure. Below are some steps commonly followed by most organisations to select the most worthy candidate :

1. Screening of applications– After applications from the candidates are received through the recruitment process, they are examined to decide which ones deserve to be considered and followed up. The job advertisement may mention the particulars to be given in the application. In many cases the candidates are required to apply in the prescribed form of the company which requires them to mention their name, address, nationality, religion, mother tongue, date and place of birth, marital status, education and training, employment history, job references, etc. Screening exercise involves checking the contents of the applications so as to ascertain whether or not the minimum eligibility conditions in respect of age, experience, qualifications and skills are fulfilled by the candidates. Screening may be done by a senior officer of the company or by a screening committee. The purpose of screening is to prepare a list of eligible candidates who are to be considered further. Candidates that are not eligible are thereby excluded from further consideration.

2. Preliminary interviews– Those candidates that are shortlisted in the screening may be put through a preliminary interview. Preliminary interview can be a face-to-face physical interview; it may be a telephonic interview or a video-chat interview using audio-visual applications like Skype.

The interviewee may be asked to submit all relevant data in a given format, or may be sent a format in a soft copy that has to be submitted after filling all details. This generally happens in case the applicant has the potential to be the right candidate.

3. **Employment test–** The candidates may be asked to go through various tests that to testify their skills and talents. This will enable the organisation to properly form an idea of the candidate.

Such tests can be :

(a) Written test.

(b) Psychometric test.

(c) Physical test– To test the candidates physical abilities.

(d) Proficiency test–To measure the candidate's skills and knowledge.

(e) Aptitude test– This measures the candidate's potential for a particular job. Aptitude tests can be an intelligence test to test reasoning and memory, or the candidate's intelligence quotient, etc. It can also be a personality test.

4. **Final interview–** Generally, the final interview is a face-to-face interview before an interview panel. The interview is the most important part of the selection procedure and serves as a means of checking the information given in the application form and making an overall assessment of the candidate's suitability for the job. In the interview, the candidate has a face-to-face interaction with the employer or representatives of the employer. The recruiter subjects the candidate to minute scrutiny in order to assess his full potential and suitability.

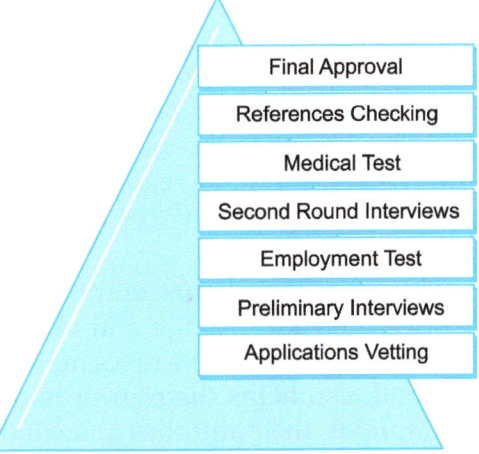

Fig. 10.3 Selection Process

5. **Medical test (not in every case)–** Candidates finally selected for the job may be asked to undergo medical examination to determine whether the selected candidates are physically fit for the job or not. A formal medical examination ensures a certain standard of health of the employees and their physical fitness which can potentially impact the organisational objectives.

The medical examination reveals whether a candidate suffers from any illness or not. Medical test is essential for certain jobs as in the case of police and army, where physical fitness is of prime importance.

6. **References–** Some organisations firmly ask the candidate to furnish the details of people who can vouch for them, certify their character and other qualifications. The next step taken by the organisation is to get the details provided by the candidate verified by cross-checking with the references or people.

7. **Final appointment–** Finally, selected candidates are offered a formal appointment letter. The appointment letter contains such details as the nature of appointment,

the terms and conditions of appointment, the work details and the scope of work that is allotted to the selected candidate. It may also contain the benefits that will come to the selected candidate. It also mentions the details of remuneration, pay scale and other terms and conditions relating to employment.

Usually, a reasonable time is given to the candidates to join the organisation. This is also set out in clear terms in the appointment letter. If the candidate does not join by the indicated date the appointment can be subject to cancellation.

TRAINING

Almost every new hire is put through training to in order to improve their knowledge and skill so that they are able to perform their tasks more efficiently. It is an organised activity for increasing the knowledge and skills of the employee for a specific purpose. Training improves the competence of employees and motivates them. Many organisations have in house training centers. Others make arrangements with some training institutions to train their employees.

Training is necessary for new employees as well as existing employees. It improves their work performance. Training helps new employees to get acquainted with the method of operation and skill requirement of the job. For existing employees, training at regular intervals helps in learning better ways of doing the work.

Training
- Maintains quality of products/services
- Achieves high service standards.
- Provides information to newcommers.
- Refreshes memory of old employees.
- Achieves learning about new things; technology, production methods.
- Reduces mistakes and minimize costs.
- Opportunity for staff to suggest improvements.
- Improves communication relationship; better team work.

Thus, training helps employees to improve their knowledge and skill and make them perform their tasks more efficiently. It also helps them in promotion and improves their attitudes and confidence levels.

Methods of Training

There are different methods of training employees. They can be divided into two broad categories :

1. On-the-job methods– In these methods, the employees learn about their jobs while doing the work. Here they are assisted by their supervisors or seniors. Such methods encourage self-learning through practice. Job instruction or coaching, job rotation and learning while working as an apprentice or as assistant to a senior, are some of the common on-the-job training methods.

2. Off-the-job methods– These methods involve training employees away from the workplace. In this method experts may conduct the training. Employees are freed from their regular duties which enables them to concentrate on the learning. Lectures with demonstration, conferences, case discussions, video shows and films are some of the common methods used here.

There is another off-the-job method of training called Vestibule Training or Simulated Environment Training. Such trainings are in specially designed workshops which are a duplication of the actual condition of the workplace. In such workshops a large number of employees can be trained in a relatively short period of time.

Need for Training

Training of employees is very important for the following reasons :

   1. **New employees have no work experience**– When new employees join, they are raw due to lack of any on-the-job work experience. They need to be trained in the methods followed by the employer. After the training, they can be expected to have the wherewithal to further the aims and objectives of the organisation.

   2. **Existing employees need refreshing**– Existing employees need to undergo refresher trainings so that they can avoid the obsolescence of skills. It also helps get rid of the lethargy that creeps into the workforce that has been there for a long period of time.

   3. **Need training for safety purposes**– Training from time to time helps the employees prevent workplace accidents and mishaps. It jerks them to consciousness and re-familiarises them with the safety precautions they must take while working. Thus, it helps to prevent industrial accidents.

   4. **To embrace new methods and technology**– Training becomes important to familiarise workers with new and changed work technology where old machines may have been discarded and new machines and manufacturing technology deployed.

   5. **Prelude to new responsibilities**– Training is required when employees are being given new responsibilities. They are familiarised with their new job requirements and responsibility sharing during the course of the training.

Importance of Training

Training is a systematic process which enables an organisation's human resources to gain knowledge and develop skills by instruction and practical activities that result in improved corporate performance. Training benefits both the employee as well as the employer. The market value of the employee goes up after training. On the other hand, the organisation benefits by way of increased efficiency as a result of a well-trained employee.

Listed below are the major benefits of training :

   1. **Brings in greater efficiency**– Training imparts a new outlook to the employees who work with renewed zest and efficiency. It increases the skills and performance both, invigorates the work environment.

   2. **Optimises use of resources**– The performance of well-trained employees is satisfactory in qualitative and quantitative terms. There is less wastage of time, money and resources when employees are properly trained.

   3. **Raises morale of the workforce**– Self-confidence and attitude undergoes a great change through training. Training brings the workforce and the management closer through training. The worker feels that the management cares for them. This makes them more cooperative and flexible to the demands of the management. All this has a positive impact on the overall working of the organisation.

4. **Reduces need for supervision–** Training reduces the need for close work supervision. Training imparts professionalism to the workers which makes them dedicated to their duty.

5. **Imparts stability–** An organisation that is well-trained becomes stable from within. It acquires a dynamism and flexibility that allows it to adapt to the changing environment and grow and expand.

6. **Increases industrial safety–** Training makes the workforce more conscious of safety procedures. This reduces incidence of industrial accidents. In other words, it means that no man days are lost through absenteeism due to injury.

7. **Economy–** Training makes the workers better equipped in handling and using materials and machinery. This in turn reduces spoilage, breakage and wastage. In terms of cost, it helps to save and economise.

8. **Career growth–** Training raises the chances of promotion of employees. It furthers their career chances, increases earnings and job security.

TRAINING AND DEVELOPMENT

Training and development are two different terms and must not be confused. Very often, the layman thinks that these two terms mean one and the same thing. The objective of training is that employees improve their knowledge, expand skill base and use that improvement towards the achievement of organisational goal. Thus, training has a specific purpose *i.e.,* improving the work performance.

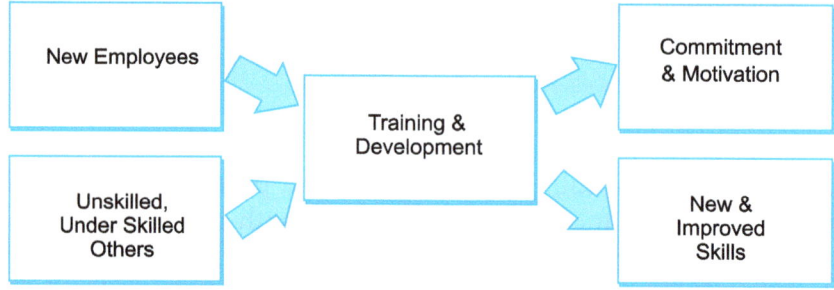

Fig. 10.4 Purpose of Training and Development

Development goes beyond mere knowledge and skills building. It aims at expanding the overall competence of employees. It seeks to make them ready to shoulder greater responsibility and handle difficult and challenging tasks in a changed environment. It seeks to equip them with leadership skills. Its scope includes the entire career of the employee. Hence, it is seen as future-oriented.

Development indicates the long-term growth of a person in terms of handling a host of situations if and when they arise at any time in future. Human resource development is undertaken with a view to work on the existing skills, attitude, abilities and performance of workers, giving them a long-term vision, responsibilities and converting them into leaders. Training, on the other hand, is about creating the mental environment that allows workers to behave in a particular way when put into certain conditions and circumstances. The condition becomes a sort of stimuli which makes them respond in a set pattern.

Objectives of Training and Development

The principal objective of training and development is to make sure there is skilled and willing workforce is available in an organisation. In addition to that, there are four other objectives : Individual, Organisational, Functional and Societal.

1. **Individual objectives**– Help employees achieve their personal goals, which in turn, enhance the individual contribution to an organisation.

2. **Organisational objectives**– Assist the organisation with its primary objective by bringing individual effectiveness.

3. **Functional objectives**– Maintain various departmental contributions at a level suitable to the organisation's needs.

4. **Societal objectives**– Ensure that the organisation is ethically and socially responsible to the needs and challenges of the society.

Difference between Training and Development

Training	Development
1. Training is the process of enhancing the knowledge, ability, talent and efficiency of an employee for doing specific jobs in a desired manner.	1. Development is the process of all around growth of the employees through promotion opportunities, bonus and other development programs.
2. Training is provided by the organisation for doing specific jobs. Hence, it is of short duration.	2. Development is a continuous process needed continuously in an organisation to motivate the employees.
3. Training is essentially concerned with the present events. It intends to solve the existing problems.	3. Development is concerned with both present and future events.
4. Training is to make the employees efficient for doing specific jobs.	4. Development intends to take optimum benefits from the existing employees.

SUMMARY

Staffing– The process of hiring, training and developing an employee and turning him into an asset for the company.

Recruitment– The process of finding and attracting suitable applicants for employment for various activities of the organisation using internal and external sources.

Selection– It is the process of choosing the most suitable person from the short-listed candidates. This involves screening the applications, holding tests, interviews, checking references, conducting medical examinations and issuance of appointment letters.

Training– The process of improving the knowledge and skill base of the employees for making them eligible to perform their duty more efficiently. The methods used for the task may be on-the-job or off-the-job.

Training and Development– Training improves the knowledge and skills of employees whereas development goes beyond mere knowledge and skills building.

QUESTIONS FOR PRACTICE

Very Short Answer Type Questions
1. Define the term 'Staffing'?
2. Write a short note on staffing as a management function.
3. Define Recruitment.
4. List any two advantages of external sources of recruitment.
5. List two limitations of internal recruitment.
6. What is Training?
7. What is Development?

Short Answer Type Questions
1. Why is staffing regarded as an all-pervasive function of management?
2. Evaluate the importance of staffing in a business organisation.
3. Does the scope of staffing extend beyond the personnel department of an organisation? Briefly state your view.
4. What methods of recruitment are used by modern organisations?
5. List three comparative advantages and disadvantages of external sources of recruitment.
6. What role is played by placement agencies in helping organisations in staffing?
7. Explain sources of internal recruitment.
8. Outline the different steps in the selection process.
9. State any two points of distinction between Recruitment and Selection.
10. What are the objectives of training and development?
11. Is the training and development of employees useful for an organisation?
12. List any three differences between Training and Development.
13. List the options available to an organisation for training its new employee.

Essay Type Questions
1. Discuss the importance of staffing as a function of management.
2. Explain steps is staffing process.
3. Explain any five sources of external recruitment.
4. Evaluate the importance of selection in the staffing function.
5. Evaluate the importance of training in an organisation.

11 Directing

> **LEARNING RESULT**
> After reading this chapter, you should be able to :
> ◆ Define Directing function of Management.
> ◆ Understand the importance of Directing.
> ◆ Identify the elements of Directing.
> ◆ Understand the meaning of Supervision.
> ◆ Distinguish between Directing and Supervision.
> ◆ Understand the meaning of Motivation.
> ◆ Describe the features and process of Motivation.
> ◆ Define Maslow's Theory of Motivation.
> ◆ Elucidate Leadership and qualities of a good leader.
> ◆ Understand the meaning and objectives of Communication.
> ◆ Identify barriers to communication and how they can be overcome.

The managerial function of directing is similar to the role of a teacher in a classroom. In order to teach, a teacher guides his pupils, maintains discipline, inspires and leads them to the desired goal. Directing helps the managers to ensure quality output by the employees and the resultant achievement of organisational goals.

MEANING OF DIRECTING

Directing is the process that involves giving instructions, guidance, motivation, help and assistance to subordinates in order to help them achieve organisational goals. In other words, it involves monitoring and correction of employee performance to focus their coordinated efforts for attaining organisational objectives. It is a management function that is performed by the directors of the organisation as well as the supervisors down the line.

According to Theo Haimann, directing consists of *"the processes and techniques utilised in issuing instructions and making certain that operations are carried on as originally planned."*

Koontz and O'Donnell define directing as *"the interpersonal aspect of managing by which subordinates are led to understand and contribute effectively and efficiently to the attainment of enterprise objectives".*

Ernest Dale says that directing is *"telling people what to do and seeing that they do it to the best of their ability."*

The importance of directing must never be underestimated. In the absence of directing, or in the absence of effective directing of the organisational efforts, the objectives or goals can never be achieved. As indicated above, directing encompasses all those activities that will make the joint organisational efforts yield desired results through coordinated harnessing departmental efforts. Thus, it will impact all the departments of a business unit. Inspiration, motivation, guidance and leadership are important inputs in directing any organisational force. Direction lies at the center of every business organisation. It is in fact the life spark of any workforce; whether it works for profit or charity. In fact, it is through direction that employees can identify their real capabilities and give optimum output.

FEATURES OF DIRECTING

Some of the main features of directing function in the sphere of business management are given below :

1. Human factor– Directing function is aimed towards human beings. It is the employees that are being directed towards certain organisational goals. The guiding, counseling, motivating and leading functions in an organisation are all directed towards human beings.

> Directing involves shaping human behaviour. It is the starting point for continuous performance oriented action. It flows from top to bottom.

2. Management function– It is an important management function carried out mainly by the managers. It aims at getting work done by the employees with the help of managers.

3. Result-oriented– Directing is a result-oriented function. The efficiency of this function is measured by the overall performance of the organisation. If the organisation continues working towards its goal achievement, it is an indicator that the directing function is being performed well.

4. All pervasive– Directing is performed at all levels in an organisation. It is the duty of all managers and supervisors.

5. Continuous nature– The manager has to continuously guide and supervise his subordinates so that they can align their objectives with the organisational objectives.

IMPORTANCE OF DIRECTING

Plans remain mere plans until and unless they are put into action. In the absence of direction, subordinates will have no idea about the work they are expected to do. They may not be inspired to complete the job satisfactorily. Implementation of plans is chiefly the concern of directing function. As a function of management, directing is useful in many ways. The importance of directing stems from the benefits it gives to an organisation. The importance of directing has been outlined below :

1. Initiates actions– Direction is the starting point of the work performance of subordinates. It is from here that the action takes place; subordinates understand their jobs and do according to the given instructions. Whatever are plans implemented are only through direction.

2. Motivates– Direction function helps in achievement of goals through the use of the element of motivation. This improves subordinate performance. It is accomplished by providing incentives or compensation, whether monetary or non-monetary. Motivation is the driving force that makes employees deliver expected output.

3. Provides stability– Stability and balance are very important factors for long-term survival of the business in the market. Directing brings stability through a judicious blend of persuasive leadership, effective communication, strict supervision and efficient motivation. Stability is very important since that is an index of growth of an enterprise.

4. Efficient utilisation of resources– Direction helps in clarifying the role of every subordinate towards his work. The resources can be utilised properly only when there is less wastage as well as duplication of efforts and performance overlap doesn't occur. Through direction, the role of subordinates become clear as manager makes use of his acquired skills to inspire the subordinates. This helps in maximum possible utilisation of resources of men, machine, materials and money which helps in reducing costs and increasing profits.

5. Helps in coping up with changes– It is human behaviour that puts up resistance to change. Adaptability with changing environment helps in sustaining planned growth and becoming a market leader. It is the function of directing that enables the organisation to cope with internal and external environmental changes.

ELEMENTS OF DIRECTING

Directing is not a single but a group of functions. The following elements fall in its scope :

1. Supervision
2. Motivation
3. Leadership
4. Communication

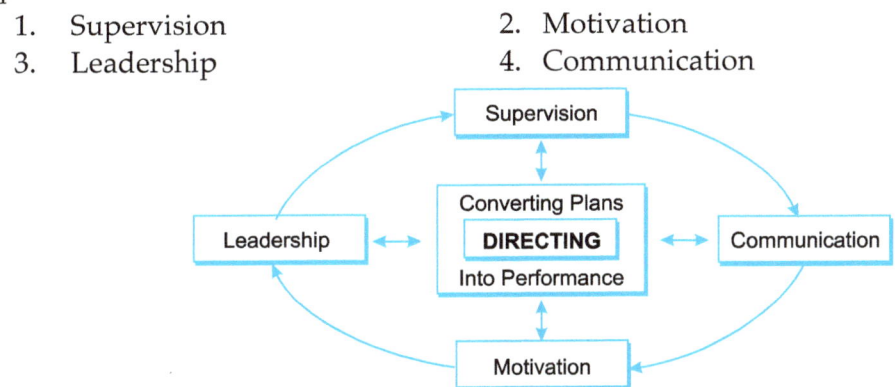

Fig. 11.1 Elements of Directing

Supervision

The word 'Supervision' can be broken down into two words where 'super' means over and above and 'vision' means seeing. Hence, supervision is an act of seeing the activities of the employees from over and above. Supervision is important to ensure that acceptable standards of workmanship are maintained and employee practices are in line with established policies. In other words, supervision can be defined as instructing, guiding, monitoring and observing the employees while they are busy carrying out their assigned duties.

Supervisors need to make sure that work is done according to the plans laid down by the higher management. As part of supervisory function, the managers must clarify instructions in case of any ambiguity, resolve problems and ensure cooperation and smooth working in their team. The supervisor has to :

> Supervision improves the working of the supervisee. It includes evaluation, monitoring and correction of performance.

1. oversee their subordinates at work,
2. look out for deviations,
3. ensure remedial means to remove obstacles, and
4. wherever required initiate training and development to see to it that the workforce attains necessary wherewithal to satisfactory job performance.

The importance of supervision must never be underestimated. Supervisors are the important link between the actual workforce and the management. They are the medium through which the management communicates with the workforce and the workforce interacts with the management. They communicate the policies, the plans and dreams of the organisation to the employees. They motivate and energize the workforce to focus its energy towards joint goals. Any miscommunication can adversely affect the organisation as a whole.

The supervisors have to raise the morale and job satisfaction level of the workers, help the workers to avoid stress while remaining focused on the goals. They have to share responsibilities with the supervisees and lead them. This highlights how important it is for a supervisor to possess leadership skills. They have to share the organisational vision with the workers and make them willing partners in the organisational progress.

Functions of a Supervisor

The various functions of a supervisor are defined as under :

1. Guiding subordinates– A supervisor's primary duty is to guide the subordinates and help them regarding the technical aspects of the job. He ensures all required raw materials and tools are made available to the workers so that their work goes on unhindered.

2. Scheduling of work– The supervisor is responsible for planning the work schedule and ensuring that production activities continue without a hindrance. He has to ensure that each work cycle is completed in time.

3. Issuing instructions– It is the supervisor's duty to issue instructions as and when necessary for the timely execution of work. The instructions may also be regarding how a particular work is to be done. He is also responsible for inducting new workers and familiarising them with the work process. The supervisor oversees the work at every stage and keeps a check on quality control.

4. Maintaining discipline– Maintaining discipline at the workplace is an important duty of the supervisor. He has to ensure that all rules and procedures are being followed without violation on part of any worker.

5. Motivating workers– The supervisor is responsible for ensuring that the morale and spirit of workers does not dwindle. This is very important for the organisation as a whole. Appreciation and recognition of good work and making sure the employees get monetary incentives for good work are some of the important duties of the supervisor.

6. Redressing grievances– If a worker experiences any problem pertaining to his work and performance he needs to approach the supervisor. It is the supervisor's duty to listen to such grievances, issues or problems and take steps to redress the wrong done. If necessary, the supervisor makes recommendations to the higher authorities. He can ask for action against erring workers and recommend rewards for the outstanding ones.

7. Monitoring performance– The supervisor is duty bound to check the daily performance of all workers in his department. He has to notice every worker achieves the targets in terms of quality and quantity. The supervisor has to keep a formal record of employee performance.

8. Reporting– The supervisor has to submit timely reports regarding the work done, the deviations in performance or targets, breakdowns (if any), anticipated problems on the shopfloor, etc. These are important inputs for the management. Additionally, the supervisor has to maintain records regarding workers attendance, leaves, late comings, etc.

9. Ensuring workers safety at workplace– This is another important aspect of the duty of a supervisor. Besides being in-charge of the proper functioning of plant and machinery kept under his supervision, he has to ensure that the safety of workers is not compromised. He plays a vital role in ensuring that industrial accidents are avoided.

Distinction between Directing and Supervision

Directing	Supervision
1. Directing is telling people what to do and issuing instructions describing how a task is to be done. It goes much beyond supervision.	1. Supervision is merely ensuring that work is done in line with the instructions issued. It is an element of directing.
2. Directing is the function of the higher management.	2. Supervision is done at the operating management level.
3. Involves giving broad directions to the middle-level managers.	3. Supervision involves the middle level managers giving specific directions to the lower level managers
4. Directing does not necessarily involve face-to-face interaction between the higher and the mid-level managers.	4. There can be no supervision without face-to-face interaction between the middle level and the lower level managers.

Motivation

Motivation is the art and the science of influencing people so that they accomplish the objectives and goals of the organisation. Motive is the force that makes human beings work towards a particular objective. It acts as a stimulant for people to work hard. This force urges human beings to work in order so that certain intrinsic wants and desires are fulfilled. The intensity of the desire plays a very important role in motivating the person towards its fulfillment.

Motivation has been defined in a number of ways. According to Dubin, *"Motivation is the complex force starting and keeping a person at work in an organsation"*.

Dalton E. McFarland defines motivation as *"the way in which urges, drives, desires, aspirations, stirrings or needs direct, control or explain the behaviour of human beings."*

According to another noted writer, William Scott, *"Motivation is a process of stimulating people to action to accomplish desired goals."*

The accomplishment of organisational goals is not possible until and unless we harness the efforts of employees to its common goal by giving them a single unified target and making them strive towards attaining that target. This becomes all the more important when we consider that a demotivated worker can demoralise the entire team and may adversely impact the performance of the entire unit. The management has to bring about an environment of motivation in the organisation. Effectively motivating employees has been one of the most important and challenging duties of the management. Because motivation is highly individualised, managers have to use a number of techniques to keep their employees motivated and happy.

Features of Motivation

The following are the chief features of motivation :

1. **Psychological–** Motivation is a personal and psychological feeling that arises from people's wants and needs. It remains there as long as the need remains unfulfilled.

2. **Continuous process–** Human wants and desires are unlimited and do not exhaust as long as he lives or unless he consciously decides to get rid of them. Thus, motivation continues to exist as long as desires and wants exist.

3. **Complex–** Different human beings have different motivational needs. These needs do not remain static; they change from time to time. Different people satisfy their wants in different ways. One person may get satisfaction by living an expensive lifestyle, while another may be satisfied with simple living.

4. **Goal-directed–** The human being, when motivated, works towards the fulfillment of his needs. His activities are directed towards the fulfillment of his desired goals. Motivation is the force that directs his activities.

5. **Positive or negative–** People may be motivated both ways. They may be motivated to work hard, get rewarded and recognised for good work. While at the same time, some people may be negatively motivated. Their negative motivation may be seen in strikes, unrest and violence at the workplace and absenteeism at work.

6. **Influenced by different factors–** Human beings are influenced by internal needs and desires, and also by external factors such as their work environment, lifestyle, culture and patterns of the society.

Process of Motivation

The motivational process can be broken down into following steps :

1. **Recognition of the need–** Motivation starts with the recognition of the human need. Recognition nurtures the need to fulfill the need.

2. **Response and action–** When the person recognises his needs and desires; he starts working towards fulfillment of the needs. He takes action to satisfy the said needs and desires. His goal is the satisfaction of the need. Thus, he sets out on this goal-directed activity.

3. **Fulfillment of the need–** Once the need in question is satisfied, the person feels fulfilled. This satisfaction leads to a reduction on his tension and intensity of desire.

4. **Eruption of new and higher desire–** Human wants and desires are never ending. As soon as a desire is satisfied, another one crops up and the person once again starts looking for ways and means of satisfying it.

Maslow's Theory of Motivation

The theory of motivation was first propounded by Abraham H. Maslow an American psychologist and is called Maslow's Hierarchy of Needs. According to the theory, human needs can be classified into five categories and arranged in order of their importance. They are :

Abraham H. Maslow

1. **Survival or physiological needs–** These are the most basic needs that are vital for the human beings survival. These are the need for water, air, food and sleep. These needs are the most basic and instinctive needs. All other needs become secondary until these physiological needs are not met.

2. **Safety or security needs–** These include the requirement for safety and security. Security needs are important for survival. However, they are not as urgent and demanding as the physiological needs. The need for employment, health care and shelter from the perceived dangers are some examples of safety and security needs.

3. **Social or affiliation needs–** These include the need for belonging, love and affection. These needs are less demanding than physiological and security needs. Affiliations, friendships, families, social, community and religious involvement help to fulfill these needs.

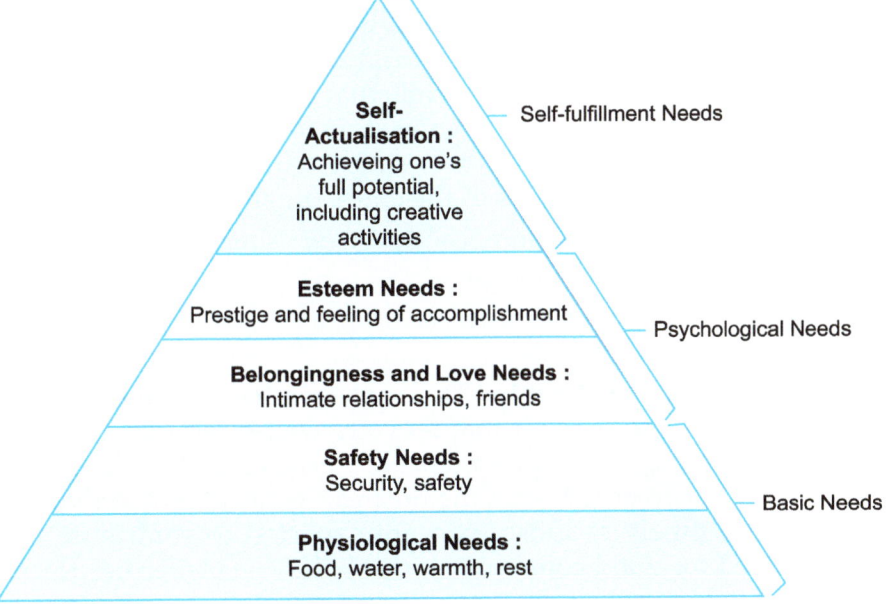

Fig. 11.2 Hierarchy of Needs

4. **Self-esteem needs–** The need to feel recognised by the society. Esteem needs become important only after the first three needs have been met. These include the need for self-esteem, personal worth, social recognition and accomplishment.

5. **Self-actualisation needs–** The need for spiritual and mental development is the highest need of all human beings.

Application of Maslow's Theory at Work

We can categorise Maslow's Theory into two broad categories specified as under :
1. **Deficiency needs**– These include safety and physiological needs.
2. **Development or growth needs**– These will include belonging, self-esteem and self-actualisation needs.

When we apply Maslow's theory to the workplace, we find that a manager's bottom responsibility is to make sure that the employees get fair and acceptable wages and a safe and secure work environment. It is the management's responsibility to give people the environment in which the employees grow, there by motivating them to deliver the best performance at work.

On the contrary, when the employees are given inadequate wages or an unhealthy work environment, it results in frustration on part of the workers and thus leads to substandard output due to poor performance.

Leadership

Leadership means influencing people and their behaviour and leading them to the achievement of certain goals and objectives. The qualities in a leader should be such that he influences and guides his followers towards the accomplishment of common goals.

Leadership is a very important aspect of management. The manager has to perform all duties as a leader and is expected to fulfill different roles that he or she may be called upon to fulfill. The leader will have to play many roles, which may be informational, decisional or even interpersonal. The basic role that the leader is required to play is to lead the organisation (or department) rally and the subordinates to a single unified line of action that resonates with predetermined objectives or goals of the entire organisation.

According to Koontz and O'Donnell, *"Leadership is the ability of a manager to induce subordinates to work with confidence and zeal."*

Louis A. Allen defines leader as, *"the one who guides and directs other people and gives their efforts, direction and purpose."*

Management includes leadership. The manager has to function as a leader by motivating the employees to see to it that they are well-directed towards fulfillment of corporate objectives. One of the requirements of effective leadership is good communication. The manager has to ensure that the business goals and objectives are communicated effectively and timely to those who are expected to contribute to those goals. Therein lays the need for good communication skills. The leader has to ensure that his message is understood with the least distortion, is received well and is acted upon. The leader has to make sure that if there is any dissonance, he is around to take effective measures and clear any misgivings that could later on have any adverse effect on the employee performance.

Guidance, empathy and encouragement are also a part and parcel of the traits of a good manager if he has to come out as an effective leader. At times conditions could be adverse to the interests of the organisation. Targets may not be met many a times. There could be other problems which may have a temporary unfavourable effect on the unit's performance. During such hard times the manager has to come forward to raise the morale of his subordinates. Encouragement and motivation go a long way in uplifting their sagging morale. A good leader has to be patient when there is no wind in the sails.

A good leader, and by extension, a good manager must be ready to solve employee problems, formal or informal. He must have the wherewithal to empathize and must be seen by employees to be a trusted person. He must be able to fire-up their enthusiasm and spur them to higher achievement. The capability of a leader or a good manager depends much on how he can influence the actions of his fellow workers. This influence has to be exerted in the right direction. When the manager acquires the cap of a leader his outlook becomes quite different; he looks at things from a long-term perspective. He scans the horizon and beyond. He has to organise the people and define them for well-thought-out jobs.

Distinction between Leadership and Management

Though leadership and management are often thought of as one and the same, there are important differences between the two that set them apart. They are :

1. Relationship– For a management we need a formal group where there is a superior-subordinate relationship. This superior-subordinate relationship cannot exist in an informal group. But a leadership requires no formal relationship or a formal organisation. Leadership can exist both in formal as well as in informal surroundings. Managers will have subordinates by definition, but leaders will have followers.

2. Focus– The manager focuses on managing people, whereas the leader focuses on leading the people.

3. Origin of influence– The authority of a manager stems from his formal appointment to the position of a manager. He is formally bestowed with the authority to direct the behaviour of his subordinates. On the other hand, a leader has no formal authority, but derives strength from the people who are his followers. He uses acceptance authority to bring about a change in the behaviour of the people.

4. Definition-wise difference– Leadership means to influence and motivate, and empower people to contribute to the achievement of goals. On the other hand, management implies directing and controlling groups and coordinating their activities towards the formal organisational objectives.

5. Distribution of rewards– The manager has the authority to allocate and distribute material or financial rewards and compensation to participating group members. However, the leader has no such authority. He can only give social satisfaction to his followers.

6. Different approach to tasks– The leader uses his guidance, inspiration and commitment for a task to motivate his followers; while the manager creates policies, procedures and strategies to achieve goals.

7. Accountability– The manager is more accountable for all managing functions. But, the leader does not have a clear-cut accountability in his role.

8. Working style– The leader generally adopts a consultative, transformational and participative style of working; whereas a manager may be autocratic and authoritative at the same time.

Characteristics of a Good Leader

A good and effective leader should have the following features embedded in his personality.

1. **Initiative–** A good leader should have the courage to initiate changes. He should be bold enough to hold on to opportunities and implement new ideas.

2. **Intelligence–** He should have intelligence to assess the problems fairly and arrive at sound judgment on the basis of observation.

3. **Integrity and honesty–** A leader should have honesty and integrity, so that the followers have trust in their leadership.

4. **Good decision-maker–** The leader has to be a good and quick decision-maker, free of bias and prejudice. He should be willing to listen to all.

5. **Emotionally stable–** A leader needs to show emotional balance when confronted with emotions and sentiments. He must display stability in the face of odds.

6. **Good communication skills–** The leader must be good at communication. He must have good persuasion skills and needs to be a good speaker able to inspire people.

7. **Sense of responsibility–** He must be a person to whom people can look up to for support in times of need. He should be able to assume responsibility and take ownership of problems and have the courage to withstand and overcome obstacles.

8. **Vision and foresight–** Leading is all about the future. A good leader should be able to anticipate the future, what the future promises for the business and how the organisation can benefit from the favourable business environment that a future may hold for it.

9. **Inspire–** The leader should be able to inspire his followers towards the achievement of goals. He must be capable of exhorting the people to exceptional efforts so that all obstacles can be overcome.

10. **Willing to take up challenges–** The leader must not be one who is not willing to take up challenges. Ability to stand up to challenges is one of the basic traits of leadership.

Communication

Communication can be defined as "the act of conveying information from one person to another, or from one person to a group. It should be done in such a way that the message suffers the least distortion on the way, and is conveyed in a manner that it is understood by the receiver exactly the way it was intended to be by the sender." Thus, communication links the different functions of management. It is the primary means by which people obtain and exchange information.

According to Mockler, "Communication is the process of passing information, ideas or even emotions from one person to another."

According to Newman and Summer, "Communication is an exchange of fact, ideas, opinions or emotions by two or more persons".

Keith Davis defines communication as "Communication is the process of passing information and understanding from one person to another."

The importance of communication lies in the fact that it links all other functions of management. Management is a joint organisational effort in which all members need to know what and where they are to focus their energy.

In today's dynamic world, communication is a vital part of our daily life. We all depend on communication, social or businesswise. The information technology and communication facilities available to us today enables us to continually exchange information, ideas, thoughts, opinions and data (business and academic) on a continuous basis. This exchange can be electronic (through the internet, TV or radio) or printed (newspapers, magazines).

Communication can be of different types, such as :
1. Oral (By word of mouth)
2. Written (Printed, handwritten)
3. Visual (Posters, charts, models, etc.)
4. Action (Body language)

Characteristics of Communication

The key characteristics of communication are as follows :

1. At least two persons– Communication involves at least two persons, one who sends the message or communication and the other who receives the communication, *i.e.,* the person for whom it is intended.

2. Continuous process– Communication is a continuous, ongoing process. Organisational activity requires a continuous exchange of information and ideas within an organisation.

3. Omni-directional– Communication flows in all directions of an organisation. In other words, it is from top to bottom and vice-versa. The managers may send information to their subordinates and the subordinates may send feedback to the higher authorities. Managers on the same level of the organisation hierarchy may also need to exchange information and feedback.

4. Influencing human behaviour– The objective of effective communication is to influence human behaviour and direct or shape organisational members behaviour by exchanging information, opinions and feelings. Communication is also responsible for converting negative feelings into positive feelings.

5. Two-way process– Communication is a two-way process in the sense that the receiver by sending the message expects a feedback from the receiver's end. This feedback may be in the form of reports or opinion, or facts and figures. The two-way exchange is a signal that the communication has been understood.

6. Multi channel– Communication can be formal or informal. Formal communication can be vertical or horizontal and vertical communication may flow upwards or downwards.

7. Multi media– Communication can be written or verbal. It can be textual or can include graphics. It can also be in the form of body language.

8. Facilitates understanding– The basic objective of communication is to enable instructions to be easily understood by the expected receiver and to elicit the required response from them.

Objectives of Communication

There could be a number of objectives of communication depending upon who is sending and to whom. A son may communicate with his parents, a student may communicate with teachers or fellow students, friends may communicate with their circle, a government may communicate with its officials, and the corporate officials may communicate within their own organisation or with other business houses. In all these cases, the objective and goals of the activity differs.

The important objectives of communication are the following :

1. To help in sound decision-making– Communication helps in sound decision making with its quick flow of information. However, this flow of information must be relevant, accurate and timely. Any information which is not timely or received late, will cease to be of any use to its receiver. In today's technological world, the flow needs to be swift, on a real time basis, and must be in a form that can be readily understood by the receiver so that the receiver is in a state to put that information to productive use.

2. To keep the receivers well abreast of developments, speed decision-making– It is the steady flow of information that connects the receiver to developments in his environment thus keeping him abreast of what may be going on in his area of interest or work. This enables the receiver to be mentally prepared for any emergency or extra input that may be required of him in order to correct emerging situations in and around his area of work.

3. To help in flow of information related to work and promote efficiency– For any business unit or entity, the information system is designed to help in the timely flow of information that will help, or is expected to help in attaining business objectives and furthering the goals of the business house. The information should be relevant to the work of area of interest of the business entity. Otherwise, it will be a waste of resource.

4. To strengthen business relations– One of the very important objectives of communication is that the information flow network must help in cementing public relations of the organisation with other entities. It is ideal to communicate the organisational objectives and goals to the employees to keep them focused on their objectives. Second, the various stakeholders such as the shareholders, the creditors and the customers need to be kept informed about the position of the organisation. This boosts their confidence in the organisation. The company needs to stay in the public limelight. It must boost its corporate or business image. This can be effectively done with a good communication system.

5. To fulfill advisory and authoritative requirements– There is a growing need to keep in touch with the staff, make them feel connected and in loop by the higher management. From time to time, the staff should be given advice on critical or emerging issues so that they are mentally prepared to deal with situations. Advisory can also be issued for bringing about improvement in the workforce and boosting their morale. At times important instructions may also be issued advising them how to address situations. All these requirements and needs can be fulfilled through a communication system.

6. To carry out the change– Communication is a very powerful medium of affecting and bringing about desired changes in opinion and thoughts of an audience.

Though both verbal and written communication can bring about this change, written or formal communication is the preferred medium to bring lasting changes in the way people think and go about doing things. A very powerful means of persuasion, it must be on a continuous basis if it has to achieve the desired result. Communication on an on-and-off basis will fail to bring about any lasting benefit. It needs to be focused and constant.

7. To educate and motivate people– Organisations publish in-house journals or forward electronic mails through which they provide a platform to bring about greater enlightenment and reinforce learning about the usage of their products and services, etc.

Communication inspires the employees to work towards achievement of organisational goals. By giving access to information about the organisation, communication helps in building workers loyalty towards the organisation. It motivates them and creates cordial relationships.

Types of Communication

Communication is of two types. Both are explained below :

Formal Communication

Formal communication is the exchange of information on an official to official basis. Formal communication becomes necessary in order to carry out the organisational duties. It is done in accordance with prescribed patterns and procedures. For example, a general manager may issue instructions to a manager who may then, in turn, issue instructions to the supervisors.

Examples of Formal Communication :
- Downward communication: instructions, directions, orders, feedback.
- Upward communication: data required to complete projects, status reports.

Informal Communication

Communication that takes place on the basis of informal or social relations among the members of the organisation is called Informal Communication. For example, there can be sharing of information between a finance manager and a production manager as they happen to be friends. This exchange of information is not along formal relationships established by the management. Instead, it is along informal channels due to friendly interaction of members of an organisation. It may be personal or related to organisational matters. Informal communication is also known as the 'grapevine'.

Steps in the Communication Process

The process of communication consists of the following steps :

1. Sender– The sender initiates the process of communication. He or she sends the message which may be in a textual or a graphic form. It may also be an audio message.

2. Message– The message, the subject matter of communication, is what is conveyed by the sender. It may consist of text or graphics, sound, or a combination of these.

3. Encoding– This is the use of the suitable language for sending the message. The subject matter of the communication is to be transmitted into a set of words or symbols understandable to both the sender and the receiver.

4. Media– The media represents the channel or the medium through which the message must pass in order to get to the receiver. This media or channel could be the telephone, internet or television. It may also be a face-to-face talk, or can also be in the form of print.

5. Receiver– The receiver is the person or a group at whom the sender directs the message.

6. Decoding– Translating or interpreting the message so that it can be understood by the receiver.

7. Feedback– If the receiver does not respond to the message sent to him, it may mean that the message has not been received. It may also indicate the ineffectiveness of the message.

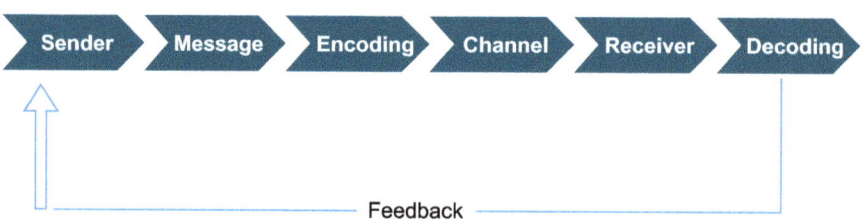

Fig. 11.3 Communication Process

Barriers to Communication

The main barriers to communication are given below :

1. Perceptual– Perception is how we see and interpret a message. Our judgement, social values and emotions often act as barriers. If there is lack of trust and confidence between the sender and the receiver it may act like a barrier.

2. Language– Language is a powerful medium for communication; yet it can also be an obstacle in certain cases. The significance of a message may be lost in translation. The meaning of the message sent in a translated language may be misunderstood.

Barriers to Communication
• Perceptual
• Language
• Cultural
• Environmental
• Organisational
• Psychological
• Stress
• Systematic barriers

3. Cultural– Culture plays an important role in deciphering the messages directed at people. The culture people belong to shapes their interpretation of a message. Many a times cultural factors are overlooked in communications which results in poor reception of the communicated messages. The culture dictates norms of social interaction in the society. These details need to be kept in mind when designing a message.

4. Environmental– If there is an environment of mistrust, fear, anxiety, then these factors will act as a barrier to effective communication. If we need a message to reach its intended target efficiently, we need to give it an environment free of these factors.

5. Organisational– Where communication is internal to an organisation, the organisational culture needs to be kept in mind while designing the message to be communicated. At times organisational work overload can cause distortion or act as barrier to communication. Meeting timelines, fulfilling targets, report generations can also be a barrier to effective communication. The size of an organisation can also affect the way communication is received. In a complex organisational hierarchy, it is likely for a sent message to get distorted.

6. **Psychological or personal barriers**– The perception and behaviour of people play an important role in their reception of messages. If people tend to resist change, it will assert influence on any message they receive. Internal bias also affects the reception of messages. People may have a bias against change, against technology, against certain superiors, or subordinates, and this may affect their reception of corporate communication.

7. **Stress**– In certain cases the receiver may be pre-occupied with work, either organisational or personal. They may also be over stressed with work. In such case, the message may not receive the attention it deserves. This inadequate attention may cause the message to be partially understood.

8. **Systematic barriers**– A poorly designed or faulty communication system acts as a barrier to communication. This can also happen if the employees are fed with insufficient about their roles and responsibilities.

Overcoming Barriers to Communication

Communication is a process that has two or more participants, one being the sender who is responsible for disseminating the message, and the second one being the receiver at whom the message is directed. There is also the channel through which the message is communicated. An efficient channel of communication is that where the message suffers the least distortion and reaches the receiver in a way the sender intended it to be received in terms of content as opposed to terms of effect or influence. More often than not, messages suffer from distortions as there may be many disturbances on its way from the sender to the receiver.

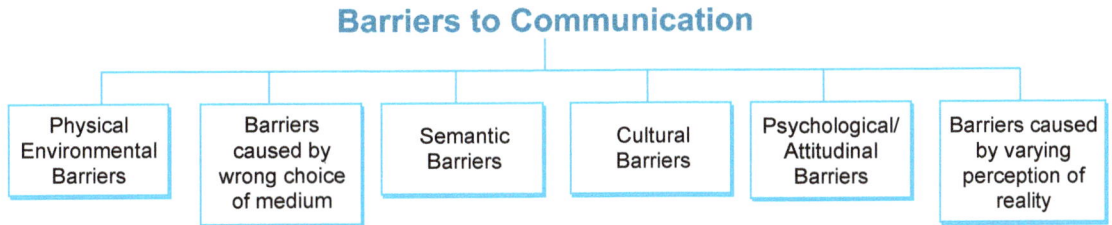

As seen above barriers to communication are of different types ranging from systematic to psychological.

An organisation that is beset with communication problems must analyse where the actual barriers lie. It must scan for signs that suggest problems in the organisation may be the result of barriers in communications. For example, an organisation may be facing problems of discipline within its workforce. It could also be due to the roadblocks in the achievement of organisational goals. What must be understood is that the inability to achieve those goals may not be the problem, instead the real problem could lie somewhere else; the shortfall in objective achievement could be an indicator that there exists a problem. The organisation must first ensure that it is able to identify the barriers to effective communication. Once the barriers are identified, the organisation can get down working on plugging the loopholes in communication.

Ways to Overcome Barriers to Communication

1. Proper language– A message can be effective if it is properly worded in a language that is simple and easily understood by the receiver.

2. Properly drafted message– If the message is properly drafted, has clarity and is concise, it will be properly understood.

3. Motivation– If a message is worded in a way that it inspires, it will motivate the receiver. Messages should be such that inspire confidence and build trust in the receiver.

4. Good listening skills– In case of verbal and telephonic communication, lack of listening skills, both on part of the sender and receiver, is often responsible for ineffective communication. Listening skills must be developed as this can greatly contribute to effective communication.

5. Employee orientation– Problems can arise in communication when people are not aware of their rights and duties and their role in the organisation. In such a scenario, the organisation should orient the members, apprise them of their responsibilities, make clear who is to report to whom and when. These measures will go a long way in ironing out the creases in effective communication.

6. Open door policy– The management must keep its communication doors open and should be ready to listen to all who wish to communicate.

7. Use of informal groups– At times informal groups play a great role in communicating through informal means of communication. They can be used as a communication strategy to achieve the organisational communication goals.

SUMMARY

Directing– It is the management function of converting plans into actual performance through the use of the human factor.

Elements of Directing– Supervision, motivation, leadership and communication are the elements of directing.

Supervision– This is the function of overseeing people at work. It includes work planning, issuing instructions, giving guidance, ensuring discipline and handling grievances. It also includes formal record keeping of the shopfloor.

Motivation– This means the process of ensuring that workers remain inspired and have high morale so that the input increases.

Maslow's Theory of Motivation– This theory states that human beings have certain intrinsic, never ending needs and wants which require fulfillment.

Leadership– This is the process of influencing people and inspiring them towards a goal. A leader needs to be a visionary, courageous and honest person willing to take up challenges.

Communication– This function means the exchange of instructions, facts and reports, etc. It enables managers to understand situations and take timely and sound decisions.

Barriers to Communication– Any factor that contributes to a message not reaching its intended recipient, or causing distortion, is considered to be a barrier to communication. They can be classified as perceptual, emotional, cultural, psychological, organisational, inattention, systematic and language barriers.

QUESTIONS FOR PRACTICE

Very Short Answer Type Questions
1. Define the term 'Directing'.
2. Name the elements of directing function of management.
3. Define Leadership.
4. What is the significance of feedback in the process of communication?
5. State any two features of communication.
6. Outline the steps involved in the process of communication.
7. Write about any three barriers to communication.

Short Answer Type Questions
1. Bring out three differences between Leadership and Management.
2. What is 'Supervision'?
3. Explain the term 'Motivation'.
4. Write a short note on Maslow's Theory of Needs.
5. Explain the importance of communication in directing function.
6. Explain any four objectives of communication.
7. Elucidate the importance of communication in business.

Essay Type Questions
1. What is the importance of directing as a function of management?
2. Explain important elements of directing.
3. What is Maslow's Theory of Motivation?
4. How does Maslow' theory of motivation impact a business organisation?
5. In order to succeed as a good manager, does one also need to be a good leader?
6. What should be the qualities of a good leader?
7. Discuss the importance of communication in an organisation.
8. What can be the potential barriers to a communication system in an organisation?
9. Examine and identify the factors that obstruct free flow of communication. Suggest feasible steps to overcome them.
10. How can we overcome obstacles to communication in an organisation?

12. Controlling

> **LEARNING RESULT**
>
> After reading this chapter, you should be able to :
> - Understand the meaning and nature of Controlling.
> - Define the importance of Controlling.
> - Identify the limitations of Controlling.
> - Explain the steps in Controlling Process.
> - Understand the relationship between Controlling and Planning.
> - Elucidate Management by Exception.
> - Understand Span of Control.

Controlling consists of the steps taken in management to confirm that plans are being implemented and results being obtained as per the expected and pre-stated standards and guidelines. Where the performance deviates from the agreed and benchmarked levels, corrective action is immediately taken.

MEANING OF CONTROLLING

Controlling can be thought of as a process of monitoring performance and taking corrective action wherever necessary to get the desired results. This will involve checking performances, comparing with targeted results, issuance of instructions and rectification of errors, etc.

According to E.F.L. Brech, *"Control is checking current performance against predetermined standards contained in the plans, with a view to ensure adequate progress and satisfactory performance."*

According to Koontz and O' Donnell, *"Controlling is the measuring and correcting the activities of subordinates to ensure that events conform to plans."*

According to Theo Haimann, *"Controlling is the process of checking to determine whether or not plans are being adhered to, whether or not proper progress is being made towards the objectives and goals, and acting, if necessary, to correct any deviation."*

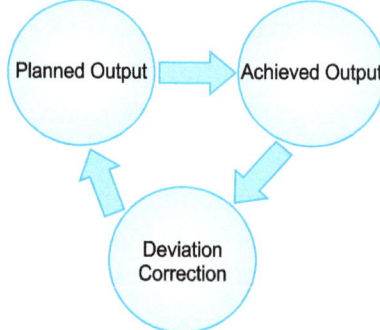

Fig. 12.1 Controlling

Given below are the two main objectives of controlling :
1. It facilitates coordination.
2. It helps in planning.

Thus, we see that controlling ensures that all actions are being carried out as per the plan, checks any deviation from the charted plan and takes corrective measures to make certain that the pre-decided course is being steered. Now, this is not as easy as it looks. For better controlling, standards of performance have to be established, information systems have to be designed to get timely feedback, areas of weakness have to be identified and worked upon, workforce has to be given required training and the actual performance has to be compared with established standard. Benchmarks have to be established or changed as and when required. All these activities have to be done on a continuing basis.

NATURE OF CONTROLLING

Controlling is one of the most taxing tasks a manager has to perform. If we look at the basic purpose of controlling, we will see that its objective in an organisation is to ensure that the people concerned have the necessary wherewithal to confront any problem and resolve it before it turns critical and results in a loss of revenue.

The main characteristics of controlling are listed below :

1. Management function– This is an important function of management. If controlling is excluded, then all other functions of management become futile.

2. Pervasive– Controlling is a function that is required at every level of the management. Extent of control may differ but the element of control will remain there.

3. Needs adaptability– Control is a very dynamic process in the sense that the changing needs, requirements and the operating environment of the firm have to be kept in view, and these may call for a change in process and procedures.

4. Continuous process– Controlling is a continuous or never ending process. There has to be a continuous monitoring of performance within the organisation.

5. Action oriented– The heart of controlling function lies in taking corrective measures against deviations. Controlling does not fulfill its purpose if it fails to correct the deviations.

6. Future-oriented– Controlling seeks to ensure that future performances are improved by monitoring the current performance and making sure that deviations are avoided in the future.

IMPORTANCE OF CONTROLLING

Controlling function is one of the four foundations of management. Its importance arises out of the necessity to ensure that tasks allocated to each department and each worker is carried out in the way it was meant to be carried out, and that the end product is of a certain quality that meets the accepted quality of the organisation.

The management, through controlling, ensures that the organisational train is running on schedule and on the right track. Controlling works according to a standard decided by the top management. The management continually monitors the organisation's performance with a certain yardstick. This ensures corrective measures against any deviations so that the major disturbances are taken care of before they take root.

The major important aspects of controlling are listed below :

1. Helps in achieving organisational goals– It is through the function of controlling that we can successfully execute plans and get fruitful and targeted results.

Timelines and targeted performances are ensured only through controlling. In fact, the secret of successful management lies in efficient controlling.

2. Optimum utilisation of resources– Controlling ensures avoidance of waste. It ensures that all avenues of wastage are plugged and resources, whether human or material, are optimally utilised. This leads to economy and greater profitability.

3. Facilitates coordination– Controlling helps in coordinating efforts towards the common organisational objectives. It removes overlapping and duplication of efforts, and by bringing in control at every level, ensures that there is organisational harmony.

Fig. 12.2 Importance of Controlling

4. Improves planning– Controlling examines every deviation and comes up with solutions. It also brings to the fore any flaw or fault in the planning. Thus, it ensures that plans are rectified and modified. In this way, it contributes to better planning, both long and short-term.

5. Eases supervision– Controlling sees to it that regular performance reports and updates are made and looked into; thus helping in identifying deviations and taking corrective measures before the issues escalate further. It thus brings efficiency to the function of supervision.

6. Introduces dynamism– Controlling keeps managers on the lookout for changes in the firm's operating environment. It helps them quickly anticipate and identify changes and how those changes could be effectively countered. It teaches the management adaptability and dynamism.

7. Brings order and discipline– Controlling seeks to bring order and discipline into the organisation by clearly defining workers behaviour in the work environment. By laying down the norms and procedures for settling workers issues, and resolving industrial disputes it ensures a congenial atmosphere.

8. Raises employee morale– By ensuring that workers issues are redressed and by rewarding performances controlling seeks to raise the employees' morale.

LIMITATIONS OF CONTROLLING

Following drawbacks have been identified in the controlling function :

1. Difficulty in arriving at quantitative standards– Controlling works well in areas where quantitative standardising is possible, like production and finance. However, it fails in areas like job satisfaction, employee motivation, etc. These are the domains where quantitative measurements don't work.

2. Employee resistance– Control fails to deliver when employees resist control measures. They consider it as an encroachment on their rights.

3. **Costly**– Often control measures are expensive in terms of overall cost and impact a firm adversely. It may also be time consuming. For smaller firms, this means cutting down their profit margin significantly.

STEPS IN CONTROLLING PROCESS

Below are the important steps that make the controlling function more beneficial for the organisation :

1. **Identifying areas of control**– The first step in controlling is to identify those functional areas that the organisation wishes to control. Therefore, the areas for control are identified before moving to the next step.

2. **Establishing standards of performance**– Establishing criteria or standards of performance is the next step towards maintaining control. The person who controls or the manager whose job is to keep an eye on performance must be able to evaluate performance in the light of standards that have been adopted as acceptable by the organisation. This requires that the organisation must establish reference points or standards which it can apply for comparisons. The standard can be the criteria of performance. The following standards can be adopted for control by an organisation :

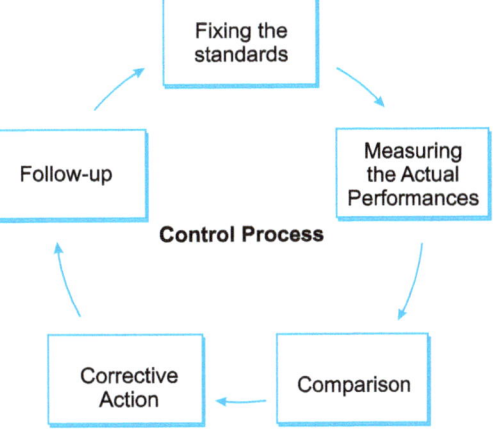

Fig. 12.3 Steps in Controlling Process

(a) Profitability of the organisation.
(b) Market share.
(c) Productivity and output.
(d) Labour relations and human resources utilisation.

These reference points or benchmarks have their origin in the overall objectives of the organisation and should be capable of being easily measured or interpreted. These performances can be in areas that an organisation thinks fit to measure.

3. **Measuring performance**– The next step is the measuring of performance in the areas that the organisation wants to control. It must be noted that controlling is an all-pervasive function and exists in all areas. Thus, performance has to be measured in all areas of the organisation. This measurement of performance should be in the terms of the established standards. Very often this can be a difficult exercise, but it has to be accomplished. The measurement needs to be accurate and timely.

4. **Comparing with accepted benchmarks**– Measuring performance in different areas of the organisation and then comparing it with targeted output or pre-stated standards facilitate knowing what is being actually accomplished. Different areas need to be measured at the same time to give an overall picture. If the yardstick or accepted standard of performance is well-defined and easily measurable, it helps in the accurate measuring and comparison of performance. This standard is the level of productivity

that an organisation accepts as a model for performance. It determines whether the performance is acceptable or not. Upon this determination will depend the next step, *i.e.*, whether the area needs corrective measures or an upward revision of targets and expectations.

    5. **Analysing deviations–** Deviations are analysed; and those beyond acceptable levels are examined in greater detail and their causes are identified. These causes maybe carelessness, environmental factors or flawed planning, etc.

    6. **Applying corrective measures–** This is the next and the final logical step wherein any or all deviations and errors in implementation are to be applied corrective measures so that things get back on the track they were intended to be. If this step is not taken, then the entire exercise and the purpose of controlling get defeated. The corrective measures could be department specific or it may also cut across several departments. It may involve the retrenchment and firing of workers, changes in plant and machinery, reconsidering the pre-decided standards of control and a possible adjustment in company goals and objectives.

RELATIONSHIP BETWEEN CONTROLLING AND PLANNING

    Planning and controlling go hand-in-hand. These are two functions of management that cannot exist on without each other. If there is to be planning in any rudimentary form, then there will have to be an exercise of control over the activity no matter how shallow it might be. On the other hand, there is no meaning of control in the absence of planning. In fact, both complement each other. The ideal situation should be that a business unit's plan must provide for a well thought out control process. Let us look at planning as the starting point of a business enterprise. It is at this point that an entrepreneur decides to produce a product to sell it to a predefined market. At this point, what is to be produced, when it is to be produced, how it is to be produced and all its allied issues are decided. The long-term aims and objectives of the business are put on paper at this point of time.

    If planning means deciding the course of action for an organisation's performance, then control can be said to be a set of control devices or processes and procedures for measuring the correctness and the direction of performance. In the event of any lack, or failure on part of planning, control procedures come into play to balance things out. Where control fails to live up to expectations, plans need to be readjusted to puts things back on the right track.

    The major thrust of controlling is to monitor progress and look out for deviations from the pre-decided route that may hinder progress and may prevent the business from achieving stated goals. It may have to take corrective actions which may differ from department to department of a unit. For example, a unit where the workforce is not performing in accordance with expected results may call for the training of the workforce; it may also call for some incentives, or penalties. In extreme cases, it may require the laying off of some of the workforce. If the sales target is not being met, reasons will have to be analysed; the quality of products or services may require some changes or improvement which will have to be brought about. The likes and dislikes of consumers may have to be enquired and products or services refocused around the new consumer choices. Any shortfall in production from the target production as planned will require to be enquired into and its causes analysed. Required plant and machinery may need to be added or modernised; new production technology may have to be deployed. Controlling means locating and pinpointing shortfalls and deviations and the causes thereof. It does not end there. It also has to come up with solutions to the problems.

Occasionally, we find there is a mindset against controlling. Certain sections assume that controlling is a function through which employee rights are curtailed and violated. Management has to see to it that what has been planned is being achieved. If there is a deviation between the planned output and the achieved output, the deviations need to be rectified and the reasons eliminated so that deviations do not recur. It is the controlling function of management that looks after all this.

Difference between Planning and Controlling

Planning	Controlling
1. Establishes objectives.	1. Establishes parameters or benchmarks.
2. Determines activities.	2. Measures and compares results.
3. Delegates work.	3. Evaluates output.
4. Allocates resource mix.	4. Evaluates optimum utilisation of allocated resources.

Another very important difference which defines the boundary between planning and controlling is that the latter checks for deviations, provides for rectification of errors.

MANAGEMENT BY EXCEPTION

In a business environment, a vast number of issues and problems crop up which keep the management busy, thus, encroaching on their precious time. Many a times, the management is kept busy on small issues when the managers should have to focus on more important issues. This eats into the managers' time. To bypass such a situation, to save management from wasting its time and resources on issues of little worth, to ensure that management is able to focus on issues and problems that need to be solved on a priority basis, the practice of management by exception is often found helpful by businesses.

Management by exception is the concept that the problem should be brought to the management's notice, only if they exceed a certain level. Only such problems are brought to the management's notice that represent a serious departure from the established or planned norm and can have a serious impact on the company's goals. The lower or the middle management measure performance and bring deviations to the notice of the higher management. In other words, a management will take no action if things go as planned and there is no deviation from established norms, or the deviation is within acceptable limits. This leaves time for the higher management to deal with strategic and tactical issues.

Certain business units have re-adapted this concept. What they have done is that while letting the higher management take care of strategic issues they allocate smaller issues to the lower level managers for resolution. These allocations are done as per established policies of the organisation.

Advantages of Management by Exception

1. Allows higher management to make productive use of time– The fact that higher management now has to attend only to issues that are of strategic or tactical importance, gives them much needed time to make better use of resources. It cuts down on the amount of data they are to review; consequently, allowing them extra time to attend to pressing issues.

2. Allows greater flexibility and initiative to middle and lower management– It allows the lower and middle management the opportunity to contribute proactively to the goals and achievements of the organisation and makes them feel an important cog in the decision making machinery. It allows them to gain firsthand experience, thereby, preparing them for shouldering higher responsibilities.

3. Reduces work load for internal audit people– As issues are resolved more and more efficiently and in numerically larger quantities, it reduces the burden on the internal audit department. They can now concentrate on larger issues rather than waste their time on all and sundry.

Disadvantages of Management by Exception

1. Centralised decision-making– Management by exception is rooted in the system of centralised management. Issues to be resolved are allocated by a central group of managers. This calls for a decentralised system of management where situations can be monitored by the local managers who can be given a wider mandate to decide themselves.

2. Dependence on financial analysts– Management by exception extensively uses financial data that is compiled by financial professionals and used by management to arrive at conclusions. We find that this concept cannot function in the absence of people who do not have an in-depth knowledge of financial side of management, who cannot decode financial statements and reports and analysis. If they fail somehow to spot the significance, misread or wrongly conclude the pattern of financial data, it may lead to a serious lapse on part of the management.

3. Debatable concept– This is a concept that focuses on high impact issues. Therefore, this concept overlooks issues which may appear minor at the beginning, but stand a good chance of snowballing into serious proportions if not looked into properly from the very start. If middle and lower management lacks the wherewithal to deal with such cases the results and output can be skewed. Thus, instead of resolving an issue it may compound it.

Secondly, it is seen that management by exception concept is applied in situations where the cost of proactive management is very high. The more a process is capable of being measured and benchmarked, the more sense this concept makes.

4. Dependence on budgets– Management by exception has an over dependency on budgets and the accuracy with which these documents have been compiled. Any inaccuracy in the compilation of these, any overambitious target setting, any irrelevancy can and will result in a waste of time of the managers concerned.

5. Works on assumption– The concept of management by exception works on the assumption that everything is proceeding according to the plan if nothing is brought to the notice of the higher management. As it has been already pointed above that major deviations could be concealed by vested interest and the higher management will rest with the assumption, though false, that since things are not being brought to its notice, all is going well.

SPAN OF CONTROL

Span of control refers to the number of persons a manager or supervisor can control. The span of control concept was propounded by Sir Ian Hamilton in the UK around 1922 out of the need to quantify the number of people one person could actually supervise or control effectively. It has been concluded that the time spent on supervision increases geometrically if the number of supervised people are higher. With each increase in the span of control there is a decrease in the effectiveness of supervision. Thus, there emerges a need to strike a careful balance regarding the number of people working under the watchful eye of a manager so that there can be effective supervision at all levels within the organisation.

Narrow Span of Control

A narrow span of control means that a manager supervises or controls a small group of persons or subordinates. When a narrow span of control is present in a medium or large organisation, there is a need for a large number of managers or supervisors so that more people get supervised for better working. Normally, a narrow span of control restricts the number of persons the supervisor or manager may interact with, thereby, making the task easier and more effective. On the flip side, it restricts the number of people in a group and may be harmful to effective communication.

Advantages of Narrow Span of Control

A narrow span of contorl can have the following advantages :

1. Under narrow span of control, every supervised person gets more attention from the supervisor with respect to his work. This leads to intensive specialisation for the subordinates.
2. The narrow span is of great utility in industries where fine workmanship and close supervision is required.
3. Due to less workload, decisions are prompt and sound.

Wide Span of Control

A wide span of control means comparatively lesser number of managers and supervisors are controlling a larger group of subordinates. This large span of control fits organisations where the job is of repetitive nature and employees are engaged in similar tasks. In such case, controlling becomes easier despite the large size of the group. Communication also becomes easy within the group.

Advantages of Wide Span of Control

A wide span of control can have the following advantages :

1. It leads to comparatively better communication.
2. Since, a smaller number of supervisors control a comparatively large number of subordinates; it leads to lower costs of supervision.
3. Supervision improves within each supervised group.

Factors Influencing Span of Control

The factors influencing the span of control are given below :

1. Degree of centralisation– A high degree of decentralisation enables a manager to supervise a large number of subordinates. This means a wide span of control. On the other hand, if there is centralisation, the manager will have to do a lot of decision-making. This is known as narrow span of control.

2. Nature of work– The span of control is influenced by the nature of work within an organisation. The more a work is specialised, the narrower will be the span of control to help in close and personal supervision. Work of a repetitive nature requires wider span of control as close supervision is not so much required here.

3. Organisational size– The size of an organisation matters when it comes to deciding the span of control. In larger organisations there is generally narrow span of control. This can be attributed to a large number of factors such as availability of resources, financial and human both to the larger organisation, nature of activities being carried out, etc. On the other hand, smaller organisations tend to have a wide span of control; the reasons being paucity of resources and nature of the activities being carried out.

4. Workforce abilities and competency– Abilities and competency of a workforce play a great role in deciding the span of control in an organisation. Where a subordinate stands up to the task delegated to him/her with little or no supervision, there is less need of close supervision. If the subordinate is qualified and experienced enough to understand his job and accomplishes it within the required time, then there is no need for a narrow span of control. However, in situations where the workforce ability and competency does not measure up to the required standard, there will be required close and near personal supervision to ensure goal achievement. In such a case, the span can be gradually adjusted as the workforce gains enough expertise and ability.

5. Communication and control techniques– In organisations that have a very effective system of communication the span of control is wide. In such organisations, the need for face-to-face interaction with supervisors is reduced. Further, the control procedures such as regular and timely reporting and the reports coming from different departments contribute to reduce the need for close supervision. As a result, the organisation can have a wide span of control.

6. Location of operations– The span of control will tend to be narrow, if the organisational operations are widely dispersed. It is easier for a manager to control a large group if it is located close to him physically.

7. Availability of specialist staff– Where the team of specialists is available, a manager can have a wide span of control as advice and assistance is readily available. But when specialist staff is not available to help in decision-making, the manager has no other choice but to make decisions on his own. This tends to put a lot of load on the manager, as a result, narrowing the span of control.

> ### SUMMARY
> ***Controlling–*** *It is the management process that ensures organisational goals are achieved through careful monitoring of performances.*
> ***Relationship between Planning & Controlling–*** *Planning is based on forecasting and controlling is measuring and evaluating past performances and then trying to improve the future.*
> ***Management by Exception–*** *This is a concept where managerial action is focused only in the event of exceptional deviations from planned and targeted performance.*
> ***Span of Control–*** *It means the number of subordinates a manager has under his effective control. There can be a wide or a narrow span of control.*
> ***Narrow Span of Control–*** *This means the manager has a few subordinates to supervise. This is common in a work environment where the work is specialised and requires close supervision.*
> ***Wide Span of Control–*** *The manager has a large number of subordinates to control. Wide span of control is common where the work is of a repetitive nature and does not require specialised skills.*

QUESTIONS FOR PRACTICE

Very Short Answer Type Questions
1. 'Planning provides the basis for control'. Explain.
2. List two limitations of controlling.
3. Write a short note on the steps involved in the process of control.
4. List any two factors determining the span of control.

Short Answer Type Questions
1. What is Controlling?
2. What are the objectives of controlling?
3. Explain briefly the various steps in the process of control.
4. Explain the essentials of a good control system.
5. List three differences between Controlling and Planning.

Essay Type Questions
1. Can an organisation carry out the functions of controlling without first establishing standards of performance?
2. How can deviations in performance be corrected through the control function?
3. Is there a relationship existing between Planning and Controlling?
4. "The essence of control is in action". Comment.
5. Explain Management by Exception.
6. It is said that management by exception overlooks minor issues that may assume serious proportions and pose problems later on for the organisation. Give your opinion on this.
7. "Controlling is an inseparable function of management". Comment.
8. "Controlling is of no constructive value if it cannot accomplish results according to pre-established plans." Comment.
9. Elucidate on "Controlling is a continuous activity."
10. Explain Span of Control.
11. What are the factors influencing the span of control in an organisation?

13 | Marketing : Concept and Functions

> **LEARNING RESULT**
> After reading this chapter, you should be able to :
> ◆ Understand the meaning of Market and Marketing.
> ◆ Explain the traditional and modern concept of Marketing.
> ◆ Distinguish between Marketing and Selling.
> ◆ Describe the objectives of Marketing.
> ◆ Identify the importance of Marketing.
> ◆ Define the functions of Marketing.
> ◆ Elucidate E-Marketing.

Traditionally, the term market means the place where the buyers and sellers gathered to buy and sell. With the passage of time, the word market came to be known as the sum total of buyers that were willing to buy a product. However, even this meaning underwent a change. Now, when we talk of a market it means all the buyers and sellers who interact with one another with the intention of buying or selling anything of value. Marketing can broadly be divided into three main parts namely; (i) Concentration, (ii) Dispersion and (iii) Equalisation.

Concentration refers to the process of procuring goods from different places and collecting them at a central point. Dispersion means the distribution of goods from the central point to ultimate consumers spread across various places. Equalisation means making sure the supply of goods is in line with the consumer demand.

Today, the term market extends beyond political and geographical boundaries.

MEANING OF MARKET AND MARKETING

To the layman, market implies the physical place where one can buy useful articles or where valuable produce can be sold to earn money. In the commercial sense, market means the entire environment in which the buyers, sellers and related factors affect the demand for a particular good or service. It includes the mechanism whereby the sellers and buyers come in contact with one another and engage in give and take transactions. This mechanism also includes communication modes like the telephone, internet, etc.

Philip Kotler, the revered and well-known author, defines market as the one that "includes both place and region in which buyers and sellers are in free competition with one another".

According to Jevons, "A market means a body of persons who are in intimate business relations and carry on extensive transactions in any commodity".

Market can be defined as the area where buyers and sellers interact and wherein a group having some wants is willing to pay for the products or services being sold by the other group that has the potential to fulfill those wants. Market need not be a physical market place; it encompasses any medium capable of providing the opportunity for these two groups to interact with each other. For instance, the print media, newspapers and magazines, telephone and the online shopping websites can be classified as market.

The meaning of market can be looked at from a number of different concepts that are mentioned below :

1. Place concept– This is the physical concept of a market and assumes the market to be a place physically associated with the selling of goods. For example, a shopping mall and the neighbourhood shop.

2. Area concept– This concept assumes the market to be associated with a particular geographical area. For example, the American Common Market.

3. Demand concept– It assumes exclusive importance in the marketing concept. In the demand concept, market is equalised with the total demand.

4. Exchange concept– This concept assumes market to be a medium or a platform wherein goods can be exchanged. For example, the Stock Exchange.

5. People concept– This assumes the market to be sum total of all the buyers and sellers.

TRADITIONAL CLASSIFICATION OF MARKET

Traditionally, the markets can be classified in different ways :

1. **On the basis of geographical area :**
   (a) **Local market–** This refers to the market present in the local area. For example, a village market, or a city market.
   (b) **Regional market–** This denotes the market relative to a particular area or region. For example, the northern India.
   (c) **National market–** This means the market or the buyers and sellers are spread across a particular country.
   (d) **International market–** This means the market encompasses more than one country.

2. **On the basis of volume:**
   (a) **Wholesale market–** In such market, the goods are sold on bulk basis for reselling or industrial use.
   (b) **Retail market–** Here, the goods are sold in small quantities and are meant for consumption by the end consumer.

3. **On the basis of exchange :**
   (a) **Commodity market–** In such market, the goods are sold and bought in accordance with prescribed rules and regulations. For example, the cotton market.
   (b) **Capital market–** These are specialised markets for providing long-term finance to business enterprises. For example, the stock exchange.
   (c) **Money market–** These are specialised markets for providing short-term finance to business enterprises. For example, banks.

4. **On the basis of position of buyers and sellers :**
   (a) **Primary market–** In this market, the primary producers sell their produce to wholesalers. This is common in case of agricultural produce.
   (b) **Secondary market–** This type of market is marked by the practice of wholesalers selling their produce to the retailers.
   (c) **Terminal market–** In this market, the retailers sell their goods to the end users or consumers.
5. **On the basis of nature of transaction :**
   (a) **Spot market–** In this market, the sellers physically transfer their goods to the buyers.
   (b) **Future market–** The purpose of this market, the main purpose is to make profit from the price fluctuations. The intention of delivering the goods is missing here.
6. **On the basis of nature of goods:**
   (a) **Consumer's market–** In these markets, goods are purchased for personal use.
   (b) **Producer's market–** In such markets, goods are purchased for further processing or industrial use.

EVOLUTION OF MARKETING

The concept of Marketing is based on the notion that human beings have wants and needs that have to be satisfied through products or services. An organisation that can spot these wants and needs stands a better chance of producing the suitable goods or providing the appropriate service to the customers at a price that will not only cover the cost of production, but also provide a justifiable profit to the company.

This marketing concept revolves around some basic facts :
1. Human beings have needs and desires of different levels and of differing intensity.
2. These needs and desires have to be satisfied at a cost.
3. These needs can be influenced by an organisation. For instance, a company can produce and supply the goods and services that have the potential of satisfying human needs.
4. By satisfying these needs and desires on a continuing basis, a producer can earn profits for himself.

People have needs that have to be fulfilled to lead a life of reasonable satisfaction and comfort. These needs can range from basic physiological needs to that meant for satisfying the self-esteem. There are basic needs for food, housing, shelter and clothes. As man progresses in life, his needs increase in complexity and intensity. The concept of marketing views these needs as opportunities for a producer to earn profit from the business by producing goods for the potential customer and presenting them as the means of satisfying human wants. This action ultimately induces the customer to buy the product.

Let us look at how the concept of marketing has been defined by different people and organisations.

Dennis Adcock defines Marketing as *"the right product, in the right place, at the right time, at the right price."*

The American Marketing Association describes Marketing "an *activity, a set of institutions, and a process for creating, communicating, delivering, and exchanging offerings that have value for customers, clients, partners, and society at large."*

The Chartered Institute of Marketing, United Kingdom defines the Marketing concept as *"the management process responsible for identifying, anticipating and satisfying customer requirements profitably."*

Going by these definitions, it can be concluded that:
1. Customers or consumers are the focus of all marketing activities.
2. Consumer needs have to be identified.
3. Consumer needs have to be satisfied at a price that the consumer accepts.

CONCEPT OF MARKETING

There are two different concepts of marketing : (1) Traditional or Production-Oriented Concept ; (2) Modern or Consumer-Oriented Concept.

Traditional or Production-Oriented Concept

In order to understand and develop an understanding of the gradual evolution of this concept, we have to look back to the time of the industrial revolution. In this period, factories were being set up, automation was relatively novel and it presented the opportunity for mass production. Sales, especially of essential commodities, was growing at a fast pace due to huge unfulfilled demand and the cost of production was relatively low. This phase can be named as the era of production or the age of production concept. Producers concentrated on selling more and more of their products to make quick profits.

This period was succeeded by what we call the era of sales, or the sales concept. In the 1930's, the number of producers, especially in America and United Kingdom, had registered a manifold increase and consequently production had risen in totality. Producers had begun to feel the heat of competition. They began to experiment new methods of affecting sales. The time had come for advertisers to enter the market and offer their services to producers who quickly saw it as a means to broadcast the need-satisfying virtues of their ware. The era of hardcore selling had begun; all focus was brought to selling as much as possible.

According to Philip Kotler, *"The selling concept holds that in the absence of marketing, the consumer will ordinarily not buy enough of the organisation's products. The organisation must, therefore, undertake aggressive selling and promotion work aimed to induce the customer to buy the products."*

Modern or Consumer-Oriented Concept

Towards the end of the 1940's another change appeared in the business scenario. The end of the World War II saw an increase in purchasing power of the consumer due to many reasons. It also brought about a change in the perception of the consumer.

Resources released from the war efforts found way into new plants and industries. Production of goods and services saw a quantum leap and the buyers realised that they had a lot of choices in the market. They began to grow more discerning about the goods and services. As a result, the producers began to react and respond to this new change. They began to think in terms of what the consumers really needed. They focused on identifying consumer needs and wants. Thus, the modern concept of marketing began to take root.

According to the modern concept, *"Marketing is the identification of customer needs and subsequent efforts of the producer to satisfy them by producing and selling the required product or service."*

According to Prof. William J. Stanton, *"Marketing is a system of interacting business activities designed to plan, price, promote and distribute want satisfying goods and services to present and potential customers."*

According to Philip Kotler, *"Marketing is the process of planning and executing the concept, pricing, promotion and distribution of goods and services and ideas to create exchanges with target groups that satisfy customer and organisational objectives".*

The concept of marketing focuses on the consumer's wants and needs and the means to satisfy them at a price that justifies the producer. This concept begins with the identification of the needs and carries much beyond the mere satisfaction of the needs.

Major Features of the Concept of Marketing

Philip Kotler states that *"marketing concept is a customer orientation backed by integrated marketing aimed at generating customer's satisfaction as the key to satisfying organisational goals."* The main features of the marketing concept are described as under :

1. Customer-oriented– This is the main feature of the marketing concept. It focuses on the needs and wants of the consumer and the ways these wants can be satisfied.

2. Dynamism– Marketing begins with the identification of the consumer needs and desires. Thus, it begins much before production. Secondly, it does not end with the sale of the product or service. It continues beyond the process of selling.

3. Marketing research– A very important part of the concept of marketing relates to marketing research which is extensively used to gain understanding of consumer needs and wants. Continuous marketing research is an integral part of marketing.

Societal Marketing Concept

The marketing concept was quickly embraced by the organisations. The producers reoriented themselves, began focusing on the consumers, looking and analysing their needs and wants and producing goods and services that tended to satisfy their needs and requirements more efficiently. The consumer had suddenly become the king. However, by now it was realised that though the producer's orientation had changed in favour of the consumer, he was well on his way to produce more and more goods without taking into consideration some harmful aspects that could harm the environment and humans in the long-term. Concerns arose about environmental degradation, senseless use of natural resources and increasing hunger and poverty around the world. Money-minded business houses were depleting the valuable resources and none even gave a serious thought to preserve the environment. Producers were still busy furthering their revenue at the cost of mother nature. There arose the question whether the organisations were really working in the long-term interest of the society and the consumers or not.

These thoughts and concerns brought about a change in the earlier concept of marketing. A new school of thought came up and became famous as the Societal Concept of Marketing.

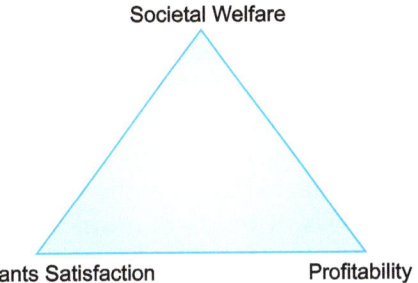

The societal concept is a variation of the modern concept of marketing. It was born out of the questionable role of traditional marketing which though focused on the consumer and his want satisfaction paid no heed to the long-term welfare of the society at large. They concentrated more on casting their consumers into different categories and then proceeded to satisfy their needs and wants by selling goods that were very similar but differently priced.

The societal concept of marketing concentrated on bridging the gap between the consumer wants and their satisfaction on one side, and the society's long-term welfare on the other side.

Prof. Phillip Kotler, the renowned authority on marketing, holds the view that *"the organisation's task is to determine the needs, wants and interests of the target market and deliver the desired satisfaction more efficiently than the competitors in a way that preserves or enhances the consumer and societal wellbeing."*

MARKETING AND SELLING : A COMPARISON

The selling concept became a rage when manufacturing organisations began all out production as a result of more and more resources being pumped into the industry. Production, especially of consumable goods and goods of necessity, rose considerably. As a result, the producers became burdened with inventory. The need arose to sell them off in the shortest period of time so as not to block the capital of the producer. The goods needed to be sold off in the shortest period of time so that the producer's capital could be released and more production affected through that capital. The producers began pushing their sales force to sell more and more products. Thus, began the practice of high pressure selling. The producer began to focus on selling his products and the product occupied the center stage.

Selling Concept

The selling concept assumed that the producer needed to influence the buyer to buy in increasingly larger quantities and with more frequency. The philosophy was to keep on coaxing the consumer with all tactics at the seller's end in order to overcome the consumer's inertia to buy. The consumer's needs, his side of the picture was not taken into consideration by the seller. The company was interested only in stimulating sales. They worked with the theory that the consumer must be made to buy what they were offering rather than they produce what the consumer really needed.

Marketing Concept

When the selling concept is compared with that of marketing, glaring differences are apparent. The marketing concept questions the earlier concepts, especially the concept of selling. While the selling concept focused on hardcore selling, the new concept of marketing addressed actual customer needs and wants. It tends to divide the customers on the basis of the nature of their needs and wants. It also takes into account their purchasing power. Once a producer analyses the needs and wants of one group of consumers, it sets out to produce goods and services that will satisfy their wants at a price that will cover the overall cost of production and also fetch acceptable profit for business. It tends to address the critical question of how best to satisfy the consumer's needs.

The differences between Marketing and Selling are listed below for easier assimilation :

1. Scope– While, selling consists mainly of ensuring sale of goods and services, marketing ensure that the goods or services sold satisfy the consumers' needs and wants, and are acceptable to the customers in every sense of the term.

2. Orientation– While, selling is product-oriented, marketing is customer-oriented.

3. Beginning– Marketing begins with the identification of the consumer's wants and needs, whereas selling starts with the production of goods.

4. End– The function of marketing continues long after the customer has purchased the goods. It gives after sales service and keeps track of how well the product satisfies the consumer's needs and requirement. However, selling ends with the exchange of product and transfer of ownership.

5. Focus– The selling focuses on the need to sell in order to increase the firm's profitability whereas marketing focuses on the satisfaction of the consumer's needs and desires.

6. Goals– The goal of selling is to maximize the firm's profits. Marketing, on the other hand, tries to address the growth and stability issues of the firm.

7. Means– Selling tries to maximize profits through increased sales volume, but marketing maximizes profits through maximum customer satisfaction.

Difference between Marketing and Selling

Marketing	Selling
1. Focuses on satisfaction of consumer needs and wants.	1. Focuses on increasing the sales volume of the seller.
2. Targets the needs of the buyer.	2. Targets the needs of the seller.
3. Marketing is consumer-oriented.	3. Selling is product-oriented.
4. Marketing seeks profit through consumer satisfaction.	4. Selling seeks profit through high pressure selling.
5. Marketing begins with identification of consumer needs and requirements.	5. Selling begins only after production.
6. Marketing carries beyond sale and transfer of ownership.	6. Selling ends with transfer of ownership.
7. Marketing seeks to build a long-term relationship with consumers.	7. Selling forgets the consumer after selling process ends.

OBJECTIVES OF MARKETING

The basic objectives of Marketing are shared below :

1. Customer satisfaction– This is the first and foremost objective of marketing. The marketer seeks to satisfy consumer needs and wants at the right time with the right good or service and at the right price. In fact, this is the secret of business success. A product only sells if it satisfies the needs and requirements of the consumer.

2. Profitability– The firm aims at profitability by creating demand and then fulfilling that demand at a price that gives it profitability. It balances the profitability and price in such a way that it wins consumer loyalty.

3. Coordination and integration– The aim of marketing is to bring about a careful balance among all its elements, like the product, the price, the promotion, and the methods of physical distribution and to integrate them in such a way that it results in the maximum satisfaction for consumers and also gives acceptable profit to the producer.

4. Service to society– Marketing seeks to contribute to the betterment of the society by preserving the environment and by sustainable development. Conserving the natural environment and keeping the society's welfare at the core, while simultaneously creating employment is the business's commitment towards society.

IMPORTANCE OF MARKETING

Marketing through various functions makes sure that consumers come to know of the existence of goods and services that can satisfy their wants and needs. It is the marketing function that sees to it that all the goods and services reach the target market.

Marketing plays a key role in revenue generation by spreading the word about the product of the manufacturer. It is important to the business for the following reasons :

1. Cornerstone of business– Inventory will keep on piling in the company warehouses and goods as well as services will not be purchased if marketing fails to keep potential customers informed about their existence. Consumption will come to a standstill if marketing remains absent from business. The success of any business enterprise depends upon the efficiency of its marketing activities.

2. Satisfies human needs and wants– A very important function of marketing is that it determines human wants and needs and the pattern of human consumption. It helps the producer to know exactly what the consumer wants; thereby enabling the producer to produce what is needed by the society. In other words, it helps avoid production of unnecessary goods, thus conserving valuable resources.

3. Generates revenue– Marketing creates demand for a product and helps to empower the business. It helps in matching production with the demand while at the same time ensuring that over production is kept in check. By matching production with demand it makes sure that the producer is able to sell the quantity that he produces at a price that is acceptable to the customers, and is rewarded with the profit margin that makes the producer stay active in the market. Thus, marketing generates revenue for the producer.

4. Creates employment– Marketing function helps create avenues of employment. It creates gainful employment for people in areas such as warehousing, distribution, advertising, selling and distribution. It widens the scope of banking and insurance.

5. Develops the economy– By creating demand, and channels of satisfying those demands, by creating employment for millions, by giving business opportunities to entrepreneurs and investors, by creating demand for consumption, marketing gives a great impetus to the economy. By utilising resources and optimising their use, marketing ensures the economic resources are put to gainful use.

6. Helps in managerial decision-making– By providing information and relevant data on consumption patterns as well as consumer needs and wants, marketing helps the management gain valuable insights that help in decision-making and formulating plans and objectives.

FUNCTIONS OF MARKETING

Marketing activity consists of a number of other activities that are very specialised and essential for satisfying human needs and wants. These activities are performed by intermediaries. Marketing functions are broadly classified into three categories defined below :

1. Exchange function– This refers to the transfer of ownership of goods and services.

2. Physical function– This refers to the function that involves the physical transfer of goods and services.

3. Auxiliary or facilitating function– All functions that assist in exchange and distribution of the goods and services.

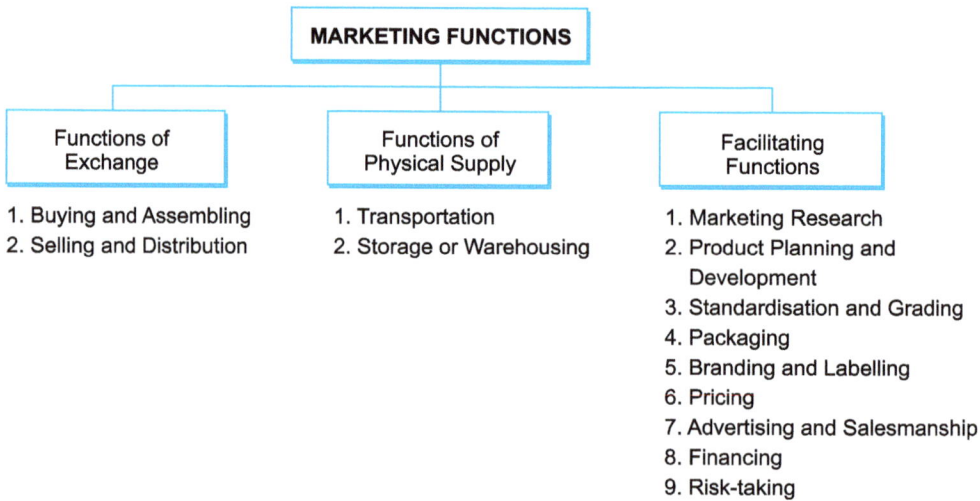

Fig. 13.1 Functions of Marketing

Marketing can be sub-divided into the following individualised functions :

(a) Buying and assembling– Successful marketing begins with buying quality raw material at economical price. The quality of the final product depends on the quality of the raw material. Care must be taken so that quality raw material is bought at a price that will not inflate the final price of the product. There are many products that require carefully purchased raw material. Still, many raw materials or unfinished raw products require technical specifications and must conform to certain specifications and tests before they can be used.

Assembling starts after the goods or parts have been purchased and is separate from buying. It involves the creation and maintenance of stock of goods purchased from different sources. When goods are purchased from different sources, they have to be collected and assembled at a place under control of the producer. Buying and assembling are two distinct processes.

(b) Selling and distribution– Selling is the basic objective of marketing. Selling generates revenue and adds to the profit of the firm. It comprises finding customers and the subsequent transfer of ownership of goods and services to them. Selling includes using many techniques and forms of persuasion with potential customers. It also includes negotiations for terms of sales, deciding on the channels to be used for physical distribution of goods and services. Channel of distribution is the path through which goods travel from the producer to the consumer. A distribution channel can also be a direct transaction from the producer to the consumer; or it may include several interconnected middlemen along the way such as wholesalers, distributors, agents, retailers, etc. Each intermediary receives the item and moves it to the next point until it reaches the final buyer.

Selling is not an easy task and requires constant communication with potential customers, tracking their material needs and formulation of strategies to counter the competition in the market.

(c) Transportation– Transportation is the act of moving the product from the place of manufacture to the place where the customer can take possession of it. This is a very important function of marketing. Transportation creates place utility. In the absence of transportation, the goods may have to be sold locally, or the firm's market may be very restricted to a small physical area. By removing the barriers of distance transportation enables a firm to expand the reach of its products, and thus widen its market. In other words, it enables the firm to serve its customers who may be otherwise, geographically widely dispersed.

Transportation may be land, sea, or air based, but while selecting means of transport, cost, speed, safety, reliability, availability and carrying capacity must be considered carefully.

(d) Storage– Marketing function includes making arrangements to safely store the products in a safe and suitable place till it is sold to the customer or the wholesaler. Keeping the goods in storage till they are sold in the market creates time utility and adds to the value of the product. It is also a means to match the demand with the supply and to stabilise the price. Storage and warehousing is becoming a very important and specialised function of marketing. Special care has to be taken to store delicate and perishable products like food grains, milk products, vegetables and frozen food.

(e) Marketing research– Conducting research on consumer wants and desires, buying patterns, consumption patterns and gathering data and information that will help management decision making. Marketing decisions are taken in the light of information that is collected through marketing research. These data and information needs to be unbiased and accurate so that realistic and sound decisions can be arrived at.

Marketing research enables a firm to estimate the potential demand for a product or service. It can also identify potential customers, their needs, wants and preferences. The attitudes of customers towards a particular product, its price, quality or expected demand can be gauged through marketing research. Marketing research enables a product to be tested before being finally introduced into the market. New use of existing products can also be found through marketing research.

(f) Product planning and development– Product planning and development is one of the prime functions of marketing. The products are planned in such a way that they satisfy the wants and desires of the customer and are so priced that they win market acceptability. Designing and building the right product is ensured by the marketing function. Small details such as color, size and the outer packing are attended by marketing because although these seem to be small details, but they have a great significance in winning customer acceptability. The role of marketing does not end here. It has to monitor older products and improve them so that they continue in the product line and generate steady revenue stream for the firm.

(g) Standardisation and grading– The products must conform to certain standards or quality stipulated by the various laws from time to time. These laws may pertain to the quantity, quality, or any other safety aspect of the product. These are the desirable features that must be present in the product. The absence of such positive attributes can result in either penal action by law or rejection of the product by the customers.

In manufactured goods there is ease of standardisation in terms of technical aspects. However, agricultural products are not of uniform quality. Therefore, they require grading and standardisation. Products like rice, wheat and fruits need to be graded on the basis on their colour, ripeness, size, quality, etc. However, that does not mean technical and other manufactured products do not require any grading. Electrical equipments are also graded according to certain specification depending on the nature of their use and duration of use at a stretch. Some equipment could be circuit breakers, heavy duty electrical cables, cables for use in the electronics industry, etc.

Standardisation and grading facilitate buying and selling by description. The customer does not need much detail in the face of the product being graded or standardised. The standardisation assures the customer of a certain level of quality and workmanship. The standardised product also commands a better price and a larger market compared to an unstandardised one. It also reduces the marketing costs by its ease of transportation and storage. ISI and ISO are examples of standardisation in India.

(h) Packing and packaging– Packing and packaging are also very important functions of marketing. Packing means the wrapping or crating of the goods in such a way that it remains safe from spoilage and pilferage, breakage, etc. The type of packing depends upon the nature of the good. Bulky materials require one type of packing while liquid or fragile goods demand another type of packing. Heavy goods may require packing in wooden crates. Whatever be the nature of the product, it has to be packed in such a way that it remains safe and can withstand the rigours of transportation and remain safe during long periods of storage in warehouses.

Packaging is distinct from packing. Packaging is the act of designing and producing the package or the wrapper or container in which a product is kept. Packaging helps in product identification. It promotes the product, acts as a business promotional tool. It helps in differentiating the product.

Packaging
- Identifies the product.
- Promotes and sells the product.
- Provides information about the product.
- Provides safety to the product.

It makes the product marketable by breaking them into small lots so that the consumer can purchase the product according to the requirements. It provides convenience to the consumer by making the product user-friendly. Packaging helps in product protection due to spoilage and breakage.

(i) Branding and labelling– Branding is the process of giving a product or service a distinctive name with the purpose of differentiating it from other competing brands. It positions the product in the view of existing and potential consumers. Branding helps to serve consumers by supplying information to them about quality, origin and value of the product or service. Ultimately, branding helps the consumer choose the product over and above others in the market.

A brand is a name, sign, symbol or design assigned to a product so as to differentiate it from competitor brands. It identifies the product and imparts a distinct identity to it. Brands include elements such as brand and trade names, trade and brand marks, and trade characters. It can also be a word, group of words, letters, or numbers that represent a product or service.

Labelling is a marketing function. It is the identification mark put on the package to inform buyers about the contents and other details. These details are the contents in terms of weight or size, the price, the date of manufacture and expiry. It also specifies the grade, quality and instructions about handling the product.

(j) Pricing– This is of prime importance in marketing. It involves fixing the price that the firm will charge for a product. The price is a very important determinant of the sales volume of any product. While, a high price may keep the customers away from the product, a low price may result in a loss of profit for the firm. The price itself is dependent upon such factors as the price of raw materials, taxes and duties, competition, firms pricing policies and overall objectives.

(k) Advertising– Advertising is a very important aspect as it is an important mode of communication chosen by the business to inform potential customers about its products and services. Advertising creates desire and demand among potential customers. It is a powerful means of persuasion. Advertising increases consumer loyalty for a product, service or idea. It seeks to maintain and then expand a company's customer base by disseminating product information and by reinforcing purchasing behaviour. Advertising seeks public recognition and acceptance of trademarks, brand names. Thus, it builds up the producer's goodwill and that of the product.

Dealers prefer dealing in brands that are well-advertised. It helps to expand and widen the market for a product. It also is a tool for educating the customers. Today a producer has numerous medium for advertising his product. He has printed media (newspapers, magazines, etc.), electronic media (TV) and the internet.

The rising importance of advertising can be judged by the fact, that in 2008, the revenue generated through advertising in India touched ₹ 221 billion and reached ₹ 300 billion in 2011. It was projected to reach ₹ 474 billion in 2015.

(l) Salesmanship– Salesmanship creates demand through interaction between the customer and the company's sales staff. This is a very important function and a skilled job. Poor salesmanship can have an opposite effect. Truly speaking, it is efficient salesmanship that brings revenue to the business organisation. The sales force is responsible for creating and maintaining demand among the consumers as well as for shaping the attitude, behaviour and buying decisions at the point of sale.

(m) Financing– One of the functions of marketing is ensuring that the revenue or sale proceeds are not blocked. In other words, it means that marketing function makes sure that wholesalers and dealers clear their bills and outstanding at the earliest. A delay in payment or blocking of revenue may deprive the firm of funds and may affect the business. Marketing ensures that the sales and credit policies are so framed and implemented that the firm does not suffer by way of delayed payments from dealers and wholesalers.

(n) Risk-taking– Risk-taking is an important function of marketing. There are innumerable risks which an enterprise has to face in the process of marketing goods. They arise on account of unforeseen events which may take place from time to time such as theft, burglary, bad debts, wars, strikes, etc. It may occur during the course of transportation or due to decay, deterioration and accident and fluctuations in the price of commodity due to changes in its supply and demand. Some of these risks can be avoided by careful handling, while others easily shifted to insurance companies or other parties.

E-MARKETING

E-marketing is comparatively a new development introduced by the development of electronic communications and widespread use of internet. E-marketing or electronic marketing refers to the application of marketing principles and techniques via electronic media, especially the internet. E-marketing is the process of marketing a product or a brand using the internet. It includes both direct response marketing and indirect marketing elements. It uses a range of technologies to help connect a seller to the buyer. E-marketing includes all the activities a business conducts via the web, aimed towards attracting new business, retaining current business and developing its brand identity.

E-Marketing
- Connects the company with its customers via e-mail.
- Enables sharing information via social media.
- Helps advertising via search engine marketing.

SUMMARY

Market– A Market is any platform that brings the seller and buyer into contact with each other for a commercial transaction.

Marketing– It means identifying human wants, needs and the way to satisfy them at a price that is acceptable to the buyer. Marketing fetches profit for the seller.

Marketing Vs. Selling– Marketing is a consumer-oriented systematic group of functions, whereas selling is a producer-oriented fragmented activity.

Societal Marketing Concept– This concept, while keeping the focus on the consumer, ensures the sustained development and preservation of the environment and the society.

Functions of Marketing– Major functions of marketing are : Buying and Assembling, Selling and distribution, Transportation, Advertising.

Storage and Physical Distribution– Ensuring goods are prevented from spoilage and damage. It also makes sure the goods are transported and reach the customers in a good and useable condition.

Marketing Research– This function seeks to collect and process information useful in marketing decisions.

Product Planning and Development– This function includes product designing to match consumer wants and needs.

Standardisation– Basic standards to which a product must conform in order to become readily salable.

Packing and Packaging– It means classifying products according to their size, volume and quantity, covering them to prevent breakage and easy identification.

Branding and Labelling– Branding is the putting of an identification mark on a product to give it an identity and to differentiate it from other competing products. Labelling is the putting of a tag or label giving information about the product's usage, its ingredients, directions about its usage, etc.

Pricing– This is the function of fixing a price or money value. The price must be such that the consumer is willing to pay and at the same time it should generate profit for the producer.

E-Marketing– It is a platform for selling by applying marketing principles using the electronic media like the TV and the internet.

QUESTIONS FOR PRACTICE

Very Short Answer Type Questions
1. Define Marketing.
2. Give one difference between Selling and Marketing.
3. Write about any main objective of Marketing.
4. Define Branding.
5. Name two physical supply functions of Marketing.
6. What do you mean by Advertising?
7. Define E-marketing.

Short Answer Type Questions
1. Define the term 'Market'.
2. Mention two objectives of marketing.
3. Explain two functions of marketing.

4. Explain briefly the assembling function of marketing.
5. State two differences between packing and packaging.
6. Write short notes on Branding and Labelling.
7. Mention any two differences between Branding and Labelling.
8. Write a short note on Marketing Research.
9. Why is buying an important function of marketing?
10. How is marketing different from selling?
11. What is the difference between a brand and a label?
12. What is product planning?

Essay Type Questions

1. Explain the concept of Marketing.
2. What do you understand by traditional and modern concept of marketing?
3. Differentiate between the Selling and the Marketing concept.
4. Analyse the societal concept of marketing showing its relevance to today's dynamic business environment.
5. Explain the importance of (a) branding and (b) packaging in marketing. Give examples to support your answer.
6. How does transportation increase the value of seller's product?
7. Distinguish between Advertising and Salesmanship.
8. What do you understand by pricing?
9. What do you understand by E-marketing?

14 Marketing Mix

> **LEARNING RESULT**
>
> After reading this chapter, you should be able to :
> - Understand the meaning of Marketing Mix.
> - Gain conceptual knowledge and understand meaning of Product (Goods and Services), Branding, Labelling and Packaging.
> - Understand the meaning and factors determining Price.
> - Understand the concept and meaning of Place, Physical Distribution and Channels of Distribution.
> - Recognise the meaning and elements of Promotion.

Marketing seeks to study consumer behaviour and his material needs as well as the nature of his needs. It tries to satisfy his needs with product or service that best suits his requirement. The marketer attempts to understand the purchasing power of the customer to arrive at the best possible price at which the product or service should be presented to the customer, the form in which the product should be presented, how it should be packaged, etc. It is the sum total of all these factors that together constitutes what we know as the Marketing Mix.

MEANING OF MARKETING MIX

According to Kotler and Armstrong, *"Marketing Mix is the set of controllable, tactical marketing tools that the firm blends to produce the response it wants in the target market. The marketing mix consists of everything the business can do to influence the demands for its product."*

Boone and Kurtz define Marketing Mix as, *"the blending of four strategic elements of marketing decision-making – product, pricing, distribution and promotion – to satisfy chosen consumer segments."*

The basic objective of the marketer is to put the *'right'* product in the *'right'* place, at the *'right'* time and at the *'right'* price. This means that an organisation must think of and come up with :

1. a plan to identify a sizeable group of customer whose wants and needs can be satisfied.
2. a thorough product (or service) that will be seen by the customers as a means to satisfy their needs.
3. a price tag that will be accepted by the customer and prove beneficial for the business owners as well.

It will now be easy to get an idea of what the marketing mix is. From the above explanations we can see that once an organisation decides to produce a 'product' it must know what that 'product' is going to be like. At the same time the business concern must know to whom it has to sell that 'something'. Once that has been finalised, the next step that the organisation must take is to decide about the price and the foolproof process to make the 'product' available to the consumer.

The organisation will have a number of choices in the above process. It will decide to embrace those choices that match its resources, objectives and philosophy. Ultimately, these choices will become a part of the process used by the organisation in bringing its product (or service) before the customer and selling it to the chosen circle.

Now, let's move on to identify the components of the marketing mix. Read through the following broadly classified sets of actions or tactics that the organisation will use in making a final choice regarding the product or service to be sold.

1. The **Product (or Service)** that the organisation intends to sell.
2. The **Place** where it intends to sell.
3. The **Promotion.**
4. The **Price.**

The marketing mix refers to the set of actions or tactics that a company uses to promote its brand or product in the market. These are listed above. In marketing terminology, these factors are known as the **4 P's of marketing**. A firm counts on these variables that are mixed in combination and proportion, to achieve its marketing objectives.

The market for any product or service consists of different classes of customers. Each class has a different set of likes and dislikes, education, culture, and preferences, incomes, etc. They are influenced by a factor in different ways. The entire market for any product is made up of smaller sub-classes of consumers and each class has different and distinct attributes. Thus, there are

Fig. 14.1 Marketing Mix–The 4 P's

different groups of customers, and each group can be considered a distinct market in itself. The marketer looks at each group differently and approaches them differently. One group of consumers may be very reactive to the quality of the product, while another group may pay greater attention and may be influenced more by the price than by the quality. Another group may buy the product to get social prestige while another group may buy the same product to satisfy their ego and get noticed in the society. The marketer adopts a different selling strategy to sell them the product. He may stress on the price and durability of the product when approaching one group but may lay emphasis on product quality when dealing with another group. Different aspects of the product such as the price, the way it is promoted, how it is presented before the customer, all comprise the marketing mix.

The marketer can create the right marketing mix in the following way :

1. His product has to have the right features. For example, the product must be attractive and work well.
2. The price must be acceptable to the consumer.

3. The product must be accessible at the right place and at the right time, *i.e.* readily available when it is demanded.
4. The customer must be made aware of the existence and availability of the product through advertisement.

IMPORTANCE OF MARKETING MIX

Marketing mix is important due to the following reasons :

1. Marketing mix enables the marketer to focus on the needs and preferences of all segments of consumers, thus enabling revenue and sales maximization.
2. It allows an integrated approach to marketing by allowing the firm to balance the various marketing elements.
3. Marketing mix makes marketing efforts dynamic by allowing selective adjustments in consonance with varying market and consumer requirements.

COMPONENTS OF MARKETING MIX

If we look into the concept of marketing mix in-depth, we'll find it consisting of the below mentioned components :

1. **Product mix–** (a) The range or line of products, (b) Quality of product, (c) Brand name, (d) Packaging and labelling, (e) After sales service and warranty.
2. **Price mix–** (a) Price, (b) Discounts, (c) Terms of credit for purchase.
3. **Place mix–** (a) Channel of distribution, (b) Distribution policy, (c) Transportation, (d) Warehousing, (e) Inventory control.
4. **Promotion mix–**(a) Advertising, (b) Personal selling, (c) Sales promotion, (d) Publicity, (e) Public relations.

PRODUCT CONCEPT

In business dictionary, the word 'product' stands for a tangible substance that has attributes like physical form, shape, colour, size, etc. along with the capacity to satisfy certain human wants and needs. The product must lend itself to storage over a period of time. Though the word 'product' is often wrongly used in place of the word 'service', the latter denotes something intangible that cannot be stored. In other words, a service has to be consumed as soon as produced. A good example of a 'service' is the service provided by a doctor to his patient and of a 'product' is the purchase of furniture or any other object.

The product is an item offered by a producer to his customer. It must be capable of performing or delivering to uphold the producer or seller's claims. In case it fails to work or satisfy the want claimed by the producer, then all his efforts may go in vain, the product will be a failure, and the money invested will go down the drain as a result.

When the producer is deciding about the product or service he should be able to answer the following questions :

1. What is the actual product or service that he intends to put on the market?
2. What are the real needs of the customer?
3. How will the product satisfy the existing need of the customer?

4. What will the product look like?
5. How does it differ (in size, shape, features, etc.) from the offerings of competitors?

However, these are not all the questions a producer will have to answer before he moves ahead in the process; there will be a lot many more. In any product or service, the features that play a very important part, besides price, are branding, labelling and packaging.

Benefits of a Product

Normally, a product gives three types of benefits to the purchaser, as indicated below :

1. Core benefit– This is the fundamental benefit because of which the customer decides to purchase the product. For example, I buy a pen to write with.

2. Expected benefit– This includes the product attributes that will provide the buyer some desired intangible benefits. For example, I expect social recognition and ego satisfaction when I buy the costly fountain pen.

3. Augmented benefit– This includes the add-on advantages provided by the seller with the product to convert potential customers into actual customers.

The Concept of Product Attributes

Product attributes can be best defined as the characteristics of a finished product. The point to be noted here is that when we decide to purchase a product, we look for its tangible as well as intangible attributes. For example, we may choose to buy a car depending on its colour, size, and design. But we can't overlook its intangible attributes such as its brand name, model and warranty to name a few. Therefore, in marketing, tangible attributes are indispensable; but it is the intangible attributes that enable the customer to take informed decisions.

Classification of Products

The products can be generally classified into two primary categories: Consumer Product and Service. While, the products have physical shape and are tangible, services are intangible and do not have any physical shape. More will be explained about services later. The products can be classified as :

Consumer Products

These are the products or goods that are required by end users or consumers. These are finished products that can be used by consumers without any commercial process. Soaps, toothpastes and television fall in this category.

Consumer products may further be classified as :

1. On the Basis of Shopping Efforts Involved

Consumer Products can be broken down into the following categories on the basis of shopping efforts put in by the customer.

(a) **Convenience goods**– Convenience goods are relatively inexpensive, highly standardised, widely advertised and require frequent purchases. There is little decision-making involved in their purchase. Toiletries and confectionery products serve as examples of convenience goods.

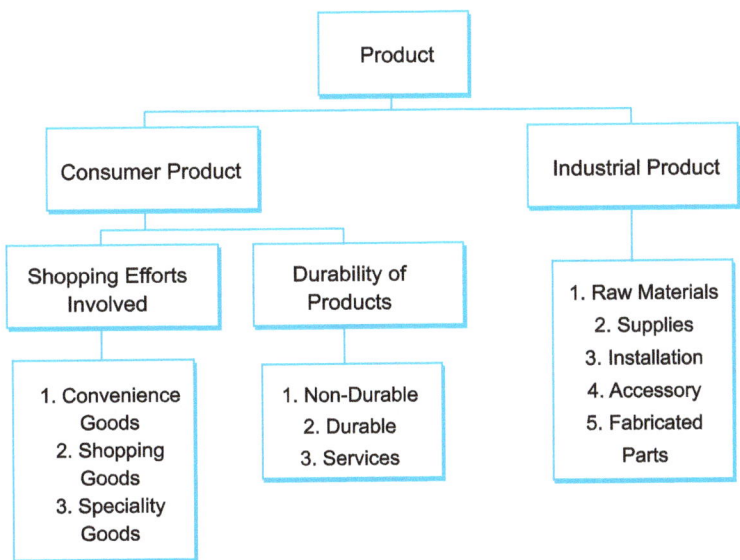

Fig. 14.2 Classification of Products

(b) **Shopping goods**– Shopping goods are products that consumers do not buy as frequently as convenience goods, yet, they are comparatively costlier. Consumers do some research and compare product features and price before deciding which brand of shopping goods to purchase. Refrigerators, washing machines, Television sets and microwave ovens are some examples of shopping goods.

(c) **Specialty goods**– Specialty goods come with unique features or branding. They represent uniqueness and consumers are ready to invest time and money to buy the kind of product they want. Designer clothes, luxury cars and antiques are some common specialty goods.

2. **On the Basis of Durability of Products**

Products can be classified on the basis of how long they can serve the consumer.

(a) **Non-durable products**– We can also call them consumable goods. These are goods that are consumed in a short span of time through continuous usage. Items like toilet soaps, toothpastes and washing powder are consumable items.

(b) **Durable products**– Durable goods are of such nature that they can be used for a long period of time. In other words, they have extended shelf life. Goods like pressure cookers, heaters and air conditioners last for an extended time period.

(c) **Services**– Services are intangible products. Unlike the physical product, a service cannot be touched or felt. It has no physical form, and hence, cannot be stored. Services are perishable and their production as well as consumption is simultaneous.

Industrial Products

These are products meant for re-use either as raw material by other industries, or as machineries for manufacturing other products. Industrial transformers used by large factories, earthmoving equipment for use in construction industry and rail freight cars can be classified as industrial products.

Industrial products may be further classified as below :

1. Raw materials– These are organic matter that will be used in manufacturing other products. To cite an example, iron ore is used to make steel, which in turn, is used in making buildings, engineering goods, ships, etc. Here, the raw material loses its original shape and form to be fashioned into a finished product.

2. Supplies– These are materials that are necessary for manufacturing a product. But they do not become a part of the product. Substances like lubricating oil for machineries and fuel are necessary in smooth working of the machines and hence can be called as Supplies.

3. Installations– These are items or equipment used as either a part of installation (Industrial chimney, etc.) or to help in the installation of machineries, factories (towers, steel pylons, etc.). Installations are of high capital value.

4. Accessory equipment– Accessory is an item of low value used as a part of another product. Nuts, bolts and screws can be regarded as accessories. The equipment like drills, lathes, etc. used to produce accessories are called accessory equipment.

5. Fabricated parts– These are parts that are fabricated or pre-produced and then adjoined to produce a finished good. Automobile tyres and buttons of jeans are some common examples of fabricated parts.

Services

There are a number of features that differentiate a service from a product. They are given below :

1. Services are intangible– Unlike a product, services do not have any physical shape.

2. Services are perishable– They cannot be stored like a product.

3. Services cannot be standardised– Since a service is intangible and lacks physical shape, it cannot be subjected to any form of standardisation.

4. Services are simultaneous–The production and consumption of service is simultaneous. There is no time lag between the production and consumption of a service.

Distinction between Product and Service

Product	Service
1. Tangible– Can be seen, touched and felt.	1. Intangible– Unseen, untouched and unfelt.
2. Durable.	2. Can be produced and consumed simultaneously.
3. Can be made as per set manufacturing standards.	3. Standardisation not possible.
4. Can be repaired and replaced in case of manufacturing defects.	4. Repairing is not possible but replacement is.
5. Can be bought in anticipation of need.	5. Cannot be bought unless the need arises.
6. Movable.	6. Immovable.

Branding

Branding is the process of giving a product or service a distinctive name with the purpose of differentiating it from other competing brands. It positions the product in the view of existing and potential consumers. Branding helps consumers by supplying information to them about quality, origin, and value of the product or service. By being suggestive of quality and status, branding helps the consumers in decision-making.

When we think of any brand, visuals of its name, design, trademark, numbers or codes and colours flash in our mind. These features help the producer differentiate his product or service from that of the competitors. They form an intrinsic part of the product. If any of these features are removed, the product or service will be considered different from the existing one. In fact, the function of branding is to serve as a powerful tool for differentiating the product/service from that of competing products. Generally, producers get their brands registered so that the competitors cannot copy them or infringe the original brand owner's rights. A partly eaten apple serving as the brand logo of Apple Computers is a good example of impressive branding.

Thus, a brand is a name, term, design, symbol or combination of two or more of these elements that seek to identify the product or service and distinguish it from its competitors. David Ogilvy defines branding as *"the intangible sum of a product's attributes: its name, packaging, and price, its history, its reputation, and the way it's advertised."*

Trade Mark

A trademark can be a word, name, symbol, device or a combination of all these. An important feature of trademark is that it enjoys legal protection by the law. Trademarks are used to prevent other companies from using similar identification marks or any such combination that might confuse the customer about the identity of the company selling its products in the market. The trade mark becomes the property of the company that gets it registered by law. Any infringement, misuse or violation of the trademark is punishable by law.

Branding Strategies Adopted by Organisations

There are about three commonly embraced branding strategies adopted by a business firm. They are :

1. **Corporate branding**– In this case the company or corporate brand name is used for all products. The benefit is that the familiar name and goodwill of the company gets prominence and readily wins over new customers. It gives instant recognition to the product. The company does not need to invest in brand recognition and advertising again and again. Brands like Sony, Panasonic, Kellogg's, Heinz, Tata and Virgin are good instances of corporate branding. However, the use of a corporate brand can also

create problems if one of the products, such as Maggi noodles in case of Nestle, gets bad publicity.

   2. **Corporate-cum-individual branding**– This is also known as Combination Branding. A combination branding strategy brings together a corporate brand name and an individual brand name. The objective here is to provide some association for the product with the corporate brand name while maintaining some distinctiveness. It gives credibility to the brand name. A good example is that of Intel Pentium and Intel i7 computer processors. Microsoft Windows and Microsoft Office in personal computing software are also good examples.

   3. **Individual or multi-branding**– In this case, the company uses different brand names for different products that it markets. These different brand names do not identify the brand with the particular company. For example, Unilever markets its soaps using different brand names like Dove, Lifebuoy, Pears, and follows the same strategy in case of other products. In multi-branding, the corporate brand name is given little or no prominence.

   This strategy is to safeguard against the harm brought about by the main corporate name. It is also a strategy to build up a distinct and strong image for each product in the company's portfolio.

   Multi-branding strategy is also possible when a company acquires a brand that already has established itself in the market and it wants to extract the best advantages from the acquisition.

Advantages of Branding

   Branding is an integral part and function of marketing and it has advantages for both the consumer as well as the marketer.

Advantages to the Marketers

   1. **Differentiates products**– Branding is a means by which a company can make its product standout from that of another company. This way a customer makes out the identity of the company that sells the product. That's how branding protects the company's target market by preventing the customer from buying the product of a rival company.

   2. **Helps in pricing**– The marketer promotes his brand as a product different from other competing products. This enables him to fix a price that denotes the individuality and uniqueness of the product. Thus, it becomes a tool for enabling differential pricing.

   3. **Facilitates advertising and sales promotion**– Brands help in advertising and building consumer loyalty. This is a way of building up consumer preference for the product.

   4. **Enables dealer acceptability**– Branding enables dealer acceptability in the market. The more famous a brand, the more dealer acceptability it commands. Where a brand is not popular, the dealers feel shy of accepting it on their shelves.

   5. **Helps in marketing of new products**– The consumers feel more confident and readily buy a new product if it carries a well-known brand name. A reputed brand readily gets consumer acceptance, while the lesser known brands have to work at building up consumer trust over a long period of time.

6. Capitalises on brand exposure– It helps companies introduce their products into new markets. Thus, the companies can tap new markets and increase revenue.

Advantages to the Customers

1. **Product identification**– Branding helps the customers readily identify the product through its unique colour, trademark, or other identification marks. This enables repeat purchases of the product.

2. **Ensures quality and consistency**– Branding conveys the company's assurance of quality and consistent products to the customer. The company becomes bound to stick to its standards of quality and workmanship. Thus, it produces products that comply with its quality standards. This builds up customer confidence in the company and increases it customer base.

3. **Displays producer's commitment**– The brand displays the commitment of the producer to its customers and the society. It may signify innovation, commitment to a clean environment and commitment to a certain cause. Another function of branding is to win customer loyalty and promote product recognition.

4. **Builds egoistical satisfaction**– Certain premium brands satisfy egoistical whims and fancies, and thus, become status symbols. For instance, high-end cars like Rolls Royce and Ferrari are sought-after by people for whom flashing the logo of luxury beamers is a sign of better social and financial standing.

5. **Brand names protect consumers**– By printing the price and other manufacturing details like the manufacturing and expiry dates on the packaging of the product, the brand functions as a tool for consumer protection.

Labelling

Labelling denotes attaching a tag or label for easy identification of anything. In marketing terms, it denotes any informational tag, wrapper, seal, whether on paper or on the outer covering or packaging of the product for the purpose of disseminating information about the product, or its use. The producer can deliver the sales message through product labelling and can communicate different type of information about the product. For example, labelling can display information about the product, its ingredients, and its nutritional content. Terms and conditions of its availability, its price, place and name, and address of its manufacturer, date of production and date of expiry can all be displayed through labelling. It is obligatory on part of a producer to display this information on the packaging.

Functions of Labelling

The labelling of a product is an important aspect of marketing. Labelling fulfills the following functions :

1. **It gives an identity to the product**– The label is the identification mark of the product and indicates the company that produces and markets it.

2. **It specifies the content**– Labels specify the contents or the ingredients of the product.

3. Labels indicate usage instructions– The labels have printed instructions and directions regarding the ways of the product's consumption or usage.

4. Statutory function– The labels are to be put on the product to satisfy legal requirements. Thus, they fulfill a statutory function.

Advantages of Labelling

There are a number of advantages of a label. These have been identified as under :

1. Prevents overcharging by seller– The price of the product is printed on the label and thus it ensures that the seller does not overcharge the customer.

2. Serves as an advertisement– A good and colourful label advertises the product and the company too. It is instantly recognised and has great recall value. It establishes a quick association between the label and the company or the producer, thereby popularising both the brand and the company.

3. Helps develop brand goodwill– The label is a stamp of guarantee of the good quality of the product. By raising the prestige and reliability of the product, the label serves as a brand ambassador thereby increasing the goodwill of the producer.

Disadvantages of Labelling

Labelling is not without its flip side. It also has certain disadvantages that are listed below :

1. Increases the cost of the product– The labelling is not a consumable part of the product. Hence, the cost incurred in labelling goes waste.

2. Requires standardisation– Labelling works only with products that are standardised. It does not confer any benefit where products are not subject to standardisation.

3. Benefit only with literate consumers– Information on labels loses its meaning if the consumers are illiterate; it is beneficial only for literate consumers.

Labelling is used to provide useful information about the product and the manufacturer. A good label should provide :
- Name and address of the manufacturer.
- Weight of the product.
- Size and colour of the product.
- Ingredients used in manufacturing the product.
- Directions of usage and cautions against misuse.
- Date of manufacture and date of expiry.
- Maximum retail price including taxes.

Packaging

Packaging can be defined as the designing and producing of the outer covering of a product so as to bring out its distinctive identification, and assist in providing an identity to the product in order to make it look different from competing products. It is an important part of the product planning and serves as a selling tool.

The role of packaging is to create a mental imprint of the product among the target market. This is expected to help in acquiring brand loyalty. Packaging is visible as the outer wrapping or container that holds the actual product. Packaging involves designing the box or wrapper that contains the product. In addition to holding and protecting the product it also functions as a powerful selling tool.

A product can have multiple packages. This includes the container such as a bottle, can or a case. This can be enclosed in a box for protection. The product may also have a case or a larger container to transport multiple products within one box. Each of these packages, particularly those that are visible at the point of sale, offers the opportunity to communicate information to consumers at a critical point in their decision-making process.

> **Packaging**
> - Identifies the product.
> - Promotes and sells the product.
> - Provides information about the product.
> - Provides safety to the product.

In the modern marketing scenario packaging is acquiring increasingly greater importance.

Levels of Packaging

There are three levels of packaging of a product that are explained below :

1. Primary package– Primary package is the package, which encloses the actual commodity. This package remains attached with the actual commodity till the product is totally consumed. For example, the tube of a shaving cream and bottle of drinking water.

2. Secondary package– Secondary package is the layer of cover added to the primary package for protection. It is removed prior to using the product. For example, many companies that sell edible food items like biscuits wrap the product in a white butter paper and then rewrap it for the second time in the final covering.

3. Transportation package– Transportation package is used to facilitate the identification, transportation, handling and storing of products. It helps to store the product for longer time and keeps it safe when it has to be transported to remote or faraway locations. This package can consist of corrugated cardboard, wood, or a mix of both. E-commerce companies deliver fragile items in a cardboard box to keep it safe during transit.

Benefits of Packaging

Packaging offers several benefits to the producer as listed below :

1. Protection– Packaging protects the product from the rigours and strains of transportation, and ensures the product reaches the customer in a usable condition. It prevents breakage of fragile and delicate products like light bulbs, electronic items, etc. It also protects the product against deterioration during its shelf life.

2. Identification– Packaging promotes a product at the point of purchase. It also differentiates the product from its competitors. For example, the Coca Cola bottle can be easily identified due to its well-recognised packaging.

3. Encourages impulse buying– Packaging serves as a powerful selling tool and stimulates impulse buying. Numerous products are purchased without any salesman assistance. Products like music CD's, perfumes and chocolates are bought on impulse.

4. Economy– Packaging makes sure that the products occupy the most economical space when they are in transit and when in storage in the warehouse or on the shop shelf. Thus, packaging helps in minimising transportation and storage costs.

5. Promotion– Packaging complements other promotional activities. Depending upon how well it is presented, it attracts the attention of the potential customers.

Features of a Good Package

Listed below are the features that are desirable in a good packaging :

1. Convenience– Package should be such that the product can be conveniently taken from one place to another and should be easily handled by middlemen and consumers. The size and shape of package also should be convenient for retailers to keep in shop or for consumers to keep at their home.

2. Attractive– The package should be attractive and capable of drawing customers' attention. It must stimulate their interest and awaken desire for the product. The colour, picture, design, size, etc., of the package can be tools for influencing customers.

3. Economical– The package should be economical and not costly. Costly packaging inflates the price of the product. High price can be a drawback in selling.

4. Protective– The basic purpose of packaging is to protect products from different risks. The packaging should be such that the quality, quantity and colour of the product does not deteriorate or gets damaged by sun, rain, insects, dust, etc. It must prevent the product from getting damaged, putrefied, spoiled or rotten.

5. Communicative– A good packaging should communicate information to the customers about the brand utility and quality of the product.

PLACE CONCEPT

In marketing terms, 'place' denotes the physical distribution of a product to the consumer for his consumption. The product must be made available to the consumer at the place of his choice and at the time he wants or needs it. This also means that the product must be stored at a place from where it can be readily made available to the consumer in the quantity that he desires. The marketer has to consider the following options when selecting a channel of distribution :

1. The channels through which the product is to be sold whether through the producer's retailing stores, or through other retailers.
2. Will there be wholesalers as part of the supply chain to sell the product? Will the product be sold through online shops? Or, will it be sold in shopping malls and supermarkets?
3. Will the company use own sales force? If yes, then the size and composition of the sales force is to be decided.
4. The producer will have to think of its sales and distribution strategy, and how it will impact its profitability and the success of the product or service.

The options specified above will have to be considered by the marketer before he can be in a position to successfully place his product in the customer hands.

Channels of Distribution

A channel of distribution is the pathway through which a product or a service is made available to the ultimate customer for consumption. We can look at a distribution channel as a chain that comprises the producer and a host of other people whose job is to move the product from the producer to the ultimate consumer. It covers all those wholesalers, super stockists, warehouses, retailers via whom the goods or services pass before finding their way into the hands of the ultimate consumer. We can call the distribution channels by other names such as marketing channel, or a supply channel.

Physical distribution takes into account all interrelated functions like all available means of transportation, warehousing and storage facilities, transportation time, cost of transportation, etc. in order to ensure that the goods reach the consumers at the right time and at an affordable cost. The functions are all interrelated because any decision made in one area has an effect on the others. For example, transporting a product by air can be very time saving and it can protect the product against the hazards of surface transportation. But, in this case, the cost will be very high and would push up the selling price. So many aspects have to be considered in relativity, and never in isolation, when selecting a particular channel of distribution.

Functions of Channels of Distribution

The channels of distribution or the middlemen play an important role in ensuring the products reach the consumers in time. Some of the functions are listed below :

1. Sorting– The distributors or middlemen sort the various products according to their nature, size, quality and quantity. This standardisation helps in quick and efficient distribution of the products.

2. Accumulation– The distributors are those people who have to ensure that the sellers always have their stocks readily replenished at the shortest possible notice. Therefore, they maintain a ready stock of goods that is supplied to the sellers on a continuous basis.

3. Allocation– Allocation is the breaking up of larger packages into smaller and manageable smaller packs that can be readily and easily handled by the sellers. The warehouses get large packages which they break and organise into smaller and convenient packages to ensure quicker movement.

4. Assorting– This function includes the supply of goods that have to be combined as per the buying needs and demands of the consumers so as to enable them to get the required products all under one roof. For example, the customers like to get their requirement for the kitchen from one shop instead of visiting a number of retailers for different utensils. Thus, the middleman ensures that he can offer an assortment of all such items under one roof.

5. Promotion– Distributors also play a role in promoting products when they take part in the promotional programs. They also promote sales through word of mouth and at times, through personal selling.

6. Negotiation– It often happens that it is the middleman who plays a vital role in finding buyers. They take upon themselves the role of negotiating the terms and conditions of stocking and selling the goods.

7. Risk taking– Middlemen take title to goods; as a result, they readily diffuse the risk between themselves and the producer. If the goods gets spoiled, destroyed, or the price goes down, the loss is borne by the middlemen.

The nature of the product plays an important role in deciding the system of distribution to be used. There are basically **three types of marketing channels** as indicated below :

1. Direct or zero level channel are the chains of distribution that are marked by the absence of middlemen. In other words, there are no middlemen in the form of wholesalers, distributors, or retailers in this channel. The producer is interacting directly with the consumer; he is selling directly to them bypassing the intermediaries. This can be rendered possible when the producer has his own sales force, sells through his own retail counters, or through mail order. Where the producer has his own sales force, the sale is generally done at the consumer's home through direct contact. In the Indian countryside context, when the farmer brings his produce to the 'mandi' and sells it to the customers, he is bypassing the village middleman. This is an example of direct selling. In this case, the seller is interacting directly with the consumer. Many producers are also using web-based applications to reach out to the ultimate consumer. Consumers can pay online or cash on delivery and have their good couriered to them.

$$\text{Producer} \longrightarrow \text{Consumer}$$

The advantage of selling directly is that by bypassing the middlemen and distributors, the producer is able to control the selling price, thereby seeing to it that the consumers get the advantage of low price. When the goods pass through the distribution channels, the end price gets inflated for various economic reasons. The longer the chain of distribution the more the price is subject to increase. One disadvantage of direct channel is that it could be more capital-intensive as the producer has to set up his own distribution network.

2. Indirect channels comprise the wholesalers, super stockists, retailers and such related middleman through whose hands goods pass, before the ultimate customer gains ownership of the goods. These middlemen or intermediaries are responsible for transferring the goods from the producer to the ultimate consumer. These middlemen take ownership of the goods in most of the cases.

Indirect channel may be one-level or two-level. *One-level channels* are normally used for durable goods and high-value products like automobiles, etc. It is also used for perishable goods. The advantage here is that by reducing the number of intervening middlemen, the time lag between the product leaving the producer and arriving at the ultimate outlet is reduced and the consumer receives the product while it is still fresh.

$$\text{Producer} \longrightarrow \text{Retailer} \longrightarrow \text{Consumer}$$

Two-level channels include a wholesaler and the retailer between the producer and the consumer. This channel is useful where the consumers are scattered over a wide geographical area and there is strong promotional support for the product. However, this increases the time for the goods to arrive from the production point to the selling or consumption point.

Producer ⟹ Wholesaler ⟹ Retailer ⟹ Consumer

One of the advantages of indirect channel is that it enables the producer to reach widely dispersed markets across vast geographical areas. This cuts down the distribution costs for the producer.

The disadvantage of indirect channel is that the producer has to give up ownership of the goods, or at least part of the marketing aspect.

3. **Dual distribution or three-level channel** means the producer has to make use of more than one channel to sell his goods to the consumer.

Producer ⟹ Agent ⟹ Wholesaler ⟹ Retailer ⟹ Consumer

This is the longest channel of distribution and three middlemen are involved here. It is used when the producer wants to be fully relieved of distribution and hands over his entire output to the selling agents. The agents distribute the product among a few wholesalers. Then the wholesalers distribute the product among a number of retailers who sell it to the end consumers. This channel is common in the distribution of industrial products.

Whether a producer uses direct or indirect channel depends on certain factors, one being the nature of the goods. Where the goods pass through different hands the end cost increases and the customer has to pay more in terms of final price. This is just the opposite in direct channels where the producer has control over the end cost as he eliminates the middlemen.

Selection of Channels of Distribution

The following factors must be borne in mind by the seller while selecting the channels of distribution for his product :

1. **Product related factors–** The product related factors that affect the selection of distribution channels are listed below :

(a) **Unit value–** If the product is expensive, then the shortest distribution channel should be adopted. On the other hand, if the product is inexpensive, then a longer distribution channel can be used. Cars and jewellery fall in to the category of expensive products, whereas toiletries are generally classified as inexpensive products.

(b) **Bulk and weight–** To minimize the cost of transportation, heavy products are distributed through a shorter distribution channel. But smaller and light weight products are dispatched through a longer channel.

(c) **Perishability–** If the product is fragile and perishable like fruits, vegetables and dairy products, then the shortest channel of distribution should be used.

(d) **Standardisation–** Standardised products are distributed through longer channels of distribution, whereas the customised products are distributed through the shortest channel since it requires closer interaction between the buyer and the seller.

(e) **Technicality of the product–** If the product is of a technical nature requiring expert advice and demonstration, the shortest channel of distribution is needed. These products can be explained technically and sold better through the marketing and sales team employed by the company rather than the distributors who may not fully understand the product's technical aspects. Further, direct distribution allows company employees to build relationships directly with customers. These relationships could possibly be stronger, and allow for better supply chain management if conducted by the company on its own.

2. **Market related factors**– The following are market related factors that play a role in deciding the selection of distribution channels.

(a) **Nature of the market**– The nature of markets affects the selection of channels of distribution. Industrial markets require a shorter channel while consumer markets have a longer channel of distribution.

(b) **Size of the market**– In a larger market longer channel of distribution is the best fit. Inversely, if the market is small, a shorter channel of distribution is needed.

(c) **Geographical location**– Geographical dispersal of the consumer plays an important part in the selection of distribution channels. The wider the dispersal of the consumers, the longer is the channel of distribution. On the other hand, direct selling can be used if the consumers are not widely dispersed.

(d) **Size and frequency of order**– If the frequency of orders placed is low but the size of the order is large, the channel of distribution can be kept short. However, if the frequency of orders is high but the size of the orders is small, the marketer will have to reach out to the customer multiple times. Thus, he will have to use a longer distribution channel to cater to the requirement of frequent but small orders.

3. **Company related factors**– The following are company related factors that play a role in deciding the channels of distribution.

(a) **Financial strength**– The financial strength of the marketer is an important factor in determining what channels it can use. If there is no paucity of funds with the company, it can create a customised distribution channel to serve its purpose. Though every company has to ultimately depend on external channels of distribution, a well-funded company can control the distribution channels more effectively than a smaller company with limited marketing funds.

(b) **Need for control**– The choice of distribution channels also depends on how much control a company needs on its distributors. If there is a need for close control then a company can opt for direct distributors so that it can closely control them. Indirect and longer channels are more difficult to control.

(c) **Scale of operation**– The scale of operations of a company also affects its distribution channels. If the scale of production is large and the product range is well extended, a company opts for a direct distribution channel.

4. **Middlemen related factors**– The following factors related to middlemen play an important role in deciding channels of distribution.

(a) **Availability of specialised middlemen**– Distribution is a specialised role and the skills and techniques of distribution vary from place to place and from product to product. Very often, absence of specialised and trained distributors compels a company to devise its own distribution system. It is also possible that existing distributors may be engaged in handling competing products and may not be ready to accept the new brand.

(b) **Attitude of distributors–** The company has to take into account the attitude and behaviour of the middleman. At times when the middlemen display an attitude not consistent with the producer's work culture and policies (*e.g.* failing to adhere to time frame, etc.), their services get turned down by the producer. Instead, the company could come up with its own distribution network. However, if the middlemen cooperate with the company, share its vision and objectives, the company may prefer external middlemen rather than bringing in its own distribution set-up.

(c) **Services rendered–** This is an important factor in selection of a distribution system. If middlemen render specialised and valuable services to the producer which would entail heavy cost in case it were to be done by the producer himself, the producer will have no option but to take the services of the middlemen.

(d) **Sales target–** The distributors need to attain certain company allocated minimum sales targets. This fulfillment of sales target becomes a criterion in the selection of distribution channels with producers preferring such channels that help in the attainment of company sales targets.

(e) **Terms and conditions–** In case the producer does not find the terms and conditions laid down by middlemen unfavourable, the former may choose not to engage the latter in distribution activities.

Physical Distribution

Physical distribution is the term given to the group of activities that help in moving the finished product from the producers to the consumers. Physical distribution includes many sales distribution channels, such as wholesale and retail. It also includes customer service, inventory, materials, packaging, order processing, transportation and logistics.

According to Professor Philip Kotler, "Physical distribution involves planning, implementing and controlling the physical flow of materials and final goods from points of origin to points of use to meet customer needs at a profit."

Physical distribution is also known as '*Supply Chain Management*' and '*Marketing Logistics*'. Its main elements are as follows :

1. Order processing.
2. Transportation.
3. Warehousing.
4. Inventory Control.

PROMOTION CONCEPT

Promotion means increasing consumer awareness of a product or brand, boosting sales and creating brand loyalty. Promotion has a very wide perspective. It includes many areas and sub-areas about which the producer thinks seriously. It includes questions such as :

1. How the producer will ensure that the product or service meets the acceptance of the buyer?
2. How to ensure that the product gets a favourable reception from the customer?
3. In what form the product is presented to an audience?

> Promotion is the communication technique a business uses, such as advertising and other promotional methods, to interest customers in buying the products.

Promotion includes marketing activities such as advertising, exhibitions, media events, trade shows, road shows, point-of-purchase discount offers, etc. It is a very important part of the marketing mix.

Basically, promotion is the method of communicating with the customer to provide information about the offered product. Promotion is either directed at the consumer directly, or it can be directed at the distributors. Promotions typically include advertising, publicity, sales promotions and other related tactics. The methods used in achieving these effects may vary, depending on the company's goals, priorities, markets and scale of operations.

The key to best results through promotional activities is ensuring that companies target the consumer who is more apt to buy their products. Promotion is a costly exercise and covers a large part of the product budget. It adds to the cost of the product. Therefore, it needs to be cost-effective. The producer has to take into account the types of promotional campaigns being practiced in the industry before finalising his own.

The sales promotion is a very important function of marketing. Without promotion the public has no means of knowing what the company has to offer to its customers. It serves, through its various components, as a very important window through which customers can look into the company's product house and figure out what offering could serve their needs and wants.

Functions of Promotion

Promotional activities have the following main functions :

1. Stimulate demand– Promotional activities are directed at creating awareness about the product and also aim to create interest among the consumer group for the product. The sum total of these activities stimulates demand for the product. Promotional efforts are the best way of introducing a new product to the potential consumers and stimulating the demand.

2. Inform and educate– Another important function of promotion is keeping customers informed about the introduction of new products. It is in the interest of the seller or producer to educate the consumer about the contents, ingredients or the technical aspects of the new product. The producer also needs to educate the consumer about the ways the new product can be used.

3. Differentiate the product– Promotion helps the consumer to identify the producer's products. Thus, it enables him to differentiate it from the other competing products.

4. Highlight the product's utility– Promotion focuses on the utility of the product for the customer. It throws light on the usefulness of the product and its role in satisfying the wants of the customer. Thus, promotion builds up demand for the product by highlighting its unique selling points.

5. Build the product image– Promotion is an image building exercise. Different functions and aspects of promotion such as advertising, public relations and publicity are used to build up a favourable image of the product and increase the sales volume.

Elements of Promotion

In a promotional exercise or campaign, a firm or business unit uses a number of different promotional techniques to ensure that its sales revenue continues pouring in. There are basically four tools in the promotional mix. These are listed below :

1. Advertising
2. Personal selling
3. Publicity
4. Sales promotion

These are also known as the elements of promotion. The firm has to determine what mix of promotional elements it wants to use to achieve its goals. All the four elements cannot be used equally because their value and utility changes according to the business environment and the nature of the product. In order to get the maximum impact of a promotion exercise the firm needs to combine multiple promotional tools in the correct proportion.

The elements of promotion are explained below :

Advertising

We can consider advertising as a paid form of non-personal communication to cultivate a positive image about a product, a service, or even a company. If the advertising is meant to improve the public image of a company, it is called Institutional or Corporate Advertising. In any case, the cost of the advertising is paid for by the company. Today, a wide range of advertising options are available for the advertiser to choose from. The selection of the media depends upon many factors, chiefly the advertising budget and the nature of the product or service. Advertising can focus on any one product or service of the seller. It can also be used to build or improve a company's image in the view of the consumer.

> **Advertising Media**
> - TV, Radio.
> - Newspaper, Magazine, Trade Journals.
> - Web and Mobile.

Features of Advertising

The important features of advertising are identified as follows :

1. A service paid for– Advertising, unlike publicity, is a service that is paid for by the advertiser. It is a paid form of communication. It ceases to qualify as advertising if its cost is paid for by anyone other than the organisation whose product or service is being advertised.

2. Impersonal presentation– It is a form of non-personal presentation directed at a wide audience rather than a particular individual. The advertiser and the consumer do not come into contact with each other.

3. Identified sponsor or advertiser– The sponsor or the company who is being provided the service gets always identifiable due to the impact of advertising. If it cannot be identified, the activity ceases to qualify as advertising. In that case, it can be termed as propaganda or publicity only.

4. Promotes ideas, goods and services– The scope of advertising is wide in the sense that it promotes not only tangible goods, but also company services and ideas.

5. Informative and persuasive– An important feature of advertising is that not only it informs consumers about the products, services as well as their benefits, utility; it also serves to persuade potential consumer to buy these products and services. It stimulates human desires, thereby generating the demand for the product.

Objectives of Advertising

There can be many objectives of advertising by a company. Some of the major objectives are given below :

1. To create demand– The basic objective of advertising is to attract potential customers and motivate them to buy the products.

2. To ensure loyalty of customers– By focusing the company's commitment to quality through advertising, the company makes certain that its existing customers do not shift their preference to other brands.

3. Introduce new product– Another objective of advertising is to keep the buyer informed about the new products and services introduced in the market. It is through advertising that customers are informed about the utility, quality, features, benefits and price of the new products.

4. To create and maintain image and goodwill– Constant and regular advertising builds a good impression, goodwill and positive image of the producer. When a brand has a good image in the market, it enjoys a prosperous business. This also creates the right marketing environment to introduce new products with ease.

5. To educate customers– Advertising seeks to educate customers regarding the proper usage of the product so as to provide maximum utility and prevent any loss, physical or otherwise, to the customer.

Personal Selling

Personal selling can be defined as the process of motivating and persuading a consumer to buy a product of the seller's choice by making use of a face-to-face interaction. In such a scenario, the consumer is in direct contact with the sales person whose aim is to convert the potential customer into a loyal consumer of the brand. It is a systematic, repetitive and measurable process. For instance, in departmental stores and shopping malls, the sales person often employs convincing tactics to lure in customers and get them buy the product.

Features of Personal Selling

Personal Selling can be better understood by the following features :

1. It is a promotional method using skills and techniques for persuasion and building relationships with potential and actual consumers.
2. Personal selling is through face-to-face meetings and contact with customers.
3. It uses a personalised approach that is tailored to meet the individualised needs of the customer.
4. It utilises aggressive sales techniques.
5. It is a multi-stage process starting with prospecting and ending with selling. This result in consumer satisfaction.
6. The salesperson who successfully performs the job of personal selling is rewarded with financial incentives.
7. The consumer is rewarded with benefits of consuming the product purchased.

Marketing Mix

Objectives of Personal Selling

Some important objectives of personal selling are as listed below :

1. **Reinforcing the brand–** Most personal selling is intended to build long-term relationships with the customer. A strong relationship can only be built over time. Meeting with the customer on a regular basis allows the sales staff to repeatedly hold a discussion on their company products and brand promotion.

2. **Building relationship–** Personal selling intends to build up an ongoing and long term relationship with the customer. The process does not end with the sales.

3. **Creating interest–** Personal selling involves person-to-person communication. It seeks to create greater interest in the product. It also encourages the spread of product awareness by sales professionals.

4. **Stimulating demand–** The most important objective of personal selling is to convince the customer to make a purchase.

Publicity

It is the non-personal stimulation of demand brought about by the positive coverage received by a product or brand. Issue of press releases, getting an honorable mention in the media, doing charitable activities for social good, taking up charitable causes, giving donations, etc. are all forms of public exercises. These are all designed with the objective of getting publicity for the organisation and its products and services.

Features of Publicity

Some basic features of publicity are defined as under :

1. **Third party involvement–** Publicity requires third part involvement for spreading information and messages about goods or services of a firm. This third party involvement becomes necessary for the promotion of business firm and its products. It imparts an element of authenticity.

2. **Publicity is free–** No fee or charge is needed to be paid to the third party for the publicity of information about goods or services or the firm. The business firm does not incur any expense for the publicity materials communicated to the general public through mass media by the third party.

3. **Wide and quick dissemination of information–** Information about the business firm and its products is communicated to a very large number of viewers and readers by the flow of news and publicity both in print and electronic form in a very short span of time.

4. **Free advertising–** Positive publicity serves as free advertising for the business firm.

Objectives of Publicity

Major objectives of publicity are listed below :

1. **Building product awareness–** The first objective of publicity is to generate consumer attention and awareness through media placements and special events. This results in increasing hype specially when a new product or service is being introduced by a company.

2. Stimulating demand– A positive news report in a newspaper, a TV news show or a favourable mention on the internet often results in significant rise in product sales. The objective of publicity is to ensure constant positive coverage and thus gain through every increase in sales.

3. Creating interest– Creating interest among the masses in the company's product or service is another objective of publicity. It is the first stage towards creating a customer base for the company.

4. Providing information– Publicity provides customer with detailed information about products and services. Publicity and information dissemination is done through newspaper articles, collateral materials, company newsletters and websites. It helps the customer gain an in-depth understanding of the product.

5. Reinforcing the brand– Publicity is a way of building brand awareness by maintaining positive relationships with key audiences, thereby aiding in building a strong brand image. A strong image helps the company build its business which can prove helpful in times of crisis.

Sales Promotion

This is another element in the marketer's toolbox to bolster the product sales. It consists of sales tactics to push-up the sales at intervals and can be directed either at the trade or the customer by creating incentives to buy the product or buy more of it. One disadvantage of sales promotion is that it cannot be conducted regularly or continuously because if this is done, the entire program will lose its sheen and customers may begin questioning the quality of products or services. Distribution of free samples, cash discounts, road shows and exhibitions are examples of sales promotion.

The sales promotion tools directed at customers are :
- Free samples.
- Sales coupons giving discounts to customers on future purchase.
- Free trials and demonstrations.
- Giving away of extras or value discount promotions.

The sales promotion tools directed at trade are :
- Giving of trade discounts, cash discounts.
- Gifts upon completion of trade targets.
- Cooperative advertising.
- Training of sales force.

The following can be considered as an additional means of promotion :
- Exhibitions and trade shows.
- Conventions.
- Road shows.
- Any other tactic used by the producer

Sales promotion is influenced by the overall marketing policies and objectives of the organisation. It is a part of a concerted effort to bring about a change in the views of the customer about the product by conveying the important or attractive elements of the product.

Features of Sales Promotion

Sales promotion has the following major features which are listed below :

1. **Supports advertising and personal selling–** Sales promotion supports advertising and personal selling. It acts as a connecting link between the two. Companies follow up advertising campaigns with sales promotion campaigns. Sales promotion gives strength and support to personal selling. The price inducements given during sales promotion help the sales force to generate sales.

2. **Stimulates sales–** A unique sales promotion feature is that it stimulates sales at the point of sale, *i.e.,* where the sale actually takes place. It appeals to the consumers, through price discounts, or other inducements, when they are in the process of buying, and induces them either to buy in larger quantity or in terms of other promoted products of the same brand. Both ways it brings in more sales revenue for the producer.

3. **Acts as a marketing tool–** Sales promotion acts as a very effective marketing tool, highlighting the qualities and unique selling points that serve as powerful magnets to draw the consumers' attention to the product. Packaging, pricing and consumer satisfaction as a result of usage of the product are highlighted by an effective sales promotion campaign.

4. **Stimulates dealer effectiveness–** Dealers are positively affected and are more supportive of brands that are frequently supported by well-organised sales promotion campaigns. The reason is that sales promotion helps the dealers in popularising brands and they are able to attain company sales targets. It assists them in getting larger trade discounts and other incentives thus increasing their operating profit.

Objectives of Sales Promotion

The main objectives of sales promotion are identified below :

1. **Product differentiation–** Use of sales promotion techniques helps to differentiate one brand from other competing brands especially where all products offer essentially the same features and benefits. A common sales promotion method is to offer products at a slightly reduced price for a short period of time.

2. **Attract customers and push up sales–** Sales promotion is used to attract customers during periods of low sales. This helps in drawing the customer attention to that product and also helps to support sales.

3. **New product introduction–** Sales promotion is used to introduce a new product into the market. By offering a new item and promoting its sale, the marketer persuades the existing customers to give the new product a try, while it also attracting new and potential customers.

4. **Phasing out a product–** Sales promotion is extensively used to sell out remaining stock of old products or brands that the company intends to phase out of its portfolio.

5. **Increase off-season sales–** Business organisations encourage the purchase of their products during off-season through sales promotion. That is why they offer

discounts and off-season price reductions of many products in the market during period of slack sales. Products like air-coolers, fans, refrigerators, air-conditioners, and room heaters have seasonal demand. Business organisations focus to maintain a stable demand of these seasonal products throughout the year.

Factors Determining the Promotion Mix

The marketer keeps the following factors in consideration when deciding the promotional mix for his product :

1. **Nature of the product**– Products differ in their requirement of promotional tools. In technical and industrial products personal selling is more effective as they need more after sales services. Consumers, especially housewives, are at times swayed by the advertising, price discounts and schemes. Hence, such consumer products require more advertising and promotional efforts, especially in and around shopping areas.

2. **Nature of the market**– If the customers are dispersed far and wide, the product requires more of advertising. Concentration of buyers in one place needs more of personal selling. Products which encourage impulsive buying like eatables and fashion wear, need more advertising and point of purchase promotional efforts.

3. **Product's life stage**– If the product is at the start of its life cycle it requires intensive advertising and publicity. If it is in its maturity stage, then again it needs more of sales promotion and personal selling. Thus, the promotional mix to be used depends on the product's life cycle.

4. **Promotional budget**– The promotional budget of the company is directly responsible for the type of promotional efforts and mix that will be used to promote a product. Higher budget with result in greater promotional efforts for a product.

5. **Timing of the promotional program**– The marketer has to consider the environmental factors that may affect the effectiveness of the promotional mix as a whole. It may also affect just one or two components of the mix but the overall effect may defeat the thrust of the promotional mix. The effectiveness of any mix will vary from time to time. Environmental factors, the economy, consumer's purchasing power, time of the year, festivals and holidays can affect the effectiveness of any promotion mix.

A General Comparison of the Elements of Promotion

Features	Advertising	Sales Promotion	Personal Selling	Publicity
Purpose	Dissemination of information about the product.	Reward for buying the product.	Face-to-face persuasion to buy the product.	Generating news or obtaining favourable media publicity.
Mode of Finance	Paid for by the marketer to advertising agency.	Rewards offered by the marketer to the buyer.	Cost borne by the marketer.	Cannot paid for by the marketer.
Reach	Advertising reaches far and wide transgressing physical distances.	Can be done only at the point of purchase, i.e. where the selling takes place.	This requires the physical presence of the customer at whom the efforts are directed.	Is done by the media, no need of presence of customers.

Evaluation	Direct impact and effect of advertising cannot be evaluated with certainty.	The volume of sales as a result of sales promotion efforts can be easily evaluated.	Amount of sales due to personal selling can be evaluated.	Sales increase as a result of publicity cannot be evaluated.
Frequency	Regular and constant advertising has a positive impact on brand and image building.	Long-term sales promotion can have an adverse effect on sales, product and brand image.	Long-term and constant personal selling success depends on the nature of the product.	Regular positive publicity can be very good for the brand and the product.
Customer Base	Advertising is directed at both potential and existing customers.	Sales promotion is rewarding existing customers and attracting potential customers.	Personal selling is directed more at those who are not brand-loyal customers and can be made to change their mind.	Publicity seeks to gain new customers by creating a positive corporate image.

PRICE CONCEPT

This is the most important of all the 4 P's of marketing. It is the most important determinant of sales revenue for a producer. Price can be the value of a product or service computed in monetary terms by its producer. It has to be paid by the buyer before any change of ownership can take place. It is the price that determines the quantity of production, distribution and consumption in the economy.

The first factor that has to be considered before fixing any price is the value of the product as perceived by the customer. Although the manufactured produce is dear to every producer, what really matters is how the customers regard it. If the customer see it worthy of satisfying their needs, the producer can charge a high price from the customer. On the contrary, if the customer views the product as an unworthy produce incapable of satisfying the needs, it will never find acceptance in the market even if the price is reduced. But, in case of an innovative product there may not be any competitor and hence the producer, as the market leader, can charge a price according to his liking. However, in a market which is populated by competitors with a niche, the producer cannot charge the price of his personal liking. In practical terms, the existing competition will have to be taken into consideration for the business to survive in such a scenario. In case of greater competition, more flexible approach to pricing will be required.

Another factor that plays a role in fixing price of a product or service is the pricing strategy of the company. A company may intentionally fix a higher price for its product as part of its marketing strategy to gain leadership of the market. It may have a higher break-even point for the product. It may even adopt a low production high price policy to ensure its product remains a premium product for an exclusive segment.

The consumer segment for which a particular service or product is targeted also plays an important role in deciding the price. If the target segment is the upper class, the producer will put a high price on the product. If the consumers are price conscious, the producer will decide on a comparatively lower price. The customers have to be profiled in terms of their social and financial status. For example, if a service provider is trying to sell holiday excursions to the Philippines, it will need to have an idea of the type of customers that will or can buy those services. The producer will form an idea of their purchasing power and willingness to pay. Only then, the producer think of putting a price tag on the ticket. The price in this case should be such that will make the customer think highly of it. If it is low, a particular segment may see it as either substandard or of little value. Thus, we see that looking into the societal status or class of the market segment is a very important factor in deciding the price for a product or service.

Determinants of Price

The price itself is determined by a number of other factors. Some of these factors are listed below :

1. **Product cost–** The cost of the product includes the cost that goes into the research and development of the product and in producing the product. The initial investment has to be recovered by the company by selling a certain number of products at a specified price.

2. **Market demand–** The price fixed by the company also depends on the nature of demand for the product or type of product. It cannot fix a price higher than what the market is willing to pay. If it prices a product too high, it may not find acceptability with the consumer. However, if the demand is high and the supply is low, the producer can fix a high price for his product.

3. **Competition–** If the number of competitors are high, the producer will have to price his product in the vicinity of what the competitors are charging. However, where competitors are fewer in number, the producer may be able to put a higher price tag on his product.

4. **Government and legal regulations–** Many a times a producer may not be able to put a higher price tag on his product due to government restrictions and legal regulations. This is very common in case of services and products that are subsidised by the government.

5. **Promotional strategy–** A producer may put a high price tag when the product is introduced and he intends to recover his investment within a short period of time. This policy applies if the producer intends to position the product in the high-end premium category. On the other hand, the producer will go in for a lower price tag if he resolves to capture a big chunk of the market in a short period of time.

6. **Customer perception–** The way a consumer perceives a product also influences the price. If a product is seen as useful and of high value it can command a higher price. However, if the consumer thinks of it lacking utility, the producer can sell the product at a lower price only.

7. **Marketing methods–** By applying thoughtful and smart marketing strategies, the producer can influence the target market and present a low-cost product as a premium, high-end product at a high price. In some cases, a high-end premium product

can fail to command a high price if it is not positioned in the right way by the marketer. Hence, the marketing techniques devised by the producer play an important role in influencing the price.

> ### SUMMARY
>
> ***Marketing Mix*** – It is the systematised combination of product, place, price and promotion in marketing a product or a service.
>
> ***Product Concept*** – Product can be a tangible object (physical product that can be touched or seen, or has colour, form and shape, etc.) or a service (intangible, that can be experienced, like a holiday package, or a cruise).
>
> ***Branding*** – A name or a symbol that gives the product an identity and differentiates it from competing products.
>
> ***Labelling*** – The label is the outer covering of the product that spells out information about the product and gives directions for usage.
>
> ***Packaging*** – It is the outer covering or container that holds the actual product. It can be a plastic container, crate, box, or can, etc. It serves the purpose of identification, promotion, protection and convenience in use.
>
> ***Place Concept*** – It refers to the channels of distribution or the path the product takes from the producer to the ultimate consumer. Different products have different channels of distribution.
>
> ***Promotion Concept*** – It is the process of persuading a prospective customer to become a consumer of a particular brand or product.
>
> ***Price Concept*** – The value of a product or service expressed in monetary terms. It is determined by the quality, demand, buying motives, etc.

QUESTIONS FOR PRACTICE

Very Short Answer Type Questions

1. Name the elements of the marketing mix.
2. Write short note on Branding and Labelling.
3. List any two features of labelling.
4. Define Promotion.
5. "Advertising is a social waste." Comment.
6. Briefly describe any two aims of sales promotion.

Short Answer Type Questions

1. What is Marketing Mix? Explain its elements.
2. How would you define a product?
3. State any two features of labelling in relation to marketing.
4. How does branding help the marketer?
5. List any three determinants of price.
6. What is a channel of distribution?
7. List three factors that influence the choice of channels of distribution.
8. Explain physical distribution.
9. Explain any three elements of Promotion Mix.

10. Define sales promotion as an element of promotion mix. Highlight its objectives.
11. A washing machine is to be launched in the market. Describe any five methods of sales promotion that can be used to do so.

Essay Type Questions

1. What is Marketing Mix? Explain the elements of marketing mix.
2. Explain the concept of price as an important component of the marketing mix.
3. What is packaging? Explain three functions of packaging.
4. What are the different levels of packaging?
5. Discuss the factors that influence the price of a product.
6. What are the different types of channels of distribution available to a producer?
7. Explain direct channel of distribution in relation to marketing.
8. What role does pricing play in the marketing of a product?
9. How can you differentiate between a product and a service?
10. What is the difference between Personal Selling and Sales Promotion?

15. Consumer Protection

> **LEARNING RESULT**
>
> After reading this chapter, you should be able to :
> - Understand the need for Consumer Protection.
> - Define the Rights of Consumers.
> - Identify Consumer Responsibilities.
> - Elucidate Methods of Consumer Protection.
> - Expound Consumer Protection Act, 1986.

It has been observed very often that the consumers are exploited by unscrupulous producers and sellers. They put misleading advertisements, charge unreasonable amount for a product, sell spurious and substandard products and exploit the consumers in any other way it pleases them. This had been largely due to the general ignorance of consumers. Underweighting, overcharging, adulteration are some of the ways consumers are exploited. Thus, there is a need for providing protection to consumers against such practices on part of the producers and sellers.

NEED FOR CONSUMER PROTECTION

The need for consumer protection arises because of the following reasons :

1. Business focuses on consumer satisfaction– The objective of business is to serve the consumers, not to exploit them for petty gains. Business cannot survive if consumers remain unsatisfied.

2. Social responsibility of business– It is the responsibility of the business to serve the interest of the society. The influence of the business on the society should be such that it benefits the society in the long-term. Consumers make the society. Their interest can be preserved by ensuring that they are protected against all types of exploitation.

3. Business ethics– There can be no real business without business ethics and moral values being upheld. A high standard of moral values can be ensured by legally ensuring that business adheres to it. Thus, consumer protection is the ethical obligation of business. A legal watchdog makes certain that high moral standards with respect to consumer protection are kept alive.

4. Self-interest– In today's environment of globalisation, the Indian business houses cannot survive the competition unless they produce quality goods and compete with foreign brands. They have to become consumer-oriented. If the business exploits consumers, it may never gain brand loyalty. Therefore, to protect the interest of Indian business, it is necessary that the business does not exploit consumers. The best way to ensure this, is through legally protecting the consumers.

5. Business as the trustee– The producer is the trustee of the social wealth and must ensure that it is used for the general benefit of all. It cannot be allowed to exploit the social wealth and millions of consumers through falsification and misleading the consumers. The enacted laws serve as boundaries to make sure that consumers get what they pay for.

RIGHTS OF CONSUMERS

As a consumer, a person has the right to know about the price, quantity, purity, contents and ingredients of a product before making a purchase. The consumer has the right to be protected against malpractices and unfair practices by the trade or the producer. Consumer rights are very important especially in a country like India where people are largely illiterate and unlettered. Trade and producer both connive with each other to work against the interest of the consumer. Often prices are not mentioned on the packaging which gives the seller a good reason to charge a price over and above the price that should have been otherwise charged.

The following rights have been legally given to consumers to save them from becoming a victim of trader malpractices :

1. Right to safety– The consumer has the right to be protected against hazardous and harmful products that can possibly endanger his life and property. They have the right to buy such products that will not put them at risk or injury. They have the right to get quality, reliability and performance. The producer has to ensure that his product will not harm the consumer in any way and is fit to be used the way it is supposed to be used.

2. Right to be informed– The consumer has the right to be informed about the quality, quantity potency, price, etc. of the product that he is buying. The producer is under legal obligation to ensure that this information is made available to the buyer. This also includes the technical specifications, date of manufacture, date of expiry, and information about methods of usage, serviceability, etc.

3. Right to choose– The consumer has the right to be allowed to choose any product. He cannot be subjected to any pressure or aggressive selling technique that compels him to buy any particular brand. He must be allowed full freedom to exercise his free choice and buy a product of his choice.

4. Right to be heard– The consumer has the right to register his dissatisfaction and get his complaint heard at the appropriate forum. He can make representation to the government regarding his complaint. The government or the forum is under legal obligation to hear him and consider his complaint.

5. Right to seek redressal– The consumer has the right to get his complaints settled against the concerned producer. Any issue arising out of any unfair trade practice or malpractice by the producer or seller has to be attended by the court concerned. The product has to be either repaired or taken back and replaced by the seller or producer. At times the consumer also has to be compensated in monetary terms by the seller.

6. Right to consumer education– The consumer has the right to acquire knowledge and become aware of his rights and the remedies available to him. This way the producer cannot plead ignorance as an excuse to get away with his malpractice.

7. Right to healthy environment– The consumer has the right to be protected against environmental pollution caused due to the manufacturing practices employed by the producer. The business is under obligation to ensure that there is no environmental degradation or pollution by the producer.

CONSUMER RESPONSIBILITIES

To be safeguarded from producer malpractices, a consumer must be aware of some major responsibilities. These are :

1. Exercise their rights– It is the duty of the consumer to exercise his rights while making a purchase.

2. Ask for full information– In case the information regarding the product is missing from the label, the consumer should ask for the relevant information from the seller. Such information can be regarding the price, or date of manufacture, or quality, etc. The seller is under legal obligation to furnish these details to the buyer.

3. Be quality conscious– The consumer needs to look for quality certification marks like ISI, AGMARK, Hallmark, etc. It is a wise way to save oneself from being cheated by adulterers and spurious manufacturers.

4. Insist on receipt– Receipts or cash memos are proof of purchase by the consumer and are needed if there is a complaint regarding the product. The consumer must ask for the cash receipt while buying the product.

5. Not be swayed by advertisements– The consumer must carefully examine the product and see to it that it is advertised the way it is. It is important for the consumer to avoid getting carried away by advertisements which at times can be misleading.

6. File complaints in case of exploitation– Last but not the least, in case of any issue with the product, the consumer must file a formal complaint with the relevant authorities or body for the speedy redressal of their grievances.

METHODS OF CONSUMER PROTECTION

Consumer Protection has emerged due to the need to look after the interests and rights of millions of consumers who buy goods and services from scores of producers and sellers around the world everyday.

Such concerns and issues led to the evolution of consumer protection movement and compelled governments around the world to enact legislations to legalise consumer protection acts and laws. In India, the Consumer Protection Act was enacted in the year 1986 with a view to ensure that consumers were well-protected from dubious and fraudulent practices and gain awareness of their rights and duties. This act covered all goods and services producers and sellers and put into effect procedures and processes for speedy redressal of complaints against erring companies and sellers. It makes sure that consumers are protected against frauds and deception and exploitation; and aggrieved consumers are duly compensated.

Business organisations have now become aware that their profitability lies in the welfare of the consumers. Consequently, they have begun adopting fair and just trade practices keeping the consumers in focus. Consumer associations have come up. They monitor trade practices keeping an eye on unfair practices and take the erring producers/sellers to court.

The methods of consumer protection are enumerated below :

1. Consumer awareness– The best method is that the consumer must be aware of his rights and responsibilities, and look for all information relevant to the product before making a buying decision. Thus, he can best protect himself against exploitation.

2. Self-regulations by business– Business houses are now increasingly applying self-regulations and are behaving in a disciplined and responsible way. Trade associations see to it that the producers do not adopt unfair practices. They serve as watchdogs of the society.

3. Consumer associations– Consumer associations and Non-governmental Organisations (NGOs) ensure that consumers are informed about their rights and responsibilities. These bodies educate and bring awareness to consumers. They also act on behalf of consumers.

4. Legislative measures– The government plays a role in ensuring that consumers are protected against exploitation. It brings in legislations ensuring protection to consumers. Some of these measures are listed below :

(a) **Consumer redressal forums–** The government provides judicial machinery for redressal of consumer grievances. It has set up the central and state commissions for settlement of consumer disputes as under :

   (i) Consumer disputes redressal forum (district-wise)– Established by the state government, also known as District Forums.
   (ii) Consumer disputes redressal commission– State commission established by state governments after prior approval from center.
   (iii) National consumer disputes redressal commission– Established by the Central Government, also known as the National Forum.

(b) **Lok adalats–** The consumer can approach the lok adalat where officials will look into the complaints and take appropriate action to redress the complaint. It is a speedy and economical system for redressal of complaints. Many government departments, like the Railways, telephone department, etc., organise lok adalat for speedy redressal.

(c) **Public interest litigations–** Public Interest Litigation or PIL can be filed in a court of law for redressal of complaints on behalf of the poor, the weak and the downtrodden people of the society, etc. Remedial action can be taken by the court.

(d) **Publicity and awards–** Government seeks to educate and encourage people to become aware of their rights and responsibilities as consumers by airing special programs on TV and radio. It also publishes journals and publications that are meant to enhance consumer awareness. The Government of India also presents rewards to people in order to encourage their participation in consumer protection.

(e) **Consumer welfare fund–** The government has organised a fund with the purpose of consumer education, training, guidance and research in consumer education.

It also has set up counseling centers, complaint handling facilities, product testing facilities, etc., to make sure consumers are not cheated.

(f) **Consumer protection councils**– These councils have been set up to look after consumer interests, which are as follows :
- Central Consumer Protection Council
- State Consumer Protection Council
- District Consumer Protection Council

THE CONSUMER PROTECTION ACT, 1986

The Consumer Protection Act was passed by the Indian Parliament in 1986 and came into force on July 1, 1987 to empower consumers and consumer organisations with the authority to take on business organisations that were bent on taking advantage of hitherto ignorant consumers. Its objective is to provide speedy redressal to consumers and to protect their rights and interests.

The Consumer Protection Act, 1986 seeks to provide for better protection of consumer interest, and to make provision for the establishment of consumer councils and other authorities for the settlement of consumer disputes and for matter connected therewith. It aims to promote and protect the rights of consumers.

Mentioned below are some rights that consumers are entitled to under the act :

1. The right to be protected against goods which are hazardous to life and property;
2. The right to be informed about the quality, quantity, potency, purity, standard and price of goods in order to protect the consumer against unfair trade practices;
3. The right to be assured of access to goods at competitive prices;
4. The right to be heard and to be assured that consumers interests will receive due consideration at appropriate forums;
5. The right to seek redressal against unfair trade practices or unscrupulous exploitation of consumers;
6. Right to consumer education.

Under the Consumer Protection Act, 1986, the following remedies are available to the aggrieved consumer :

1. Refund of price paid to the seller.
2. Removal of defects in the goods or services bought.
3. Replacement of defective goods with new goods.
4. Payment of compensation by seller for loss incurred by consumer.
5. Withdrawal of hazardous goods from the market.
6. Discontinuance of unfair and restrictive trade practices.

The Consumer Protection Act, 1986 sets up a three-tiered system of consumer protection which is given below :

1. **District forum**– This is the district-level forum which each State Government is to set up in every district. It has the authority to redress complaints and settle disputes of

transactions whose value does not exceed ₹ 20 lakhs. The law entitles it to the power of a civil court and is under a chairman and two other members one of whom should be a woman. They are appointed by the concerned State Government. It has the authority to test products, issue directions to the defaulting party, implement redressal and order payment of compensation. It can summon witnesses, examine them under oath and call for evidence, etc. An appeal against the order of the District Forums can be filed in the State Commission within 30 days.

    2. **State commission–** Each State Government is to set up the State Commission whose jurisdiction is restricted to the boundaries of the concerned state. It consists of a President, who either is a sitting or a retired High Court Judge and two other members, one of whom should be a woman. They are appointed by the concerned State Government. It hears complaints in cases wherein the value of the transaction or compensation claimed exceeds ₹ 20 lakhs but does not exceed ₹ 100 lakhs. It also hears appeals against the orders of any District Forum.

It has the power to :
(a) summon the parties concerned.
(b) send the goods for testing.
(c) issue orders directing the concerned party to replace the goods.
(d) return the payment, or pay compensation for loss or injury incurred.

Parties can appeal against the order of the State Commission within a period of 30 days to the National Commission.

    3. **National commission–** The National Commission represents the third and the topmost forum for redressal of consumer grievances. It is set up by the Central Government. It consists of a president, who either is a sitting or a retired Judge of the Supreme Court and four other members, one of whom should be a woman. All are appointed by the Central Government. It hears all complaints where the consideration involved exceeds ₹ 100 lakhs and appeals against the order of any State Commission. The powers of the National Commission are similar to that of a Civil Court. It can order recall and replacement of defective or unsafe goods, order compensation payment and take any other action to redress grievances. Appeals against the order of the National Commission can be filed in the Supreme Court within 30 days.

Who is a Consumer ?

The consumer can be defined as any person who buys goods or hires a service for consideration, paid in full, in parts or promised, as under an installment system. This definition extends to the user other than the actual purchaser where the approval of the buyer has been taken.

But this definition does not extend to the reseller or the person who avails the goods for a commercial purpose.

Who can File a Complaint ?

Under the Consumer Protection Act of 1986, the following persons or entities can file a complaint :
1. any consumer;

2. any voluntary consumer association registered under the Companies Act, 1956 or under any other law in force at that time;
3. the Central Government or any State Government;
4. any consumer or more than one consumer having a common interest; or
5. legal heirs or representative of a deceased consumer.

Against Whom can the Complaint be Filed ?

Any aggrieved consumer or any of the above mentioned entities can file a complaint against the below mentioned bodies or institutions under the Consumers Protection Act, 1986.

1. Manufacturer– A person who manufactures or provides the product, or claims to have manufactured the product, or puts his trademark or brand name on the goods even though someone else may have manufactured the product. In effect it means that even if the goods are assembled by someone else, the manufacturer, under the legal definition, will be the one whose trademark is on the product.

2. Supplier of the service(s).

3. Trader– The one who distributes or sells the goods.

ROLE OF NON-GOVERNMENT ORGANISATIONS (NGOS) AND CONSUMER ORGANISATIONS

Today we see a number of voluntary organisations have joined the fight against consumer exploitation. They are playing a vital role in ensuring that consumers are safeguarded against exploitation and defrauding by the manufacturers and sellers. Their outstanding roles are listed below :

1. Making consumers aware of their rights and responsibilities.
2. Educating consumers about available remedies for safeguarding their rights.
3. Publishing journals and disseminate information on consumer affairs.
4. Coordinating seminars, conferences and workshops on consumer affairs and issues.
5. Providing counselling and guidance to the consumers on a regular basis.
6. Filing complaints, petitions and helping in legal action against the trader on behalf of consumer.
7. Testing products, publishing data, etc.

List of Some Prominent NGO's
- Consumer Utility and Trust Society (CUTS), Jaipur.
- Consumer Guidance Society of India (CGSI), Mumbai.
- Voluntary Organisation in Interest of Consumer Education (VOICE), Delhi.
- Consumer Education and Research Center (CERC), Ahmedabad.
- Common Cause, Delhi.

> **SUMMARY**
>
> ***Definition of Consumer–*** *A person who buys goods or services for personal consumption.*
>
> ***Consumer Rights–*** *These include: right to safety, information, choice, heard, seek, redressal and education, and a healthy environment.*
>
> ***Consumer Protection Measures–*** *These include self-regulation measures by the business itself, legislative measures initiated by the government, and the efforts of non-governmental organisations and consumer associations.*
>
> ***Consumer Protection Act–*** *It safeguards and protects the consumer against manipulation, frauds and unfair trade practices. It also seeks to compensate the aggrieved consumer through a three-tier system of safeguard mechanism.*
>
> ***NGOs and Consumer Organisations–*** *These are non-governmental bodies that volunteer to help consumers fight exploitation and malpractices on part of traders and manufacturers.*

QUESTIONS FOR PRACTICE

Very Short Answer Type Questions

1. Why the need for consumer protection arises ?
2. Define a Consumer.
3. Explain the consumer's 'Right to Information' as per Consumers Protection Act 1986.
4. List any two responsibilities of a consumer.

Short Answer Type Questions

1. What are the rights of a consumer?
2. Write briefly about the Consumer Protection Act, 1986.
3. Write four methods that help in achieving the objectives of consumer protection.
4. Write briefly about Public Interest Litigation.
5. List any three legislative measures promulgated by the government for the protection of consumers.
6. Name any three non-governmental organisations engaged in helping consumers.

Essay Type Questions

1. Is there really a need of consumer protection? Bring out your case either for or against the topic.
2. What rights does a consumer enjoy under the Consumer Protection Act 1986?
3. What options does a consumer have in the event of an infringement of the rights?
4. Briefly describe the multilayered system of consumer protection set-up through the Consumer Protection Act, 1986.
5. What are the remedies available to an aggrieved consumer under the Consumer Protection Act, 1986?
6. How do non-government organisations help the consumers?
7. Discuss the role of the state commission in providing protection to consumers in India.

Project Work

Project No. 1

A Comparison of Marketing Strategies by Apple Inc. and Samsung

This is a comparative study of the marketing strategy practiced by the two leading sellers of mobile phones, Apple and Samsung. Both claim to be the market leaders in their field. The comparative study is along the basic areas of marketing, *i.e.,* the product, place, price and promotion.

Marketing Strategy Concerning	Apple	Samsung
Product Mix	(i) Reliance on heavy emphasis on research and development. (ii) Packed its products with new and innovative technology features. (iii) Targeted its products for the rich and the upper middle class. (iv) Apple tried to create an 'Apple lifestyle' that was supposed to improve life of consumers who bought its mobiles. (v) Invested heavily in research and development.	(i) Focused on products that come with exciting features. (ii) Introduced innovation. (iii) Targeted its products for those who considered themselves 'young'. (iv) Aggressively pursued consumer needs and desires. Introduced products whose features could satisfy consumer needs. E.g. Phablet- an astounding success. (v) Invested heavily in market research.
Price Mix	Apple introduced products that carry a higher price tag.	Samsung made higher end products available. But they also marketed products meant for consumers who could not afford expensive products.
Place Mix	Apple had a futuristic, diverse and very well managed supply chain that complimented its marketing.	Samsung ensured more product presence and availability than that of Apple. Like Galaxy S4 was available on 36 per cent more carriers and in 55 per cent more countries than the iPhone 5.
Promotion Mix	(i) Apple placed a heavy emphasis on creating brand loyalty. (ii) They tried creating consumer excitement towards the brand. (iii) Apple focused on creating an image in the consumers' mind of the 'Apple lifestyle'.	(i) Samsung focus was on the features of its smart phone. (ii) They emphasised on innovative technology and its exciting features. (iii) Samsung invested heavily in advertising and promotion, more than what Apple spent.

	(iv) Apple ensured product placement in movies to get publicity.	(iv) Through ads Samsung created an atmosphere that emphasised on the need for Samsung smart phone and created the impression that life will be rendered easier and more exciting by using Samsung products.

Project No. 2

Consumer Protection

Case No.	Rights Violated	Redressal Mechanism	Outcome
2004-CPC2 TN	Complainant bought a bus ticket for the journey. The bus broke down on the way. The passenger was stranded. He approached the court for redressal.	District Consumer Forum	It was held the incident was no act of God. The transporter was ordered to pay compensation of ₹ 5,000 to complainant.
2011(2) CPC 63 HP	Complainant consumed contaminated bottle of soda. He fell ill as a result.	District Consumer Forum	Awarded ₹1,00,000 compensation paid for by the seller of the soda.
Feb. 28, 2012 National Insurance Co. Vs. Mohd. Ishaq	Insurance claim not settled by insurance company due to adverse surveyor report.	District Forum/State Commission/National Consumer Dispute Redressal Commission	The district forum, state commission rejected the surveyor's report and ordered compensation, national commission upheld the decision.
Nov. 9, 1990 P. Nabhushanrao Vs. Union Bank of India, Andhra Pradesh	Delay in return of fixed deposit money by bank.	State Forum, Hyderabad, Andhra Pradesh	The forum declared that the bank was guilty of negligent service and delay in return of the money. Immediate payment along with adequate compensation was ordered by the forum.
April 2011 Kailash Vasdev Vs. Bajaj Electricals, Mumbai	Delay in repairing under warranty microwave oven.	Consumer Forum for Fair Business Practice (CFBP), Mumbai	The forum compelled the sellers to replace the defective microwave oven.

Project No. 3

Procedure of Opening a Savings Account
UCO Bank

Procedure of Opening a Bank Account

The procedure of opening a bank account is listed below in steps :

1. **Submission of application in the prescribed form–** The person desirous of opening the bank account has to apply to the bank on the bank's prescribed form. The application form is available at the bank branch and is available on request free of cost. The form has to be duly filled out by the applicant. It requires the applicant's personal details along with his email address and his mobile number. The applicant also has to fill in the nominee's name.

2. **Introduction of the applicant–** The bank insists on having the new prospect introduced by an existing account holder who will vouch for him. The introducer will have to sign on the applicant's application form giving his own account number and name.

3. **Submission of proof of address–** The applicant then has to submit evidence authenticating his address that he mentions on his application form. This is accomplished by submitting the copy of his/her Driving license, Aadhar card or Passport.

4. **Photographs–** The applicant also has to submit a photo identification proving that he is the person in the application. So, two photographs of the applicant are required to be submitted which will be pasted on the applicant's form for photo identification.

5. **Specimen signatures–** Once the bank is satisfied with the introduction and references it proceeds with the opening of the account. The applicant is asked to give three specimen signatures on a separate form which is prescribed for the purpose. This form also has the applicant's photograph affixed. This is filed by the bank and the specimen signature is used to verify his signature as and when the need arises.

6. **Initial deposit–** The applicant has to make an initial deposit of ₹ 1,000 towards his account for opening it.

After these formalities the bank sends him an SMS next day informing him that his account has been opened and gives him his account number too. Bank calls him after two days for giving him his passbook, cheque book and the ATM card.

Agency Functions

UCO Bank offers following services as part of its agency functions :

1. **Collection and payment of credit and other instruments–** UCO Bank collects and pays cheques, bills of exchange, and promissory notes. It also makes payment of income tax, fees, insurance premium etc. on behalf of its customers.

2. **Purchase and sale of securities–** It purchases and sells various securities like shares, stocks, bonds units and debentures. etc., thus functioning as a broker.

3. **Remittance of funds–** UCO Bank remits funds on behalf of customers from one place to another through cheques, drafts, mail transfers, etc.
4. **Issues letter of references–** UCO Bank furnishes information about economic position of its customers to domestic and foreign traders for business transactions.
5. **Purchase and sale of foreign exchange–** UCO Bank buys and sells foreign exchange on behalf of their customers and help in promoting international trade.

General Utility Services

UCO Bank offers following general utility services to its customers. However, this is not an exhaustive list.
1. **Locker facilities–** UCO Bank provides locker facilities to their customers.
2. **Letters of credit–** UCO Banker issues letters of credit to certify the credit worthiness of its customers.
3. **Acts as underwriters–** It underwrites the securities issued by joint stock companies for a commission.
4. **Traveller's cheque–** UCO Bank issue traveller's cheque to their customers to avoid risk of taking cash during their journey.

Project No. 4

Interest Rates of Fixed Deposits

Sr. No.	Name of Bank	Interest Rate			
		1-2 Years	2-3 Years	3-5 Years	5 Years or More
1.	Allahabad Bank	9.05 %	9.05 %	9.05%	8.75 %
2.	Punjab & Sind Bank	9.00%	9.00 %	9.00 %	8.75 %
3.	HDFC Bank	8.75 %	8.75 %	8.75 %	8.25 %
4.	Kotak Bank	8.50 %	8.50 %	8.50 %	8.25 %
5.	IDBI	8.25 %	8.25 %	8.25 %	8.25 %

Procedure and Formalities of Opening a Fixed Deposit Account.
1. Ask for the fixed deposit application form available in the bank branch.
2. Fill in the pay-in slip available in the branch.
3. Attach the photocopy of your Permanent Account Number (PAN) card.
4. Submit the amount of money through cheque.
5. Fill in the Form 15 G regarding the deduction of TDS, if you don't want the bank to deduct tax at source (TDS) from the amount of interest.
6. Collect the FD receipt from the bank.

Procedure for Closing the Fixed Deposit Account.
1. Sign the FD receipt after affixing the revenue ticket and mentioning the fact that you want the FD encashed.
2. The bank will either credit your savings account with the FD amount and the interest thereon, or issue you a cheque.

Project No. 5

Investment in Companies

Investment

Sr. No.	Company	Opening Price (in ₹) (as on 1 Dec., 2014)	Opening Price (in ₹) (as on 31 Dec., 2014)
1.	Arti Drugs	1,330·25	1,345·75
2.	Abbot India	3,936·15	3,960·75
3.	ABG Shipyard	199·00	206·75
4.	Infosys	2,258·15	2,278·15
5.	Flexituff	195·00	232·00

Profit/Loss

Sr. No.	Company	Amount Invested (in ₹)	Profit /Loss (in ₹)
1.	Arti Drugs	19,953·75	232·50
2.	Abbot India	19,680·75	78·75
3.	ABG Shipyard	19,900·00	775·00
4.	Infosys	20,323·35	180·00
5.	Flexituff	20,085·00	3,811·00
	Total	99,942·85	5,077·25

Project No. 6

Share Prices of Nifty and Sensex Companies

Company	Share Price (2015) (in ₹)						
	Day 1	Day 2	Day 3	Day 4	Day 5	Day 6	Day 7
Infosys	2,300·00	2,328·00	2,294·00	2,290·55	2,280·30	2,299·60	2,280·50
Kalyani Investment Co. Ltd.	1,763·50	1,760·00	1,762·90	1,760·00	1,763·00	1,763·00	1,763·00
SML Isuzu Ltd.	1,091·70	1,091·00	1,091·00	1,092·00	1,093·00	1,092·70	1,091·00
OCL India Ltd.	589·75	589·75	590·00	590·00	590·50	590·50	592·00
Arti Drugs	1,330·25	1,330·25	1,330·75	1,332·00	1,332·50	1,332·00	1,333·00

Project No. 7

A Comparative Study of the Recruitment and Selection Procedure of two Business Organisations

Area – Information Technology and Communication

Sr. No.	Source of Recruitment	Atlanta Communications	Dynamic Informatics
1.	Newspaper Advertisements	√	×
2.	Company Web Page	√	√
3.	Placement Agency	√	√
4.	Walk-in	√	√
5.	Referrals	√	√

Sr. No.	Selection Procedure	Atlanta Communications	Dynamic Informatics
1.	Preliminary screening and vetting of applications received through sources cited above	√	√
2.	Initial level interviews by middle level HR personnel	√	√
3.	Written and hands-on skills test	√	√
4.	Interview 1 by GM-HR	√	√
5.	Interview 2 by CEO	√	√
6.	Verification of documents, certificates, character and police verification	√	√
7.	Letter of appointment	√	√
8.	Orientation	√	√

Project No. 8

Capital Plan for a Hypothetical Business

Beater Packaged Drinking Water Company

Type– Manufacturing

Product– Bottled drinking water

Target market– Hotels, restaurants and home consumers in the middle income group bracket

Targeted production (per month)– 1,00,000 litres per month

Plans for raising capital–

(a) 10 lakh Equity shares of ₹ 10 each		₹ 1.00 Crore
(b) 10 lakh Debentures of ₹ 10 each		₹ 1.00 Crore
	Total	₹ 2.00 Crore

Justification–

(a) High rate of return–A minimum estimated 30% per annum.

(b) Clean packaged drinking water is in great demand across all consumer brackets.

(c) All debentures can be redeemed within 2-3 years.

(d) Tax holiday for packaged drinking water units set up within government-designated economic zones.

Comparative Study of Organisational Structure of Two Business Firms

The subject of this project is the comparative study of organisational structure of two business organisations *i.e.,* The electrical engineering sector producing consumer electrical equipment.

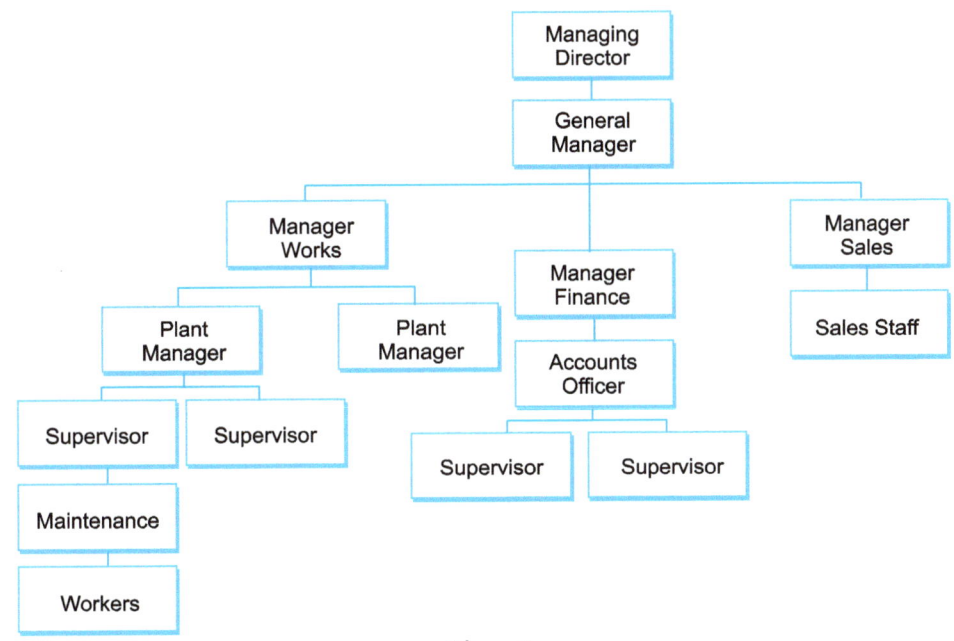

Firm 1

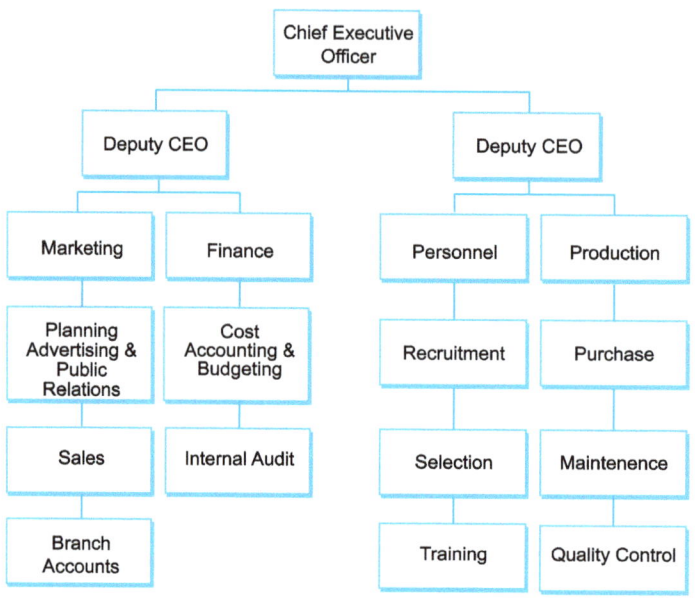

Firm 2

Sr. No.	Area	Firm 1	Firm 2
1.	Hierarchy	(i) There is hierarchical arrangement of authority. (ii) It is suitable for the small organisation.	(i) It is a combination of line and functional structures. (ii) Is logical and reflection of functions. (iii) Follows principle of occupation specialisation.
2.	Centralisation/ Delegation of Authority	(i) Lines of authority are vertical *i.e.* from top to bottom. (ii) Specialist staff absent.	(i) Evidently authority is more decentralised compared to Firm 1. (ii) Authority delegated through departmental heads.
3.	Flow of Information (Scalar Chain)	(i) The flow of information is quick and bottlenecks are not created.	(i) Reduced information flow at functional level. (ii) Flow of information is such that it can reduce coordination between functions.
4.	Span of Control	(i) Department is self contained and works independently. (ii) Easy to control as the managers evidently have direct control over their subordinates.	(i) Span of control narrower than in Firm 1. (ii) However, we can expect better intra-departmental control.

| 5. | Channels of Communication | (i) Communication is fast and easy as there is only vertical flow of communication. (ii) Horizontal channel of communication is at the upper level. | (i) Efficient communication may be slowed down. (ii) Choking and conflicting communication can be evidently possible. |

Project No. 10

Study of Business Undertaking

Name of the business– Hotstuff Restaurant

Nature of business– Food-dining and takeaway

This is a family restaurant specialising in very good North Indian, South Indian, Chinese, Italian and Continental food.

Type of ownership– Private

It is a family-owned private company where the top management is controlled by the family. The day to day running is supervised by a professional manager. The kitchen is supervised by a professional chef while the assistant chefs are young men and women who have good exposure to the type of foods that the restaurant provides.

Capital–

Land & Building		₹ 2,75,00,000
Furniture		₹ 15,07,500
Equipments		₹ 3,10,05,900
Working capital– Cash in hand and bank	₹ 27,96,000	
Raw materials	₹ 3,15,000	₹ 31,11,000
	Total	₹ 6,31,24,400

Profitability–

The business operates on an operating profit margin of 37.21 %.

SWOT Analysis

Sr. No.	Strength	Weakness	Opportunity	Threat
1.	Reputation for good, delicious, hygienic food.	Recruitment of experienced chefs at affordable terms and conditions difficult.	More and more families dining out.	New and bigger restaurant coming up in the neighbourhood.
2.	Owners have a long experience in food business.	Lack of adequate dining space.	Growing fondness and affinity for non-indian food.	Competition by existing restaurants in immediate vicinity.

3.	Very good public relations.	Premises needing renovation.	Increase in purchasing power with the younger generation.	Rising costs of maintenance eating into profit.
4.	Experienced, loyal and dedicated staff.	Kitchen equipments outdated.	–	–
5.	Very good relations with corporate and business houses.	–	–	–
6.	Reputed as a good family restaurant.	Lack of adequate parking facilities for patrons.	–	–

www.ingramcontent.com/pod-product-compliance
Ingram Content Group UK Ltd.
Pitfield, Milton Keynes, MK11 3LW, UK
UKHW050418240426
12048UKWH00014B/693